DOUBTS AND CERTAINTIES

DOUBTS AND CERTAINTIES

A Personal Memoir of the 20th Century

FRED DAINTON

Baron Dainton of Hallam Moors

If a man will begin with certainties, he shall end in doubts; but if he will be content to begin with doubts, he shall end in certainties.

Francis Bacon (1561-1626)

Sheffield Academic Press

A Continuum Imprint

To
John, Mary and Rosalind
and
Penelope, Harriet and Anna

Copyright © 2001 Barbara Dainton

Published by
Sheffield Academic Press
Mansion House
19 Kingfield Road
Sheffield S11 9AS
England

http://www.sheffieldacademicpress.com

Typeset by David Porteous Editions,
Newton Abbot

Illustrations and dust-jacket originated
by J.W. Northend Ltd,
Sheffield

Printed in Great Britain
by Bookcraft Ltd,
Bath

British Library Cataloguing in Publication Data

A catalogue record for this book is available
from the British Library

ISBN 1-84127-168-3

CONTENTS

1O DOWNING STREET

If only there were more people like Fred Dainton to call upon: not only able, and quietly efficient, but so kind and thoughtful. He can size up and understand a situation so quickly and find a constructive way forward.

As a Vice-Chancellor and as a Professor of Chemistry he really did carry out what I have always regarded as the true tasks of university life: teaching and transmitting his knowledge, to give every student a good basis for the future; undertaking research to unlock the unknown; and making time to talk to undergraduates so that all feel a part of the community of a university, which is one of the greatest privileges our society can offer.

Fred is always ready to take tough decisions - for example, on how to allocate a budget. He knows the realities and he doesn't run away from them. He is a a leader in everything he undertakes. How I wish we had more Freds to do all the things that he does so well.

But at least he will still be around, still be involved, still be helpful and still be optimistic about the future he has done so much to create.

Margaret Thatcher

October 1985

FOREWORD BY
LADY DAINTON

Fred drafted this personal memoir during 1996 and 1997, the last two years of his life: I was later asked to prepare the text for publication, whilst also adding an appendix about my own background and career. This book is the result.

Each time I read the text I am conscious of the fact that many of the people and events shaping our lives have not been mentioned, or have been given only brief coverage. Like Fred, I found that for the book to remain 'a reasonably short read' this was inevitable, but selecting what was to be included or omitted was always painful. Four categories have been sadly neglected.

The first is the family, and especially the extended family, all of whom have meant so much to us. Like most families we have had our problems and even our tragedies, but overall we have been a close-knit group of real friends who, for me anyway, have been enormously supportive in good times and bad.

Secondly, only a few of Fred's collaborations with those in other universities and colleges even receive a mention. We made many memorable visits to higher education institutions in the UK and overseas, during which we met old friends and made new ones. Some of the honours Fred received are listed in Appendix 1, but unfortunately it has not been possible to do the same for all the talks and invited lectures that he gave.

The third category encompasses the rewarding trips we made, either together or separately, to schools and colleges for speech days, or to open new buildings, or to talk to sixth forms. They were all distinctive and enjoyable, keeping us in touch with young people even after our own children had grown up.

Lastly, I must mention the many research students and post-doctoral fellows who worked with Fred, especially in Cambridge and Leeds. They form a large group of people, now scattered around the world, who have kept in touch and who entertained us royally on his 75th and 80th birthdays; it has again been a sorrow that so few can be mentioned by name.

Fred's decision to include only a little information about his scientific work was made because the book is aimed at the general reader. However, the science – and some of Fred's colleagues – figure to a greater extent in the Biographical Memoir of the Royal Society prepared by Professors Ken Ivin and Peter Gray, who worked with Fred as members of the Physical Chemistry Departments in both Cambridge and Leeds.

I would like to acknowledge the support given by the various friends and colleagues who read at least parts of the first draft, and encouraged me to proceed with the book. All made helpful suggestions which were invaluable in making me think about the text, though I remain responsible for the mistakes and deficiencies which I am sure must still exist.

A special vote of thanks must go to the University of Sheffield, which has helped to finance the project, and to those there who (like our daughter Rosalind) have helped to check and correct the text. Roger Allum and John Hawthorne have undertaken the lion's share of the editing, and in addition relieved me of much of the work of selecting photographs and preparing them for publication – something which I would have found hard to do without their professional expertise.

Lastly, I must thank Sheffield Academic Press for publishing the book: this is certainly the agency Fred would have chosen, and I am very grateful to everyone concerned for taking it on.

Barbara Dainton
Oxford

PREFACE

From time to time I have been urged by friends to write a book about my life. The representations have generally been made on the grounds that I have been involved in a wider range of issues than is common for most who have launched themselves on an academic career, especially in science. However, certain people, knowing that my father was born in 1857 and had almost no schooling, suggested that the story of his life and mine could be used to illustrate in human terms a crossing of class boundaries, in a time when Britain's national moods and values changed markedly from those of a self-confident, imperial, Victorian society to those less absolute and more relativistic ones which characterise modern Britain. When I pointed out that there must be many others in a similar position my friends stuck to their guns, but at least did not buttress their argument with flattery, for example saying that I wrote well; for they knew, as well as I, that this is simply not the case.

Why then have I written this book? Partly it is a thank-offering in recognition of those who have helped me on my way. To that extent it is a glad acknowledgement of the debts which I owe, and cannot repay, to many individuals: some still alive, some, alas, now dead. Partly it is to leave a record for friends, and particularly for my family. Yet another reason is to try to increase my own self-knowledge, by making an appraisal of my acts and opinions with that degree of detachment which comes more easily to the old.

Looking back over what I can remember of the eighty-plus years of my life, I have discovered no general plan; indeed, I do not recall ever thinking in such terms. But I have gained a strong impression that, when faced with the necessity of making a choice, I frequently considered not merely the intellectual arguments and those of immediate expediency, but also wondered how, faced with similar circumstances, my parents would have tackled them; and in so doing began to perceive what seemed to be an underlying principle which informed their lives. I doubt whether either of them would have identified this *leitmotif*, let alone put it into words as a personal credo. In their case, their actions certainly spoke louder than words. The nearest I can come to what I believe they instinctively felt is expressed in a phrase which I discovered in the spring of 1933 when, having already gained entry to an Oxford college, I was teaching myself sufficient Latin to secure formal admission to the University itself. The phrase is *Vita data est utenda*: 'Life is given to be used'. I cannot recall the writer but I have never forgotten the words, and to ensure a permanent record I arranged that they should be inscribed on the silver medal made by Kevin Coates to commemorate my service as Prime Warden of the Worshipful Company of Goldsmiths. My parents' lives exemplified this maxim; but the reader will have to be the judge of whether mine does.

Fred Dainton
Oxford

CHAPTER 1

STEEL CITY CHILDHOOD

Parents first season us; then schoolmasters
Deliver us to laws; they send us, bound
To rules of reason.

George Herbert (1593–1633)

My Home in Ranby Road

The house where I was born in 1914, and which I left in 1933, still stands. It is 66 Ranby Road, Sheffield, one of an unbroken row of terrace houses made of brick, with stone windowsills and steps and slate roofs. They were arranged in pairs, each pair sharing a common roof. Because the district is hilly, the side elevation of the roof ridges resembled a shallow staircase. The pavement was made of stone flags with a granite curb, and for all the time I lived there the road surface consisted of stone setts to enable the hooves of the dray horses to gain a secure purchase, particularly in the winter. I still recall vividly the clip-clop of those splendid animals, especially when they were hauling four-wheel drays bearing many one-hundredweight sacks of coal for domestic use, and I admired the horses' instant response to the quietly uttered instructions of the drayman. It always struck me as remarkable that, when going uphill and told to stop, a horse would, without any further command, turn the front wheels into the road and then allow the dray to slip back until the steel-tyred nearside wheel became wedged against the kerb. In this way the horse gained a temporary respite from its labours while the coalman unloaded and emptied his sacks of coal. Such resting horses were willing recipients of a sugar lump proffered by a small boy.

Each pair of houses was identical and presented a front elevation designed to give the illusion, from a distance, of the grandeur of a double bay-windowed villa with a central doorway. In our case such pretentiousness was reinforced by the inscription over the entry: 'Pretoria Villas'. The ground floor of the house included the front room, called 'the parlour' in most households; the room where meals were taken, usually known as the back room; and a further room that served as scullery, kitchen, laundry and bathroom. There were two bedrooms on the first floor and a small attic with a skylight on the second floor, whilst beneath the parlour was a coal cellar into which the coalman, after removing a grating in the passage, would deftly and accurately shoot coal from the sack over his back. A ton of fuel was usually delivered in this way, generating an enormous amount of dust which left a black layer over every horizontal surface. That same coal had, of course, to be duly hauled up the steep cellar steps when it was required.

Houses of this kind were typical of many constructed in Sheffield at the turn of the century, and were built for renting to the occupants. The principal breadwinner would usually consider himself a cut above the labouring classes in that either he had an identifiable craft, requiring a long apprenticeship to acquire the necessary skills, or he supervised the work of others. The homes they favoured were indeed a distinct improvement on the back-to-back houses occupied by the working class who lived nearer the city centre, but they were not much larger. My recollection is that our parlour measured about 12 feet by 12 feet, sufficient to accommodate an upright piano and stool, a glass-fronted bookcase, a table supporting a hand-wound gramophone, a settee and a couple of chairs, a mantelshelf with a wooden-cased mirror and, proudest boast of all, one or more well-scrubbed aspidistras in the bay window, seeming to challenge the passing neighbours to dare to assert that their aspidistras were either bigger or in better condition. In the spring, bowls of daffodils, hyacinths and tulips would compete for places in the bay where they were not obscured by the spiky, tough aspidistra leaves.

In many ways the parlour was wasted space, being put to family use at most on Sunday nights for singing round the piano after chapel. It was also the venue for family parties and games, such as whist, hunt the thimble, finding the ring on a string circle held in the hands of many people, blindfolded pinning of a two-dimensional tail onto a two-dimensional donkey, or simply for unpacking Christmas or birthday presents. Such under-use by the family was for me a godsend, since at other times the parlour was a quiet, if somewhat cold (the fire was not lit except for parties) haven for study, homework or just reading.

The back room – it was never aggrandised by being called the dining room – was the real family social centre. Of similar dimensions to the parlour, but having a simple wooden sash window looking onto the backyard, it was generally thronged with people sitting at a meal, round the fire, or just passing through it on their way to other destinations. This back room contained a dresser, table and chairs, and one armchair known as 'Father's chair' and invariably occupied by him after tea, which was the evening meal taken around 5.30 to 6pm. In that chair he could sit comfortably and warmly, feet to the fire, smoke his pipe and be read to if he was resting. Otherwise he might use the table as a desk to translate architects' plans into 'working drawings' for his men to use in the days to follow. Winter and summer alike, there was always a bright fire in the three-barred, black-leaded grate, the hot gases from which were often deflected to heat an oven. On the other side of the fire was a hob, on which stood a black kettle ever ready with hot water for a cup of tea, the standard offering to any visitor, day or night.

My mother's cheerful, bustling activity always seemed to have its focus in this room. First thing in the morning the grate was cleaned, ashes emptied into the midden outside, coal brought from the cellar, the fire laid and lit. These were Father's tasks, after which he would shave in the scullery using an old-fashioned 'cut-throat' razor of the sort much favoured as personal weapons by members of the 'razor gangs', which were prominent in the east end of Sheffield in the inter-war years. Meanwhile, Mother laid the table and prepared breakfast, and also filled a basin with something for Father's midday break; he could reheat the food on a stove at work. After his hasty departure to catch a tram to the masons' yard where he was in charge, those children still living at home were washed, fed and dispatched to school or work as the case might be. Then Mother set about cleaning of a kind unknown to today's housewife – for example, scrubbing with a brush and hot soapy water the top of the plain deal table at which we ate, clothes washing (as I shall describe), and dress-making using a treadle Singer sewing machine. It was a matter of pride for housewives that their windowsills and doorstones were gleaming clean and for this they were washed, scrubbed and 'donkey stoned'.[1] Most of my

---

1. So called because the scouring blocks had a donkey stamped on them and were hawked from small carts drawn by donkeys. I think each stone cost ½d, but the hawker would frequently accept payment in kind (for example, bones and old clothes).

mother's regular chores were performed while the family was away at work or school, but she preferred to do clothes-mending in the evening – beside the fire in winter, but always in company with others because it permitted her to converse without moving from room to room. Her shopping tended to be purely a local affair, involving short visits to specialist 'corner shops' such as the grocer, greengrocer, butcher and baker, located at intersections of nearby roads. Some of the owners of these corner shops also held an off-licence, entitling them to sell ales, wines, spirits and tobacco within prescribed hours. The proximity of the local shops removed the necessity of holding a large stock of food at home, and the lack of a particular item was easily remedied by sending a child out on an errand.

Though sometimes an unwelcome interruption if I was absorbed in another activity, especially reading, for a variety of reasons I found performing such errands a generally interesting experience. The nearest corner shop, only some four houses distant, was the butcher's. I was always fascinated by the skill of the owner as he wielded his cleaver with unerring accuracy, and with just enough force to carry the sharp edge through the carcass to the surface of the solid table without making more than the slightest incision in the thick wooden top; and how he would then skilfully dissect chops or whatever with knives, the blades of which had been eroded from their original shape by repeated sharpening on a 'steel' after each use. I admired his blue-and-white-striped apron and the leather belt from which his fluted steel was suspended. I marvelled at the deftness with which his left hand found the handle of the steel without his eyes looking for it, and brought it into position for a few quick strokes with whatever knife he had in his right hand. If I was especially lucky the hand-powered sausage machine, which pushed the minced meat into the skins, might be in operation and I would see how little knots would be tied at each end of every sausage. He would answer clearly and in a matter-of-fact way questions about where carcass parts such as kidneys, liver, tripe and so on were to be found in the body, and what function they performed. I suppose I must have gained from his replies a more objective, unsentimental view of my own body, which has made me more ready to accept medical treatment and to enjoy first-aid work. He also endeared himself to me by giving me a short ride in his motor car; I think he may have been the first person I knew to own one.

A visit to the baker's was less exciting because mother made all her own cakes and scones, but the smell inside the shop was quite delicious and was wafted out onto the road when there had been an early-morning bake. By comparison, green-groceries were dull places, and in any case the loads of fruit and vegetables were undesirably heavy and voluminous, often not fitting well in the basket I had brought. Whether it was Burgon's or the Co-op, an errand to a grocer's had many attractions. First there was the bacon or ham-cutting machine, called a Berkel. Here the meat was securely pressed to a flat bed which moved horizontally towards a rapidly rotating, vertical, steel wheel whose circumference was kept very sharp. It cut slices of ham or bacon with great precision and of any desired thickness, the possibilities being displayed vividly in a diagram facing the customer, who would choose by reference to the number associated with each thickness. What fascinated me was the skill with which the grocer peeled off the slices as they were being cut and laid them neatly on greaseproof paper on the weighing machine, an Avery if I remember correctly, and also the indescribable but unforgettable 'swoosh' as the blade cut the flesh. Second in fascination was the wielding of the ribbed wooden butter pats, which were always kept moist by immersion in water. With these, a slab would be cut from a huge lump of butter, carried between the pats and dropped onto a piece of greaseproof paper placed on the pan of the weighing machine. Smaller portions were removed or added to get the required weight and then the butter was patted into an immaculate brick, the greaseproof paper was folded over and, untouched by human hand, the result was given to the customer before the pats were returned to the water. Finally, the grocer we patronised kept boiled sweets and lumps of toffee in large glass bottles and usually I was given one, or if I bought 'a penn'orth please' was allocated a generous measure.

There was a regular weekly rhythm to many household activities. Monday was washday, and in the morning the action centred on the scullery. This small room contained the only water supply in the house, a simple cold tap emptying into a large, shallow, stone sink in the corner, adjacent to the window. It was also the site of the washing up of dirty dishes, a minor social occasion involving one to wash, two to dry and put away, and a great deal of conversation and banter. Adjacent to the sink was a built-in metal boiler, shaped like a large orchestral tympanum, known as the 'copper', which had to be heated by a fire below and from which hot water could be drawn through a tap and taken in a jug for use elsewhere in the house. In the corner of the scullery facing the door into the backyard was a large iron mangle with two big wooden rollers. The washtub was stored underneath when not in use. The routine on Monday morning after breakfast was first to fill the copper and light the fire beneath it. Then hot water was poured into the washtub and shredded soap was added. Dirty garments followed and were 'dollied', which is to say a 'dolly', comprising a wooden post with a crossbar handle and three legs at the bottom, was placed with the legs and part of the shaft in the tub and then oscillated manually round the shaft, using the handle. This process was continued until the articles of clothing were judged to be clean. If they were very dirty, the clothes might then be rubbed on a fluted washboard, which was sometimes made of wood and sometimes corrugated zinc, using plenty of soap until the stains vanished. Then the tub was emptied of its soapy water, clean hot water added, dollying repeated to ensure residual soap was removed, the tub emptied and, after the clothes had been given an initial 'wring' by hand, the water was squeezed out by passing them through the mangle.

All this hard physical work had of course to be followed by clothes drying. In summer, if the weather was clement, this involved pegging the garments onto an outdoor line in the yard. In winter they were hung on a clothes-horse placed round the fire in the back room, or on a clothes-rack made by my father which could be hoisted up to the ceiling. When I came home from school on a winter Monday afternoon the atmosphere seemed to be like that of a steamy tropical greenhouse. The following day was for ironing, the iron itself heated over the coal fire and the ironing board being the kitchen table.

Friday also had its own ritual, because Friday night was always bath night. The copper was brought into service again. A two-handled zinc bath, in which a man could only sit with his knees drawn up to his chest and which normally hung outside the entry to the water closet, was brought into the scullery, placed in front of the mangle and charged with hot water. Each member of the family bathed in turn – myself, being the youngest, first – all rubbing ourselves down with the distinctively smelling carbolic soap. As a child I was taken out of the bath, wrapped in a large towel and dried in front of the back room fire. This, and a cup of hot cocoa at about 8 or 9pm, ensured that a small boy, warm inside and out, went happily to a cold bed, to be tucked in by a parent or elder sister, and given a goodnight kiss before the burning candle at the bedside was extinguished.

Although there was no larder, my father had constructed numerous shelves alongside the steps down to the cellar to accommodate many home-made foodstuffs like orange wine, cakes and preserves. The presence of these shelves made access to the cellar less easy, and was a constant irritation to my father because that was the only place he could keep his tools and a workbench. I should also mention that there was no indoor water closet; the lavatory could only be reached by leaving the house. It was cold, unlit and primitive, and exclusion from it of vermin could not be guaranteed, though they were said to be deterred and the sanitary conditions improved by regular lime-washing of the walls. The itinerant lime-washer's cry was 'Sixpence a lavatory. Only good Buxton lime.'

Old-fashioned town gas, generated locally from coal, was piped to all houses in the road, but there were only four outlets in ours (all on the ground floor): in the centre of the ceilings of the parlour and the back room, plus a little batwing burner and later a small gas oven in the scullery. The fittings in the parlour and back room gave out an easy and comfortable mellow light, but to me the striking feature of both lamps was that the light was emitted from a fragile Welsbach gas mantle which had a greater luminosity than that of the flame which heated it. I was puzzled by this, but had to wait for an explanation of the riddle until 1939, at a Faraday Society Discussion in Oxford!

In retrospect, the lesson that I draw from comparing life 70-odd years ago in Sheffield with that of today's labour-saving homes is that life was extremely hard for housewives then. It seems to me that women have been liberated from the drudgery of those early days more by advances in scientific knowledge (and their application) than by any other single means. At the time, of course, I had no inkling that such a future was possible.

I turn now to the rooms upstairs. Each of the two first-floor bedrooms accommodated a chest of drawers and a double bed, that in the front room having a canopy while the larger back room also contained a wardrobe and was my parents' bedroom. Neither had gaslight, and we went to bed by candlelight. For three reasons, the front bedroom had a special fascination for me. First, it was possible to climb out through the open sash window onto the roof of the downstairs bay window and, by lying on my stomach, I could watch the world go by undetected. The knowledge thereby gained had no practical value, but its appeal to me was that whatever happened was known only to me and the actors themselves. I used to invent all kinds of stories to account for the perfectly ordinary movements of people in the road, who came into and passed out of my sight. I was never detected by anyone in the street but my silent vigil was brought to an abrupt end when my shocked mother, fearing I would fall off the window top, summoned my father who applied his strap to my body with good effect. Secondly, there was a lamp-post on the pavement just outside this bay window. It too was fired by gas, and every evening at dusk the lamp-lighter made his lonely journey, armed with a long pole bearing at its upper end a wax taper and a short sideways-projecting metal stud. He would push this contraption upwards through a trap door in the base of the lamp housing and engage the projection with a tap, allowing the gas to escape and be ignited. In a few seconds the mantle glowed brightly and a patch of the road was suffused with light. More importantly as far as I was concerned, the upper wall of the bedroom was illuminated: by interposing my hands I could cast moving shadows, and by using paper cut-outs I could create bright images. I think it must have been in this period that I accepted that light must travel in straight lines because when, years later, that proposition was put to me by a physics teacher, I needed no convincing and felt I had known this for a long time. Thirdly, because of the hilliness of the terrain many district highways, which were also tram routes, were within sight. Consequently the flashes of the tramcar trolleys, as they passed under the insulated holders of the overhead wire, were easily visible and the dark night above Sheffield twinkled deliciously.

Neither of these rooms was where I normally slept. I had to ascend a further curving staircase to the small attic. Until he married, I shared this room with my elder brother Ernest, whose kindness to me I have always remembered. But the room itself was gaunt and unfriendly: nothing but the sky could be seen through the skylight and in winter the unheated room was very cold, while in summer, being under an uninsulated roof, it was unbearably hot. Nonetheless, after my brother left home it was still 'a room of one's own'. I could read by candlelight, or with the aid of a flash-lamp, to my heart's content, not to say my mother's dismay as she feared for damage to my sight.

So much for the house itself, for whose construction my father, with his discerning master mason's eye, had little regard, declaring it to be 'jerry-built'. Certainly the walls separating our house from the adjoining one were not soundproof, and the wooden gutters under the eaves, the windows and the doors needed constant attention. The backyard also had little to be said for it, as it was much too small to play games with others; the only play that was possible was skipping or throwing a ball against the wall and catching it. There was a tiny area of earth which my mother, with her green fingers and love of flowers, made glow with colour throughout the summer months. Most games with other children – for example, cricket, rounders, 'tag', marbles and even ball-kicking – necessarily took place in the street, unless there were enough of us to go to Endcliffe Park, just opposite the end of the road, a venue which always bore the risk of interference in our games by groups of larger boys.

Although the house, its meagre backyard and Ranby Road itself had little to recommend them, the suburb of which they formed a tiny part was singularly well placed. This was because of the topography of the western side of Sheffield, which is dominated by the eastward-flowing streams draining the high moorlands and cutting valleys in the grit and shales of the underlying terrain. The northernmost of these streams turns to flow southwards and is joined in turn by eastward-flowing rivers – the Little Don, Ewden, Loxley, Rivelin, Porter and Sheaf (from which Sheffield takes its name) – all eventually forming the River Don, so that the pattern resembles the stern of a Venetian gondola. Having received these tributaries, the Don does a U-turn in the centre of Sheffield and flows to the north-east through the coal measures. The steeply cut valleys of these feeder rivers have all been dammed in the past to provide both water reservoirs and power to drive machinery, albeit later supplanted by steam. The river valleys are in many places too steep for housing, and so the inhabitants of Sheffield have easy access to leafy glens and tumbling streams. Walking through such a landscape is a delight, and after only a few miles the pedestrian comes to the source of the stream on the heather-covered moors, generally some 1,500 feet above sea level. The Porter Brook, which rises on Hallam Moors, is typical. Along some three miles of its length within the city of Sheffield it contains eight dams, and its banks now form a series of delightful public parks. Two of these – Endcliffe Park and the neighbouring Bingham Park – were my free and welcoming gateways to Hallam Moors and the delights beyond, such as the gritstone crags of Stanage Edge and High Neb and the views they provide over Edale and the Kinder Scout plateau, the latter the highest ground of the so-called Dark Peak region. I can think of no other city more delightfully situated or affording such excellent opportunities for healthy, interesting outdoor pursuits. This simple geographical fact was to have a powerful educative effect on me, particularly in the second decade of my life.

The Family and the Youngest Child

In my lifetime there have been endless discussions about the roles of nature and nurture in the development of a child. It seems to me that to attempt to weigh the one influence against the other is unlikely to be productive of much useful outcome. This is because while everyone accepts that nature is the genetic component and considers that nurture is something acting on the individual from outside, it is often forgotten that nature and nurture are not completely separable. Nurture has several constituents, some of which are inculcated by parents who are themselves the sole determinants of nature. These components include the habitat, which is why I have attempted to give a clear picture of what in my early years seemed to be the permanent environment, namely the house in which we lived, its immediate geographical setting and the human activities which had to be carried out in it to sustain life. I am sure that it is this, and the memory of it, which give me a sense of 'belonging' to Sheffield, as well as my ineradicable feeling of 'going home' whenever I visit that city. Yet another component of the nurture is, of course, the interaction with the other human beings in the habitat, and I must therefore now describe the members of the household at 66 Ranby Road.

My father, George Whalley Dainton, was (I believe) born in Knutsford, Cheshire, in 1857, the year of the Indian Mutiny. He was the son of John Dainton, described in official documents as a mariner, and he attributed his middle name Whalley to a near relative named Captain Mann Warrington Whalley; precisely why this should be so I have never discovered. There are no records of my father's early life and I do not know who his mother was. I believe the family was extremely poor, and he repeatedly told me that it had only been possible for him to have a few weeks of formal school, for which a fee had to be paid. This was because the Forster Education Act, which made primary school education free to all in England, was not introduced until 1870. Consequently, to the end of his days my father read with great difficulty and slowness, and both that and writing were torture to him. I have heard him say that at the age of nine he was doing odd jobs and then obtained a post of stable lad to a doctor in Wavertree, a suburb of Liverpool, where he said he lived over the stables and was given a hammer and chisel which he used to embellish some of the stonework. He was obviously much attracted to this craft and it was evident to me that he had a lifelong passion for working with stone. He therefore became apprenticed to a mason but, as he would often describe, the building trade was seasonal and in the bad weather he did other jobs, including playing bit parts in one of the Liverpool theatres. His somewhat jaunty air, and the way he wore his clothing when he was cutting a figure, certainly gives credence to the notion that he had a touch of the thespian about him. From his other characteristics I would describe him as a 'card', in Arnold Bennett's sense of that word. Despite his lack of formal education, which caused him so much frustration, he taught himself to make plans, elevations and sections of buildings and, as he described it, to 'lay out' work for other men to do. He rose steadily in his trade, soon becoming a foreman mason and in his fifties and sixties a clerk of works for buildings all over the country, including the Sheffield Town Hall (1897), its extension which opened in 1923, the Sunderland General Post Office and many church projects in Lancashire and Yorkshire, including the remodelling of Ecclesall Church, a few hundred yards up the hill from where we lived.

In this work he served many well-known architects, including E.W. Mountford who, having won the open competition for Sheffield Town Hall in 1890, designed several London buildings, most notably the Central Criminal Court at the Old Bailey; and Temple Moore, a pupil and friend of George Gilbert Scott Jr, who was a pure gothicist responsible (among other buildings) for many churches, the nave of Hexham Abbey and the chapel of Pusey House, Oxford. As I write I have in front of me moving testimonials from these architects, and they all testify to my father's practicality, conscientiousness, good management of men, general capability and, above all, his energy.

A few years ago I learned for the first time how my father's employees regarded him. The way in which this information came into my hands is an excellent example of how a voice from the past may suddenly be heard again, with most pleasurable consequences. Early in 1990 Dr John Padley, Registrar and Secretary of the University of Sheffield, produced a rusty tool and asked me to tell him what I thought it was. I had no hesitation in recognising it as a mason's chisel, and thinking that there was nothing remarkable about that, told him so. He then asked me to look at it more carefully and I noticed that, stamped on the shaft but barely discernible, were the letters 'G. Dainton'. In surprise I exclaimed, 'That must be my father's! How did you come by it?' He then told me that the firm of Charles Gibbs and Sons, Builders and Stonemasons, had done a considerable amount of work for the University, and that the Managing Director, John Gibbs, had taken some University document home to show his father, Charles, who lived in the Old Vicarage at Grenoside. Seeing my name on the document, Charles exclaimed to his son, 'That must be young Fred!', meaning that I was the son of the master mason to whom he had been apprenticed in the early 1920s.

My immediate reaction was that I must meet Charles Gibbs, and so we arranged to visit him at his home. Our meeting proved to be one of the most enjoyable occasions of our lives. Charles turned out to be a charming, fresh-complexioned early octogenarian, and he and his equally delightful wife Alice welcomed us very warmly indeed. Soon he began to tell me about my father, how he was my father's last apprentice and how he knew me when I was just a lad. He explained that my mother had taken a particular interest in all my father's apprentices and that he, Charles, was particularly fond of her. As he talked, and all of us fast became friends, I realised he had an insight into my father's character which really should be recorded. I therefore asked the University to send someone as near Charles' age as possible, and born and bred in Sheffield, to talk with him about his apprenticeship and his relations with my family. Peter Linacre, retired Academic Registrar of the University, admirably filled this role and Charles talked to him freely. We have in our possession both the tape of that conversation and the transcript. Rather than dilute Charles' words, I have included below some excerpts from the interview which explain more about my father than I knew myself:

> In answer to a question as to whether George Dainton was a hard man, Charles said: 'Well, he was very keen ... he was a good boss for a boy to be under, you had a good start but he was strict, there was no skiving, messing or larking about ... not when he was there anyway. He was on the ball all the time. I was lucky I had a bloke like Dainton to set me off'.
>
> Asked how he was regarded and what sort of work he did in George Longden's masons' yard, Charles replied: 'Although he was always addressed as Mr Dainton, everybody called him GWD when he wasn't there. Some people called him "Full Size Detail" because he always liked to set out in full size. He used to make full-size sections on zinc sheet (enlarging from the architect's drawings), so that the mason had a zinc template from which to cut the stone. He was a stickler for detail. Everything had to be 'spot on'. He was sharp on the uptake; he didn't miss much. He was always well dressed and put a good face on. He used to come in, particularly on Saturday mornings (he worked a 56-hour week), with his breeches and leggings highly polished and wearing a stetson-type hat'.

Concerning the character of my mother, Charles said: 'Mrs Dainton was a smashing person', to which his wife added warmly: 'She was a lovely lady; she had a big smile and rosy cheeks.'

Referring to my mother's gift to him of my father's tools when he died, Charles said that he had always treasured them: 'I had to get a barrow to push them back home. But they were jewels to me; being a young lad and having a box of tools with everything in it! Normally you would have to buy a few when you could afford it. It wasn't just tools. There were set squares, scribers, dividers; everything a mason wanted. I was cock-a-hoop when I got them. I hadn't to go begging chisels to do different jobs, like the other lads did!'

Charles then showed me the box, which still contained many of my father's tools, including his mallet. With characteristic generosity, he insisted that they should come back to me for safe keeping. Knowing that these tools had been used on many prominent buildings in Sheffield – including the Town Hall at the turn of the century and an extension in the 1920s, the City Hall in the early 1930s and the post-war extension to the Cathedral, not to mention numerous churches – my immediate reaction was that the proper place for them was in the Ruskin Museum.[2] However, I could tell at once that Charles was not best pleased with this notion. He would obviously have preferred them to be under my control as a kind of return gift to me, an expression of what he owed to my father's tutelage and my mother's care. After a discussion we came to a splendid compromise, which was that the tools would be on display in a fine oak case situated beneath my portrait in the Chancellor's Room of the University of Sheffield. There they are and there they will stay as a permanent memorial to two skilled individuals who valued and made best use of the master–apprentice relationship.

My wife, Barbara, and I decided it would be fitting if there could be a small ceremony marking the handing over of these tools, and this was arranged to be carried out on 14 July 1990, after one of the Annual Degree Congregations in the

2. The Museum was set up by the Guild of St George, a body founded by John Ruskin. He wanted to display works of art, beautiful books and manuscripts, and products of the craftsman's work on metals, minerals and precious stones. Ruskin's argument for establishing a museum in Sheffield was that he wanted things to be available to be seen by workmen and labourers, and especially cutlers whom he regarded as 'the finest tradesmen in the land'. Sadly, because of lack of interest after the Second World War, the original museum was closed and some of its collections dispersed. Happily, however, in recent years the Ruskin Gallery has been re-established in Norfolk Street, close to the theatres and the Public Reference Library, in an area very familiar to me. [It has now been incorporated into the city's new Millennium Gallery (BHD).]

University. Appropriately enough, that was the ceremony at which graduating architects were admitted to their degrees. Following the congregation there was a tea party in the Chancellor's Room, at which Charles, Alice and John Gibbs were our guests. I know that day has given them a great deal of satisfaction, just as it has to my wife and myself. After tea we made a tour around some of the buildings in the centre of Sheffield, for which either my father or Charles Gibbs had a responsible role as masons. To hear Charles, with his hand on my forearm, say while pointing to a building, 'Now, Fred, your father did that' was indeed a moving experience and one I shall always cherish. We have remained in contact with the Gibbs' and greatly value their friendship.

My father did not attend church or chapel, and I have often wondered why. It could have been embarrassment over his inability to read the hymnbook or the prayer book, or maybe some deeper motive such as the perceived irrationality of belief. Whatever the reason, the fact was that while all the children on Sundays were busy with various services and Sunday school, he would spend the day at an allotment which we leased some three-quarters of a mile away from the house. There he grew a range of vegetables and also some flowers, and he had a little shed in which he kept his gardening tools. I have a mental picture of him working hard on that allotment; occasionally I would see him sitting with the shed door open, his pipe alight, thinking I knew not what. But in later years I used to believe it had been his way of achieving peace by a kind of communion with nature. On many Saturdays when I was young I would accompany him to the allotment, where my special task was to fetch water from a spring about 250 yards away. The spring came to the surface by Ecclesall Church, which my father had to pass on his journeys to and from home, and sometimes I still wonder whether his mind ever went back to 1907 when the foundation stone was laid for the great extension of that building, designed by Temple Moore. I have included in this book a photograph of that occasion: it shows my father as clerk of works in a characteristic posture, surrounded by the clergy and notables but clearly himself supervising the laying of the stone, in a manner which must have indicated beyond doubt to all those present that it had to be done to his personal satisfaction!

Eventually I decided I would try to find the foundation stone in the church, and during one of my visits to Sheffield I managed to locate it in the vestry. This puzzled the officiating clergy, who asked what my interest was, and I explained it.

This incident had two sequels. The first was a request from the vicar, the Reverend Dr Peter Williams, for me to write an article for the parish magazine, which I gladly did. The second occurred in 1995 when the 1914-18 war memorial was refurbished and rededicated on VE Day. The vicar kindly invited us to go to the church and the dedication, and to take lunch in his house. He explained that he wished us to be present because the parish records showed that when the war memorial was erected in 1920 this project was also placed under the supervision of my father, who had been called in to give guidance to the monumental masons who had constructed it. As in the case of Charles Gibbs, we were once again struck by the natural generosity of the folk and the institutions of Sheffield, as well as their thoughtfulness in trying to reconnect us with my family's past.

My mother's father, John Bottrill, was born in 1833 and became the toll clerk and lock-keeper of the Watford locks on the Grand Union Canal. These locks are discernible on the east side of the M1 motorway, just north of the Watford Gap service station. The lock-keeper's house on the lowest level is still there, as is the lock into which he fell and was drowned on a frosty Boxing Day night in 1889, while he was closing one of the gates. He had three sons and three daughters, and my mother – Mary Jane – was the penultimate child, born in 1873. When her father died the lock-keeper's house had to be vacated and the family moved to a very small cottage at the end of a row of four within Watford village. I well remember the fortnight's holiday which our family spent there, every August until my mother's mother died in 1921. In order to enhance the depleted household income after her father's untimely death, my mother entered service first as a daily at Henley Court, the big house of Watford village, and later as a residential maid at Overslade, which was a preparatory school to Rugby.

The eldest of my mother's siblings was Sarah, whom my father married on 14 September 1881. I believe she was under twenty years of age at the time. I have no idea how they met but I do know that they had five children. After the birth of her fifth child Sarah died, and my mother went in due course to keep house and look after the motherless young family. The relationship must have developed from there, because she was married to my father in St Barnabas' Church, Herschell Road, Sheffield, on 3 June 1895. An intriguing aspect of this marriage is that the Tables of Consanguinity at that time should have prevented the solemnization of the marriage between the deceased wife's sister and the widower. Nevertheless the union was duly consecrated and four children of alternating sexes followed, so that I was the last and ninth child of my father.

With only one breadwinner it cannot have been easy to raise such a large family, and it is not surprising that I had the only real educational chance. That all the others deserved such an opportunity is beyond question. For example, 'big brother Bill' (George William Bottrill Dainton), though he went straight from school to be apprenticed to my father, showed he had talent and character. He enlisted in the East Yorkshire Regiment in the First World War and rose to the rank of sergeant. He was three times wounded, and thereafter – convinced that Europe was in decline and, compared with Mesopotamia where he had served in the war, had a very unattractive climate – took a job in Shanghai. Though not qualified as an architect, he had a successful career there designing buildings, including Bubbling Wells Road Fire Station, which, because the original names had been changed to commemorate heroes of the Revolution, I failed to locate on a visit to China in 1982. He was wounded again during a rising of the warlords, when they attacked the 'foreign' settlements. When the Japanese invaded Manchuria in the mid-1930s he foresaw that China would be no safe haven and moved to Singapore. Before that city state was overrun he ensured that his wife and son got out to Australia and he himself escaped some time later, catching up with his family in Brisbane. He then started an entirely new career and, according to his widow whom I saw there in 1959, ended his life as chief engineer on the Queensland State Railway.

My elder sister Mabel, who was the most senior child of the 'second family', was clearly talented. She went to Derby Training College and came home to be a schoolteacher in Sheffield, only retiring from this when she married. My brother Ernest, to whom I have already referred, did not have the chance of anything more than an elementary school education. At the age of fourteen he went off to the Sheffield Testing Works as a laboratory assistant, while at the same time studying by night school for his 'matric' (the equivalent of today's GCSE). After five more years of hard work in the evenings attending courses in the University of Sheffield, he was admitted to an Associateship in Metallurgy, while at the same time making progress in the laboratories of various Sheffield steel works, such as Vickers and the English Steel Corporation. Then came the economic depression and, although he had studied a foreign language (French) by night school and correspondence courses, and had been appointed his company's representative in Belgium, the rationalisation policy adopted by his employer during the depression led to him losing his job. Today he would have been declared redundant and entitled to some severance payment. Then there was nothing, and after a period of unemployment he had to build up his life again, joining another firm, Jesse and Civilise, which had a reputation for special steels and was later taken over by the BSI Company of Birmingham. His younger and my elder sister Gladys was also able, and at the age of eleven secured a place in the Central Secondary School for Girls, where she obtained her matriculation. However, she did what was expected of most girls of her age and rejected the possibility of higher education, instead gaining employment in the General Post Office.

I was born some four months after the outbreak of the First World War, on the same day that the Australian cruiser *Sydney* sank the marauding German warship *Emden*, which had wrought havoc among the merchant shipping on the seas around Australia. I was told that this induced my patriotic father to give me the middle name of Sydney, he having previously chosen Frederick because of his admiration for Frederick the Great (though I doubt whether he would have been willing to disclose this reason to his workmates at the time that I was born, so high was patriotic feeling then running).

It is small wonder that my most enduring memories of early childhood are of a crowded and busy house. I slept between my father and mother in the back bedroom, my two sisters slept in the front bedroom and my two brothers in the attic; I was moved there when my elder brother went to China. I have only two clear recollections of the war. The first is of 'big brother Bill', at that time a sergeant, coming home on leave. I was terrified of him. He was so large in his khaki uniform and greatcoat, and carried an immense amount of baggage which seemed to fill up the whole of the back room downstairs. I could not understand the things he was telling my mother and father, any more than I could comprehend the reasons behind the war; but that he was at risk was clear and was confirmed in my mind when, as I well remember, I was taken to visit him in Nether Edge Hospital, where he was a patient after being wounded for the third time.

That actual danger could reach us at home never crossed my mind, and yet my second memory was of just such an event. One night, to my bewilderment, I was hastily removed from my bed, bundled up in a blanket and taken downstairs, not just into the back room but into the cellar. There was a good deal of commotion in the road, unintelligible to me, and then there were some dull, heavy thuds. We stayed down in the cellar for some time and I remember my vocabulary was increased by the word 'Zeppelin', though whether this was on first hearing it, or because I was told the story many times subsequently, I do not know. What I do know is that there were several raids by Zeppelins on Sheffield and this can only have been the last one, which I think was in 1917, since I have no real memories of anything in life much earlier than that. Later on I was often to hear from parents and siblings alike that, in answer to my question 'How do the Zeppelins stay up there?', I was told 'Well, they are filled with gas like balloons'; to which I said 'Well, our balloons don't stay up. They always fall down. We have to hit them up again.' The explanation I was given several years later, that Zeppelins are filled with a gas lighter than air, seemed much more convincing, especially when I was shown that a rubber ball held under water rose up rapidly when released.

The end of the war was marked by characteristic celebrations on the part of my parents, and Armistice Day 1918 is imprinted on my memory. At that time, which was also my fourth birthday, I was ill with some kind of fever and had been moved to the front bedroom which was heated by a fire in the small grate. To my surprise, my father arrived home early from work and proceeded to climb onto the top of the bay window where I had been forbidden to go. His intention was to string bunting across the road from our house to the one opposite to celebrate Armistice Day, and I recall so clearly my mother expostulating with him in these words: 'The poor lad will catch his death of cold' – the poor lad being me. There then ensued an argument which ended in compromise: my father hurriedly made the fixings at our house and the window was duly shut before I died! From then on Armistice Day meant to me the two minutes' silence at 11am, during which period I hardly knew what to think about, and a half-day's holiday from school, which seemed an entirely acceptable thing to happen on a birthday.

In the decade or so after the war the life of the family underwent a number of significant changes, as one after another of the children left home on marriage. This may have lightened my mother's burden but it did not change the routine of her workaday life, although it must have decreased its intensity. As I went to infant, elementary and secondary schools in succession, so my life became less home-centred. But for many years, two days – Saturday and Sunday – retained their character. For me the weekend began on Friday night: initially with the meeting of the Cubs at St Augustine's Church, and latterly with the Banner Cross United Methodist Church Scout Troop. For my father, and those brothers and sisters still living at home, the weekend did not begin until after they had returned from work at lunchtime on Saturday. While I was a Cub, Saturday morning was often given over to a long walk with the Cub pack, of which the most favoured was along the southern ridge of the Rivelin Valley, where I had my first real glimpse of gritstone crags; and then the path would take us on to Hallam Moors, where I saw my first adder. I confess now to being scared stiff. In retrospect, I marvel at the devotion of the Cub mistress who gave up so much of her time to a lot of unruly lads. Despite all the curious ritual, which I quite enjoyed, we did learn many useful things – for example, about first aid, the countryside and its plants and animals. On Saturday afternoon my father, with perhaps my mother and myself, would go to the allotment if the weather was suitable and there were jobs to be done. Alternatively he would work at home. Sometimes he would help me in getting prepared for the Cub handicraft badge. But there were also high days when my mother would take me out into the part of the Peak District she liked best, known as the White Peak because it is based on the limestone where, of course, the flowers are much more abundant than in the Dark Peak. Her great delight was Lathkill Dale, up which we would wander, have some tea in the meadows and return home, I am now ashamed to say, grasping wild flowers.

Not all my mother's pleasures were rural. There were summer evenings when I would be taken to a park, either the nearby Endcliffe Park or Weston Park, to listen to a band playing popular melodies or to enjoy an entertainment offered by a group of white-faced pierrots and pierrettes. At the cost of a penny, a portable park seat or deckchair could be rented from those arranged in concentric rows round the elaborately decorated bandstand. My memory of these occasions is what decorous affairs they seemed to be: no litter, no rowdyism, much polite applause and yet no heavy-handed authority, only the friendly park-keepers. It was all innocent pleasure, enjoyed for itself in a spirit of neighbourliness. If there was a darker side I was never aware of it.

Sunday was a steady routine of an 11 o'clock service at the local Methodist chapel and Sunday school at 2.30pm, for which 'golden texts' had to be learned and then recited to the class teacher. Accurate repetition Sunday after Sunday of the chosen golden text brought its own reward of a Sunday school prize, in the form of a book. So began my tiny library. The golden texts themselves were quite simple pieces from the Bible, a hymn or some straightforward maxim. When I was a vice-chancellor dealing with radical students, I acquired Chairman Mao's little red book (their bible) and I found that there was a surprising resemblance of his aphorisms to the golden texts I had had to learn almost fifty years earlier – an observation which, when made to the radical students, was not particularly acceptable! Also, as a Sunday school pupil I had to sign the pledge, because the United Methodists at that time were total abstainers from alcohol in any form – at least so they claimed. But I remember my mother making orange wine which she would proudly proclaim to be made only of sugar and orange juice and left to stand, and when she served it in tumblers about a year later she said innocently, 'It makes the party so jolly'. It was some time before chemistry revealed the mystery of this process to me. Her insistence on my signing the pledge annually was something with which I complied, though I was puzzled because I was brought up to believe that having once given your promise you never gave back word. Sunday school finished around 3.30pm and then one would walk with one's friends in the streets or the neighbouring parks, getting home about 5 o'clock in order to have high tea before departure for the 6.30pm service in chapel. After this there was often another walk, and so back home to bed.

The great event of the Sunday school year took place on Whit Monday. Children, Sunday school teachers and some of the elders of the chapel assembled after breakfast and formed a procession, led by a large standard proclaiming 'Banner Cross United Methodist Church Sunday School'. Everyone was dressed in their best clothes because it was a time for new frocks and bonnets, new suits, new shoes, indeed new hopes for the coming summer and year. The standards were large, generally about seven or eight feet square, and were carried on two vertical poles, with a cross member and with fore and aft ropes attached to the top of each. The base of each upright would be hoisted into a special leather holster by a strong man, and men would take the ropes to prevent this large object being so affected by the wind that it could not be kept vertical by the two main weight-bearing members of the team. Then the children and their teachers would be mustered and led forward, sometimes by the Minister and Sunday school superintendent, and sometimes by a Scout band or the Boys' Brigade band. The march would then proceed to one of various places in the city where many Sunday schools could meet. Our venue was the grounds of King Edward VII School, but by far the largest assembly area was Norfolk Park where tens of thousands would be gathered. There then followed an open-air service which was largely singing, and in Sheffield's case naturally the stirring hymns of James Montgomery or Ebenezer Elliott would be sung, not because of their quasi-revolutionary flavour but because of local patriotism. The other local churches took little part in these Whit walks. After the mass hymn singing we paraded back to chapel, where most of us disbanded to get home for dinner, as we called it, and put away our finery, only to reassemble at about 3pm in a field which had been rented for sports day. There would be all kinds of games and races, and at the end of the day tea, ice cream, cakes and sandwiches would be provided. It was always a memorable occasion but, alas, is no more.

Until I was ten the only places I knew outside Sheffield were parts of the Peak District and Watford village in Northamptonshire, where we would go for our fortnight's stay with Granny in her cottage, or latterly as guests of the lock-keeper. The thrill of those holidays still remains with me. There would be a great deal of preparation. Old leather cases would be filled and we would go to Sheffield Victoria Station (now non-existent) by tram. The agony of hauling a heavy case up the steep approach road still lingers. Then there would be the exciting journey to Rugby by way of the Great Central line. On arrival we went by horse-drawn cab to what seemed to me the huge Midland Railway Station, whence a slow train would take us on to Watford station (later called Welton station). It was a delight to walk in the fields or to play with the village children, and perhaps swim in the canal. I have vivid memories of conversations involving farming folk, villagers and my mother, who in their eyes had news to bring them from the great city. On one memorable occasion, in 1924, we took part in a day-trip to the British Empire Exhibition at Wembley. This was breathtaking for me. The highlight was not so much the evidence of the Empire, but the opportunity to get into the driver's cab of a 4-6-2 type locomotive; my interest in steam engines had been aroused by watching from my holiday bedroom window the London expresses thundering through Watford station. My father generally could only manage a week away from his work, and when he came the expeditions tended to be more wide-ranging. He would persuade someone to let him have the use of a horse and trap so that he could once again experience the pleasure of driving a horse and showing his equestrian skills. Apart from this fortnight in August, I can remember only one holiday, when we went to the seaside; and that was made possible by the fact that my elder sister's college friend's mother ran a boarding house in Scarborough, and we went outside the season at no charge. It was a thrilling time for me; I wondered where all the ships were going and how long it would take them to make landfall.

First Steps in Formal Education

There was a school at the top of Ranby Road but it had no infant department, so my first school was Hunter's Bar. It took its name from the last of the turnpikes in Sheffield, and one of the things we were told was that the entrance to neighbouring Endcliffe Park was guarded by the two stone posts across which the bar was slung when tolls were exacted from traffic coming into Sheffield. My clearest recollection of Hunter's Bar School is of the excruciating noise of slate pencils on pieces of slate set in a wooden frame, one of which was issued to each pupil. Each slate had sets of three horizontal lines, and on these we learned a strict drill of letter-forming. From slates we graduated to paper similarly marked, and we were issued with pens with steel nibs and a little inkwell to lodge in a hole in the right-hand corner of the top surface of the desk. There I learned reading, writing and elementary arithmetic, but what fascinated me most was a blackboard round the room, between three and six feet from the floor. Some enterprising teacher had made it a pageant of English history, beginning with the English tribes, then their Roman conquerors, and so on down the ages, culminating at the end of the third side of the room with an aeroplane. It would have been a delight to have had all this explained by the charming Mrs Winter, but alas she was preoccupied with the much more mundane teaching of over sixty children.

The two or three years I spent in this school were punctuated by an event which for me is particularly memorable. Being conducted by my mother to school, I slipped on a banana skin and hurt my left arm. In due course I was taken to the doctor because it was so painful, and he referred us to the Children's Hospital. They said that it might be broken, so we were then dispatched to the Sheffield Royal Infirmary. This was housed in several lovely buildings erected around the end of the eighteenth and the beginning of the nineteenth centuries, but to my eyes they were all black with dirt and the reception was abominable. We were herded like felons onto low benches and called in turn. I was only five at the time and I can recall holding my mother's hand very firmly until it was my turn to be X-rayed. I was taken into a room and made to sit down against a table, on which was placed a glass plate in dark paper. I was instructed to put my left arm on the plate and, to stop me fiddling about, my hand was weighed down with a sandbag. Then a nurse positioned over my arm what appeared to be a large glass bulb, suspended from an overhead gantry, with some protuberances a bit like a cow's udders. Looking back, I recognise this was a modified Crookes tube, descended from the tube which Wilhelm Konrad Roentgen had shown just twenty-five years earlier could emit X-rays when activated by a discharge through the attenuated gas. The nurse went behind what appeared to be a glass screen, pulled a switch, there was a slight noise, and it was all over. From my vantage point of chairman of the National Radiological Protection Board some sixty years later, I do not think I would have approved the arrangement from the point of view of health and safety! A break in my elbow was duly identified, and quickly mended itself.

A couple of years later I was transferred to the school at the top of Ranby Road, called Greystones School. Like its name, and like Hunter's Bar, it was constructed of grey stone and had a large schoolyard in which games were played. I have only two outstanding memories of this school, both associated with the headmaster, whose signature I can see now – Chas. T. Gould – a man of less than benign appearance and a strict disciplinarian. From him I received repeated canings for unpunctuality and talking in class, and a severe caning when it was discovered that I was doing homework for other pupils for a modest fee – generally in kind, for example, an apple. At that time to do this seemed to me to be perfectly natural and in no way immoral. Nowadays, I suppose there would be some who would positively approve of the introduction of the market-place philosophy into the primary school classroom.

My performance in this school was variable. I knew this from the fact that if one did well one occupied a desk at the back of the class, but if one did badly one was moved to the front, so the teacher could keep a closer eye on the work being done. I seemed to oscillate from day to day between the front and back rows. Fortunately for me the source of the trouble was identified at a medical inspection, when it was found that I was shortsighted. This accounted for the fact that I could answer dictated questions correctly, but when sitting at the back had some difficulty with those written on the board.

There was only one good thing about this school, and it was that for one afternoon a week we travelled over the hill through Bingham Park to Nether Green School, which had a basement room fitted out as a laboratory. There I was introduced to the pneumatic trough and saw an experiment in which a teacher transferred a piece of glowing white phosphorus in a deflagrating spoon into the air space above the water, and I observed the glow die out after the water had moved up one-fifth of the volume. This was the clearest possible demonstration that air was not a single substance; that one-fifth of it could react with phosphorus and the remainder not. Many other interesting experiments were performed there, making the walk home less wearisome as I had so much to think about.

In May 1925 I took a written test in arithmetic and English known as the Scholarship Examination, which was for those children whose parents wished them to go on to a secondary school. I had little notion of what this meant, other than leaving Greystones School and being asked whether I would like to put the Central Secondary School ahead of Firth Park Grammar School and King Edward VII School. Since I knew nothing about any of them, the matter was settled for me and the Central School was placed first, although King Edward's would have been closer to home. Fortunately for me, I was accepted for my first school; and was also given an Ecclesall Bierlow Scholarship of a few pounds a year.

In September 1925, still aged ten, I began as a pupil at the Central Secondary School for Boys in the centre of the city. It was an event that was to shape my life. It is ironical that the Forster Education Act of 1870, which came too late to allow my father to have much education, was the Act which led to the establishment of the school I was to attend with so much pleasure and profit.

The Central Secondary School, Sheffield

When the Forster Education Act was passed, largely due to the unremitting pressure of A.J. Mundella (the far-sighted radical MP for Sheffield Brightside), the first chairman of the Sheffield School Board, Sir John Brown, a steelmaster and churchman, promoted the formation of Central Higher Grade Schools, to which able pupils from the elementary schools could go to receive a sound scientific and technical education. Mundella added his weight to this cause, and the idea was to place the new school adjacent to the site where another steelmaster, Mark Firth, imbued with Methodism's notion of self-improvement, proposed to construct a University College (which later developed into the University of Sheffield). In this way there could be a natural progression up the ladder, from free elementary education via higher grade elementary education to university level. This notion ignored the fact that higher grade elementary education was supposed to stop at fifteen years of age. The decision of the School Board was therefore one in which they exceeded their legal powers, but this did not make them hide their light under a bushel. On the contrary, the school was opened on 10 July 1880 by the Education Minister of the day with a good deal of pomp and ceremony, and the attendance of local and national notables, including the Archbishop of Canterbury.[3]

The school got off to a fine start, appointing as the first headmaster Alexander McBean, assisted by a staff of eleven masters and four mistresses. The flavour of the school, its effectiveness and its ethos is best given by the following quotation from a piece by an anonymous writer in the school magazine, *The Sheaf*, of March 1930, when the Golden Jubilee was celebrated. He wrote:

> They [the Sheffield School Board] were successful in their search for the right kind of headmaster. The appointment of Mr Alexander McBean was fully justified by the results. I remember him as a tall, burly Scot with sandy hair and beard. His personal demeanour gained for him the respect of pupils and staff. To many of the more sensitive boys, including myself, a feeling of awe was added. His roughish hair and beard and his commanding personality gave him a Rob-Roy-ish appearance, although his build was somewhat of the heavy and bulky type. However, his broad, freckled features were often lit up by a smile which reflected his good nature and good humour. He introduced the 'tawse' – a broad leather strap with one end cut into strips – an implement of punishment brought over from Scotland...
>
> Mr McBean was a fine disciplinarian, and the school made good progress under his direction. We certainly felt his loss when he was elected head of the famous Heriot's School in Edinburgh. He was 'canny' enough, sometime later, to send for Mr Cash, one of the assistant masters who was an exceptionally capable man, exceedingly popular with the boys. Mr Cash had been a Volunteer, was as straight as a ramrod and was looked up to in more ways than one (he was over six feet tall), and we delight to talk of him to this day. It was he who started the Rambling Club. Mr Cash made a great reputation in Scotland, where he resided until his death.

---

3. No history of the school has been written, but the *Sheffield Morning Telegraph* printed a special supplement on 21 March 1980, to mark the school's centenary.

Mr McBean was succeeded by Mr Arthur Newell, who had already made a name for himself in Birmingham. Our own Central School, of which we Old Boys are all so proud, was even in those days visited by many distinguished men: Cabinet Ministers, Members of Parliament, and foreign visitors were constantly being trotted round to see what a fine lot of lads we were, and incidentally to learn something of Sheffield's up-to-date administration of higher elementary education.

Mr Newell was of a type absolutely different from that of Mr McBean. He was from Yorkshire where his father had been a schoolmaster. However, he showed no trace of Yorkshire accent or mannerisms. When he came to us he had, though only forty years of age, a white head and beard. He was a tall, handsome and scholarly man, who at once made an impression in Sheffield. He showed an active interest in cricket and football, and encouraged Mr Cash to get the older boys into the country on Saturday afternoon. He developed the 'English' side of the school's curriculum, taking a special interest in the Debating Society. In short the school made considerable progress...

The importance of science as a part of the education of young people was quite naturally recognised by steelmasters such as Sir John Brown, and from the outset accommodation was provided in the school for a workshop and a chemical laboratory. Indeed, by 1885 the whole ground floor had become a technical school, which was so admired by the Royal Commission on Technical Instruction that it reported that the Central Higher Grade School was 'the finest thing of its kind in the country'. Assisted by the provisions of the Technical Instruction Act of 1889, the Town Council was able to subsidise technical and scientific education by diverting the product of a penny rate ('whisky money'), and the School Board set about extending its provision. New laboratories and workshops were also resourced through sponsorship by local manufacturers.

In 1898 the School Board appointed as Principal J.W. Iliffe, a lecturer from Cambridge who remained headmaster for twenty-four years. Soon after he was appointed the inclusion of a science department in an elementary school was declared illegal under the 'Casperton Judgement', and the position of the school became precarious. Happily Sir John Gorst MP, the last Vice-President of the Committee of the Privy Council on Education, was anxious to encourage the school to have a perfectly free hand in drawing up its own curriculum, the standard of which could be as high as the school could make it; and Michael Sadler, then Professor of Education in Manchester, who had been invited by nine local authorities to investigate secondary education, recommended that the school should be granted secondary school status. This became effective in September 1904. Within a few years the higher grade and higher elementary school functions had disappeared and there remained the secondary school with 30 to 35 in a form, just half the numbers that were permitted in higher grade schools. The institution flourished, numbers increased and it was decided to hive off the girls into a separate school. Mr Iliffe had a striking personality and a belief that everything was possible, which was communicated to the senior pupils. It was not long before A.L. Atkin secured an open scholarship to St John's College, Oxford, and from then on school pupils frequently won open awards at both Oxford and Cambridge. The local University of Sheffield was not neglected either, as is shown by the fact that up to the year 1922 every Sheffield graduate in the honours school of mathematics was an old boy of the Central Secondary School.

A Central Secondary School Boy, 1925–33

In September 1925, when I entered the school, it had been so successful it had already outgrown its original buildings. All the first year and two forms of the second year were accommodated in the Quaker Meeting House at nearby Hartshead, which was most unsatisfactory for this purpose. But the deficiencies did not matter, because of the quality of the masters who taught us and the sense of purpose they brought to their work, as well as the standards that they expected the pupils to attain. The staff of the school were very able, partly because jobs for graduates were hard to come by and a teaching post was highly prized, but also because some of the facilities of the main school were quite remarkable. There was a tiered physics lecture theatre and two physics laboratories; a tiered chemistry lecture theatre and three chemistry laboratories; a biology laboratory; a room where geology could be taught; a raked machine drawing lecture theatre and a practice room; and metal and woodwork shops. We were also encouraged to make our own apparatus. Another attraction of the school for well-qualified, capable staff was that they might augment their income by teaching part-time students at night school for external degrees of London University. It is no surprise that the staff included two PhDs, several MScs and an LLB. The headmaster in my time, W.I. Moore, had MA, BSc and DLitt degrees. One master, J.M. Brown, himself an old boy of the school, was renowned for his entomological researches and his classes were notable for their absolute quiet, because of the way in which he interested the boys. I will allow myself three examples of how I was treated, each of which had a powerful effect on my attitude to life.

In 1926 it became evident that there was a strong likelihood of a general strike, and if that were to happen then the school would be closed because many boys came from far afield. The geography master, Mr Campbell, addressed me in these words: 'Dainton, I see in you all the signs of incipient idleness. I am particularly anxious that you shall not waste your time if there is a general strike, and therefore I would ask you to map out whatever interesting features you can find in the Porter valley.' The Porter valley was, as I have mentioned, adjacent to where I lived, at least in its lower reaches. There was indeed a strike and I spent the time happily mapping out all the dams and the one working water-driven mill that still remained. With the aid of the public reference library, I was also able to identify the house owned by Thomas Boulsover, the inventor of Sheffield plate in 1742. This discovery not only added to my interest in the history of Sheffield but also gave me an insight into the craft of silversmithing.

The second example occurred a year later. It had been predicted that there would be an eclipse of the sun by the moon which could be seen from the Yorkshire Dales. The school decided to have an excursion for those who were interested. Each boy had first to make a soot-darkened glass plate to protect his eyes while looking directly at the sun. The day came when we were walking up Ingleborough in the West Riding, but alas the golden orb was already obscured by cloud. However, that did not diminish the impressive effect of the actual eclipse itself. It was not so much that the world darkened for some minutes but that the darkening was accompanied by complete silence. It seemed as if the animals were equally stupefied by the extraordinary nature of the eclipse. Perhaps of greater importance was that we came down from Ingleborough via the perched blocks of Norber. These strangely shaped rocks were formed of blocks of Silurian slates and grits brought down from the Lake District by advancing ice, and left there stranded on a limestone base. They had then become toadstool-like by the erosive action of the soft rainwater dissolving the supporting calcium carbonate, except where the cap gave shelter. The explanation of this phenomenon given to me by Mr Campbell, the same man who had set me off looking into the history of the Porter valley, also gave me a lifelong interest in geomorphology.

The third example came from the sixth form, when I was asked whether I would like to make some cysteine, a compound which can be obtained by the hydrolysis of keratin. Since it was said to be important biologically I accepted the challenge, but was a little taken aback when I was told that the first thing I had to do was go round barbers' shops and collect two sacks full of hair clippings. Over the next six weeks I managed to acquire the requisite amount of material, and in due course ended up with some pristine crystals. The master sent them to the university for microanalysis, and it was accepted that I had achieved the objective. To this day I can remember the feeling of personal triumph: here was I, probably the only boy in the city of Sheffield who had seen, let alone made, pure cysteine! I was in fact enjoying a foretaste of the delights of discovery.

Much happened at school outside formal teaching. There were numerous societies in which senior boys and masters met on more or less equal terms. These included activities like chess, debating, science, natural history and rambling, a literary and debating society, and, most important of all because of the time it took up, a Shakespeare Society. This remarkable society staged a five-day performance of a Shakespeare play in the school hall just before Christmas each year. Rehearsals took place after school every Friday until the production began, but every minute was worth it in terms of pleasure, companionship and an introduction to the Bard's writing. For these rewards I was willing to walk to and from school, a combined distance of five miles, five days a week, thereby saving fivepence in old money, which was the cost of a hot supper in the school canteen on Friday night.

As my life became more centred on the school and its extramural activities, inevitably it became less focused on home; and the narrow regime of Sunday, especially attendance at Banner Cross chapel, began to lose its appeal. There was little I could do about the latter without giving unnecessary offence to my parents, and so I said nothing about my doubts in relation to Christian belief. In any case, more pressing circumstances were arising. The first was external in the form of the Wall Street Crash, which initiated a worldwide depression, this in turn having a devastating effect on employment in the manufacturing industries of Britain. Then in September 1930 my father died in the third year of his retirement, at the age of 73. The cause of his death was carcinoma of the stomach. During August he went downhill very rapidly and an effect of the disease on him was to warp his attitude, so that he could not bear his wife to see him in his deteriorating condition. As a result I was the one who had to do some of the elementary nursing tasks associated with the advanced state of his illness, until a week before his death when he was finally admitted to hospital.

The time I spent caring for my father left its mark on me, and I felt I could not go back to school. I would have to seek employment. One of my sisters drew my attention to an opportunity to become a bank clerk at 26 shillings a week (£1.30), hardly riches beyond the dreams of avarice but worthwhile having until we knew what the financial situation was going to be like. About ten weeks after I had begun work my mother received a letter from the headmaster of my school to say that a small sum had been found from a charity, and this could be mine if I would come back to school. My mother insisted that I should do so, and she decided that we could manage if a second allotment was taken on. She proposed to work the allotment herself, notwithstanding the fact that she was 57 years old. This state of affairs only continued for a year, because by that time lawyers had decided that everything my father had left was to be my mother's, and she concluded that one allotment would be sufficient for our needs. I often wonder what would have happened to me if the decision to return to school had not been taken. When I look at my subsequent career in the light of that fact, I realise how much I owe to the farsightedness and generosity of my mother at that difficult time.

In the early 1930s the depression appeared to gather momentum in Sheffield, and I can remember the tell-tale signs as small knots of men gathered at street corners with nothing to do. If it was raining I would see in the reading room of the public library more of these men, who seemed to have about them an aura of utter despair. Nor was my own family immune from the effects of the depression. As I have already mentioned, my next eldest brother Ernest was made redundant by the English Steel Corporation, a most serious blow for a newly married man whose wife was not working because of the principle of not employing married women as teachers, however well qualified they were.

We had always lived frugally at home and the belts were tightened a little more, but I do not recall any sense of personal deprivation. In part this was due to the fact that my mother, elder brother and two sisters never wavered in their belief that continuation at school was the right thing to do. Expediency was also part of our lifestyle: for instance, walking to and from school meant that after two terms I had saved about ten shillings (50p) – not a negligible sum in those days. Although holidays of the kind we had taken when my father was alive were out of the question, school trips were not barren of enjoyment. At Whitsuntide the school organised a camp for a week at Howstrake near Groudle Glen, north of Douglas in the Isle of Man. For a very small cost we travelled by train to Liverpool and then boarded an Isle of Man steam packet boat to Douglas, after which we enjoyed a week of sailing, swimming, walking and other communal activities.

Anglo-German Friendship Schools

During those last few school years I came to know the White and Dark Peaks of Derbyshire much better, reaching them either on foot or on a bicycle borrowed from my brother. Often this was in company with schoolfriends and the question which we constantly discussed, because it was prompted by the evident misery engendered by unemployment, was how political systems could deal with these matters in a better way. For me there was suddenly a new light shed on European politics. This arose from the fact that at the end of the first year at school I was asked whether I wished to study Latin or German as a second language, alongside French. I chose German, for reasons that I cannot now remember, but again it proved to be a wise choice. Not only did I enjoy it, but it enabled me to become one of twenty Sheffield sixth-form boys chosen to live with twenty German boys of similar age during the summer holidays in Anglo-German summer schools, held either in Sheffield or in the small village of Hohenlychen, 100 kilometres north of Berlin amid the Brandenburger Lakes. I believe the concept was the brainchild of Dr Lloyd Storr-Best, a linguist who was headmaster of Firth Park Grammar School, and he persuaded the Magistrat of Berlin and the City Council of Sheffield to underwrite all the expenses of the scheme. It was hoped that by living and working together the boys would benefit both linguistically and culturally, and thereby enhance Anglo-German understanding. I was fortunate enough to attend one school in Sheffield, and the following year one in Germany.

I can vouch for the fact that the schools had their intended effect on us, as far as personal relationships were concerned. We became friends with our overseas colleagues, and many of us corresponded with the German boys in later years. The experience in Germany also had an unintended outcome. My memories are particularly sharp because it was my first journey out of the United Kingdom and, from the moment of getting on the boat at Parkeston Quay at Harwich, I was especially watchful of everything that happened. I can still remember many of the details of the journey by rail through Holland and Germany, and our late arrival in Berlin, where we stayed overnight before making a three-hour bus trip the following morning. For that part of the journey we drove through delightful forests, rather like the Breckland, and round the shores of numerous shallow lakes. Our first surprise was to be met not by a group of German boys but by forty girls, half of them French, half of them German, who were attending a Franco-German summer school nearby. After disembarkation we went across to an island in the centre of the lake. It was here that we met twenty German boys and three German masters, at a sanatorium which was to be our home.

On the next day no time was lost in getting down to work, which in the morning comprised a pre-breakfast swim followed by two hours of language study, one of physical training and one of singing English and German songs. The afternoons were free, but unless there was an excursion planned we stayed on the island reading, writing or even playing games. I got to know the oarsman who ferried the passengers over to the mainland quite well, because he had been a prisoner of war in England in the First World War: just as I liked to practise my German, he liked to resurrect his English. The German boys seemed exceptionally strong swimmers and oarsmen and they were all tanned by the sun, so that we looked weak, puny, white-skinned townees by comparison. However, we proved to be much better at team games than they were. The first excursion, which I think was to Warnemünde on the Baltic coast, nearly began in disaster. We were ferried over to the mainland in small numbers and told to wait until the party was complete, which we duly did, but we were quite unprepared for the action of the gym master (Turnlehrer) who wanted us to march along two by two singing soldiers' songs, such as:

> Wann wir schreiten Seit' an Seit'
> und die alten Lieder singen,
> und die Wälder widerklingen,
> fühlen wir, es muss gelinge
> Mit uns zieht die neue Zeit.[4]

---

4. This can be translated along the lines of 'When we march side by side and sing the old songs, and the woods reflect them back, we feel success is sure; with us the new age is coming.'

The English boys mutinied, thereby generating near apoplexy in the Turnlehrer. But we won our point. As the days sped by it became clearer to us that this teacher was very likely a Nazi: I think this was perceived by the English masters with us, who shared our dislike of him.

A three-day visit to Berlin was planned so that we might see notable buildings like the Palace of Sans Souci, the airport at Tempelhof, the Ufa-Palast am Zoo and the Allgemeine Elektrische Gesellschaft, the equivalent of the British General Electric Company. All were most interesting and enjoyable experiences. However, on the first evening we English boys wanted to go out after dinner to see the lights of the Kurfürstendamm and, if possible, to ascend the Rundfunkturm (the tall radio mast). The Turnlehrer forbade this, insisting that we must be in bed by 9.15pm. However, we were ready for him and duly complied with the instruction, so that just before 9.15 we were all safely tucked up in our beds in the youth hostel, and at 9.15 precisely we all rose fully dressed and walked out past the Turnlehrer, bidding him good evening. He was speechless. After that life was never the same between us, although we returned in good order well before 11pm, in conformity with the rules of the youth hostel. His reaction was to try to institute some form of punishment, and I am afraid that this led to lengthy confabulation between the English and German masters until some kind of agreement on disciplinary matters was worked out. The German boys, who were somewhat older than us, were amazed by our behaviour. Despite the fact that they were, in many ways, more mature intellectually, they appeared to accept rules without question.

Travelling round Berlin in those three days was not a cheerful experience, because of the graffiti all over the walls. I well remember 'Juden raus' (Jews get out), 'Deutschland erwache' (Germany awake) and others in a similar vein. We got the message. But that message was rammed home to me in a particularly disagreeable way. I wished to take home a few presents for my family, and one of the German boys said that his sister would assist with the shopping expedition. She was extremely helpful and took me to a department store in the district of Neukölln. I am very easily bored by shopping and was looking out of a window on the third floor when, on the other side of the road, I saw people emerging from what appeared to be an office block and running in terror through two lines of brown-shirts, who were beating them unmercifully with short sticks. Parked close by was a Berlin police lorry, out of which policemen had climbed in their characteristic greenish uniforms, equipped with all the means they needed to disperse these bullies; yet they stood by doing nothing while this brutality was perpetrated.

These events radicalised one young English sixth former, and I suspect many more. They were very much the topic of our conversations on returning home, and I read the news bulletins in the papers with more understanding than I would have done if I had not been to Germany. I was convinced that if Hitler came to power he would have to be stopped. The failure of the British and French governments to bar him when he marched into the Rhineland in March 1936, when they had the military power to do so, and then not to make proper objection when his 'Condor Legion' assisted the rebels in Spain and his air force destroyed the Basque town of Guernica, reinforced my radical views. I became convinced that the British and the French governments either were not serious about opposing Hitler, Mussolini and Franco, or were totally unprepared militarily.

A Sixth Former Choosing a Future

On my return to school in the autumn I found I had become a prefect. The sixth form was divided into two sections – VI Science and VI Modern – but these divisions did not betoken a narrow curriculum. For my own part, I studied maths, additional maths, physics and chemistry at what would now be called A-level (and was then called Principal Level of the Higher School Certificate), and also English, French and German as subsidiary subjects. In addition, we had discussion periods in which plays were read, issues were thrashed out and there was plenty of time for debate; half a day a week was spent at the playing fields. That breadth of curriculum was something I hoped to achieve later for others, through the committee I chaired into the flow of science candidates into higher education, which in 1968 produced government paper Cmnd. 3541, known colloquially as the 'Dainton Report on the Swing Away from Science'. But it seems that what the secondary schools thought suitable over sixty years ago was too far advanced for the educationalists and political masters of the 1960s or, for that matter, today.

By this time I was clear that I would like to go to a university, and I therefore had to choose what subject I wanted to read. That question was settled for me in a rather curious way. First and foremost was the influence of my friends. I was immensely impressed with the erudition of a schoolfriend named F.J. McQuillin, who won an open scholarship to Christ Church, Oxford, and ultimately became a professor in the University of Newcastle upon Tyne. More important, I think, was the fact that with the exception of nuclear physics, which was developing in an exciting way at Cambridge, physics appeared to be really about as dead as one could imagine. Everything seemed predictable on the basis of classical ideas (and I think now how wrong I was!). The only thing that could be said about heat, magnetism, properties of matter and mechanics was that they were laid out quite adequately in the textbooks. Chemistry, on the other hand, seemed at that time to have an enormous number of unexplained phenomena, and to be a much more interesting subject to pursue.

Unfortunately for me, as I entered the second year of the sixth form we had a new senior chemistry master named Percy Lord, who came to Sheffield from a school in Oldham. Despite a first class honours degree in chemistry at Manchester University, he had minimal understanding and even less interest in the subject. I suppose he could not have been actually unintelligent, but he was very cynical and if asked an awkward question he would give a reply that was inadequate and dismiss the matter. Perhaps it is not without significance that he ultimately became the rather undistinguished Chief Education Officer for Lancashire, and was knighted![5] I therefore cut his lessons and instead went along to my temple of knowledge, the Public Reference Library in Surrey Street, some three minutes' walk from the school. My absences naturally led me into some conflicts with school authority, but I survived these and the most important benefit, outweighing all the disadvantages, was that I came across two books which made me determined to go to Oxford to read chemistry. The first was the 1929 edition of Sidgwick's *Electronic Theory of Valency,* which made sense of the periodic table and a great deal of inorganic chemistry which for me had previously been rote learning. The second was Hinshelwood's *Kinetics of Chemical Change in Gaseous Systems.* I think it was the second edition and it seemed to me to link together for the first time, on the one hand the fact that we knew that molecules moved about in gases and liquids, and,

---

5. My only later encounter with Percy Lord was in the early 1960s when, as Chief Education Officer for Lancashire, he came to give evidence before the planning committee for the new University of Lancaster, of which I was a member. His paper, and his presentation of it, made a singularly unfavourable impression upon the committee. I recall with pleasure his ill-disguised shock and irritation on being questioned once again by his erstwhile pupil.

on the other hand, that they had to meet one another if they were going to react. I did not fully understand Hinshelwood's book at the time, but the fact that both men wrote so well and were at Oxford made me feel that this would be the right place for me. The future was beginning to take shape.

Percy Lord gave me absolutely no encouragement, and used his sarcastic tongue to hide his ignorance of Oxford chemistry. Fortunately, however, the school had also appointed another first class honours graduate of Manchester University to teach chemistry: he was Alfred (Alf) E. Ridler, a man of an entirely different character. He was genuinely interested in his subject and devoid of personal ambition: if one asked him for an explanation and he could not give an answer he would say 'I don't know. Let us try to find out.' So I caught the spirit of enquiry from him. He became a lifelong friend, who to my delight was one of the guests at a splendid dinner given by the University of Sheffield in 1994 to celebrate my eightieth birthday. Alas, illness prevented me from joining his ninetieth birthday celebrations at the end of October 1995.

To go to Oxford required money, and that meant I must secure either a State Scholarship or a college award, or preferably both. The second week of December 1932 therefore saw me travelling by train to Oxford, where I was accommodated at Christ Church in huge rooms in the Meadow Building, a place such as I had never dared to dream about. The theoretical papers were taken in University College Hall, starting at 9.30am and broken by coffee brought in at 11am and tea at 3.30pm. Practical examinations were in laboratories which seemed to me to be inferior to those at school. I was absolutely stunned by the beauty of Oxford and I spent most of the time immediately after lunch wandering round the colleges on my way to the afternoon paper at University College. If, as seemed likely, this was to be my one and only visit to Oxford, I felt I must use any available hours of daylight to visit as many of the colleges as possible. I therefore decided to take the last direct train back to Sheffield, which left Oxford about 7pm on Saturday, and spent all the time after what I thought was the last paper on Saturday morning just walking about and letting the beauty of Oxford in the weak winter sunshine work its magic on me. It did, and I boarded the train with my mind full of pleasurable thoughts. However, my daydreams were shattered when, as the train drew out of Banbury station, I began to look at the question papers I had been set and the instructions I had been given. Perusing the latter, I discovered to my horror that there was an additional mathematics paper scheduled for Saturday afternoon. It was optional, but I had elected to take it, and I had missed it. All my hopes were dashed. The more I tried to think of ways in which the obvious consequence of this lapse on my part might be avoided, the more I became convinced of the impossibility of doing so. I could not tell my mother and family that, by my own folly, I had destroyed any prospect of success; and I knew that I could not ask for more money for rail fares to have a second chance in March, for another group of colleges.

The next ten days at home and at school were agony, repeatedly brought to a focus as my friends asked me how I had fared in the examinations. I distracted myself by filling my time at school with the innumerable small but necessary chores which fell to my lot as the Honorary Secretary of the Shakespeare Society, in preparation for a performance of *Macbeth* scheduled for the week before Christmas. Then, ten days after my return from Oxford, there arrived a letter from Mr A.L. Poole, Senior Tutor of St John's College, informing me that I had been elected to an Open Exhibition of value £80 per annum, but also that in order to be admitted to the University of Oxford I must gain exemption from something called 'Responsions' by passing an examination in Latin, a language of which I knew not a syllable. He added that the entrance fee for this examination would be £1 10s and that it would be advantageous if I would also take the Preliminary Examination in Science before coming into residence the following October, and concluded with the dates of these examinations. The following day I received similar information from Claude Gordon Douglas, described as Tutor in Natural Sciences, who turned out to be a charming and well-known respiratory physiologist and inventor of the 'Douglas bag'. This news seemed little short of miraculous and in my euphoric state I took the duplication of information to signify a warm welcome to St John's, rather than administrative inefficiency, a conclusion which my later acquaintance with both men was to prove correct.

I did not answer these letters immediately, because I was aware that £80 per annum was insufficient and that other resources had to be found; so I immediately applied to the City of Sheffield Education Department for assistance. After a long delay I was awarded a £40 grant and a £40 loan per annum. Anxious to ensure that its loan, which over four years of study would come to £160, was not at risk whatever happened to me, the Education Department required me to take out an endowment insurance policy for this amount, which would mature in fifteen years.

The annual premium of £10 5s 11d is permanently engraved in my memory, because it inevitably reduced the cash available to me from Sheffield, from £80 to £69 14s 1d – beaurocratic meanness that has rankled ever since. Somewhat unsure as to whether £150 per annum would be sufficient, but arguing that for twenty-four weeks of actual residence in Oxford each year it represented roughly £6 per week, and further reflecting that on retirement in 1927 my father's weekly wage was £7 and that had proved sufficient for a household of five, I felt I was justified in accepting. Reaching this decision took a few months, which meant that my replies to the Tutor and Senior Tutor were delayed and I could not be a candidate for the Responsions Latin examination in the following March.

The Shakespeare Society

A second and less substantial reason for procrastination was my preoccupation with the affairs of the school's Shakespeare Society, which formed an important element in the life of the school. The Central Secondary School for Boys Shakespeare Society was founded in 1907. It met after school hours on Friday evenings under the leadership of W.B. (Benny) Marshman, a geography master who had a remarkable flair for infecting others with his own enthusiasm. The first play given in the school hall was *A Midsummer Night's Dream* in December 1909. Thenceforth the Society's Christmas plays became an important annual event in the life of the city, and had a great effect on the school.

I can do no better than quote from the book *All Right on the Night*, edited by G.W. Keeton, an old boy of the school and later the distinguished head of the Department of Law at University College, London. This book was published in 1929 to mark the coming of age of the Society, and the headmaster of the time, Dr W.I. Moore, wrote a piece entitled 'The Society as I knew it'. In it he described how, as a new incumbent unaware of the activities of the Society during his first term in 1923, he was captivated by the performance of *Twelfth Night*, being increasingly impressed as the play progressed 'by the skill shown in production, by the high level of acting and diction, by the light-hearted earnestness with which all and sundry worked with a will to make the play the success it was'. He quietly joined the enthusiasts. Later in his article he asked how it was done, and to my mind gave himself a true answer. I quote:

The answer was simple – Mr Marshman – Mr Marshman who knew what he wanted, whose enthusiasm for Shakespeare and genius for play production and for inculcating a spirit of good fellowship have made the Society what it is. Nothing was too much trouble for him. Only those behind the scenes knew of the labour put into, say, *Othello*, before production could even be thought of. No detail was too small for his consideration, no minor enthusiast too small for a kindly word of encouragement, no pompous incompetent too august to be the butt of his happy, nimble wit. In public he 'ragged' the members one and all; in private he never tired of singing their praises. He made them work as they had (many of them) never worked before; and they loved him for it and asked for more. That was how it was done.

He then expatiated on the Society's service to the school and the city, and said of the former: 'It has been the means of binding its members for over twenty years into a fellowship, the fellowship of those who have served disinterestedly to achieve an ideal and a corporate aim – the study of Shakespeare and the production of next year's play. The Society as I knew it had become the most potent factor in the social life of the school. It demanded real service of its members and they acquired, in return, that feeling of confident comradeship which only service freely rendered for a common cause can give.'

I joined the Society in 1925 as a humble violinist in the orchestra, when the play *Richard II* was produced on the nights of 18 to 23 December inclusive. I remained a member until I left school, never having a speaking part but much involved in jobs such as stage manager and electrician until finally, in 1932, I became Honorary Secretary. I was amused to find that there was a strictly observed convention concerning this office, in that all correspondence to me began 'Dear Mr Secretary'. Like my predecessors, I found such an archaism quite pleasing. The play that year was *Macbeth*, and the amount of work that had to be undertaken by the office holders was prodigious. A stage with proscenium arch and an apron complete with arrangements for curtains, scenery changes and lighting had to be constructed at the eastern end of the school hall. I still have the Stage Manager's Book which gives details of the procedures to be followed for the whole process. It bears on its cover two maxims: 'Experience teaches fools to be wise' and 'Experience is by industry achieved; and perfected by the swift course of time'. (The latter comes, appropriately enough, from *Two Gentlemen of Verona*, a play my knowledge of which was to come to my aid in a difficult interview in 1937 with Sir

Cyril Norwood, the President of St John's College, Oxford.) Costumes had to be ordered from theatrical outfitters for the actors, and this was the one area in which masculinity had to give way to the superior knowledge of women: a female wardrobe mistress and helpers had to be recruited to help us in this task.

Correspondence was vast and much of it was handwritten by the Honorary Secretary who, among his duties, had to secure an exemption by HM Customs and Excise from the otherwise statutory requirement to pay an entertainments fee. Membership cards and programmes had to be devised, printed and distributed; letters had to be written to prominent citizens of South Yorkshire and North Derbyshire, inviting their attendance (these invitations frequently being accepted), and to many tradesmen. Bills had to be paid and accounts kept. The range of transactions is evident from the stubs in the cheque books of the Society for 1929, 1930 and 1931 which I still have. Management of sales of complimentary tickets, of lowest-price tickets to schoolboys, of adult unreserved tickets and of higher-priced reserved tickets was quite a complicated business: there was an attendance of about 2,000, spread over five nights. The income was of the order of £100, the equivalent of several thousand pounds today, and every penny had to be accounted for. These were only a few of the essential tasks, which had of course to be fitted in alongside ordinary school studies. That this complicated system worked within a matter of twelve weeks was a tribute, as Dr Moore has recorded, to the colourful Benny Marshman and the ability and devotion of successive generations of members of the Society, for whom it was not only a powerful educative experience but also the source of some lifelong friendships.

A characteristic of the Society was that it was not just inward-looking and merely school-oriented. Having accumulated some financial resources, it had inaugurated an annual Shakespeare Festival on the Bard's birthday. This was open to the public, originally in the Victoria Hall and latterly in the City Hall's Memorial Hall. The programme included performances and readings from Shakespeare's works, music associated with him and an address by a national figure. Among those speakers I remember the writers and dramatists Alfred Noyes, Laurence Housman, and R.C. Sherriff – whose play *Journey's End*, based on his experiences in the trenches during the First World War, was an immense success and a useful corrective to the absurd romantic notions of the soldier's life still common amongst those who had not actually fought. He spoke with great modesty, whereas Hilaire Belloc gave a speech which matched in flamboyance and self-centredness the honorary doctor's red robe which he chose to wear. One of the remaining cheque stubs shows that Mr Sherriff was paid thirty guineas for his services.

Towards the end of the school year 1932-33 I was summoned to a meeting with the headmaster, Luther Smith, the successor to Dr Moore and himself an old boy of the school, who, according to his eulogistic entry in *All Right on the Night*, was an admirer of the Society. He announced baldly that the Society would have to close forthwith. I was flabbergasted. When I had recovered a little of my composure I asked why, to which he gave the feeble response that the school would be moving to a new building in a suburb during the approaching vacation. This I knew, but it did not seem to be an adequate reason for terminating a society which had given so much to the school, and if allowed would continue to do so. Moreover, I was aware that the school's new buildings would contain a large hall with a permanent stage, very well suited to theatricals. The headmaster then demanded that I hand over the cash balance standing in the Society's account at the Yorkshire Penny Bank, a request which I could not accept – not least because financial transactions required the signature of another person whom I must consult. I also could not see how, if the Society had had this account over so many years, the school could claim title to its financial assets; so I asked leave to think about the matter, and also to consult Mr Marshman. The latter was intensely irritated, as well he might be in the light of his 25 years of devoted service, including a notable contribution after he had retired. I do not know, but I suspect that there was a hidden reason behind Mr Smith's attitude. It might simply have been the not uncommon envy which smaller men frequently have for those of larger personality.

In this situation there was very little I could do but play for time, claiming preoccupation with my imminent Responsions and Higher School Certificate examinations, but I knew the headmaster had the whip hand because he would have complete control over the uses to which accommodation in the new school could be put. In the end, after I had gone to Oxford but through no action of mine, the matter became public. An article appeared in the *Daily Express* of 20 October 1933 under the headline 'Shakespeare Society to Die: Plays by Boys at a Famous School', which rehearsed the facts and ended by quoting Mr Marshman's regrets, also recording that the headmaster 'declined to make any statement on the matter'. *Sic transit gloria scholae!*

Farewell to School

Looking back on my years at the Central Secondary School for Boys, I have remarkably few reservations; those that I have relate to odd personalities, who are bound to be found in any large organisation. I am (and always will be) indebted to it for an excellent formal education and, through its out-of-school activities, much else besides. I have already mentioned that one of its strengths was the high quality of the staff it attracted; another was that it was an intellectually selective but socially comprehensive school. A few boys were brought in from outer suburbs by their parents' cars even seventy years ago, while at the other end of the income spectrum boys like myself would walk to save a halfpenny tram fare. But within school such differences of wealth and class had no meaning and did not inhibit friendship. I gained a great deal from such friendship, especially with boys whose homes were places of music, conversation and books.

One example of this was the Turner family. The father had come to Sheffield from Kent to work as an Admiralty Inspector; his wife, like my mother, had been in service, but in her case with the parents of the distinguished public servant Sir Stephen Tallents. The Turners had five children of whom four were boys, all in their turn pupils at the Central Secondary School. The oldest boy, like my elder brother Ernest who knew him well, took an Associateship in Metallurgy at the University of Sheffield by night-time study. The three other sons all won open awards at Cambridge colleges – Selwyn, Sidney Sussex and Peterhouse. They were a lively and welcoming family and my visits there were always memorable for music and conversation on any matter under the sun, and for long walks, especially with the youngest, Tom, with whom I was especially friendly. They enlarged my horizons immensely. So too did John Buckatzsch and his sister Marna (who was at the Central Secondary School for Girls). They were the children of two gifted people: John went up to Balliol a year after I went up to St John's and had a brilliant career, which was sadly cut short after the war by tuberculosis. I felt his loss enormously. It was all the more tragic because only a few years later therapy became available which would have saved his life.

A rather different schoolfriend who greatly enriched my life was Robert Thompson, an historian with whom I went on a memorable walking holiday at the end of my school career. We took the train to Seahouses on the Northumbrian coast, toiled along the stony beach to Bamburgh and turned inland to Wooler, where we spent an uncomfortable night in a railway station waiting room. Next day we walked up the Harthope Burn and the Cheviot, returning by interminable bog-trotting to Alnham, whence a few lifts and a bus took us south to Hexham and so by walking along Hadrian's Wall to Gilsland youth hostel. There I met a demonstrator in chemistry from Imperial College named J.S. Anderson, some seven or eight years older than I, who was to become my professorial colleague in Oxford nearly forty years later. We next went by bus via Alston to Penrith and a brief tour of the Cumbrian fells, before catching a train home from Coniston. Three things stand out in my memory. First, the average daily cost excluding fares was 3s 4½d, such a low price being made possible by the Youth Hostels Association, of which I therefore became a lifelong supporter. Secondly, I was greatly impressed by the possibilities for solitude in Northumberland's 'wilderness' country. Thirdly, and most importantly, I was fascinated by the historical and classical erudition of Robert Thompson, by which he illuminated our travels and enlarged my perceptions – for which I now offer belated but sincere thanks.

I have mentioned that my period in the sixth form coincided with the worst of the economic depression, and so our pleasures had to be cheap. Our play and exercise ground away from school was the Peak District, so easily reached on foot or on bicycle, either on solitary excursions or with the Rambling or Natural History societies. We were not alone in looking for refreshment in these hills. Many young unemployed people from the conurbations on each side of the Pennines sought an outlet for their energies in the High Peak. Some of them pioneered notably difficult gritstone and limestone climbs; and some, like Joe Brown of Sheffield, achieved international distinction for their technical skill, not just in the Peak District but in the Alps and elsewhere. However, there was one fact that irritated all my generation. This was the hostile attitude to walkers and climbers alike of some of the grouse-moor owners, including public utilities such as the Derwent Water Board, who denied access and employed gamekeepers, often augmented by casual hirelings on Saturdays and Sundays, to enforce this restriction. To us schoolboys, who felt that walking on the high tops of Bleaklow and Kinder Scout could do no more damage to either the grouse or the watercourses and reservoirs than the grouse shooting parties themselves, this situation was a natural challenge. We took pride in outsmarting the gamekeepers, and in so doing of course had to learn much about the terrain and the cover it could afford. This certainly sharpened our wits and honed our survival skills. For others it was not always thus. There were ugly encounters which caused a number of clubs to organize mass rallies and mass trespasses. Today, however, the Peak District National Park authorities have negotiated virtually unrestricted access and it is hard to see what harm can come from such innocent pleasures as walking the hills. It is another story as far as motorcycle climbs and mountain bikes are concerned.

Happily, my interest in the Peak District brought me into contact with some of the staunch pioneers of access, both men and women. One who became a friend and with whom I stayed at Edale was the charming and redoubtable Fred Heardman, in his later years owner of the Nag's Head and the Church Hotel in that hamlet. Small of stature, he was a champion among men. It was he who kept Brown, Bayley's steelworks out of delectable Edale, and he has been host to many a Pennine Way traveller over the years. One of the best days of my life was spent with him, Anthony Rowlinson (son of the Bishop of Derby and later Second Permanent Secretary at the Treasury) and the Reverend Ernest Turner (vicar of the plague village of Eyam), when we undertook a great 'grind', as Fred called it, from Edale – a splendid hike which encompassed Bleaklow and Kinder Scout.

My final year at school was a very happy one. After Christmas I was teaching myself Latin with occasional guidance from the helpful Latin teacher, Mr Russell, and I much enjoyed that language's logical structure and the insights it gave me into my own tongue. Moreover, after my battle with Percy Lord I spent a lot of time in the Public Reference Library. In this facility Sheffield was ahead of many mercantile and manufacturing cities, having established a reference and lending library at municipal expense in 1856, and in my last school year a splendid new building was being erected for it. I owe much to that library. I used it a great deal during university vacations in the next six years, and they generously accorded me a study carrel for my own use after I had successfully defended my need to the formidable City Librarian, J.P. Lamb. I am not the only member of the science side of the sixth form to sing the praises of the Public Reference Library: a few years ago Juda Hirsch Quastel FRS, the distinguished biochemist, who entered the school fifteen years before I did, sent me a reprint of Chapter 6 of *Selected Topics in the History of Biochemistry: Personal Recollections* (Elsevier, 1983). In it he wrote the following words, which express my sentiments precisely:

...the Sheffield Public Reference Library where I became one of its most frequent visitors. There I read, at my leisure, all the forbidden literature. I studied the elements of anatomy, physiology, zoology, botany, but more than this I learnt much that was known at that time about growth and reproduction, about sex and genetics. Biology became open to me in a most unexpected manner. I also found advanced textbooks of chemistry, physics and mathematics, which later I found to be of the greatest help for my scholarship examination. I began to appreciate the wonders of the arts, to learn about the great creator artists, Rembrandt, Leonardo, Michelangelo, about the scores of great writers. I dimly realised how much I had missed in my formal education at school. I owe the Sheffield Public Library a great debt which I know I cannot repay and all I can do is to acknowledge it with gratitude.

The library was advertised as being open on Sunday afternoons. Much as I would have liked to do so, I did not choose to visit it then. As I have already indicated, Banner Cross United Methodist Church and what it stood for had begun to lose its appeal and credibility. But I knew I could not cease going, and in particular resign from being a Sunday school teacher, without wounding my mother's feelings. The fact was, of course, that the range of interests at school and elsewhere which commanded my attention was inevitably diminishing the experience I shared with her. I knew I was not growing away from her in any deep emotional sense, but I could not deny that I was growing away from my home background and the lifestyle under which I had been reared. Knowing that my departure for Oxford would provide a natural excuse to make a break with the chapel, I saw no point in declaring my changed views and thereby hurting my mother's and her chapel friends' feelings. In retrospect, I think I may have made a presumptuous mistake, for she had an intuitive inner wisdom and sense which would have understood and accepted the situation. As things turned out, my intellectual position had to be disclosed to the Sunday school superintendent because he, puzzled to know why my class of eight-year-olds was so quiet and attentive, discovered that my pupils, whom I had trained to have a near perfect record in learning golden texts, were being told stories which were far from biblical. I did not deny this and he, good man that he was, agreed that a simple parting without fuss when I left Sheffield would be a solution we could both accept.

On 27 June 1933 I travelled to Oxford for the second time in order to take the Responsions Latin examination the following day. Memories of that visit were evoked recently when I came across an envelope containing a receipt, dated 29 June, for half a guinea paid by me for battels – that is, for dinner, breakfast and lunch. This was my first visit to St John's College, which had escaped my attention in the preceding December, and I revelled in the glories of the Canterbury Quad and the College gardens. They bore signs of some recent festivities which, with hindsight, I assume must have been connected with the patronal festival of St John the Baptist just three days earlier. There was another candidate sitting the Latin examination at St John's named H.K. Fowler, with whom I compared notes and with whom I was to become firm friends for life. We both passed the Responsions Latin and for me there remained only the one further hurdle of the Science Prelims, which I successfully negotiated in September. With that completed, my family began to present me with gifts, chosen for their utility rather than their beauty; for example a dressing gown, a good fountain pen, a College blazer and tie, and, the best gift of all, a large Revelation expandable leather case which I still possess and which is still in working order. The claim that it was made to last – a claim no longer made by many manufacturers today – has been fully justified.

Thus it was that at Victoria Station, Sheffield, on a day early in October 1933, I boarded a through train to Oxford, feeling quite uncertain what being an undergraduate at St John's College would entail. If I had been told that Oxford would be my home not just for the ensuing four years but also for the last third of my life, I would have dismissed the notion as moonshine. In the event it was a fateful day, and many surprises lay ahead.

CHAPTER 2

PRE-WAR OXBRIDGE, 1933–39

The King, observing with judicious eyes
The state of both his universities,
To Oxford sent a troop of horse, and why?
That learned body wanted loyalty;
To Cambridge books, as very well discerning
How much that loyal body wanted learning.

Revd Joseph Trapp (1679-1747)

Oxford: The Initial Shock

Though nothing had been prearranged, I half expected to meet on the Sheffield Victoria station platform some of the old boys of the Central Secondary School who, like me, were going up to Oxford for the first time or who were returning after the long vacation to resume their studies. In the event there were no Centralians, as alumni call themselves, waiting to board the train; but walking down the corridor I did see two boys from King Edward VII School, one of whom I recognised as having attended the Anglo-German School at Hohenlychen. The other, Evans, turned out to be reading chemistry at Jesus College. They invited me into their compartment and introduced me to another Old Edwardian, whom I later discovered was Edgar ('Bill') Williams; he was to become Field Marshal Montgomery's chief of intelligence in the last war but was then a Postmaster (i.e. Scholar) of Merton College reading history and, I think, entering his final year. He was the unwitting beginning of my Oxford culture shock. Of smallish stature, impeccably dressed in a suit, he seemed, in manner of speech and bearing, to be the embodiment of Dorothy L. Sayers' amateur detective, Lord Peter Wimsey. He was so polished, assured and Oxonianly allusive and elusive in his speech that I found it difficult to visualise him as a Sheffield 'tyke', let alone the son of a dissenting minister in that city. On arrival at Oxford station he persuaded us to share a taxi with him which, given my exiguous resources, I regarded as an unnecessary extravagance. The taxi dropped me at the top of Beaumont Street, near St John's, and when I offered to pay Bill forbade any contribution from me. As I was to learn from our frequent contacts during the last twenty-five years of his life, the sharp wit, ellipsis of speech and generosity he then exhibited were characteristic. Whether these mannerisms were acquired at Oxford and Balliol, where he became a Fellow, or whether indeed they were the product of early nurture I have no means of knowing.

Entering the main gate of St John's, I was directed at the Porter's Lodge by a dark-haired, saturnine man to a staircase in the front quadrangle. There I ascended two steep flights of stairs, which brought me above the Bursar's offices to a corridor on the top floor. I proceeded to the right, passing on my left a small cubby-hole which I later learned to be the headquarters on that floor of the scout (i.e. servant), and his boy (i.e. assistant), William; finally I faced a door bearing my name on the lintel. On entry there appeared to be no less than two rooms, the first being a sitting room with a dormer window and window seat overlooking St Giles and the Taylorian Institute. To me the appearance was breathtaking. The furniture consisted of a desk and chair, a table, two easy chairs, a bookcase and some table chairs, and the fire was already laid in a fireplace which was less utilitarian than the one in the back room at home, though of comparable dimensions. A door on the right led to a small bedroom replete with washstand and equipped with a bowl and a basin, a bed and a chair. There was a small window in the roof but, alas, the parapet on that side of the building precluded any real view of the quad. Though not as grand as the vast rooms I had occupied in the Meadow Building of Christ Church some ten months earlier, when taking the scholarship exams, the accommodation was sufficient to meet what I thought would be my needs; in fact it was more than ample, without being in any sense intimidating.

As I was familiarising myself with my new home and slowly unpacking, there entered a man who, in build and moustache, was very like Alf Garnett of TV fame; he introduced himself as my scout Robbins. Never having had, or dreamed of having, a personal servant I was at once deferential, rose from my chair and paid careful heed to all he said, much of which I later discovered could be ignored. I had not seen anyone like him before, but I am sure he had seen many innocents like me.

Afterwards I found he was president, chairman, or at any rate held some high office in the Oxford University and College Servants' Association, and was well endowed with the wiliness and quick appraisal of other people which a successful small-time politico needs. He explained how he would awaken me and bring hot water before breakfast, which he would serve in my room, and would lay and light the fire, tidy and clean through, and return in the evening to repeat some of these domestic chores. To me it all seemed very grand and he most helpful. What he failed to point out was that my choice of foods would be recorded by him and duly entered in my battels, that is, my bill for services provided by the College kitchens. It took a little time to restrict his wishes to serve me to a level in keeping with my financial status, following which his ministrations were reduced, to my pleasure as much as his. When he had gone I explored the other part of the corridor, discovering that the first door on the left bore the name H.K. Fowler. That seemed, and proved, to augur well for the future, because he was the agreeable contemporary I had met in June when taking the Latin examination. The next room belonged to someone called K. Grayston, whom I later found was the Open Scholar in Chemistry elected at the same time I was elected Exhibitioner. I believe his father, or his father's family, came from Sheffield, but Grayston had been at Colfe's Grammar School, Lewisham. He later abandoned chemistry for theology, moving after graduation to Cambridge where he got a first in the Theological Tripos and, after a spell as assistant director of religious broadcasting at the BBC, had a distinguished career in Bristol University which culminated in the Chair of Theology.

The next few days are rather a jumble in my memory. I know I had to acquire a gown, to discover something of the College rules and those who administered them, to learn the customs prevailing at Hall dinner and to locate my fellow Centralians at Corpus Christi College, Christ Church and St Edmund (Teddy) Hall. However, a few incidents in those early days are indelibly imprinted on my mind: the first was making the acquaintance of my tutor in chemistry, H.W. Thompson.

This came about because Dr Thompson, whom we all called Tommy, had put up a notice asking the freshmen reading chemistry to call on him at specified times, armed with a copy of the *Oxford University Gazette*, lecture list edition, price 3d. Tommy was at that time a young bachelor of immense energy, living in rooms at the top of what was then the most north-westerly staircase in College. He had an attractive sitting room containing a grand piano and photographs of the Oxford

University Association Football Club XI. He had been a soccer blue and later in life was to be the prime mover in establishing Pegasus, the remarkably successful Oxbridge Amateur Soccer Club; he ultimately became Chairman of the Football Association. There was also a signed photograph of Max Planck, the originator of the Quantum Theory in 1900, with whom Tommy lived as a guest during the year he worked on his PhD in Fritz Haber's laboratory in Berlin. Only six years older than I, Tommy came from Sheffield and was educated at King Edward VII School. He plunged straight into the business in hand, along the lines of 'Only go to a few of Soddy's lectures, to see the apparatus he used to get the data on which the radioactive disintegration law was based; go to Sidgwick's but not to Hammick's... of course you will come to mine'. Next he turned to the sub-faculty of physics, drawing my attention to the presence of German and Austrian émigrés such as Erwin Schrödinger, the London brothers and Franz Simon, and urged me to go to their lectures. He then told me that my practical work would be divided between the Old Chemistry Department, where inorganic chemistry was carried out, and the Dyson Perrins Laboratory for organic chemistry, and that I should present myself at particular times in each of these laboratories. In the momentary pause that followed I asked what textbooks I needed to buy.

'What for?' he responded.

'To go with the course', I said, meaning by that the syllabus.

'What course?' he replied.

By now somewhat perplexed, I said, 'For a degree in chemistry'.

He replied, 'I don't know if there is one'.

On seeing my baffled look he said, 'Let's look', and took down a paper-backed book entitled *Excerpta e Statutis*, found chemistry in the index and the relevant page, which showed that the only words were 'the principles of chemistry'.

Later in life I was to be grateful for this succinct specification and the inherent flexibility it gave to adapt the teaching to the individual educational needs of the student, but at the time I was completely bewildered and enquired what books he recommended. Tommy then said, 'You write your own. I want you to write me an essay on gaseous chemical reactions. Drop it in to my room next Thursday, and your tutorials will be at 9am on Fridays.'

At least this was something definite to do and, guided by my familiarity with libraries as storehouses of knowledge, I went to the Radcliffe Science Library and looked at the titles on the spines of the books in the physical chemistry section for words which would now be called the 'keywords in context'. I chose some which I thought should be consulted, including Hinshelwood's book which I already knew, and set about producing an essay of some ten pages of close-lined foolscap paper; and delivered it, as requested, on time. At the tutorial next morning Tommy told me to read my essay. I demurred, saying it was too long, but he insisted. After a few paragraphs he mystified me with the comment 'I see you agree with me'. Seeing no proposition with which I could agree or disagree, I remained silent. Then came the words 'You want to vomit', which stung me to defend myself by saying, 'It is not as bad as that', at which point he dissected all I had written, said what structure the essay should have, gave me references to original scientific papers which I must read (one in a German journal), and told me to resubmit next week another essay on the same topic, as well as one on the determination of the atomic weights of the elements. Feeling that my life depended on satisfying him, I did not visit a laboratory in the next six days but worked at the Radcliffe Science Library and the College Library. The two essays were duly handed in, and this time were found to be acceptable.

I have often wondered how this kind of treatment would be described in the jargon of modern educational theorists. I fancy it would not be approved. For all that they might say, I know that in two weeks at Oxford I had learned invaluable lessons: how to use a research library; to seek, find and digest original papers; to construct an essay with a beginning, middle and end, drawing attention to still unresolved issues. I also learned how to cope with Tommy. It was a kind of minor victory, not so much over him as over my own lack of self-confidence and, in a curious way, I am grateful to him for that. Without his demanding so much of me, I doubt whether I would have discovered that I had the capability.

When I have described this experience to others, some have disapproved of Tommy's handling of his students. One of Tommy's pupils after my time, more worldly wise than I, asked the help of the undergraduates a year ahead of him when given similar treatment. They could provide this because they had been given the same topic twelve months earlier, and so he was able to produce the required essay without being the recipient of Tommy's opprobrium. On reflection, I think that though my innocence of the ways of the world was a weakness, I nevertheless gained some valuable chemical knowledge and self-knowledge, probably more than if I had known and followed another student's course of action. Moreover, though a physical chemist primarily interested in various forms of spectroscopy, Tommy had a broad, deep and synoptic view of all branches of chemistry (except crystallography) that was sufficient to steer me in the right direction, and to cover the essential 'principles of chemistry' and how to apply them.

Attendance at lectures was voluntary, and although attendance records were kept for practical work in laboratories, I know of no serious action taken against any delinquent student – certainly not in my case – and there were quite a few occasions when I chose the Radcliffe Science Library rather than the Old Chemistry Department. I did act against Tommy's advice by going to Soddy's lectures, and never regretted the decision. Through his lecture bench demonstrations, when Soddy used devices like the gold leaf electroscope, one felt a real linkage with the early giants of radioactivity, the Curies in Paris and Rutherford in Montreal and Manchester. Moreover, although Soddy was not an engaging personality he had a fine, uncompromisingly honest face. It surprised me to learn over a year later that this distinguished man, Nobel Laureate of some ten years' standing, had personally redesigned the teaching laboratories in the Old Chemistry Department and supervised their refurbishment. He could quite often be seen striding through the first floor, unsmiling and seemingly oblivious to others, but on one occasion when I was doing qualitative analysis he came up to me and blurted out, 'What is this doing here?' The 'this' in question was a new grey rucksack which I had just bought because of a pending foray into the Cairngorms. At my reply he smiled and began to talk about the Scottish hills, sharing some of his memories in a very friendly way. A couple of days later he lent me a book by Seton Gordon, to be returned after my trip. The incident made a lasting impression on me of a man who, however odd or wrong-headed he might seem to many, was in important matters a person of real integrity. More than sixty years later I enjoyed reading his biography, which was written by a graduate student in the University of Sussex.[1]

When I was quite young my brother Ernest had taught me to swim, an activity which I greatly enjoyed. In the winter, in company with other boys from school, I used to go regularly to the municipal baths in Glossop Road. One visit, costing 2d,

---

1. Linda Merricks, *The World Made New* (Oxford University Press, 1996).

would last an hour and was a mixture of exercise in the swimming pool and conversation in the warm slipper baths. In the summer I often used to take a free dip in a rather muddy, rough-and-ready pool in Endcliffe Park, at the bottom of Ranby Road, and on Saturdays would occasionally visit the much better pool in Millhouses Park – usually with an older and better swimmer, George Hills, who lived nearby. He became an Open Scholar in Chemistry at Corpus Christi College and used to accompany his moral tutor, the mathematical physicist Dr F.B. Pidduck, in a morning swim in the Cherwell at Parson's Pleasure, the dons' bathing place, at 7.45am throughout the year. Before I went up to Oxford, Hills persuaded me to join them. In my first day at St John's I read a notice to the effect that the Junior Dean, who turned out to be Tommy, would supervise a roll call in the College Hall between 7.45 and 8.15am; I also gathered from Grayston that he had to read in chapel from time to time, and I gained the impression that the exhibitioners might also have this duty. Obviously, in such circumstances I would need permission from the authorities to swim at Parson's Pleasure.

I went to see the Senior Tutor, Austin Lane Poole. He had a rather dark office on the ground floor, lined with bookshelves, and I asked him if I might be excused from roll call and reading in chapel. I was taken aback by his question in response: 'Are you an atheist?' I said I didn't really know what I was, but religion had nothing to do with it. He then explained that exhibitioners were not called upon to read in chapel, and asked again why had I made this unusual request. I told him about my promise to Hills and Dr Pidduck and the clash with roll call, to which he replied, 'It is now October. I assume you will desist in November'.

I disagreed, which caused him to comment, 'Next term the river sometimes freezes'. My only answer was to explain that I had given my word and then, using Yorkshire idiom, I said, 'I can't give back word'. He then asked me to repeat my request. Why he did this I never knew, but I have the clearest recollection of taking a deep breath to steady myself and then speaking very slowly and deliberately. When I had finished there was a pause and Poole said, 'You must be mad. Permission granted.' This was my first, but not my last, significant example of his skilful and humorous approach to flexible administration.

Pidduck was a lonely, quirky, bachelor don of Corpus who lived in rooms overlooking the Corpus Fellows' garden. He was enormously kind to his tutees and, because of my daily swims with him, I shared in his largesse. On Sunday mornings

I returned from the swim, not to St John's but to Corpus to partake of a large guest breakfast consisting of grapefruit, porridge or cereals, and a main course of a mixed grill or fish, completed with toast or Ryvita and preserves. When the scout had cleared away, there came a surprise. Simultaneous heaves at each end of the table raised its surface by about eight inches, into which position it could be locked, and the mahogany leaves covering the top could then be removed to reveal a billiard table. Some of us played, including me, but because of his poor eyesight Pidduck rarely did, preferring instead to play classical piano works on his pianola, when he displayed a rhythm more metrical than musical. Then we would drift away in ones or twos, George Hills and I sometimes going for a cycle ride together.

Pidduck had marked likes and dislikes. The latter caused him never to dine at High Table. He had unbounded admiration for J.S. Townsend, the Wykeham Professor of Physics, in whose laboratory he was a demonstrator, and a very low opinion of F.A. Lindemann (later Lord Cherwell), the Dr Lee's Professor of Experimental Philosophy. Pidduck had written a *Treatise on Electricity and Magnetism* which I had used and admired at school, but in the 1930s he was mainly concerned with collisional processes in gases, work which attracted the admiring attention of Chapman and Cowling in their classic work on kinetic theory.

It is fair to say that Pidduck's reputation was higher outside Oxford than within it, and I had a dramatic demonstration of this in the 1940s. Pidduck had been invited to Cambridge to give seminars in the Cavendish Laboratory and the Electrical Laboratory in the Engineering Department. I was working in the Department of Physical Chemistry at that time, and when I learned of his visit I naturally invited him to stay with my wife and me. Because of his extreme short-sightedness, I felt I ought to give up the whole day to steer him around the city, and therefore I attended both seminars. I was greatly impressed by the respect with which he was received in the two departments, and some years later I commented on this to Sir Harold Jeffreys, the Plumian Professor of Astronomy and Experimental Philosophy. He said, 'Well, you know that just after the First World War we wanted him here in Cambridge, but he wouldn't come'.

Although alienated from many of his fellows in Corpus, to his pupils and friends Pidduck was generous to a fault. He would take (and if need be pay for) students on mountaineering holidays in the Alps or his beloved Lake District, to which he retired and where he died. All we could give him in return was friendship.

Near the middle of my first term I had another meeting with the Senior Tutor, having been notified by him that I was on the list for low battels. I went to see Poole in a rather belligerent mood since there was plenty of visible evidence that my contribution to the kitchen revenue was not really essential to ensure the financial viability of St John's College, which quite clearly was not short of a bob or two. I was taken aback when Poole asked me what I was eating. I explained that I found it necessary to shop in the Cornmarket for milk and cereal, and to use other similar expedients to save money. He then enquired into my finances and concluded by saying, 'You don't have enough to live on' – a fact of which I was only too well aware, since all those around me had told me that £230 a year was the minimum needed and I had only a £120 grant and a £40 loan, from which just over £10 was to be deducted each year to cover the insurance premium. We then discussed what other means there might be of augmenting my income. Nothing was in view for that year other than the Grocers' Company, which awarded exhibitions provided the applications were in by the end of the calendar year. I prepared a 'Memorial to the Master, Wardens and Court of Assistants of the Worshipful Company of Grocers', but early in 1934 I received a curt statement that I was 'not among the candidates selected for one of the Grocers' Company Exhibitions', with an even more curt duplicated postscript: 'This debars you from making a further application'.

Meanwhile, however, Poole had been at work, and before the end of the Michaelmas term I learned from him that the Rustat Fund had awarded me a further £30 a year. From then on it seemed to me that the College found every possible pretext for granting me money – for example, on the results of Collections (the examinations at the beginning of term). I was also invited to sit for the Casberd Scholarships examination although I was ineligible to receive a scholarship, just so that they could award me a £10 book prize. Moreover, in the summer of 1934, when facing the College governing body, I was asked what I was going to do in the long vacation. I said that I had applied to the A.C. Irvine Travel Fund for financial help to explore the Cairngorms. The President then infuriated me by saying he thought all young men should visit the Continent, something which was far beyond my means; but followed this up by passing an envelope across the table. On opening it later I found a clean £10 note.

I sensed that the Senior Tutor's 'fine Italian hand' was behind all this, and towards the end of my first academic year he excelled himself. He sent for me again and said I ought to be looking for further sources of financial support. He pointed out that the Goldsmiths' Company also gave exhibitions to those who sat a competitive examination. It appeared that these were potentially open to everyone at the University of Oxford, in all subjects. I remember saying that I thought I would have little chance in competition with people in their second and third years, to which Poole replied, speaking very slowly and deliberately, 'It can certainly be said that if you don't apply you won't get one'. With that I left him, thought it over, applied, and was fortunate to be awarded an exhibition. Whether benign hands were working behind the scenes on my behalf I cannot tell, but I still treasure the letter of notification dated 18 April 1935 from the Clerk of the Company, Walter T. Prideaux, a delightful man I later came to know. It was a charming and friendly letter, pointing out that the exhibition would be backdated to the previous January and was 'awarded to enable you to complete your degree course and tenable until the end of the normal degree course'. There was a final sentence which cheered me beyond belief: 'It is also granted on the understanding that any scholarships or allowances which you at present hold are not withdrawn or reduced in consequence of this award'. When I reported my success to the City of Sheffield Education Committee they immediately said that my grant would be withdrawn. I then sent them by registered post a copy of the letter from Walter Prideaux, and several weeks elapsed during which, I think, the Goldsmiths' Company must have pressed my case so that in the end the city, whilst cancelling the loan, left the grant unaffected. So it was that after four terms at St John's I found myself with some debts, but now with £220 a year without borrowing any further money. The practical concern which the Senior Tutor and his colleagues showed for my financial position did not end there. At the earliest date I became eligible to apply for a Casberd Scholarship I was reminded to do so, and was duly awarded one which raised my annual income to £240 a year.

I have recited these details of my financial affairs while an undergraduate simply to illustrate how skilfully Poole took a hand in my welfare. Not only did he arrange for my funds to be augmented, but he did so in a manner which gave the appearance that I had earned the increase, and thereby preserved my own dignity. I was not a mere beggar.

There were 49 freshmen in 1933, of whom eight were from overseas. Some were Rhodes Scholars and many later achieved eminence in their own countries: for example Fritz Caspari, who became a well-regarded German diplomat; Burke Knapp, who held high office in the World Bank; and J.G. Ruttan, who became a respected judge in the Province of British Columbia. In the first few days one could distinguish two groups among the British freshmen: those who came from day schools and those from independent boarding schools. The latter had more self-assurance, while the former seemed to be more mature. However, as the term wore on such differences mattered less and less, and individuals were judged more on their intrinsic qualities (although among the public school boys there were certainly some who, in these meritocratic days, would not have been admitted to Oxford). There were rowdy parties from time to time, mainly given by former independent schoolboys who had considerable means, but Evelyn Waugh would have found it difficult to base his *Decline and Fall* on St John's.

Looking back, I am surprised how a college of about 200 students, including postgraduates, supported so many clubs. In addition to the usual clubs for various team games, there were frivolous ones with nominal activities to justify convivial dining, for example the King Charles Club, celebrating the College's Jacobite connection, and the Archery Club. There were also serious, high-minded, exclusive clubs like the Essay Society, whose members read papers to one another from time to time after imbibition of mulled claret; and there were the Mummers, who produced an annual play with actors sometimes drawn from other colleges and often including Helen Highet, wife of the Latin don Gilbert Highet. She later gained fame under her maiden name of Helen MacInnes, the detective story-writer.

I have noticed great changes in college life over the last sixty years. Disregarding the trebling of the numbers of both Fellows and junior members and the admission of women, several differences loom large. The first is the small number of dons for whom college is their home. When I was a freshman, in addition to the President seven Fellows (just over one-third of the total) lived in college, a much higher proportion than now, and they were often very hospitable to undergraduates. Now even bachelor dons usually choose to live out of college, because it seems only prudent to buy one's own property when house values are increasing faster than salaries. Consequently, discipline and security are now more the responsibility of the porters than the dons, and something valuable may have been lost. St John's is not unique in this respect, nor in the proportion of under-graduates who go away at weekends, following a tendency which began earlier in the big civic universities. It follows that *in statu pupillari* is more of an empty archaism than a reality, as indeed it was bound to become after the lowering of the age of majority to eighteen. The Senior Common Room, on the other hand, still retains many of the old customs, such as dining in black tie on Sunday evenings and having three evenings each week of formal dessert.

By the middle of my first term, then, I had an improved but still unsatisfactory financial position which induced a certain gloom, only partly dispelled by the evidence of the Senior Tutor's interest in my welfare. I had established a base in the laboratories, become familiar with the usages of the College and Radcliffe Science libraries, got to know some of my fellow chemists from other colleges, and other freshmen in St John's. My schoolfriend F.J. McQuillin, the Scholar of Christ Church reading chemistry and in his second year, was especially helpful in elucidating the mysteries of the chemistry laboratories, only two of which seemed to belong to the University whilst four (Christ Church, Balliol and Trinity, Jesus, and Queen's) were independent college facilities. Taken altogether, it could be said that I was well on my way to having settled into Oxford. I had even learned to play squash, a game I relished. The ritual of dinner in Hall, for five of which we were forced to pay each week and which, therefore, I never missed, was becoming intelligible and I had once witnessed the effects of sconcing.[2]

I had nothing like the self-confidence or articulacy of many of the freshmen of St John's who had been at boarding schools, and who handled the College servants in a manner which sometimes had an element of disdain (the latter, however, did not seem to resent it: perhaps they expected it of the 'young gentlemen', but it was a practice that was alien to me). I soon discovered that their confident, articulate expression of opinions did not always mean that those views were unchallengeable

---

2. The College possessed several large silver cups, sometimes with a cover, which would hold over three pints of any fluid. These were the sconces. It was the right of the senior scholar dining at the separate scholars' table to send a note to any undergraduate who he thought had infringed one of the ancient rules of etiquette: for example, if the student had put his commoner's gown on inside out, a very easy thing to do, he might receive from the senior scholar a little note which would read *"Te sconsam posco quod togam reversum est"*. The recipient then had to decide whether to provide, at his own expense, a full sconce pot of ale for the scholars' table, or to challenge the scholar, accept the sconce and without removing the cup from his lips down the contents in one long swallow. The President of the College told me recently that the admission of women undergraduates to St John's was the trigger for the abolition of what some regarded as an unworthy or even barbaric tradition.

or ultimately correct. At the same time, some of my own preconceptions were rightly shattered by the conversations which I had. The best of these were often over coffee in one's own room after dinner, and they could be protracted. I also found the Junior Common Room a very agreeable place. This occupied two rooms on the first floor and could be approached from the staircase in the south-east corner of the front quad, or the staircase in the south-west corner of the Canterbury Quad. It was presided over by a genial scout called Dudley, who would provide tea and toast – plain, buttered or anchovy – and cakes for what seemed, even then, to be a ridiculously low price. There was a small writing room and a larger sitting room which contained ample daily and Sunday papers and magazines. It was a natural focal point for undergraduate life.

The last four weeks of my first term passed with amazing rapidity, and ended with two surprises. The first was what we undergraduates knew as 'the Don Rag', but which I believe was officially known as Collections. Throughout the last day of term the President sat at the centre of the High Table in the Hall, with Fellows on either side wearing gowns but not in 'subfusc' (the collective noun for the clothes worn by an undergraduate in addition to academical dress and defined by the Proctors as 'a white tie, collar and shirt, a black coat, a dark waistcoat and dark trousers, a dark blue suit, dark grey suit, or a dark brown suit with black shoes or boots and dark socks'. Non-compliance could lead to exclusion from buildings and even from examinations, as I remember – but not from my own experience). At the Don Rags the undergraduates wore their gowns and carried a mortarboard, and were summoned in turn from the body of the Hall to sit opposite the President. The scene always recalled to me that well-known painting of a Cavalier child standing before his Roundhead inquisitors, which bears the caption 'When did you last see your father?' When it came to my turn Tommy, who was sitting at the end of the High Table, read aloud his report on my progress during the term. Unaware that a response was expected from me, I remained silent. The interview soon ended with a reminder to come up to Oxford no later than the Thursday in January immediately preceding the beginning of full term, and then to be ready to take one or two (I forget which) three-hour examination papers in the Hall (these papers were also, rather confusingly, called Collection Papers). It was an entirely novel concept to begin rather than to end the term with an examination, but it was one which I have come to regard as admirable because it made crystal clear that the intervals between terms were regarded by the College as an opportunity for students to carry out personal, unsupervised study. When I was a professor in Leeds nearly twenty years later I found this idea, which I tried to introduce, quite unwelcome to my students. Though admittedly the terms at Leeds were of ten weeks' duration against the eight at Oxford, I sometimes felt that I was fighting a losing battle in encouraging the Leeds students to use their vacations in this way!

The second surprise was a notice in the College library pointing out that books could be borrowed for the whole of the vacation. I took full advantage of this, taking home not only several chemistry books but also a philosophical work by R.G. Collingwood, the title of which, *Speculum Mentis*, fascinated me. I read it in the Christmas period and it was a revelation, leading me into realms of knowledge as different from chemistry as could be imagined. I was glad to find in recent years that Collingwood's work, which tended to be ignored in Oxford after the Second World War, has been reinstated in esteem by many academics, especially those in the United States.

My return home for Christmas was just as much a family event as my departure two months earlier. I arrived on a Saturday just after midday, and at 5.30pm there was high tea for seven, which included my brother and two sisters. It was a jolly party and they were immensely and touchingly interested in what I had been doing, but the most moving moment came after they had dispersed. My mother was washing the dishes in the low sink in the scullery, and I was drying and putting things away. She had spoken least of all during tea, and for her this was unusual at a family gathering. Suddenly she stopped washing and rested her hands on the side of the stone sink; with her bent back, she epitomized one of Millet's tired peasant women. Turning her head to me she said simply, 'You've not changed a bit, lad', in a way that betokened both relief and disappointment. There was nothing I could say. I knew in that moment that she both hoped that Oxford would improve my chances of moving up out of our class and feared that such a change would inevitably weaken, perhaps even break, the bond between us. We never spoke about it again, but I hoped a chance would come so that she could see at first hand something of the life I lived in Oxford, and feel a part of it.

That Christmas vacation was in marked contrast to those of earlier years. The Central Secondary School had moved that summer from the city centre to handsome new buildings in the suburb of Bents Green, close to where we lived, but sadly there was no Shakespeare play because the headmaster had closed the Society down.[3] However, there were still walks, talks and visits to be enjoyed with boys who had left school when I did and were now at other universities and colleges.

I found Sheffield very depressing: the grimy pavements and blackened stone of the buildings were in such marked contrast to Oxford. The smoke, laden with sooty dust particles (it used to be said that you could always spot a Sheffield tyke from the slightly projecting lower lip, the product of repeatedly blowing smuts up off the nose), in which we used to take such pride as evidence of the virility of strong craftsmen teeming steel from furnaces or crucibles, now seemed unhygienic, and certainly was the cause of much respiratory disease. Worst of all was the spectacle of many people out of work. The unemployment rate was about one-third of the labour force, whereas the national figure was about one-fifth. Moreover, unemployment benefit, the 'dole', was time-limited and means-tested. The despair on men's faces, and their poor condition, were plain to see. Coming from Oxford, the contrast was tragic and painful and was a powerful incentive for me to give what I could to the Hunger Marchers, some of whom later passed through Sheffield on their trek to London to awaken the conscience of the nation. I was doubly thankful for the proximity of the moors and dales into which, as well as walking, I made several trips on my brother Ernest's 'sit up and beg' Raleigh bicycle, equipped with a Sturmey Archer three-speed gear. He now lived on the other side of the city, with little opportunity to use the machine, and in due course he kindly gave it to me. From April 1934 onwards it was my means of locomotion between Oxford and Sheffield, a journey of approximately 133 miles. I managed to accomplish this on every occasion, except one, within the day and without any help. The exception came one Easter when I encountered snow in Chatsworth Park, and had ahead of me a long climb up to about 1,400 feet which I just could not face; I therefore took the train from Grindleford through the long tunnel to Sheffield.

Most of my reading and writing was done at home in the front room or parlour after I had, quite illegally, made some modifications to the electrical circuit in the house. Electricity had arrived in the 1920s. There was no earth wire, only two cotton-covered wires carrying current. These were encased in two channels in a

---

3. In 1940, seven years after the move from the city centre, the school changed its name to High Storrs Grammar School.

wooden conduit plugged onto the wall, to which access was very easy. I was able to rig up new leads to get electricity through a small electric fire and table lamp. These arrangements, which the modern Health and Safety Executive would have insisted on removing as unsafe, sufficed for four years. However, despite this adequate study space, I felt the need to go to a good science library from time to time. I made for my old friend the Public Reference Library, only to find the services somewhat restricted because of preparations to move the stock into the splendid new building, which was nearly completed. So I had perforce to seek help from the University of Sheffield. I was cordially received, both in the main Edgar Allen Library, now the administrative centre of the University, and in the small Chemistry Departmental Library. I was already familiar with the chemistry laboratories, having twice suffered Higher School Certificate practical examinations there, and got to know some of the staff. One morning I was reading a paper in a bound volume of a journal when a shortish, dark man came in, looked along the bookshelves, could not find what he wanted and came to the tables, finally peering over my shoulder and saying, rather peremptorily, 'You've got the volume I need'. Naturally, as a guest I apologised and pushed it over. He read what he wanted and then returned it to me and said, perhaps prompted by an awareness of his own churlishness, 'My name is Dr Glasstone. Who are you?'

'Oh', I said, 'I have read your book on recent advances in physical chemistry, and also your book on recent advances in inorganic chemistry', and then I told him who I was. Over the next three years, on my occasional visits to that library, I came to know him as well as anyone could, and on one occasion I asked him who the 'V' was to whom his books were invariably dedicated. He told me that this was his wife, whom he had met rather romantically because he had seen a portrait of her at the photographers Ramsay and Muspratt, the Oxford branch of which was then in Cornmarket Street. She was a botany student at St Hilda's College. Having seen the picture he managed by various devious means to get to know the young lady, and subsequently married her. It all seemed a highly improbable story, quite out of character with his somewhat cold, rational personality, at least as it appeared to me, but it enhanced my regard for him.

Just before the war Glasstone moved to the Frick Chemical laboratory at Princeton, New Jersey, where he did little research and devoted himself almost entirely to textbook writing. For many years his *Textbook of Physical Chemistry*

1. A touch of the thespian: my father, George Whalley Dainton, in his early sixties.

2. My mother, Mary Jane Dainton, as I remember her from my childhood.

3. My first official photograph, in the family christening robe, 1915.

4. Another studio portrait, this time when I was aged 3.

5. Ranby Road, Sheffield, at around the time I was born. Number 66 is on the left side of the street, just hidden by the cart: the nearer houses are of the same design. The corner shop is still an off-licence, but the gas lamp has gone.

7. Holding the reins: my first seaside holiday, Scarborough, 1922.

6. Five years old, having just started at
Hunter's Bar School.

8. With my mother in Lathkill Dale, showing off my brand new
uniform for the Central Secondary School.

9. In the backyard of 66 Ranby Road, with
Flossie my dog.

10. Watford Locks on the Grand Union Canal in Northamptonshire, where my grandfather, John Bottrill, drowned on Boxing Day, 1889.

11. With my parents at the locks, while I was still at Greystones School.

12. My brother Ernie, after admission to his Associateship in Metallurgy at the University of Sheffield in 1927.

13. My mother on 26 August 1942, the night before my marriage to Barbara. Our photographer friend was so taken with her that he used up all his film before the ceremony!

14. The last photograph of my father, taken at Ernie's wedding in the Isle of Man, June 1930; it was his one and only 'overseas' trip.

15. Laying the foundation stone of the Ecclesall Church extension, 27 June 1907. My father is on the extreme left, hands on hips and clearly in charge of the proceedings.

16. Hunter's Bar School. My formal education started here in 1919.

17. Greystones School, where I received a memorable caning for doing other pupils' homework.

The Building News. Oct 17 1879

FIRTH COLLEGE, SCHOOL BOARD OFFICES AND CENTRAL SCHOOLS, SHEFFIELD.

FLOCKTON & ABBOTT AND E.R.ROBSON, JOINT ARCHITECTS.

18. My love of education was kindled at the Central Secondary School. This engraving, reproduced from a copy of *The Building News*, shows the boys' and girls' schools on the left and Firth College – the forerunner of the University of Sheffield – on the far right, with the School Board Offices in the centre. The city's Education Department later occupied all of the buildings.

19. Sixth-form pupils in the school year 1931-32. On the far left of the back row is F.J. McQuillin, who went up to Oxford in 1932, and whose example encouraged me to do likewise. I am standing near the centre of the middle row.

20. The staff in 1931-32: headmaster Luther Smith is seated in the centre of the front row. At the back are Alf Ridler (left), who inspired my chemistry studies and became a lifelong friend, and geography master Fred Campbell (centre), who fostered my interest in the natural world as a preventative for idleness.

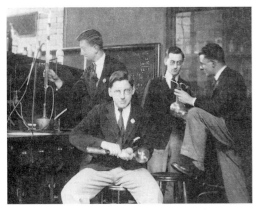

21. Messrs. Keyworth, Dainton, McQuillin and Wilde, carefully posed but rather blurred, in the science lab, June 1932. The same four appear again in the crumpled press cutting reproduced on the right.

22. Also in 1932, a wreath from 1,000 past and present members of the Central Secondary School Shakespeare Society was presented at the opening of the Royal Shakespeare Theatre in Statford-upon-Avon.

23. Members of the 1932 Anglo-German Summer School at Schloss 'Sans Souci', Berlin. I am tucked away near the back.

24. Central Secondary School prefects with the Headmaster in 1932. Dainton, Keyworth and Wilde are together again, in the back row.

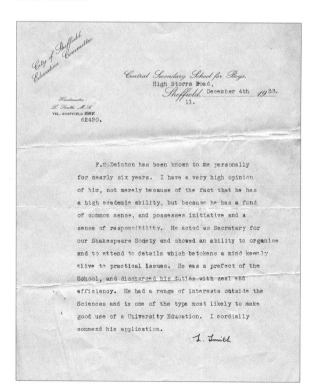

25. Headmaster Luther Smith's letter in support of an application for a Grocers' Company Scholarship during my first term at Oxford. Pleasing words, but not persuasive enough.

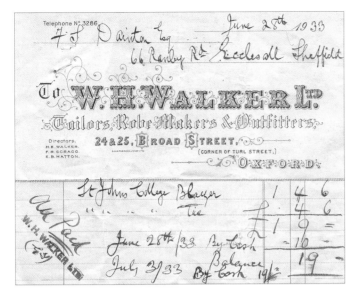

26. Family presents to kit me out for Oxford, as purchased…

27. …and as worn by a very new undergraduate, autumn 1933.

28. First year at St John's College: in the front row, extreme right, is proof that my hair would curl if grown long enough.

29. *Above:* The Canterbury Quadrangle of St John's College, Oxford, drawn in 1936 by Muirhead Bone.

30. *Right:* My tutor 'Tommy' Thompson in later life (1978), when he had become 'rather grand' and was Chairman of the Football Association.

31. *Below:* Matriculation, in October 1933. My Christian names reflect the lack of the letters K and Y in Latin.

OXONIÆ, TERMINO *Mich.* A.D. 1933
Die VII Mensis Oct.

QUO die comparuit coram me
Fridericus Sidneus Dainton
e Collegio *Di. Jo. Bapt.*
et admonitus est de observandis Statutis hujus
Universitatis, et in Matriculam Universitatis
relatus est.

Vice-Cancellarius.

32. Scotland, September 1937: just before taking up residence as a PhD student in Cambridge.

33. The front of the University Chemical Laboratory on Downing Street, Cambridge (from a journal reprint of 1928).

34. Intent on my researches! Gleaming in the background is the temperature controller/recorder which I borrowed from Lord Rutherford on behalf of my supervisor, Professor Ronald Norrish.

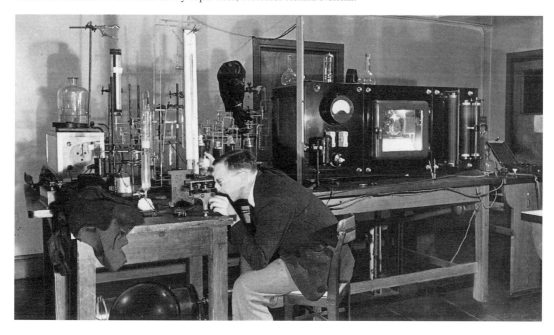

35. In the Cairngorms with Botany colleagues, summer 1938. I am lurking in the back row, second from the right.

36. 'Three Wise Monkeys' – hearing (FSD), seeing, and speaking no evil in Cambridge.

37. August 1940: proof that there was work as well as play during my three years as a postgraduate student.

38. An early foray into government service, albeit under wartime conditions.

39. The fire squad which I commanded in Cambridge, with the pump which enabled us to extinguish a blaze in Pembroke College.

40. Barbara Hazlitt Wright as a zoology research student in Cambridge, 1941: the nearest we have to an engagement photograph. I first met Barbara in 1938 when she was an undergraduate at Newnham College, and we married at Trumpington Parish Church in 1942.

41. In 1941, when this photograph was taken, I was teaching intensively for the Natural Sciences Tripos as well as conducting research for the Ministries of Supply and Aircraft Production.

42. On honeymoon in the Cotswolds.

43. Outside our first home, 53 Woodlark Road, Cambridge, which we rented for £50 per annum. My gas mask can be seen to the left of the bicycle lamp.

44. In 1948 the Queen became the first woman on whom a Cambridge degree was formally conferred: prior to that their degrees were merely 'titular' and women were not even full members of the University. Barbara is fifth from the left in this group of former students being presented by Dame Myra Curtis, Principal of Newnham College.

The Master's Lodge,
St Catharine's College.
Cambridge.

Dec. 16, 1944

Dear Dr. Dainton,

For some time we have been considering the necessity of strengthening the science side of the College teaching staff, in view of
the increasing number of men reading science subjects, and I am
writing to ask whether you would consider the possibility of
accepting a fellowship here to help us in dealing with the problem
of science direction and teaching.

As regards emolument, we have recently introduced a new scale
under which a newly elected fellow will start at a basic stipend of
£350 per annum plus £100 per annum for the performance of any
college duty which he may be asked to undertake, in this case,
directorship of science studies. This advances by 5 year increment
of £50 of both basic and additional payments. I am not quite sure
at what point you would enter the scheme, but this may be adequate
information to give you an idea of the prospects which could be
further discussed in an interview, if you are able to go further
into the subject.

We cannot make an election forthwith in your case, as you would
thereby lose your fellowship allowance for this year; but we could
pre-elect in April with a view to your formal election in October
1945. The reason for this procedure is, that should you be unable
to entertain the proposal, we should then have more time to
consider other possibilities.

I hope, however, that this will not be the case. I can assure you
of a warm welcome here from every member of our Society and I
think that you would find life both interesting and agreeable.

Yours sincerely,

45-47. I was a Fellow of St Catharine's College,
Cambridge, from 1945 to 1950. The view above shows
the gateway onto Queen's Lane; my rooms (below)
dated from 1634.

48. Staff and research students of the Department of Physical Chemistry at Cambridge, July 1948. Ronald Norrish, as Head of Department, is seated in the centre of the front row, and I am on his left. Peter Gray (back row) and Ken Ivin (middle row) were among those who became long-term colleagues and friends. George Porter (front row) went on to become Director of the Royal Institution and President of the Royal Society, as well as a Nobel Laureate (jointly with Norrish, and Manfred Eigen of Göttingen in Germany).

had complete primacy in that field. He also wrote jointly with Professor Henry Eyring and Professor Keith Laidler another classic, *The Theory of Rate Processes*. His reputation for producing clear accounts in difficult fields led to him compiling just after the war a most useful handbook, called *Source Book of Atomic Energy*, for the newly established US Atomic Energy Commission. I met him twice thereafter and on the first occasion he tried to persuade me to go to the USA permanently, believing that Britain was finished and that no self-respecting physical chemist should continue to live there. To my great surprise, my next and final contact with him occurred when I was Dr Lee's Professor of Chemistry in the University of Oxford, when I received an airmail letter, I think about 1972, announcing his intention of bequeathing some of the financial gains from his scientific writings to that institution.

Oxford: Four Years of Paradise

I enjoyed my vacation at home enormously but, equally, found I was glad to be back in Oxford in the New Year. Soon the succession of terms, with their regular rhythm of activities, seemed to be the main part of my life. As time went by this focused more and more on Oxford, where I was making new friends, notably Henry Fowler, and where I was finding many satisfactions. There were, for example, various scientific societies in which I became involved. The first was the 'Junior Sci' or, to give it its proper title, the Oxford University Junior Scientific Club. Founded in 1882, it met fortnightly, the members reading papers among themselves, and of course it had included people such as Sidgwick, Moseley, Haldane, Soddy and J.S. Huxley. It also had a Boyle Lecture and an enormous conversazione; it even published a journal called *The Transactions*. By the time I arrived in Oxford science had become much more subdivided into specialisms, and the Junior Sci was having to find a new role because the reading of papers by junior members on their pet subjects had been taken over by specialist clubs. In my case the appropriate body was the Alembic Club.

I became a junior member of the Alembic Club as soon as I could, despite its annual subscription of six shillings (30p!). Its rules were a model of clarity and practicality, and in my experience served the club very well. There were senior and junior members, each group of which met separately at 8.30pm on five of the eight

Monday evenings during full term. These were called 'ordinary meetings' and were held in the college rooms of one of the members, when they heard and discussed a paper given by one of their number; minutes were kept by the Honorary Secretary. The remaining three Monday meetings were called 'general meetings' and were open to senior and junior members alike. They were usually held in the lecture theatre of the Sir Leoline Jenkins Laboratory of Jesus College, and were addressed by distinguished outside speakers. The minute books would make fascinating reading today, to judge from the termly programmes I have for the academic year 1936-37, when I was the Honorary Secretary of the senior section.

The annual dinner was an especially grand black tie affair of six courses, held at the Randolph Hotel at the end of the Hilary term at a cost of 8s 6d (43p) exclusive of wine. After the loyal toast there were three other toasts: to the club, the guests and the victims. By tradition the last toast was proposed by the chairman of the examiners in chemistry and the response was rendered by the Junior Vice-President. On 7 March 1936 I was that respondent, and in more than one sense it was for me a salutary experience. To give me Dutch courage my friends had sent me drinks and I have no clear recollection of what I said, though I am told it was quite adequate. After dinner there was general conversation and then we were supposed to disperse around 10.30 to 11pm. An old friend doing research, knowing that I played chess, asked whether I would like to go for a game or two at a house in North Oxford. Though well aware that I must be in my lodgings by 11pm, and even so would face a gate fine, I readily agreed because to be playing chess late at night seemed to me the most natural thing in the world. The result was that I arrived at my landlady's home early in the morning, and when I went into College on the Sunday I found a note inviting me to go and see the Senior Dean, a law don called Edwin Slade. He interrogated me about breaking the rules, and enquired as to the cause of my delinquency. My reply that I was playing chess in North Oxford seemed utterly incredible to him, and he told me that I would have to see the President. The following morning I was duly summoned to meet this august personage, Sir Cyril Norwood, a man of considerable pomposity who wore a black jacket, black waistcoat and pinstripe trousers every day of the week. (On Sundays he wore a silk gown when, accompanied by his wife, he went to church at St Mary's, following which they would parade through the College garden.) By the time I had to see him my friends had told me that the matter would be dealt with just by a fine, so I had better have a few pounds in my pocket. Thus armed I went to see him, told my tale and to my astonishment he gave me a long lecture on the virtues of punctuality and the duty of scholars to set the standards. I was deeply embarrassed and just wanted to get away. Another incident, which I will relate later, confirmed for me his lack of understanding of young people, despite the fact that he had been Master of Marlborough and Headmaster of Harrow.

Undergraduates at St John's had two years' residence in College and then, depending on the length of their course, one or two years in lodgings. In our second year Henry Fowler and I moved to more commodious rooms in the North Quad: he to a staircase built in the late nineteenth century overlooking St Giles, and I to one erected just before the First World War and backing on to the President's drive. The third term of that year was free of examinations after Collections at the beginning, and this, together with my improved financial position, led me to decide that Oxford must be enjoyed. The pleasure of deliberately achieving this is not to be underestimated. I indulged in punting and canoeing on the Cherwell, cycling in the Cotswolds and tennis at the College sports ground. I enjoyed to the full the celebration of the Silver Jubilee of the Accession of King George V, marked by a feast in Hall and fireworks in South Park, on the flank of Headington Hill. I also found this period a good opportunity to give time to my family, and first of all to invite my brother Ernest, who had given me his bicycle, to visit me. He stayed two nights in the guest room in College and enjoyed every minute, particularly dining in Hall. Secondly, I invited my mother and my elder sister Mabel to come and stay a couple of nights in a family hotel on the Iffley Road. I was proud to show off Oxford to them and almost walked them off their feet, but undoubtedly the high point of their visit was the lunch I was able to have served to them in my rooms. I must confess to some trepidation beforehand, and some shame afterwards. I was concerned that my mother, with her humble origins, might not know how to behave and might let me down in the eyes of my scout. Not only were these unworthy thoughts but I need not have entertained them at all, because her service in Henley Court meant that she knew the manners of the gentry better than the gentry themselves, and she positively oozed confidence to the manner born.

I did not entirely escape work, because I had to complete some physical chemistry experiments in the Balliol and Trinity College laboratory. One morning, while engrossed in this task, I heard a voice say in a broad Worcestershire accent,

'I say, that's a bloody dull experiment'. I looked round and saw a young man dressed in tomato-coloured plus fours, who went on to say, 'Come with me and we will do some experiments on hydrogen peroxide'. The young man was the charming E.J. (Ted) Bowen, and I spent the next six weeks in another room with him, decomposing hydrogen peroxide on a platinum sol made by Bredig's method. The results were not reproducible but the experience was valuable, in that I learned much more about myself and the atmosphere of a research laboratory, as well as the kind of camaraderie that can develop within it.

Bowen was Junior Proctor at the time, and included among his duties was that of patrolling the streets and certain public houses to which undergraduates were forbidden entry. For this he was appropriately dressed and accompanied by two 'bulldogs', that is, members of the University police. One evening, in company with two friends, I was enjoying a glass of beer in the buttery of the Clarendon Hotel in Cornmarket Street (now sadly replaced by a glitzy shopping mall) which was out of bounds to us, when in walked Bowen in whose laboratory I had been working that very afternoon. Clearly I could not escape detection and I awaited the inevitable as he 'progged' my companions, that is, noted down their names and colleges. Then, looking me straight in the eye (and there must have been a twinkle in his, though at the time I was not aware of it), he said, 'You're not a member of the University, are you, Sir?' I did not deny his statement, but merely marvelled at his benign and flexible use of authority. Bowen became a firm friend, and when I was a professor at Leeds and used to take my students on study trips to Malham Tarn Field Centre, I would invite him to come along. He was the life and soul of the party, being a natural geologist and full of lore about the countryside. He also became a kind of favourite uncle to my family.

At the end of the second year I went up to Scotland again, in the company of a fellow Centralian, Ken Brooksbank of St Edmund Hall, when we made a 1,200-mile cycle tour. This took us up through York, across the Roman Wall, and into Northumbria and the Border country, with visits to the abbeys of Melrose and Galashiels. From there we went on to Edinburgh, across the firth into Perthshire, and so to Aviemore for a stay in the Cairngorms before exploring the northern part of the Great Glen. We then went west into Wester Ross and Sutherland, and back down through Argyllshire, Glasgow and the Lake District, and so home. It was a memorable trip in many ways, not least for being preached against in Ullapool because we arrived unsuitably clad – in shorts – on a Sunday morning just before service time. We did not hear the sermon, but were told about it in the youth hostel. Oddly enough, my wife had a similar experience there in 1927 when caravanning with her parents. After a few days in Ullapool camping near the shoreline they broke camp on Sunday, only to be upbraided by the local minister for moving on the Sabbath; exception was also taken to what was then considered equally shocking – my future wife, aged 11, likewise clad in shorts. Her parents were very upset about this, for though they had long outgrown such strictures, it was in keeping with their upbringing that they deeply regretted giving offence.

My third year at Oxford was spent sharing digs with Henry Fowler in a semi-detached house in Victoria Road on the northern side of the city. Our lugubrious landlady, appropriately named Mrs Moody, delighted in serving us 'a nice glass tongue', which gave me a lifelong revulsion for that dish. There is little to remember about that final year except that, first, I was unable to swim with Pidduck, and secondly there was yet another thoughtful and kind act on the part of St John's, which elected me to a further Casberd Scholarship. I remember that on the day this happened I received scathing comments from my tutor Tommy on an essay I had written, and for which I had chosen the topic 'colour'. I had apparently irritated him by making no mention of science, but had discussed colour in music and painting, and the emotional reactions it could evoke.

By the Christmas of my third year I knew that I wanted to do research, but tried to hide from myself the seemingly impossible ambition of becoming a don. What was certain was that I must do sufficiently well in the Final Honours Schools, and in the research year which followed, to be awarded a first class degree. I prepared myself as well as I could for the examinations and arrived in good fettle, if somewhat tense, at the Examination Schools for the first paper. To my dismay, after about an hour I was violently sick and had to be taken out by one of the invigilators who, thank God, was the kindly E.J. Bowen. He gave me some mixture to swallow, but I lost about three quarters of an hour before I could get back into the examination room. I was in despair at lunchtime, and instead of going back to College I went across to St Edmund Hall to have lunch with Ken Brooksbank. He cheered me up, and convinced me that even if I had blown my chances there was nothing I could do about it – the only option left to me was to make the best of the remaining five papers. Happily, either Bowen's nostrum or Ken Brooksbank's advice seemed to do the trick, so that I left Oxford (after also taking the practical examinations) feeling I had acquitted myself reasonably well. I then had to return in late August to begin research with Tommy for Part Two. Henry Fowler was staying on to do a Diploma in Education, and we moved into lodgings at 15 Walton Street, near the centre of the city, whence I was able to resume my swimming at Parson's Pleasure. We shared those lodgings with two other members of St John's: Cyril Reed, who was also taking a Diploma in Education, and Jack Linnett, two years my senior and like me a physical chemist. Jack remained a close friend and ultimately became Master of Sidney Sussex College and Vice-Chancellor of the University of Cambridge, where he died in office. It fell to me to give the address at his memorial service in 1975.

That Part Two year was a very happy one. The pressure was off, in that there were no lectures – one just got on with one's research. It had been my intention to work with Robert Robinson on an organic topic and he had accepted me, but I was dissuaded from this by Tommy, and I cannot remember now why I changed. The topic I actually worked on was the photochemistry of the alkyl nitrites, something which will have little meaning for most readers. Let me just say that I enjoyed the work enormously, though by modern standards it would have been regarded as rather elementary. However, it did produce some publishable results and the first paper appeared in the *Transactions of the Faraday Society* in 1937. It was a great satisfaction to me to receive a letter from Sir Derek Barton in 1979 enclosing a reprint of a paper which he had written for the *Journal of the Chemical Society, Perkin Division,* on the eponymous Barton Reaction. On the cover he wrote 'Good work is never wasted: see page 1164'. I duly did and found the reference was to this first paper of mine, so after a lapse of over 40 years I had the pleasure of knowing that my earliest work had contributed significantly to a famous chemical process devised by a Nobel Laureate.

My research was carried out in the 'Abbot's Kitchen', a part of the Old Chemistry Department modelled on the building of the same name at Glastonbury Abbey. This location not only gave me an unrestricted view of the forecourt of the University Museum, but also meant that the light of my high pressure mercury arc lamp illuminated the Warden of Keble College's study. The Warden, the Reverend B.J. Kidd, objected strenuously, and the ensuing verbal exchange when I went to see him brought enlightenment (*sic*) to us both.

As I knew he would be, Tommy was a slave-driver and kept us hard at it. At the time there was a Rhodes Scholar called Milton Meissner, a proficient high-jumper, who was also doing research with Tommy. His work was on the decomposition of gaseous ethylene oxide, for which he had to have an apparatus in which the reaction vessel was maintained at a constant temperature inside an electric furnace. The temperature control of this furnace was achieved by the manual moving of a simple slider on a rheostat. Meissner not only appeared late in the laboratory, which caused Tommy great irritation, but he was very tall and, sitting on the laboratory stool manipulating this rheostat slider, his body was bent in a way which made him look extremely idle, possibly even asleep. This was too much for Tommy and one morning he said in irritation, 'Meissner, why can't you settle down to work properly?' Without changing his posture, Meissner raised a lazy eyelid and said out of the corner of his mouth, 'Say, wha'd'ya expect me to do? Knock the molecules apart?' By silencing Tommy in this way, Meissner gave untold pleasure to us humbler occupants of the laboratory.

Despite the pleasures of independent research, and agreeable friends in the same lodgings, I could not help being concerned about what would happen next. Sometime near the end of the academic year Sidgwick sent for me and indicated that I was likely to do well and that there was a possibility that I might get a Department of Scientific and Industrial Research award, of which two or three had been allocated to Oxford. With this at the back of my mind, I quite cheerfully refused an invitation from M.P. Appleby, Tommy's predecessor in the Fellowship at St John's, to join the staff at ICI's Billingham Division. A little later came the news that I had got a first, and Tommy told me it was likely that I would be offered a senior scholarship by the College.

I imagine that most people would have felt very content with this situation, but although I had had four years of paradise at Oxford I knew in my bones that it was important for me to get away and test myself somewhere else. I indicated to Tommy that if I were offered a scholarship I might well refuse. He could not shift me from this position and suggested, nay commanded, that I go and see the President. From my previous experience I did not think that this would be a particularly agreeable meeting: however, it was worse than I expected because Sir Cyril began by patronising me, asking questions such as 'Have you not enjoyed your four years at Oxford? Has it not lived up to your expectations? Is the chemistry school not good enough for you?' and so on. I just could not get him to see the point that I was neither dissatisfied nor discontented with chemistry in Oxford, but really needed a change. My answers clearly did not satisfy him and there suddenly came back to me, from my experience gained through the Shakespeare Society at school, the words of Valentine to Proteus in *The Two Gentlemen of Verona* (Act 1, Scene 1), which I quoted:

> 'Home keeping youth have ever homely wits...
> I rather would entreat thy company
> To see the wonders of the world abroad,
> Than, living dully sluggardised at home
> Wear out thy youth with sleepless idleness.'

That seemed to silence the President, but whether it was the convincing nature of my argument or whether it was surprise that a scientist should quote Shakespeare to him, I shall never know.

I left that interview feeling I had burned my boats, but evidently my good fairy was at work again, because a short time later I received a letter from Professor R.G.W. Norrish in Cambridge asking me if I would like to go and work with him on a grant he had obtained from ICI Explosives Division at Ardeer on the Ayrshire Coast. I also had an invitation from Sidney Sussex College, Cambridge, which had become twinned with St John's College, Oxford, some few months earlier. I went over to see Norrish as soon as I could, and also called on Canon George Arthur Weekes, Master of Sidney. I then managed to fit in a trip to Paris with an old Sunday school friend, Ralph Bainbridge, who had gone to the University of Sheffield to read a general science degree.

Looking back at these pages, I think I may have given the reader a false impression that life was entirely centred on Oxford during these four years, from 1933 to 1937. That could not possibly be the case for anyone with any sensibility living at that time, and particularly for one who had been to Germany and seen signs of the coming horror of Nazism. If I had not already known about the political problems in Britain, and the growing international tensions, I would have been made aware of them by John Buckatzsch, who for the last three years had been living in Balliol and whom I often used to see, both in Oxford and during the vacations. I was also mindful of the refugees who came to Britain, even to Sheffield as well as to places like Oxford, where I attended their lectures. There was great concern among young people about the inertness – later to be called appeasement – of

Britain against the background of these rising forces, obviously bent on domination. After my return from Germany I had studied reports about that country in the newspapers with some care, reading about Hitler's rise to power and his appalling behaviour against the Jews and against all liberal-minded people. At the end of my third year in Oxford, when I had just completed the practical examinations for my degree, the Spanish generals, who controlled most of the regular army, rebelled against the Popular Front (elected earlier that year) but were held at bay by the factory workers whom the Republican government had armed. Young people in Britain were nauseated when Fascist Italy and Nazi Germany sent military aid to General Franco, and we felt out of tune with the British Establishment, which seemed to have no regard for the duly elected Spanish government. We considered the non-intervention agreements in the years that followed to be merely an excuse on the part of the French and the British to let the Fascists, Falangists and Nazis rearm themselves for what we felt would be the ultimate aggression. So in due course I went to Cambridge with mixed feelings, delighted at the change of environment but distinctly doubtful about the prospects politically.

A Research Student at Cambridge

Cambridge was not entirely unknown to me, at least by repute, because more Centralians went to Cambridge than to Oxford and many of them had told me about it when we met in Sheffield during the vacations. Moreover, I had stayed for a weekend in 1936 with Tom Turner, a history scholar of Peterhouse. It was an unforgettable weekend because I stayed in college and had been invited to attend a meeting of the Peterhouse Sex (short for sexcentenary) Club, of which Tom was an officer. The members of this society read papers to one another and occasionally had guest speakers. On this occasion the meeting was to be addressed by F.R. Leavis: I was eager to hear him, because his reputation as a literary critic and thinker was then in the ascendant. So I was in an attentive and respectful mood, anxious to learn what I could.

My hopes were dashed by the actuality. After dinner in Hall we repaired to someone's rooms; Leavis was introduced and invited to speak. He first removed his tweed jacket and secondly his red tie, and then requested that the electric lights be replaced by candlelight because harsh electric light would be inappropriate for the poetry he intended to read. After some delay candles were brought in and he began to speak in the dullest near-monotone, using sentences which seemed to me to be highly contrived and convoluted. I had just read the book *The Meaning of Meaning* by I.A. Richards and C.K. Ogden, which my Oxford friend Henry Fowler had had to study and which, by comparison with Leavis' talk, seemed to me to be a model of clarity and insight. I could not help wondering how this man, whose spoken English on this occasion was so turgid and laboured, and who was so prone to dismiss with contempt those whose views he did not share, could attract such a reverential following. In the light of that evening it did not surprise me when, nearly thirty years later, Leavis made a venomous attack on C.P. Snow's Cambridge Rede Lecture *The Two Cultures*, and I remember thinking that Richards would probably have been much more perceptive of Snow's purpose.

This early experience of Cambridge was totally against the grain of my preconception of that university as a centre of scientific excellence and calm, rational discussion. However, on my first visit after the Peterhouse weekend I was reassured. This was early in August 1937, when I went to be interviewed by Professor Norrish and Canon Weekes (as mentioned earlier). I stayed the night before my interviews in a house in Drosier Road, near the old Perse School for Boys, occupied by John Turner (elder brother of Tom, and a University Demonstrator) and David Valentine (Research Fellow of St John's College), both botanists. They jointly owned a splendid grand piano and that night they invited in a few friends for coffee, conversation and music. It was a wholly delightful and civilised evening; a good antidote to the Peterhouse fiasco. The following morning I visited the Department of Physical Chemistry and found that, even in early August, it was a hive of activity. It transpired that the natural science dons used five weeks of the Long Vacation to offer short lecture programmes and sometimes laboratory courses, mainly for Part One of the Natural Sciences Tripos. Norrish showed me the room in which I would work, and to my delight I found that I would have for my exclusive use a whole table abutting a service console. He also introduced me to E.J. Buckler, who had the adjacent bench and who was to be an invaluable help to me in the next twelve months; he was an admirable voluntary chemical mentor. My next call, on the charming Canon Weekes, was also most agreeable. After a short conversation, and to my great surprise, he offered me rooms in Sidney Sussex College for 1937-38, which I accepted at once.

These tasks accomplished, I spent a few hours walking around Cambridge to get a feel for the layout and architecture of the college and University buildings. In many ways the similarity to Oxford was obvious, and yet in others subtly different. For example, compared with Oxford the architectural styles were more miscellaneous, there was a much greater use of brick, and the layout of many of the colleges seemed to have been dictated by the river (which they adjoined). This gave a coherence to their western aspects, and a feeling to the observer that they were all part of the same institution. Cambridge seemed to wear its architectural heart on its sleeve, whereas Oxford's collegiate beauty was not so easily accessible and could only be fully enjoyed after going through small doors in large entrance gates.

I enjoyed the railway journey back to Sheffield, admiring Ely, Peterborough and Lincoln cathedrals with their towers picked out in the evening sunshine, and wondering what further pleasant surprises Cambridge might have in store for me. I could not but contrast my euphoria on this occasion with the sombre depression I experienced at Banbury nearly five years earlier when returning to Sheffield from Oxford, convinced that my carelessness was sure to destroy any hope of being admitted to that university. So on my return home I cheerfully went off to Paris with Ralph Bainbridge, thankful for the opportunity to relax in one of the great cultural centres of Europe. The year 1937 was marked by the great Paris Exposition and I have never been able to erase from my mind the dominant image of the Eiffel Tower framed by the two massive Soviet and German pavilions, brutally glaring at one another from either side of an elegant flight of steps, symbolising architecturally an implacable enmity which the Nazi-Soviet pact, negotiated in 1939 by Ribbentrop, could not disguise. The outbreak of war soon demonstrated that the pact was just a cynical deal by Hitler to protect his eastern flank while he attacked in the west, and Stalin for his part gained time to prepare Russia's defences against what he believed would be the inevitable German onslaught.

The pre-war years in Cambridge were delightful, despite the shadow of imminent war. My rooms, on the top floor of the red-brick Garden Court building of Sidney Sussex College, were commodious and convenient. Though technically a non-graduate, I was permitted to dine at the BAs' table where there were many agreeable Cambridge research students, some of whom became friends for life. My fanciful preconception that, being Cromwell's college, Sidney Sussex would be greatly different from Laudian St John's proved false. The dons were equally friendly, especially Tommy Knox-Shaw (University Treasurer); Kenneth Riches, the Chaplain, with whom I played squash and who later became Bishop of Lincoln; and Austin Robinson, an economist with a shy but warm smile. The College had a strong physics tradition: C.T.R. Wilson was in his final years as Fellow and Jacksonian Professor of Physics, and P.I. Dee and J.A. Ratcliffe were Fellows, the last going out of his way to entertain research students. But there was no chemist other than the Professorial Fellow, Sir William Jackson Pope, whom I saw only once in Sidney Sussex, and once in the University Chemical Laboratory, before he died about two years later.

The close resemblance of the Cambridge collegiate organisation to that of Oxford made settling in to Cambridge very easy, but it also obscured what I later realised was an important difference: namely, that the balance of power between the colleges and the University was tipped more towards the University in Cambridge. My first inkling of this was the receipt of an invitation to lunch with Dr J.T. Saunders at Christ's College. He was secretary to the University's Board of Research Studies (or some such title), and it was clear that Cambridge felt a real concern for the welfare of graduates of other institutions, and made an effort to introduce them to their peers and also to the ways of the University.

There were, of course, many University clubs and societies through which social contacts could be extended beyond the college and the laboratory. Some of them, such as the Cambridge branch of the Association of Scientific Workers, had serious purposes, but that which suited me best was the YHA (Youth Hostels Association) Rambling Club, which I joined in my first week because of my frequent holiday use of youth hostels. Every Sunday morning in Full Term those members who wished to explore the country on foot met at Drummer Street bus station to board a coach, commissioned to carry these walkers to their departure point and to meet them on return at the tea place designated in the programme as marking the end of the ramble. The Lent Term card for 1938 shows these termini to include Eltisley, Newmarket, Saffron Walden, Houghton Mill, Royston and Brandon. Compared with the Peak District, or even the Cotswolds, the countryside was tame indeed, but the club had many interesting members, including research students such as the future cosmologist Fred Hoyle; Austyn Mair, later Professor of Engineering; A.J.C. Wilson, a red-headed Canadian crystallographer; and Edward Miller, the mediaeval historian, subsequently Master of Fitzwilliam College. It also welcomed undergraduates into its membership. After returning from a ramble many of us would take a simple, cheap but filling meal in the Blue Barn near Portugal Place. This was run by a colourful émigré American who produced excellent stews and hot Chinese dishes, and considered second helpings to be *de rigueur*. From there we might repair to someone's college rooms for coffee, when the opportunity would be taken to plan future walks and discuss whether there should be an Easter expedition to, for example, the Lake District. But increasingly the conversation on those Sunday evenings was taken up with the inevitability of war, not least because some of us were actively concerned in helping refugees from Europe. I particularly remember going to Martin Ryle's parents' home (his father was Regius Professor of Physic, in other words medicine), where they kept open house for refugees from Spain. At the same time there was a Cambridge anti-war group whose blandishments were easy to resist for anyone who, like myself, had been to Germany or knew refugees. And of course there was at that time excellent music, theatre and cinema in Cambridge, with prices more easily within my means than was the case when I was in Oxford.

Although I had no formal knowledge of botany, I came to know many of the members of the Botany Department through the hospitality of John Turner and David Valentine, and I also learned something of their research in bogs and breck-lands and on photosynthesis (where the effect of intermittent illumination was of particular interest to me). I was also included in some of the botanists' social activities: one occasion I specially remember was when a group of about fifteen people visited the Theatre Cinema, adjacent to Emmanuel College, because it was there that I first met Barbara Wright, who was to become my wife four years later. She was one of two Newnham friends of Kaye Jones, to whom John Turner had become engaged to be married. All three girls were reading for Part One of the Natural Sciences Tripos. John had just been appointed to the Chair of Botany in the University of Melbourne in Australia at the early age of 28, and it had been arranged that Kaye would follow a year later when she had graduated. He asked me if I would supervise her studies in chemistry during that year, and help with any other problems that she might have. I willingly agreed. I will never know if it was he who, in gratitude for my compliance with his request, engineered the invitation which the botanists gave me to join the Cambridge University Botany Department Expedition to study the sub-arctic flora of the north-facing flanks of the

Cairngorms. Alternatively, it may have been because the botanists thought my knowledge of those hills would be useful. It was certainly a delight for me to spend the last two weeks in June 1938 living at Glenmore Lodge on the shores of Loch Morlich, enjoying those splendid mountains once again.

July saw me back in Cambridge to experience and contribute to my first Long Vac Term, which was somewhat truncated by the Annual Meeting of the British Association for the Advancement of Science. As soon as my bank was open on the last day of the conference I cashed a cheque for more money than I knew I had credit for in my account and, together with Einar Stenhagen from Uppsala, I was driven by A.E. Alexander (Alex) – a Fellow of King's with whom I had become friendly – to Parkeston Quay, Harwich, to catch the ferry to Esbjerg in Denmark. As the ship sailed away we could not fail to notice three large steel towers at Bawdsey, the purpose of which was unknown to any of us, but which later became famous as part of the early radar aircraft detection system which was of vital importance in 1940. On arrival at Esbjerg, Einar Stenhagen left us and Alex and I then hitchhiked through Denmark via Ribe to Copenhagen, where we visited J. N. Brønsted's laboratory and of course, the Tivoli Gardens. We took the ferry to Malmö and proceeded to Lund to see part of the University science departments, and so onward by hitchhiking via Nässjö and Linköping to Stockholm for a couple of days before reaching Uppsala, where we slept in Professor Theorell's Biochemistry Department and saw Svedberg's ultracentrifuge. Leaving Alex to his research in Uppsala, I went on a magnificent railway journey (which was also very cheap) to Abisko in Lapland for an ascent of Sweden's highest mountain, Kebnekaise. Here I narrowly escaped being entirely devoured by midges. I had hoped to travel on to Narvik in Norway, but the news was bad: Hitler threatened an invasion of the Sudetenland, Chamberlain was about to visit him in Bad Godesberg, and the impression was that this time Britain and France would stand by the Czechs against the Germans. For me, the key item in the news was that important buildings in London were being protected by means of sandbags. This signified to me that Chamberlain's claim to have gained peace was empty rhetoric, and therefore I felt it was necessary to return home as rapidly as I could.

Internationally the situation worsened over the next twelve months, but although there was a sense of a background worry, overseas news made little impact on the daily lives of young research students in Cambridge. However, the signs of preparation for the inevitable conflict were clear. The names of those working in laboratories were entered on a National Scientific and Technical Manpower Register, created to ensure that the special knowledge of scientists was used for the war effort and that they were not merely drafted into the armed forces as ordinary combatants. Some of us took first aid classes, began air raid precaution (ARP) training and, in my case, also fire service training, but otherwise we worked as usual. I was even able to enjoy another fortnight in the Cairngorms with the botanists in June 1939, this time in company with P.G. Ashmore, of whom more later. In some ways the keenness of our enjoyment of the present was the greater because the future looked so bleak.

Science in Cambridge was very different from that in Oxford. The Cambridge laboratories were larger and better equipped, and none were owned or operated by the colleges. The students reading natural sciences (including medicine), mechanical sciences (i.e. engineering), agriculture and mathematics comprised more than half the total student body, and the distinction of Cambridge in research in most scientific fields was, throughout the nineteenth and early twentieth centuries, generally superior to that of Oxford. Furthermore, the whole structure of courses was more varied and more closely defined than in Oxford, and called for more centralised teaching. The Natural Sciences Tripos involved two years of study of three or four subjects, at least one of which – for example mineralogy with crystallography, biochemistry, physiology – was not in any school curriculum and therefore had to be dealt with *ab initio*. There were examinations at the end of the first and second years, with the results divided into classes according to the standard achieved. Students would then choose to study one subject, or even only a part of one subject, more intensively throughout the third year before taking the final examination (Part Two).

The consequences of the Cambridge structure, and those variations from it which were permitted, were predictable. The graduates were more broadly educated than those of Oxford, and could defer their choice of final specialisation, but there were also disadvantages. The range of subjects which could be taken necessitated highly complex timetabling of lectures and practical classes for Part One, and there was an abundance of programmed work for undergraduates which gave them little time for their own personal development. Moreover, the examination at the end of each year took place in the middle of the third term, so that there were no more than

20 teaching weeks instead of 24, and the four weeks in the third term were of little value because students tended to revise in this period. Another disadvantage was the fact that the level attained at the end of Part One in chemistry was not very much beyond that of the Higher School Certificate, and consequently Part Two, taken in the third year, had to be narrowly specialised if there were to be any depth. Furthermore, most colleges expected students to attend supervision for one hour a week in each of the subjects they were studying for Part One of the Tripos. These supervisions were nothing like Oxford tutorials, but were usually small classes in which students were coached in answering Tripos questions. Consequently the Cambridge students, even at the end of their second year', had not acquired any method of delving into a subject for themselves, or of writing in a way that could subsequently be criticised constructively. I soon realised that my own understanding of chemistry was much more profound across the whole subject than that of Cambridge graduates, though on the other side of the coin I was not as strong as them in mathematics and physics. I tried to remedy this deficiency by going to Part One lectures in mathematics, and to some of the Part Two specialist lectures that were offered in physical chemistry.

At the end of my first term I was asked by Emmanuel College if I would supervise some of their Part One students in chemistry. I set my face firmly against the prevalent Tripos training sessions and found to my pleasure, and I think the students' benefit, that they enjoyed writing brief essays which I would mark and discuss with them, as well as trying to deal with questions which arose out of their lecture or practical work experience. From Part One I graduated to supervision in Part Two specialist physical chemistry, where the Oxford method worked extremely well – in terms of both the development of the individual pupil and his or her success in the Tripos examination.

It took me some time to understand how chemistry in Cambridge was organised at the university level. The substantial University Chemical Laboratory, fronting onto Pembroke Street, accommodated mainly organic chemistry and also some metallurgy. The head of this laboratory was Professor Sir William Pope, who was rarely seen and who had done very little research in the last ten years. So moribund was Pope considered to be that when his death was announced to Dr Moelwyn Hughes (one of the University Demonstrators) in 1939 he at once commented, with characteristic wit, 'How did they know?' With the exception of a few dons, teaching and research in organic and inorganic chemistry seemed very dull. But lively and important work was being carried out in the three separate departments of Theoretical Chemistry, Physical Chemistry and Colloid Science, all of which contributed to teaching and research. E.K. Rideal was head of the Colloid Science Laboratory and his lectures were notable for the immense number of ideas which were thrown out by him, the total disorganisation of the content, and the fascinating personality of the lecturer. He had many lively junior colleagues, including Alexander (of whom I have written), Schulman, Melville, Bosworth, Twigg, Eley, Bolland – all migrants from other universities, and all engaged on interesting new lines of investigation. Physical Chemistry had Norrish at its head, with a fine reputation as a photochemist, and F.P. Bowden, an electrochemist, as Humphrey Owen Jones Lecturer, just starting work on friction and lubrication which later was to become famous.

There were two University Demonstrators. W.C. Price, who was educated as a physicist, was one of the best researchers I have ever known and equally one of the very worst lecturers, except to the most able students. The other, whom I have previously mentioned, was E.A. Moelwyn Hughes, a Welshman educated in Liverpool, who had spent several years in Oxford with Hinshelwood and a year in Germany. I regarded him as a tragic case because he was a classic example of a highly intelligent man, the full flowering of whose intellect was inhibited by a somewhat immature personality, who was easily offended and who believed that Norrish did not appreciate him and that Hinshelwood had not been fair to him. His work on reaction kinetics in solutions, which had been good while he was in Oxford, had become pedestrian and was being outstripped by that of Ingold, A.G. Evans, and their colleagues.

Working with Norrish in Cambridge was totally different from working with Thompson in Oxford. Norrish was an excellent experimentalist but shaky on theory. Correspondingly, his Part One lectures were splendidly illustrated by successful experiments which enthused some students, but were distinctly unmathematical in a subject which is highly quantitative. Norrish visited his research laboratories every day he was in Cambridge and 'directed' the research students to do things. In self-defence we got into the habit of keeping him out of date with our news and making counter-suggestions to him for work that we might do because we thought it would be productive, when in fact we had already done some of it and knew that this would be the case. By nature competitive and combative, he was a hard taskmaster but very convivial, and for years I played squash with him every Friday night at Portugal Place, followed up by drinks at the Union Society.

Also housed in the Physical Chemistry Department was a highly effective group led by Dr G.B.B.M. Sutherland, a physicist and Fellow of Pembroke College, who held no University office. He attracted able colleagues from other universities, including G.K.T. Conn, E. Lee, Mansel Davies and C.K. Wu, whose research was concentrated on the measurement and interpretation of infrared spectra of small molecules, using largely home-made equipment. Alas, they played no part in the teaching. This group, and that led by Tommy Thompson in Oxford, were to play an important role in the development of infrared spectroscopy for analysis and structure determination, especially of the components of enemy aviation fuels during the war. There was a good laboratory spirit: we had a cricket team jointly with Colloid Science, and once a year we would have a sports day at the Emmanuel College grounds, to which academics, research students, technical staff and their wives came in large numbers.

As stated earlier, my research was supported initially by ICI, together with Nobel Industries Ltd. The idea was to try to discover how oxides of nitrogen left behind in mines after the firing of explosive shots affected the spontaneous ignition of fire damp, that is, methane. The obvious first step was to find out what had been published on this subject, for which I needed a science library. I soon exhausted the limited resources of the Physical Chemistry Departmental Library (housed in the Perse Room, which was the upper part of the Hall of the old Perse School), and all the books and serials in the University Chemical Laboratory seemed to be forbidden territory, treated as Professor Pope's private property. So I trekked across Clare Bridge to the splendid new brick edifice called the University Library, the construction costs of which had been partly defrayed by the Rockefeller Foundation. In marked contrast to the smooth efficiency of Oxford's Radcliffe Science Library, also a copyright library, I found not a card index in the central hall but huge leather-bound volumes in which cards adhered to every page. Furthermore, science books were shelved in a far wing, seemingly grouped contiguously by size rather than by chemical affinity. Eventually the books led me to references in chemical journals which were held on an upper floor in the opposite wing. I looked in vain among the bound volumes for the *Journal of the*

American Chemical Society for 1935. None was available after 1934, so I tentatively concluded these were either at the binders or held on shelves for unbound parts. Retracing my steps to the ground floor I approached a library clerk, who directed me to a pamphlet on a table, though I have no doubt he knew the answer to my question. From this pamphlet I learned that the University Library had ceased to take this most important journal in 1935 because a science department (I have forgotten which, but not a chemistry department) had started to buy it. I never entered that library again, and readers will understand why I felt no remorse when, in the summer of 1938, I inadvertently tipped the University Librarian and his lunch into the River Cam when I dived off the Swimming Club's springboard.

Enquiry in the Physical Chemistry Department suggested that I should use, on payment of a fee, the Science Periodicals Library owned by the Cambridge Philosophical Society and located nearby. This was much more convenient, and after background reading there I decided that, before tackling the methane system, I would try to get some results from what I thought would be the intrinsically simpler investigation of the effect of nitrogen dioxide on the hydrogen-oxygen reaction. Oddly enough, at that time the only publication on this was one by Hinshelwood and H.W. Thompson. I found that their data were grossly in error, and this was the beginning of my appreciation of the fact that the experimental techniques in Cambridge were far superior to those in use in Oxford.

Having shown that nitrogen dioxide would indeed sensitise the ignition of methane-oxygen mixtures, which satisfied ICI, I wanted to be free of the constraints of an industrial research grant. Happily the Goldsmiths' Company once again came to my aid and offered me £250 a year, without any strings. This was not riches untold, but it was enough to live on. Augmented by what I was earning in supervision and demonstrating to students in the laboratory, the grant enabled me to meet all my bills, which of course included the cost of chemicals used and particular items of equipment which were not returned to the store in good order. This new source of funding also allowed me to contemplate and execute more basic research than the original problem would have provided, and I decided to investigate carefully the thermal and photochemical sensitisation of the hydrogen-oxygen combustion, both by oxides of nitrogen and by nitrosyl chloride. Such processes were bound to be chain reactions, and therefore the first thing I did was to spend part of the prize which St John's had awarded me for a good result in finals to buy

N.N. Semenov's classic *Chemical Kinetics and Chain Reactions,* published just two years earlier, every page of which I read with great enjoyment. The subject became a lifelong interest and his book both influenced my own work and prompted me, some nineteen years later, to write a shorter monograph for student use. I first met Semenov in Moscow in 1965, when we had several conversations: I then became acquainted with his daughter Lyudmilla and son-in-law Vitalii Goldanskii, also an Academician. Both were extremely helpful when I had to write Semenov's biographical memoir for the Royal Society. I shall always regret that it was impossible for me to attend the conference held in Moscow in 1996 to commemorate the centenary of his birth, though my absence did not prevent the Russian Academy of Sciences from awarding me a Semenov Centenary Medal.

For my intended research I needed glass or silica reaction vessels, maintained at an elevated temperature within an electric oven, to which I could admit the reagents and sensitiser. Norrish had heard that George Kent of Luton, instrument makers, had constructed a 'Multelec' temperature controller and pen recorder which they had presented to Lord Rutherford. Believing that it would be an asset to his laboratory equipment and that I might find it useful, Norrish sent me to Lord Rutherford to see if I could persuade him to lend it to me. What was noteworthy about the encounter was Rutherford's directness, his uninhibited adverse comments on chemistry in general compared with physics, and his contempt in particular for Cambridge chemistry. His forcefully expressed doubts about physical chemistry made me indignant and caused me to answer back with some spirit. Paradoxically, that seemed to please him, and after commenting that chemists make inaccurate measurements on pure compunds, while physicists make accurate measurements on impure compounds, he dismissed me with instructions to collect the instrument. In the event, the temperature recorder did not prove to be particularly useful but Norrish, who saw no use for the apparatus in Rutherford's laboratory, had once more got his own way.[4]

It was a salutary experience for me, and I was fascinated by Rutherford's personality. I had another glimpse of it before he died when, shortly after I came to Cambridge, Niels Bohr was passing through on his way to work with John Wheeler

---

4. This incident is neatly described on page 564 of David Wilson's biography, *Rutherford: Simple Genius* (Hodder & Stoughton, 1993).

at Princeton on the Bohr-Wheeler liquid drop model of the nucleus. Rutherford asked him to give a colloquium in the Cavendish Laboratory, which I attended. Rutherford, then only a few weeks from his death and suffering from a hernia, fell asleep during Bohr's quietly spoken lecture but was awakened by the applause, and immediately began to ask questions. Bohr, who had worked in Rutherford's laboratory in Manchester back in 1913 and loved him as a son loves a father, was a very patient man, but even he was moved to say in his quiet way, 'Professor Rutherford, if you would only read the literature you wouldn't ask some of these questions': whereupon Rutherford, with his famous stammer, said, 'D-D-Damn it Niels, I am so-so-so busy writing the literature I have no t-t-time to read it'.

I have drawn attention to differences between Oxford and Cambridge, but these are differences mainly of emphasis and are relatively trivial in comparison with what they have in common. What I did not realise about these two universities until I was in my mid-forties was that to be a student at either Oxford or Cambridge confers on an individual a unique benefit, which lasts throughout life. It is not that the student is studying under the tutelage of some of the best minds in the United Kingdom; indeed, I can think of some departments in other universities which can surpass their counterparts in Oxford or Cambridge. Nor is it the social graces which one is likely to acquire in Oxford and Cambridge which make one more readily acceptable to the British Establishment. An Oxonian or Cantabrigian is often assumed by representatives of that Establishment, many of whose members are themselves drawn from the ancient universities, to be more likely to share their values and their implicit belief in certain British institutions. They are predisposed to declare an Oxbridge graduate as 'sound', their highest accolade. Joining Oxford or Cambridge, therefore, is similar to being enrolled in a network which confers advantages, especially within the corridors of power.

I have never been happy to be referred to as an Oxford (or Cambridge) man, for such labelling diminishes individuality. Others more easily pigeonhole us, adding to or detracting from our intrinsic worth according to their prejudices about either university. However, I believe that belonging to both universities has worked to my advantage to a degree far beyond my just deserts, for I can think of many persons I have met who, not being Oxbridge graduates, have greater talents and would have performed some of the tasks I have been given better than I, but who have not been asked. The country is the poorer for this. I would be more depressed by this situation were it not for the expansion of higher education in this country in the last thirty years, and therefore the inevitable decline in the proportion of university graduates drawn from Oxbridge. So the walls of Jericho are bound to crumble, without any sound of trumpets, and Britain will be stronger for it – as will Oxford and Cambridge, which will have to look to their laurels.

At the head of this chapter I quoted a verse by the Reverend Joseph Trapp, Oxford's first professor of poetry, who also knew Cambridge and received its MA degree by incorporation. In it Trapp wittily conjoins the two commendable qualities of loyalty and learning, but attributes only the former to Cambridge and the latter to Oxford. This attracted a riposte, also in verse, from the Cambridge medical graduate Sir William Browne, later President of the Royal College of Physicians. Browne's lines neatly turn the tables on those of Trapp, and it therefore seems fitting that they should be the final words of this chapter. The reader may also feel, as I do, that the compositions reveal that each eighteenth-century versifier shares with the other certain values which can only be categorised as the Oxbridge ethos, and will make his or her own judgment as to how much survives to this day.

> *The King to Oxford sent a troop of horse,*
> *For Tories own no argument but force;*
> *With equal skill to Cambridge books he sent,*
> *For Whigs admit no force but argument.*
>
> Sir William Browne (1692-1774)

CHAPTER 3

CAMBRIDGE

My patience is now at an end.

Adolf Hitler, September 1938

The War Years, 1939–1945

After the Sudetenland fiasco in September 1938, the question in the minds of most Cambridge people was not 'Will there be war?' but 'When and how will war break out?' Most were uncertain what action they should take. Eric, the technician who served the research laboratories where I worked, had already joined the RAF Volunteer Reserve and qualified by part-time training as a sergeant pilot. The scientists got on with their teaching and research, observing with interest the planning of air raid precautions (ARP) for university buildings, including their modification to provide easy access to roofs and upper floor windows, identification of places where voluntary wardens would have their overnight bases in individual laboratories, and a central control point for, among others, the whole of the New Museums Site (which included the Cavendish Laboratory, the Chemistry, Physical Chemistry, Colloid Science, Metallurgy and Zoology Departments, the Examination Schools, and the Science Periodicals Library of the Philosophical Society). Training in first aid, firefighting and wardening continued, and many participated. But few of us knew what was likely to be in store for us when the war began.

In the late spring of 1939 some of this uncertainty was removed when five of us in the Department of Physical Chemistry were nominated to go to the Royal Aircraft Establishment (RAE) at Farnborough, which was the major Air Ministry research establishment. The five comprised W.C. Price (later FRS, then a University Demonstrator), T.P. Hughes, Fellow of Caius, who was looking after the group F.P. Bowden had left when he went to the USA and Australia (ostensibly on a lecture tour, but he did not return until 1945), and three research students including myself. We arrived at the RAE in, I think, early August, found digs in the Farnham area and reported to the chemistry department, which seemed somewhat unprepared for us and slightly embarrassed to know what to do with us. Only Bill Price found work where he could make a real contribution to the war effort. This was because he was a very accomplished experimental spectroscopist: although his primary interests were in vacuum ultra-violet spectroscopy, he saw scope for infrared spectroscopy in the analysis of hydrocarbon mixtures, especially enemy fuels, and in fact he spent most of the war working at ICI on Teesside.

My experience was, I think, more typical. My first shock came on seeing a man, whom I later discovered to have a PhD, stirring a bucket of black paint which he applied to pieces of the material used on the underside of Wellington bombers. He then measured its reflectance to white light, as a means of determining which type of paint would give the least chance of a bomber being picked out by enemy searchlights. Having seen the Bawdsey array just a year earlier, and having learned from chance conversation that there was a part of the non-visible electromagnetic radiation spectrum which could be reflected by aircraft, with the returning signal used to determine their direction and range, I thought it likely that the Germans would also have such aircraft detection systems. By contrast, the application of black paint was, to say the least, primitive and in any case not effective against radiation outside the visible spectrum.

The first task I was given was to use the inclined glass plate method to assess the suitability of a range of oils as lubricants. This involved placing a drop of the liquid on a clean glass or metal plate, and then measuring the angle of tilt of the plate at which the liquid drop began to flow downhill. On the face of it this seemed to me to give little information about how such a fluid would influence the coefficient of friction of one metal surface on another and, after making a number of measurements, I tried to write a brief paper relating the angle of tilt to the density, viscosity, wetting angle and size of the drop. I was disappointed to find that my observations were not particularly welcome to the permanent staff, who clearly found my approach too theoretical!

Possibly because the RAE already knew that my research was on the combustion of hydrogen-oxygen mixtures, I was then asked to find a chemical which, when added in small amounts to hydrogen in the barrage balloons, would render the latter immune to inflammation when punctured. *A priori* arguments based on what was known about the chemistry of this reaction, and of the flame propagation limits of hydrogen-air mixtures, convinced me that it was very unlikely indeed that such a substance could be found – a view which was strengthened by a visit to Cardington, the barrage balloon station near Bedford. Once again my masters were not well pleased, and they asked me to justify my pessimism by direct experiment. I accepted the challenge but as I could not do the necessary work effectively at the RAE, I returned to Cambridge. Having found somewhere to live and obtained Professor Norrish's approval, I started on this task with a new research student, P.G. Ashmore (later to be Professor of Physical Chemistry at UMIST), to help in studying what happened when a membrane of balloon fabric separating hydrogen from air was penetrated by a high voltage spark. Ashmore and I found that some additives would narrow the composition range of hydrogen-air mixtures which could be ignited by a spark (the best was the evil smelling diethylselenide), but we could not believe that this would afford any significant protection when a large hole had been blown in a barrage balloon by either a high explosive or an incendiary bullet, both of which we knew the Germans had available.

The outbreak of war was an enormous anticlimax in Britain, though not of course in Poland, which was swiftly overrun. But the Germans made no move towards the west, and there was no immediate mass bombing of British cities. It seemed that I could achieve more by staying in Cambridge to contribute to the teaching and demonstrating that was necessary if the students, now enrolled on intensive shortened courses, were to be dealt with adequately, given the shortage of staff (three of whom – Bowden, Price and Moelwyn Hughes – had left or were leaving the Physical Chemistry Department); Norrish and Rideal were putting a great deal of pressure on me to do this, and I acquiesced. An added advantage was that I could get my PhD thesis written at the same time, and I succeeded in doing so by the following Easter.

The next five years, from the fall of France to the end of the war in Europe, were probably the busiest and hardest of my life. In addition to the intensive schedule of lecturing, demonstrating and supervising students studying for Parts One and Two of the Natural Sciences Tripos, and coping with my ARP responsibilities, I became involved in a lot of extra-mural research for the Ministry of Supply, the Ministry of Aircraft Production and other bodies.

During this period I was paid by the University as a Departmental Demonst-rator, on terms similar to those of a University Demonstrator, and contributions towards my salary came from the government departments for which I was doing extra-mural research. The students were often equally hard-pressed. Many had duties in the University Officers' Training Corps, and a large proportion were required to take compulsory courses in the Tripos which had never been offered before – for example, in electronics – since it was expected that many of them would go off into radar, in either research or operational work. Despite these preoccupations, they worked hard and I had some splendid students. Among my supervisees were people like Norman Sheppard (FRS), Don Ramsay (FRS), R.R. Baldwin, J.C. Bevington and K.J. Ivin (all later appointed to chairs), Herchel Smith, afterwards a notable benefactor of the University, and many others. Predictably, they did very well in the Tripos examinations and I am afraid that much of the credit for their success was attributed to me when in fact they were so good that no supervisor, however bad, could possibly have ruined them.

I also derived great benefit from having to lecture on every conceivable branch of physical chemistry, for both Part One and Part Two, the main course for the latter being shared with Professor Rideal. I had never lectured before and the memory of my first experience, in the large Number One Lecture Theatre of the University Chemical Laboratory, is still engraved on my mind. This was a lecture for Part One of the Natural Science Tripos and was accompanied by a number of demonstrations, for which I had the able assistance of a very experienced labora-tory assistant called Fred Smith. I had prepared every word with great care and rehearsed the demonstrations with Fred. I ought to have been quite confident, but nevertheless I was terrified when faced with an almost full room. I began to speak but after a few words my voice seemed to desert me – I imagine through sheer nervousness. Fred was completely prepared for such a situation, which no doubt he had witnessed many times before. He tactfully pushed in front of me a beaker containing water and said, 'Drink this, Sir, take a deep breath and start again slowly'. I did precisely as I was instructed and my voice came out, but I made one mistake. I began by saying, 'I hope you can all hear me'. A reply came from a student in the first occupied row, whose identity I do not know (if he happens to read this book perhaps he will declare himself). He said loudly and clearly, 'I can hear you, but I am prepared to swap places with someone else'. This produced a great roar of laughter throughout the lecture theatre. Its effect on me was to set the adrenaline flowing and make me determined to succeed, so thenceforward I made little reference to my notes, relied more on my understanding of the subject matter, and spoke naturally, thereby winning Fred Smith's approbation.

During this period I was in charge of a fire squad of six people who initially comprised Moelwyn Hughes, whose Welsh stories kept us greatly amused; Morris Sugden (T.M. Sugden, later FRS, Head of Shell Thornton Research Laboratories, Master of Trinity Hall and, I think, the most able student I ever encountered in Cambridge); Jack Dainty, a physics graduate who later became Professor of Biophysics in the University of Toronto; and a couple of technicians drawn from a pool consisting of Johnny Dear (who had been J.J. Thomson's laboratory assistant and had endless stories about him), Fred Webber, Ted Webb and Jack Eyles, all from the chemistry laboratories. Our first duty was to check that the individual air-raid posts in every department were properly manned and that each fire-watcher had his equipment and either a piece of cheese and two biscuits, or sixpence 'in lieu thereof'. That inspectorial and clerical work completed, and the communication lines thoroughly tested, we would occasionally have a drill with hose and fire pump. In our case this was a mobile unit which could be hauled by two men and which delivered a powerful jet of water after coupling up to the mains. We had many amusing episodes, and one evening distinguished ourselves by dousing a fire which had started in Pembroke College and which could not be quelled by the Auxiliary Fire Services sent from the nearby fire station. I realised that if we could get our pump into the lift in the Chemical Laboratory, and connect it to one of the main risers on the top floor, we might then be able to send a jet of water across the street and onto the burning Pembroke College on the opposite side – something which the Fire Services, not having a turntable and high ladder, were unable to achieve. This we did, and it turned out to be very successful. The result was that the following morning I was summoned to see the Master of Pembroke College, Sir Montague Butler, who not only thanked me but gave me a letter of appreciation, which I still have. Despite the obvious hazards I enjoyed firefighting and the ideas behind it, and I suppose that it was my known interest which resulted in my being appointed an Honorary Fire Observer. In that capacity, I went to various fires in the Cambridgeshire area and sometimes further afield, for example to Stevenage to attend a spontaneous blaze in a paper mill.

By Easter 1940 I was getting rather restive, particularly as Sandy Ashmore had decided to go off and join the Royal Air Force. My eyesight was sufficiently bad to preclude actual military service, so I tried to get a job where my chemical knowledge might be of some use. I made one application, for which I was interviewed, to join the contemporary Bristol Aeroplane Company, and another to what was then the Anglo-Iranian Oil Company and is now BP. Both turned me down, but by the time the rejections came the Germans had turned their attention to the western front and the fall of France was imminent. The first impact on me came during the evacuation of Dunkirk, when Sir Will Spens, then Regional Commissioner for East Anglia, summoned myself and Dr J.H. Schulman from the Colloid Science Laboratory. He told us that within his area of jurisdiction there were many underground petrol dumps of considerable size, that it was essential that these dumps should be made useless to the Germans should they invade, and that we as chemists must surely be able to identify some marvellous additive which, in small amounts, would do this trick. Expense was no object, so we each arranged for the use of a car, and in my case I also asked Sandy Ashmore if he would help once again. Our research involved adding a chemical to the petrol tank of the car and seeing what effect it had on a test run, and this frequently necessitated siphoning out old fuel and filling up again with new. At that time rumours abounded to the effect that German parachutists dressed as nuns were descending from the sky to perform their knavish tricks on the innocent civilians of East Anglia, and our suspicious roadside activities would swiftly have led to our arrest had we not each carried a magic piece of paper which gave us immunity.

The work was purely empirical, except for one thing. Everybody told us that the way to put petrol out of action was to deposit sugar in it. Of course that is not effective – the sugar is not soluble, but sinks to the bottom and therefore would not readily be delivered to the fuel tanks of any enemy vehicles (and in any case none of their vehicles had a gravity feed from the fuel tank to the engine). Therefore the petrol had somehow to be altered. In the end Sandy and I did find a chemical substance, phosphorus oxychloride, which polymerized the unsaturated hydrocarbons in the petrol: this led to a progressive gumming of the petrol pump valves, so that the fuel failed to get to the engine. Having found that small quantities of this worked, I then went to Albright and Wilson, the phosphorus manufacturers at Oldbury, and told them I had the authority to commandeer their supplies, as needed, without telling them the purpose. My meeting with them would have been an absolute disaster but for the happy chance that one of the directors present was an ex-Oxford chemist, Brian Topley, who saw the point at once.

That was the end of my part in the affair, but there are two further comments I must make. First, many years after the war I learned that the Regional Commissioner for the London Area had put exactly the same question to Alexander King, then a lecturer in physical chemistry at Imperial College, London. (He later became an international figure, first in UNESCO and then in the Club of Rome, where he was responsible for the publication of the seminal book *Limits to Growth*.) He found that shredded rubber is swollen by petrol, and therefore has the effect of clogging up petrol supply lines. The other comment relates to the fact that after the war I became interested in what is called cationic polymerization of unsaturated hydrocarbons. In this reaction the catalyst is a halide – like boron trifluoride or, in our case, phosphorus oxychloride – which reacts with the water as a co-catalyst in the slightly damp petrol to produce an acid, which can release the cation H^+ to start the polymerization. It was not until much later that I realised that this reaction was as old as the hills, in that nearly two centuries earlier Richard Watson, while still a Fellow of Trinity College, Cambridge, had mixed oil of vitriol with oil of turpentine and got a dark gum.[1]

Yet another problem which proved very interesting, on which I worked for the Ministry of Aircraft Production, was the mysterious, spontaneous inflammation of fuel in the petrol tanks of British aircraft after attack by German fighters.

---

1. Richard Watson, born in 1737, studied mathematics at Cambridge and was elected a Fellow of Trinity College at the age of 23. Four years later he was appointed Professor of Chemistry although, as he records in his memoirs, he knew not a syllable of the subject. This was not much of a prize because no stipend was attached, and the Duke of Buckingham had to intercede with the King in order to ensure a modest salary, half of which Watson used to employ an Italian laboratory assistant to teach him his trade. When he wished to experiment himself, he would ask the assistant to bring his 'laboratory in on a tray', which suggests that his equipment was of the simplest kind. Nevertheless he did some interesting experiments in chemistry, including the one referred to in the text.

When Watson was 37 the Regius Chair of Divinity became vacant. As he again records, it had long been the secret object of his desire to occupy what he regarded as the most important chair of this kind in Europe: however, he lacked the necessary primary qualification of a degree in divinity. Conveniently, that was accorded to him just before the election took place in the Senate House. He did not then abandon chemistry, but continued to work at it and to write about it until various clerical preferments came his way, culminating in his appointment, at the age of 45, to the Bishopric of Llandaff. Watson appears not to have visited his diocese often, because he went to reside at Calgarth House in the Lake District, just outside

Sometimes damaged tanks did not inflame in the cold air, but did so on reaching the ground. The reason for this was that the Germans were using phosphorus-filled incendiary bullets, and with Dr J.C. Bevington (later a professor at Lancaster University) I reinvestigated Boyle's early work on the effect of hydrocarbons on the combustion of white phosphorus. This led to a simple remedy to a practical problem: namely, to flood any petrol tanks which on landing appeared to have been pierced by a bullet, and which were largely empty of fuel, with nitrogen to displace the air, and then remove all the petrol. When the war was over I turned again to the mechanism of the oxidation of white phosphorus to which, as I have mentioned, I was introduced at the age of nine in Nether Green School, Sheffield. This resulted in the publication of three papers, although the mechanism of the reaction is still not completely understood.

When it became known that the Germans were developing jet propulsion, using low grade kerosene fuel which is not easily inflammable, a problem arose as to the sort of 40mm anti-aircraft shell filling which would be necessary to cause ignition. I therefore found myself, with a colleague named McMullen, involved in the study of how drop-size distribution in a spray of AMVO (Air Ministry Vaporising Oil) affected ignitability. Yet another problem was that of improving the efficiency of the 'candles' used for laying down smoke screens.

These various experiences added little, if anything, to my scientific knowledge. They were nonetheless valuable in many other ways. I learned how to relate to people of very different backgrounds, including many whose concerns were not with the 'how' and 'why' something worked but with ensuring that a device functioned properly and rarely failed, or who had to train others to use potentially lethal devices with safety and efficiency. One example will suffice. When I first saw smoke candles labelled 'ROB' (rate of burning) as so many seconds per inch, my purist, scientifically-trained mind recoiled, for all rates must

---

Bowness-on-Windermere. In fact, it was while sheltering from the rain in the early 1950s, during a holiday in Windermere, that we wandered into Bowness church and almost the first thing that caught my eye was a marble tablet commemorating in Latin *Ricardus A Watson*. Watson was a man of many parts, much given to writing tracts of a controversial kind, covering not only religious issues but also political matters: he even took on as his antagonists the redoubtable Edward Gibbon and Thomas Payne. It is said of him that he did not visit his diocese more frequently because he was so busy writing tracts denouncing absenteeism among the Anglican clergy, but I have not been able to find any actual evidence for that statement.

by definition be expressed as quantities per second, minute or hour. A moment's reflection, however, showed me how much more useful the first (unscientific) label is to the Royal Engineer sergeant commanded to lay down a smoke screen for a stated period of time. I then began to look at other instructions in military manuals, and gained a new respect for their practicality and the people who had written them. I resolved that as a university teacher I should always keep in mind the real utility to my students of what I was trying to teach.

I also learned a good deal about the behaviour of people, each with their own private goals, both as individuals and in formal groups – the latter nowadays given the pompous name of group dynamics. This happened in part because I was, for a considerable period, secretary of a committee concerned with military pyro-technics, incendiaries, fuses and initiators. Some of the members were especially sensitive about how I recorded their verbal contributions: their punctiliousness in this regard, it seemed to me, was designed to bolster their self-importance rather than to advance the debate. There were lessons to be drawn from this experience too, which have stood me in good stead in my later academic life!

The autobiographer's trap is to over-emphasise his own work, and I must try to redress the balance: there were several other groups of scientists remaining in the Department of Physical Chemistry whose work may well have been more important than that with which I was involved. One such group was the one led by Dr G.B.B.M. Sutherland, who had been brought back from other duties to develop a spectroscopic service for identifying the components of enemy aviation fuels (to which I have already made brief reference). The ultimate benefits of this work were manifold, not least in enabling the most crucial enemy oilfields and refineries involved in producing these fuels to be identified, and targeted for attack by the Allied bombers. In this investigation Dr Delia Simpson, Fellow of Newnham College, had an important documentary role.

Dr C.H. Bamford was probably the best of the 'classical' photochemists who worked with Norrish and were responsible for identifying the various types of decomposition which are possible when aldehydes or ketones absorb ultraviolet light. He ran a group charged with making incendiary mixtures for a variety of purposes, including use by saboteurs in enemy-occupied countries. I have already mentioned Dr T.M. Sugden who, having obtained an outstanding First in Chemistry Part Two in two rather than the usual three years, had begun research with Dr W.C.

Price in 1940 on the measurement of ionization potentials by electron impact. For most of the war he, in collaboration with D.W.E. Axford, another former Cambridge student, investigated the nature of gun muzzle flash with a view to its suppression, to deprive the enemy of this clear indication of the location of artillery. This group developed fast techniques for studying a range of processes occurring in the propellant gases, including ionization using optical and microwave techniques. They became expert in timing circuits, and these were subsequently important in devising the flash photolysis techniques for which Norrish and Porter were to be awarded a share in the 1967 Chemistry Nobel Prize. The fourth group was led by Dr T.P. Hughes and concentrated on friction and lubrication.

In 1942 we had two notable visitors to the laboratory: George B. Kistiakowsky (Kisty) and E.W.R. (Ned) Steacie. Kisty was at that time working in the US Navy ordnance laboratory at Bruceton, near Pittsburg, and afterwards became head of the explosives division of the Manhattan Project (which developed the first atomic bombs) at Los Alamos. Ned was head of the Chemistry Division of the National Research Council of Canada, of which he was later to become President. Both were attractive characters whom I was to get to know very well after the war, and each was interested in the mechanisms of gaseous chemical reactions. Both also deserved a book to themselves: one has now been published about Ned, and I have written a biographical memoir for the Royal Society about Kisty. I mention them here simply because Kisty asked me what I was going to do after the war. I raised the question of photochlorination and, with a marvellous smile on his face, he directed my attention to an important paper which he had written and which I had overlooked. When I met Ned Steacie for the second time, which I think was towards the end of 1944, he mentioned something about 'Tube Alloys', of which I knew nothing except that one or two people in Cambridge were said to be employed by a firm of that name.[2] I told Ned that I was already fully occupied with work in Cambridge and that no move would be possible. Immediately after the war, however, he arranged for me to visit the Chalk River nuclear research centre in Canada, which gave me an experience (described later in this chapter) which was influential in determining my choice of post-war areas of research.

2. It was in fact the cover name for the British atomic research programme.

The most important event in my life, and a constant cause of rejoicing, took place when Britain's fortunes were very low. I mentioned earlier that I met briefly in 1938 a zoology student from Newnham College named Barbara Wright, two of whose friends I supervised in chemistry during 1938-39. At the time France fell she was taking Part Two of the Natural Sciences Tripos examination in zoology, after which she went on to carry out research with James Gray, and later C.F.A. Pantin. When she was a research student, Barbara was required to do fire-watching in the Zoology Laboratory and, since I was responsible for arranging the fire-watching rotas, I soon ensured that my duties coincided with hers on a more regular basis than those of any other person on the site. We were married on 27 August 1942, the hottest day of the year, by Bishop Kempthorne, the retired Bishop of Lichfield, at the delightful Trumpington Parish Church. We chose Trumpington because Chaucer's Reeve's Tale describes how there was a miller there who 'bore a Sheffield thwytel in his hose', the earliest literary reference to the cutlery trade in that city. This is not the place to go into the many and varied satisfactions of a rather rich married life, but two things which subsequently gave me great pleasure were to receive an honorary ScD degree from Trinity College, Dublin – the same award that my father-in-law, W.B. Wright, had earned as a research geologist – and an honorary degree from Manchester University, which institution had also awarded my mother-in-law an honorary MSc many years earlier.

Barbara and I managed to find a tiny house to rent in Woodlark Road, backing onto some college playing fields, and settled in with very little furniture – a mixture of what we found in second-hand shops and what friends gave us. Our stock was augmented a year later when we were given coupons and bought a 'utility' wardrobe under the newly introduced wartime scheme. There was enough garden at the back to enable us to grow vegetables and we had that rare possession, a telephone, which was installed because of my status as an Honorary Fire Observer liable to be called out at any time to visit a suspicious fire. We both remember those early years with pleasure, despite the fact that there was little time for recreation and, indeed, little opportunity for it. But we had many friends and there was a widespread feeling of togetherness, of being united by our experiences of the war; as it says in the Epistle of St Paul to the Ephesians, we were all members one of another. The only great sadness was the death of my mother in 1943, and therefore the end of 66 Ranby Road as the focus of my family.

Recovery and Renewal, 1945–50

Much has been written about the extraordinary and deeply held sense of community of the people of the United Kingdom throughout the Second World War, which my own experience confirms. There were, however, many changes of national mood, especially following news of adverse events. These were noticeable after, for example, the fall of France in 1940, and the setbacks in the Mediterranean and the Far East in 1941 and 1942. The turning point for me, after which I was less prone to gloom, was 22 June 1941 when BBC radio announced that the German armies had invaded the Soviet Union. I remember thinking that where Napoleon had failed it was unlikely that Hitler would succeed. Nevertheless, although the German advance was slower than expected they were at the gates of Moscow by early December, before they were stopped by the Soviet armies. However, in the same month Japan attacked Pearl Harbour, and Hitler and Mussolini declared war on the USA. It then seemed to me quite impossible that the Allies could ever lose the war. This certainty of ultimate victory was sufficient to allow influential people and institutions to begin to consider the kind of Britain its citizens might wish to build after the war was over.

From my experience in ARP, fire-watching and other activities which brought me into contact with non-academic citizens, it seemed to me that most wanted a society in which burdens and benefits were more equitably distributed than was the case during the inter-war years. This impression was confirmed by the reception given to the Butler Education Act of 1944. Other more far-reaching proposals were articulated, notably Sir William Beveridge's plan for universal social security, and many voices were raised to urge the nationalisation of industries such as coal and the railways, where there was evidence of mismanagement by the owners. Whether such views corresponded with the wishes of the majority of the British people, and whether the Conservative Party or the Labour Party would have the better programmes and the will to reform, was unknown. All that was certain was that the existing government had not been constituted for any such purpose of radical change: only a general election could settle the matter. This took place on 5 July 1945 and resulted in a large Labour majority in the Commons.

What few of us, certainly not myself, realised was the high economic cost of the war to the United Kingdom. The country was, in fact, effectively bankrupt. The new government nevertheless pressed ahead towards full employment, the passage of the National Health Service Act, and the nationalisation of certain industries. The full New Jerusalem was inevitably postponed, in the sense that austerity was even more stringent than during the war and that food, clothing and furniture continued to be rationed; all manufacturing effort was directed at producing goods for export. However, although to many young dons it soon became apparent that they would not enjoy the lifestyle of their pre-war counterparts, that house and car ownership would be long deferred, and that universities would be significantly underfunded, there were many powerful mitigating factors which made the immediate post-war period a cheerful one, in which the continued shortages were merely a trifling irritation. In my case some of these mitigating factors were peculiar to me; others were of general applicability, and some a mixture of both.

Of central importance was my connection with St Catharine's College. I had supervised undergraduates of that College for about three years during the war, and in 1944 the College kindly allocated a set of rooms in the Hobson's building, where I could keep a few papers and books and conduct supervisions with one or two pupils. To my great pleasure and surprise I received a letter in December 1944 from the Master, asking me whether I would 'consider the possibility of accepting a Fellowship ... to help us [the College] in dealing with the problems of science direction and teaching'. I eagerly accepted, was formally elected in May 1945, and assumed office on 1 October. It was the beginning of five very happy years. The Master had assigned me rooms in a building completed in 1634 and later demolished, together with the old SCR, to make way for the present dining hall. My set was number 3 on what was known as E staircase: it became my College base on 6 November 1945 and was commodious, containing a large wood-panelled sitting room with windows looking out onto Walnut Tree Court on one side and Queen's College, across Queen's Lane, on the other. There were attractive ornamental wood carvings over the fireplace and the four door lintels; happily these carvings have been preserved within the College. There was also an ample bedroom, a simple kitchen and a small gyp room.[3] Many of my former pupils will remember with varying mixtures of pleasure and pain the supervisions they experienced there, but

---

3. 'Gyp' is the Cambridge equivalent of the Oxford 'scout'.

I expect only a few realised that this early building was made possible by the bequest of the Bull Inn and its yard from the Master of Caius, one John Gostlin, who died in 1626. I have often wondered whether the present Master of Caius still encourages his Fellows to drink sadly 'to the unhappy memory of Dr Gostlin, who was such a goose as to leave the Bull to Catharine'.

The main positive factor in St Catharine's was the great sense of common purpose, which reinforced a pervasive collegiality. A high proportion of the students were ex-servicemen who, after six years of war, were eager to learn (and therefore a pleasure to teach) and to enjoy to the full the opportunities offered by Cambridge. They also had a sense of the permanence of the fundamental values which higher education should serve. I well remember the riposte of a former RAF officer in his mid twenties, whom I had asked why he, as a man who had had to meet the ultimate test in battle, did not find it irksome to be forced to wear a gown in the street after dusk. Tugging at the front of his own gown he said simply, 'I think this is the gown that Newton wore' – words that I have never forgotten. Another example was when several mainly ex-service undergraduates reading natural sciences, not all of them from St Catharine's, expressed to me their longing for something which would speak to the affective, as distinct from the cognitive, side of their nature. I spoke to the English don and senior tutor of St Catharine's, Tom Henn, and he arranged lectures for them in the Long Vacation. These attracted very large audiences indeed, which not only surprised him but stimulated him to write a delightful book, *The Apple and the Spectroscope*, and then to make a notable collection of scientific writings.

I saw much of the junior members because I was Praelector, which meant that among other things I presented graduands for their degrees, and I was also the 'link man' between the SCR and the JCR. I enjoyed every minute of my work with the junior members, and their names and faces still come readily to mind with great pleasure. By and large they were committed to their work and to their College and, of course, they had much to teach me.[4] There was a parallel commitment to

---

4. I do not wish to imply that the undergraduates, whether ex-service or straight from school, were over-serious. Quite the contrary was the case. There was some light-hearted flouting of the rules which it was the duty of the pernoctating Fellow to apply. I tried to apply the rules with discretion, based on the idea of flexible rather than rigid administration from which I had benefited when an undergraduate at Oxford.

collegiate life from the senior members. Only five of them lived in College, but the others would frequently pernoctate and, as with the other Fellows, their rooms were the natural and welcome foci of enormously diverse social, literary, scientific and musical activities. Of course there were differences of opinion from time to time, sometimes strongly maintained, but our debates were always civilised and I was constantly aware of the firm adherence of the Fellows to the principle that St Catharine's should be a place where the common aim was to develop the latent talents of intellect and personality of every junior member. Even the question of the admission of women to full membership of the University, of which I was an active and public proponent, caused much less schism in the College than it did in many others. I am reminded of St Catharine's junior and senior members on every day that passes, not least because in July 1945 I had the misfortune to have a laboratory accident which removed the index finger of my left hand, causing me to undergo a succession of operations in Addenbrooke's Hospital. The kindness and attentiveness of both the Fellows and the undergraduates is something I shall never forget. In this context I must mention one person particularly. He is Sir Peter Hirsch FRS, who was then studying for Part One of the Natural Science Tripos and who went out of his way to visit me regularly. That surgical experience was an important basis for my later interest in medical education.

Life in the Physical Chemistry Department was equally happy. Once France had been liberated ultimate victory in Europe seemed secure, and even the flying bombs of September 1944, against which we had no defence, did not shake this view. By March 1945, when the Rhine was crossed, we all knew that the outcome

---

Sometimes the police became involved, and in my experience they always telephoned the College to inform the duty Fellow of their apprehension of any undergraduate in his care who they judged had committed an offence and might be charged. In one case in which I was involved there was an amusing denouement. At 2am I was awakened by a telephone call from the police informing me that they had taken a student into custody and were considering charging him with disorderly behaviour, and inviting me to come and act as his 'friend'. I was sure he had no malicious intent, so despite the inclement weather I proceeded to the police station. There I was shown the young man sitting in a room, looking rather the worse for wear and holding his head in his hands. A chair for me was placed opposite to him; after some unproductive thought, in which I wondered how A.L. Poole would have coped with the situation, I rather weakly said, 'Hello, X'. He looked up, studied my face carefully through somewhat glazed eyes and, when the light of recognition dawned, said with disarming simplicity, 'Good God, Sir! How did you get here?' I averted my eyes in time to catch those of the smiling policeman in attendance, and reflected that although an Oxford education may teach one much, it did not provide manuals of suitable responses for occasions such as this. I remained silent.

could only be delayed by a matter of weeks, and we could begin to think and plan for teaching and research when the war was over. I had drawn up a list of physico-chemical problems I wanted to investigate and Professor Norrish, aware that W.C. Price would not be returning, and wishing to do some high intensity photospectroscopy using a searchlight as an intense source of light, decided to reorganise the accommodation in the laboratory. This reorganisation provided me with better facilities, sufficient to begin on some of the problems I had in mind.

It has always been my view that a supervisor should try some preliminary experiments himself to assess the feasibility of a particular project before offering it to a research student for thorough investigation. To this end I had already carried out some experiments in photochlorination, which led me to believe that this would be a fruitful field. I wanted to study addition polymerization reactions, particularly in relation to a totally inexplicable phenomenon called the ceiling temperature effect, and it was during these initial studies that I had the laboratory accident. But other projects were arising from some of the wartime investigations, so that by the beginning of the 1945-46 academic year the main concern was not experimental ideas but the resources to pursue them, in terms of research students and equipment. The latter was a particular problem, and financial support had to be secured from outside bodies such as the Chemical Society and the Royal Society.

My pocket diaries for the immediate post-war years are revealing. My average teaching load in the form of lectures, laboratory supervision, demonstrating and the tutoring of undergraduates (but excluding time for preparation, and that devoted to research students) amounted to 22 hours per week. Also, during Full Term space had to be left for College committee meetings and for University bodies like the Faculty Board of Physics and Chemistry, the Chemical Engineering Syndicate, the Committee on the Duties and Stipends of University Teaching Officers and the Local Examinations Syndicate. University and College duties therefore took up six days a week throughout Full Term. Outside the University, I was involved in a little industrial consultancy work, and sat under the chairmanship of C.P. Snow on interviewing boards for the Civil Service Commission, to select people for posts in the Scientific Civil Service.

During the vacations the emphasis switched to research, still on a full-time basis. Furthermore in St Catharine's, which was a poor college, Fellows would sometimes be asked to help in the management of conferences which the College hosted in order to generate income during the vacation. It was the responsibility of the Fellows assigned to a particular conference to live in College and deal with any difficulties which could be remedied by some swift administrative action. I think it was in the Long Vacation of 1947 that I acted in this capacity when the Society of Motor Manufacturers and Traders held their summer school. All seemed to go extremely well, and having heard the Society's conference organiser express his appreciation to me I mildly suggested that perhaps, if that were the case and the industry was prospering (which it was, through large exports), the Society would care to make a gesture which would assist the College in its general work, for example by establishing a scholarship or fellowship.

At breakfast the following morning, when the matter had entirely disappeared from my mind, I was greeted by his remark 'I have got your money', and was told that the Society would like to establish the Kenward Memorial Fellowship, preferably in some branch of economics, perhaps related to the motor trade. I reported this to the Fellows, who were rather taken aback, as indeed was I. In due course the gift was accepted, and the first Fellow to be appointed was a young ex-serviceman who had been captured at Dunkirk, taken an external London degree while a prisoner of war, used his gratuity on demobilisation to take a first in Modern Greats at Christ Church, Oxford, and was then a research student at Nuffield College, Oxford. His name was Fred Mulley. He arrived in 1948 and departed in 1950, having been elected Labour Member of Parliament for the Park constituency of Sheffield. In due course he became Secretary of State for Education and Science when, in my capacity as chairman of the University Grants Committee, I had dealings with him to which I will refer later. Subsequently he became Secretary of State for Defence. His successor Fellows were also well known: Aubrey Silberston, who became Professor of Economics at Imperial College, London, and John Vaizey, later Lord Vaizey, who effortlessly and unblushingly made the easy transition from the left of the Labour Party to the right of the Conservative Party.

A Brief Interlude in North America

In that first post-war year the immediate future seemed to be quite secure and agreeable. Aged thirty-one, I had a College Fellowship and a University post, and my wife had completed her PhD. Sheffield had receded from my consciousness with the death of my mother two years earlier, and Cambridge was where we hoped and expected to live for a long time (and to be very content in so doing). However, two things were to disturb this placid prospect. First, Professor Norrish, largely for domestic reasons, decided to go on a tour of the United States of America, beginning in March 1946, and left me in charge of the Department. This was an awkward situation for me because in academic seniority I was behind two other staff members. It was also a period in which men were being demobilised from the services, sometimes with degrees and wishing to begin postgraduate work. That temporary stewardship was an educative process for me, requiring both tact and firmness. Even more significant was the fact that, probably due to Ned Steacie's initiative to which I have already referred, I was invited to go as a British Scientific Civil Servant for three months to the Chalk River laboratories, 130 miles up the Ottawa River valley from Ottawa itself. It was an invitation I felt I could not decline, because I had never worked overseas and the only voyages I had made away from England were brief holidays in the Isle of Man and Paris, plus the Anglo-German Summer School. I left Southampton by boat on 28 June 1946 and returned just three months later to Heathrow, then merely a series of fields with a runway and some wooden huts, on 28 September. The whole experience was an immense culture shock: fortunately I have kept some of the notes, journals and letters that I wrote on this trip. There is room here merely to record briefly what life was like in Canada, something of the flavour of two trips to the USA, and how the work at Chalk River gave me both problems of choice and also a new subject of research, the pursuit of which proved to be particularly fruitful.

Early in the morning of 1 July, after a very warm night spent on the non-air-conditioned Canadian National train from Windsor station, Montreal, I alighted at Chalk River station with a few other passengers. I was unsure as to what to do next, other than feeling that I must get to Deep River, which was where most of the staff based at the Chalk River plant lived. Fortunately my appearance attracted the attention of one or two of the other passengers who had alighted – possibly because I was dressed in the highly unsuitable garb of a tweed plus-four suit and the temperature was already in the upper seventies. I was therefore delighted when one of them said to me, 'Are you going to Deep River?' Getting an affirmative answer, he said, 'Come with us'. Off we all sped in a station wagon, partly over dirt roads, and arrived at Deep River village, where I and my baggage were delivered to the

Staff Hotel, pleasantly situated just a few yards from the southern bank of the Ottawa River. After taking possession of the room which had been reserved for me, and eating a magnificent breakfast, I unpacked and wondered what to do next. Since it was a glorious Monday morning I decided to get my bearings in the village before catching a bus to the plant, which was some miles away to the east and also on the banks of the Ottawa River. Although my arrival was expected it seemed that nobody had given much thought to what I should do, certainly not the rather opinionated head of the Chemistry Department, a Canadian named Dr Cook. However, at lunch on that first day I had the good fortune to see a number of familiar faces, including Dr Maurice Lister, who had read chemistry a year or so ahead of me at Oxford, and whose wife Lois (née Dunkerley) had been at Girton and was a fellow member of the Cambridge Rambling Club; Dr A.G. Maddock, who had been working with the Tube Alloys project in Cambridge and was later to succeed me as Fellow in Chemistry at St Catharine's; and three delightful persons who described themselves as radiation chemists: Dr F.H. (Kim) Krenz, Dr Nick Miller and Dr Colin Amphlett. There was space for me to work in Dr Miller's laboratory, and he made me feel welcome. At that stage I did not really know what radiation chemistry was, but Nick sensed my ignorance and kindly gave me a copy of his excellent *Short Handbook of Radiation Chemistry*. Dipping into this, I realised that my lack of knowledge was even greater than he had expected. Therefore I started off by doing some background reading in the library before tackling his manual, and then consulted the only book which seemed to deal specifically with radiation chemistry – S.C. Lind's *The Chemical Effects of α-Particles and Electrons*, published as long ago as 1928. I spent the next ten days immersed in the literature, a fact which greatly displeased Dr Cook who considered I ought to be doing experiments at once, although he had no concrete suggestions to offer.

I decided to focus on what actually happened to water when it was irradiated. Until 1944 most people assumed that irradiation caused water molecules to be 'activated', and that such activated molecules reacted with solutes or solids which they encountered during their short lives, to bring about chemical change by unspecified means. But in 1944 J.J. Weiss of King's College, Newcastle, proposed in a letter to the journal *Nature* that the activation was a splitting of the water molecules into hydrogen atoms and hydroxyl radicals – a notion which I later discovered had been suggested by Otto Risse in Vienna nearly twenty years earlier. The evidence for this seemed to be largely circumstantial and some direct proof was needed. Page 85 of my laboratory notebook lists six possible experimental ways by which the hypothesis could be confirmed or refuted. I went back to the laboratory and within three weeks had what seemed to be a positive result, confirming that water was broken up into two free radicals H and OH, each of which could initiate polymerization of a suitable dissolved compound.[5]

It was about this time that J.D. Cockcroft (later Sir John), who was living at Deep River and had been designated as Director of the UK Atomic Energy Research Establishment to be located at Harwell, made one of his periodic visits to the chemists. He took me aside and said he was very keen that I should join his new team. He offered me a Senior Principal Scientific Officership, the starting salary to be arranged but certainly not less than £1,000 per annum – considerably more than my existing Cambridge income. But just a few days earlier I had received a letter from Norrish to say that the Appointments Committee of the Faculty Board of Physics and Chemistry had decided to appoint me to the Humphrey Owen Jones Lectureship in Chemistry the following October, provided funds were available. I found the choice a difficult one, but as I thought over the matter I realised that I had had nearly six years of largely *ad hoc* applied work and that my real enjoyment came from teaching and academic research, so I told Cockcroft that I must regretfully decline his offer. He understood at once and offered a consultancy at Harwell instead, to be paid *pro rata*.

Fifty years later, I now see that my three months in Canada provided an important scientific experience; apart from the fact that Barbara was not with me, it was a most enjoyable period both intellectually and physically. Canada, as seen by someone who had spent the past seven years in Britain, seemed to be a land flowing with milk and honey. The Canadians I met were all very friendly.[6] The location of Deep River allowed plenty of sport and exercise in delightful country, and absence from the heavy routine of Cambridge gave me time to think and decide what it was that I really wanted to do.

---

5. Later we had to revise the conclusion to recognise that the precursor of H was the hydrated electron.

6. Some of the Canadian chemists, notably R.H. Betts who was at Chalk River with me, and others who worked there later, including Tom Hardwick and John Davies, subsequently came to Leeds for one or two years. They were all agreeable and effective. There were also some striking personalities, including

Norrish's letter to me had emphasised that, if I were to accept the lectureship, I should clearly understand that I must not conduct research in any field in which he was currently active. When I first read it this irritated me because I saw it as a 'keep out' notice, which seemed to me to be the antithesis of the relations which ought to exist between scientists; I never discerned Norrish's motive in making this condition. In the event the prohibition had a beneficial effect in reinforcing my independence, and I returned to Cambridge at the end of September with renewed zest for teaching and plenty of ideas for research.

Part of the stimulus arose from the fact that the authorities at Chalk River were perfectly prepared for me to make visits to scientists elsewhere whose work could be considered either directly or indirectly germane to the research in which I was engaged. This meant that I was able to go to the University of Notre Dame for conversations with Milton Burton on radiation chemistry and Charlie Price on polymer chemistry; the US Bureau of Mines to meet Bernard Lewis and Gunther von Elbe; Harvard and MIT, where I was splendidly entertained by Charles Coryell and the effervescent George Kistiakowsky; and the Frick Chemical Laboratory at Princeton, where I was made most welcome by H.S. Taylor, Dean of the Graduate College and Head of the Laboratory, who had graduated from Liverpool University and warmly welcomed all visitors from Britain. Just before I returned to the UK I attended the annual meeting of the American Chemical Society, held in a hotel in Chicago: there was a section devoted to radiation chemistry, and my attendance enabled me to meet and listen to several more of those who had been working in this field during the wartime Manhattan Project.

The warmth of the welcome I received in North America, the ease of social relationships, the openness of the scientific community, the size of the country and the variety of its topography were all factors which, added to the success of the

---

A.J. Cipriani, a health physicist and amateur herpetologist, and Bruno Pontecorvo, a highly intelligent theoretician who had worked in Rome with Enrico Fermi. He was convivial, an excellent tennis player and seemed to have an uncomplicated boyish enthusiasm for life – not quite grown up. How wrong I was, for he later defected to the Soviet Union. Others even more colourful appeared at the beginning of August, having witnessed the A-bomb tests at Bikini Atoll at the end of July. At the other end of the temperamental spectrum was Harry Thode, a quiet mass spectroscopist whom I liked immensely. He was a professor at McMaster University and later its President, and in the late 1960s we found that we each had the responsibility of founding new medical schools. Our daughter Mary took part of her medical elective at McMaster, which Thode had transformed from a sleepy college into a prominent Canadian university.

experiments at Chalk River, contributed both to my sadness at departure on 27 September and to the strengthening of my resolve to return to North America whenever opportunity offered. (The first such chance was to come just ten months later, when I accepted an invitation to attend the first Radiation Chemistry and Photochemistry Conference at the University of Notre Dame – the proceedings of which were fully reported in the *Journal of Physical and Colloid Chemistry*.)

If I was sad to leave Deep River, particularly at 6am without breakfast, I had much to think of on my journey back to Cambridge. The original arrangement was for me to fly from Montreal, but this was changed at the last minute and I found myself leaving the train at Ottawa, taking a taxi to what was euphemistically called Ottawa Airport (not much more than a modest shed and one runway) and there boarding an old Douglas DC3 (the ubiquitous but uncomfortable Dakota) which slowly found its way down to La Guardia, stopping at many small airports in New England and New York State. I spent the night at the Commodore Hotel and next day boarded a fine new Lockheed Constellation, scheduled to stop at Gander and Prestwick, and arrived at London Heathrow around midday. Barbara was among the dozen or so people waiting near the wooden huts which did duty as Heathrow terminal, who in those days were allowed to walk to the plane to greet the passengers. I think she found me disoriented by the time change and overexcited, partly because I had so much to tell her and partly because I had been able to organise some food parcels and other things which would make our lives, and those of our friends, a little more pleasant in austere Britain. Even the short time left to prepare for the next term did not quench my feeling of well-being.

Fortune continued to smile on me, for in the spring of 1948 my research student Ken Ivin and I arrived at the explanation of the ceiling temperature phenomenon. This opened up a veritable goldmine of useful information relating the kinetics and thermodynamics of addition polymerization to one another, and to the structure of the monomer. In addition, my colleague Joseph Mitchell (Professor of Radiotherapeutics and Director of the Radiotherapeutic Centre at Addenbrooke's Hospital) agreed to let me use one of his 250 kilovolt X-ray machines when he did not need it for radiotherapy or for his own research, so that I could continue some of the experiments begun in Canada. Lastly Harry Eméleus, Professor of Inorganic Chemistry at Cambridge, asked me to prepare a special report on aspects of radiation chemistry, which gave me an incentive to study the literature even more thoroughly than I had previously done. I also gained a better understanding of the subject by consulting a book published in that year by Douglas Lea, called *Actions of Radiations on Living Cells*. It set out all the basic principles needed to comprehend the primary physical processes, and having read the book I made contact with him at the Strangeways Laboratory in Cambridge. He was a quite remarkable person who, alas, died young. After his death I was given access to his notebooks, and found that he had been teaching himself some principles of chemical thermodynamics and reaction kinetics. Indeed, he had carried out experiments in chemistry which he never published but which deserved a wider audience, and I was able to get this work included posthumously in the *Transactions of the Faraday Society*. Through him I also met his friend L.H. Gray, whose fundamental work in radiation biology was recognised by naming a unit of absorbed dose after him.

Unsettling Thoughts and Events

At Cambridge my life was dominated by teaching and research. I believe that these two functions lie at the heart of every good university, and the resources which it secures should be dedicated to serve this end, and this end alone. Two key constituencies of such a university are the older, experienced academic and the young researcher who, by definition, is much less experienced but who has a fresh and lively mind and for whom the future has infinite promise. Nowadays, however, the whole ethos of developed countries is to see universities as businesses and students as customers. Plain language has given way to jargon, and every university produces each year a document which is a monument to standardised illiteracy – an 'Annual Report' which opens with a 'Vision' and a 'Mission Statement', succeeded by a 'Statement of Aims, Objectives and Goals' (never use one word where three synonyms will do) and pomposities such as an 'Action Plan' and an 'Implementation Plan', then a section on 'Performance Monitoring' in which quality and quantity are invariably confused. Finally, and worst of all, the resources which the state provides are allocated under the delusion that universities can be described in these terms. It becomes important to re-read the works of real thinkers, such as Alfred North Whitehead, philosopher, scientist and educationalist of extraordinary range and wisdom. In an address to the American Association of Business Schools, for example, he presented the following thoughts:

The justification for a university is that it preserves the connection between knowledge and the zest of life, by uniting the young and the old in the imaginative consideration of learning. A university imparts information, but it imparts it imaginatively. At least, this is the function which it should perform for society. The university which fails in this respect has no reason for existence. This atmosphere of excitement, arising from imaginative consideration, transforms knowledge. A fact is no longer a bare fact: it is invested with all its possibilities. It is no longer a burden on the memory: it is energising as the poet of our dreams, and as the architect of our purposes.

Whitehead further saw that:

Youth is imaginative, and if the imagination be strengthened by discipline, this energy of imagination can in great measure be preserved through life. The tragedy of the world is that those who are imaginative have but slight experience, and those who are experienced have feeble imaginations. Fools act on imagination without knowledge; pedants act on knowledge without imagination. The task of a university is to weld together imagination and experience.

He neatly summarised the object of the organisation of a university in these words:

The whole art in the organisation of a university is the provision of a faculty whose learning is lighted up with imagination. This is the problem of problems in university education; and unless we are careful the recent vast extension of universities in number of students and in variety of activities – of which we are so justly proud – will fail in producing its proper results by the mishandling of this problem.

Have the universities and funding councils of the United Kingdom forgotten this elementary truth? Whitehead saw an essential prerequisite combining imagination and learning, and also wrote:

The combination of imagination and learning normally requires some leisure, freedom from restraint, freedom from harassing worry, some variety of experiences, and the stimulation of other minds diverse in opinion and diverse in equipment. Also there is required the excitement of curiosity and the self-confidence derived from pride in the achievements of the surrounding society in procuring the advance of knowledge. Imagination cannot be acquired once and for all, and then kept indefinitely in an ice box to be produced periodically and stated quantitatively. The learned and imaginative life is a way of living, and is not an article of commerce.

With all its hardships and austerity, the Cambridge of the five post-war years – at least those parts which touched me – seemed to come as near to the ideal as was possible in the circumstances; and that was the fundamental reason why it was such a happy period. The reader is therefore entitled to ask why I left in 1950, particularly in view of the fact that in 1949 we felt able, with the help of a mortgage, to buy a larger house on the southern side of Cambridge to accommodate a family which had now grown by one son, with a second child expected. As is often the case, there was more than one reason for our decision to go. In the first place, I had been slightly unsettled by an approach of an informal kind from King's College, London, which was beginning to consider a successor to the chair of physical chemistry shortly to be vacated on the retirement of Professor A.J. Allmand. My antipathy to living in London quickly ruled out this possibility. However, one day in the Lent Term 1950 there was a knock on my College room door at 11 am, just after I had said goodbye to two students whom I had been supervising. The visitor declared himself to be Charles Morris of Leeds (a statement which had no significance for me) and asked if he might come in and have a word. I was quite glad to have a break and a coffee with a person whom I quickly saw had great charm, though his sentences were often more allusive than direct, which gave him an air of mystery. I was perplexed as to the purpose of his visit and offered to show him the College, which he politely refused. So I then came out bluntly with the question, 'What do you want of me?'– to which, opening his hands in an expansive gesture, he smiled and said simply, 'We want you in Leeds', and also revealed himself as the vice-chancellor of the university in that city.

This immediately struck me as an entirely different proposition, worthy of serious consideration: firstly because Leeds was in the West Riding of Yorkshire, to which I still had a strong attachment; secondly because the School of Chemistry had an excellent reputation and was well housed; and, thirdly, because I was aware that physical chemistry was especially well developed under the leadership of M.G. Evans FRS (who was in fact well known to me, and was coming to Cambridge a few days later so that I could consult him on another matter). Therefore I told Charles Morris that I would give his offer some very careful thought. To help my deliberations I wrote to Ned Steacie in Ottawa, who was strongly supportive of the idea, and I also resolved to have a word with Alexander Todd, Professor of Organic Chemistry in Cambridge, who had previously spent six years as a professor in

Manchester and therefore had a full understanding of the nature of what were known as 'redbrick' (later 'civic') universities.

I also sought Todd's advice for another reason. About two years earlier he had brought a proposal to the Faculty Board of Physics and Chemistry, then sitting under the chairmanship of Sir John Lennard-Jones, to reform part of the Natural Sciences Tripos Examination, because he saw how feeble was the content of the chemistry required to pass in Part One. The chairman turned to myself and Jack Ratcliffe, who were acknowledged as ground rules experts on the complicated structure of the Tripos, for our views. To my undying shame I remember that I approached the problem as anyone teaching in Cambridge would be likely to do, which is to say that I started from the proposition that the Natural Sciences Tripos had been given to Cambridge by God and one doesn't interfere with divine gifts. Therefore I began to list all the reasons why no change should be made. Todd's face got blacker and blacker, and finally he interrupted by saying, 'It is ridiculous for Dr Dainton to attempt to stultify the development of organic chemistry in this university'. His remark did not fall happily on the ears of the majority of the members of the Faculty Board, some of whom laughed outright. However, two or three weeks later I had a private chat with Todd, in the course of which he convinced me that the Tripos did indeed merit reform.

When I talked with Todd in 1950 he simply made the point that if I had ideas in teaching or research, or both, which I wished to pursue, then I should move to a university where tradition was less respected as a valid argument against change than it was in Cambridge. The inference was clear. This advice, combined with what M.G. Evans told me, convinced me that I should indicate to Leeds my willingness to be considered, provided that Barbara felt able to face such a change and a second house move within twelve months. To my delight she readily concurred. Moreover, her childhood as a daughter of parents closely associated with Manchester's academic and scientific communities meant that she was much better placed than I to assess what effect the change would have on our domestic and social lives. So after due process in Leeds I was appointed as Professor of Physical and Inorganic Chemistry, the other such professor being E.G. Cox, a physicist turned chemical crystallographer. My later experiences confirmed both the correctness of the decision to move and my earnest belief that curricular change might be effected more easily in Leeds than in Cambridge.

Our last academic year in Cambridge was not only a watershed in our lives, it was also extremely busy because of our need in 1949 for a larger home as the family expanded. Just before the Michaelmas Term began we moved from rented accommodation to the house which we had bought. Barbara had her hands full with our two-year-old son John and was pregnant with our daughter Mary, who arrived just four months later. So busy was I that when a telegram arrived from the President of the University of Toronto inviting me to give one of the inaugural lectures for the opening of the Wallberg Memorial Laboratories, and mentioning a fee of $1,000, I merely placed it on the mantelpiece in the sitting room as an irrelevance to my preoccupations and forgot all about it. Two days later a second telegram arrived from Andy Gordon, head of the Chemistry Department, which opened ominously: 'Disregard President Smith's telegram' and continued more propitiously to the effect that the fee would be $1,500 dollars and would I stay on for ten days as a visiting professor. I waited for several multiples of two days in the hope that this raising of the ante was just the beginning of a trend, but unfortunately Andy Gordon's telegram was the end of the matter! Nevertheless, I got leave of absence for the second half of the Michaelmas Term and had another splendid trip to Canada in wintertime. I again went by boat, because I had to have some time to prepare the lectures I had undertaken to give. It was in every way a memorable trip because Toronto ceremonial occasions called for white tie and tails, and it was planned that I should sail from Liverpool on a Canadian Pacific liner, *The Empress of Canada*, and travel first class. The journey could not have been more different from that on the Cunard steamship *Aquitania* in the more austere conditions which had applied four years earlier. I had a splendid cabin to myself in which I could work, as well as the use of the ship's library. We left Liverpool just after sunset on 23 November and apart from one day, 27 November, when there were very rough seas, the most adverse weather we had was a moderate swell.

I found my table companion was L.H. Dudley Stamp, the social geographer who founded the Land Utilisation Survey of Britain and was a professor at the London School of Economics. He was an entertaining fellow and we got on famously. In the course of our many conversations he told me that he was en route to visit an island which he owned off Victoria in the Province of British Columbia, and that he would be flying from Halifax to Vancouver. I explained that I would be taking the train from Halifax to Toronto and we should therefore be saying goodbye. I was a little taken aback when, just before our disembarkation on 29 November, he approached me and said he thought he had insufficient dollars to buy his airline ticket to Vancouver: would I lend him $100? I had a difficult decision to make, because in fact I had the means to lend him the cash but I had a strong feeling that I might be one of Mark Twain's 'innocents abroad', and wondered if I would ever see the money again; and, if not, how I would recover it from him on his return to the United Kingdom. As it turned out he did forget, but a reminder produced an immediate apology and reimbursement.

In my time I have attended a large number of opening ceremonies for university buildings, but I cannot recall any which quite matched in grandeur the one I attended in Toronto. The formal opening of the complex was performed by his Excellency the Governor General of Canada, Field Marshal Viscount Alexander of Tunis. A dinner in his honour was held in the Great Hall of Hart House, to which we were bidden to attend in full evening dress. Alas, neither the food nor the drink lived up to the sartorial splendour: in common with the rest of the campus, Hart House was 'dry', and because so many people were present it was impossible to do anything except serve a standard menu. However, such things did not detract from the pleasure of the evening for me, because I found myself sitting next to Lady Alexander, with whom I had a splendid conversation, and the Governor General himself was in sparkling form.

It was also a great joy to me to be able to entertain to lunch in the Park Plaza Hotel a number of my former students who had travelled to Toronto just for this occasion. They were also the manifestation of a scheme which Ned Steacie and I had talked about in 1946 over half a bottle of Canadian rye whisky in the Staff Hotel at Deep River. The idea was to give young Canadians the opportunity to travel abroad, or to a centre of excellence such as the National Research Council of Canada; and young foreign scientists might likewise apply for postdoctoral fellowships to improve their own experience by association with outstanding research leaders on the staff of the National Research Council. In 1949-50, the second year of this scheme, 24 of the 32 Fellows in Chemistry were from the United Kingdom, no fewer than four were my old pupils, and three were graduates from Leeds.

December was an entirely hectic month: I gave seven lectures in Toronto, fitted in one at McMaster University in Hamilton, and then went on a tour including the University of Rochester and three days in New York visiting a polymer centre at Brooklyn Polytechnic. I then travelled to Harvard, MIT, Ottawa and Chalk River, concluding with Christmas in Kingston, Ontario, with Walter Macfarlane Smith and his wife (he having been a post-doctoral student in Cambridge just before the war, and one of the members of the Rambling Club). Alas, this left no time for a leisurely sea journey home, but a non-stop flight to London instead.

Much of the Long Vacation in 1950 was spent in moving to Leeds, clearing my College rooms and the laboratory, and making arrangements for those research students who would be coming to Leeds with me from Cambridge, as well as for new arrivals from overseas. We alarmed our neighbours in Leeds by our resolute determination to install central heating in our house, notwithstanding their dire warnings about the probable adverse effect on the health of our children. In the end, more by good luck than management the move was effected smoothly, without the benefit of any motor car, and an entirely different kind of academic life began.

CHAPTER 4

AN OLD CIVIC UNIVERSITY: LEEDS, 1950–65

Et augebitur scientia
University of Leeds motto

First Impressions of Leeds

Both Barbara and I had lived in northern cities, she in Manchester between the ages of four and eighteen and I in Sheffield from birth to eighteen. Each of us was therefore conscious of the presence of a university bearing in its title the name of its home city. Nevertheless nearly half our lives had been spent in Oxford and Cambridge, where the university was not just an institution close to being the largest, if not the largest, economic unit in the city, but was correctly perceived by the majority of the citizens as the sole reason for its international prominence. Inevitably this later experience, together with the loss of family homes, had dimmed our memories of the North. Our first impressions of Leeds were a curious mix of surprises and resurrected memories: we had much to learn.

Reminiscent of our origins and visually obvious were of course some monuments to Leeds' civic pride and utility: the Town Hall, the Civic Hall and other public buildings including libraries, and the municipal transport services, still significantly reliant on trams, which were boneshakers compared with the Sheffield 'Rolls-Royces'. We were not surprised that the north-western suburbs were hillier and had much more open space and better-class housing for the bourgeoisie than those lying in other directions, which contained the factories and the back-to-back dwellings of their workers (all so evocatively described by Richard Hoggart in *The Uses of Literacy*) or new housing estates. The house we had bought from a retiring member of the Chemistry Department staff was in West Park, one of those north-western suburbs just within the Leeds Ring Road and with many open spaces close by, such as Beckett Park, Lawnswood playing fields and Meanwood Beck. All of these were just a short walk for us and beyond, within easy car driving distance, were the beauties of Wharfedale.

Our new home was a semi-detached brick villa with adequate space to raise a family, for me to capture one of the six bedrooms for a study and another attic bedroom for a workshop and storeroom, and still to accommodate an au pair. Since I had completed the purchase without Barbara having seen the house I was apprehensive of her reaction, but happily it proved to be favourable. When I bought it the only heating was from coal fires and, since neither of us relished the idea of attending to the needs of eight firegrates, we installed central heating. Though this was primitive by North American standards, being wide bore and relying on convection rather than an electric pump for circulation, it worked well, even attracting approval and consequent frequent visits from Canadian and US students and post-doctoral fellows. However, as I have mentioned, it was regarded by some neighbours with deep suspicion as being fundamentally unhealthy for our children. There was a large, well-built outhouse which easily accommodated in separate sections a second-hand car, which we acquired in our first twelve months, a generous store of solid fuel and an assortment of garden tools and bicycles. The garden was adequate for growing vegetables and flowers as well as for children's play, and the house was to serve us well for fourteen years.

Of course we were aware that Leeds, like Sheffield and Manchester, would be dirtier than Cambridge and we were not surprised by the blackness of the stonework of the buildings in the centre of the city, or the darkness of the brickwork. However, we were not prepared for the volume of airborne dirt which was deposited on every external horizontal surface and which penetrated the house and added enormously to the housework. It also led to the most horrendous fogs whenever there was a temperature inversion. If we commented on this to our neighbours, they would usually reply 'But this is Bradford muck'. Though much of the pollution must have been due to domestic chimneys, there was no denying that there was a measure of truth in this statement because the prevailing wind was from the south-west; but it was of little consolation to us, since the deposition of dirt could not be prevented without abolishing Bradford and, in any case, I am convinced that a large proportion of it was emitted from a solid fuel electricity generating station which lay in a valley between the two cities. It is small wonder that one of the champions of clean air policies, and a pioneer in measuring particulate pollution, was J.B. Cohen, the first Professor of Organic Chemistry in the University of Leeds.

Both of us were particularly reassured to find that the ordinary folk with whom we had to deal had lost none of the endearing north country characteristics which we both remembered from our youth. They were friendly, helpful, enjoyed a pawky sense of humour and made their conversational points directly and pithily. A day or two after we arrived the local policeman called on us and explained that as part of his regular beat he checked up on houses that had been unoccupied, and now wanted to make himself known to the new occupants. He clearly also wanted a chat, and because I wished him to regard us as friends I indulged him in this. After a few exchanges he volunteered, 'There is a mint of money hereabouts'. Aware of my somewhat dirty and dishevelled appearance and therefore feeling unworthy to be so categorised, I responded with what I considered to be self-deprecating humour: 'It looks as if we got in by mistake then'. Putting his notebook back in a pocket and carefully looking me up and down, he commented in all honesty and without a touch of malice, 'Aye. Like as not.' I could not respond but there was no need to do so, for the same hand that put away the notebook pulled a cigarette case from another pocket in his tunic and extracted a cigarette. As I was then a smoker myself I was quick to produce matches and to offer him a light, at which he said, 'Ah! A sprat to catch a mackerel, eh?' and duly offered me a cigarette. He guarded us faithfully for several years, and although he came to call me 'professor' never disguised the fact that titles cut no ice with him.

The neighbours and tradespeople with whom we had dealings were equally helpful and friendly, and we quickly began to feel that we belonged and were accepted. We settled into a routine which continued with minor variations as the children grew older and their schools and friends changed. It was one that meant Barbara was much more tied to the house and children than I, who would disappear to the University at about 8.30am and reappear between 6.30 and 7pm. But at least I was not burdened with college duties, and when there were social occasions in the University which I had to attend these, more often than not, included invitations to Barbara. Saturday afternoon and Sunday were the times when we used to explore the countryside *en famille,* almost invariably using the car to carry us by back roads to the remoter parts of the Dales; our pre-war Morris brought us great joy, also bearing us frequently to our friends in the Lake District for summer holidays based in cottages on the west shore of Lake Windermere or at the northern end of Buttermere.

When the Burma campaign culminated in the surrender of the Japanese forces to Lord Mountbatten, my St John's College friend Henry Fowler, who had been a prisoner of war working on the notorious railway, was released. After repatriation and a period of recuperation, followed by service in the British-occupied zone of Germany, he decided to seek his future career in education. Following a short period as a teacher he became an administrator in Leeds, and to our delight he and his wife Charmian bought a house in Roundhay, not far from ours. In addition to exchange visits between houses we would occasionally arrange to dine out together. Not only could we forget work, but our wives could escape briefly from their heavy duties as mothers, since we both had young and growing families. Fortunately for Barbara she had the help of first a Swedish au pair (Majlis) and then two French girls (Michele and Jacqueline), followed by Joan, the perfectly admirable daughter of one of the St Catharine's College porters named Bob Frost. She had just the right temperament for handling the children and was absolutely reliable and trustworthy, so Barbara and I were able to go out together in the evenings much more frequently. After Joan had been with us for a couple of years we encouraged her to take a nursery nurse course in Leeds, and she continued to live with us until she had qualified. She remains a friend to this day.

One of the positive factors I mentioned in our favourable consideration of the move from Cambridge to Leeds was that it and Sheffield were then both in the West Riding of Yorkshire (though, since the creation of South Yorkshire, this is no longer the case). The distance by road from West Park in Leeds to Ecclesall in Sheffield was about 40 miles. The journey was not one we made as often as we would have wished, partly because work occupied so much of my time; partly because of family commitments (and the conventional wisdom of those days was that the young should experience a regular routine, following the precept 'early to bed and early to rise makes a child healthy, wealthy and wise'); and partly because, with no motorways and an increasingly temperamental car well over ten years old, the journey to and fro took a good deal of nervous energy and time. However, we used to manage one or two visits a year.

On a couple of tragic occasions our relative proximity to Sheffield did prove helpful to my brother Ernie, with whom I felt a special bond. The first was when his elder daughter Sylvia developed nephritis, for which there was then no known cure: kidney transplants had yet to be pioneered, and dialysis was not available. At his request, and after consulting the much respected Leeds nephrologist Leslie Pyrah, I went with Ernie to see the consultant in charge of Sylvia's limited treatment. I came away feeling I was of little use as a comforter, though possibly helpful as an interpreter of the consultant to an anguished parent. I had little to offer by way of hope, not least because I recalled that a few years after he was married my brother had himself suffered from a fever, which was followed by albumen in his urine, a sure indication of kidney malfunction.

Worse was to follow in 1956, the year of the Suez crisis. By that time Ernie had moved to Hall Green in Birmingham. One evening he telephoned me in great distress; he was not very coherent, except that he begged us to come and see him. After managing to obtain a little extra petrol (the Suez crisis had by then led to fuel rationing), Barbara and I drove to Birmingham and found Ernie, his skin flaking, showing all the signs of what Leslie Pyrah described as toxaemia due to failing kidneys. He was able to give us his family doctor's name, address and telephone number, and when we made contact the doctor told us that he had prescribed medication which, given Ernie's acute condition, could only be palliative, but that he knew it was not being administered. More to the point, he stated his belief that Ernie knew he did not have long to live, and would not get the necessary nursing at home. Again with Pyrah's help, a bed was found for Ernie at the Queen Elizabeth Hospital, Birmingham, where he died with dignity and free of pain.

The whole sorry story was slowly unravelled, and that my brother should have fared so badly was one of many tragedies to be laid at the door of that vile cult Christian Science, which has no justifiable claim to either of the words in its title. I first became aware of its existence when a friend of mine, Leonard Kemp, an only child, fractured his leg in a sledging accident. It became gangrenous and amputation was then the only life-saving course of action. However, the parents, who had come under the influence of a Christian Science practitioner, refused to allow this, and Leonard died. Notwithstanding this tragedy my sister Mabel, when faced with a difficult problem, also succumbed to the teachings of the same practitioner and then, when Sylvia was ill, persuaded Ernie's wife to accept their false tenets – a fact hitherto unknown to me – with these dire consequences for my brother later. This insidious cult still spreads amongst vulnerable and often desperate people by offering false hopes and flying in the face of objective, incontrovertible knowledge about physiology and pathology, obtained by years of patient, painstaking research by able, dedicated and properly qualified people whose sole object is to add to knowledge in the hope that it can be used for the alleviation of human suffering. How fortunate I am that my wife is a biologist and that our views on these and other matters are so similar.

I was of course concerned how life in Leeds, with all the cares of a young family, would suit Barbara. Happily, with Joan's help and a diminution of the need to ferry young children to and from school, it slowly became possible for her to do other things, such as part-time biology teaching in a secondary school and, during our last two and a half years there, research in the Department of Zoology of the University. With the acquisition of our first reliable car, a new Vauxhall for which we had put our names down about seven years previously in Cambridge, it became easier for us to take the children abroad for holidays. We first went to Ireland, where we became regular visitors to a delightful guest house in County Wexford. It specialised in family parties and had the added advantage of enabling us to introduce the children to the surviving Irish members of Barbara's family, so they learned something of their roots and had enjoyable holidays in the company of other children. Latterly we also went to Europe by car, so that they could see there was more than just the English way to lead the good life. On such visits and excursions we often wondered to ourselves whether the diverse experiences would have any lasting effect on the children, but from what they have done and said as adults we are left in no doubt about the positive impact of the trips.

En Famille in Canada and the USA

Most memorable of the family travels, and possibly most influential on our children's development, was that of living for five months in 1959 in Wellesley Hills, Massachusetts, when I was Arthur D. Little Professor of Chemistry at the Massachusetts Institute of Technology (MIT). Our friends at MIT and Harvard, especially Professors Stockmayer, Bartlett and Kistiakowsky, had found us a detached wooden-frame house in an older part of Wellesley Hills, within walking distance of the station so that I could commute to MIT by train or car. Within MIT's friendly Chemistry Department I also had a thoroughly enjoyable and profitable time scientifically, managing to write up some papers and plan a book on radiation chemistry as well as making visits to some New England universities, including among others Yale and Brown.

On 22 January 1959, leaving our house in the safe hands of a Canadian research student, Gene Cherniak, and his wife Vivienne, we boarded a Trans-Pennine Express train at Leeds City Station. On arrival at Liverpool we embarked on the Cunarder *SS Sylvania*. On this first family visit to the USA it was a constant delight to observe how the children coped with the different customs, ideas and practices. The time abroad was powerfully educative for us all: we were constantly reminded that the United States and England are divided, as much as they are united, by a common language. However, given patience, tolerance and a sense of humour, the differences can serve to emphasize that all human beings have the capacity to work and live together in harmony, if only they have the will to do so.

The journey across the Atlantic by sea (something quite hard to achieve nowadays) was enjoyed to the full by the children, and contained one highly evocative experience. In mid-Atlantic we ran into a gale which delayed us by a day. Fortunately we are all good sailors and so did not suffer as some passengers did, but suddenly Barbara realised that she had not seen John for some time. I was not about, so she put the girls into someone else's care and ran all over the ship looking for him. She found him leaning over the railings on the top deck: he turned and said simply 'I would not like to have come across on the *Mayflower*'.

The day we arrived at our temporary home in Laurel Avenue, Wellesley Hills, we were greeted by a lady bearing gifts from the neighbours (the Welcome Wagon tradition). The same generosity was shown by the schools, which adapted their normal practices to suit the children's needs. At home John was a pupil at Bradford Grammar School, an independent school renowned for its high standards of formal education. The Headmaster, Canon Newell, did not disguise his view that for John to miss one term there would not be compensated by his experiences in an American Junior High School, access to which I had already sought from the Superintendent of Schools at Wellesley Hills. He finally relented when he realised that we were determined to take John with us, but on the condition that his mother would teach him the Bradford Grammar School syllabus when he came back from school each afternoon: he would then sit the school examinations three weeks after we returned home. Barbara duly worked hard to fill in the gaps in her own education each morning and John studied with her after tea, though it was always apparent that he was much more interested in American history than in the English mediaeval period or the journeys of St Paul in the Mediterranean.

John's attendance at the Junior High School posed a problem because he was only eleven and the normal age range was thirteen to eighteen. The Superintendent advised us that the matter could only be resolved by the Principal of the school, so in due course I presented myself and John at the Principal's office. While I was shown round the establishment by a charming senior pupil, a Miss Whittemore, John underwent an interview. Returning after a pleasant half hour with Miss Whittemore, I saw at once from John's mulish expression that something was seriously wrong. The Principal took me aside, explaining that the two ladies who were present in his room were guidance counsellors, a term which carried little meaning for me, and went on to say in the nicest possible way that they and he considered John to be untruthful. It emerged that the evidence for this was that a boy of such tender years could not possibly be studying, as he had stated, Latin, French, algebra and some science. I think I reassured the Principal but not the guidance counsellors, who had been brought into the conversation. In the end the matter was only resolved when I said I was perfectly prepared to set John some unseen examination questions in the subjects concerned, but added the proviso that the disbelieving guidance counsellors should also be required to take the same papers. That argument proved conclusive.

Once accepted, John could not have been better treated. He was generally placed in classes where the subject work was as nearly as possible equivalent in standard to that which he had attained at Bradford, and in beginners' classes in, for example, American history. His experience in the latter exposed a difference of outlook which would be valuable later: when Dr A.E.R. Westman of the Ontario Research Foundation – who had been a mature student of mine in Cambridge – came to visit, John regaled us with how the wicked British had burned the White House in 1812. He was immediately corrected by our Canadian friend, who explained that this was a just retribution by the British on the Americans for the sacking of Fort York, today's Toronto, by the wicked Americans. *Quot homines tot sententiae*! We were immensely indebted to the Junior High School, which even encouraged John to draw a small Union Jack on the blackboard, where it remained until he left. In return he seemed to be perfectly willing to swear allegiance to the flag of the United States of America, even if occasionally substituting the last line of his pledge by the words 'With coffee and doughnuts for all'.

The girls were just as sympathetically treated in elementary school; indeed one teacher, perceiving Rosalind's backwardness in reading compared with her arithmetic, sought our permission to give her special one-to-one tuition after school. The result was startling and gratifying: in two weeks Rosalind was happily reading, and never looked back.

By this time we had become well known and accepted in the local community. I was asked to judge the individual science projects that pupils had submitted for a science fair at a well-known and much respected high school in a nearby township. The judging actually took me a good deal of time and was a fascinating task. I concluded that the best effort was that in which a pupil had studied the fauna of a nearby pond by sampling the water and identifying the organisms visually, in some cases with the aid of a borrowed and not very good microscope. The account of this work was admirable in its accuracy and I was favourably impressed by the way in which the pupil drew attention to matters which she did not understand, proffered a few explanatory ideas, and suggested how they might be tested. It was also clear that her effort was unaided. I was somewhat taken aback when, following the announcement of the results, the rather bossy mother of another child approached me to dispute my decision. It was true, as she claimed, that her offspring's work was well presented; indeed I had already noted this, but considered it both a little too glossy and somewhat overstocked with words which could not possibly have been fully comprehended by a child of that age. However, I was unprepared for the argument which the mother advanced: 'But she has been advised throughout by Professor So-and-so (a colleague of mine at MIT), and has done all that he said', words which in her mind were conclusive evidence of my incompetence as a judge.

Lectures at MIT

My lectures at MIT were on Mondays and Wednesdays at 1pm. There was a pleasant air of informality, and the audience comprised mainly graduate students who did not hesitate to ask questions at any time during the lectures, a custom which I quite liked although it could disrupt the flow of argument. Even so, it was not unusual for one or two students to have further discussions after the lecture hour was over, and I often found this as beneficial for me as I hoped it was for them. Other than this my duties were quite light. I shared a room with Emeritus Professor George Scatchard, a delightful man who had many a tale to tell. He was a willing conspirator in a scheme to bring some dignity into the proceedings of the Harvard-MIT Joint Chemical Seminar, which we both agreed with mock seriousness had become somewhat ribald. When I was due to give the next talk, our plan involved my wearing George's gown and mortarboard and speaking the first few sentences of my talk in Latin. The composition of those few sentences took me over an hour, and my request to an assistant in the MIT library for an English–Latin dictionary produced some raised eyebrows.

I was unprepared for the full effect of our little plot. The impact on the audience was as we had hoped: stunned surprise, followed by applause when I reverted with relief to the local vernacular. However, there were two other unforeseen effects. The first was a flash of light before my talk was over, and a few days later the Harvard *Crimson*, the student newspaper, carried a photograph showing my unusual garb. The second consequence, which was good for my humility, was the initiative of Bruno Zimm, whom I had got to know during my consulting work at General Electric. He had been in the seminar at Harvard, and when a few weeks later it fell to him to introduce me as the speaker at another meeting, he did so in Greek! Of that language I knew not a syllable, and so my bluff was called. In passing, I should mention that Bruno drove me to Yale to give a talk and I stayed overnight in one of two bedrooms which shared a common bathroom on the top floor of the Sterling Chemical Laboratory, the other bedroom being unoccupied. By some mischance I locked myself out of my own bedroom but could get from the bathroom into the second bedroom, and so through its door into the laboratories. I had no idea who to phone for assistance, and decided to look for advice and help from any chemist still at his bench. At 10.30pm there was only one laboratory which had a light in it. Wrapped solely in a bath towel, I asked if anyone was there. A female face appeared, registered shock, and had to be reassured that my intentions were honourable before I could be rescued. I began to feel that any more events of this kind and someone would be writing a sensational article on the wanderings in New England of an Old English chemist.

Thanks to the kindness of the MIT library staff I could usually hide away in a study carrel out of earshot of 'garrulous George', so that I got a lot of useful reading and writing done and felt quite justified in spending a little time consulting in the area and visiting institutions such as the Brookhaven National Laboratory, Brooklyn Polytechnic, Princeton and Columbia. Whenever the opportunity arose and school programmes permitted, I would try to involve all the family in these excursions. Three of them were especially memorable.

Before the snow in Wellesley Hills showed any signs of a thaw we visited Washington DC, where the ground was clear and the weather was most clement. It was wholly delightful to see the children completely absorbed in the new experience, enjoying urban open space on a scale they had not seen or envisaged before. Their reactions varied from silence to bright chatter, but tiring as it must all have been from time to time, the dreaded word 'boring' never once fell from their lips. Two weeks later, when the snow in Wellesley Hills was turning to slush, I left for visits to Stamford, Brookhaven and Brooklyn, joining the family at the Biltmore Hotel in New York City. The next seven days were equally memorable, particularly for me, because we traversed much of the same ground I had covered on my first trip thirteen years earlier, and I could study the reactions of Barbara and the children without being distracted by the spell which the Big Apple casts over the newcomer. I wondered then what long-term effect such visits might have. I can prove nothing, but the fact that John spent part of an Oxford Long Vacation working at General Electric, Mary took her medical elective period in Canada and Rosalind spent a pre-university year as an American Field Service Scholar in Plano, Illinois, suggests a connection.

After three nights in New York we went to Princeton, where H.S. Taylor and his successor Don Hornig insisted on putting us up in their homes – the boys with Hugh Taylor, the girls with Don and Lilli. It was a most enjoyable weekend, with a dramatic climax. On the Queen's birthday, 21 April, I was driven to the station, boarded my train and was allocated a seat by the conductor. I moved to the door to wave goodbye to the children, who were staying in town while I went to Columbia to give a lecture, when we were all surprised to hear the siren of what proved to be a motorcade, out of which emerged a bearded, khaki-uniformed giant. He was no less than Fidel Castro, who had just gained total power in Cuba and was on his first official visit to the United States. The party proceeded to move into the train and the conductor came along to say he had instructions to move me. Since this seemed to me to be totally unnecessary, and maybe because it was the Queen's birthday, I refused; and to my astonishment the conductor did not see why a passenger should be so disturbed. There was a good deal of conversation at the back of the carriage in a language entirely incomprehensible to me, but I was left in peace. I was thus able to prepare my lecture as planned, but in the event it was curtailed because when I went to Columbia in the afternoon there were literally thousands of people around the entry yard, all hoping for a glimpse of my competing peripatetic speaker: I was over half an hour late for my talk, and I do not think that my audience was of comparable magnitude to Castro's! Barbara and the family arrived in Boston two days later, and I met them at Logan Airport. I shall never forget the look of intense excitement on John's face as he came off the plane after completing his very first flight.

On our third trip we were independent of public transport, because shortly after our arrival in Wellesley Hills I bought an old second-hand Plymouth sedan which served us well, not just because a car was becoming essential for shopping but also to enable us to visit friends and colleagues in the Boston area and to show the children some of the historically significant places in New England. After a winter's night in the unheated garage 'Plymouth' was a brute to start until I had sprinkled a little ether on the air intake filter: at this she would roar gleefully into action and from then on was a joy to drive. This trick is probably the only useful bit of information I gained when I was in the Chemistry Department at the Royal Aircraft Establishment in 1939.

By the time spring was over and the buds had burst, Plymouth was feeling much more sprightly and took us on a splendid tour. After my last lecture at MIT on the afternoon of 6 May I dashed back home, where the car had already been loaded and the children were ready. We travelled north on the Massachusetts Turnpike to Concord, and then north-west to Schenectady to stay at the Hotel van Curler. I consulted at General Electric in the next two days, whilst the rest of the family were splendidly entertained by friends, and then we moved on to Buffalo and Niagara, which can never disappoint. On this occasion Niagara excelled itself by displaying a magnificent rainbow, and the bridge of that name did even better by enabling the children to stand with one foot on Canadian and the other on American soil. Furthermore, as we walked back to our hotel a figure approached us from the opposite direction. He was Dr J.E.B. Randles, lecturer in electrochemistry at the University of Birmingham; there could not have been a more striking example of the statistics of rare encounter.

We went on to Toronto to stay with the family of my Cambridge mature student, Dr A.E.R. Westman, for two days in which work and pleasure were apportioned as in Schenectady – the former to me, the latter to Barbara and the children. An easy ride on the Queen Elizabeth Highway brought us to Ottawa and many friends of long standing, including old students, Canadian post-docs who had worked with me, and National Research Council colleagues – far too numerous to list. Nothing could have been more delightful. Nevertheless we were glad to spend half a day cruising slowly up the almost empty road on the east side of the Ottawa River, until forced to cross at the last covered bridge. And so on to Deep River for four days, spending the Saturday and the Sunday swimming, walking and generally enjoying the countryside with which I had become so familiar thirteen years earlier. Though to me Deep River had lost its newness, its adventurous spirit and the sheer vastness of the Canadian Shield must have had their impact on the children.

It was with some sadness that on Whit Monday I turned Plymouth's nose back down the Ottawa River valley for the 220 miles to Montreal and the ever-welcoming McGill chemistry faculty. They not only gave us a splendid lunch in the Faculty Club but allowed me to talk to two of their best PhD students (Nelson Wright and Dave Wiles) as potential post-doctoral fellows at Leeds. Bidding farewell to Montreal on 22 May, we decided to make the most of the drive south through Vermont and New Hampshire back home, treating it as a holiday. We knew that we had only three more nights at Laurel Avenue in which to clear up our affairs, pack, dispose of Plymouth and board a train for New York for an overnight stay before embarking on the *Queen Elizabeth* for Cherbourg and Southampton.

Barbara and I found the return sea trip greatly relaxing: no chores, only rest, read, eat and swim. Our stop at Cherbourg provided us with a surprise. We had time to go ashore for a couple of hours: it was a beautiful spring day and we rejoiced in the higgledy-piggledy multicoloured architecture of comprehensible human dimensions, the chaotic traffic, and especially the open market with its bustle and delicious aromas of wine and cheese and fresh farm produce. To our horror, the children's immediate verdict was adverse: they rejected the untidiness and the smells as unhygienic. No doubt they were recalling with infinite trust the North

American toilet statements 'This seat has been sanitized for your protection', whereas I, having often seen hotel chambermaids' dirty grey damp cloths whisked round once at lightning speed, had a more sceptical attitude to their disinfective power. To confound us still further, as soon as we set foot on English soil reanglicisation proceeded rapidly, so fast indeed that we wondered if the 'American experience' was not just an easily eroded patina. We were wrong, of course. Children have immense absorptive power and long memories, but also a great capacity for adaptation to their surroundings. The drive in the hired car from Southampton to Leeds by way of Oxford (marked by no divided highways, let alone turnpikes) was accepted for what it was, just part of the way they and everyone else lived in England.

There have been many occasions since 1959 when we have reflected on the enduring effects this visit had on each of us. Of course, it is always a pleasure for parents to witness the often unpredictable and immediate responses of their children to entirely novel situations, and I had the added satisfaction of seeing how Barbara's reactions in some cases resembled and in others differed from those I had experienced on my first trip alone. However, I was quite unprepared for the way in which the children's behaviour so often seemed to remove the scales from my inward eye, and to reveal with an engaging freshness some new and enriching feature of a situation which I had missed on my own first sight. That the effects were long-lasting on the children in their attitudes to the USA and to other countries only really emerged many years later.

For me the pleasure of being free from administrative duties was immense. It was bliss to arrive at MIT and not be faced with a day broken up by letter answering, meetings or telephone calls: being able to devote four hours at a time to one task, either in the library or in the office, allowed much more real work to be accomplished. It was also a delight to be lecturing only to graduate students, and to be able to attend some of the lectures given by other members of the department. It seemed to me that I got more from MIT than I gave to it and I therefore had mixed feelings of guilt and gratitude, which have recurred on every subsequent visit. My last one, some thirty-six years later, was made in my capacity as chairman of a sub-committee of the House of Lords Select Committee on Science and Technology. On that occasion we met faculty members all morning, and as the lunch given by MIT was coming to its end I rose to thank them for their hospitality and cooperation, only to be pulled down by my jacket back into my chair before I could say more than a few words. Then a trolley bearing a large birthday cake and champagne was wheeled in, so that all could celebrate my eightieth birthday. That I was remembered so long after my earlier visits was for me very moving and heart-warming.

Being a Professor

Readers may be puzzled to know why I have jumped almost a whole decade from 1950 to 1959, nearly two-thirds of the total period spent in Leeds, and yet have written not a word about my working life and the institution in the service of which it was spent. This is in some measure deliberate, because just as the children experienced a culture shock in going to the USA to live, so Leeds University was a comparable shock for me as someone who had spent the previous seventeen years in Oxford and Cambridge. To an extent this was because those mediaeval seats of learning are collegiate in organisation: the colleges are independent, self-governing corporations, charging their own fees for membership, tutorial tuition and residence, and retaining the sole right to present students for admission to degrees of the University. The colleges also have their own significant endowments.

Oxford, Cambridge and the four ancient Scottish foundations (in date order St. Andrews, Glasgow, Aberdeen and Edinburgh) were for half a millennium the only universities in the United Kingdom. Thereafter, the first wave of higher education expansion began in the nineteenth century and led to the foundation of the University of London (a loose confederation of colleges), the University of Durham, the Queen's University of Ireland, and colleges in some of the larger mercantile or manufacturing cities. The latter institutions had all gained independent charters by the early years of the twentieth century and form a relatively homogeneous group in history, organisation, ethos and purpose, becoming known as the old civic or 'redbrick' universities. Leeds is typical, having sprung from the amalgamation of the Leeds School of Medicine, founded in 1831, and the Yorkshire College of Science, which opened in 1874. The resulting body combined with University College, Liverpool, and Owen's College, Manchester, to form the federal Victoria University in 1887, finally getting its own charter as an independent university in 1904, when it had about 800 students. By

1950 the number of students had reached 3,000, and architecturally and constitutionally it could not have been more different from Cambridge.

The main entrance at Leeds led into the recently completed Parkinson Building, clad in Portland stone like a miniature University of London Senate House and approached up a grand set of stone steps. Passage through the great doorways revealed a large concourse which served no particular purpose other than as a circulation area and an entry to the Brotherton Library, which seemed to be modelled on the Great Round Reading Room at the British Museum. To the north it led into similar Portland stone-clad buildings, which housed the Departments of Chemistry, Physics and Mining. Most of the remaining buildings were of brick, some being the old Yorkshire College of Science. The centre of the city was a mere ten minutes' walk away, and there one found the Leeds General Infirmary and the University Medical School. Most of the students who did not live at home were in lodgings or scattered in the single-sex halls of residence lying to the north-west of the city. There was no purpose-built refectory or senior common room, but merely an adapted terrace house and wooden huts where lunch could be taken. One room was called the Professors' Room and was restricted to those holding that title, unless the professor was a woman, in which case she was excluded – a sad denial of the original concept of the College that it should be open equally to men and women. Chemistry was probably the best housed of any department and as such attracted the envy of others, the usual jibe being that it had a room for every element. It certainly seemed superior to the Cambridge department in size and convenience, and there was ample accommodation for my research group.

Social life in Leeds was quite different from that in Cambridge, where the major focus had been St Catharine's College. In Leeds there was no comparable social unit which crossed subject boundaries; instead there was the occasional Senate Dinner, to which the Vice-Chancellor would bring a guest from outside Leeds to open a post-prandial discussion. There were of course other lunches or dinners associated with lectures by visiting speakers, but the main University-wide functions were the rather grand receptions in the Parkinson Hall attended by the Chancellor, where white tie and full academic robes were *de rigueur*, for example when honorary degrees were awarded.

Coming from Cambridge to Leeds was also a transition from an academic democracy in which the coordination of varied and often autonomous parts was difficult, but could occasionally be creative, to a much more integrated structure. The supreme governing body of Leeds University, like that of most of the civic universities, was named the Court: it included members from public institutions, schools and industrial associations, together with all the members of the Council (which was the executive governing body). The Court met infrequently – no more than twice a year – and its meetings were purely formal, while the Council met monthly, except during the vacations: it too was dominated by lay members, the remainder being elected academic staff, mostly professors. Whilst Council was recognized as the *de facto* ultimate authority over finance, estates and buildings, and was in the strict sense 'the employer' of both academic and non-academic staff, the other key body was the Senate. This was the academic authority: it could express a view on any matter, and its opinions were naturally treated with great respect by the Council. The membership of the Senate in those days was restricted to professors, plus one or two elected non-professorial members.

The Chancellor, then HRH the Princess Royal, was the Chief Officer of the University. The statutes laid down that she should preside over meetings of the Court and the Council, but custom decreed that the Pro-Chancellor would take her place were she to be absent, which was always the case in the fifteen years that I was there. The crucial figure in the life of the University was the Vice-Chancellor, who was the paid, full-time, ex-officio chairman of the Senate and a member of the Council and Court. He, the Registrar and the Bursar were the three permanent senior officials. They were at the centre of the web of communications, and the nodal points integrating the work of the various University departments.

Each of the three departments in the School of Chemistry made an annual case for funds, which ultimately would appear in front of the Finance Committee of Council. The bid would be based on a programme which had to be in conformity with current academic policy, as formulated by the Senate and approved by the Council (the body at which considerations of academic policy and resources came together), after it had been reviewed by the Faculty Boards and any ad hoc committees set up for specific purposes. Once the process was completed, each head of department would be informed of any additional posts for his area, and of the financial resources for equipment which would be at his disposal in the following year. Curricular matters were almost entirely in the hands of the Board of Chemical Studies, which consisted of all the established members of Chemistry staff, although its recommendations had to proceed upwards for approval by Senate after passing through the Faculty Board of Science and Technology. Although, on the face of it, I appeared to have less autonomy than I would have done as a head of department in Cambridge, in fact this was not the case and in many ways change was easier to accomplish in Leeds than it ever was in Cambridge – as Todd had predicted on the basis of his experience at Manchester.

My first term in post was a heavy one, not just because of my slowness to adapt to an entirely different system of university governance, but also because no one had been found to replace me in Cambridge and therefore that university asked me to continue to give my lectures there: I compressed them into about a fortnight at the end of the Michaelmas Term. By the end of my first year in Leeds I had begun to understand the mechanism of operation of the University and had also come to know something of the Vice-Chancellor, the same charming Charles Morris who had called on me in St Catharine's College early in 1950.

Charles Morris was Vice-Chancellor of Leeds from 1948 to 1963, one of a group of remarkable and progressive vice-chancellors in the redbrick universities which included his brother Sir Philip Morris (Bristol, 1946-66), Sir Eric (later Lord) Ashby (Belfast, 1950-59), Sir Robert Aitken (Birmingham, 1953-68), Sir James Mountford (Liverpool, 1945-63) and Lord Stopford (Manchester, 1934-56), with whom must also be included John (later Lord) Fulton (Principal of University College, Swansea, 1947-59, and the founding Vice-Chancellor at Sussex, 1959-67). They were all very influential in the Committee of Vice-Chancellors and Principals (CVCP), and collectively did much to prepare the ground for the expansion of existing universities and the establishment of new ones in the 1960s. In a period when the total cost of university education in Great Britain increased enormously, as also did the proportion of it borne by the state, there were inevitable pressures for the State to intervene more and more in the universities' affairs, on the grounds of public accountability and social audit. That this was successfully resisted was due in no small measure to the reputation for personal unselfishness and integrity of these vice-chancellors, and the symbiotic relationship which existed between the universities and the University Grants Committee (UGC).

When I arrived at Leeds, Charles Morris was 52 and had been Vice-Chancellor for two years, having previously been Headmaster of King Edward's School, Birmingham, and for the whole of the inter-war years a Tutorial Fellow in

Philosophy at Balliol College, Oxford. He was also Chairman of the CVCP, and in great demand to give public service at home and abroad; even after his retirement from Leeds he helped the new Universities of Bradford and Lancaster. My initial impressions of him were conflicting. He was very friendly, a great supporter of science and technology in the University,[1] but in argument he was sometimes elliptical and frequently more allusive than direct – a trait which I often thought was a general characteristic of the discourse of Balliol philosophers. His advice was invariably sound, but also delphic. When I gave the address at his memorial service in Balliol on 27 November 1991, I was moved to say:

> The seeker after advice was never told *what* to do. Many of us at Leeds found this kind of response perplexing. I remember once leaving his room not just puzzled, but actually irritated. I had sought his guidance on a difficult matter affecting the welfare of my department. He listened patiently as I expounded the nature of my dilemma and then, after a long pause in which he contemplated the passing tramcars, turned and said simply 'I trust you – absolutely'. Pleasing as this observation was, it seemed of little use to me in my predicament. But on reflection, and in the light of other experiences, I came to realise that it was a fundamental part of his belief that individuals should not be told what to do, but should make their own decisions based on certain fundamental human values and principles, which he was prepared to defend and debate at length, as well as on the best information available. The effect on the questioner is, of course, to make him or her more self-reliant, more capable of coping with new, as yet unforeseen, difficult situations. In that moment I saw his attitude as that of the true teacher, the antithesis of the mere didactic purveyor of compulsory lectures which deaden rather than quicken the mind.

---

1. On only one occasion did he fail to achieve any objective which we both shared. Early in 1962 I realised that if Leeds was to maintain its strength in chemistry and not lose outstanding persons to the new universities at that stage being planned, we must anchor some key people by offering them personal chairs. The two I had most in mind were Peter Gray in physical chemistry and Durward Cruickshank in inorganic chemistry. The idea of divisions within the School which were multi-professorial did not appeal to Basil Lythgoe in organic chemistry, nor to Harry Irving in the inorganic department. I went to talk about the proposal with Charles Morris, who, after discussion, sympathised and commented that the problem was one of tactics. 'I can get one but not two chairs out of Senate' were his closing words. That left me with a very difficult choice between two good candidates, both of whom were later elected FRS, and I agonised over the decision for several weeks. Happily, J. Monteith Robertson, head of the chemistry department at Glasgow University, then telephoned me to say that the Glasgow Senatus had agreed to establish a new (Joseph Black) chair in chemistry, to which he would like to see Cruickshank appointed. I was sorry to lose him, but relieved that the new principle was established for Leeds.

Charles Morris showed his progressive attitude in many ways. He ensured that the University had a development plan, which had the effect of making it ready and able to take maximum advantage of UGC money for buildings and equipment when this became available. He was receptive to the idea of a School of Chemistry in which the headship was held in turn by each of the three established professors and, in the 1960s, he responded positively to the notion of more *ad hominem* professorships. As the University continued to grow he foresaw that its system of governance would need to change, and about two years before he was due to retire he set up a working party to examine and report on this issue. Uncharacteristically, however, he then made an unwise decision. He became so determined to effect the changes proposed by this group before he retired, that he would not see the force of the argument that the vice-chancellor-elect, who after all would have to operate the new system, should be drawn into the discussions before conclusions were reached, or at least that debate on the report of the group should be deferred until the new vice-chancellor arrived.

How well I remember, with great sadness, the date 3 July 1963. There took place on that day the last meeting of Senate over which Charles Morris presided before his retirement, and one item on the agenda was the approval of the working party's report. I was aware that there had been several groups of professors opposed to its recommendations; indeed, I had been present at a meeting of one such group and had agreed to the suggestion of others that I should speak against any motion for acceptance. At the same time I had pointed out to the dissidents that, because the University was growing rapidly and was likely to continue to do so, the existing composition of its major committees would not remain appropriate for long, and change was inevitable. When the time came for this item to be debated I was miserable at having to frustrate the good intentions of a man whose work, both within and outwith the University, I had admired for so many years. It came as no great surprise that the report was rejected, and I felt deeply for him. The situation was all the more poignant for both of us because, later that day, Senate gave a farewell dinner for the Vice-Chancellor. I had been asked to make a speech, which at least gave me a chance to remind everyone of the great work he had done for Leeds, and to put the afternoon's proceedings into a proper perspective. It was typical of Charles Morris' generous nature that our friendship was unaffected by that potentially divisive Senate decision.

In the two immediate post-war decades the esteem in which scientific research in Great Britain was held, both at home and abroad, was very high. In that period Britons were awarded six Nobel Prizes in physics (all between 1947 and 1954), six in physiology or medicine and nine in chemistry. Within Britain memories of the role of radar in aerial defence during the war, of penicillin, the great healing antibiotic, of the invention of practically useful polymers such as polythene, terylene and perspex, of the jet engine, and many other advances convinced both Labour and Conservative governments that 'what is good for science is good for Britain'. This widespread enthusiasm for science was acknowledged by politicians and the 'white heat of the technological revolution' is remembered (albeit a little inaccurately) as a Wilsonian electioneering slogan.

On gaining power in 1964 the Labour government established a Ministry of Technology with Patrick Blackett, one of the Nobel Laureates in Physics, as its chief adviser. The same enthusiasm was reflected in the government's willingness to support its Department of Scientific and Industrial Research (DSIR), the Medical Research Council and the Agricultural Research Council. All these bodies awarded research grants, fellowships and studentships to individuals in university science departments, which were themselves also recipients of money for research through the UGC's institutional block grants.[2] At the same time the science and technology-based industries such as chemicals, pharmaceuticals, aeronautics, power generation, and so on were prospering, and recruiting all the graduate applicants of good quality who were produced in these subjects.

There were other factors influencing higher education. First was the decision to raise the school-leaving age, which increased the proportion of the age group going on to sixth-form work and presenting for A-level examinations. Secondly, there was the 'Anderson' agreement that possession of two A-levels and acceptance by a university would guarantee that a student's tuition fees would be paid and a maintenance grant, subject to a parental means test, would be awarded if the student had been resident in the United Kingdom for not less than three years.[3] There

---

2. The arrangement was known as the Dual Support System for academic research.

3. This important principle was set out in 'Grants for Students', the report of a government committee chaired by Sir Colin Anderson (Cmnd. 1051, published in 1960).

was therefore no impediment to increasing the number of students in universities studying scientific, engineering or technological subjects, or to supporting those worthy to undertake research for higher degrees. I was particularly aware of the situation because I was a member (and later chairman) of the DSIR committee that had to allocate a number of studentships which university chemistry departments could then award to meritorious graduates for postgraduate research. This work began in 1953 and concluded in 1964, after which DSIR was replaced by the Science Research Council (SRC) as a result of the passage of the 1965 Science and Technology Act – one of the earliest pieces of legislation enacted by Parliament following the election of the Labour government in October 1964.

It was in this national context that Leeds, like other civic universities, was expanding rapidly. Thus the signs were all favourable for a new, young professor of chemistry. Moreover, I had a splendid colleague in E.G. Cox, a man some nine years older than me who had been appointed a professor some five years earlier.[4] He was a physicist by training whose research was in X-ray crystallography: he had worked with W.H. Bragg at the Royal Institution and, after appointment to the staff of Birmingham University chemistry department, had elucidated some important organic chemical structures. He had established an X-ray group in Leeds, which was a particularly appropriate place for this kind of study because not only had W.H. Bragg been Cavendish Professor of Physics at one time, but there were active X-ray research teams in several departments, for example Physics (Brindley), Botany (Preston) and Biomolecular Structure (Astbury).

Of greater significance for me was Cox's personality. He had willingly made room to accommodate the influx of seven researchers who came with me from Cambridge, and others from Canada and Ireland, and also arranged that one of the students graduating with first class honours in Leeds in 1950 should join my team: my research was quickly re-established. In the ten years that we were colleagues I particularly admired how he accepted the steady growth of my own group, and the groups of other members of staff I had appointed to physical chemistry, which, to a lesser and more jealous person, would have seemed like a threat. I have never known a man so free of envy.

---

4. Cox resigned his chair in 1960 to become Secretary of the Agricultural Research Council.

My Chemistry Research

Simply stated, research compulsion is an overriding desire to satisfy curiosity about the nature of the world we inhabit, by systematic enquiry into those natural phenomena which are not at all (or only partially) understood. My own major preoccupation has always been to gain a better understanding of the underlying mechanisms of the movement of the atoms or electrons in molecules which are undergoing relatively simple reactions in the gaseous, liquid or glassy states, brought about by the absorption of heat, light or ionizing radiations. The results of of this work have, somewhat surprisingly, proved to be relevant to matters which touch many people with no knowledge of science. Such mechanisms may underlie the production of plastics, the alteration of their properties for certain purposes, or the means of protecting the public from nuclear radiations. To attempt to make my researches comprehensible to all readers would occupy so much space that it must be rejected. I have therefore compromised and devote only a few paragraphs, which inevitably employ chemical terms and symbols (but no equations), to a rough explanation of what my researches were about, whilst letting the emphasis fall more on the relations with my research colleagues, the international nature of the enter-prise and the effects on myself. I hope this recipe works, although I confess to doubts; however, the reader will be the judge.

Well over half my adult life has been spent in university teaching and research, two activities which I have greatly enjoyed. Scientifically, my fifteen years in Leeds were probably the most productive and happy. The photochlorination problem was completely elucidated and, from purely kinetic arguments, we established the life of chloroethyl radical activated complexes as being of the order of a nanosecond, that is, a thousand-millionth of a second, and possessing more than one exit channel. General methods for studying isotopic effects on the rate of abstraction of hydrogen or deuterium atoms from CH or CD bonds by CH_3 or CD_3 radicals in the gas phase, or by OH radicals in water, were successfully developed. Electron transfer reactions surrendered some of their secrets: notably, we were able to provide the first direct kinetic evidence of the bridge-activated complex mechanism, when we showed that azide-catalysed isotopic exchange of iron-59 could only occur rapidly through the complex $(FeN_3Fe)^{4+}$. The detailed mechanism of the polymerization of water-soluble vinyl compounds, such as acrylamide and methacrylamide, was revealed by a combination of classical steady-state methods and pulse radiolysis. Nor were cationic and anionic polymerization in non-aqueous media neglected, a field further developed by Ken Ivin. During a year's stay in Leeds, Henry Taube of Stanford University (later a chemistry Nobel Laureate) showed me how dissolved ozone in water could be dissociated by light to release oxygen atoms in a particular electronic state (designated ^1D), which could insert between two atoms joined by a single covalent bond in a molecule. I thought that nitrous oxide, N_2O, might similarly be decomposed by light of a shorter wavelength to produce the same oxygen atoms, but with the advantage that every atom so formed would be accompanied by a stable molecule of nitrogen: measurement of the total amount of nitrogen could thus be used to count all the oxygen atoms in this ^1D state produced in any experiment.

Meanwhile, two other major research themes flourished. The first was the investigation of the kinetics and thermodynamics of addition polymerization, which had emerged from our early success in solving the ceiling temperature phenomenon and which led us into developing an isothermal, adiabatic calorimeter for determining enthalpies of polymerization. The comparison of experimental data with values calculated from the known structures and internal vibrations and rotations of monomer and polymer molecules led to useful guides to the polymerizability of unsaturated and cyclic potential monomers, based on the details of their structure. In due course Ken Ivin and I summarised this and related work in an article published in *Quarterly Reviews* in 1958.

Much later – twenty years or more – I heard from Gene Garfield that this particular paper was the 'most ever cited' in, I think, polymer chemistry but it may have been polymer science. My gratification at receiving this information from Dr Garfield, who had created citation indices, quickly gave way to some alarm at the thought that Dr Ivin and I would be credited with too great a degree of originality in this paper: in fact it was nothing more than a compilation of ideas, some of which were ours but many the work of other people. This immediately caused me to think how dangerous it is to use crude measurements, such as citation indices, as an indication of the intrinsic intellectual quality of scientific work, though they may give some clues about utility. This is not an idle concern on my part. At a time when assessment of 'research quality' is being demanded as part of the public audit of the work of universities, it would be only too easy to use high citation scores of published papers as part of the basis of a claim for a quality ranking which would attract more funds. To those who would advocate such measures I would simply say two things. First, scientists are not fools, and once aware of such factors they would be tempted to change their practices and cite each other's work more frequently, thereby raising the score unjustifiably (and if such practice varied from subject to subject, that alone would to lead to injustice). Secondly, if I were still in the publishing business, I could almost certainly beat my own record by producing a paper with a deliberate error in it, thereby guaranteeing citation by all those clever people around the world who would spot this error and feel called upon to draw everyone else's attention to it!

The other major research theme was that of radiation chemistry. Here our preoccupations were with understanding how energy absorbed primarily by the solvent, whether in liquid or solid form, from incident ionizing radiation, that is, α, β-, γ-, and X-rays, brings about chemical change in the solutes. Our principal concerns were with solutions of these solutes in water, or in aqueous glasses at low temperatures, but we also made similar investigations using other solvents, mainly organic materials. We used three main experimental methods. The first and classical method was simply to irradiate the chosen system and analyse what new products were formed by a known dose of radiation, and in what quantities. Any conclusions about the intermediate steps could only be intelligent conjecture based on a general knowledge of chemistry, except of course that it was possible sometimes to say that the entities first produced from the water had particular characteristics. We had inferred by this means that the primary products were free radicals, unstable species each having an odd number of electrons. It was nevertheless possible to establish by the method I have described (sometimes called the steady state method) that one of these free radicals had unit negative charge and, in the case of water, could therefore only be a single electron surrounded by suitably oriented water molecules, which preserved it for almost a thousandth of a second. Broadly similar conclusions were reached for polar organic solvents.

The other two methods were to use either fast reaction techniques, in our case pulse radiolysis, or matrix isolation. The first approach is simply to deliver a lot of energy in a very short time, a nanosecond or less, and to use fast sensitive methods to detect any species which are produced in that time and die away after the pulse. By this means rates of reactions of the primary species with the solutes can be determined accurately, and in the case of the hydrated electron more is now known about this simplest chemical entity, despite its short life, than about many chemical compounds that can be contained in bottles on the shelf. Matrix isolation is quite different. This relies on making a transparent glass of the solvent in which the solutes cannot move around, and then irradiating the system at very low temperatures but not necessarily in a very short time. The intermediates so produced are then held, as it were, in cold storage and can be examined at leisure by spectroscopic methods, usually optical or magnetic. When the glass is softened by warming the intermediates begin to react, but much more slowly than in the liquid, so that fast detection methods are unnecessary. These two methods are of course mutually confirmatory, and by such means it was possible to investigate the basic radiation chemistry of a whole range of systems and to elucidate the parts played by free radicals, solvated electrons and excited states.

Because living cells in mammals are about 85 per cent water, work of this kind is relevant to an understanding of how radiation can affect processes in living cells, and therefore to both radiotherapy and radiation-induced disease – two areas of considerable public concern. This fact, combined with the need to have a very powerful source of radiation, led to a particularly interesting and unique development.[5] Cookridge Hospital in Leeds was the prime radiotherapy centre for West Yorkshire, and the northern centre of the National Radiological Protection Board. Shortly after my move to Leeds I was made aware that our radiation chemistry studies had been drawn to the attention of Gerard Pomerat, then a representative in Europe of the Rockefeller Foundation. He visited me to ask if there was any way in which the Foundation could assist my work. My immediate and obvious need was for a powerful, small-sized source of γ-rays, which I knew could be produced in the high neutron flux of the Chalk River reactor to which I have already referred. I therefore asked him for help to purchase a cobalt-60 source, which was speedily forthcoming, and a thousand-curie source was ordered from Canada. This, with its essential heavy shielding, could not easily be housed in the Chemistry Department in the University but, having realised that it could provide all the radiation that we needed in a few hours a day and for the rest of the time could be used for radio-

---

5. This story is an abridged account of the contribution which I made to *The History of Cookridge Hospital 1867–1972*, published by that hospital in 1997.

therapy, I approached F.W. Spiers, the Professor of Medical Physics, with a proposition that an arrangement for shared use should be worked out. A small committee was formed, and we decided that Cookridge Hospital was a suitable location for the venture. Further financial help was received from the Yorkshire Council of the British Empire Cancer Campaign, the University and the Board of Governors of the Leeds General Infirmary, and this allowed us to build a laboratory and accommodation for the source, with irradiation rooms for patients and for chemistry. This co-operative effort was typical of Leeds, and the new buildings and installations were formally opened on 15 May 1956 by HRH the Princess Royal. Of course, as the subject and the techniques developed we needed to build other facilities there, and in 1964 we were fortunate in securing a grant of £100,000 from the DSIR to install a 3MeV Van de Graaff generator, which would deliver very short pulses of very energetic electrons. Thirty years later, on 27 May 1994, I was delighted to open a new wing at Cookridge commemorating Professor Spiers, an occasion which gave me a welcome opportunity to express my indebtedness to him and to others in the city.

My fifteen enjoyable years in Leeds would not have been possible without good support from the centre of the University and the very fair consideration given to our applications to DSIR for special resources. Most important of all were the many good research students and post-doctoral fellows who studied with me. I do not have a complete record of all who worked in this group, but from memory I have been able to identify 110 persons from the USA, Commonwealth countries and Europe (including those from behind the Iron Curtain), and from the Far East, whose presence greatly enriched the educational development of the British students. We are still in touch with many of them.

We also could not possibly have managed all this without splendid help from several colleagues, notably Dr Ivin, Dr Ayscough, Dr Collinson and latterly Drs Buxton, Salmon and Wilkinson, many of whom had their own independent research groups as well. Financial support came from the British Research Councils and also from industry: there were grants for research under my direction from the American firms Monsanto, General Electric, Dow Chemicals and Grace Chemical Company, and in this country from the Atomic Energy Authority, Hedley's, the Distillers' Company, and the Anglo-Iranian Oil Company (which became BP). In all cases except one the initial approach came from the companies, asking if I would act as a consultant on either an ad hoc or a regular basis. Contact with such firms was valuable, not only because of the resources for research which it brought in, but also because I gained knowledge about what aspects of reaction kinetics and mechanisms were of importance to industry, and how new information could be turned into industrial applications or, to use the current jargon, into wealth creation. That kind of knowledge was useful in many ways, not least in providing illustrative material to students in the course of lectures and discussions. Moreover it was possible for me to accumulate research funds, held by the University, for use at my complete discretion. Several of those who worked in Leeds in this period had financial problems which could be resolved by a grant from this source: for example, I can remember two students who graduated with indifferent first degrees but whose laboratory performance was superb. There was no chance of them getting awards from DSIR but I was prepared to stake each individual to a year's support, to give them the chance to prove themselves as researchers: if they succeeded, I would support their applications for a DSIR award for a further two years. In due course one became a professor, and the other a university reader.

Gaining this extra money was sometimes absolutely crucial, but there was a considerable price to be paid in terms of my time and energy. One example must suffice. I became a consultant to Unilever, which involved me in many visits to Port Sunlight and Colworth House in this country, Vlaardingen in Holland and Edgewater in New Jersey. However, the contacts I made enabled me to apply to Unilever for financial help to complete the chemistry quadrangle with a new five-storey building costing, in 1955, a mere £85,000. Unilever responded to my appeal with a gift of £30,000, which was the critical sum needed to ensure that the project went ahead.

Although there were problems from time to time with individuals, I think the morale of my collaborators was generally high. One reason for this was that the group regularly spent a few days away in September in the Yorkshire Dales, for example at Malham Tarn Field Centre. The mornings and evenings would be devoted to the presentation of papers by those who had work to report, and the afternoons were spent walking in delightful country. There was a marked tendency among some of my European colleagues to be very formal in their initial relations with me: this formality soon disappeared when they saw me slip under Gordale Scar and be drenched with water, or take part in scrambles up and down the hillside with much younger people. I also made a habit of inviting old friends from other universities, such as E.J. Bowen and R.P. Bell from my Oxford days, and Sandy Ashmore from Cambridge after he had become a professor in the University of Manchester Institute of Science and Technology.

Entertaining Visitors

I tried to entertain all our foreign research workers at home as soon as they had arrived, which imposed an immense strain upon Barbara, particularly when the children were young, but it seemed to be much appreciated. Inevitably we had some near-catastrophes. I especially remember a charming American and his wife, whom we had invited to dinner on a Friday night immediately after their arrival, and for whom Barbara had cooked beefsteaks to make them feel at home. Alas, it turned out they were devout Catholics; and because we had ourselves just returned from the USA the larder was nearly empty of permissible alternatives to meat. A quick telephone consultation with a Catholic colleague of mine, Ted Caldin, suggested that a word in the ear of the Bishop of Leeds might procure a special dispensation: fortunately it did, and the evening was saved. We also had overseas people, who had nowhere to go, as guests for lunch and dinner each Christmas Day, which would provoke amusing letters from the children. On one occasion Mary (aged seven) wrote ambiguously to her grandmother, 'Thank you for my present. We had a Pole and a Canadian for lunch and an Australian and a Czech for dinner'.

There were, of course, a lot of academic visitors who came for one, two or three nights, sometimes longer, often under the auspices of some institution such as the British Council or the Royal Society. Ned Steacie used to visit whenever he was in England and Kondratiev, the Soviet Academician, spent several days with us, as did many others including Wilhelm Jost, Frank Mayo and Cheves Walling. There were some colleagues who would come for a whole year, such as Henry Taube and R.M. (Dick) Noyes when he was a professor at Columbia.

The visitors who were in Leeds for a day or two liked to talk to research students, and sometimes they heard more than they should. I remember one occasion when my guest and I were conversing in the corridor just before I was going to take him into a room containing four research students, with whom I knew he would like to have a discussion about their work. As he spoke I turned the handle and opened the laboratory door about two inches. Immediately I heard a familiar voice say, 'When's that old bugger Fred coming round?' I shut the door as silently as I had opened it, explaining to my visitor that I was not upset by what I had heard and that the noun applied to me was not to be taken literally but, if anything, carried a rather friendly connotation in Yorkshire parlance.

The most surprising of all these visitors, both in the manner in which he came and in the long-term effect which he had, was a man named Osman Achmatowicz. One Friday in August 1957 I was alone in the house because Barbara had taken the children off for the weekend to see their grandmother on the western side of the Pennines. It was a splendid opportunity to have some quiet time working at home, but before long I was disturbed by a telephone call which I answered by saying 'Dainton, Leeds 56194'.

The reply came, 'Here is Achmatowicz'. That meant nothing to me so I repeated my first statement, to which the voice then said 'I am Polish and I come see you Somaday'.

Somaday was pronounced as if it were spelt Summerday, from which I was puzzled to know whether it was some future day, Sunday or a French Saturday. I realised I was unlikely to get a clear answer to any question of this kind so I then said slowly, 'Where are you speaking from?' The voice replied, 'It is British Council', and I countered with 'I will meet you at Leeds station whenever your train arrives'.

I immediately telephoned the British Council, who made it clear to me that Achmatowicz would be arriving on the afternoon of Sunday, that he was the Polish Minister for Science, and that part of the purpose of his visit was to place the first government-supported post-doctoral fellow in chemistry with Lord Todd at Cambridge and the second with me in Leeds. As soon as I had said I would meet him and put the phone down I realised I had no car. Fortunately I was able to persuade Peter Gray to lend me his Rover, and I met Achmatowicz as arranged, deciding that the best thing I could do was to take him out into the Dales, give him dinner at the Harewood Arms, and lodge him in his hotel ready for talks on Monday. As we drove to the Harewood Arms he said to me, 'This is a very good car' and added in terms of reproach suggesting that I did not deserve a car of this kind, 'Even I think it is better than Sir Todd's car is good'. I explained that it was not mine, but accepted the implicit reproof and assessment of my position in the

British chemical hierarchy, and we drove on to a pleasant dinner. Our discussions went well and the first of these post-doctoral fellows to arrive was one Jerzy Kroh, who was extraordinarily good. He took an excellent PhD in 1960, returned to his own country and established a first-class laboratory of radiation chemistry in Lódz Polytechnic University, became its Rector and retired only in 1994. In September of that year there was a celebratory meeting in his honour which took place partly in Lódz and partly in Zakopane, to which Barbara and I went.

The Varied Benefits of Keeping in Touch

Receiving visitors from other countries was something I especially enjoyed, and when we could persuade them to see particular research students and to give a talk or colloquium, I think we got great benefits from them. Having so many parallel topics of research, I tended to be invited to scientific meetings in many locations, and to my great pleasure I was from time to time asked to give named lectureships at various universities. I have already referred to MIT, and in 1961 I spent September to December as George Fisher Baker Lecturer at Cornell University, a very worthwhile experience in which I hoped to finish off the text of the book I had begun at MIT. Alas, my visit was marred by persistent illness which frustrated my good intention. I had other visits, but of shorter duration, to the University of Notre Dame in 1952 and the University of Alberta in 1962.

I always felt that North America, either Canada or the USA, was a second home which I knew better than Europe, while the Pacific anglophone countries were at that time a closed book to me. This deficiency was duly remedied, beginning in 1959 when, within a few weeks of returning from MIT, I took off for an eight-week visit to the Antipodes at the invitation of the Royal Australian Chemical Institute and its New Zealand analogue. From the moment of my arrival I loved both countries: I visited most of the universities, making friendships which have lasted to this day and stimulating a flow of students and post-doctoral researchers to Leeds. For example, out of the Australian visit came Don Stranks, whom we were able to appoint to the first university lectureship in radiochemistry; he stayed for some five years before returning to Australia and a meteoric career, culminating in the position of Vice-Chancellor of the University of Adelaide (in which office, sadly, he died). It fell to me to give the first Stranks Memorial Lecture on a further visit to Australia in 1988. Another visitor, D.L. Baulch, came to Leeds, stayed for ever and rose through the ranks to become a professor.

Visits to Europe tended to be of shorter duration. Some were to big international conferences, such as the International Union of Pure and Applied Chemistry meeting in Moscow in 1965, following which, through the generosity of the Soviet Academy of Sciences, I was able to spend four days in Leningrad (now once more St Petersburg). They were delightful days in one sense, but they also exposed some of the deficiencies of the Soviet system. Many of my other European visits were to Paris, where there was a strong tradition of radiation chemistry dating back to Madame Curie's days; indeed, one of the meetings was held to celebrate the fiftieth anniversary of the discovery of radium, somewhat delayed from the actual Golden Jubilee because of internal disagreements as to who should run the event. This meeting terminated in a marvellous dinner given by the Municipality of Paris in the restaurant on the second level of the Eiffel Tower.

The least useful meetings were large set pieces run under the auspices of some grand organisation such as UNESCO or OECD and often having meaningless titles, for example 'Atoms for Peace', bringing together everybody who had any connection with the use of radioactive material. Such government-sponsored meetings did, however, have a secure financial base: attendance, once approved, would automatically attract adequate travel and living allowances, and the social events could be delightful. I shall never forget Elisabeth Schwarzkopf singing for us in Vienna in 1956, the year in which that city was celebrating the end of four-power occupation. I know of no scientific society, national or international, which on its own could have commanded her magnificent voice at that time.

Very occasionally the *ennui* I often felt at the formal meetings had its surprises. I well recall an OECD meeting in Nancy in 1954 where a speaker was droning on, determined to read every word of his paper although he must have known that everyone present had a copy. We had simultaneous translation into four languages and were provided with earphones and a selector switch to tune in to the language of choice. In my case I had chosen the chairman's channel, knowing that this would be silent and I could doze undetected. I distinctly remember that I was wondering where Sadi Carnot, inventor of the 'Carnot thermodynamic cycle' which has tortured many a schoolboy, had lived in the town and how he had come to his idea, when my reverie was broken by a rasping noise. I was astonished and puzzled as I looked round until I saw our chairman, a rather hirsute individual, using a small pair of scissors to trim the long hairs protruding from his nostrils. That done, and blissfully unaware of how the sound of each cut was being magnified and broadcast, he applied the scissors to his ears – an equally noisy but rather more dangerous procedure, in my judgment at least. I wondered whether I was the only amused witness of this performance.

Occasionally something of scientific value could be derived from these events, such as the rare meeting with someone who, though nominated by government, actually knew something of technical interest. I recall the grandiosely named Second United Nations International Conference on the Peaceful Uses of Atomic Energy in Geneva in 1958, when I and Dr B.K. Blount, then Deputy Secretary of DSIR, decided to play truant and went to a nearby lido. We were sunbathing and quietly resting when we were joined by a rather corpulent person who spoke no English but had some German, in which language he politely enquired if he might join us. We began to talk in the only language common to us all, and it appeared that he was involved with radiation chemistry. I declared my own interest and he drew my attention to some work by Proskhurnin and Chernova on nitrous oxide, the anaesthetic commonly known as laughing gas. What he said they had demonstrated sounded so implausible that on my return to Leeds I asked a US National Science Foundation Fellow, Don Peterson, to repeat the experiments. The outcome of his work was that nitrous oxide turned out to be an ideal reagent for distinguishing hydrogen atoms, with which it does not react at room temperature in water, from hydrated electrons, with which the molecules can react at every encounter to form nitrogen and a hydroxyl radical – a reaction of great utility. Remembering this and similar surprises in my scientific life, I endorse Pasteur's famous words, *'Dans les champs de l'observation le hasard ne favorise que les esprits préparés'*, usually shortened in translation to the aphorism 'Chance favours the prepared mind'.

The scientifically most valuable meetings, in my experience at least, are those in which relatively small groups of specialists are brought together to discuss the latest theoretical and experimental work in their own field, or even just a part of the field, to the exclusion of all else. Here two distinct forms of meeting are discernible. The first is that which the Faraday Society pioneered over ninety years ago and called 'General Discussions', in which some twenty or so pre-printed scientific papers of publishable form, some solicited and the others proffered, are circulated to the known participants well ahead of the meeting. The meeting rarely lasts more than three days and, because it is assumed that all the participants will have read the papers beforehand, each author is allowed only five minutes in which to highlight the most important features of his or her work – thereby leaving, at the discretion of the sessional chairman, up to five times that period for discussion from the floor. All the observations made, and the authors' replies, are recorded and printed, together with any supplementary written contributions and responses. The published proceedings make a fascinating record for the specialist and the historian alike, as they illustrate the cut and thrust of debate and hence something of the personalities involved and how ideas develop.[6]

In the second form of specialist meetings the papers are not pre-printed, nor are the proceedings subsequently published. They therefore take much longer to cover the same ground, and there is little or no benefit to those who do not attend. The earliest and best of this kind are the American 'Gordon Conferences'. While at Leeds I went to many such conferences on radiation chemistry or polymer chemistry, and greatly enjoyed them because they were quite leisurely, with the afternoons free, and were held in the delightful rural surroundings of such institutions as Colby Junior College or New Hampton School in New Hampshire. Both Faraday and Gordon meetings have their imitators and variants, and sometimes they are incorporated as parts of the annual conferences of large professional scientific societies. I have done my best to encourage these developments and, indeed, was much involved in establishing the series of Miller Conferences on radiation chemistry (in memory of my friend Nick Miller, whom I first met at Chalk River), and also in promoting the concept of the Euchem conferences. One recently introduced feature of many meetings which I greatly welcome is the opportunity for young researchers to display their work in 'posters' and explain it to any enquirer. For them this is less intimidating than having their work criticised in front of a large audience; and it is also useful to their interlocutors, who can spend more time probing details of particular interest.

Primacy of place in my affection still goes to the Faraday Discussions. My recollections of these meetings go back sixty years and include not only new ideas

---

6. Many of the new ideas of scientific importance are recorded in the *History of the Faraday Society, 1903-1971*, published by the Faraday Division of the Royal Society in 1996.

of scientific importance, but also incidents and encounters of a more personal kind. For example, the first event to be held after the last war was in September 1945. The subject was oxidation, the venue University College, London, and those attending included Professor F.G. Donnan, the doyen of British physical chemistry; but what impressed me was the large number of colleagues from Europe and the USA, whom most British chemists had not seen for six years. The meeting was a celebration of the renewal of contacts between old friends, and a moving reaffirmation of the international character of scientific endeavour.

A second example comes from a big radiation chemistry discussion held in Leeds in 1952. As I write I have in front of me a photograph of the 200 or so participants standing in front of the Parkinson Building, and memories come flooding back. Seated in the front row are two Frenchmen of Russian extraction (Moise Haissinsky and Michel Magat) who did not have happy experiences in German-occupied France, and Joseph Weiss, an Austrian Jew forced to leave his own country by the rise of the Nazis. During the meeting I was talking with Karl Friedrich Bonhoeffer, a noted physical chemist whose brother Pastor Dietrich Bonhoeffer had been executed following the failed assassination attempt on Hitler in July 1944, when we were joined by the other three. Listening to their conversation, I was immensely impressed by the extraordinarily dignified way in which all four of them conducted themselves; their lack of personal rancour, and their firm adherence to civilized values and rejection of all that the regimes of Hitler, Franco and Mussolini represented. It was a moving and heart-warming experience.

I shall never forget the last morning of that conference, towards the end of which I was due to present my own paper: several conflicting personal and professional concerns had to be reconciled. The morning began inauspiciously with three telephone calls. The first was from Milton Burton, complaining that his room in Devonshire Hall (a men's hall of residence) was painfully cold and asking me to rectify it, which was beyond my power. The second was from Professor Challenger, my organic chemistry colleague, demanding that I instruct the 'delegates' to refrain from using his private lavatory. I ignored this request because there was no evidence that anyone could gain entry to this unremarkable facility, the door to which was always locked. The third was from Barbara, heavily pregnant, announcing that she thought she had labour pains and what should we do about Harry Eméleus, whom we had invited to come to lunch at home – to which my response was to urge her to 'hold on'! As soon as my paper was over, the goodbyes had been spoken and the meeting concluded I took Harry home to eat a splendid lunch, got him to the station and drove Barbara to St James' Hospital, where she spent the night in the labour ward. The next day she was delivered of a daughter, some six weeks premature but in good health. The hospital staff were shocked by our subsequent delay in selecting a name, which in part was due to our debating jocularly whether she should be called Radiation, Radical, Radiance or some variant thereof, these matters having been uppermost in my mind for the preceding three days. We preserved the alliteration by calling her Rosalind.

All professions have their hierarchies, with greater power given to or assumed by those in the higher grades. Even when that higher position has been justly earned through past achievement, there is a danger of authoritarianism which can lead to pedantry and, worse still, can quench the imagination of the young. One example from my travels often comes to mind. In 1952 I was at the Argonne National Laboratory near Chicago to give a seminar, and came to a point at which I suggested that the precursor of the hydrogen atom generated by the absorption of ionizing radiation in water could be the electron, which might survive by being solvated in the same way that the electron in ammonia was known to be solvated. Unfortunately for me, sitting in the front row were the Nobel Laureate James Franck and Bob Platzman, Professor of Theoretical Physics at the University of Chicago. They interrupted almost simultaneously to say that that was impossible, the electron could not survive for more than ten million-millionths of a second, giving a well-known argument in support. I felt crushed, expunged the idea from my mind and did not do definitive experiments until seven years later: as mentioned earlier in this chapter, the results proved that I was correct and they were wrong. In this context there often comes to my mind the maxim of the science fiction writer Arthur C. Clarke: 'When an elderly and distinguished scientist tells you something is impossible, he is almost certainly wrong.'

Creativity and Credentialism

Travel, I have suggested, is educative even within one's native country. Whilst at Leeds there were few university chemistry departments I did not visit, either as an external examiner or to lecture, and I learned a number of valuable lessons. The first of these concerns the perennial argument about 'standards' of British university degrees. People with little or no experience of university life, especially politicians, are inclined to use this much misunderstood term without defining it. They often appear to believe that there can be a set content or curriculum for each particular subject, and that the grade of a degree can be determined by the numerical aggregate of the candidate's performance in the various parts of it. While this approach can work in some vocational subjects, it is wholly inappropriate in disciplines where the content is vast and constantly expanding, so that no more than a fraction can be accommodated in any three- or four-year course. Many of these are the traditional subjects of universities, where curricula which are different in content can legitimately be regarded as equivalent in standard, provided they all give the student a grasp of general principles and how to apply them to novel situations, and inculcate habits of clear and logical thought.

By the same token there can be no standardised model of a good lecturer or tutor. An ability to purvey information clearly is certainly an asset, but the best teachers are those who, by their own enthusiastic, lively and irreverent questioning manner, based on deep knowledge, stimulate their students to want to know more themselves. Students thus inspired will be far better able to deal with the rapidly changing work environment which will be their future than those who, by rote-learning on a fixed curriculum, have achieved some specified arbitrary 'standard'. Darwin was right: the survivors are those who have the wit and flexibility to adapt.

Those who espouse the notion of absolute standards are also prone to fall into the trap of credentialism, by which I mean that a person is typecast by a particular examination result or qualification which becomes the sole criterion for selection to enter the next stage. The error is that this approach makes no allowance for individual variability of background or circumstances, or for the fact that young people are by definition still developing, so that predictions based on the achievement of a particular 'standard' are liable to be faulty. I recall one classic example of this when I was at Leeds and still had the time to take part in interviewing candidates for admission to the School of Chemistry. One person who had applied from a school in Lancashire attracted adverse comment from his headmaster as being uncooperative and strong-willed. That was enough for me to wish to see him. The candidate, a large, gangling youth, somewhat awkward in his manner, arrived late. I taxed him with his tardiness, and he explained that he had taken three buses to get to Leeds. When I asked him why he had taken buses when there was a perfectly good train called the Trans-Pennine Express, he said he wanted to have an opportunity to observe the landscape in certain parts of the Pennines which he had not seen before and which could only be reached by bus. This led us to discuss the characteristics of limestone and gritstone country, their morphologies and flora. I then put in front of him a crystal of copper sulphate and asked him to describe it to me. This was a common ploy I used with candidates: high scorers in A-levels from schools where students were well prepared often gave as their response 'It is copper sulphate, sir', to which my reply could only be 'You have not answered my question'. The awkward candidate sitting in front of me said, 'It's blue and it looks like a cube pushed over on one side. Does it dissolve in water?' When I said it did he said, 'Is the solution blue?' and so on. I knew I had in him a man who was curious, who could observe and infer, and who wanted to find out more. Satisfied that he had mathematical ability, which is essential for all scientists, I accepted him. He got a very good degree, insisted on going away to do his national service, and returned to achieve an excellent PhD. Rigid application of standards and credentialism would have excluded this man, and the country would have been the poorer for it.

Branching Out Beyond My Subject

Another important lesson which travels at home and abroad taught me is that able people will usually manage to do good work, even under relatively adverse conditions. Of course they will do better if they have all the resources they need, but it does not follow that a unit with lots of resources will produce good results if the quality of the people is indifferent. For this reason it seemed to me that my major duty as head of physical chemistry in Leeds was to attract first-class creative people, and to ensure they had the right conditions for them to do the work they wished to do. To achieve this it was necessary to attain a standing in the University, and a familiarity with the decision-making processes. This meant service on over fifty bodies within the University, and external appointments as the University's representative; though the most awkward task which the Vice-Chancellor assigned to me was, to use his own words, to 'keep an eye on the Department of Botany'. At the time this department included on its staff several eminent people, later to become Fellows of the Royal Society, but could not be described as a happy family. My task was achieved, but not made easier by the fact that the most distinguished member of the department, Professor Irène Manton, was an old friend of Barbara's, having been her 'sitter in' when she was a child in Manchester; moreover, her sister, Sidnie Manton, had been Barbara's supervisor in Cambridge. The two sisters were both elected FRS, but were not on speaking terms.

Inspecting old pocket diaries is not something which I had ever done before I came to put these reflections down on paper, and needed to check my recollection of events. I shall not do it again if I can avoid it, for the perusal of these daily records evokes a curious range of emotions. The first is sheer amazement that so much was packed into each day at Leeds. This is quickly followed by regret that I cannot sustain that pace now, and finally I wonder how I did it without any particular tiredness that I can recall. I then remember that I was never bored: the sheer variety of my activities ensured that. Indeed, the stimulus of suddenly changing from one activity to another completely different one seemed to heighten my interest in both, rather in the way that parts of a symphony, with their different keys, rhythms and tempos, produce changes of mood which intensify the listener's perception of each.

Despite the above, life would surely be unendurable if it were only a constant froth of small events. It is essential to have some periods in which sustained attention can be given to a single problem or field, and fortunately this is usually possible in academic life. I was particularly lucky in that I also had the added dimension of many invitations to go overseas. Even if the invitation was simply to give a single lecture or talk, there would still be the benefit of making time to prepare the material (which always engendered new thoughts), and then the bliss of escaping for a period from the humdrum daily tasks which are necessary but not stimulating. Moreover, there was always the added stimulus of talking with foreign colleagues with whom one shared a common scientific interest.

Charles Morris encouraged his staff to become involved in the life of the region and I think it must have been a great shock to some of them, who had not got my Yorkshire background, to face the kind of audiences which the West Riding could then produce. I give only two examples of this. The first arose out of the fact that one of the divisional officers for the West Riding Education Committee was a man named Edward le Fèvre, who had been an undergraduate at St John's College, Oxford, in my time. He persuaded me to give a talk to the Brighouse and Raistrick Mutual Improvement Society (or some such title). I had chosen the subject 'Universities at Home and Abroad', adding 'to be illustrated by colour slides'. This was 1951 and, aware of the friendly but amateurish nature of local societies in the Pennine valleys, I prudently forearmed myself by taking along my own projector and screen. It was as well I did, because in the event such apparatus was not provided. At my request I was admitted to the room in which the talk was to be given, to set up the screen and projector, when there arrived a spotty-faced youth who asked me if I was the lecturer. I said yes and enquired as to who he was, to which he replied 'I represent the Huddersfield... ', giving the name of a regional paper which I have forgotten. Immediately I felt flattered by the attention of the press and asked him what he required of me. 'May I ask you a few questions?', he replied, indicating that an article would appear in his paper. Vanity made me acquiesce at once, and he then asked with typical Yorkshire directness, 'Exactly what are your qualifications for giving this lecture?' This did more for my humility than my ego, but also made me feel at home.

The second example involved Edward Boyle, then Minister of Education. He was opening some buildings at Huddersfield College, and I was sitting on the platform next to a governor who had only ever expressed two sentences to me. (The first of these had been in answer to my question as to what he did, to which he had replied, sticking his thumbs in the armholes of his waistcoat, 'I'm a butcher by trade'. Wishing to keep the conversation going I had asked a supplementary question, 'What is the butchering trade like nowadays?' to which the response was prompt and doubtless accurate: 'When I wa' a lad there were nowt but choice cuts. Now there's no choice cuts.') When Edward Boyle's turn came to speak he, Baronet, old Etonian, graduate of Christ Church, Oxford, a man immensely knowledgeable about music, chose to speak on Poulenc. This seemed to me a somewhat eccentric choice of subject, and I wondered how his words would be received. A few sentences produced a dig in my ribs from the butcher, followed by the words 'Eh, what's he on about?' There are some things that lecturers should not hear and I never told Edward of this remark, although later in life I got to know him well and discovered that he simply had the refreshing quality of assuming that, on any subject, he was as ignorant or knowledgeable as everyone else he met.

There were also increasing demands on my time from national institutions in London. *Inter alia* I served on committees for the Ministry of Supply concerned with non-metallic materials for the Services, on the Council of the Royal Society, and on its national committee for chemistry. In addition, I had become involved with the University Grants Committee, initially because I thought that its equipment grant policy did not adequately recognise that an institution's need for new equipment depends on student load and the research activity that is being carried out, rather than on the nature of the buildings occupied.

Resisting the Thought of a Move

It was in the early 1960s that a number of things happened which led me to conclude that some person or persons had put my name to that group of influential people within the Establishment who make recommendations for public and academic appointments at the national level. All I know is that the UGC asked me to serve as a member of the planning committee for the new University of Lancaster, which I did (but made it clear to the chairman of that committee, Sir Noel Hall, in answer to his enquiry, that I did not wish to become the founding vice-chancellor). My answer could be prompt because slightly earlier I had been approached by a representative of the appointment committee set up by the University of Leicester to find a successor to Sir Charles Wilson, who was moving to be Principal of the University of Glasgow, and then also I had made it clear that I was not interested in becoming a vice-chancellor. When serving as one of the Senate's representatives on the selection committee for a successor to Charles Morris at Leeds I had told the Registrar, Dr Loach, that my hat was not in the ring. I somewhat softened my attitude when approached by the planning committee for the new University of Warwick, and went to see them, and likewise the University of Liverpool, where I also met the appointment committee. However, in both cases I withdrew, believing that the right thing to do was to stay in Leeds for a further seventeen years – up to retirement age – since we were so happy there.

I thought such matters were settled, until I was invited by Lord Rothschild to go and have lunch with him in London. It was an indifferent lunch, with none of the famous Rothschild vintages on offer, and Victor came straight to the point: 'I would like you to head the Shell Thornton Research Laboratories. I will pay you twice what you are now getting.' I was affronted by his cheek and said, 'You don't know what I am getting', but he replied, 'I do', in a manner which only he could command, and which I knew would reflect the truth.

I told Victor plainly that I intended to stay in Leeds, where I believed I had a very good department which could be made yet better. As I was developing this theme he interrupted and said, 'I will pay you two and a half times as much'.

I was getting rather annoyed by now, and said that the answer must be a firm 'No'. 'Why?' he asked, and rather than offer him any circumlocution I gave him a short, direct, truthful answer. I said, 'Well, Victor, there is you and there is me' and then left, because it was quite clear that he could not see the inwardness of that remark. Neither of us knew that in eight or nine years' time we should be crossing swords again, and indeed Victor was a man who never gave up. A few months later, when he was either a member or chairman of a Cambridge University Committee on the organisation of the chemistry departments, he sought my advice – which was simply that there should be not several but one department of chemistry. In the course of our exchanges he said, 'Will you come to Cambridge when Norrish goes?', and again my reply was negative.

We were so settled in our intention to stay that when the University of Leeds – discovering that the incoming Vice-Chancellor, Sir Roger Stevens, did not wish to live in Charles Morris's house – offered us that property to rent, we decided we would accept. So in September 1963 we moved into 18 North Hill Road, an enormous house which we subdivided: the whole of the attic floor was let to visiting professors, other members of University staff, or even research students. The house was ideally located, in that I could walk to the University across Woodhouse Moor and our two daughters could easily reach Leeds Girls' High School at the bottom of the road. It was no more difficult to get John to the station to go to Bradford Grammar School than it was from West Park. The house was also adjacent to Devonshire Hall and there were many University folk living in the houses around, so that we were in the midst of an agreeable community. We were content to see ourselves living there until retirement, and were made to feel all the more settled because Barbara had been appointed a Research Assistant to Professor J.M. Dodd in the Zoology Department.

CHAPTER 5

A VICE-CHANCELLOR'S LIFE: NOTTINGHAM, 1965–70

The duties of a permanent vice-chancellor are arduous.

Sir James Mountford, 1966

We resolve to stay in Leeds

By mid-July 1963 many decisions appeared to be behind us. We were clear that I would not become a vice-chancellor or the director of an industrial research laboratory. Instead I would continue teaching and research, and Barbara, after a gap of sixteen years, would resume research. The obvious place to achieve both without disturbing the children's school education would be Leeds. We were eagerly looking forward to living in a house with direct access to the Meanwood Valley, so that we could walk through woodlands to Adel and beyond to lower Wharfedale and Harewood. So it was with especially light hearts that we drove to Southend, took the ferry to Ostend and were soon heading southwards along the 'Romantische Strasse', stopping to visit delightful mediaeval towns en route for two weeks' holiday in Austria, the first to be spent on the Achensee and the second in the hills, almost in sight of the Bavarian Zugspitze and Hitler's mountain retreat. Then we drove south to Varenna on Lake Como, where I taught for a couple of days on an international course on radiation dosimetry, under the auspices of the Italian National Research Council and its Physical Society. The setting on the lake shore was enchanting, and we lived in a delightful villa. We would gladly have stayed longer, but had to work our way northwards through Austria and Germany to call in at the Karlsruhe Kernforschungs Zentrum, making a brief detour to observe the reality of the impermeable boundary separating East and West Germany.

The last fortnight in August was spent in Leeds, largely in planning research with the new 3MeV accelerator which the splendid £100,000 grant from DSIR would enable us to install at Cookridge, and so begin a new phase in our radiation chemistry research. This time for thought was a useful prelude to taking part in the second Faraday Society Discussion on Radiation Chemistry, to be held in the first week in September in the University of Notre Dame, Indiana, the inaugural conference having been held in Leeds eleven years earlier. With many other things to be accomplished before the University term began on 1 October, the house move on 30 September seemed to be a relatively minor incident in our lives and, of course, it is always easier to move into a larger house. Planning ahead, I agreed to give a series of lectures in northern Italian universities in May 1964, to spend two weeks in the United States in July of that year and, looking even further into the future, I intended to visit Padua in early July 1965 and thereafter to spend twelve days in the USSR. When term began I had much committee work on hand, both in the University and in the wider world outside, and was about to take on the chairmanship of the Association for Radiation Research. Happily, two of my colleagues had been promoted and the independent research work of the other members of staff was proceeding so well that I felt I could begin to pass on to others more of my administrative work, and thereby find time to complete some unfinished business (notably the book on radiation chemistry begun at MIT in 1959). The only slightly discouraging feature of life at Leeds was that applications from school-leavers to read chemistry did not show the usual buoyancy, which had allowed the annual intake to quadruple in the twelve years we had been there. I had no idea then that this was the local manifestation of a national problem which I would be asked to address in a few years' time.

In May 1964 I received a letter from Sir Francis Hill, President of the Council of the University of Nottingham, inviting me to discuss the possibility of my moving to that university as Vice-Chancellor in succession to Bertrand Hallward. I drafted a brief note of refusal, suggesting that it was pointless to meet the selection committee because I had no intention of becoming a vice-chancellor anywhere. When I showed it to Barbara she said at once, 'You can't send that.' Her objection was that the letter was too curt and dismissive and that I owed Sir Francis the courtesy of an explanation of why I could not accept. A few days later I wrote and explained my position, emphasising that despite my belief in the importance of civic universities in the expansion of higher education, which government wanted to see, I was unwilling to waste the time of the committee; adding for good measure that DSIR had recently awarded me a very large grant for research in Leeds. I thought that this would satisfy Sir Francis, but I had seriously underestimated him. In the middle of June, when I was busy acting as an external examiner in the universities of Hull and Birmingham, I was summoned by the new Leeds Vice-Chancellor, Sir Roger Stevens, to whom I had not said anything about this approach because I considered the matter closed. He showed me a copy of a letter from Sir Harry Melville, then Secretary of DSIR, to Sir Francis indicating that a move to Nottingham would not affect the grant, provided I continued to direct the work. Having belatedly explained the position to the Vice-Chancellor, I returned to my laboratory – only to find an urgent message to telephone a Lincoln number, which I knew to be that of Sir Francis. My respect for his pertinacity was growing rapidly! I did telephone him and was persuaded to meet him for lunch at the White Hart in Lincoln, although we soon established that because of other commitments this could not be until late in July.

No Decision is Final!

The moment I set eyes on Sir Francis Hill I took an instant liking to him. The most notable features of his face were his bright eyes, which I discovered were matched by a quick intelligence. He summed me up rapidly and, knowing my interest in medical education, played his trump card: that it would shortly be announced that Nottingham would have the first new medical school to be established in the United Kingdom since 1893.

Largely as a result of my own experience of surgery in Addenbrooke's Hospital in Cambridge, and a period as Medical Director of Studies in my College, I had long believed that the medical curriculum was in need of reform (and in particular the integration of the preclinical and clinical parts of the course). My service on the medical curriculum committee of the University of Leeds, which began in the late 1950s, had convinced me that the forces against reform in many existing medical schools were overwhelmingly strong, particularly where those schools were dominated by the clinical part-timers, who thought first in terms of bed allocation rather than the needs of the students. I considered that to found a new medical school successfully would be the best way of spreading new ideas, since these would be copied elsewhere as soon as the new entreprise appeared to be attracting high-quality teachers and students.

I decided to have a look at the Nottingham campus, and what I saw there was very attractive. In particular, Highfield House appeared to me to be the best vice-chancellor's residence I had ever seen in this country. So, as I travelled the next afternoon to the Plastics and Polymers Research Laboratories of ICI at Runcorn, my mind was in some turmoil. Barbara and I talked over the matter in great detail and we agreed that Nottingham was a distinct possibility, provided that I was able to secure an agreement from the University of Leeds that the Cookridge laboratories could be called a High Energy Radiation Research Centre, that they could be independently financed, and that I could remain as honorary director. As far as Nottingham was concerned, I wanted an explicit approval of my continuing involvement with Cookridge. I also felt it was absolutely essential that I should be a member from its inception of Nottingham's Medical School Advisory Committee, because I was particularly anxious that the new medical school should feel just as much a part of the University as any other faculty, and that it should get the greatest possible benefit from interaction with the science departments. Getting the agreements, particularly at the Leeds end, seemed to take an unconscionably long time. I finally got the consent from Leeds on 6 November 1964 and immediately informed Sir Francis, who arranged that Barbara and I should visit Nottingham on the rather inauspicious date of Friday 13 November.

Remembrance Day that year fell on Sunday 8 November. It was a day which I spent walking with colleagues and research students over the Langdale and Coniston Fells in the Lake District. I took two of them in my car from North Hill Road, leaving early in the morning and arriving at the Yorkshire Ramblers' hut in Langdale for coffee. I felt constrained because I was not free to tell anyone that I was leaving, and I was greatly saddened that in all probability this would be the last of these excursions for me.

My appointment was unanimously approved by the University of Nottingham Council, to take up office on 1 October 1965. At my request, I was also made a member of the Medical School Advisory Committee with immediate effect. That committee, set up only a few days previously, had as its chairman Sir George Pickering, Regius Professor of Medicine in the University of Oxford; about half its members were distinguished clinicians from other universities, and half were drawn from the University of Nottingham. We held our first meeting on the afternoon of 10 December 1964 and thereafter met almost at weekly intervals, often with full-day meetings and with one memorable Ditchley Park weekend in February 1965, when we were joined by distinguished medical scientists from overseas. My membership of this committee was a refreshing and stimulating experience, as well as a liberal education in the art of chairmanship, Pickering style. We saw an immense number of witnesses, encompassing administrators, clinicians, preclinicians, students and members of professional and learned societies. Our final report was issued in June 1965.

Meanwhile life went on in Leeds, but naturally I was viewed in a different light after the announcement of my impending departure. Fortunately I was far too busy to have second thoughts, and once term had ended there was the USSR visit and a fortnight's holiday with our two daughters in Scotland. We moved to Nottingham in August 1965, the outgoing Vice-Chancellor, Bertrand Hallward, having gracefully retired a little earlier to enable me to have the whole responsibility of planning the medical school. He and his wife could not have been more accommodating or welcoming. However, there were still things to be done in Leeds and elsewhere: in September I had to give the promised lectures in Padua and also, as President of the Faraday Society, to chair the General Discussion on Intermolecular Forces held in Bristol.

I had resolved to go to Nottingham because at the time I thought it was the most important academic decision of my life, even though I knew that I would have much less teaching contact with young people, which I very much enjoyed. I could not then foresee the consequences of another development, when in December 1964 I was invited to become a member of the newly established Council for Scientific Policy (CSP), set up to advise the Secretary of State for Education and Science on his responsibilities for science (which included the size of the science budget and its allocation to the Research Councils, the Natural History Museum and the two Royal Societies, as well as general policy issues and many other matters). I imagine my appointment was made because of my long service as chairman of the DSIR committee which allocated postgraduate studentships in chemistry, but, whatever the cause, membership of the CSP was to lead to an ever-increasing involvement in public affairs.

Thoughts on the University System

In his famous phrase *Nam et ipsa scientia potestas est*, Francis Bacon enunciated a profound and enduring truth: 'Knowledge itself is power'. Human beings are empowered, both in personal development and as an economic unit, to the extent that they can gain knowledge and learn how to use it. For early human beings that knowledge – for example, of fire or of the lever – was purely empirical, but that did not preclude its use for practical purposes. As knowledge developed, it became possible to connect observations in a systematic way. The resulting generalisations are known as 'laws' and can be used to predict the behaviour of inanimate materials when subjected to a change of circumstance, thereby further extending mankind's power. The major step forward, which enormously increases that power, is when human beings successfully develop a 'theory' and thereby gain an understanding of why the laws exist, by invoking some fundamental idea or principle or abstract concept such as gravity, force, or heat. The theory then has great predictive force, and in the physical sciences can be applied to invent devices to further extend our practical and intellectual capacities.

However, curiosity continually drives us to seek more knowledge by experiment, both mentally and physically, whether in the laboratory or by the observation of natural phenomena on earth or in the heavens. Frequently the purpose is to test accepted theories. When theories are refuted, that is, they fail a prescriptive test, they must be modified to accommodate the new facts; if that proves impossible, a new theory must be devised which brings the new facts into a consistent harmonious relationship with the older information. The progress of science – public objective knowledge about ourselves and the world we inhabit – is therefore measured by the development of fewer theories of greater comprehensive and predictive power than those which they replace. We must also remember that there are other kinds of knowledge which are no less important but are as yet less well understood, like the way in which the human psyche operates – including affective and emotional reactions as well as the cognitive function, as some of my Cambridge undergraduates recognised after the war.

The success of a society or an individual is not easily defined or measured. For some people the possession of power to dominate or resist domination by others is important, while other persons may have quite different priorities, for example to attain an inner peace, or to live harmoniously with other human beings and be free from external compulsions. What is certain is that all individuals, whatever their aspirations, will be confronted by complex situations and the necessity of making choices and decisions. Furthermore, whatever the correct measure of success, that success will be enhanced if existing knowledge is understood, tried, extended and applied. Pasteur's famous aphorism about the prepared mind makes the point succinctly. It follows that essential to the well-being of all human societies are those institutions where individuals can gain the knowledge necessary for their own and society's progress, and where existing knowledge can be scrutinized, tested and advanced by research. At the post-school level these institutions include, *par excellence*, the universities, and other centres (which may be embedded in universities or stand alone) with research as their primary role. It is also true that the more developed a country, the more dependent it becomes on research and development, particularly that concerned with objective knowledge.

Universities develop their own individual cultures and policies, which often vary over time. If institutions do not change in this way they will stultify, become mere purveyors of a predigested pabulum of existing (or even out of date) knowledge, and their students, and society as a whole, will be the poorer and less effective thereby. In this context the problem facing all countries is how to manage the university sector to achieve the optimum result. Universities cost a great deal of money for capital and recurrent expenditure, and this now normally comes from a wide variety of national and international sources. The only secure basis for success is an arrangement in which the teachers and researchers, who are *ipso facto* the best informed, are able to deliberate and decide what should be taught and researched in the university to which they belong. This is why academic freedom is so important. On the other hand, providers of funds also have duties that may restrict their freedom of action in the disbursement of monies to universities, and may require that conditions be attached to an award. For example, an industrial firm must satisfy its shareholders that all expenditure is incurred in the financial interests of the company. Those interests may be general and long term: thus the firm may quite reasonably take the view that it is of general benefit to itself to facilitate high-quality teaching and research in particular disciplines at the university level. This was, for example, an immediate post-Second World War policy of many large chemical companies in Britain, and it found expression in the establishment of scholarships and fellowships in chemistry, to be gained through open competition, and in the provision of means to purchase specific items of equipment. I have never known any difficulties arise in such cases, where the company acts like a charitable body, and it is not surprising that some firms set up separate charities for such purposes. However, private enterprises may also wish to commission specific pieces of research, the outcome of which may significantly affect their profitability, and in such cases the interests of all parties – the university, the academic and research staff, and the firm – must be protected in legal contracts which may cover issues such as confidentiality, patent applications, intellectual property rights, publication, or the sharing of revenues from licensing a product or process. Such contracts can be complex, and it is wise to provide for the arbitration of disputes. On one such occasion I was asked to be an arbitrator and before accepting I read carefully and commented upon the articles of agreement, which were so well drawn up (and the parties so reasonable) that my services were never called upon – and that was the best outcome of all!

It might be thought that government departments with specific missions such as defence, transport, and agriculture are very similar to private enterprises. To a certain extent this is true, and it seems to me to be perfectly proper for them to seek contractual arrangements with a university in, for example, employing it to design a specific piece of hardware. But in many instances the findings of the research are likely to be of general benefit, and might well influence public policy. This is quite often the case in the sphere of public health and environmental matters, and here I believe that wherever possible the knowledge gained should be in the public domain, open to wide scrutiny and to challenge by peers. Restrictive contracts are inappropriate in such cases, and are likely to lead to less good quality work. Nevertheless I do know of cases where government departments have tried to censor or suppress the publication of work falling into this category.

The reader may think I exaggerate when I maintain how insidious and pervasive the contract culture has become. In the 1970s it invaded educational thinking to the extent that the government bill to set up a Universities Funding Council to replace the University Grants Committee at the end of that decade used the word 'contract' to cover monetary awards to individual universities for general teaching and research, in place of the time-honoured word 'grant'. This was symptomatic of the government of the day's overt or subconscious wish to control the style and content of the work that goes on in universities, and it is bizarre that it fell to the House of Lords, an unelected body of outmoded constitution and composition, to be the defender (not for the first time) of academic freedom. Of course, to be granted this freedom brings to the universities an obligation to exercise it responsibly.

The best device invented so far for accommodating the two desiderata of accountability and academic freedom is that of a buffer body between the universities and government, to which the latter appoints the members on the basis of their experience and wisdom. Government should also assign terms of reference which confer flexibility on the body in its work of promoting the adaptation of the universities to changing circumstances, without interfering unproductively in the details of style, content, and choice of teaching and research activities. Public accountability for the use of funds voted by Parliament for education and research properly rests with that body, which should be able to use its judgment of the quality of work done in a university to augment or withhold funds.

Between 1889 and 1919 the proto-UGCs, and from 1919 to 1989 the UGC itself, satisfied these conditions. The final terms of reference given to the Committee in 1946 exemplify the point:

> To collect, examine and make available information relating to university education throughout the United Kingdom; and to assist, in consultation with the universities and other bodies concerned, the preparation and execution of such plans for the development of the universities as may from time to time be required in order to ensure that they are fully adequate to national needs.

These are exemplary words, and there is no doubt that until the early 1970s the independence of the UGC from government was accepted as a reality. The UGC was also trusted by the universities. An important element in the winning and retention of that trust was that no vice-chancellor was ever appointed to membership of the committee, and any member who was on the staff of a university was automatically excluded from discussions or visits of any kind relating to matters concerning his or her own institution. Another source of trust was that there were regular quinquennial 'visitations' of the UGC to each university, which involved discussion between the whole committee (except any member from the institution being visited) and every element of the university: the Council, the Senate, representatives of the students, representatives of the non-academic staff, and others by agreement. These visits were most informative to both sides: they were preceded by an exchange of papers, and each side could question the other on policy matters of any kind. Of equal importance were the visits of UGC subject sub-committees, which likewise allowed (at the level of individual faculties or departments) a free exchange of ideas and arguments, the removal of mis-conceptions, and an appraisal of staff quality. On such visits Research Council representatives were always welcome as assessors. The information gained was again valuable in helping the UGC to make the judgments necessary when the quinquennial block grant for each university was determined. Nowadays assessments are made on a notably different basis involving fewer face-to-face meetings and a much more mechanistic approach to quality, in which numerical scores or grades are awarded. How reliable these assessments are is an unresolved question: in the case of research at least, they leave much to be desired but may carry very significant financial bonuses or penalties. What is certain is that the system has a distorting effect upon the choice of research topics, causing academics to favour the safe rather than the speculative. In nearly all scientific disciplines British papers are now less often cited than used to be the case. It is also true that this country's 'hit rates' for Nobel Prizes in physics, chemistry, physiology and medicine have fallen greatly, although these prizes are so rare that they cannot really be regarded as sound indicators of general quality.

Why have these and other adverse changes come about? The answer is partly the good intention of wishing to make the process of allocation more transparent (which is particularly important when, as has been the case in Britain, the unit of resource has been steadily declining), and partly the sheer size of the system. It has been argued that formula funding becomes the only possible practical mechanism when there is a change from an elite to a mass system of higher education. I must say that I do not find that argument convincing because Wales and Scotland have their own funding councils, each of which has fewer universities to support than the old UGC, yet they slavishly use similar formula-funding methods.

I mention these matters because I am often asked for my views about the suit-ability of particular individuals to become vice-chancellors. Many of my interlocu-tors suggest that since vice-chancellors are now designated as 'accounting officers' – that is, each holds a Treasury certificate which makes him or her personally accountable for the expenditure of public funds – the job of academic leadership must have changed, along with the qualities which are necessary for a vice-chancellor to succeed. I am inclined to doubt this last proposition. Of course it is possible simply to regard a university as a business and the vice-chancellor as its chief executive, appropriately endowed with executive powers to 'direct' its scholars and scientists. However, such an arrangement is no adequate substitute for genuine academic leadership of the kind which each of those vice-chancellors I named in Chapter 4 possessed in abundance.

The term 'leadership' carries with it various connotations. At its best it implies that a particular person has the power of persuading intelligent individuals to follow a specific course of action. It is not that such persons possess immutable attributes: as a colonel is reputed to have written about his subaltern, 'Mr Smith can be said to have leadership qualities in that his men will follow him anywhere – if only out of a sense of curiosity'. In the academic setting it means an ability to achieve a clear consensus on the basis of frank and rational argument in which everyone has access to the facts, with decisions openly taken and recorded, and then implemented in a transparent manner by due process. The most important qualities of a vice-chancellor, given reasonably good intellectual abilities and competence in chairmanship and related techniques, are not academic distinction (though that helps to ensure acceptance by the purists), but honesty, fair-mindedness and openness. A vice-chancellor whose colleagues are satisfied that he or she has these qualities will be trusted, backed up in difficult situations and given a degree of freedom to act on their behalf. In other words, he or she will have been chosen as their leader by colleagues whose own commitment to the purposes of the university will also have been strengthened in the process. In this context 'colleagues' include not only office-holders and members of the Council and Senate, but all those with whom the vice-chancellor has dealings. By contrast, leadership which relies on power conferred by external authority may be of short-term utility, but without trust it will be of little avail in the long run.

The First Term in Nottingham

One of my first tasks at Nottingham was to visit my colleagues in their departments to hear all that they had to tell me, both collectively and individually. It was an assignment that I was never able to complete but the intention was acknowledged, even if my performance fell short because of other demands on my time. I also invited lay committee members and students to Highfield House, which proved to be an ideal venue for entertaining and informal discussion. In our first year, when Mike Hanson was the Students' Union President, we were often the guests of the Union Officers – a courtesy we reciprocated – and Barbara was invited to membership of a Union committee which thereafter met at our home.

Similar considerations led me to believe that I should also make contact with local institutions and people who had an interest in the University. While certain members of the Council were obvious channels of communication, I thought that there should be more direct links with both the County dignitaries and other leading citizens. I realised that this would take time and needed careful planning if it were to become more than mere socialising. In fact the first approach was made not by me but by the Lord Mayor, Alderman Derbyshire, and it took rather a surprising form. My secretary, Miss David, told me he wanted to speak to me on the phone and added that once I had met him I would not forget him. This proved to be the case because he had a large moustache, like that of Jimmy Edwards, and wore a toupee. The conversation started well enough, with an exchange of greetings and a welcome to Nottingham. He then went on to say, 'I am sure we can talk like man to man, Vice-Chancellor', and there followed a great deal of circumlocution. I finally divined that he wanted me to remove from membership of the City of Nottingham Education Committee a certain professor, whom I had never met, whose views did not coincide precisely with those of the Lord Mayor. He concluded his remarks by saying, 'I am sure we understand one another and I can rely on you'. I responded that I certainly understood what he was saying, but that under the Statutes it was not within my power to appoint or remove anyone as a representative of the University without going through due process, which in this case meant a recommendation from the Senate. I therefore promised that I would report faithfully to the Senate, as near verbatim as I could, all that he had said to me. The conversation closed with him saying, 'That will not be necessary, Vice-Chancellor', and that particular ploy was never tried with me again.

The first person we felt we must have as our guest at Highfield House was Sir Francis Hill. We talked about his outstanding career at Cambridge and his busy life in the public service, during which he had also been building up a successful solicitor's business and still found time to do scholarly work. Several volumes of his history of Lincoln, where he lived, were published by the Cambridge University Press and were of such a quality that they earned him the LittD degree. No vice-chancellor could have wished for a better President of Council than Sir Francis, and the depth of our mutual understanding increased over the years.

I also felt it was worthwhile to entertain those who for one reason or another were critical of the University. One of the earliest examples was when we invited the Treasurer of the University, Cyril Cripps (later Sir Cyril), and his family to Sunday lunch because we had been told that he had made several benefactions to the University but had been so offended by Senate's rejection of one scheme, which Bertrand Hallward had proposed and Cripps was prepared to support financially, that he let it be known that no further money would be forthcoming. As Cripps' married son Humphrey followed him and Mrs Cripps through the door there was instant recognition on both sides of a common interest in chemistry, Humphrey having read that subject in the Natural Sciences Tripos at St John's College, Cambridge. It was a very successful lunch in that mutual confidence was quickly established and the Cripps Foundation later agreed to extend Cripps Hall, to fund a new student health centre (also named after Cripps) and to defray the cost of a link to the large regional computer in Manchester University. A few years afterwards Cripps came to the financial rescue again when we wished to build an indoor sports centre; to everyone's pleasure we were able to acquire a structural steel frame for this for a knock-down price at an auction of surplus Air Ministry equipment, it having previously done duty as the skeleton of an aircraft hanger.

The academic powerhouse of the University was the Senate, and I was anxious that it might consider that I (having been a member of the Pickering Committee) would be too partisan a defender of the fledgling Medical School's interests, to the detriment of other academic activities. Fortunately, I knew that the distinguished mediaeval historian Dr Kathleen Major FBA was planning to take early retirement from the principalship of St Hilda's College, Oxford, and intended to live in Lincoln and to continue her scholarly work. Knowing her well through our joint membership of the UGC's University of Lancaster planning committee, I ascertained that she would be delighted to serve as a part-time professor in the History Department. Having secured the enthusiastic agreement of the History professors, I put my proposal to Senate and it was agreed with acclamation. One senator, not an historian, went so far as to observe during the tea break, 'I didn't know you cared about the humanities'. Dr Major's appointment would have been useful just for registering that point in Senate's mind but, more importantly, she was a powerful influence for good in the department and in Willoughby Hall of Residence, where she became Chairman of the Hall Council and was a rock of common sense during the later student troubles.

Senate also approved two initiatives I took over the conduct of its business, both of which had quickly been accepted by the Senate Steering Committee (to which I initially presented them). One was to divide the Senate agenda into two parts: the items in the first part, judged by the Steering Committee to be non-controversial, would normally be agreed without discussion (though the right of any member to ask for and secure a debate was preserved). This simple device, not my own invention, expedited business. The second was to include in the agenda, immediately after the confirmation of the minutes of the previous meeting, a state-ment from the Vice-Chancellor in which I would share with Senate knowledge I had gained from external sources such as the Committee of Vice-Chancellors and Principals (CVCP) or its committees, or government bodies on which I served. I thought this would provide helpful background knowledge of the national scene, and might inform Senate's attitudes to our local issues. This approach was particu-larly valuable because the government made attempts during the late 1960s to bring public expenditure under tighter control, which dislocated our own planning procedures (not least in relation to the Medical School building programme).

Also uppermost in my mind was a quinquennial visitation of the UGC, planned for the eighth week of my first term. The fact that I would have to assume the role of the University's principal advocate in these discussions was an additional impe-tus to learn all I needed to know very speedily. In this regard I owe a great debt of gratitude to a number of people, in particular Professor Norman Haycocks, whose knowledge of the workings and personalities of the University was prodigious. He possessed immense patience and calmness, was utterly devoted to the institution, and proved a staunch friend throughout the five years we were at Nottingham.

Medicine and Other Developments

The University had little endowment income but its situation and facilities were good, and it had a high ratio of applicants for entry to places available. It also had the challenge of planning the new Medical School, using the Pickering Report as the academic basis of much of that planning. There was a great deal to be done: a Dean and foundation professors to be recruited; the site for the teaching hospital to be secured, which involved many of us in a time-wasting public enquiry; architects to be appointed; physical planning of the site and buildings to be carried out as quickly as possible; good working relations to be established with the Regional Hospital Board (RHB); and, in cooperation with the Board, plans to be drawn up for the governance of the new University Hospital. Arrangements had to be made for clinical teaching in other local hospitals, not just until the new teaching hospital was built but even after it had been completed; and of course it was also necessary to find teaching accommodation for preclinical students. Fortunately we were able to recruit a splendid Dean (David Greenfield, Professor of Physiology at St Mary's Hospital Medical School, London) and a good Assistant Registrar for Medicine (Mr R. Graham OBE, who was just leaving the Colonial Civil Service). These two persons, splendidly supported by the representatives of the RHB – Dr Jim Scott and Mr John Dann – did excellent work for the University, although accommodated rather inadequately in huts known familiarly as 'the cow-sheds'. To add to our problems in the Medical School, the financial goalposts were always being moved as the Labour government tried to cope with what seemed an endemic economic crisis. Inevitably I was drawn into these matters, and so was Barbara, as she made Highfield House a haven for harassed foundation medical professors and helped to keep up their morale.

Apart from the challenge of the Medical School, Nottingham University was so comfortably placed that it could easily have become self-satisfied and inward-looking to an unhealthy degree: and some claimed they could see signs of such a tendency. I have always held the view that in modern society a university should be outward-looking to a point well beyond extra-mural education; that links with industry should be strengthened, and new activities established on the campus to facilitate this. That is why I persuaded the Wolfson Foundation to finance an Institute for the Study of Interfacial Phenomena, created an Industrial Liaison Office, induced the University to appoint part-time professors who were also the holders of senior posts in companies such as Unilever and Rolls-Royce, and, aware of the looming crisis in mathematics teaching, coaxed Shell into endowing a chair in mathematical education. Although such developments are now commonplace, in the 1960s they had a distinctly pioneering flavour.

With love from Fred

49. Looking at this photograph, taken during our time in Leeds, Barbara said I was becoming tight-lipped and committee-minded!

50. In my office as Professor of Physical Chemistry at Leeds, holding a photochemical switch developed with Ken Ivin during the war.

51. The University of Leeds in the 1950s: the Chemistry Department is on the right, next to the Parkinson Building – Leeds' answer to London's Senate House.

Sarnia Visited by British Scientists

Top ranking British scientists, members of the Faraday Society of Great Britain, toured Polymer Corporation's Sarnia installations yesterday. Among those present, left to right: Sir Charles Goodeve, Faraday Society president (hand to head); Professor F. S. Dainton, Elof Christensen, Polymer engineer.

52, 53. Canada, September 1952, during the first meeting of the Faraday Society to be held outside the UK. *Above,* I appear to be giving the president a headache; *below,* with a relaxed Ronald Norrish (centre) and Dr H.L. Williams of the Polymer Corporation.

54. The chemistry wing of the Radiation Research Centre at Cookridge Hospital. Opened in 1956, this was a joint development between the University of Leeds and the Leeds Regional Hospital Board.

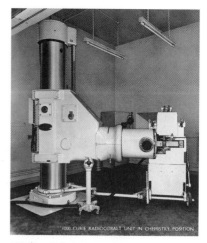

55. The Cobalt-60 source from Chalk River, Canada, which I obtained with the help of the Rockefeller Foundation. The unit was mounted on a modified drill press so that it could be aligned for patient treatment or chemistry research.

56. In May 1994, I had the great pleasure of declaring open the Spiers Wing and the Dainton Building at Cookridge, successors to our 1956 development – a particularly enjoyable circularity.

57. With John and Mary, Easter 1952, after a winter of measles.

58. Christmas 1955: in the garden at 16 North Parade, Leeds, with our daughter Rosalind and Whiskers the marmalade cat.

59. The family on board the old *Queen Elizabeth* liner in 1959, returning from my six-month appointment as Arthur D. Little Professor of Chemistry at MIT.

60. Dressed up for the wedding of one of my research students, Gerry Lawrence, who married Laurel in 1955. Mary is flanked by Rosalind and John.

61. In 1965 I became Vice-Chancellor of the University of Nottingham. The British Association for the Advancement of Science held its week-long Annual Meeting on the campus in September 1966, and Prime Minister Harold Wilson came to open the new science and engineering complex. In this photograph the Duke of Portland, Chancellor of the University, confers the honorary degree of Doctor of Laws on him, watched by Sir Francis Hill (President of Council) on his right and myself on his left.

62. Nottingham's new Medical School was the first to be established in England in the 20th century, and its creation was a major factor in my decision to take up the Vice-Chancellorship.

63. The formal opening of the Queen's
Medical Centre in Nottingham (the
University Medical School and University
Hospital) did not take place until the Jubilee
Year of 1977. By then I was Chairman of the
University Grants Committee, and was
invited to be part of the occasion.

64. Whilst we were at Nottingham, Lódz
Polytechnic University in Poland awarded
me my first honorary degree (in 1966).

PUNCH 21–27 JANUARY 1970
TWO SHILLINGS & SIXPENCE

Punch

STUDENTS LAID BARE

Dickinson

red blob 6d

GOODBYE FREDDY

—AND GOOD RIDDANCE

SENATE BOARD † SENATE

65. *Punch* epitomises on its front cover the cultural and sartorial differences between radical students and senior university officers (in this case, Alan Bullock, Vice-Chancellor of Oxford).

66. *Red Blob*, the radical students' mouthpiece at Nottingham, purported to see a sinister motive behind my introduction of a Senate Board – intended to involve students in all Senate discussions except for areas of 'reserved business'.

67. We found Highfield House, the Vice-Chancellor's residence at Nottingham, ideal for its purpose – even down to the grass tennis court!

68. The Yorkshire Dales remained a favourite haunt for our weekend walks.

69. Outside the gates of Buckingham Palace with Barbara, John and Mary, after my investiture as a Knight Bachelor in 1971.

70. The old Radcliffe Observatory, one of the loveliest of Oxford's buildings and a stonemason's delight in its detailing and choice of materials. I treasure this engraving, from Ackermann's history of the University of Oxford, published in 1814.

71. I went back to Oxford in 1970 as Dr Lee's Professor of Chemistry. The Physical Chemistry Laboratory was opened in 1941 as a two-storey building and was subsequently much extended.

72. The original teaching laboratory, largely unaltered until 1991 when it underwent major refurbishment.

BUT ROTHSCHILD IS NOT DAINTON

There has been a curious response to a call for publication of a report by Sir Frederick Dainton examining the quality of fundamental research in universities, the effectiveness of the five research councils which spend nearly £100m supporting this and work in their own institutes, and other matters related to the development of science and higher education. The report was completed earlier in the year, but has languished since in the files of the Cabinet Office. Repeated requests for its publication were lent urgency last week when the chairmen of two research councils, in comment highly critical of Whitehall, described the crisis of confidence in the scientific community caused by uncertainties about the future.

Our Political Editor has reported that the Government intend to produce the long awaited White Paper being prepared by Lord Rothschild as head of the central policy review staff of the Cabinet Office. This is good news indeed, for the review is expected to embrace many aspects of organization of the executive, including many vexed questions connected with the vast Government expenditures on research. Emphasis is very

rightly expected to be placed on getting a more direct relationship between the fruits of much of this research and industrial development. But to put it bluntly, Rothschild is not Dainton. The issues they have examined, which may look superficially so alike, are in fact poles apart.

Perhaps the clue to this fracas, which could so easily be remedied, lies in the advice a former senior scientific civil servant gave to a scientific conference last month. He warned of the danger of equating the sociology of the university laboratory with the sociology of the Whitehall department. This may seem a blindingly obvious statement.

Yet the past few days have established that a clear lack of rapport exists between Whitehall and the scientific community. The money spent by research councils is of course a fraction of the vast sums of Government money spent on former defence research establishments and other laboratories. The arguments for reshaping and harnessing all these resources for industrial benefit were indisputable.

As is to be expected, many of the research workers who make a profit

for industry learn their skills as postgraduates sponsored by grants from a research council. Naturally, a research council has a prime responsibility for underwriting the quality of postgraduate scientists produced through its support. This extends to ensuring that the conditions are the best available to stimulate good research work. Unless there is strict adherence to producing quality, the health of the country's scientific resources will be undermined. It makes little difference to that whether the work in hand is of academic interest, or of direct obvious application to industry, medicine, or defence.

So whatever proposals come from Rothschild for turning huge stagnant Government resources to industrial riches, the successful continuation of such schemes would have to be secured by the attention to quality produced through the more financially modest resources reviewed by Dainton. Ebbing confidence in the scientific community reached crisis with the unprecedented public criticisms from the research councils. The publication of Dainton would go a long way to clearing the air.

---

73. Between November 1970 and May 1971 I chaired a working party of the Council for Scientific Policy, which looked at the effectiveness of the Research Councils in supporting pure and applied research in universities and specialist institutes. Publication of our report was deferred by the Cabinet Office pending the outcome of the concurrent enquiry by Victor Rothschild, head of the Prime Minister's Think Tank, into how government departments could best exploit scientific research for their own use. The story is told in Chapter 8: as this *Times* leader of 6 October 1971 makes clear, the delay in publishing our proposals fuelled a good deal of public debate and concern.

74. A cartoon by Horner which appeared on the front page of the *Times Higher Education Supplement* two days after the publication of the White Paper 'Framework for Government Research and Development' in 1972. Victor Rothschild tries to convert me to the customer-contractor principle, while Prime Minister Edward Heath looks on with wallet in hand.

THE TIMES
Higher Education
SUPPLEMENT

UGC abandons new projects to save university budgets

THES 8.3.74

by Laura Kaufman

The national univ... year will be about ... in 1973-74 after th... the December Bu... the former Chan...

The University... has used its enti... rent grant and a... tary grant for 19... universities in g...

Projects for c... universities an... graduate a... courses, and p... development... now been aba...

According... UGC to uni... rate of infl...

THES 1.10.76

Mr R. E. Macpherson, said that Cambridge expected to receive much less than 100 per cent and was pleased ... the allocation.
...ived £267,000 in-
...cent.

since we are an expanding university anyway."

Sussex has received no grant against inflation either.

● Universities have now lost between £114m and £175m from ... budgets for 1974-77 since th... ... Budget and the sub... ...d by the

Universities face 4 per cent cut in resources next year

by Peter Scott and Frances Gibb

Universities are likely to suffer an effective cut of about £25m in their recurrent grant for 1977-78 compared with the present year. In cash terms they will probably receive only about £9m more next year than this.

In a letter sent out to universities at the end of last week Sir Frederick Dainton, chairman of the University Grants Committee, warned that the total resources available to universities next year, from both grants and tuition fees, would fall by about 4 per cent compared with the current year, when measured in constant prices.

The UGC letter con... figures for next... Frederick ...

Sir Frederick Dainton: "continues existing economies."

Chancellors and Principals, said "The implications of the UGC statement are alarming. The universities have always made clear their willingness to take their fair share of economies during a period of economic crisis and they will naturally have to consider the ment decisions in the context of govern of public er... ...le are...

...s a c...
...und
...ems.
...sec...
...U...
...n...
...B...

Student expansion set back 50,000 after £100m cuts

by Brian MacArthur

As universities and polytechnics surveyed the wreckage of their quinquennial expansion plans this week, it became clear that student expansion may fall short of the 1976-77 targets agreed by the Government a year ago by 40,000 to 50,000.

University budgets for the next three years have been cut on the most optimistic count by at least £100m and starts on about £150m of new university and polytechnic building have probably been post... ...ed. Many polytec...

Higher Education and the Crisis

which compensation is based, may show a 9 to 10 per cent rate ...

The view in Whitehall, as well as at the UGC, is that student targe... cuts will not achieve significan... savings. The serious spending, it i... pointed out, is generated by sta... appointments, equipment and buil... ing.

Sir Hugh Robson, chairman of the Committee of Vice-Chancellors and Principals, said that the announce-ment of the cuts by the Government on Monday had confirmed the universities fears that they would be severe.

THES 25.1.74

75. These cuttings, from various *THES* front pages, give a hint of the pressure on the University Grants Committee during the time I was its chairman.

There are two aspects of our lives in Nottingham to which I must refer again at this point: the external activities into which I was increasingly drawn (initially by way of the Council for Scientific Policy), and the Cookridge Radiation Research Centre at the University of Leeds. I have already described the arrangement by which I became honorary director at Cookridge, and its negotiation was one of the critical factors which changed my hitherto resolute resistance to leaving Leeds for any other university, no matter what the incentives might be. Apart from my personal interest in the work there, I had two main objectives in this matter. The first was to use what influence I could to ensure that the accelerator was well installed and that resources were available to enable it to be used as required, thereby justifying the confidence which DSIR had shown in making such an unprecedentedly large grant to a research chemist. Subsidiary reasons were that I could be helpful to the *de facto* director, Arthur Salmon, and the two other permanent academic staff in their dealings within and outside the University of Leeds, and that my continued association would help to maintain the flow of able persons into the Centre, especially from overseas. The latter hope was realised but the former was more difficult: although the University of Leeds had accepted the idea of an advisory committee with external as well as internal members, there was one person whose understanding of the work carried out (and its significance) was minimal, and who would much have preferred to uncouple the University from the Cookridge enterprise. Fortunately his was a minority voice.

A further reason for wishing to maintain my involvement with Cookridge was to send a signal to staff and students in Nottingham that their Vice-Chancellor really cared about research as a vital function of a good university. It did no harm for them to know that by 7.30am on Saturdays I would be travelling 70 miles to Leeds for just this purpose. As for myself, despite driving 140 miles in the day, I found that several hours spent sitting down with young people trying to understand particular chemical problems which they faced, and in which I was much interested, was a stimulating and refreshing experience after a week of seemingly endless meetings in Nottingham and London. In the Christmas vacation the researchers at Leeds used to come to Nottingham for a whole day's symposium, in which those whose work was at a stage for reporting would make presentations for discussion. The proceedings were only broken by a celebratory lunch in Highfield House, and it was always an enjoyable and scientifically profitable day.

There was also an entirely unforeseeable benefit which both I and the University of Nottingham derived from my Cookridge commitment. This arose during the period of student unrest. One Friday evening I was working in my office in the Trent Building when, at about 9pm, two students knocked on my door. They explained that a general meeting of some body whose status was somewhat hazy had decided that a series of 'non-negotiable demands' should be presented to me. I heard them in silence, and when they had finished speaking I maintained that silence. Plainly perplexed, they asked what I was going to do, to which I replied 'Nothing', adding that the adjective 'non-negotiable' made their statement into an ultimatum which would allow no discussion and left room only for me to remind them of the University rules of which they would be in breach. 'But we have been mandated to "sit in" tomorrow if you don't accept', they said. The ensuing long pause was eventually broken by one of them asking me what I was thinking about. I replied truthfully that I was wondering whether I would not leave a little earlier than usual to start my journey to Cookridge the following morning, and then explained why I believed a vice-chancellor should symbolise the value of research and demonstrate his conviction by his own acts. Then they left and I resumed my work. Just as I was leaving my office to go back home they reappeared and informed me that the body of students whom they represented, and to whom they had described their meeting with me, had decided that as I would not be in Nottingham there was little point in having a sit-in. My parting comment, 'So now you see the value of research', evoked no response and I fear its irony eluded them.

London Calling

The inaugural meeting of the Council for Scientific Policy took place early in 1965, and was memorable for two reasons. First, it was attended by the new Secretary of State for Education and Science, Michael Stewart, and his Minister for Science, Lord Vivian Bowden. The former was there to welcome us, the latter was signalling his intention to attend our meetings but fortunately was prevailed upon not to do so. Though a delightful person, he saw the Council as a body which would merely advise him on how best to execute his own preconceived policy, whereas our duty was also to proffer to the Secretary of State our views on what his policy for science should be, for him to accept in whole or in part, or simply reject. Secondly,

I was sitting just a short distance from the Secretary of State and, as he was making his speech of welcome, a messenger entered the room and presented an envelope bearing a red 'Urgent' label to his Private Secretary, who opened it, blanched and gave it to his master as soon as he sat down. Having read it, Michael Stewart excused himself and left. That was the last the CSP saw of him: unknowingly, we were witnessing the consequence of the exercise of prime-ministerial power, for the next morning the newspapers announced that Harold Wilson had appointed him to be Foreign Secretary.

The CSP met on Fridays at roughly monthly intervals, and quickly identified a number of particular problems requiring detailed investigation by special committees or working groups. Some of the matters studied had arisen at Research Council level, whilst others had been flagged up as a result of the CSP's own discussions. Typical of the issues arising from discussions held by the Research Councils was a proposal that the Conseil Européen pour la Recherche Nucleaire (CERN) should build a 300 GeV particle accelerator at a cost estimated to be about £150m, of which around a quarter would fall to the United Kingdom as one of the major member states of CERN. Thereafter its running costs were likely to consume about 10 per cent of the Science Research Council's annual budget, and if past experience was any guide there was a distinct possibility of considerable cost escalation. The CSP was aware in early 1967 that the SRC was considering the matter and felt that, being responsible for allocating money to the Research Councils, it should also look independently at so important an issue. Therefore the CSP set up a working party for this purpose under Michael (later Lord) Swann. By July 1967 the SRC, having considered this problem carefully, advised Tony Crosland (who had succeeded Mr Stewart as Secretary of State) to support the proposal when it came before the CERN Council. However, two greatly respected members, Sir Ronald Nyholm and Sir Ewart Jones, objected to this conclusion and issued a contrary minority report. This was one of the early classical examples of a clash between, on the one hand, the advocates of 'big' science – often nuclear physics or astronomy – and, on the other hand, the advocates of 'little' science, in which smaller sums are spent (as Jones and Nyholm put it) on 'projects which offer some prospect of material advantage to the community and at the same time serve to train useful (*sic*) scientists and technologists'. 'Big' is very expensive but can yield data of immense fundamental scientific significance about the constituents of the atomic nucleus and the forces holding them together, and about cosmology, that is, knowledge of the universe. This division is one of the perennial problems of science policy, more recently illustrated by the US project to build a 'super-conducting supercollider' in Texas at a cost of several billion dollars: even after a considerable proportion of this sum had been spent the US government reversed its earlier decision and stopped the construction.

The CSP group under Swann worked rapidly, so that it was able to issue its advice only twelve days after that of the Research Council. As so often happens in politics, however, it was an adventitious event which was the determining factor – the devaluation of sterling, which resulted in the British government deciding it could not enter into an international commitment on the scale envisaged. The issue arose again in my first year as chairman of the CSP, when a revised proposal was put forward. After much agonising it was endorsed, but on the condition that the cost was contained within the SRC's nuclear physics budget. The government concurred, and happily for everyone Dr J.B. Adams, a founder member of CSP and Director of the Culham Laboratory of the Atomic Energy Authority, was appointed director of the new project. He was outstandingly successful: rarely is it the case that such a vast project is finished completely satisfactorily, ahead of schedule (in March 1971) and at less than the estimated cost – a real tribute to Adams.

My continuing concern over the decline in well-qualified applicants to read chemistry at Leeds, first noted in 1964 and confirmed in the spring of 1965, led to a few enquiries of other universities which showed that this concern was also manifest elsewhere. I suggested rather hesitantly at the second meeting of the CSP that this problem might be investigated: the Council agreed, and a working group was set up with me as chairman. From then on I seemed to be cast in the role of 'Mr Scientific Manpower Studies' of the CSP and was later drawn in as a member of other bodies with kindred interests, such as the committee (again chaired by Michael Swann) on the flow into employment of qualified engineers, scientists and technologists. I also became a member of the Committee on Manpower Resources, set up under the joint aegis of the Department of Education and Science and the newly established Ministry of Technology.

My own committee began its work in March 1965 and issued two reports: an interim one in February 1966 (Cmnd. 2893) and a final one two years later (Cmnd. 3541), under the cumbrous title *Enquiry into the Flow of Candidates in Science and*

Technology into Higher Education. In the press and in the context of 'swinging London' in contemporary youth culture, it quickly attracted the sobriquet *The Swing Away From Science*. The latter was the better description because the most striking fact that emerged was that, although the fraction of any given age group staying on at school beyond O-level was increasing, the proportion of pupils in the science echelon – those whose A-level subjects gave them a *prima facie* claim for acceptance into higher education courses in science, engineering or technology – was steadily declining. The adverse effect of this on the number of actual applicants in the late 1950s and early 1960s was partly offset by the concomitant increase in size of the relevant age groups. However, the age-group size peaked about 1963-64, a demographic change associated with the high post-war birthrate, then declined by about 20 per cent to a flat trough some three years later. Undoubtedly, the decline in applications for chemistry at Leeds was the local manifestation of this national trend. The committee foresaw that the situation would get worse and that the plans for the expansion of university capacity in science, engineering and technology then being implemented would lead to 'vacant places' and would therefore be sure to attract adverse comment, as in fact occurred. Likewise it led to questions about the effectiveness of the University Grants Committee, as I shall describe, at the time when I was its chairman.

It was crystal clear that what needed to be done was to have a broad span of subjects studied to school-leaving age – both on general educational grounds and in order to defer premature specialisation – and to amend university entrance requirements and courses to encourage these changes in schools. The relevant bodies in England and Wales, from the Department of Education and Science downwards, failed to grasp the nettle and have consistently fudged the issue in the so-called reforms embodied in the numerous Education Acts of recent years. The result is that, in a period of increasing global dependence on science and technology education, compared to our competitors the youth of England remains relatively disadvantaged and scientifically illiterate. Most disappointing to me was the attitude of the universities and the Schools Council, which should have been pace-setters of progress. Instead the Committee of Vice-Chancellors and Principals referred the matter to its Standing Conference on University Entrance, which joined forces with the Schools Council to recommend the N and F levels for school certificate examinations; being milk and water when strong drink was required, these never really had a chance and have probably passed out of most people's memories. We would serve our youth much better if we adopted the International Baccalaureate as a basis for school education, with the acquisition of those skills embodied in the Diploma of Achievement now offered by the Oxford and Cambridge Schools Examination Board.

Further discussion of the CSP must wait, because my reference to the CVCP prompts me to explain how much of my time as a vice-chancellor was taken up by that body. At the meetings before Christmas 1965 I made no contribution to the discussions, but merely tried to get the feel of the committee and its principal actors while it was in the period of growth – from the pre-war membership of around 25, a size which gave it a club-like atmosphere, to almost double that number as vice-chancellors from the new universities and the transformed Colleges of Advanced Technology were added. I noted with interest that the vice-chancellors of Oxford, Cambridge and London, all of whom had limited tenure and to that extent could not be considered 'professional' vice-chancellors like their namesakes elsewhere, had their 'minders' with them who provided the necessary continuity. Oxford and Cambridge were accompanied by their Registrars, London by the Principal, Dr Douglas Logan (a Scot with a large body and an equally firm opinion, based on his long experience, which he fancied gave a final authority to all he said).

In the spring term of 1966 the CVCP met at the University of Manchester, following the installation of Andrew, Duke of Devonshire, as Chancellor of that institution. It was expected that the business on the Friday morning would be non-controversial and that we would get away quickly after lunch. Unfortunately, one of the items was the report of a committee which had been considering how best the University Grants Committee could allocate money for equipment. In the report it was recommended that grants should be provided whenever a university department occupied a new building. Having acted as an assessor for the UGC for many applications of this kind, I knew that this proposal was a nonsense because the needs of a department for equipment are determined not by the newness or otherwise of the fabric of the building occupied, but by the number of staff and research workers and the nature of their research, as well as the undergraduate student load. The chairman, Sir Charles Wilson, Principal of Glasgow University, put the whole report to the committee in the obvious expectation that its proposals would be accepted. I demurred for the reasons given, which not only caused consternation but brought down on me the Johnsonian wrath of 'Jock' Logan. It was difficult to refute my arguments, however, and at the end of the debate the recommendation was rejected. Instead, Charles Carter, Vice-Chancellor of Lancaster (who did not share my view) and I were deputed to hold discussions with the UGC. In due course the logic of my argument was accepted by the UGC, something for which I was most grateful when I later became chairman of that body.

Whether it was for that or for other reasons, soon afterwards I was appointed a member of the CVCP Steering Committee: I was glad to accept, because the Steering Committee was the effective motor of the CVCP, which certainly found it useful to have someone on its steering committee who was also a member of the CSP. One of my concerns on both the CVCP and the CSP was the need to bring British industry and British universities closer together, so that the former could contribute to shaping the education of future scientists, engineers and technologists, which would give the country a long-term benefit. Industry would also gain from closer contact with academics and their research. Having expressed some of my views on such matters I was made a member of the joint CBI/CVCP Universities and Industry Committee, and a couple of years later became its alternate chairman. There I met Denning (later Lord) Pearson, Chief Executive of Rolls-Royce, and this enabled me to start a link between Nottingham and Rolls-Royce Engines Division, then busy with developing the RB211 engine. As a result, Alex Smith came as Special Professor in the Engineering Faculty and we also acquired on a permanent basis their expert on carbon fibres. Alex Smith astonished me by asking if he might attend a few meetings of the Senate, to which I agreed, and he later left Rolls-Royce to become Director of Manchester Polytechnic. That he should do so after attending Senate meetings was my only reason for doubting his judgment!

New Technology, Old-fashioned Courtesy

One area in which I saw an opening for Nottingham was the development of computerised information databases (in chemistry, for instance, the *Chemical Abstracts* of the American Chemical Society, on which all chemists rely, was already being mechanised). Two factors worked in my favour. First, DSIR had set up a division under Harry (later Sir Harry) Hookway, a chemist like myself, concerned with scientific and technical information: this had an advisory committee which I was asked to chair, thereby enabling me to learn quickly about present actualities and potential future applications. At the same time the Chemical Society in London was interested in this matter, in so far as it affected chemistry, and wished to place itself in a leading position in Europe in this field. Moreover Jack Barrett, Research Director of Monsanto UK, whom I knew well, had taken this idea under his wing and in due course we agreed that the Nottingham campus was a good place to locate the Society's Chemical Information Retrieval Unit. By a further lucky chance a member of staff of the Zoology Department, Dr Tony Kent, was already interested in scientific applications of computing. Nottingham University thus became the nursery of what is now a much bigger operation, located in the large Information Services Division of the Royal Society of Chemistry at Thomas Graham House in Cambridge.

Though very busy, the remainder of the academic year was also enjoyable because we were made to feel so welcome in departments, halls of residence and the Students' Union, and also among the ancillary staff, those splendid people on whose backs all academics march and who, more than anyone, showed their unshakeable loyalty during the later student troubles. I felt honoured when I was asked to be a vice-president of the Non-Academic Staff Bowling Club, and I actually played for them in one match.

Because the third academic term is one in which students and staff are preoccupied with examinations, it was possible to squeeze in two overseas visits. One of these involved eight days in Poland as guests of the government, doubtless arranged by Dr Achmatowicz: the whole visit was delightful once I had discharged my duty of advising Dr Minc, the Minister for Higher Education and Research. We managed to see something of the country, including the charming city of Cracow with its Jagellonian University founded over 600 years ago, the castle of Wavel and the Collegium Majus, where I found and was able to correct a slight error in the labelling of one of the exhibits. Conversations which we had with our various hosts and interpreters gave us the clear impression that the Poles were by conviction patriots first, Catholics second and communists a very poor third. We were greatly touched to see how well the old town of Warsaw had been reconstructed after its savage destruction by the Germans in 1944; and in the house of the Polish Chemical Society, with its echoes of Marie Sklodowska Curie, we noted with pleasure how British chemists had helped to restock the library.

Polish values were clearly Western rather than Slavic, and the Poles had kept their identity despite having been ruled at various times by the Prussians, the Russians and the Swedes. We became convinced that their survival as Poles, despite their hardships, owed much to a pervasive sense of humour, a strong feeling for the comic and the incongruous, and often a touch of gallantry. We both remember a charming man who was our main guide on this visit, and who was particularly courteous in a manner reminiscent of a cavalry officer of the *ancien régime*. When we had visited the Lazienka Palace in Warsaw and were walking down the steps into the park, he characteristically stood aside for a lady to come by and it prompted me to say to him, 'I notice your great courtesy, and in particular the way in which you are always careful to kiss the hand of a lady as a form of greeting or departure. Why do you do this?' With a twinkle in his eye he replied at once, 'Well, you see, we have to begin somewhere' – to which there was no answer.

A Policy for Tertiary Education?

Once the die was cast to leave Leeds for Nottingham I felt I ought to try to find out more about how the university 'system' in Britain worked, by which I meant learning where crucial decisions concerning size and general lines of development were taken. I knew, of course, something about the UGC's role in encouraging or discouraging developments in those universities which qualified for grant aid. But I also knew that in recent years that number had increased: the Colleges of Advanced Technology had become Universities of Technology, two entirely new universities – Sussex and Keele – had been created and more were emerging, which everybody seemed to attribute to the deliberations of the Robbins Committee (a view which I regarded with some scepticism because, from my own experience, I knew that the UGC's decision to establish a planning committee for the University of Lancaster predated the publication of the Robbins Report). I also found it hard to believe that an 'arm's length' body like the UGC would have the power to enlarge the university sector to the extent envisaged. Moreover, local authority colleges prepared significant numbers of students for external degrees of the University of London, or degree-equivalent qualifications of professional bodies. I wanted to know who decided that this arrangement should persist for some institutions, while others became university colleges and later universities.

At first I found it impossible to get clear answers, but in any case my initial thoughts were superseded by Tony Crosland's famous speech at Woolwich establishing the concept of a 'binary line' dividing the autonomous universities from 'a vocationally oriented non-university sector which is degree-giving'. This speech led to much comment in the broadsheets and the educational weeklies, much of it from aggrieved vested interests. The whole brouhaha had the effect of making me wonder who had advised the Secretary of State on this matter, and what were the arguments that he heard. In the event, the answer came to me from his own lips not much more than a year later.

In June 1966 I was invited to Mr Crosland's home in London for drinks and a discussion about higher education matters. Once acclimatised to Crosland's cigar smoke I could pay full attention to the exchange, which was a free-for-all. At this first meeting I decided just to listen to what was being said by commentators more fluent (and certainly more self-confident) than me. It was heady stuff. I was however somewhat embarrassed because here was a group of intelligent people, well disposed to higher education, but some of whose comments showed a lack of awareness of how universities actually work, particularly the civic universities which in fact catered for the vast majority of UK students. A further cause for embarrassment was my feeling that Sir Charles Wilson, Chairman of the CVCP, should have been there rather than myself.[1] So at the first opportunity I told Charles in confidence what was going on, and that I was prepared to withdraw if he considered my presence at these discussions inappropriate. He did not, so I continued and took more part in the conversation, quickly developing a liking for the lively, speculative mind of Tony Crosland and the courtesy with which he received and treated everyone's contribution. This was very different from Dick Crossman's hectoring, particularly of his own staff, which I had witnessed in discussions with him over the Nottingham Medical School. At a later meeting at Tony Crosland's house I expressed my view that all degree level education should be dealt with nationally rather than by local authorities, because a degree confers national and international mobility on the holder. In my opinion, this kind of education should properly be the province of two types of institution: one primarily professional, the

---

1. One possible reason for my invitation was that the DES must have been well aware of my efforts, made partly under its auspices, to identify and examine the swing away from science.

universities, and the other primarily vocational. I firmly believed that the latter institutions should not be deflected from their vocational emphasis, and therefore urged that there should be an overarching national council for higher education in the UK, which would be responsible for advising on overall policy matters and for determining the appropriate division of purpose and resources between the two wings (with the latter being allocated to individual institutions by two grants committees, one for the universities and the other for the vocational institutions). Nothing in my later experience has caused me to change my mind, so that when the Oakes Committee was set up in 1977 to reconsider the general issue, although I had not been asked for views (which struck me as bizarre, since I was then chairman of the UGC) I wrote a paper to Sir Philip Rogers, the secretary of that committee, advocating this solution.

Diversions in Europe and North America

As well as the visit to Poland which I already mentioned, the third term of my first academic year at Nottingham also accommodated a quick trip to give a main sectional talk at the American Chemical Society meeting in Cleveland, Ohio. Although the total time away from Nottingham was only 65 hours, it was possible for me to fit in a visit to Case Western Reserve University Medical School, which had been a pioneer in the design and use of multidisciplinary laboratories for preclinical medical students. These had been urged on me as a cost-saving device we might adopt in Nottingham, but I was not wholly convinced. Here I also had an unforgettably vivid illustration of changing attitudes to marriage in the United States. I was invited to have lunch at a downtown hotel with an industrialist friend of mine. When I arrived I was surprised to see that with him was the wife of another (academic) acquaintance. We chatted quite happily for a few minutes while we drank cocktails, and I noted that when the waiter came in pushing a trolley he prepared a table for only three people. I was on the point of asking about the spouse of my host when he greatly embarrassed me by explaining that she was neither unwell nor attending another function: there had taken place what was in essence a simple wife-swap, and he rendered me speechless by describing how 'we talked about it like mature adults'. From that day on the abbreviation MA has had for me a connotation beyond the purely academic.

Two days after my return from America I was off again to an International Association for Radiation Research meeting in Italy, from which I returned to a busy July, including a visit to Cookridge to show the Secretary of the Medical Research Council, Sir Harold Himsworth, what we were learning about the radiation chemistry of water. Then, after the final University Council meeting of the session, Barbara, Rosalind and I left Nottingham for a long break in New England, the older children having gone off on other excursions. It was a wholly delightful trip, with the right blend of rest and stimulus. After a week of lazy life we drove to Schenectady in New York State, where I consulted with General Electric while the other two were entertained by old friends, following which we had five days at a Gordon Conference on radiation chemistry at New Hampton.

At the end of the conference Barbara and Rosalind departed for Boston and home while I moved on to the University of Michigan at Ann Arbor to give the plenary address at the International Symposium on Free Radicals in Solution. Organised by the Organic Chemistry Division of the International Union of Pure and Applied Chemistry (IUPAC), the symposium commemorated the centenary of the birth of Professor Moses Gomberg, who discovered the first long-lived free radical: triphenyl methyl. It was appropriate that I should talk about the simplest free radical – the electron in water – which stands at the other end of the timescale, being the shortest lived. At the banquet the President of the University of Michigan, Harlan Hatcher, introduced me along the lines of 'It is a great pleasure for me to invite Dr Dainton to respond to this toast, though it is much less of a pleasure, and certainly more difficult, to know how to describe him. He is listed in the programme as Vice-Chancellor of the University of Nottingham. That academic office is not one which is common in this country, but I imagine it is a post of great authority as well as distinction, and to give expression to that understanding I propose to refer to him tonight as the Deputy Sheriff of Nottingham'.

According to IUPAC, Phillips Petroleum had sponsored my visit, and so it was suggested that I should visit Bartlesville, Oklahoma, where most of the research and development work of that company was carried out. I was glad to comply with this request, not least because it was in those laboratories in 1935 that two researchers discovered the ceiling temperature phenomenon, the elucidation of which by Ken Ivin and me yielded so much fundamental kinetic and thermodynamic information about addition polymerization.

The First Year Ends

The day after I returned to Highfield House the 1966 Annual Meeting of the British Association for the Advancement of Science opened in Nottingham. Most of the activities making up this very large event took place on the campus, and we had seven hectic days of meetings, exhibitions and receptions. Added to this, we received the Prime Minister and Mrs Wilson on Saturday 3 September in order to confer an honorary degree on him and for him to ceremonially open 'Technopolis', as the science and engineering buildings were sometimes called. It seemed entirely appropriate that a man so committed to 'the white heat of the technological revolution' should undertake this task. Mary Wilson proved to be a delightful companion and I was much touched when a few days later we received a photograph of the opening of the Trent Building which had been taken by her father, the Reverend D. Baldwin, a free churchman who had studied at a theological college then on the Nottingham campus and named after the eminent Congregationalist minister and educationalist, the Reverend J.B. Paton.

The rest of September was fully occupied with visits to Cookridge to start off new researchers, a radiation chemistry conference in Newcastle and a meeting of the Faraday Society (of which I was in my term as President) on colloid stability. It had been a typically busy year, but I did not feel tired because it had been worth while. We felt very happy doing work which, though demanding, suited us and was eliciting a favourable local response. The only real disappointment was that the Professor of Zoology, E.J.W. Barrington, did not relish the idea of the Vice-Chancellor's wife working at a bench in his department, albeit for no pay, so that Barbara's *Xenopus* work was discontinued. However, she was soon afterwards appointed to the magistracy and in this role demonstrated that a partially deaf person with an efficient hearing aid was not cut off from Court proceedings any more than a person with normal hearing, thus setting a precedent which others have been able to follow. She was also made a member of the House Committee of the Nottingham General Hospital, which later led to other cognate appointments. So began her long association with the National Health Service. The girls had settled in at Nottingham High School and John had continued at Bradford Grammar School, staying with friends; to our joy he had been awarded a place at Merton College, Oxford, to read physics, beginning in the Michaelmas term 1966.

It is not my intention to continue describing our life at Nottingham and nationally in such detail over the next four years of our stay. Suffice it to say that each year was equally busy and in the main just as happy for both of us, despite the problem of student unrest to which I shall return in the next chapter.

London Calls Again: Science and the National Libraries Committee

The calendar year 1967 was again very full, with the Council for Scientific Policy or its preparatory group meeting fortnightly, and the CVCP (which also spawned subgroups in which I was involved) meeting on a monthly cycle. Solly Zuckerman had left his post as Adviser to the Secretary of State for Defence, Denis Healey, and had been appointed Chief Scientific Adviser to the government. I surmise that there was an element of slight push and marked pull in this appointment because it was becoming evident that, although the government was still keeping faith with science and technology in the sense of increasing in real terms the money which was allocated on the advice of the CSP, most science-based industry (and certainly the engineering and manufacturing industries) were not performing very well. The government evidently felt there was a need for a Central Advisory Council on Science and Technology, and this was set up under Solly's chairmanship.[2] To my surprise I found myself a member. We met monthly in the Cabinet Office throughout the three years (1967–70) that the Council existed. I am not sure that it served much purpose, except symbolically, because Solly was always a loose cannon; but it was useful for me to know what Ministers and Permanent Secretaries, who occasionally came to these meetings, were thinking about. In 1970 I got clear indications that there were moves afoot to do some restructuring of the Research Councils, a matter to which I shall refer again later.

The Michaelmas Term of 1967 seemed to be especially demanding, particularly as the committee on 'The Swing Away From Science' was finalising its report. I have a clear recollection that on one Saturday evening I was exhausted and went to bed rather early. The telephone rang about 10pm: my first inclination was to ignore it, but it was close to my ear, and in any case experience had taught me that

---

2. The terms of reference of CACST were 'To advise the Government on the most effective national strategy for the use and development of scientific and technological resources'.

few people would telephone on a Saturday night without some urgent matter which they thought justified my attention. I answered it, and at once recognised the speaker as Sir Herbert Andrew, Permanent Secretary at the Department of Education and Science, whom I knew and liked. (In fact he was a Manchester Grammar School boy who had been a pupil of Dr Pidduck, the mathematical physicist at Corpus Christi College with whom I used to swim at Parson's Pleasure when I was an undergraduate.) It appeared that he had been trying to get me earlier in the week without success, and that he wanted to settle a matter rather quickly. As usual he was brief and to the point, explaining that the government was concerned about the effectiveness and interrelationship of a number of large libraries which it funded, directly or indirectly. He was aware that some of the libraries were themselves unhappy with the current situation and that the latest Secretary of State for Education and Science, Patrick Gordon Walker, considered that the whole problem required thorough investigation by a competent committee, and that I should be that committee's chairman; and finally that he, Andrew, shared his master's views.

I was so tired I fear I was somewhat abrupt and, knowing that the following year was already likely to be very full, not least with a long trip to Australia, I refused on the spot. I remember saying to Barbara the next morning that I did not expect Herbert Andrew to give up so easily and, as he was a devout man, it would not surprise me if he were to telephone again after he had been to church. If so my stance would have to be much less dismissive, but I would propose a number of conditions for acceptance, any one of which I thought would actually be unacceptable to the Secretary of State.

True to form and courteous as ever, Sir Herbert rang between half past twelve and one o'clock and I signalled to Barbara that she should pick up the other telephone. Herbert listened to my various conditions. The first was that, were I to take it on, the committee should be small, with members appointed for their competence rather than representativeness, but between them experienced in all the main subject areas for which the libraries had holdings. I could speak for the science and technology side and also, from my experience as chairman of the Advisory Committee on Scientific and Technological Information, cope with the effect which new information technology would have on libraries; others should be able to cover the arts and humanities and the social sciences, and it would be a good idea to have someone acquainted with the running of large organisations, preferably from entirely outside the library world but sympathetic to the aims and purposes of libraries. I added that I would be ready to suggest names and would not take it well if they were turned down. I made the point that a small committee moves more rapidly and I could only give fifteen months at the most of my spare time to this activity, and so therefore we should be adequately staffed by good civil servants who had all the resources they needed. Finally I said that I did not wish to see a draft report go before the Secretary of State with any expectation that he would want it altered from its final typescript form. There was a slight pause before Herbert uttered the single word 'done', for which, knowing him well, I imagined he had to remove his smoking pipe from his mouth.

The next step was to meet Patrick Gordon Walker, whose kind nature was hidden behind a somewhat dolorous facial expression. Alas, he had resigned before we finished our work and died in 1968, so that our report was presented to his successor, Mr Edward Short, just sixteen months after the first meeting was held. We were given a committee room in the old building of the DES in Curzon Street, where the choice was either to die by asphyxiation or to open the windows and be unable to hear one another speak because of the traffic noise. After a few meetings, however, we were given space in the charming and beautifully panelled library at Richmond Terrace.

Sir Herbert and the Secretary of State were as good as their word. The membership of the committee was ideal, and the Department had produced three names which I had not thought of but which were better than my own suggestions. In the end, in addition to myself, we had an academic publisher, Sir John Brown of Oxford University Press, by training a zoologist; a social scientist, originally Professor Sir Roy Allen, who had to resign after some six months due to ill health and who was replaced by the economic historian John Habakkuk, recently appointed Principal of Jesus College, Oxford; the Vice-Principal and Professor of Art History of the University of Edinburgh, Professor Talbot Rice; and Sir Bernard Miller, Chairman of the John Lewis Partnership, who had had a distinguished undergraduate career as an historian at Jesus College, Oxford. The leading civil servant was an Under Secretary, Noel Thompson, who had been a lecturer in metallurgy at the University of Birmingham and was therefore able to supplement my limited knowledge in the technological field. From the very beginning the committee 'gelled' and the work proceeded swiftly.

The problem was essentially a simple one. The British Museum Library grew out of the bequest of the President of the Royal Society, Sir Hans Sloane, who died in 1753 at the age of 92. His literary and art collections were bequeathed to the nation, and the government of the day decided to house them (with other mediaeval manuscripts and state papers which had been given 'for public use and advantage') in Montagu House, a former ducal mansion in Bloomsbury. When Sloane died Parliament passed the British Museum Act, and the Board of Trustees provided a reading room where the collections could be studied without charge by 'all studious and curious persons', thereby effectively creating the first free public library in Britain. Many other gifts and bequests came to the British Museum in the latter half of the eighteenth century, including the Royal Library, amassed during the long lifetime of George III, and the Trustees decided to build a new east wing to Montagu House to contain what is now known as the King's Library. The next major step forward resulted from the appointment of Antonio Panizzi as keeper of printed books. Described as 'the Prince of Librarians', he transformed the Museum into a great cultural repository, and the Library Department became *de facto* (but not *de jure*) the national library of Britain. It was he who achieved the great domed reading room which has attracted so much public attention over the years.

During the next century the accrual of books by 'legal deposit' and by purchase accelerated, so that despite the construction of new buildings on the island site behind the classical facade, additional accommodation had to be sought. The Trustees out-housed the newspapers in a specialised library at Colindale in the 1930s, and they moved about three million volumes to the old Royal Woolwich Arsenal in East London, but material continued to arrive in ever greater quantities: for example, in 1960 the Trustees acquired what is now the Science Reference Library, which had its origins in the great surge of enthusiasm for science and technology following the Great Exhibition of 1851. Parallel with this growth came an increasing demand for higher and adult education, and with it the need for a library to lend books to mature students. This was partially met in 1916 when, with the aid of grants from the Carnegie United Kingdom Trust, a new library was established and slowly developed into the central clearing house of inter-library lending. It was incorporated by Royal Charter in 1931 as the National Central Library and in 1966 was rehoused in purpose-built accommodation in Store Street, about a quarter of a mile from the British Museum.

However, after the Second World War the output of scientific and technical literature grew so explosively that some entirely new developments were necessary. The first came from the recognition that the sheer volume of scientific literature would be self-defeating unless the needs of an individual user could quickly be identified, located and produced. An Office of Scientific and Technical Information was set up under the aegis of DSIR to see how scientific literature could be codified and made accessible by means of the computer, and also to carry out research and development work on library and information systems. A second development was the creation (again by DSIR) of the National Lending Library for Science and Technology, to meet the needs of scientists and technologists for a postal lending service – primarily for individual articles or monographs. It was intended that this library should provide the quickest possible service, and be specially designed for the lending function by eliminating as far as possible waiting lists and delays due to binding. The site chosen was at Boston Spa in Yorkshire, from which virtually all parts of the United Kingdom could be reached by post within 24 hours, and it became fully operational in August 1962.

Almost inevitably, this piecemeal growth of libraries resulted in an administratively and geographically chaotic system, with numerous buildings scattered over London and one in Yorkshire. The first thing the committee had to do was form a clear picture of the size and nature of the holdings of all the libraries concerned, of the clientele who used them, and of the ways in which they used them. In this task we were helped by the Economic Intelligence Research Unit. It quickly became clear to the committee that the unification of these diverse libraries into a National Library under a Board of Management was absolutely essential if good services were to be given right across the field of knowledge, and if a sensible policy for development was to emerge. By the end of October 1968, when the committee met for three days in Nottingham, our ideas were firm and much of the draft was written. The final report was presented to Edward Short on 27 November and published in 1969 as Cmnd. 4028.

For many reasons I found the work of the committee most enjoyable. First, there was the sheer quality and dedication to the task of the other members, and also the secretary and his assistants. Secondly, once the facts about each of the libraries had been teased out, and the different needs of the various categories of users identified, it was not difficult to propose an organisational structure which would reflect those needs better than in the past. Thirdly, I had no difficulty in persuading my colleagues that, although strictly it was outside our terms of reference, we should emphasise the absolute necessity of housing the vast and valuable national collections in accommodation which was purpose-built and environmentally satisfactory, to ensure their future survival and availability. Our hope was that, at the very least, this would break the log-jam which had developed over the proposed new building for the British Museum Library (Patrick Gordon Walker had by October 1967 formally rejected both the original Martin-Wilson project of 1962-64 and subsequent attempts to modify it). Fourthly and finally, I owed so much to the Sheffield Public Reference Library that I had a feeling I was helping to repay a debt, which gave me a good deal of personal satisfaction.

In due course first the Labour government, and then the Conservative government which succeeded it in 1970, responded positively and the British Library Act, which gave expression to most of the committee's recommendations, was passed in 1972. Against this background, it was a great and welcome surprise for me to become associated with the British Library Board six years later.

America Once More, and Some Bread on the Waters

Early in 1969 I was asked by the English Speaking Union if I would join a study tour to the United States in the autumn of that year. Like so many other forays in the 1960s, it was intended to examine questions in which American practice seemed superior to British. I think the person behind my invitation was Eddie (later Sir Edwin) Nixon, the Managing Director of IBM UK. It proved to be a very interesting trip, both from the composition of the British party and the distinction of the Americans whom we met. The timing was perfect from my point of view in that it allowed a visit to New England during the fall, which I always enjoy, followed by a couple of days in Washington. There, with Sir Harrie Massey, chairman of the CSP (whom I was to succeed a couple of months later), and Jack Embling, a Deputy Secretary in the Department of Education and Science, I was able to meet Dr Lee DuBridge, Chief Science Adviser to President Nixon, and the staff of the Office of Science and Technology. I also spent a day at the National Institutes of Health (NIH), which I certainly wished to see because in Britain Sir Harold Himsworth had conceived the idea of a Clinical Research Centre based on the NIH model, and this was in the process of being incorporated into the new Northwick Park Hospital then under construction at Harrow. I knew that any background knowledge I was able to acquire at NIH would be helpful in making judgments about progress with the Clinical Research Centre, as well as being of value to the Nottingham Medical School specifically.

The British party comprised a mixed bag: the two MPs John Biffen and Michael Heseltine; the Tyneside local politician T. Dan Smith, who later gained considerable notoriety; a Treasury official; the Executive Head of the Electrical Trades Union, Les Cannon, who had earned that title after a chequered career in which he began as a communist, then reformed both himself and the Union; a cluster of academics, including Lord Penney of Imperial College, Sir Harry Melville of Queen Mary College and Walter Perry of the Open University; Andrew Shonfield, Chairman of the Social Science Research Council; the Industrial Director of the CBI, Lord Byers; and other industrialists such as Eddie Nixon. The English Speaking Union had laid on some remarkably distinguished people for us to meet, drawn from such organisations as the Ford Foundation, AT&T, IBM's major research laboratory at Yorktown Heights, Chase Manhattan Bank, the Hudson Institute, MIT, and the Harvard Business School.

The experiences of the tour were also varied. I still carry in my mind vivid images of the unscripted monologue leading us to the year 2000 delivered by the corpulent, intelligent, arrogant Herman Kahn of the Hudson Institute, who would brook little contradiction from anyone. In a conference room on the sixteenth floor of the Chase Manhattan Bank there was a perfectly splendid confrontation between the chain-smoking Les Cannon and a very 'with it' cleric, the Reverend Malcolm from Columbia Theological Seminary, who came dressed in regulation proletarian costume and delivered a highly idiosyncratic piece on the US student movement, an issue which seemed to be preoccupying a lot of people in business, academe and politics at that time (which in my view gave it too great a significance). I am not sure what the others took away from this trip, but I certainly returned with a lot of interesting notes and impressions.

I was particularly fortunate on one occasion to be placed next to Dr Emmanuel ('Mannie') Piore, Vice-President of IBM worldwide and previously its first Director of Research. We had a long and interesting talk, neither of us aware that his mantle would one day fall on Lew Branscomb (at that time Director of the US

National Bureau of Standards, which I was to visit eight days later). This chance meeting was to prove fruitful in the mid-1980s, when Oxford University Press was looking for resources to enable it to computerise the next edition of the *Oxford English Dictionary*. After it had turned to me for help, my first act was to persuade Kenneth Baker, then Minister for Information Technology, that it would be a good thing if his department were able to contribute some pump-priming money. My second act was to spend the best part of a day with Lew Branscomb when he came to Oxford, and during it to ask whether IBM would give some computer hardware and know-how to the project. I was able to show Lew his father's college, and I am sure that his support, with that of Eddie Nixon, was absolutely crucial in securing the very significant gift which IBM made to the University, without which the new dictionary could not have been produced on time and with so few errors.

During the study tour Eddie Nixon and I had several talks, and I formed a high opinion of him. Some years later, when I was chairman-elect and a member of the UK selection committee for Harkness Fellows, I had no hesitation in recommending that he should become a member. His industrial and academic experience were of great value in this role.

CHAPTER 6

STUDENT UNREST:
A VIGNETTE OF A LOCAL ABERRATION

Youth is the season of credulity.

William Pitt the Elder (1708–1778)

Background: The Media and the Reality

No chronicler of the history of any British institution of higher education during the late 1960s and early 1970s can or should avoid reference to student unrest. This is not because the phenomenon produced any major long-term change in how universities are run, nor because the disturbances were anything more than the palest imitation of what happened in the universities and on the streets of some European countries, notably France and Germany, or in the United States of America, where lives were lost – as, for example, at Kent State University. By contrast, the British scene requires consideration because it illustrates how even the most benevolent university system in the world is not immune from disruption by a tiny minority of students if they are absolutely (albeit incoherently) committed to some ideology, are well organised, have few qualms about manipulating others, and know how to attract media coverage.

In some ways, by the 1960s Britain had become notable for its manifestations of youth culture, and the media paid great attention. In the early 'swinging sixties' they gave much coverage to the so-called 'liberation' from the lifestyle of earlier generations of students, made possible by the contraceptive pill, the lowering to 18 of the age of majority and the increasing use of psychedelic drugs, whilst later in the decade their attention switched towards the attempts by a handful of students to disrupt the work of the universities. Furthermore, while there were undoubtedly some ugly and violent scenes in a few institutions, the picture portrayed by the media exaggerated both the magnitude and the importance of the phenomenon, and in so doing performed a disservice to British higher education. It is not surprising that one of the main tactics of the activists was to secure publicity: to this end they cultivated the newspapers and television, which responded by reporting fully the theatre of the absurd while making no reference to the fact that the vast majority of students were indifferent to the antics of their radical contemporaries. I remember many times while in Nottingham trying unsuccessfully to get some balance into the reporting by pointing out that the number of students who were regularly engaged in doing socially valuable work with the infirm, old folk and the underprivileged was much greater than the total of active 'revolutionaries'. In this lack of balance the media were no different then (and are no different today) from at any other time: I recall the saying of an eighteenth-century divine who remarked perceptively, 'He that cometh to persuade the multitude that they are not well governed shall not lack a large and attentive audience'.

An honourable exception to the above was the attitude of Desmond Wilcox, who used his BBC *Man Alive* television programme to involve students, parents of students, vice-chancellors (including myself) and particularly the radicals in discussion, both alone and together, and did so in a manner that honestly tried to get to the root cause of the phenomenon in a way that would genuinely inform the public. It was often especially interesting to observe the failure of the militant students to make any convincing points. One reason for this was the discipline imposed by the television studio. After a while the students became aware that they were unlikely to be heeded unless they controlled their febrile movements and language, stayed in position and spoke in a manner comprehensible to ordinary folk, rather than one loaded down with socio-political jargon; in general, however, I thought they failed notably to connect with the audience. Although my views were formed as a participant, I later found them confirmed by a large majority of the home viewers with whom I talked.

The deleterious effects of this undue publicity, with its consequential exaggeration of the unrest, worked on the collective mind at two levels. The first was that which concerns the public at large, who were led to believe that something was seriously amiss in the running of our universities. The most eloquent testimony to this pervasive misconception which I experienced was when, at the request of the chairman of the East Midlands Coal Board, Mr Wilf Myron, I was a member of a 'brains trust' at a gathering of miners and their wives; I think it was at Hucknall. There were four main topics for discussion, which were reflected in the expertise of the members of the platform party. I was there to deal with student disorder, and was so bombarded with questions that I am afraid the other panel members had to accept totally minor roles. The burden of the complaints of the miners and their wives could be summarised in the frequently articulated question, 'Why should we pay taxes to support universities which should be educating the rising generation and not allowing this major task to be interfered with by so-called students, whose fees we pay?' This was the authentic voice of the working class into which I was born, and indeed such questions echoed the views of many of the non-academic staff on the Nottingham campus.

The other level, where the effect was much more damaging, was that of Whitehall and Westminster. There, civil servants and parliamentarians alike showed justifiable concern over the reported disruption of the work of the universities; indeed the House of Commons established a committee which, in the 1970s when I was chairman of the UGC, visited various institutions and by so doing fell into the ancient trap of enhancing the visibility and importance of the radicals. Unaware of the realities which university staff dealt with on a regular basis, the committee was led to propose impracticable courses of action to control the extremists: this damaged morale and did no one any good.

By far the most damaging high-level effect, and again one of which I had direct experience at the hands of both Labour and Conservative politicians, was that specious reports of student unrest were taken at face value and seen by politicians as evidence of maladministration. The apparent problems became in their minds a cogent argument for responding less generously to bids for resources, which in any event were under pressure in a period of financial retrenchment. Perhaps of greater long-term significance was an increased impression that universities could not manage their students and, to that extent, the behaviour of the radicals in the 1960s and 1970s was an invitation to government to interfere by legislation in the detailed running of institutions. Future historians may well conclude that the dissidents succeeded in damaging academic freedom, by provoking a reaction which opened the door to direct state intervention in the work of British universities, so evident in the Education Acts of the 1980s and early 1990s.

The details of what happened in Nottingham have been faithfully recorded by Dr Brian Tolley in preparation for his history of the University.[1] As he summarised it in discussion, 'Nottingham was relatively untouched by violent action and displays of aggressive behaviour towards the authorities. Yet all the characteristic signs of student unrest were present, including demonstrations, sit-ins, the occupation of major buildings and the vilification of those officers responsible for the management of the institution.' To understand the situation and how it affected us, it is essential to know the attitude towards students which Barbara and I had when we came to the University.

Our Relationship With University Students

I must begin by saying that with very few exceptions, no more frequent than would be found in any cross-section of society, I have always found it easy to establish good relations with students; many of those whose work I personally supervised became friends for life. I felt that as a teacher my task was to help them to gain the knowledge and skills they required, not merely for the professional careers at which they were aiming, but in a much wider sense. I hoped that my approach and attitudes, the way I treated them and assisted and assessed their work, would constitute 'an attractive invitation to learning' which would stay with them all their lives; that it would help them to enlarge the general capability of their minds and so discover and develop their latent powers of intellect and personality. Of course I never put it to any of my students in such explicit terms; that would have struck them as too pompous and intrusive. But I always hoped that sooner or later they would come to see our relationship in the same light.

In this context it was important not to be too didactic, but to offer students plenty of opportunity to be aware of the limits of my knowledge, letting them realise that I too was a 'learner' like them and would remain so to the end of my days. This is one of the reasons why active participation in research or scholarly work is such a vitally important activity for a university teacher. As Rabindranath Tagore movingly wrote, 'The teacher who has come to the end of his subject, who has no living traffic with his knowledge, but merely repeats his lessons to his

---

1. B.H. Tolley, *The History of the University of Nottingham 1948-1988* (Nottingham University Press, 2001).

students, can only load their minds; he cannot quicken them'. Moreover, there is a reciprocal relationship between the tutor and the student. I learned much from my students when, during our discussions, they would identify flaws in my arguments or ask searching questions which often became the starting point for new lines of enquiry. So it was that we helped each other in our common enterprise of learning. I always felt deeply that this lay at the heart of the relationship between the older teacher and the younger student in the university, the former bringing knowledge and the latter imagination. I felt and still feel that universities have a wholly honourable place in society, which was beautifully expressed by the poet John Masefield on the occasion when he was given an honorary degree by the University of Sheffield. This happened in 1946, when all around us was grim evidence of the destruction and misery which the Second World War had brought about in our great industrial cities. He then said:

> There are few earthly things more splendid than a University. In these days of broken frontiers and collapsing values, when the dams are down and the floods are making misery, when every future looks somewhat grim and every ancient foothold has become something of a quagmire, wherever a University stands, it stands and shines. Wherever it exists, the free minds of men, urged on to full and fair enquiry, may still bring wisdom into human affairs.
>
> There are few earthly things more beautiful than a University. It is a place where those who hate ignorance may strive to know, where those who perceive truth may strive to make others see; where seekers and learners alike, banded together in the search for knowledge, will honour thought in all its finer ways, will welcome thinkers in distress or in exile, will uphold ever the dignity of thought and learning and will exact standards in these things.
>
> There are few earthly things more enduring than a University. Religions may split into sect or heresy; dynasties may perish or be supplanted, but for century after century the University will continue, and the stream of life will pass through it, and the thinker and the seeker will be bound together in the undying cause of bringing thought into the world.

This was in essence the guiding ethos which Barbara and I brought to Nottingham University, and which had served me well in all the previous posts I had held. It was indeed the basis of the unexpressed, but nonetheless real, 'social contract' which I believed should exist between myself and my students, and why I have always regarded myself as an advocate of the real interests of the student body. It was what impelled me to make changes in the governance of the halls of residence (which I had previously canvassed and seen implemented in Leeds), and to persuade colleagues that students had something worthwhile to contribute to the deliberations of many university committees – although I was always clear that students had little to offer in the formulation of course content or the appointment and promotion of academic staff, the selection of applicants for admission or the assessment of their academic progress, from which processes I therefore felt they should continue to be excluded.

Reacting to the First Signs of Unrest

With this as our background it came as a great shock to find that in late 1967, for the first time in our lives, there were students banded together in various groups – labelled as Maoists, Socialist Workers, Anarchists, and so on – who, without know-ing anything about myself and my wife as people, or my past history or what I stood for, regarded me as their natural enemy. I found this very wounding at first, and it took a few weeks for me to realise that while it was still possible to have some quiet reasoned discussion with a student on a one-to-one basis, however radical his or her views might be initially, this was not possible with groups of students already committed to some extreme view or policy. Indeed, that was probably the reason why such students were so reluctant to engage in ordinary conversation with me. Perhaps the most revealing comment came from the daughter of middle-class professional parents (a disproportionately large fraction of the student activists came from this class: I think working-class students had more sense). This young lady expressed her measured criticism of me in these words, 'You are making it very difficult for us [radicals] to see you as a symbol of repressive authority'. I was in fact delighted with this verdict on my actions, but since it was intended as a rebuke I did not dare show my pleasure!

Because the radical students claimed that universities were the complicit agents of a repressive state, I welcomed the idea of setting aside a Saturday for a discussion of the purposes of a university, which anyone could attend. In passing, I should say that we had to use the pervasive vocabulary of the time and refer to it as a 'teach-in'. I took the challenge seriously and went to some trouble to prepare a paper which would be fit to put before any departmental seminar. Indeed,

I considered that to do less than this would have been to debase those university standards which Nottingham should uphold. However, I was deeply disappointed with the outcome. My efforts were a complete waste of time. What most of the students who attended had to offer was not thought but sloganising, and their ignorance appalled me. In response to a question from a student I made a point about the way in which scientific knowledge can powerfully influence society, and illustrated it by citing Faraday and his discoveries; but, from the glazed look in his eyes, I realised he was not following my argument. Not knowing whether this was from sloth or from the blindness of an ideologue, but not believing that it could simply be from ignorance, I asked, 'You do know who Faraday was and what electromagnetic induction is, don't you?' Alas, he was indeed unaware of even the most basic scientific facts, and worse still appeared to be content with his condition. He later revealed to me in conversation that he was an 'intellectual' because he was concerned with society, whereas I, as a scientist, could not be so concerned and therefore was merely an 'intellect worker'. Pity the poor Newtons, Einsteins, and Darwins who have no place in his 'intellectual' pantheon!

Most irritating and depressing of all were the attempts of the radicals to shout down platform speakers. One example of this behaviour will suffice. At the beginning of each academic year a week was set aside to introduce new students to Nottingham (both the City and the University). In the course of this there would be a large meeting in the Portland Building, addressed by the Lord Mayor, the President of the Students' Union and the Vice-Chancellor, who spoke to them respectively about the City, the Union and the University. Questions would then be taken. I enjoyed the first three of these annual 'Week One' events, as they were called, and felt they were of some service to the incoming students. However, on the fourth such occasion I was constantly interrupted and shouted down by small groups of students strategically placed in the audience. I was deeply ashamed of their behaviour in front of the Lord Mayor, and the only redeeming feature of the evening was when I heard the familiar voice of my son John, about to return to Oxford for research after gaining a First in his physics finals, who was attending the meeting out of curiosity. He simply said words to the effect, 'What about the right of free speech? Let us hear the speaker.' He did not return home to Highfield House until very late, having joined some of the radical students who evidently thought they had a new recruit; and he did not disabuse them of this belief.

The Only Possible Response

Incidents like the above convinced me that there was no room for sentimentality, either about myself or about the militants. They represented ignorance and the University was the symbol of knowledge and truth: as its chief officer, I was bound to be their natural enemy. This small minority of misguided, unthinking persons, whose only language was the slogan, and whose aim was to seize power in the Students' Union, must not be allowed to triumph. Such strength as they possessed was derived from their own discipline and determination, and a Union constitution containing rules of quoracy which enabled a small number of committed students to establish Emergency General Meetings almost at will. Inevitably, these would be poorly attended by the other students, who were relatively apathetic. By such devices they could manipulate the Union for their own purposes, and the radicals could call on battalions of like-minded colleagues from other universities whenever some action or a vote was required. To be too heavy-handed in response could easily have won them adherents in the name of student solidarity and victimisation; so (for example) there existed an arrangement by which the police would not come on to the campus to disperse crowds unless summoned by myself, or a senior officer authorised by me – though the students were not aware of this. However, one thing which as bigots the activists did not possess, but which the uncommitted students did, was a sense of humour.

Having concluded that the disruptive elements must not succeed in their dastardly conduct, the question was to decide what means were available for us to deal with them without wasting too much time and energy.

The Earliest Significant Manifestation

Unknown to me, the first 'assault' of the radicals on Nottingham was planned for the summer term of 1968. The first I heard of it was a telephone message from Barbara after dinner on Saturday 15 June, when I was attending a weekend meeting of the Committee of Vice-Chancellors and Principals at Downing College, Cambridge. One of the main items on our agenda was the role of students in university governance; I had been asked to give a paper which, as it happened, contained the major points later incorporated in a concordat agreed between the

National Union of Students and the CVCP. The gist of Barbara's message to me was that fly-sheets had suddenly appeared all over the Nottingham campus, trumpeting the following clarion call:

5000 Students

500 Staff

50 Administrators

ONE VICE-CHANCELLOR.

Where does the power lie?

Where should the power lie?

Join in the assault on the future.

Establish the Free University of Nottingham

In the Senior Common Room in the Portland Building,

Monday 17 June.

I could hardly believe that such absurd pretentiousness carried any real interest for most students, and I had no idea who was behind this anonymous poster. But within the hour John Harris, Vice-Chancellor of Bristol University, on return from dinner at Christ's (his old college) announced to us all that 'Bristol is next', and said that his Registrar had telephoned him with a message that posters of a similar wording had just appeared in Bristol. It was then that I realised the disturbances in various universities were so alike in their timing and content that some national organisation was clearly orchestrating them; that therefore the Nottingham poster was probably the signal for some disruptive action and should be taken seriously; and that some pre-emptive strike should be made. I did not know on the Saturday what should be done, but decided that the Registrar, the Bursar, Professor Haycocks (lately Deputy Vice-Chancellor), the President of the Students' Union (who I could not believe was a party to this anonymous plan) and I should meet on the Sunday, as soon as I returned to Nottingham. During the drive back from Cambridge I became satisfied in my own mind that to ban the proposed meeting would simply be interpreted as confirming their image of me as a typically reactionary, repressive and therefore loathsome authoritarian, which this unknown group would exploit to the full, and would also give them the apparent importance which they were undoubtedly seeking. On the other hand, if I allowed the Senior Common Room – the venue they had selected – to be used for a limited number of days by them and posted notices stating that the SCR lounge was reserved by the Vice-Chancellor for FUN (how grateful I was for that happy acronym which the militants had unthinkingly made available to me!), we might avoid the sort of confrontation the radicals were trying to engineer.

This combination of ridicule and exposure of silliness led to the swift demise of the enterprise, earning for me the sobriquet of 'second-rate Machiavelli' – which I could only welcome as an acknowledgment of their defeat, even if I objected to the adjective and had my doubts that any of those occupying the Senior Common Room had ever read *The Prince* or *The Art of War*. I did not visit the occupation until a few days had elapsed, when I was urged to do so by the Bursar, John Maddocks, who told me that the radicals had some wild plans to take over a large hall in the city where I would be arraigned for my as yet unspecified misdemeanours. I found this difficult to believe, but clearly if it in any way approached the truth it could bring no credit to the University and must be stopped.

My visit to the Senior Common Room lounge proved to be an unforgettable experience. As I entered I saw a young man lying on his back on a sofa and looking up to the ceiling. At intervals he exclaimed rhetorically, 'What is Society?', his arms swinging widely as if imploring an answer. Alas, the ceiling seemed unable to provide one. Meanwhile my presence at the entrance had been noted, and heads slowly turned towards me. A moment of silence was reached and I felt some statement was called for, so I simply said that I had been told of their plan and, since no one denied it, added 'It is my duty to tell you that no one other than myself, or someone I authorise, can hire a hall for any purpose in the name of the University of Nottingham'. They looked crestfallen. What I had heard of their so-called discussion had convinced me that probably many of them needed counselling, so I relented and softened my manner a little; I said that if any of them had problems with which I might be able to help I would always be willing to see them, subject only to them making an appointment through my secretary because I led a busy life. To my surprise a number of students did come to see me, but each tended simply to make statements and to be rather unwilling to engage in dialogue. I did my best with the first few but was distinctly irritated and disillusioned to find that the underground newspaper, grandly named *Red Blob* (a copy of which was regularly and mysteriously delivered to Highfield House), contained totally distorted accounts of what had passed between us. I then felt that if I were to go on trying to be helpful there must be a witness to my conversation with each student, and so the Registrar accompanied me at all future meetings.

Bathos and pathos were often evident in such interviews. One young man, whose name I shall suppress, was particularly memorable. He was adorned in the customary proletarian fashion and wore a hat of his own construction, to which he had stapled a peacock's feather. It turned out that the feather was a symbol of compassion, but only of a generalised kind in which I did not feel I was necessarily included. Having invited him to sit down, I enquired what he wanted to talk to me about. This evoked the surprising statement 'All your actions are sexually motivated'. I confess to being at a loss as to how to reply. My mind was racing for a suitable response from my past experience, but my only persistent thought was whether I would have made the same remark to the Vice-Chancellor of the University of Oxford, the Reverend Dr Lys, Provost of Worcester College, when I matriculated in the Divinity Schools in October 1933; and, if so, what he would have replied. Unfortunately, no inspiration came, so I simply said, 'Is it just me?'

'No,' he assured me earnestly, 'it is everybody'.

Evidently the student was a determined generalist rather than a particularist, but this did not help me with my reply until I suddenly thought of and put the following question to him: 'If it applies to everyone, would you kindly explain to me what was the precise sexual motive which brought you here to make this statement?' He had no answer for this, and since I saw that we were not going to make any progress I asked him if he had anything more to say. Fortunately he had not, but evidently he had something to write because, I think at his inspiration, I was classified in print as 'a bourgeois, liberal, rational obscurantist'. Eighteen months later *Punch* (21–27 January 1970) amusingly depicted on its cover the sartorial as well as the cultural gap between the radical students and others such as myself.

Encounters of this kind made me realise that my time was being wasted by such students, and that it must be turned to more urgent and worthwhile matters. These included coping with endless delays in getting the Medical School building started, largely due to uncertainties over funding and the difficulty of acquiring the proper site. The latter involved a Public Enquiry and, after that had been decided in favour of the University, the threat of litigation from the owners of nineteen acres across the Clifton Boulevard – Messrs Simms, Son and Cooke – who amongst other ploys had tried to circumvent the district valuer's assessment. It was clear that while I could not abdicate ultimate responsibility for student affairs, Norman Haycocks, an inveterate pipe smoker like Herbert Andrew, would be both a more patient listener and a match for them in loquacity. Regular weekly meetings with him were arranged and his conduct of what became known as 'Haycocks' Half Hour', after the lugubrious comedian Tony Hancock's TV show, became legendary and was extremely valuable. This was only one of many occasions on which I was thankful for Haycocks' loyalty, patience and wisdom: without him the containment of the radical students, so necessary for the preservation of the values and peaceful working of a true university, would have consumed much time and energy that I just could not spare whilst seeking to meet more effectively the needs of the genuine students who wished to learn.

In my early years at Nottingham I was confident that those who were voted into membership of the Students' Union Council, or who became Union Officers, were truly representative of the students who comprised the electorate. This was because there was a guild system which essentially divided that electorate into constituencies, each choosing one of their own number as a Council member: this person, by definition, would be someone they knew well and saw often. When that structure was changed to the more usual single-constituency arrangement, genuine representativeness became harder to maintain and a determined group of political activists could create a great deal of mischief.

Revolution and Change

In May 1968, rioting students in Paris not only brought the government to its knees but were also able to activate sections of the working class. Even though their uprising was defeated in a few weeks by the government, this was a remarkable achievement and I have no doubt that it was seen by some British radical students as an inspiring paradigm of how they too might achieve their true aims. I was aware from the press of what was going on overseas, but I was so busy that I could not pay detailed attention to it or take alarm that it might infect our students at Nottingham. One reason was that the 'Swing Away from Science' report had been published in

February. This involved me in additional lectures in Nottingham during the year, and further special lectures in London and Edinburgh as well as in dealings with the Schools Council, the CVCP and other bodies to which I have already referred. Moreover the CVCP and the Council for Scientific Policy, and their steering and preparatory groups, took up much time, and Barbara and I had planned a six-week world tour taking in the Commonwealth Universities Conference in Australia. On that journey, which also included eastern and western Canada, plus California (where the Berkeley troubles were at their height), the preoccupation of university administrators with student revolt was only too evident. They all reported experiences which, though they varied in the degree of violence involved, showed many common characteristics irrespective of country.

I also had another matter to think about. On the Friday afternoon immediately before our departure on Sunday 28 July, I was attending a meeting in London when I was summoned to see the Secretary of State for Education and Science on a matter of great urgency. No one at the meeting seemed to know why, and I had to wait until I saw Mr Short who, in his characteristically direct and economical way, stated baldly that he wished me to be chairman of the University Grants Committee in succession to Sir John Wolfenden, who would retire in the autumn. This was a complete surprise. Although he wanted a quick answer, I knew I needed time to consider the matter carefully and that this could not be achieved in the next 36 hours, all that we had left to prepare for our imminent circumnavigation of the globe. During the trip Barbara and I discussed the pros and cons. The only pro was that to accept would have released me from the tedium of the unproductive work caused by the student unrest, and would have placed me in a position where I could have given more effective support to other hard-pressed vice-chancellors by explaining the realities of the situation to government, thereby helping to prevent any heavy-handed intervention in the affairs of individual universities. On the other hand, there was one absolutely conclusive counter-argument. This was simply that I had been induced to go to Nottingham by the promise of the Medical School. To leave after only three years (as I would have to do) would place all concerned with that School in an impossible position and would put the whole enterprise at risk. I do not recall even telling anyone at Nottingham of Mr Short's invitation, except Sir Francis Hill and Paul Granger, who had succeeded him as President of the Council; for obvious reasons, both supported me in declining. Once the decision had been taken I was much relieved, and hoped to be able to concentrate on the University – as I did, apart from my ongoing work with government committees and my chairmanship of the National Libraries Committee.

In the fifteen months which followed our return from foreign travel a good deal was accomplished. Although in March 1969 the Senate rejected the report of a sub-committee which had recommended, in line with my paper to the CVCP, that students should be represented on Senate for the discussion of all items except those falling into the 'reserved areas' category, I was able to convene a special meeting after Easter to consider a variant of this proposal. The principle suggested was that Senate would discuss all items, except those in reserved areas, with six elected student members present, and for that purpose would call itself the Senate Board. After the students had departed, the first act of the Senate would be to accept the report of the Senate Board, and then it would proceed to deal with the reserved business. The then President of the Union, John Dunford, and his fellow members of the Union Executive found this arrangement quite acceptable. However, just when the matter seemed settled, they were attacked from the rear by a singularly unstable radical student called Tim Smith, whose purposes were purely political and wholly destructive of the notion of a university as an institution motivated by the ideals of Whitehead and Masefield.

Greatly to the surprise of many academics who knew Smith and his total unsuitability for any post of responsibility, he was elected to succeed John Dunford, whom he abhorred, and began a campaign to repudiate the reserved areas limitation on business, which had been working reasonably well.[2] In this he was encouraged by the example of the National Union of Students which, under the leadership of Jack Straw, disowned the concordat agreed with the CVCP; this was the nadir of relations between the Administration and the Students' Union in Nottingham, and occurred just after I had, with the President of the Council's permission, accepted

---

2. In 1969, the year in which Smith was Union President, the Nottingham Socialist Society boasted that it was 'the Society that controls the Union'. It made no secret of its three aims, *viz.* student power, anti-capitalism and anti-imperialism, nor of its methods (or 'revolutionary praxis' as it was grandiosely named), both within the University and outside (for example, in Nottingham schools). *Red Blob* was its undated, irregularly published, four-page broadsheet. Though overtly supporting 'academic equality and democracy', its members made a practice of interrupting and rendering inaudible the expression of contrary opinions by anyone else.

Mr Edward Short's invitation to become chairman of the Council for Scientific Policy from 1 January 1970.[3] I undertook this task because I was aware of (and wished to counter) some forces inimical to the Research Councils, bodies which I regarded as vital to the health of government-supported basic and strategic research in science, engineering and technology. As the student unrest worsened I foresaw that I would not be able to discharge effectively my duties as chairman of the CSP if I had constantly to deal with the destructive antics of Smith and his cronies. Fortunately, however, at this point Smith called a Special General Meeting of the Union to endorse his motion that the Trent Building, which contained the administrative offices, should be 'occupied' until Senate accepted his demands for full membership and thereby access to reserved areas. Widespread cancellation of lectures and laboratory classes by my academic colleagues enabled large numbers of students to attend the meeting, and Smith's motion was rejected: he resigned and was replaced by David Knowles-Leak.

It was around this time that I was telephoned by Sir Folliott Sandford, Registrar of the University of Oxford and a man of few words, who baldly invited me to withdraw from membership of the Board of Electors to the Dr Lee's Chair of Chemistry in that University. Although I was just aware that I was a member, I had had no recent contact with the University and none with the Board, which had not been convened during my term of membership. I was much taken aback by this terse request: indeed, I was slightly annoyed and felt that if this conversation were typical of the Board's conduct of its business, I was well out of my membership.

Several days later I had another telephone call from Oxford. This time it was from the Vice-Chancellor, Alan Bullock, whom I had met when he was chairman of the Schools Council. His message was equally simple, and to the effect that the Electors to Dr Lee's Chair had met and it was their unanimous wish to invite me to become Professor. I was greatly surprised and sought time before giving an answer.

---

3. Jack Straw had entered the University of Leeds to read Law just before I left that university and became President of the Union, where he earned the distrust of Sir Roger Stevens, the Vice-Chancellor. Between 1969 and 1971 he was President of the National Union of Students and he became MP for Blackburn in 1979, in succession to Barbara Castle. The year before he became President the NUS revoked its own constitutional veto on making political statements, and thereby opened the door to its own politicisation and that of affiliated student unions. Jack Straw became Home Secretary after the 1997 General Election [and then Foreign Secretary in 2001 (BHD).]

The more Barbara and I thought about this matter the more acceptance seemed to be the right course because, if seen by civil servants and ministers as the occupant of this prestigious chair in science, I would be able to be more effective as chairman of the CSP. Moreover, I was by this time confident that, despite all the setbacks we had experienced, the building of the Medical School and teaching hospital would certainly go ahead: a new science complex could be used to teach some medical students beginning in October 1970, and so the whole project was secure. Furthermore, earlier in 1969 and armed with all the authority which fell to the chairman of the National Libraries Committee, which had produced a widely acclaimed report, I had approached Ken Berrill (who had succeeded Wolfenden as chairman of the UGC when I declined the post) for funds to build a proper Arts and Humanities Library at Nottingham; and the case had been accepted. So to leave Nottingham at this particular juncture would be to leave a university which was well found in essential teaching, learning, sports, health service and residential buildings, and ready to make a distinguished contribution to medical education in the future. Nobody could possibly accuse me of dereliction of duty.

Red Theatre in the Great Hall

Despite the resignation of Tim Smith the radical students had not capitulated. He and his conspirators, with the support of like-minded people in other universities, notably Warwick, had espoused the so-called 'secret files' issue as one which would have popular appeal (the claim being that administrative records routinely contained adverse comments which could be invoked to the detriment of the student concerned). What happened has been scrupulously recorded in Dr Tolley's history, so here I will touch only on those matters that affected us personally.

On 6 March 1970 Brian Flowers, chairman of the Science Research Council, gave a lecture in the University. As we walked back after dinner in the Portland Building to Highfield House, where he was staying the night, I was astonished to see lights and signs of activity in the Trent Building, but I forbore to comment. A little later Knowles-Leak, as President of the Union, called to tell me of the 'occupation', which turned out to number some 300 young people. From the gear they left behind, for example blankets bearing institutional ownership marks (which we later returned to their rightful owners), it became clear that some of the protesters came from other universities. I was able to confirm this when I walked round the building, as also did Norman Haycocks and the Bursar, who kept himself remarkably well informed as to what was going on. Between us we were able to identify about a dozen of our own Nottingham students, whose names were taken after they had been told they were in breach of University regulations. It then appeared that Tim Smith was chairing some kind of 'general assembly' of the revolutionaries in the Great Hall under the glare of spotlights, with red shirt and Mao book from which he read; indeed, all the theatrical aids he could muster to enhance the sense of drama and maintain the level of excitement. This was all heady stuff for young people ushering in, as many of them thought, some brave new world.

Alas, reality rarely matches such high hopes. On 10 March an Emergency General Meeting of the Union took place. There was a very large attendance, again made possible by suspending lectures and laboratory classes, and part of the audience had to be accommodated in several additional rooms equipped with loud-speakers relaying what took place in the Great Hall. The meeting was addressed by Harry Lucas, the much-liked and trusted Warden of Cripps Hall, who explained what the University was prepared to do in granting students access to their own records (under safeguards), but never to those of a fellow student. He spoke very effectively, a motion to end the occupation was carried by a majority of three to one, and the Union agreed to pay for any damage which had been caused. Characteristically the students, quite naturally wanting to forgive and forget, also asked that no disciplinary or legal action should be taken against any individuals. In effect they had voted for an amnesty.

Taken together, I considered these events to be rather a sad episode in the life of the University. I was dismayed by the way in which the students could be so easily misled by the specious arguments of demagogues who played on their credulity, ignorance and prejudices. In my wanderings through the Trent Building when the 'sit-in' was in progress, I was particularly struck by the unreality of some of the views expressed to me. One student claimed that society should be completely free. When I reminded him of Burke's famous phrase, 'Liberty, too, must be limited in order to be possessed', he, though stating he was a philosopher, was either unwilling or unable even to discuss such a proposition. Another third-year student (reading politics) could not grasp the simple fact that if Parliament, which votes the money for universities, considers that they can not manage themselves, central government will take over. Barbara, who continued her friendly habit of talking to students, not knowing or wishing to know whether or not they had taken part in the sit-in, was solemnly informed by an apple-cheeked young chemist to whom she identified herself, 'We know that he [the Vice-Chancellor] spent his early life making money out of chemistry, and that is why he is going to Oxford'. Presumably to counteract the collapse of the sit-in, an issue of *Red Blob* which was published about this time claimed that the radical students had not failed, since they had got rid of the Vice-Chancellor!

In contrast to these students' behaviour, the loyalty of the non-academic staff of the University – particularly the porters, technicians and cleaners – was quite exemplary, and their common sense and matter-of-fact approach had a salutary effect on the mishmash of ideological claptrap which characterised the remarks of the occupation leaders. I remember going to my office in the Trent Building early on 9 March to collect some papers, just as an elderly cleaning lady arrived on her bicycle. Students are not by nature early risers and the occupying forces had certainly stayed up late, no doubt enjoying the diversionary entertainment provided by Tim Smith. An unkempt lad was just stirring on the floor in the hall outside my office. The cleaning lady took one look, sized up the situation and said in firm tones, 'You're dirty. Go away and get washed.' Without a word he meekly rolled up his sleeping bag and left the building.

There is a sideline on the press coverage of the disruption which I should add here: namely that while in the FUN episode I had been generally regarded as a 'dove' among vice-chancellors, the press later achieved the ornithologically impossible feat of converting prey into predator by dubbing me a 'hawk' because of my behaviour during the 1970 sit-in. I should however emphasise that my experiences of student unrest were not comparable in difficulty with those faced by other CVCP members, especially the Director of the London School of Economics and the Vice-Chancellor of Essex.

When the summer term (which was my last term) began, I hoped that I could generally tidy up affairs and leave to my successor a calmer university than I had recently experienced. Alas, the good name of Nottingham was blemished again by the militants, who disrupted an honorary degree congregation on Saturday 2 May by climbing onto the roof of the Great Hall, in which the ceremony was taking place, and banging metal dustbin lids, thereby creating a cacophony which made some of the orations quite inaudible. I was truly ashamed for the University, particularly as one of those being honoured was the distinguished Trinidadian veterinary embryologist Emeritus Professor Emmanuel Amoroso FRS, who had had a tremendous struggle against poverty and prejudice and who was always a friend of students and the underprivileged. He of all people present did not deserve that his oration should go unheard, drowned by the noise of the barbarians. As the guests were led back to lunch, through an underground tunnel in order to avoid any unwelcome attention from these vandals, I drew a little consolation from the fact that earlier that morning I had been able to deflect some who had intended to come to augment the disturbance. They had rather ingenuously telephoned my secretary in order to discover where the 'demo' was: I directed them through her to Trent *Bridge,* where the South African cricketers were playing, something for which I thought I really did deserve Machiavellian approval.

A Backward Glance

Over thirty years later, when universities are almost totally free of disturbances and students seem entirely preoccupied with other matters and show little interest in protest, the phenomenon of the student unrest of the 1960s and 1970s still calls for some explanation. Purely from my own experience, as a vice-chancellor and later as chairman of the UGC, I find myself not wholly satisfied with the views of those sociologists and others who have given their attention to the matter. Since this is a personal memoir I can proffer my own untutored views.

It is important to say at the outset that there have been, and always will be, issues over which university students will feel dissatisfied. Those which are concerned with curricular matters should be resolved within the institution, preferably at the departmental level. Others which relate to the rules of behaviour of students while on university premises – whether teaching, research, sporting or residential – must not only satisfy the needs of the university for good order and discipline and for it to be protected from wilful damage to its property, but must also take account of the law of the land as it affects the rights of individuals and their safety while on the premises; and, of course, where there is a contract between the university and the student over residential accommodation, the ordinary tenancy laws must also be obeyed. In my experience, all such problems can generally be settled by formal or informal methods provided there is goodwill and common sense on both sides, and for the redress of wrongs access to fair and open mechanisms which follow the laws of natural justice. However, when the concerns of students (or for that matter of anyone who works in the university) lie outside the range that I have described, they cannot necessarily be resolved internally.

The sense in which I have used the words 'student unrest' implies that the issues raised by the students involved in unrest lie outside the above range, and that their motives are ulterior. The university is then simply the stage chosen by those whose views go far beyond any real concern for the institution or their fellow students, and who wish to pursue other ends. The reasons for which they choose the university as their platform probably include the hope of capturing the hearts and minds of young people who may be tomorrow's leaders, and who are seen as naive and possessed of tender consciences, ready to enrol – often unthinkingly or romantically – under the banner of 'student solidarity'. These young people are often too inexperienced to realise that they are being manipulated and that the results of their actions may damage those very institutions where free minds, honestly pursuing truth, can bring light and progress to the world. Student unrest of this kind thus plays into the hands of the reactionaries.

It matters not that the militant leaders may be impelled by what were originally worthy motives. Protest about American involvement in Vietnam or about racial discrimination, for example, should have been on the streets where the people were, and should not have been directed at any university unless it had unfair discriminatory policies. To disrupt the working of institutions whose mission is the pursuit of objective knowledge is to harm the very cause espoused, because no issue can be resolved if it is not exposed to the twin searchlights of truth and reason. I have talked with radical students in many countries, and this experience has provided me with ample material to illustrate the points I have made. From my observation of French and German universities, for example, I would say that if I had been a student in either country thirty years ago, I would have been active in trying to remedy the damaging consequences of poor conditions for study, with professors so hierarchically grand that they had little concern or time for the welfare of undergraduates – who often had a raw deal pedagogically, absurdly long and ill-contrived courses, little pastoral care and negligible staff–student relations. From what I know I consider that all the agitation of university students in these countries, all the damage and mayhem inspired by the Red Army Faction or Danny Cohn-Bendit, actually had little beneficial impact on the real student problems.

In Britain the situation was totally different. There were less demanding student–staff ratios, shorter undergraduate and postgraduate courses that were more carefully structured and had low failure rates, much small group and tutorial teaching, excellent careers counselling and medical services, a good provision of residential accommodation, and finally an acceptance by successive governments of the 'Robbins' principle that would-be students who had established a good claim on academic grounds should be provided with a place,[4] and of the Anderson Committee's earlier proposal that students who had been admitted to a university and had a UK residence qualification exceeding three years should be eligible for generous financial help. How, one might ask, in such circumstances could students in the UK be justified in attacking their own universities? There is no adequate answer. The fact is that when I put this question to *enragés* at Nottingham the reply was usually to the effect that the university was not really free (that word being undefined) but was the instrument of an oppressive or capitalist society or of the 'military–industrial complex', or other variants of these terms. When I asked 'If you are so disapproving why do you remain a student, and what would be the intellectual principles of the institutions you would establish to replace existing universities?' there was rarely any answer. One student did say that I was an 'arch-manipulator' and that the reason for this assertion was that my concern with the flow of young people into science and technology showed that I saw individuals merely as cogs in an industrial society. I thought he had a partially defensible argument there, but he would not debate it with me.

I think that much of the evidence, and certainly all my own experience, overwhelmingly points to the conclusion that the student activists' real objectives had little to do with achieving improvements in British universities. Their goals were extraneous to the purposes of universities, which just happened to be the places where they congregated. They simply emulated the actions of their contemporaries in other countries and, in so doing, adopted subversive gurus like Marcuse and R.D.

---

4. This was proposed in the report 'Higher Education' from a committee under the chairmanship of Lord Robbins (published in 1963 as Cmnd. 2154). The 'Robbins Report' foreshadowed a substantial expansion in student numbers, starting in the 1960s, and the establishment of several new universities.

Laing. We older people also paid too much attention to them and that fuelled rather than quenched their conviction of the correctness of their views, as well as encouraging them to believe that university administrations were 'soft' and would ultimately collapse. The ease of entry into higher education during the period of expansion of student numbers, and the generous financial subsidies for which many were eligible, led to an overvaluation of their own importance – something which was frequently not subject to correction by living among ordinary working folk with down-to-earth concerns about jobs, welfare, health and housing. Indeed it was notable that Glasgow University, where the great majority of the student population lived at home, was the least affected by student unrest.

My conclusion is that the student agitation experienced in nearly all British universities during this period was a great illusion for the participants, and for the vice-chancellors a great distraction, while for the country as a whole it simply harmed the cause of an important and civilising estate – the universities.

> *We must learn ... from all who know, no*
> *matter who they are. We must esteem them*
> *as teachers, learning from them respectfully*
> *and conscientiously. We must not pretend*
> *to know when we do not know.*
>
> Mao Tse-tung, 30 June 1949

CHAPTER 7

A MUCH-DISTRACTED CHEMIST
AT OXFORD

His daily amusement is chymistry. He ... sits and counts
the drops as they come from his retorts, and forgets
that whilst a drop is falling a moment flies away.

Dr Samuel Johnson (1709–1784)

In Transition Again

The third term of the English academic year has always been the close season for
student revolutionary activity, simply because it includes the end-of-year examinations for undergraduates. This concentrates the minds of virtually all students;
even the most radical are unlikely to wish to jeopardise their own chances and they
mostly have not the heart to damage fellow students' prospects, while the latter are
not in any frame of mind to man the barricades. Even after the examinations are
over, the mood is relaxed and many students enjoy a relatively carefree period away
from university until the results are published.

For the teaching staff it is a busy time of examining and then planning with
their colleagues the programmes to be offered in the next academic year, and they
eagerly look forward to a long vacation which will give them an opportunity for
relatively undisturbed research. Administrators' lives are normally less affected by
such annual rhythms. However, Barbara and I were making a double change in our
lives, leaving Nottingham and also changing back from university administration
(though not from national science administration) to the life of an Oxbridge
professor. We were also leaving a 'tied cottage' – if one is permitted to describe so
derogatively the lovely Highfield House, so perfectly suited in location and

architecture to its function – and seeking whatever accommodation we could buy in or around Oxford. Happily, for the children the change of house in 1970 came at what was probably the least disturbing moment of their lives. John, who graduated in 1969, had already completed one year of research for his DPhil degree in nuclear physics in Oxford; Mary was in the middle of her undergraduate medical course at St Hilda's College, Oxford; and Rosalind was due to enter Bristol University to read physics, but had not yet gone up.

There was also a non-human member of the household to be considered. When our marmalade cat, Whiskers, died we considered that a dog would be an appropriate replacement (we had already tried gerbils and found them less than endearing – though good for exemplifying the facts of life). Therefore, in 1968 we had acquired a black and white Welsh Border collie whom we named Shep. He proved to be an intelligent, obedient and loyal friend. Although he could get plenty of exercise on the campus, where he became well known, and in the adjacent Wollaton Park, I felt he must have continuing experience of hills and sheep to satisfy his natural instincts. This was the pretext I used to escape early on Sunday mornings to the Peak District of Derbyshire. Shep was in his element on those hills and so was I, and four to six hours of hard walking was a great rejuvenator for facing the coming week.

In leaving Nottingham I was in fact moving to two major jobs. The first, that of Dr Lee's Professor of Chemistry, did not trouble me intellectually: I knew I could do what lecturing and administration was required, and that I was still sufficiently equipped to supervise research in my usual fields. However, I also knew that the demands of the chairmanship of the Council for Scientific Policy would make it necessary for me to have a young colleague who could act as a lieutenant; I also needed certain equipment which was not available in Oxford. Some time was therefore spent in attending to these matters, and I had the good fortune to be able to appoint Dr Mike Pilling, a Research Fellow of Churchill College, Cambridge, to the staff of the Physical Chemistry Laboratory. I do not think I could have coped in Oxford without him and Paul Gore, the laboratory administrator, who had all the virtues of a former colonial civil servant.

It was difficult for Barbara and me to get away together to inspect houses, but in the end we found what we wanted some four and a half miles from Oxford station. The house, Fieldside, was large enough for our books and children, and since it was surrounded by fields it suited Shep, for whom a suburban street would have been a form of imprisonment. Fieldside served us well for 23 years.

We moved in September and were helped to settle into the house by Rosalind, who had just returned from a summer in the United States and proved herself to be a fast-working interior decorator. As soon as we were installed we drove up to Stirling to join Duncan Davies, head of ICI's central R & D planning unit, who had arranged for several of his colleagues to link up with some of ICI's consultants (including myself) for a few days of brainstorming – by no means restricted to chemistry. As a result of this it occurred to me that the Oxford chemistry experience would be enhanced by inviting guest speakers, sometimes chemists but not always, to visit the laboratory and broaden our horizons. When I tried it the students voted with their feet, and the attendances were good. Indeed in February 1972, when the speaker was Shirley Williams (who had just written a *Times* article headed 'For scientists the party is over'), the main lecture theatre was full to overflowing and we had to relay her talk into another room as well. Three students and one post-doctoral fellow from that time, with whom I am still in contact, have often said to me how important those talks were as a watershed in their thinking about what they might do in the future; indeed, all four of them have enjoyed very good careers in fields that are outside chemistry.

Oxford Rediscovered

Apart from the larger number of pedestrians and the great increase in traffic, Oxford was superficially much as I remembered it before the war – even to the extent of many shops with familiar names still occupying the same sites. Of course the University population was about two and a half times that of the Oxford I had left: new undergraduate and postgraduate colleges had been established and many old ones had been extended, often at some distance from their central sites, whilst the science area was also greatly enlarged. But within the quadrangles life appeared to have kept its traditional pattern, an impression seemingly confirmed by the retention of ancient customs at my old college of St John's (where, as an Honorary Fellow, I occasionally dined) and at Exeter College, where as the holder of Dr Lee's chair I was automatically a non-stipendiary Fellow. In reality very significant changes were still occurring, not least the fact that the men's colleges were in various stages of considering the acceptance of women as members. The rhetoric expended on this issue was followed by a Gadarene rush which was not altogether lovely to behold. As our friend Oliver Franks (the former British Ambassador to Washington) took a wry pleasure in telling us, it was not many years since his college had taken an inordinate number of meetings to agree to the principle to be observed in inviting women as guests for dinner at high table – an extremely weighty matter! (The motion finally accepted was that a Fellow might be permitted to invite a woman as his guest, provided that the woman was the kind of woman who would have been invited had she been a man.)

For my own part, I found life as a Fellow of Exeter College very similar in its customs and procedures to those I had experienced in St Catharine's, Cambridge, nearly a quarter of a century earlier. During my time as a Fellow, Sir Kenneth Wheare retired as Rector and a successor had to be elected. I noted with some pleasure that, although the procedure and some of the arguments were very similar to those I had experienced in Cambridge on equivalent occasions, they worked somewhat more smoothly at Exeter, and the matter was concluded on time and without acrimony.

Other colleges were most welcoming to us both, and my diary shows that we attended twelve dinners between the end of November 1970 and the beginning of June 1971. Quite frequently the conversation would turn to the transition which I had made, from vice-chancellor back to academic: in other universities such a change was regarded as highly unusual but, believing that there was no better place than Oxford, most Oxonians found my choice entirely reasonable. Sometimes this view was accompanied by a degree of condescension, which was precisely expressed at St Hugh's in the Trinity Term of 1971 when the Principal, the distinguished archaeologist Dame Kathleen Kenyon, gave a private dinner party for us in her house. At one point during the meal she turned to me and said, 'How nice it must be for you, Professor Dainton, to come back to Oxford from the provinces'. I felt sure it was well meant but it stung me, and I responded by saying that I found the transition from the provincial to the parochial interesting. This was not an original thought, but nonetheless I do not think I have had a remark like hers made to me in Oxford since that date. Whether that is down to pure chance or is real evidence that the University retains the close-knit character of old-style village life in which gossip still flourishes, I have no idea.

Less than two years later I found the same degree of self-assurance in another distinguished archaeologist. The subject of archaeology sits awkwardly between the British Academy on the one hand and the Royal Society on the other, and in order to clear my mind as to what would be the better location, and more importantly what would be the best Research Council to assume responsibility for its funding, I entertained Sir Mortimer Wheeler to lunch at the Athenaeum. Though in his early eighties, his erect carriage and mane of hair gave him a striking leonine appearance. Having sat down at a table and ordered food, I called for a half bottle of wine. Before the waiter could leave, Sir Mortimer said 'Make that a whole bottle'; I did not countermand the order. As we proceeded through lunch I came to the point and put the question as to what kind of a subject was archaeology. Gazing at me with great affability, no doubt partly engendered by the wine, he put his hand on my forearm, looked benignly at me and said, 'Dear boy, archaeology is not a subject. It is a *vendetta*'.

It is a matter of regret for me that I had little contact with the undergraduates of Exeter or indeed any college, apart from in the laboratory, but on several occasions I was invited to middle common rooms (which minister to the needs of postgraduate students), and there I found the conversation refreshing and delightful. The young people were talented, drawn from varied backgrounds of country, social class and subject, and willing to discuss any issue in a totally open manner.

The Laboratory and Related University Matters

Even if I cannot entirely echo Samuel Johnson's words at the beginning of this chapter, chemistry was to me a solace and by the end of the Michaelmas Term 1970 I felt well settled into the Physical Chemistry Laboratory. I was made to feel very welcome by my departmental colleagues, some of whom I had known for many years. My undergraduate tutor and Part Two supervisor Tommy was now rather grand, being Professor (*ad hominem*) Sir Harold Thompson, Foreign Secretary of the Royal Society, which gave him many enjoyable opportunities for travel and involvement in international scientific affairs. He was also a big wheel in the Football Association, ultimately serving as Chairman between 1976 and 1981. He accepted my role as his 'boss', as he expressed it, with good grace. Leslie Sutton of Magdalen and John Danby at St John's were familiar friends, and of course Ted

Bowen, at least five years retired, was still his irrepressible, enthusiastic, sunny self and a regular attender at our Monday colloquia. The majority of the other staff were young and I knew them by repute rather than personally, though we had given a lunch party for all of them, and their wives, in Trinity Term 1970 during one of our house-hunting forays. I owe a great debt to Richard Barrow, long-time Fellow of Exeter, who proved to be an unselfish and wise guide, philosopher, friend, interpreter and demystifier of post-war Oxford. So too was 'Tim' (Sir Ewart) Jones, Waynflete Professor of Chemistry, whom I had come to know and like in his Manchester period. The third departmental head was Stuart Anderson, Professor of Inorganic Chemistry, whom I had first met as long ago as 1931 when staying in the Gilsland youth hostel.

I must say that I was shocked to see three totally independent chemistry departments in Oxford at that time, all involved in providing courses for the same students for the same degree. There seemed no desire to give undergraduate teaching a coherent intellectual framework, which would enable students to gain from the lectures a broad synoptic view of the subject; I saw no sense in not having one unified chemistry department. Having worked hard to persuade IBM to give a considerable sum of money to establish a chair of theoretical chemistry at Oxford, it was a great disappointment to me that the first incumbent, my old friend Charles Coulson, opted for another separate department. His decision was both wasteful of resources and intellectually the antithesis of the symbiosis which should exist between theorists and experimentalists in all science. Happily, the theoretical and physical chemistry departments have since been amalgamated, although the subject as a whole still has divisions.

To be back in a laboratory, sharing in the common purpose of teaching and research with able people of all ages, was a welcome change from the life of a vice-chancellor, and I approached each day's tasks with pleasure. Within the laboratory reason generally prevailed, and in the final analysis those involved in University politics were predominantly concerned with securing the best outcomes for the institution. It was plain to see that whether the task was to find a professor of the history of science, to which chair Margaret Gowing was appointed in 1972, or to identify a successor to Leslie Sutton in magnetic resonance, for which we were able in 1973 to persuade Ray Freeman to return from the United States, the same considerations motivated all those charged with the responsibility of choice. Added to these pleasures was the constant flow of visitors. Some were friends of long standing, such as John and Priscilla Magee of California who stayed for three months. Others, such as Dick and Win Noyes from Oregon and Huw Pritchard from York University, Toronto, stayed for a whole year. All these people taught me a great deal. Other old friends welcomed me back to the Gordon Conferences in New Hampshire and to a Deutsche Bunsengesellschaft meeting in Jülich, concerned with the electron in condensed media. I was always invited to give a paper at these meetings, which restored my self-confidence and was an added incentive to re-learn my subject: I soon discovered that re-education was still possible, even after five years of almost complete neglect.

Among the short-term visitors was Benjamin Levich, a Corresponding Member of the Academy of Sciences of the USSR. He came to Oxford for about two weeks and was especially interested in John Albery's work on solution kinetics. During his stay he revealed his wish to leave the USSR permanently with his wife and two sons, and go to live in Israel. It was explained to him that the Soviet authorities would be unlikely to permit so eminent a scientist to emigrate, though they might allow him to bring his family to Oxford to take up a special fellowship for a limited period. Then, once the whole family was in Britain, a move to Israel ought to be possible. Within Oxford, Levich's untiring champion was Dr John Yudkin, a lecturer in biochemistry and Fellow of University College, who enlisted the support of leading London-based Jews such as Greville Janner. I was brought into the discussions at an early stage because the obvious scientific departmental base for Levich would be the Physical Chemistry Laboratory, and therefore these plans required my concurrence. With my undying memories of Germany some forty years earlier, and the resulting tide of German-Jewish immigrants to the UK, I agreed without a moment's hesitation. When the time came I dispatched an official letter to Levich, inviting him to work in the laboratory for twelve months and stating that living accommodation would be available for him and his family for that period. The consequences of this action were terrible: Levich lost his privileges as a member of the Academy, he was debarred from work in his institute, and his telephone was tapped. His son Yevgeny, who suffered from a weak heart and diverticulitis, was called up for military service – from which he had previously been excused – with predictably adverse medical consequences. I felt as if the spirit of the odious Lavrenti Beria, executed twenty years earlier, still lived on in the

Kremlin. All that we could do at a human level was try to keep in contact by telephoning Levich at pre-arranged Moscow telephone numbers. One Sunday evening in November 1972 there was a public protest meeting in the Oxford Union Society. I made one of these telephone calls, and the conversation was relayed to all those present: it received good press coverage. Given the unforgiving but efficient memory of Soviet bureaucracy, I was somewhat surprised that when Barbara and I visited the USSR ten years later, in company with Sir Arnold and Lady Burgen, we received our visas without difficulty.

Barbara in Oxford

Barbara left Nottingham University with few regrets. Her first term had set the tone in the sense that she was regarded as a mere appendage to me, not even being provided with a seat at the ceremony when Sir George Pickering (of Medical School Advisory Committee fame) received an honorary degree: she had to ask for a ticket, and then was given a place at the back of the hall. This had been preceded by Professor Barrington's refusal to agree to her even attending lectures in the Department of Zoology. It was all in marked contrast to Oxford, where Dame Helen Gardner quickly arranged for her to have dining rights in St Hilda's College; and where, shortly after we moved, John Pringle (Linacre Professor of Zoology) invited us to dinner and at the end of the evening whispered in her ear, 'Would you be willing to come and help us with some teaching in the lab?' Barbara was surprised by this suggestion because she had not taught in a university for over twenty years, but nevertheless was sufficiently attracted by the idea to welcome it without fully considering its implications. Some three or four weeks later John asked her to demonstrate on the animal kingdom course, and to give lectures on molluscs. After a couple of years doing this rather demanding work a vacancy for a lectureship arose at St Hilda's; she was appointed, later being made a supernumerary Fellow and a member of the College's governing body.

Barbara had been active on hospital management committees in Nottingham, and was also a magistrate there. Appreciative of what she had achieved, both the NHS and the bench made it easy for her to take up similar activities on moving. She was appointed to the Oxford bench three months after our arrival, and served on the Oxford Regional Hospital Board (later the Regional Health Authority) for eight years, longer than the normal period because of the reorganisation of the NHS in 1974. By the time she retired from the Authority she had been on almost all its sub-committees, and had served as chairman of some of them.

Unavoidable Diversions from Chemistry

Before leaving Nottingham I had succumbed to the blandishments of the charming Keith (Lord) Murray, a former chairman of the University Grants Committee, to be a member of the committee which he was to chair enquiring into the governance of that vast academic conglomerate, the University of London. This work was very time-consuming, in large measure because we interviewed too many people at too great a length. Keith took the view that if our findings were to prove acceptable, then those who proffered evidence must be given a courteous hearing and a feeling that their views were being carefully considered by the committee. In the event the document we finally produced was broadly accepted by the University, though in my view it was far too bland and I had substantial reservations about it. What London needed was a radical solution which recognised that the two original colleges – University College, founded in 1826, and King's College, founded in 1829 – were now multi-faculty institutions, worthy of the status of a civic university (and, many would say, more distinguished than a lot of them). Queen Mary College on the Mile End Road was also moving in that direction, while the two monocultural institutions – Imperial College of Science and Technology, as it then was, and the London School of Economics and Political Science – were of exceptional distinction. Added to these large institutions were various smaller colleges such as Bedford, Chelsea, Royal Holloway, and the Wye College of Agriculture; a range of advanced institutes such as Archaeology, Art (the Courtauld), African and Oriental Studies, Slavonic and East European Studies; and a number of distinguished medical schools associated with national specialist hospitals (including the Royal Postgraduate Medical School at Hammersmith).

When I moved to the UGC, I learned that it built up the grant of the whole University of London (apart from Imperial College, which was dealt with separately) by aggregating what it had decided to allocate to all these individual institutions. The total sum was then notified to the Court of the University, which proceeded to subdivide it in its own way – a seemingly capricious process that sometimes led to infuriating results. If I had been aware of this difficulty at the time, I think I would have gone to the length of putting in a minority report which would have held, as its basic proposition, that the independent institutions of substantial size should receive their block grants directly from the UGC, which in any case visited them as it did normal universities elsewhere. I did not take that action, partly because I was so busy that I had not attended as many meetings as I should have done. Twenty years later this is precisely what has happened: those independent institutions that are directly supported by the Funding Council still remain members of the federal University of London, and buy what services they require from the centre as and when they need them.

Ever since my days as a research student I had been a member of the Faraday and Chemical Societies, and in due course the presidency of both those learned bodies fell to me, the latter for two years beginning in 1972. This proved to be a particularly demanding task because it came in the period leading up to the complex amalgamation process which ultimately produced the Royal Society of Chemistry. I had been involved in some of these negotiations from the other side, representing the Faraday Society, and now it was my turn to help the unification along from the alternative camp. The extra work, however, was well worth while and had a pleasing outcome for Barbara and myself.

The Annual Conference of the Chemical Society in 1972 was held in the University of Manchester. Barbara came there with me, and the renewal of her acquaintance with that institution was made doubly pleasant by the fact that I was awarded an honorary degree, just as her mother had been before the war. At the conference dinner I found myself sitting next to the Chancellor of the University, Andrew, Duke of Devonshire, whose installation I had witnessed some six years earlier. When I had thanked him for the splendid arrangements which had been made to accommodate the conference, I thought it would be rather fun to confess publicly in my speech that, from my childhood, I had trespassed over his extensive lands at Chatsworth and also at Bolton Abbey in what is now North Yorkshire; and to suggest that since I had accepted an honorary degree from his university the time had come for me to seek forgiveness, and to pay any due penalty for these mis-demeanours. In his response he rose splendidly to this challenge, granting me and my heirs and successors in perpetuity the right to range over his lands as freely as we wished. He made no mention of expiation for past offences, which I thought was extraordinarily generous of him. Then a few weeks later I received a letter from him in his capacity as chairman of the governors of Trent College, near Nottingham, inviting me to be the guest of honour at the annual prizegiving on 30 September 1972 and thereafter to open a new science block. Evidently, forgiveness and expiation were properly balanced in his mind! Since then we have had a long association, in various spheres: life is full of circularities.

The scholarly and scientific strength of the United States of America has grown enormously over the last hundred years, and it has increasingly become the Mecca of young scholars and scientists from many countries. I was conscious of the value of such postgraduate and often post-doctoral experience, all the more so because the war had prevented me from applying for any fellowship myself. As mentioned in Chapter 3, I colluded with Ned Steacie in 1946 to devise a scheme of post-doctoral fellowships for the National Research Council of Canada; and I had always encouraged my own students to follow Valentine's advice to Proteus in *The Two Gentlemen of Verona*, 'to see the wonders of the world abroad', which I quoted to Sir Cyril Norwood in 1937 and which has been a guiding precept in my own life.

Among the most prestigious and intellectually challenging awards available to young Britons are the Harkness Fellowships, created by the Commonwealth Fund of New York and tenable in a wide range of subjects and institutions. They have the unique condition that the holders should travel widely in the United States, which has a powerful educative influence on the Fellows. It is not surprising that the applicants are always of very high quality. Towards the end of my period in Oxford I was approached by the chairman of the British selection committee, enquiring whether I would be willing to become a member. Before giving an answer, I felt I needed to know more about the way in which the committee operated and who its members were. On consulting a directory of Harkness Fellows and Commonwealth Fund Fellows, I found that the chairmen of the selection committee over the first fifty years of its existence were all prominent vice-chancellors or chairmen of the University Grants Committee. Suitably reassured, I allowed my name to go forward. It was a decision I never had cause to regret: it was always highly enjoyable to select some of the most able young people in the land and then watch their progress, not just while they were Fellows but thereafter. The directory itself is a roll of honour of people who, after holding the Fellowship, have gone on to enjoy distinguished careers all over the world and to make a significant contribution to progress in the countries in which they have made their homes. I later became chairman of the selection committee myself, and this led Barbara and me to travel round the United States again from time to time, visiting some of the Fellows during the tenure of their awards. This was hard work, but thoroughly rewarding.

Finally, I must mention another educational body – the Courtaulds Educational Trust. Samuel Courtauld, who was the descendant of Huguenot immigrants, was the creator of the well-known firm bearing his name and a public benefactor in his own right. The Courtaulds Educational Trust was primarily directed towards the support of education, research and development in the fields of chemistry and engineering. The Trustees at the time of my involvement included Sir Frank (later Lord) Kearton, chief executive and chairman of the Courtaulds firm, Viscount Eccles, Lord 'Rab' Butler (who could claim a direct connection with Samuel Courtauld, having married his daughter, Sydney, and some five years after her premature death married her sister-in-law Mollie). I always imagined that I had been recommended by Frank Kearton, who was some four or five years ahead of me reading chemistry at St John's College, Oxford, and had followed a common path of St John's chemistry graduates in going first into ICI. I knew him briefly during the war, and afterwards when I was a consultant for ICI and for British Nylon Spinners, then jointly owned by ICI and Courtaulds. At our meetings it was inevitable that Frank and I would play a major part on the technical side, but there were amusing interjections and entertaining discussions over lunch, often involving the two distinguished politicians. I was greatly taken by Rab's sense of humour and a few years later, when I had dealings with him over the troubles at the University of Essex, of which he was Chancellor, I found him a very wise and kind person.[1] That kindness was manifested to me again when I was admitted to an honorary degree in Cambridge in 1979. Though he was far from well at the time and was not a guest at the official luncheon, he took the trouble to come to Cambridge solely for the purpose of seeing me receive the degree. I was greatly touched. We had a brief conversation during which, knowing of my Methodist upbringing, he noted with wry pleasure that another person honoured in the same ceremony was Archbishop

---

1. On receiving a life peerage Rab chose to sit on the cross benches, and he did not contradict me when I commented, 'It suits you'. I too came to sit on the cross benches in due course, and was honoured to follow Rab as Chancellor of the University of Sheffield, a post he had held for eighteen years.

Basil Hume, leader of the Roman Catholic church in Britain. What Rab did not know was that after the conferment, when we processed from the Senate House to Jesus College where the official luncheon was held, people had crossed themselves and bowed as the Archbishop passed. I could not help thinking as they did so that the finery in which we were both dressed would have given credence to Lloyd George's quip about the Catholic Church being 'salvation through haberdashery'.

The Major Distraction: National Science Policy

In the preceding chapter I mentioned that a major consideration in accepting the Oxford chair was that I would be better able to discharge my duties as chairman of the Council for Scientific Policy than I would have been as a vice-chancellor. However, in taking on that chairmanship I had been aware that it would involve more work on my part than had been the lot of my predecessor Harrie Massey. One reason for this was that I saw a need to get the people who were affected by the decisions which arose from the work of the Council, which in turn had a bearing on the Research Councils' strategies, to understand how such decisions were made. My experience had been that most of those affected – mainly academic staff of universities or research institutes – were largely ignorant of even the most elementary facts, let alone the considerations, which are involved in the formulation of science policy. Furthermore, this was one sector of public expenditure which for many years had increased in real terms, but which I knew could not continue to do so unquestioned – even though the Labour government was committed, in Harold Wilson's famously misquoted phrase, to 'the white heat of the technological revolution' – when other publicly supported sectors, including the universities, were not being sheltered so completely from the vicissitudes of Britain's economic policy and fortunes. The Council therefore arranged to hold meetings with nominated representatives of the universities to discuss these issues, based on position papers presented by both sides ahead of time. So it was that two-day meetings were held in January 1971 and 1972 in the Universities of Manchester and Strathclyde respectively (and evidently judged to be successful by those who wrote to me). I also attended some of the Research Councils' private weekend meetings.

Another reason for the expectation that my duties as chairman would be heavier than those of my predecessor came from my awareness of a growing mood among some Permanent Secretaries that it was inappropriate for research in fields relevant to the work of their departments to be funded by a Research Council, and that such research should instead be resourced and controlled by the department most concerned.[2] This opinion was also held by some members of the Central Advisory Council on Science and Technology, and one of them, Victor Rothschild, was even more radical in his views. Early in 1970 I found that the Department of Education and Science was unaware of this body of opinion, which could affect its responsibility for science and might become influential. I sought to inform Mr Short but was politely referred to Shirley Williams. She at once saw the issues clearly, and we had got to the point of some serious discussions when the General Election of 18 June was announced and all politicians' minds turned away from routine business. This at least allowed me time for thought, during which I reflected that it was just five years since the Science and Technology Act of 1965 had created three new Research Councils (the Natural Environment Research Council, the Social Science Research Council, and the Science Research Council, this last carved out from the old Department of Scientific and Industrial Research) and nearly six years since the CSP itself had been founded. There was therefore a good case for taking stock, assessing any progress made in that period and identifying any weaknesses of organisation or mechanism. To do this would need the concurrence of the CSP itself, but the review would carry much greater weight if the incoming Secretary of State gave a directive that it should be done. This would not only add authority to the enquiry, but would also give a public signal that the government was taking science policy seriously.

The first meeting of the CSP at which this proposal could be discussed and agreed was on 9 October 1970, less than two weeks after I began as Dr Lee's Professor. On 27 October I had my first meeting with the new Secretary of State, Mrs Margaret Thatcher. I began to lay out the problem for her and to describe the CSP's proposal, of which she had been forewarned.[3] I had not got very far when she

---

2. This view came to a sharp focus in the concrete proposal that the Agricultural Research Council should be transferred lock, stock and barrel to the Ministry of Agriculture, Fisheries and Food (MAFF).

3. She may have already discussed it with her Cabinet colleagues, because about that time an announcement was made that all Ministers were reviewing the function of their departments, including their research and development activities.

interjected with questions. This happened two or three times, and I could see my allotted time dwindling dangerously. Moreover, as Dr Lee's Professor I did not expect and was not accustomed to interruption by any former Oxford student of chemistry, however eminent.[4] So I mildly suggested that we might both save time if I could first cover the whole issue before we had questions and answers. There was a very long pause during which I contemplated the possibilities, and my future, and then she agreed. I must record here that from then on I had her full support, from the publication of the CSP's report in November 1971 and throughout the following eight months, in which there was a great deal of public discussion about science policy issues and much intra-governmental argument – in a considerable part of which I was involved.

As we embarked on the review, which turned out to have time-consuming consequences, I enjoyed a brief but splendid distraction in the form of a visit to Paris and Grenoble with Jack Embling, Deputy Secretary responsible for science in the DES. For several years a proposal had been on the table that the UK should have a high flux neutron beam reactor at Harwell. It would have been expensive to construct and run, and agreement to proceed was withheld. Meanwhile, the French and the Germans had collaborated to build the Institut Laue-Langevin at Grenoble, and in 1970 it had been agreed that the UK should become a third partner. This decision was fully justified by the outcome, in the sense that the UK got excellent value for money and in addition provided three directors – J.W. White, Brian Fender and Peter Day, all academic chemists from Oxford. The purpose of our visit was to see this laboratory and the work going on in the institute, and to hold discussions on how neutron-scattering techniques could be turned to industrial use. All went well on the first day, but then on 6 November a telegram was received by Professor Louis Néel, the noted French physicist, informing him that he had been awarded a Nobel Prize. No more serious work was done that day. There was a magnificent lunch, which began about 1.30 in what appeared to be a chateau on a hilltop. Wine of the highest quality flowed in abundance, and the food was excellent. Speeches began around 3 o'clock, and I recall some time afterwards being prodded by Jack Embling to say something. I believe I did, in my faltering French,

---

4. There is a persistant canard that I had taught Margaret Thatcher chemistry. In fact, when she was a student in Oxford I was already a don in Cambridge.

and that it was a success, but by that time anything anyone said would have been received with acclamation. It was a memorable day, and we returned to Heathrow very late: it was not surprising that the next day I fell asleep during the Bodleian Oration, an unforgivable sin on the part of one of Bodley's Curators.

What I thought would happen when the CSP began its enquiry was that our conclusions and recommendations would be sent to the Secretary of State and treated as an internal departmental memorandum, on which she would form her own opinions and take decisions which affected only her own department. At the outset I did not think there would be many recommendations which would go beyond her powers to implement, and I was not prepared for the interest which would surround the publication of our report. The story is told in detail in the next chapter: suffice it to say at this point that the interest partly reflected the fact that, at exactly the same time, the Central Policy Review Staff (newly established by Prime Minister Edward Heath, under the directorship of Victor Rothschild) chose as its inaugural project a wide-ranging review of national science policy. It was soon known that substantial transfers of resources – from the Research Councils to government departments – were to be recommended in that exercise.

After some delay a decision was taken, I know not by whom, to publish our report and Victor's side by side in a government Green Paper, which is essentially a discussion paper designed to attract informed comment. When this appeared as Cmnd. 4814 in November 1971 there was a huge debate in the media, with leading articles and much correspondence in the quality broadsheets and the weeklies, including those that were not exclusively devoted to science, as well as in professional journals. I was surprised by the extent of the furore, but I had little time to ponder its origins: I was too busy dealing with its consequences, which involved meeting scientists, professional bodies and learned societies such as the Royal Society and the Institute of Biology, as well as the media, political party groups, a House of Commons Select Committee, the Committee of Vice-Chancellors and Principals, and foreign science correspondents and attachés – and even making some overseas television appearances.

Concurrently with all this excitement, a great deal of serious work had to be done away from the public gaze. Much of this concerned the magnitude of the funding which Victor Rothschild proposed to shift from the Research Councils to government departments. As described in Chapter 8, all Victor's proposals were ultimately whittled down significantly, but only after lengthy negotiation and, as regards the Medical Research Council, the passage of some nine years.

The sense of activity and excitement which began with the publication of the Green Paper was given a further boost when, on 19 July 1972, a White Paper (Cmnd. 5046) was published setting out the government's final decisions. One of the outcomes, in concordance with the recommendations of the CSP review, was that the Council was dissolved and replaced by a new Advisory Board for the Research Councils (ABRC), of which I was designated the founding chairman.[5] The CSP's demise was then marked by a lunch at Brown's Hotel towards the end of the year, hosted by the Secretary of State; and the members of the CSP dined with their secretariat on that same evening at the Athenaeum. These were very pleasant occasions, at which we could acknowledge warmly all the help we (and myself in particular) had received from our colleagues.

Science Policy Discussions Overseas

As I left the Club I wondered if there would now be an opportunity for me to make room for more chemistry. However, the publication of the White Paper had further stimulated interest at home and abroad in science policy, which led to even greater demands on my time and energy to the detriment of my professorial duties. Among other things arising from the debate, I had to make visits to various countries overseas and these all gave me much food for thought, though I will comment here on only a few of them.

I well remember discussions with Hans Leussink of Germany and Pierre Aigrain of France, who had been closely watching developments in Britain. It was not easy to discern the reactions of researchers in universities and other institutes in these countries but, by a stroke of luck, I had been invited by the University of Göttingen to give a lecture just at this time, to mark the opening of a new Institute of Physical Chemistry. There I found no sense of anxiety among the chemists or the visitors from other universities over the question of funding, which was perhaps to

---

5. It was obvious to me from the outset that the workload of the ABRC would grow rapidly, and with it the burden on its chairman. The chairmanship became full-time in 1990, during Sir David Phillips' period of office – much too late to affect me.

be expected because the West German economy was growing much more rapidly than that of the UK and other European countries; in real terms, there was a steady increase in the money available for basic research. Thought had already been given to government support for the exploitation of applied research, which found wide expression in the establishment of Fraunhofer Institutes to facilitate science and technology transfer for practical ends. I learned much from the wise comments of my German colleagues on the British situation, although enthusiasm for science in German universities was not fully shared by the students. Some of the senior faculty were worried that there might be a disruption of my lecture: with my Nottingham experience behind me I said I could deal with that all right, even though my German was limited.

Canada, which I visited twice at this time, had shown a considerable interest in the British debate and a willingness to learn from our experiences. I was invited to consult with the Science Council of Canada, a strange general advisory body which seemed to me to be toothless, and I also talked with senators who were interested in the issue for political reasons. Later on I attended a memorable meeting in Quebec City organised by the Canadian Institute of Chemistry, where I felt that I was the 'hired gun' invited to fire critical shots at the policy of the federal government with respect to science. I had received a clear explanation of that policy, if as such it can be described, during a morning spent with some assistants of Madame Sauvé, then Minister of State for Science and Technology and afterwards Governor General. I found the experience depressing because none of the persons I met was a scientist, although there was a loquacious social scientist who had absolutely no understanding of the world of natural science, engineering and technology. The depths of his ignorance were only matched by (and could be the sole justification for) the views which he so confidently propounded. As he strove to lighten my darkness, Edmund Burke's claim that 'the age of ... sophisters, economists, and calculators, has succeeded; and the glory of Europe is extinguished for ever' came repeatedly to mind, but I held my peace and did not speak about him even when I was quizzed on television. There are, of course, many problems peculiar to Canada and in particular the different economies of the various provinces, some of which were then strong enough to have research councils of their own – receiving significant provincial financial support – whilst others were relatively poor. The most powerful actor on the science policy front in Canada was the National

Research Council, where for many years after the war the prime mover was the remarkable Ned Steacie, to whom I have already referred. The NRC received its money from the federal government, and used it in the maintenance of laboratories considered vital to the country's non-defence scientific needs. At the same time it also provided resources for research in universities in any province, although the mainstream funding for them came from the provincial governments. The NRC had succeeded in raising the standard of scientific work in Canada remarkably in the years since the Second World War.

Things were quite different when I had discussions with Ed David, who had succeeded Lee DuBridge as Nixon's science adviser in Washington; Phil Handler at the US National Academy of Sciences; and Guyford Stever, head of the National Science Foundation. All three had a clear grasp of the British situation and each could match it with experiences of his own, illustrating that some of the difficulties with which we were grappling were not unique to the UK. I came away with a clear feeling that Nixon was not much concerned with science, but assumed that its standing in the highest levels of the US government was secure. Consequently I was quite unprepared for the information which Ed David gave me over dinner when he was in England during November 1973: he was no longer chief presidential science adviser, having come to his office one morning and, in common with all the other members of staff, found a notice on his desk declaring that his office was shut with immediate effect. He commented wryly, 'At least the President was sufficiently interested to take that action!' It might in some ways be argued that the US was fortunate that Nixon's interests were elsewhere in the next two years, and that the success of that country in space observation and exploration, while using up much of the federal budget for science, produced a mood in government and among the people that still rejoiced in the success of science and did not call for any soul-searching on that account.

Mostafa Hafez was a Sheffield University chemistry graduate with whom I had developed a friendship before the war. By the early 1970s he had become influential as a scientist in the service of the Egyptian government. He and his superior, Dr M.K. Tolba (who was a botany graduate of Imperial College and at that time held the post of President of the Council of Scientific Research and Technology) kept a sharp eye on British science policies, and were responsible for inviting me to Egypt to discuss some of their problems. Thus it was that Barbara and I found ourselves at Heathrow boarding an EgyptAir Ilyushin jet for Cairo just before Christmas 1972. Never having visited the Middle East we had no idea what had been arranged, except that I was to discuss trends in science policy in North America and Europe with whomsoever the Egyptians put before me. For this I had equipped myself with many factsheets and guides.

It was a real joy to see Mostafa's smiling friendly face the following morning, and he and his wife Ann could not have been more helpful to us. He took us to the Academy which he had had a major role in creating, and there we encountered a great number of ragged, unshaven, ill-shod smiling doormen, perched on what seemed like laboratory stools, who when approached would stand up smartly and salute (British army style), open the door, and close it afterwards. This struck us as immensely wasteful of manpower, but of course we were looking at their situation the wrong way round: menial as their task was, these men had the satisfaction of feeling employed, and their self-esteem was much enhanced thereby. Our second shock was to see windows pasted over with strips of brown paper in a trellis fashion to reduce the danger from flying glass should there be an air raid, a precaution which we had come to know well in Britain during the last war. There could have been no more powerful reminder of the tension which existed between Israel and Egypt at that time, and in fact nine months later Egypt launched the unsuccessful Yom Kippur war with the intention of recapturing Sinai, which had been overrun by the Israelis some sixteen years earlier.

Mostafa and his colleagues had arranged a full programme of meetings with the heads of institutions, the Minister of Higher Education and government officials, as well as visits to see a range of laboratories in the major universities. They were facing a desperately sad situation: because of the government's apprehension over the intentions of Israel and its desire to recover lost territory, a disproportionately large amount of the small per capita revenue was spent on defence, and this left very little money indeed for desirable social purposes such as health and education. Moreover, as a result of the Suez crisis and various trade agreements with communist-bloc countries, the USA and Britain had withdrawn their offers of aid. The result was a disaster for higher education: university laboratories were dirty, poorly equipped and in many ways a danger to the health and safety of those who worked in them. In Cairo University the library was pathetic, the equipment was often covered in dust and unusable, and the student–staff ratio was horrifyingly large. At

Alexandria University, which had eight faculties and 55,000 students (including 2,000 postgraduates), the academic staff numbered only 1,000 and the budget was four million Egyptian pounds, of which little more than one per cent was available for equipment purchase each year. I met many Egyptian scientists who had been trained overseas, and some who had come from the Soviet bloc as 'experts' to teach the Egyptians in fields like corrosion and colloid science. They confessed to me freely how difficult it was to get things done with such a great lack of resources. At the same time I was astonished to be shown, with much pride, a 400KeV Cockcroft-Walton particle accelerator. Such an attempt to ape western science seemed bizarre when the basic deficiencies were so apparent. In particular, there was an all-too-obvious need to deal with health problems such as bilharzia and to control the rapid growth of the population. Yet I could understand the desire of able people to imitate the west, which had been so successful in developing and using modern scientific knowledge. I have not the slightest doubt that some of them, especially Dr Tolba, appreciated the conflicts precisely.

One small institution stood out from the rest in the high quality of its teaching and research. That was the private American University in Cairo, where many of the expatriate staff from America and Britain were of good standing and their laboratories were reasonably well equipped. Of course that university could only minister to a small fraction of those who deserved such an education, and even then they had to pay considerable fees.

The bad state of the Egyptian universities was matched by that of some of the museums, which was all the more tragic when one considered the treasures they contained. This was in marked contrast to the great monuments of Pharaonic Egypt which we were privileged to visit in the Valley of the Kings and elsewhere: the perceptive way in which these tremendous artefacts were displayed by *son et lumière* left one with a real sense of awe at the accomplishments which had followed the unification of the kingdoms of Lower and Upper Egypt under the Pharaohs some 3,000 years before Christ. Everywhere we were reminded of the enormous power which can be wielded without machinery if simple principles are understood, projects are well designed and the workforce is disciplined.

As our home-bound aircraft cruised above the Mediterranean on 3 January 1973 we felt great sadness that a country with such a magnificent record of inventiveness and achievement over so many years, especially in agriculture, architecture, irrigation and crafts, was faced at the end of the second millennium AD with these intractable problems. Our concern for the Egyptian predicament was all the deeper because everyone had been so generous and welcoming to us.

Six weeks later I was in Japan, experiencing another culture shock but one of a very different kind. The programme for my visit had been carefully constructed; the British Ambassador and his staff were most welcoming and helpful; and the Japanese officials whom I met went out of their way to provide information and to emphasise how much the British had contributed to scientific development in their country (for example, by providing funds for young Japanese to study in the UK). In the course of my stay I took part in extended discussions with senior staff in Monbusho, the analogue of our Department of Education and Science; with the chairman of the equivalent of our Committee of Vice-Chancellors and Principals; and with the makers of science policy in the Science and Technology Agency, an administrative organ under the Prime Minister's office, rather like our Office of Science and Technology. (I was surprised to learn that some 200,000 scientists, engineers and technologists elect 210 people to membership of the Science Council of Japan, a sort of science parliament whose resolutions are passed to the Prime Minister's office, but I could not discover what effect those resolutions had on policy.) I also had spirited discussions over dinner with members of the Japan Academy (average age 81, but not a wrinkle on any face) and with several other groups. Most of my formal encounters were scheduled to last about one and a half hours, but they often overran by at least an hour because the issues raised were of great interest to both sides. They included such questions as: What percentage of the GNP should be spent on research and development? How is technology assessment best carried out? How can the interaction of scientists and politicians be optimised? What is meant by technology transfer, and how is it achieved? And, of course, the perennial and unanswerable question, what is the best kind of organisation for fostering the development of science policy, and for its management?

To my surprise, many of the Monbusho officials were plainly discontented with some features of higher education in Japan. Their principal complaint, expressed very delicately, was that there were rigidities in academic structures and attitudes which made the educational and organisational arrangements of the universities inflexible, and therefore difficult to adapt with sufficient speed to meet the changing needs of the country.

I did my best to make recompense for all the hospitality and interest shown by giving illustrated talks at the Tokyo Institute of Technology, government departments including Monbusho – which was housed in a singularly unprepossessing building and, for gadget-addicted Japan, had surprisingly poor projection facilities – and also in other cities such as Osaka, Kyoto and Sendai. There was scarcely a moment to spare.

In its population density, gridlocked freeways, advanced manufacturing technologies and so on, Japan bore all the hallmarks of an overcrowded, thrusting and competitive capitalist society (except that it was more disciplined than most, and had very few indigenous natural resources). I soon learned, however, that there were other aspects to Japanese culture. In the intensely crowded residential areas women in traditional dress were not a rarity, and many small workshops were to be found – especially in Kyoto, where, for example, cherrywood was carved with infinite loving skill as part of making beautiful woodblock prints (two of which I managed to purchase). Everywhere there was evidence of a strong attachment to traditional music and theatre, and my hosts took me to several performances. Well-attended temples, with the prayer papers of the devout attached to trees and fluttering in the breeze, testified to the importance of religious observance. I longed to know more about the people as individuals, and how they accommodated working as disciplined operators in an automated environment alongside their simultaneous adherence to traditional beliefs and customs. Did such a juxtaposition not induce schizophrenia? How did it affect personal relations? These and similar questions came to my mind, but most were never answered.

Throughout my visit I was shown great kindness, and on two notable occasions I was made aware of very warm personal feelings towards me. The first of these arose out of my trying to meet the parents of a Japanese research student, Shigeo Tazuke, who had worked with me in Leeds. I had telephoned their home in Kyoto, only to discover that the father – 75 and rather frail – was in hospital for a check-up on his malfunctioning heart. I therefore concluded, with regret, that a meeting was impossible. However, early on the following morning the hotel receptionist announced that Mr and Mrs Tazuke were waiting patiently for me in the hotel lobby. I went down at once to find them, and was enormously touched that they had not only made such an effort to see me, but had brought with them presents for me to take home. My mind went back to 1960 when Shigeo had gained his PhD degree, and his father had laboured long to write in English a letter which accompanied two gifts: a sword guard for me which had been in the family for 250 years, and a string of pearls for Barbara.[6] His respect for his son's teacher was expressed quaintly but movingly at the end of his letter '...and so, dear Professor Dainton, my son Shigeo is yet but a mere green youth and I hope you will continue to give him many spankings over the ocean'. Shigeo and his wife Hiroko were already receiving my circular Christmas letters and I added to the list Shigeo's parents and also his sister, with whom we still correspond.

The second occasion when I felt I was being allowed into the intimacy of family life was on the evening of my departure for home. I was invited by a Mr Chiga, a wealthy industrialist, to come to the Festival of the Girls (*Hina Matsuri*). It was a delightful occasion during which dolls were placed in stepped array on a table at one side of a large room. There was a splendid buffet, following which presents were given to all the girls, who I presumed were granddaughters under the age of puberty. When the formalities were over he asked me if I would like to see the rest of the apartment, and if so where he should begin. I asked to see the bathroom, knowing what a central role it was reputed to play in family life. It lived up to my expectations in size and complexity. Then without my asking he conducted me to his bedroom. It was a compact 'two mat' room which had a thin, rolled-up mattress on the floor and a headrest. Otherwise there was nothing except, in a rectangular alcove, a beautiful small vase illuminated by a hidden light. I thought it might have contained the ashes of an ancestor, but hesitated to put the direct question. However, there was no other object in the room which could command my attention, so I continued to study it. Mr Chiga then said simply, 'I sit and look at it for a quarter of an hour or so before I go to bed at night, and immediately on rising in the morning'. A picture flashed through my mind of this wealthy man, who had already told me he had recently bought a mineral mine in Western Australia for around $200m, going through this routine in the morning, no doubt contemplating the infinities and the inscrutable, and then getting up from his meditations to make a commercial deal by telephone which might involve many millions of yen. It seemed another remarkable dichotomy.

---

6. After the Second World War the Japanese were not allowed to keep complete swords. Long before that, however, decorated sword guards were valued and kept as works of art in their own right.

Chemistry Finally Gives Way to the Inevitable

While in Egypt I had made a New Year resolution, based on my thoughts as I left the final CSP meeting a few weeks earlier. This was to control my engagements outside Oxford to make more time for chemistry, and I had already begun to jot down in my pocket book some possible research problems. I had also started to reject invitations to give popular talks to general audiences in favour of lectures on chemical subjects. However, as the weeks passed I seemed to have made little if any space for myself, and again I felt beleaguered by circumstances beyond my control. I was troubled, because to resign from the public duty I had undertaken would not have served science well when new arrangements had to be bedded down, and yet I could not do justice to the performance of my duties as a professor. It was this feeling, and the sense I was not serving Oxford as I ought, that made me decide to cut my losses and accept an invitation from Mrs Thatcher, early in 1973, to succeed Sir Kenneth Berrill as chairman of the University Grants Committee – the post I had turned down in 1968. This time I accepted, which of course meant that I would have to resign my Oxford chair. I had intended to report my decision to colleagues in the Physical Chemistry Laboratory and in College just before the official announcement was made; however, so acute were the antennae of journalists that the news leaked out while I was presiding over the Annual General Meeting of the Chemical Society in Swansea.

The immediate effect of my decision was actually to add to my distractions from chemistry in the time remaining, because, as part of my familiarisation with the UGC's workings, I accepted Ken Berrill's generous invitation to accompany the Committee on its quinquennial visitations to Sheffield and Hull universities, so that I could meet other members of the Committee and key figures in the secretariat. So much for good intentions!

Barbara and I were now once more facing a major change of direction, soon augmented by Rosalind's announcement, following her First in physics at Bristol University, that she was not going to pursue research for a higher degree in that subject but was joining Voluntary Service Overseas to work in Tanzania. As we drove back from leaving her at Heathrow on 30 August we realised that for the first time in 26 years we should henceforth see our children only occasionally. Fortunately, there was little time for wistful longings for the past and we knew that we must prepare for the future, much helped by our attendance at the week-long eleventh Quinquennial Conference of the Universities of the Commonwealth in Edinburgh, where many old friends welcomed us warmly 'back into the fold'. So it was that after a brief holiday on the Adriatic coast near Dubrovnik we found ourselves with only four working days in which to move my things out of the Physical Chemistry Laboratory; negotiate the lease of a flat in Prince Albert Road, London; have lunch with Brian MacArthur, the Editor of the *Times Higher Education Supplement*; and give lunch to John Polanyi, Professor of Chemistry at the University of Toronto. That meal gave a pleasing symmetry to my time as Dr Lee's Professor, since John's father had been a distinguished professor of physical chemistry in Manchester, as well as an economist and philosopher, and had given us an excellent lunch and good advice almost exactly three years earlier, appropriately enough on the patronal festival of St Frideswide. What could have been more authentically Oxonian?

The following Monday, 1 October 1973, I arrived at the UGC believing that for once I would be able to devote my energies to the main task, and that the King of France's words in *All's Well That Ends Well*, 'But to the brightest beams distracted clouds give way; ... the time is fair again', would prove to be true. I little knew what shoals I would have to negotiate.

CHAPTER 8

SCIENCE AND THE STATE: THE UNEASY BUT UNAVOIDABLE RELATIONSHIP

Nam et ipsa scientia potestas est: Knowledge itself is power.

Francis Bacon (1561-1626)

Preamble

The proportions of the tax revenues spent on the government departments charged with the responsibility of delivering satisfactory national defence, healthcare and education, or financial help for the weak, aged and unfortunate, are all very large and the tasks which these departments perform are broadly comprehensible to every citizen. But science, on which only some two per cent of gross domestic product is spent, is perceived quite differently by the public, most of whom are ignorant of its true nature and indifferent to the government's policies towards it. At the same time there are extreme attitudes at either end of the spectrum, ranging from a blind belief in science as a nostrum for all the ills to outright distrust of it as an instrument applied to exploit selfishly and irreversibly the work of a benign nature. I fear that for a long time a large fraction of the population – and indeed its rulers – will continue to misunderstand the nature, power and limits of science. It is disadvantageous to the nation as a whole that the educational system leaves so many pupils scientifically crippled and, worse still, distrustful of science.[1] When

---

1. This is not a new phenomenon. The late Professor Sir Cyril Hinshelwood used to tell a story about Professor F.A. Lindemann (later Lord Cherwell, Churchill's scientific adviser), whose university education was not in Britain but in Berlin before the First World War. Following his appointment as Dr Lee's Professor

I express my concerns on such subjects, it is often suggested to me that the lack of awareness of science in the population is matched by its ignorance of much serious literature, music and art. That fails to console me, as does the argument that science is complex: although science can indeed be difficult to comprehend, it is extremely pervasive and powerful in its action and its effects. The knowledge it represents is essential to all the departments of government I have mentioned and it is vital to the success of many industries, the efficacy of professional procedures, and the understanding of how the human race can achieve a satisfactory equilibrium with the environment which it shares with other species.

Science is also one of the means by which human beings seek to discover their identities, to find out where they come from and where they might go, what are their constituent parts and how they operate, what is their potential and what is their relationship to the planet they inhabit (and the planet's relationship to the cosmos). Though science makes great demands on the purely cognitive side of human nature, it also speaks to the affective side. We can apply to particular pieces of scientific work – whether conceptual or experimental – such adjectives as profound, beautiful, elegant, prophetic, majestic, humbling, and so on. Science is the stuff of our dreams. To achieve a significant advance in science makes just as great a demand on the intellect, imagination and personality as does the work of creative writers, poets, painters, sculptors and composers.

Science, therefore, has an unusual combination of qualities. It is public and objective knowledge, accessible to all, and it can be tested and if necessary refuted. It helps the human race better to define itself, and the high predictive power of its theories encourages people to identify possible futures. It assists individuals to progress towards satisfying their instinctive curiosity to know and understand a

---

of Experimental Philosophy at Oxford in 1919 he was widely entertained (just as we were some fifty years later). At one college he was sitting next to the wife of the Head of the House, who was a philosopher, and she asked him: 'What is your chair, Mr Lindemann?'

'Dr Lee's Chair of Experimental Philosophy', he replied.

She responded gushingly, 'Oh, how delightful it must be to be studying philosophy in Oxford'.

A little coolly Lindemann explained, 'In other universities they call it physics'.

Not a whit abashed she said, 'Ah, physics. That's waves and things. And that's science. My husband says that every educated person should know something about science, and indeed any intelligent person can learn all he needs to know about science in a fortnight'.

Lindemann is reputed to have replied after a considerable pause, 'What a very great pity your husband never had a fortnight to spare'.

great deal of what they experience through their senses and their imagination. Most importantly, the application of science can considerably enhance human physical and mental powers. It is therefore essential to understand more clearly what it is, how it influences so powerfully the way in which we live, and how it can be used to shape the future. And yet, in common with many other developed countries, we in the United Kingdom continue to debate endlessly about the appropriate level of resources to be allocated to science by government, and the way in which they should be managed. To understand why this is so we need to define more precisely the terms we use and to say something of the historical background of the interaction of science and the state, before examining in greater detail how the situation in this country has developed and is still developing.

What Does the Word 'Science' Comprise?

The etymology of the word 'science' links it firmly to the Latin word *scientia*, meaning knowledge, and that is the sense in which Bacon used it. But within the English language it has come to carry the more restricted meaning of systematic knowledge of the animate and the inanimate worlds. For my purposes I wish the definition to include three distinguishable parts: natural science, engineering, and technology, each of which is susceptible to more precise interpretation.

Natural science is self-defining. It is a body of established facts about the natural world. I employ the adjective 'established', which to a grammatical purist would seem redundant, to emphasise that the facts concerned have so far resisted refutation by direct experiment or new observation. As I have pointed out in Chapter 5, the aim of scientists is not just to establish facts but to systematise and summarise them in laws, and to understand such laws in terms of theories which frequently embody abstract ideas like force, energy and so on. Such theories have two great advantages. First, they relieve human minds of the immense burden of memorising otherwise disconnected facts, and secondly they are a means of predicting the unknown from what is known. This latter feature is both their strength and their weakness. It is their weakness because it contains the seeds of their destruction: one new, established fact, which should but does not fit in with theory, invalidates that theory – which then has to be modified to accommodate it, or abandoned and replaced by another which can satisfactorily encompass more facts than the older one. Progress in natural science is thus evidenced by the replacement of existing theories by a smaller number, of greater power, and readers should not be surprised when told of the aspirations of theoretical physicists to seek an elusive 'grand unified theory' of strong and weak forces.

Engineering, as its name implies, deals with the design and management of engines. Early engineering devices – such as the wheel or the lever – were based on a correlation of cause and effect without any understanding of why the connection existed. Nowadays, empiricism has almost entirely given way to the application of mathematics and science, so that the properties of matter and the sources of energy in nature are well understood and codified by theories, facilitating enormously the design and operation of static or moving structures. We all take it for granted that we can travel anywhere, by land, sea or air at high speed, and that intelligible verbal messages and visible images can be transmitted at the speed of light. Every time a citizen actuates an electrical device in the home – whether it be radio, TV, computer, washing machine, mixer, vacuum cleaner or telephone – he or she is benefiting from products devised by engineers. This is true not only for the domestic device itself, but also for the machines which convert the potential energy of water stored in high reservoirs, or nuclear energy, or the free energy of combustion of coal, oil, or natural gas into the rotational energy of turbines which generate electricity, and the systems which distribute and deliver the current.

All around us is evidence of the use of engineering to enhance humankind's feeble physical strength. My birthplace, Sheffield, exhibits dramatically the effect of growth in scientific knowledge and engineering skills: what was once an extremely grimy city has had clear skies for upwards of forty years, fish swim in its formerly polluted streams, and yet it still makes more steel per annum than at the height of the First or Second World War – but does so cleanly, and with a fraction of the earlier labour force.

Technology involves the systematic study of the processes and knowledge that are required for the production of objects necessary for human sustenance, health and comfort. As such it is close to engineering and applies it to these ends, along with natural scientific knowledge. On this definition the study of agricultural practice, even of medical and veterinary practice, may be regarded as being as much a part of technology as the extraction of oil and gas, the building of roads or the manufacture of consumer goods.

Although I have tried to distinguish clearly each of these three components of science from the other two, I should emphasise that the edges separating them are not sharp and that views may differ on how to classify some subject areas: for example, where does chemistry, part of natural science, end and chemical engineering begin? Such questions are unimportant when compared with the fact that natural science, engineering and technology as I have defined them can be placed in a loop (Figure 1), where each element interacts with its neighbours. New knowledge in natural science about (let us say) spectroscopy, which explores and interprets the patterns of absorption of elecromagnetic radiation by atoms and molecules, creates a demand for instruments (in this case spectrometers) which will be designed by engineering physicists, with colleagues in technology organising the manufacture and assembly of the parts at the lowest reasonable cost. The availability of better, quicker acting instruments enables natural scientists to work more effectively in making measurements, and thereby to advance their knowledge faster. Likewise, since engineering is no longer based on empiricism but on natural scientific principles, both it and the technology it potentiates will benefit and be advanced. Progress in each of the three fields is measured by clockwise movement round the circle, and it is self-evident that such a loop has the potential for auto-acceleratory progress.

In the particular example I have chosen above, the initial impetus for the work was the curiosity of chemists – natural scientists – to know more about the interaction of light with matter. But the starting point can be elsewhere. For example, ophthalmologists may need a new biocompatible synthetic polymer to replace an eye lens that has a cataract; orthopaedic surgeons may need a better hip or knee prosthesis; engineers may need to measure the flow of fluids in opaque pipes. One can think of many possible and real starting points in each of the three sub-fields, and each could be represented by entry at the appropriate point on the circle.

In short, the chief lesson to be drawn from the circle is that the more that fundamental science can tell us about the properties of animate and inanimate matter, whether at the macro or the molecular level, and about the energy changes accompanying chemical transformations, the more engineering will be likely to succeed, and with it technology; and the more they succeed, the more dependent they become on natural science (in which, at the same time, they facilitate research). The symbiosis is complete.

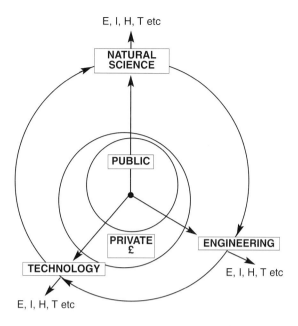

E = Energy   I = Industry   H = Health   T = Transport

Figure 1. The Virtuous Circle

Of course, the work done at any point on the circle has to be paid for. If money is not forthcoming, movement round the circle will not occur. However, each activity may generate income. Indeed, in a competitive world the sole *raison d'être* of technology is to do that successfully: technology generates wealth, often creating at the same time a requirement for more knowledge. Basic natural science and regulatory science, which I shall define later, are for the most part less well placed to generate wealth directly, and must seek their financial support from elsewhere. This is the area in which state subsidies are most needed, and there is much to learn from the history of how government support for natural science, engineering and technology has evolved in this country.

Government Support for Science in the United Kingdom up to 1965

Although Archimedes is reputed to have sought financial help in 200 BC from King Hiero of Syracuse – when the king asked him to determine (by non-destructive testing, I assume) whether his crown, meant to be of pure gold, contained any silver, and Archimedes proposed to do it by suspending the crown in water to ascertain its density – the principle of state support for science was not generally applied until over two millennia later. In the Enlightenment of the seventeenth, eighteenth and nineteenth centuries, eminent natural scientists either used their own resources (like Boyle), or were employed for other purposes (like Leibnitz, Librarian to the Elector of Hanover, or Joseph Priestley, a Unitarian minister, or Gregor Mendel, a monk), or were part of a community of scholars in a university (like Newton). By the twentieth century the situation had changed and scientists in all but the last of these categories had virtually disappeared, their places taken by those who earned their living by pursuing their subjects in universities, industry or research institutes funded by various means. How this came about throws light on how government became involved in science in the United Kingdom.

Today the Royal Society values its connections with the Royal Family, and in remembering Charles II's willingness to grant its Charter in 1662 (albeit at no cost to himself) perhaps forgets that the same King Charles was equally ready to upbraid Isaac Newton for engaging in 'childish diversions'. The state at first assisted only the science it judged would benefit the nation in economic or military terms. The expansion of trade in the sixteenth and seventeenth centuries focused attention on navigation, exploration, terrestrial magnetism, astronomy and meteorology, and the governments of the western world began to take an interest in and patronise science for the useful results its application in such spheres was expected to produce. This kind of argument induced Charles II to found the Royal Observatory: part of the cost was met by the sale of spoilt gunpowder, but even then the Crown provided so little financial means that the first Astronomer Royal, John Flamsteed, was forced to buy some of the equipment out of his own pocket! Similar considerations persuaded Parliament to establish a Board of Longitude in 1714 and, under pressure from Royal Navy captains, to offer a prize for a reliable means of ascertaining longitude at sea. However, the monarchs and Parliament could hardly be blamed for their indifference, because their lack of interest in science was matched by that of England's only two universities, Oxford and Cambridge.

The early years of the nineteenth century were notable for the fact that advances in pure science were made mainly outside those universities, either by teachers such as Dalton in dissenting academies or by those employed by the Royal Institution, such as Davy and Faraday. Davy was particularly outward-looking, and saw the implications for the common weal of a more widespread knowledge of chemistry and its applications. He gave lectures on agricultural chemistry to large audiences and he also reflected on the Napoleonic wars, commenting that science had given Britain the power that defeated Napoleon by enabling '...Britain to display power and resources ... infinitely above what might have been expected from the numerical strength of its population'. Yet in 1830, shortly after these words were written, Charles Babbage of Cambridge – the inventor of the first calculating machine – published his *Reflections on the Decline of Science in England*, pointing out that the French had learned their lesson in the recent war and had begun to organise and support science and higher education on a national basis. He predicted that French nationally-organised science would ultimately overtake British individualistic science, and he attacked the Royal Society for its inertia and for neglecting what he conceived to be its duty of pressing reforms on the government. The general discontent (especially with the failings of the Royal Society, also pungently articulated by Sir John Herschel) was probably one of the key influences which led to the establishment of the British Association for the Advancement of Science in 1831, at first almost as a rival learned society. By this time, concern about the universities was also being expressed by others (including Sir William Hamilton of Oxford) who pressed for their reform, urging the truly revolutionary idea that they should become national institutions. When the British Association met in Oxford the following year, there was a debate on the place of science in the University, at which the Savilian Professor of Geometry drew attention to falling attendances at lectures in mathematics, chemistry and experimental philosophy – surely the shape of things to come.

Despite such publicly expressed anxieties, the government remained broadly apathetic towards science in the first half of the nineteenth century, apart from founding the Geological Survey in 1835 and the Inland Revenue Laboratory in 1848. In the first case the government's action was prompted by the need for a survey of geological resources to safeguard its interests in mining royalties, while in the second the politicians' motive was to protect customs revenue by detecting adulteration. It is little wonder that after visits to England, Justus von Liebig wrote to Faraday that the country was not a land for science because 'only those works which have a practical tendency awake attention and command respect, while the purely scientific works which possess far greater merits are almost unknown ... in Germany it is quite the contrary'. Liebig was in every way a remarkable man and is known to chemists as the creator of the first big school of organic chemistry at Giessen, to which he was appointed professor at the age of 21. Though devoted to pure science he was not in any way narrowly academic, and saw very clearly the desirability of maintaining the closest possible scientific links between academe and industry. Largely because of Liebig's example and advocacy, such connections were more widely forged in Germany than in Britain: however, on a personal level he was also highly regarded by British chemists, and his visit to England in 1842 was one of the events underlying the development of the Royal College of Science (to which, on his recommendation, A.W. Hofmann was appointed as the first professor of chemistry). It was in this institution that the elder W.H. Perkin was later to synthesise indigo, which could have been the basis of a highly successful British dyestuffs industry. In fact the opportunity to create a strong organic chemical industry based upon dyestuffs was seized by Germany rather than Britain, something which the latter country had considerable cause to regret when the First World War erupted in August 1914.

Britain is frequently cited as the father of the Industrial Revolution. Her undoubted economic success rested on privileged access to the raw materials of an expanding empire as well as captive markets, together with the application of engineering knowledge to shipbuilding and railways (which enabled manufactured goods to be exported widely). It was this success which was celebrated in the 1851 Great Exhibition. However, Britain was slow in emulating Germany in the industrial use of natural science with the result that, despite the expansion of its empire, before the end of the nineteenth century Britain was overtaken by other nations in the value and volume of its exports.

It was fortunate for Britain that the Prince Consort, himself of German origin, was interested in trying to establish in the public mind that further progress depended upon the advancement and application of science. It was at his suggestion that the redoubtable Lyon Playfair visited Europe to study methods of technical education. Playfair emphasised that any lack of contact and cooperation between practical and scientific men is harmful, and that their collaboration would be highly beneficial. Some progressive steps were taken, such as the establishment in South Kensington of the Royal Colleges of Science and of Mines, and the City and Guilds College; and the government did set up a few agencies of its own to carry out particular functions, like the Meteorological Office (founded by the Board of Trade in 1854). However, most of these acts were undertaken piecemeal and they could not possibly be described as parts of a consistent policy to develop natural science, engineering and technology.

The arbitrary way in which the government allocated money to scientific enterprises was brought to public attention by Colonel Alexander Strange in 1870. He argued for the creation of state science laboratories, for a science museum and for public help to the universities and university colleges: his pressure resulted in the establishment of the Devonshire Commission some two years later. That body endorsed his approach, but its recommendations, although making excellent sense, were ahead of their time. The public and the government were not ready to accept the idea of state science or research grants to private scientists, the establishment of a Ministry of Science and Education (that had to wait until after the Second World War!) or the radical reform of secondary education. The only positive outcome was a government grant of £4,000 per annum to the Royal Society, specifically to fund meritorious research projects.

At the time the Devonshire Commission reported a young Edinburgh graduate, Richard Burdon Haldane, was studying philosophy at Göttingen, whither he had been sent by his canny Scots father to avoid acquiring the idle habits of the Oxonian. While there he became interested in the German organisation of science and retained his interest in this field on his return to England, when he became a lawyer and entered politics. The South African wars revealed serious deficiencies in British weapons, and the politician Haldane was drawn into the problem of the use of science by government. In 1905 he was appointed Secretary of State for War, and reorganised the Army. In so doing he found that he needed to mobilise research for the development of new 'scientific' weapons, especially aircraft. This was the first British organisation of government scientific research in the modern manner. Haldane was a truly remarkable man, understanding science though not a scientist, liberal in all his instincts (holding office in both Liberal and Labour governments), and a powerful advocate for the cause of higher education: it was he who shaped one of the precursors of the University Grants Committee. In the area of science and the state he proved to be the right man in the right job at the right time, always encouraging the government to follow successful German practice, such as in the creation of a national physical laboratory. Under his enlightened guidance an Advisory Committee for Aeronautics was established and there came into being a

Development Commission aimed at promoting agriculture, rural industries and fisheries. With an eye on the long term, Haldane encouraged this commission to spend much of its money on agricultural research and education, and on the assistance of grant-aided research stations.

However, Britain still lacked a coherent policy for science and a proper organisational structure to administer it. Both were to emerge through the work of two men. The first was Christopher Addison, Arthur Jackson Professor of Anatomy in the Sheffield Medical School. The quality of his scientific work was quite outstanding and he rapidly made a name for himself, not simply as an anatomist who produced work of great intellectual merit but because his surface maps were of great utility to surgeons, and in particular those who needed to know the position of the underlying abdominal organs. When he was only 32 years old he was invited to become Hunterian Lecturer of the Royal College of Surgeons: no clearer indication could have been given that a new and bright star had arrived in the medical firmament. He moved to London and a meteoric career was predicted for him, but while he was working at St Bartholomew's Hospital he became acutely aware of the ill health of the poor East Londoners, and saw how a great deal of this was attributable not just to low wages and bad diet, but to insanitary housing and poor environment as well as very limited access to proper medical care. The turning point in Addison's life came when he realised that only a two-pronged attack on this problem – namely, the provision of a freely accessible health service and also better housing and sanitation – would enable a solution to be reached. He embraced the cause, deciding that he could do more to improve the lot of the poor and needy by entering Parliament than he could as a doctor. He was elected as the member for Hoxton in a by-election in January 1910, and increased his majority at the general election in December. Lloyd George then sought his help when trying to introduce his controversial National Insurance Bill, which had attracted fierce opposition from the British Medical Association (BMA): he thought that Addison would be the ideal person to mediate between the government and the BMA, and the powerful lobby it could command, because his patent integrity and plain speech made him singularly respected and effective.

One section of the eventual National Insurance Act provided that the government should reserve one penny per insured person per annum to be spent on medical research. This initially amounted to some £57,000 and it was through

Addison's influence that a Medical Research Committee, the terms of reference of which he framed, was established to ensure that the money was well used. Addison was a member of the new body, and belonged to a group in it which wished to encourage able people with good ideas and a proven record of making advances in scientific knowledge. He himself achieved rapid political promotion, ending up as Paymaster General and Lord Privy Seal; he became Minister for Munitions in 1915 and Minister in Charge of Reconstruction in 1917, and he was appointed the first Minister for Health in 1918. As such he found himself in a very interesting intellectual position. On the Medical Research Committee he had shown himself much in sympathy with the idea that the national policy for medical research, and its implementation, should be in the hands of a body independent of government departments. As Minister of Health he nevertheless must have been tempted to take control of such research for the country, and there were many who urged him to do so on the grounds that this was logical and necessary. But Addison had already given considerable thought to the problem and, indeed, during the passage of the Ministry of Health Bill in the Commons he had proposed an amendment which contained the following words:

> A progressive Ministry of Health must necessarily become committed from time to time to particular systems of health administration ... a particular Minister may hold strong personal views on particular questions of medical science or its application to practice. A keen and energetic Minister will quite probably do his best to maintain the administrative policy which he finds existing in his department, or imposes on his department during his term of office. He would therefore be constantly tempted to endeavour in various ways to secure that the conclusions reached by organised research under any scientific body, such as the Medical Research Committee, which was substantially under his control, should not suggest that his administrative policy might require alteration ... It is essential that such a situation should not be allowed to arise *for it is the first object of scientific research of all kinds to make new discoveries, and these discoveries are bound to correct the conclusions based upon the knowledge that was previously available and, therefore, in the long run to make it necessary to alter administrative policy.* This can only be secured by making the connection between the administrative departments concerned, for example with medicine and with public health, and the research bodies whose work touches on the same subjects, as elastic as possible, and *by refraining from putting scientific bodies in any way under the direct control of Ministers responsible for the administration of health matters* [my italics throughout].

During those same years Haldane was also developing his views on research. He supported the establishment in 1915 of a committee of the Privy Council, chaired by the Lord President, 'to develop and organise the knowledge required for industry, to keep in touch with other departments concerned with science research, to undertake research on behalf of other departments and to stimulate the supply of research workers'. The following year the Department of Scientific and Industrial Research (DSIR) was formed as the committee's executive instrument. To assist the Lord President in developing the work and policies of the committee and DSIR, he appointed eminent scientists to a special Advisory Council. These were all steps in the right direction, but did not result in any coherent philosophy on the interdigitation of science and government which could serve as a guide to policy and action in the future. That came as one of the by-products of a report issued in 1918 by a Committee on the Machinery of Government, presided over by Haldane himself. This committee classified the business of government into a number of categories, which included that of 'research and information'. Its discussion of this item led it to enunciate an explicit statement about the organisation of government research, which was even more profound than was appreciated at the time. With remarkable prescience, a distinction was drawn between the research and development necessary for a department of government to discharge its own functions, which the committee considered should be 'supervised' by that department, and 'research work for general use', which it considered could be best administered by 'research councils' independent of government departments and therefore free from immediate political or administrative pressures. It gave force to this policy by a specific recommendation that if, as was expected, a Ministry of Health was set up then the Medical Research Council (MRC) should be constituted under a Privy Council committee after the pattern of the DSIR, rather than as a body under the control of the Ministry of Health.

This congruence of Addison's and Haldane's ideas gave the seal of approval to the Research Council idea. In the forty years or more before this concept came up for further scrutiny, both DSIR and MRC played notable parts in the development of British science and its application to particular problems. Their success made the later decision to create an Agricultural Research Council (ARC) both logical and widely acceptable. These three bodies gained in stature and influence during the inter-war period and the Second World War, whilst their success did not impede the development by individual government departments of additional research facilities for their own use. The esteem in which science was held by government and the people was very high, and even in 1959 the science vote was still increasing in real terms: there was also a Minister for Science and Technology of Cabinet rank (at that time Quintin Hogg, later Lord Hailsham), assisted on policy matters by an Advisory Council on Science Policy. But certain strains were becoming evident and questions were raised as to whether the Industrial Research Associations (partly funded by DSIR) still performed a useful function; whether the Privy Council should continue to be responsible for the Research Councils; and whether higher education and research ought to be brought into closer relationship with one another.

To examine these and kindred questions, a Committee of Enquiry into the Organisation of the Civil Service was set up, chaired by Burke Trend (later Lord Trend). Its report, published in September 1963, reaffirmed the Haldane principles and applied them to DSIR, recommending that a new Science Research Council should be established to take on the function of allocating research funds for general use, whilst responsibilities for industrial research associations should be detached and incorporated elsewhere in the government machine. The committee further recommended the establishment of a new entity, the Natural Resources Research Council, but argued that there should be no major change in the functions of either MRC or ARC: it also proposed a new body to replace the Advisory Council for Science Policy, to assist the Minister for Science.

Soon afterwards another government came to power and Parliament passed the Science and Technology Act 1965, which embodied most of the Trend recommendations. Thus ARC, MRC and two new Research Councils – the Science Research Council (SRC) and the Natural Environment Research Council (NERC) – were brought under the jurisdiction of the Secretary of State for Education and Science, and were also given the protection of Royal Charters. The Council for Scientific Policy (CSP) came into being to advise the Secretary of State on policy, and on the allocation of resources to the four Research Councils and to the Royal Societies of London and Edinburgh. This body became responsible for the Natural History Museum and six years later for the funding of the Social Science Research Council (SSRC), which had also been established under the Science and Technology Act (as a result of recommendations from the government's Committee on Social Studies, chaired by Lord Heyworth).

This structure had a number of advantages, including that of bringing under the same government department the provision of grants to universities (to cover their mainstream needs in teaching and research) and funding for the Research Councils, which between them covered the whole topic range from pure science and medicine to engineering and the environment, plus the social sciences. Only an Arts and Humanities Research Council was omitted, for reasons which need not concern us here. The rationale was simple: the universities were the source of qualified manpower in natural science, engineering and technology. The staff who taught in the universities were the major workforce for basic research in those subjects. The research students whom they trained would be supported on studentships provided by a Research Council, and the staff would be able to seek Research Council funding for individual projects, the criteria for the acceptance of which were timeliness and promise. The Councils were also able to initiate programmes of research by proffering specific grants to individuals or groups in universities.

The arrangement was known as the Dual Support System, and for it to work well it was essential that the bodies advising the Secretary of State on universities generally (the University Grants Committee) and on science generally (the CSP) should work closely together. This was achieved by ensuring that the chairman of the UGC was ex officio a member of the CSP, and that representatives of Research Councils in particular subjects would be attached as observers to the specialist committees of the UGC when these visited the universities.

The 1970s: A Period of Reconsideration

I was a member of the CSP and related bodies for some fifteen years, in several cases as chairman, and was subsequently chairman of the UGC for five years. I therefore have good reason to know how well the Dual Support System served this country. It managed to protect the autonomy of academic teaching and research from government interference and heavy-handed bureaucracy, and to do so through some very difficult financial periods, and yet at the same time ensured that the universities responded to national needs as articulated by the UGC or the Research Councils. It was greatly admired in other parts of the developed world. I shall explain what happened to the universities in the next chapter: what remains to be done here is to outline some of the changes that have taken place in the last thirty years and, in particular, to consider why there have been such frenetic and repeated reorganisations of the arrangements for carrying out scientific research in this country, and for shaping scientific policy.

In the first two decades after the last war the growth of per capita GDP in Britain was much slower than in other developed nations. By 1965 it had been overtaken by that of Germany and was about to be surpassed by that of France. The 'white hot technological revolution' ideal epitomised the commitment of Harold Wilson's government to science and technology as one of the important levers which would help to improve Britain's dismal economic performance, and that commitment found expression in many ways. For the first time a Ministry of Technology was established and C.P. Snow – scientist, novelist, critic, Civil Service Commissioner for the recruitment of scientists, who had attracted widespread attention through his Rede Lecture, *The Two Cultures*, and subsequent publications – was appointed a Parliamentary Secretary and given a seat in the House of Lords. At the same time, the Nobel Laureate in Physics and former naval officer Professor P.M.S. Blackett, a man for whom I had an immense personal regard, became Scientific Adviser in the same ministry, of which he had been a principal architect while the Labour Party was in opposition. To set the seal on this commitment, in 1965 Sir Solly Zuckerman was made Chief Scientific Adviser to the government, the first holder of that post in peacetime, and, as I mentioned in Chapter 5, the scientific input was strengthened in 1967 by the formation of the Central Advisory Council on Science and Technology (CACST).

The initial effect of these changes was to generate a good deal of euphoria, not just among the 'pure' science community but also more widely in the media. The pure scientists' satisfaction was understandable in that the expansion of the universities recommended by Robbins continued apace and the annual growth rate in real terms of the 'science vote' for the CSP (the key responsible body), though declining in magnitude, remained positive. But the economic clouds were gathering: British productivity was falling behind that of other countries, while inflation was only sporadically restrained by the government's orthodox economic response of quick-acting curbs on public expenditure, such as deferment or cuts in capital spending of the kind we had experienced in Nottingham with the Queen's Medical Centre. Furthermore, the universities were not delivering the planned cohorts of qualified scientists, engineers and technologists who were to carry forward the technological revolution. Instead the young, caught up with the 'swinging sixties' and with full employment beckoning irrespective of qualification, voted with their feet against science. There was a steady decline of one per cent per annum in the fraction of those studying mathematics and science in the sixth forms of secondary schools. Also augmenting this trend, and related to widespread youthful revulsion over the Vietnam war, was a growing (if mistaken) perception of science, engineering and technology as the compliant ally of the 'military–industrial complex', which brought concomitant student unrest. Not surprisingly, the first euphoria began to give way to disillusionment and the basic assumption that giving high priority to government expenditure on science and technology would automatically lead to national economic success, which should have been subjected to critical scrutiny, was never examined thoroughly.

While inflation soared, all that senior civil servants could do was seek to remedy what they perceived as flaws in existing arrangements. I became aware of this through my membership of the CACST and, in so far as the views I had heard affected the ARC, I felt I had a legitimate concern. By the beginning of 1970 I was beginning to think that in any case the arrangements which had established the CSP and brought the Research Councils into the new DES were due for reappraisal. I have described in Chapter 7 how, with the support of Margaret Thatcher, the CSP set up a small group to do this, starting at the end of 1970. At that stage I envisaged that our recommendations would ultimately be treated as an internal DES memorandum, having been submitted to Solly Zuckerman for comments *en route*; and that we would engage in a series of discussions which might be troublesome but would nevertheless be manageable. (Solly could be difficult but was by then approaching 67, long past the normal age of retirement of a senior civil servant, and in 1971 he was succeeded by Sir Alan Cottrell, with whom I knew that any proposals would be calmly and rationally discussed.)

What no one had foreseen was that Edward Heath, the Prime Minister, would choose this moment to establish a new advisory body in the Cabinet Office to consider and give advice on any problem, in any sphere of government, which was either referred to it by the Prime Minister or chosen as important by the advisory body itself. The new body was officially called the Central Policy Review Staff (CPRS) but rapidly became known to everyone as the 'Think Tank', and its first Director General, who assumed office on 1 February 1971, was Victor Rothschild (an appointment which rather surprised those of us who remembered his well-publicised decision to join the Labour Party just after the war).

I already knew Victor slightly. As mentioned in Chapter 4, he had twice tried to persuade me to leave Leeds, though I had first encountered him in my Cambridge days: at one time he had occupied a room in the Zoology Department near to that in which Barbara was working. In common with many others, Victor, himself no mean sportsman, had been a great admirer of Barbara's prowess as North of England figure skating champion for two consecutive years. Given his background at Cambridge (and in industry at Shell), it was entirely reasonable for Victor to choose as the first project for the Think Tank the investigation of science policy in Britain; as he told me himself, the decision was his alone. The subject was of intense interest to him, and he was already aware that the CSP was initiating its review of problems in and around the DES.

A few days after Victor's appointment became known, Michael (later Lord) Swann, who was Principal and Vice-Chancellor of the University of Edinburgh and who had been a member of the CSP for four years, telephoned me. It was a conversation I shall not forget easily. The burden of his message was to remind me that he knew Victor Rothschild well, having collaborated with him in joint research, and that he was sure Victor would wish to be involved in any discussion on the future of the Research Councils. To this I lightheartedly, but also tactlessly, said, 'If it be Allah's will, so be it', whereupon Michael said that Victor was not to be trifled with and that if he took up science policy he would wish to interrogate me 'in an iconoclastic manner'. I replied that this would not worry me if the questions were pertinent and fair, and that if they were neither it wouldn't butter any parsnips with me. With hindsight I decided that Michael was anxious that two of his friends should not disagree, and wanted to create platforms so that each of us could speak publicly. In my case the opportunity came at a meeting of the Royal Society of Edinburgh. Many years later the passage of a Higher Education Bill through the House of Lords in 1989, in which we were both involved, gave us an opportunity to reminisce and he confirmed his admirable intentions.

The small working party set up by the CSP consisted of Dr Tom Cottrell, Vice-Chancellor and Principal of the University of Stirling, a chemist who had worked at ICI; Dr (later Sir) John Kendrew, an X-Ray crystallographer and Nobel Laureate, a prime mover in the establishment of the European Molecular Biology

Organisation and Deputy Chairman of the CSP; Dr (later Sir) Percy Kent, for many years chief geologist of British Petroleum; Dr (later Sir) Alec Merrison, Vice-Chancellor of the University of Bristol and a distinguished particle physicist; and lastly myself as chairman. It was a deliberate decision that no member of this working group should have any official connection with a Research Council, because it might be argued that such a linkage could lead to biased judgment. Although the heads of the Research Councils were excluded, they presented papers and entered into discussions at a later stage, when we hoped to get their agreement to what the CSP might become. The task of the working group was to prepare, after detailed study, a draft report for consideration and (if all went well) endorsement by the CSP before its presentation to the Secretary of State.

We first met over the weekend 13-14 November 1970, at Abingdon. I well remember the agenda and discussion. I had decided that the situation called for a radical reappraisal and that we should tackle head-on whether we needed five separate Research Councils. I therefore ensured that the agenda included the pros and cons of replacing them, and the CSP, by a single executive body such as a National Science Board. The arguments in favour of such a proposal were obvious: better coordination and policy-making, because boundaries between subject divisions could easily be adapted to meet changing circumstances of knowledge or need; a larger purse would allow easier deployment of money at the margins, so essential to realise change quickly and effectively, and similarly to fit in long-term expensive projects (whether national or international); the coordination of interdivisional policies to deal with new interdisciplinary developments would be easier to implement; administrative benefits could accrue from economies of scale and better staff development; and finally, enhanced status both within and outwith the UK would make it easier to maintain the concept of the unity of science, and render the whole system less easily open to the predatory tendencies of other government departments (of which the Osmond Committee's activities were an example).[2] The usual counter-arguments were advanced: that monolithic structures imply bureaucratic hindrance; that specially valuable relationships which some Research

---

2. Paul Osmond was a Deputy Secretary in the Civil Service Department, where ideas for the transfer of the ARC from the DES to the Ministry of Agriculture, Fisheries and Food were developed – of which I became aware through my membership of the Central Advisory Council on Science and Technology.

Councils had developed with the users of their knowledge, for example the Medical Research Council with the doctors, would be lost; and that necessary but different policies concerning research units and institutes, research grants and studentships might tend to disappear. To my mind, both logic and comparison with experience overseas argued in favour of unification and overwhelmed the arguments for the status quo. I have seen nothing in the subsequent twenty-five years which has caused me to change the views I held then about the desirability of bringing the Research Councils together. Indeed, the present arrangements, which put great power into the hands of a single person – the Director General (ominous term) of the Research Councils, who has no formal advisory or executive council at his back – shows how easily supposed autonomy can disappear, and how readily a vacuum of informed advice can develop.

As the weeks passed it became clear that the Research Councils would not willingly surrender their Royal Charters, which they mistakenly thought afforded them some protection (whereas, of course, whatever the legalities, any organisation can disappear simply through financial starvation). Given that the threats faced were not seen as sufficient to make really fundamental change acceptable, the working party decided that the only way forward was to strengthen the CSP as a coordinating body, or to replace it by a new body with greater powers, in the meantime making a careful analysis of the existing Research Council programmes and policies. In the end we agreed to report that 'to retain the advantages of the Research Council system while providing for stronger links with the needs and policies of government departments, and for the possibility of adjustments of responsibilities between Councils and the transfer of specific activities both into and out of their field, we propose the replacement of the Council for Scientific Policy by a new chartered body, here referred to as the Board of the Research Councils, responsible to the Secretary of State for Education and Science'.

We considered the maintenance of strong links between scientific research and higher education to be vital, and so we recommended that the new Board should have among its members a vice-chancellor, the chairman of the UGC, and the President of the Royal Society; and for similar reasons, to reflect the more applied activities of the Research Councils, we deemed it essential to have members drawn from the most relevant government organisations, as well as assessors from other government departments as necessary. We also proposed the appointment of some independent members, and felt that the heads of the Research Councils should be full members of the new Board, where they would act in many ways like the executive directors of commercial companies.

Our detailed programme analysis, plus members' own experience, led us to subdivide scientific activity paid for by government into 'basic', 'strategic' and 'tactical' categories, covering in the same order the spectrum from exclusively pure, curiosity-oriented research to applied research and development work. We concluded that whereas tactical science always has by its nature a demand pull, that is, there is a part of the government machine which needs the results and probably needs them urgently for its own purposes, and should therefore pay for them using any contractor it wishes to employ – whether a private organisation, a university or a Research Council – basic and strategic science are rarely of direct and immediate interest to a single government department and are best managed on the arm's length principle, namely, by the Research Councils themselves.

Victor and I met several times during the review period, usually in his St James' Place flat or in the Cabinet Offices. He used these occasions primarily to quiz me about the CSP's line of thought and, when he had our report, to examine me on our arguments, but without giving me any inkling of what was in his own mind. He also saw all the heads of the Research Councils, singly and once (when I was present) collectively. At these meetings my attempts to probe his thoughts elicited little response, which did not worry me because I thought our report would stand or fall on its merits. I was however aware that Lord Jellicoe, Lord Privy Seal and Minister for the Civil Service Department, whose approval would be necessary for the diversion of any funds from the DES to other departments, considered (which meant he knew!) that Victor was likely to propose such a transfer. Lord Jellicoe wanted me to tell him what I thought would be the effect, but since I was not aware of the magnitude I could make no useful comment.

Whereas the focus of the CSP working group was simply on the effectiveness of the Research Councils, the Think Tank began with the general problem of how all government departments could make the best use of science to serve their purposes. Victor Rothschild felt strongly that many of those who were his most severe critics in the debate after the reports were published had failed to take account of this major difference between the starting points of the two enquiries, and I think there was some justification for his complaint. He considered that government departments other than the DES required almost exclusively applied science, and that this should be purchased from whomsoever could best supply it. This was the customer-contractor principle which he had operated at Shell and therefore valued, but it was not one which Percy Kent, with much longer experience at BP, endorsed. Another consequence of Victor's Shell experience was that he accepted that a contractor was entitled to make a 'surcharge' of about 10 per cent above the actual costs of what he called 'general research'. This overhead charge helped to fund activities necessary to maintain the expertise of a contractor; the induction costs of new staff who were not yet earning their keep; basic research in fields relevant to the applied task in hand, which could not be performed elsewhere; and time and materials for good staff to try out new speculative ideas of their own. Victor also saw that the customer-contractor relationship would not work properly unless the customer recognised that he had a duty to be a good customer, that is to say, to be clear in his objectives and about what he expected from the contractor. He further discerned that a government department could not be a good customer without having a Chief Scientist organisation staffed with knowledgeable people, personally experienced in relevant branches of science.

Victor Rothschild's spectrum of scientific activity ran from 'pure' through 'applied' to 'research and development'. There was no place in it for the 'strategic' category which we had proposed, although his pure was like our basic, and our tactical class would have come somewhere within his applied or research and development ones. He was firmly of the opinion that these latter parts of his spectrum should lie within the government departments, and it was therefore not surprising that he should examine the programmes of the Research Councils to find out what parts of their work fell into his governmental categories: these he recommended should be removed from the Research Councils' control and transferred, with their monetary equivalent, to the appropriate departments. In this exercise he must have been considerably helped by the prior analyses carried out by the CSP's working group. The main issues relating to these financial transfers, and what happened to them, are described below.

The CSP and Rothschild reports became public in the second half of November 1971, appearing – as I have explained in the previous chapter – as appendices to a government discussion paper (Cmnd. 4814). I reproduce below paragraphs 3-6 of this Green Paper, which express clearly the government's intention:

3. The Government has now received reports from both Lord Rothschild and the Council for Scientific Policy, and has decided to publish both of them in full as a basis for consultation on the future organisation of Government research and development. They are included as appendices to this Green Paper.

4. The Government welcomes the recommendation in the report by Lord Rothschild that applied research and development commissioned by the Government should be controlled in accordance with a 'customer-contractor' principle which has already been applied in certain areas. The report also considers the implications of adopting this principle for the Science Budget of the Department of Education and Science and the work of the Research Councils. The Government notes that the report of the Council for Scientific Policy is not at variance with this principle.

5. The Government endorses the 'customer-contractor' principle and considers that it should be implemented in respect of applied research and development carried out or sponsored by the Government, whether by the Research Councils or elsewhere. The Government believes that, subject to this principle, it would be right to preserve the Research Councils under the sponsorship of the Department of Education and Science. It is also the Government's view that it would continue to be desirable for a body of authoritative advice to be available to the Secretary of State for Education and Science in the allocation of her Department's Science Budget.

6. Before reaching decisions on the detailed application of the 'customer-contractor' principle, the Government intends to allow time for wide public debate and to discuss the issues involved with the scientific community. Discussions will therefore be held with the Royal Societies, the Council for Scientific Policy, the Research Councils and the appropriate Staff Associations. The Government will aim to complete these discussions by 29 February 1972 and to publish its final conclusions in a White Paper as soon as possible thereafter.

The government's initiative was well rewarded by the flood of correspondence and articles which followed publication of the reports: I suspect Victor was as taken aback as I was by the intensity of the public debate, much of which centred on the customer-contractor principle and the validity of its application to the work of the Research Councils. Amongst the many activities that took up my time in the aftermath of the Green Paper, I was involved in numerous intra-governmental meetings – either alone or in company with some of the Research Council chairmen. Not unnaturally, discussion at these tended to concentrate on whether the transfers of funds from the Research Councils to the government departments proposed by Victor Rothschild were justified, either in principle or in magnitude. The sums involved are shown in Table 1, in which the first column of figures represents the grants given to the Research Councils by the DES in 1971-72, the second column shows the amounts that would be paid after the transfers recommended by Rothschild had been deducted,[3] and the third column shows the government's decision concerning the funds actually to be made available.

Changes in DES funding of the Research Councils				
Research Council	(a)	(b)	(c)	(d)
SRC	50.9	50.9 (100)	50.9 (100)	
SSRC	2.2	2.2 (100)	2.2 (100)	
ARC	18.7	4.2 (22.5)	8.7 (46.5)	
MRC	22.4	16.8 (75.0)	16.9 (75.4)	22.4 (100)
NERC	15.3	7.7 (50.3)	10.8 (70.6)	
Total	109.5	81.8 (74.7)	89.5 (81.7)	95.0 (86.8)

£m in 1971. Figures in parentheses = % of those in column (a)

(a) Expected for 1971-72 if no changes made
(b) Proposal in Rothschild Report, 1971
(c) Government decision
(d) MRC funding after 1981, when DHSS returned the money transferred in 1972.

Table 1. Changes in Funding of the Research Councils by the DES

There are several comments to be made here about the Rothschild proposals. The first is that while SRC and SSRC were to be unaffected, more than three-quarters of the ARC funds were to be transferred to the Ministry of Agriculture, Fisheries and Food (MAFF), some 25 per cent of the MRC income diverted to the Department of Health and Social Security (DHSS), and about 50 per cent of the NERC money to be reallocated, largely to the Department of the Environment and the Department of Trade and Industry. Although the transfers were to be made progressively over three years, and it was expected that the departments which received the funds would reinvest them in the Research Councils (at least initially),

---

3. In fact the figures in the second column represent a significant reduction from Victor Rothschild's initial ideas, due to persuasive voices raised within government before the publication of his report. However, many knowledgeable people considered the figures in column (b) were too small, and there were numerous meetings and discussions with Lord Jellicoe, with his Permanent Secretary Sir William Armstrong and with Mr Frank (later Sir Frank) Cooper, trying to arrive at more realistic and satisfactory proposals.

they ultimately represented a very significant loss in the control which the three Research Councils could exercise over their own activities. The ARC was the worst affected, but even so Victor made no secret of his agreement with the Osmond Committee's view that ARC's prime task was its engagement in applied research and development, and therefore that it should simply have been transferred to MAFF.

The pressure to reach an acceptable accommodation was intense, and I well remember a Saturday lunchtime at our house in Oxford on 14 December 1971, when Sir William Armstrong and I looked over some draft notes which I had made less than three weeks earlier at a lunch with him at the Athenaeum. In brief, Victor had wished to transfer more than 30 per cent from the Research Councils' total of funds, but had been persuaded to reduce the demand to about 25 per cent before publication of his report. The government's White Paper, issued in July 1972, further reduced that sum to 18 per cent of the total. The last word on these transfers must be that nine years later the DHSS and MRC agreed that the £5.5 million which had been removed from MRC should be returned, suitably inflated, thus reducing to 13 the overall percentage transferred from the Research Councils. In this case experience was the best teacher: both the Chief Scientist of the DHSS and the Secretary of MRC had agreed that the resources could be better used if it was MRC that made the decisions on their allocation.

The government accepted some but not all the recommendations of the CSP's working group. On the proposal to reconstitute the Council, the White Paper said:

> The Government recognises the valuable work that has been done by many eminent scientists who have served on the Council for Scientific Policy. It does not intend to interpose any executive statutory body between the Secretary of State for Education and Science and the Research Councils. However to advise in future on the allocation of the science budget of the Department of Education and Science between the Research Councils and other bodies, and on the structure of the Research Council system, the Secretary of State will, in the autumn, replace the existing Council for Scientific Policy with a new advisory body. Its membership will include the chairman or secretary of each of the five Research Councils, the chairman of the University Grants Committee, senior scientists from departments with a major interest in the work of the Research Councils, the representative of the Chief Science Adviser to the Government, and independent members drawn from the universities, industry and the Royal Society of London. One of the independent members will be appointed as a part-time chairman.

I have already indicated that the new body was the Advisory Board for the Research Councils (ABRC), and I was its founding chairman.

With the perspective of twenty-five years I look back and wonder why many of the commentators in the media seemed to dramatise the situation, and cast Victor and myself in the role of gladiators in the scientific arena. It is true there was a great deal of difference in our backgrounds: he with a privileged upbringing, a member of a powerful, wealthy family, and myself from much more humble origins. But in things that mattered I think we had more in common than separated us. In particular, we were both given to discussion and dissection without fear of or favour towards the arguments which the other would advance, so that there was mutual respect. But I could no more have worked for him than he for me, as the two episodes I have described earlier illustrate.

Because of our similarities, I was genuinely sorry when Victor decided to leave the Think Tank (where I also felt that the disturbance he caused his political masters was perhaps more beneficial in the long run than the polite acquiescence normally expected of civil servants). So when Victor retired I wrote him a note, expressing my regret at his departure. As I rather expected, I got a short reply stating crisply that he found it impossible to serve a country which was making the wrong decisions. I had some sympathy with those sentiments because I was just beginning my second year of office as chairman of the University Grants Committee, which involved dealing with 30 per cent inflation (the product of Tony Barber's 'dash for growth') and trying to ensure that no university would go bankrupt. There was a postscript in Victor's small handwriting: 'Anyway, you defeated me in the end'. I was astonished at this, since I had never seen the matter as a battle between two individuals – though looking back on Michael Swann's words, and recalling what people had said and written during the public debate, I began to realise that many had personalised it, possibly subconsciously, in their own thinking. But in my judgment the government's decision (as is so often the case) was actually one in which each protagonist of a different point of view got something, but none got as much as he had originally sought. There had also been an acceptance of several points on which we both agreed, such as the importance of Chief Scientist organisations in government departments.

After my musings I could not resist telephoning Victor to ask him the meaning of his characteristically cryptic remark. Unusually, he was in a chatty frame of mind and said that what prompted him to add the postscript was that he strongly disapproved of appointments which he knew I had suggested in 1972. The appointments in question were those of Professor (later Sir) William Henderson as Secretary of ARC in succession to Sir Gordon Cox, and that of Dr (later Sir) Charles Pereira as Chief Scientist of MAFF. I was only too ready to defend my position, because I believed they were the two best men for the jobs in question and that if the new relationship of customer and contractor between MAFF and ARC were to work well, then it were better that the two principals – who had to negotiate with one another – understood and respected the views that each must hold. As our conversation progressed I became more and more puzzled, until he said, 'But you knew they were *friends*'. Since then I have long pondered that remark, and do not even now fully understand its significance. One explanation might be that Victor liked a certain tension in relationships, and believed that this contributed to the creation of more productive outcomes. Certainly his own manner, even when giving evidence before a House of Commons Select Committee, demonstrated his penchant for curt, almost dismissive, answers to questions.

Back to Basics: Who Should Pay for What?

A point which many people overlooked in Victor's paper was the stress he laid on accountability. One could speculate that this quality was bound to feature strongly in the upbringing of the son of a family with such a long and famous banking tradition. Whatever the origins of this emphasis, it became clearer to me in our telephone conversation that his view was that work would not be properly done if money did not change hands. Also he felt strongly that 'he who pays the piper calls the tune', namely, that control is only adequate when there is a possibility of money being withheld. What he could or would not concede is the Addison view that within government there is always a temptation to buy work which will buttress existing policies, and to look less favourably on work which might call them into question.[4] A mature democracy ought, of course, to have arrangements which minimise such dangers. Addison's solution was to move control of the MRC away from

---

4. There are well-known cases of suppression or distortion of research findings in the private sector for just this reason, e.g. in relation to tobacco.

76. When I became chairman of the British Library Board in 1978, the heart of the Library was still Panizzi's Great Round Reading Room at the British Museum in Bloomsbury *(above)*. This was a marvellous space, but the Library as a whole was fragmented and had completely outgrown its existing scattered accommodation.

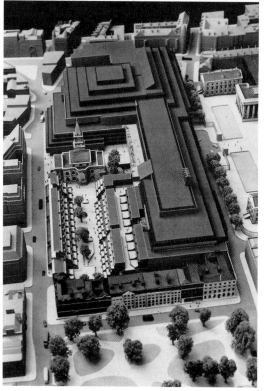

77, 78. Before my time at the British Library Board, plans had been developed for a new library complex in front of the British Museum. The original proposal (*above*) involved the closure of Great Russell Street and the erection of new buildings either side of Nicholas Hawksmoor's St George's Church. Although it was approved by the Conservative Government in 1964, the incoming Labour Government bowed to conservationist pressure and the project was deferred. A revised version, modelled in 1972 (*left*), proved impracticable because the accommodation requirement had doubled whilst the site area had been reduced substantially.

SERVICE OF BRITISH LIBRARY

From Sir FRED DAINTON and Lord TREND

SIR–In recent weeks reference has been made in *The Daily Telegraph* and other national newspapers to a letter written by Prof Hugh Thomas and others to the Chancellor of the Duchy of Lancaster.

This letter expressed the view that the great Panizzi-Smirke reading room in the British Museum building should continue in use as one of the main reading rooms of the British Library, that books which could not be stored there should be outhoused in some unspecified place or in a warehouse at Somerstown and that these actions would remove the necessity to construct a new building for the British Library (at Euston).

While we have great sympathy with those who have found the ambience of the Panizzi room greatly to their liking and must accept their statement that this is conducive to their work, there are important contrary arguments which have not yet been brought to wide public notice and, with the unanimous support of our respective boards, we seek the hospitality of your columns to do this.

In the first place the great Panizzi room, which is justly admired, is not at risk. When it is vacated by the British Library the trustees of the museum intend that it should be used by their museum in ways which will display this glorious architectural space more effectively and to more people than has been the case hitherto.

Secondly, the British Library has a duty to give the best possible service to scholars who use the books and manuscripts which form part of its reference division. This service is much less good than it ought to be because of the dispersal of the holdings and ancillary services over 17 different buildings in London. Only the juxtaposition of readers, holdings, staff and services in one building can enable the British Library to give the service which a nation properly expects to receive from its national library.

Thirdly, the British Library has a duty not only to scholars today but to scholars in the future and must therefore conserve the material it already possesses and will later acquire for their use.

The conditions under which the stock is now held do not protect it against deterioration and some of it is not far from being beyond repair. The best and cheapest way to retard the deterioration is to keep the material at a constant temperature in an atmosphere free of pollutants, such as the dioxides of nitrogen and sulphur, and at a constant humidity.

This cannot be done in any of the present buildings, least of all in the British Museum. Moreover it is no answer to store most of the material in an air-conditioned place and withdraw items to the Panizzi Room as required by readers. This would subject fragile material to damaging environmental stresses and to the hazards of transport and increase the delays between order and receipt by the reader.

Fourthly, it must be remembered that the British Library is much more than the Department of Printed Books. The reference division includes an official publications library, maps, music, manuscripts, oriental material and stamps. It also contains the science reference library with many tens of thousands of serial titles and over 19 million patents.

This library is a uniquely comprehensive source of scientific, technological and commercial information and is therefore a vitally important national asset. Though it is very inadequately and inconveniently housed on three widely separated sites, those requiring its services were prepared to make over 160,000 visits last year. The same arguments about unification and conservation apply to these holdings.

Fifthly, the British Library has many other activities such as bibliographic services, research and development which benefit readers and other libraries both overseas and at home and some of these services, together with those provided by our (unique) lending division generated nearly £5 million income last year. To be brought to the highest pitch of efficiency these services and their staff (excluding the lending division) need to be brought under a common roof.

Finally, it is worth pointing out that both the museum and the library do not look exclusively to the taxpayer for support and they attract gifts in kind and money from many who understand the value of their custodial roles and as national resource centres in their respective fields.

A dispassionate examination of the present position shows that a new building for the library is desperately needed so that a proper service can be given to the world of learning and the world of industry and commerce now and for the future. Without it there can only be retrogression.

FRED DAINTON, Chairman, British Library Board;
TREND, Chairman, Board of Trustees, British Museum.
London, W.C.1.

---

79. The idea of moving the British Library away from Bloomsbury was strongly opposed in some quarters, largely by people who did not understand the real issues involved. Lord Trend and I felt it necessary to make our own contribution to the long-running media debate in this letter published in the *Daily Telegraph* on 27 July 1979.

80. As Secretary of State for Education and Science, Shirley Williams (who had originally asked me to chair the British Library Board) was very supportive of the Library's development plans. In 1978 she authorised a start on the new building which had been designed for a site alongside St Pancras Station.

81. The St Pancras building project was frozen when the Conservatives came to power in 1979, and it was necessary for me to make the case again, directly to Margaret Thatcher as Prime Minister. The go-ahead for the first phase of construction was finally given at the end of 1980.

82. Prince Charles unveiled the foundation stone for the new British Library in 1982, several years before it was actually put in place: my father would have approved of the quality of the craftsmanship. To mark the occasion, I presented the Prince with a copy of Carl Jung's book *Man and His Symbols*.

83. The British Library Lending Division at Boston Spa, near Leeds, started life in 1961 as the National Lending Library for Science and Technology. As Chairman of the Board, I was delighted to host a visit by the Duke of Kent in September 1981, when he opened the third stage of the Urquhart Building.

84. Colin St John Wilson, as project architect since 1962, once memorably described the battle for the new British Library as 'The Thirty Years' War'. I was touched when he gave me this drawing, which faithfully depicts his marvellous design for the St Pancras site. The bricks were carefully chosen to match those of Sir George Gilbert Scott's famous station hotel (in the background).

85. In terms of public use, the reading rooms are the core of the British Library. The main Humanities Reading Room (*above*) is on three levels and is largely devoted to study space.

86. The total cost of the enterprise was a little over £500 million, of which about half was spent on the infrastructure needed to conserve the collections and keep the building operational *(right)*.

87. One of my pleasures as Chairman of the Board was to receive official gifts on behalf of the Library – in this case a collection of historical Japanese texts.

88. All good things come to an end, and I retired from the British Library Board on 30 November 1985. I was 'seen off' from our temporary boardroom in Novello House by numerous colleagues and friends who attended my farewell party. Barbara unveiled the portrait which had been commissioned from Trevor Stubley: an impression of the new building appears in the background.

89. On retiring I was moved to be given a beautifully-bound volume of 'appreciations' from the many distinguished people with whom I had worked on behalf of the Library. Here I am reading a message from Margaret Thatcher, which is reproduced at the beginning of this book.

90, 91. Towards the end of 1985 I also retired from the chairmanship of the National Radiological Protection Board and was presented with a splendid hi-fi system. Board Secretary Roger Clarke, and behind him his deputy, Peter Thatcher, seem to be concentrating hard on my vote of thanks!

I also received a commemorative medal fabricated in the NRPB's Chilton workshops by Maurice Holding (far right in the photograph below). The Board Director, John Dunster, is standing next to Barbara.

92, 93. I joined the Council of the Royal Postgraduate Medical School in 1979, later becoming chairman and then president. The School is based at the Hammersmith Hospital *(above left)*, and its Wellcome Library houses a fine stained-glass window by Ethel Lewis *(above right)*, symbolising the Hippocratic Oath in its worldwide context and made with the help of the School's own workshop.

94. In the spring of 1983 Sir Cyril Clarke, as chairman of the British Heart Foundation, presented the School with a cheque for half a million pounds. In the photograph below, he looks as pleased to be giving it as I am in accepting it.

95. My association with the Worshipful Company of Goldsmiths dates back to 1935, when I became one of its Exhibitioners whilst an undergraduate at Oxford. In 1971 I was invited to become a Freeman of the Company, and in due course I was elected to the Court of Assistants. By tradition, a goblet is made for each new member of the Court: mine was created by the silversmith Brian Asquith. The design of the stem is based on the sheaf of arrows which forms part of the coat of arms of my native city, Sheffield.

96. This portrait medal, designed by Kevin Coates, was commissioned by the Goldsmiths' Company to mark my service as Prime Warden in 1982-83. The leopard's head on the reverse of the medal is the emblem of the London Assay Office.

97. In July 1982 the Goldsmiths' Company organised an exhibition in its Livery Hall to celebrate fifty years of the craftsmanship of Leslie Durbin. I was privileged to host a visit by the Queen Mother, who owns several works by Durbin and is seen here admiring a casket which he created with Laurence Whistler.

98. One of my many pleasurable duties as Prime Warden was that of laying the foundation stone of an extension to Guardians' Hall in the Sheffield Assay Office, one of only four such offices in the United Kingdom. On my immediate left is Billy Ibberson, a much respected figure in the Sheffield cutlery industry.

99. In 1983 Oxford University Press asked me to take part in its project to produce the *New Oxford English Dictionary*, by computerising the former *Oxford English Dictionary* and its supplements. This involved the creation of the world's largest language database, and was achieved with generous financial and technical help from IBM and the University of Waterloo in Canada. The photograph shows members of the Advisory Council, with senior executives of Oxford University Press, at the first project meeting. This was held in the Clarendon Building in Oxford: the 300-year-old pewter and glass inkwells (always in place but never used) formed a pleasing counterpoint to the matters under discussion.

100. As the Immediate Past President of the British Association for the Advancement of Science, I was much involved in its sesquicentennial celebrations at York in 1981. Mischievous colleagues, seeing this photograph, have been known to make jokes about 'pulling the strings'.

101. Barbara's involvement with the British Association dates back to 1927, when she attended her first conference at the age of 11. Photographic proof was produced when we went to the British Geological Survey at Keyworth in August 1987, to open its new library.

WANTED

F.S. DAINTON
(Answers to the name of Fred)

Last seen circa 1946 in the vicinity of Chalk River.

For information leading to the whereabouts of this notorious **FREE RADICAL** we offer a REWARD of $1.50 or 1 - 3 years hard labour at the University of Leeds.

Pembroke P. D.

102. My first professional trip overseas was to Chalk River, Canada, in 1946. I have lost count of the number of times I have been back to North America, but my reputation has evidently lingered on. 'Free radical' is a chemical in-joke: the poster was presented to mark my 75th birthday in 1989.

103. Poland is another country we enjoy visiting. This photograph dates from 1983, and was taken in the Rector's Office at Lódz Polytechnic University. The Rector at that time was Jerzy Kroh, who had worked with me in Leeds as a government-sponsored Research Fellow.

105. On behalf of the British Library, I presented a framed facsimile of part of the Magna Carta to Minoru Kishida, Director of the National Diet Library in Tokyo.

104. Yuko Yoshimi acted as interpreter during our visit to Japan in 1979, and remains a great friend to this day.

106. The face of a handsome 18th-century sword guard presented to me in 1962 by the father of my research student Shigeo Tadzuke. The gold and silver inlays depict white peony and cherry blossoms.

107. With Barbara on our trip to Korea in 1979. The mountains in the background are part of the 30-mile-wide demilitarised zone between North and South Korea.

108. A conference break at the University of Queensland in November 1988.

109. In 1992 we visited the Australian nuclear research station at Lucas Heights, near Sydney, where this group photograph was taken. I was delighted to see again so many of my former colleagues and research students.

110, 111. Barbara and I always enjoy our visits to Singapore: the picture on the left was taken in 1997, when the Prime Minister, Lee Kuan Yew, entertained us in his home. He has also been kind enough to refer to me as the 'father' of his country's two universities, where I have had many speaking engagements over the years.

112. Making friends in Juray Bird Park, Singapore, to which we were taken by our colleague 'S.T.' Lee. The park has over 8,000 birds, representing more than 600 species.

the Department of Health. Haldane gave his support to the Research Council idea for the additional reason that government departments would be reluctant to provide support for scientific work 'of general use'; indeed, expenditure of that kind might well attract the criticism that a department should not pay for 'research and information' which is not necessary for it to discharge its own functions.

A few years ago I began to put together some thoughts on such issues because it occurred to me that, whereas in the non-governmental world it is easy to identify purchasers and providers of knowledge, in the realm of government-supported science such clear-cut identification is more difficult, as is the achievement of accountability and control (though in some cases 'control' should not be exercised). I began by asking myself who is the ultimate beneficiary of government-funded science, in the hope that this would lead me to answer the questions 'Who should pay?' and 'Who should make the choice of which work should be undertaken?' I soon found that Victor's classification into basic, applied, and research and development was insufficient as a discriminator, and that my own categories also had defects and therefore needed to be extended.[5]

The only rational and fair method of deciding who should pay – whether a private individual or enterprise, or government acting on behalf of the people – is to find out who will benefit from the research, and whether the work is done for public good or for private gain. Here we encounter our first difficulty, because the ultimate beneficiary is not always apparent to those who hold the purse strings at the time when the opportunity to carry out the necessary research and development presents itself. Nevertheless, some progress in this discrimination can be achieved by considering the rather crude table forming Table 2 overleaf, which I have called *Classification by Objectives*. Although it is largely self-explanatory, I shall emphasise a few points in the paragraphs which follow.

I define 'basic' science as work chosen by individual scientists with the sole object of advancing knowledge, with no practical end in view. Other adjectives have been used from time to time which may be more familiar or more evocative, depending on the reader's background. They include 'self-chosen', 'curiosity-driven', and 'blue sky' research. Whatever term one employs, the important feature

---

5. The remainder of this section is based on, and in part taken from, a lecture I gave to the American Philosophical Society at the end of March 1995.

OBJECTIVE	SHORTHAND DEFINITION	TIMESCALE TO SUCCESSFUL OUTCOME	WHO DECIDES?	BENEFICIARY	WHO SHOULD OR DOES PAY?	EXAMPLES
Advance knowledge	Basic (self-chosen, curiosity-oriented)	Unpredictable	Scientist(s)	Public	State Charity Industry	Penicillin X-rays
Meet immediate need	Tactical (improvement of process or product)	Controllable	Customer	Customer	Customer	Dosimeter Ballpoint ink Aircraft windows
Advice to legislature	Regulatory	Variable	Independent statutory body	Public	State	Health and Safety Executive, National Radiological Protection Board
New knowledge, may be applicable in future	Strategic	Very dependent on subject	Forum of pure and applied interests	Unknown at inception, may be public or private	Research Councils and some industry	Polymers Molecular biology

Table 2. Classification by Objectives

is that the choice is not part of any plan other than that within the investigator's mind, and the outcomes are uncertain both in kind and in the amount of time they take to attain. There is always the potential for practical benefit, but basic science is uncontrollable in the accountant's sense because no one knows what discoveries will be made, or to what applications they may lead (or when). What we do know is that science is one of the great creative activities and in a very deep sense part of human culture: for that reason alone it is a public good and merits support, as also do bodies such as the Arts Council and the great national museums, which need resources beyond the capacity of private individuals or institutions.

In Britain the major paymasters for basic science are the various Research Councils as agents of the state, but there are also wise charities and large-scale industries which take a long-term view and will therefore support basic research. The main practitioners of this research are to be found in the universities, and its management is easy because the determination of its direction generally lies in the hands of individual scientists or small teams of them (except in the case of large national or international laboratories). When a project is completed the only gesture that can be made towards accountability is to make some assessment of quality and significance (although true indications of worth may not emerge until long after an investigation has been finished). I consider the best way to achieve this is by peer review, rather than by crude mechanistic methods such as citation counts.

Much 'tactical' research is characterised by the fact that some practical objective is clear at the outset: there is a person or enterprise requiring an improvement in a product or a process, and it is known that the work can be done by the application of current knowledge or by the acquisition, using existing methods, of (targeted) new knowledge. There is a definite customer who is prepared to pay, and there are people able to do the work. The customer-contractor relationship is applicable, management is relatively straightforward, and accountability is readily achieved. It is often the case that timescales have to be short and progress cannot be leisurely. Research for particular governmental purposes is more likely to fall into this category than is that for general use.

There is also a category of work I have called 'regulatory'. It is largely tactical and is best managed at arm's length from government, because it is the basis of advice on regulations to safeguard or improve the condition of the people, who must therefore have trust in it. That trust can only be gained if the regulatory body is seen to be neither the creature of any particular government nor that of any private interest, but one which acts entirely in the public interest. How else can we address such sensitive matters as setting permissible levels of exposure to ionising radiation, or ensuring the safety of medicines? One can give a hundred examples. Work so clearly and exclusively undertaken for the public good can (and should) only be financed from the public purse, not least because it may well have a powerful influence on the enactment of legislation.

The final research category is 'strategic', a term (first suggested by the late R.J.H. Beverton, the renowned marine biologist) which I adopted enthusiastically in 1971. This comprises work that is clearly liable to yield results of great practical significance even though, when the decision is made to invest resources, the precise nature of the outcome and the time of its appearance cannot be foreseen (and therefore the ultimate customers are not identifiable). A classic British example of this occurred just after the last war, when the distinguished X-ray crystallographer Sir Lawrence Bragg was so impressed by the work of his young colleagues Max Perutz and John Kendrew in Cambridge that he persuaded a far-sighted Medical Research Council to establish a research laboratory for molecular biology there: fifty years and ten Nobel Prizes later, the beneficial ripples of this decision continue to circle the globe – because the discoveries made have provided both an impetus and a means for learning more about living organisms, and in addition new weapons for dealing with human disease.

Yet More Reconsiderations

Seven years after publication of the 1972 White Paper on future funding principles, the Civil Service Department conducted a review of the way in which the changes recommended in that paper were working. Its verdict was that 'while it is too early to make a firm judgment, they appear to have strengthened the government's research and development machinery'. The Department further urged that sudden changes in the pattern of research expenditure by the Agricultural, Medical and Natural Environment Research Councils should be avoided, and clearly endorsed the Rothschild view that if the customer-contractor principle was to work well, commissioning departments must learn to act as 'enlightened customers'. It evidently felt that the Department of Health and Social Security had not reached that stage vis-à-vis the Medical Research Council, and it decided to review that relationship six months later. This was the trigger that afterwards led the Public Accounts Committee to recommend the abandonment of the formal commissioning arrangement and, as a consequence, the funds transferred from MRC to the DHSS over the period 1973-76 were returned in 1981, as I have already mentioned. The Civil Service Department considered that the Advisory Board for the Research Councils had become well established and useful but that, after its (necessary) pre-occupation with the problems arising from the transfer of funds had ended, its attention should be turned to its own *modus operandi* over the allocation of funds to Research Councils, as well as to a consideration of big issues akin to those which the old Council for Scientific Policy had addressed.

The ABRC was, however, becoming even more concerned about the deleterious effects of the financial stringency which had begun in the early 1970s in the wake of high inflation and the 'oil crisis'. This in turn had led to the imposition of cash limits on public spending departments and the removal of compensation for inflation, which severely constrained those departments and made them ever less willing to commission work from the Research Councils. ABRC asked Sir Ron Mason, who was on the point of leaving the post of Chief Science Adviser to the Ministry of Defence, to investigate the problem. His report was published in November 1983 and recommended allowing the Board a stronger role, much in the style proposed in the CSP report, with a full-time chairman and 'an adequate secretariat'. However, seven more years were to elapse before this twice-recommended essential step was taken, and ABRC was itself swept away only three years later, in 1993, following yet another reorganisation.

Most of the scientists working at a Research Council or university laboratory bench were preoccupied with shrinking budgets, the decline of government expenditure on science as a fraction of GDP, and the efforts being made to reduce public expenditure. Policy at the centre was hard to discern, though it was noticeable that when Labour assumed office in 1974 it had done so without carrying a banner proclaiming the 'white hot technological revolution' which had been its clarion call ten years earlier. Those scientists who did observe the changes of policy and personnel largely interpreted them as a downgrading of science at the heart of government. It is true that when the Conservatives came back to power in 1979, Mrs Thatcher proclaimed the importance of science by recreating a central advisory council for science and technology in the form of the Advisory Council for Applied Research and Development (ACARD), replaced in 1987 by the Advisory Council on Science and Technology (ACOST). Both of these bodies reported to her, a fact which seemed to signal that she, as an erstwhile chemist, had created a place for science at the centre and under her wing. But the reality was that the chairmanships of these advisory councils were no more than very part-time appointments, of people who also held busy private sector jobs. They had no executive strength; nor could the officials, worthy as they were, pull any great levers of power. Gone for ever were the heady days of 1971-72. Among those who had experience of science policy and a continuing interest therein, the view began to develop that the cause of science would go by default unless the government recognised the need for a Minister of Science with adequate trans-departmental coordinating power, and an appropriate staff with some proper executive authority.

It was somewhat of a surprise to myself, and I believe to a few others (all having interests in science policy), when we were invited to put our views before the next Prime Minister, John Major, on 28 January 1992. We found him to be an attentive and courteous listener, but left without any great expectations. It was therefore even more of a surprise when, a few weeks later, it was announced that William Waldegrave was to vacate his post as Secretary of State for Health to become Chancellor of the Duchy of Lancaster and Minister for Public Service and Science, and that the Chief Scientist in the Cabinet Office, Professor W.D.P. Stewart, was to become Chief Scientific Adviser to the Government. That there were once again to be a Minister for Science and a Chief Scientific Adviser with assured access to the Prime Minister, and that both were to have seats at the table of the Ministerial Committee on Science and Technology, was taken to be a sign that the government of the day recognised that science should be at its centre. It was also pleasing to note the inclusion of a specific requirement for the new ministerial team to be advised by ABRC and ACOST.

However, disadvantages were also evident in the new arrangements. The major drawback was that responsibility for funding the Research Councils was to be taken away from the DES, in consequence of which that department was renamed the Department for Education (DfE).[6] In future, the Councils' resources would

---

6. Later still it was subsumed into the new Department for Education and Employment (DfEE).

be provided through the Office of Science and Technology (OST). In one stroke the much admired Dual Support System – which had worked well for many years, particularly in the difficult financial period of the 1970s, and which symbolised the fundamental interdependence of university teaching and research – was sundered. It was the end of an era.

Many observers were intrigued by the prospect of the collaboration which might develop between the Minister for Science and the Chief Scientific Adviser, two people so disparate in background: the patrician Minister, educated at Eton, Oxford and Harvard, a distinguished Mods and Greats graduate and a long-time Fellow of All Souls, former member of the now defunct Think Tank and possessed of a rich and subtly deployed vocabulary; and the botanist of humble origin and plain, unvarnished speech, educated on the Isle of Islay and at Glasgow University, who had become a professor at the age of 32 and transformed an unpromising department at Dundee into a thriving teaching and research centre which was soon a magnet for able people. But what disarmed most critics, however captious, was the new Minister's positing in mid-1992 of twelve questions, each having an important bearing on determining what might be the critical factors for achieving the optimum benefit from the deployment of public money on science (as defined at the beginning of this chapter) and its distribution across the various areas. These questions are set out in Table 3 overleaf. The Minister invited organisations and individuals to provide him with answers: they responded in their hundreds, because from the manner of his presentation they had been convinced that their opinions would be treated seriously. It was the first time that their views had been canvassed, and it not only had a tonic effect but permanently raised the level of interest in science policy throughout the country; and it did this in a much more constructive way than the fierce polemical debate which had taken place twenty years earlier. The country had moved on. A year later the respondents were rewarded with the publication of the White Paper 'Realising our Potential: A Strategy for Science, Engineering and Technology' (Cm. 2250). This stated that in future (amongst other things) a central plank in the government support of science, engineering and technology would be 'the enhancement of the quality of life and the creation of wealth' – a phrase which has since shone out from the pages of many a document, with comparable frequency to that about the now largely forgotten 'technological revolution' which had been so much in vogue thirty years before.

1. Why does the United Kingdom seem to be less successful than its competitors in translating inventions to the marketplace?
   Why is this more so in some industries than others?

2. Do we have an agreed measure of the capacity of an industry, or a firm, to innovate?
   Do we really know whether our firms are getting better or worse at innovation?
   Do technology-based innovative firms survive longer?
   Is the alleged lack of innovation a lack of good ideas, or finance, or what?

3. Do we need more or less planning in Government science and technology?

4. Do we get optimum benefit from our international collaborative programmes, especially in the European Community, and do they complement our national programmes well?

5. Does the United Kingdom get the very best value for money from the Government's considerable expenditure on science and technology?

6. Are the spending priorities right or would the Government be better advised to spend money in other areas of science and technology than the ones it funds at present?

7. Does the Government have the right advisory structures at its centre to help it take decisions on priorities?

8. How can we best ensure that the strong upward trend in industrial R&D expenditure in the United Kingdom will continue and gather pace in the years to come, so that our record is as good as the best of our international competitors?

9. Could the links between academia and industry be improved to encourage maximum exploitation of the science base?

10. Is the United Kingdom working in areas of basic science which have made less marketable derivatives than those on which our international competitors concentrate their efforts?

11. Is there scope for improved training opportunities in science and technology?

12. What steps do we need to take to improve the status of scientists and engineers?

Table 3. William Waldegrave's Twelve Questions

Some Personal Conclusions

In my experience, the two words 'science' and 'policy' often mean different things to different people. 'Science' certainly does, and that is why I have always been at such pains to define it as comprising the whole field of natural science, engineering and technology. 'Policy' is also an ambiguous term. It may imply a statement of vague and virtuous aspirations which, much as I dislike 'management speak', is better served by the simple noun 'vision'; or it may mean a definite statement of principles and programmes devised to achieve a particular desired end. In using the two words together, confusion can arise as to whether the meaning of 'national science policy' is a policy for science, that is, a plan to ensure that science in Britain is in a healthy state, or a policy for the application of science to serve the ends of government specifically.

Many scientists are employed by private enterprises which must pay them and provide them with the equipment they need, and in general a firm's policy for science will just be to use it to help ensure its own profitable survival. The government, conversely, has to pay for studies carried out either by scientists it employs directly in wholly government-owned laboratories or indirectly at arm's length in other agencies, or by those in university or private enterprise laboratories. This is a use of science to serve public policy directly, and as we have seen it casts most government departments in the role of customers paying contractors for the services they deliver. For the most part, but not exclusively, the activities involved can be classified as applied research and development (Rothschild) or tactical research (Dainton). The work to be done is usually easy to identify, manage and monitor. However, as in all our affairs, the present is the future of the past, and none of tomorrow's science will be possible without an adequate supply of able people educated to the highest standards today; and the requisite high quality of awareness will only be possible if their teachers are also actively pushing back the frontiers of knowledge in their fields.

Since private enterprise cannot be expected to pick up the bill for this part of science, the government must devise a national policy which will have three elements. The first of these is necessarily a scheme for the education of future scientists in the requisite numbers and disciplines; this in turn implies arrangements for supporting the institutions in which they are educated. In science, to the end of the first degree course and for part of the postgraduate period, the responsibility lies with the Department for Education and Employment. This element really should not be difficult to organise, but I remain dismayed by the quality of school science education – in the sense that it does not provide school-leavers with a sufficient understanding of science to make good judgments about personal choices for future careers or study, or for them to have an adequate appreciation of public issues in which science now plays, and will increasingly play, an important part. This deficiency has obvious knock-on effects for higher education, and ultimately the economic strength of the nation.

The second part of a national policy must relate to science for the use of government departments. Government ought to have little difficulty in allocating resources for this element, because the overall need is the summation of the amounts each department judges necessary to further its own objectives, and is prepared to fund from its own resources.

Thirdly, there must exist a plan concerning the range and extent of basic scientific activity appropriate to the country's needs as a civilised and developed nation wishing to play its full part in the world's affairs. Such a policy must take proper account of the need to encourage the sciences for their own sake, as being essential to human development – something that is still often overlooked.

Programmes to implement these three policy strands carry their own price tags, and will be competing with other government requirements for money. At this point it is essential to remember again that any lowering of standards of education or basic science today will detract from national scientific performance across the land ten or twenty years later.

By far the most difficult decisions are connected with the determination of the policy for, in my terminology, 'basic' and 'strategic' science. It is quite clear to me that the best way of ensuring that these activities flourish is through the Research Council mechanism. The apportionment of the science vote to the Councils, and the coordination of their activities, should be the principal tasks of a Board of the Research Councils with a full-time chairman, working in close cooperation with the other bodies responsible for higher education. It is ridiculous to think for a moment that any single person can possess the range of knowledge and experience of a body such as the ABRC: nor will it suffice for any Director General of the Research Councils to respond by stating that he does indeed take advice from experts. The public has a right to know who such experts are and why they were picked; and, in any case, the interaction of experts in debate is synergistic, so that the result of a group discussion is better than the simple sum of the members' advice given separately. It is also important that the ABRC (or equivalent body) has some trans-departmental input. To embed it in a particular department of government is bound to influence decisions in that department's direction. The relocation of the Office of Science and Technology into the Department of Trade and Industry (DTI) some years ago is much to be regretted, and all the protestations that the change would make no difference to the influence of OST, or to its ease of access to the Prime Minister, have predictably encountered incredulity. If the arguments which earlier resulted in the placing of OST in the Cabinet Office, with a Minister for Science in the Cabinet, were once regarded as strong, we should be told what factors now make these arguments nugatory. The only *raison d'être* of the DTI is to make 'UK Ltd' more profitable, and, whether intentionally or not, the transfer has sent a signal to the scientific community that the government now only wishes to listen to utilitarian arguments for science.

Leaving aside questions on the organisation of decision-making, one can understand why the 1993 White Paper 'Realising our Potential' might specify as objectives of science the creation of wealth and the enhancement of the quality of life. However, this brings real dangers in relation to 'basic' science – not least because the stress put on financial justification leads to its intrusion as a criterion of choice between areas of fundamental research, something which is bound to result in less than optimum outcomes.

I have absolutely no objection to research foresight studies, however conducted, delphic or otherwise. They are, after all, merely systematic ways of collecting the opinions of informed people. I am glad when the conclusions of such exercises are published, together with their evidence, because they can form a valuable part of everybody's general scientific education, as well as being beneficial at the applied research and development end of the spectrum. For that reason I am also glad that some have appeared under the banner *Technology Foresight*. There is ample international evidence from the last twenty-five years to show that companies selling products and services based on advanced technology grow and create new jobs which are well paid, whereas companies based on 'low' technologies shed jobs and their unskilled workers find great difficulty in obtaining new employment. The forthright conclusion is that society must continue to give proper support to free and open long-term research, driven by curiosity, because this will always remain an invaluable source of new knowledge.

Major changes in society can be caused by far-reaching advances in basic science, of a nature and magnitude to justify the use of the overworked term 'discovery'. Examples might include DNA studies with their medical and forensic applications, or semiconductor developments which have given us ever more powerful and pervasive computers. How are such advances made? We do not know. *A fortiori* no scientist can be instructed to make a discovery, let alone a particular discovery. The history of natural science, engineering and technology shows that a great many important discoveries were made by able people who simply wanted to understand something which did not fit in with existing scientific knowledge, and was puzzling them; they could not foresee where the quest would lead them. We also know the social environment in which the discoverers flourish. As in other fields of endeavour, it is one in which creative persons – having curiosity, imagination and insight based on knowledge – are allowed the freedom to follow up their own lines of thought; where they can be subject to the views of informed colleagues worldwide; and where they are allowed to continue, even in the face of adverse criticism, if they have just one good argument or hunch which merits further investigation. The ideal location for this kind of enquiry is the university as described by John Masefield (Chapter 6) or the independent research institute.

Significant major discoveries are very rare, but they more than pay for their own costs. For example, E.P. Abraham's elucidation of the structure of the powerful antibiotics, the cephalosporins, produced revenues which paid for the whole of the National Research and Development Corporation for many years, as well as permitting Abraham to establish a generous charitable foundation. But it remains the case that discoveries can only be made by those who can recognise them for what they are, which means that they must have a trained mind. If there is an element of chance in making a discovery, then Pasteur's statement that 'chance favours the prepared mind' is also true.

It is said that when questioned about the use of one of his inventions Edison replied, 'Damned if I know, but sure as hell they'll tax it one day'. Faraday's response to a similar enquiry was to ask what is the 'use' of a newborn baby. Sir Michael Atiyah, in his anniversary address to the Royal Society on his retirement from the presidency in 1995, saw the danger of the application of utilitarian criteria to basic science, and therefore how difficult it is for government to get the right balance in the allocation of resources to basic and applied science. He said:

> There is no doubt that getting the balance right between the unfettered pursuit of pure science and the harnessing of science for the benefit of society continues to be a major problem. In times of economic difficulty or financial stringency (and these seem to be perpetually with us) governments have a natural tendency to push, nudge or cajole scientists down the utilitarian path. Interestingly enough, this attitude is not supported by many leaders of industry, who see a clear distinction between the role of government in supporting our basic infrastructure and their role in building on that full industrial application. This view is widely held in other countries, and in the United States sixteen chief executives of major industrial companies recently issued a public statement to this effect.

John Polanyi has said in the same vein that the applied sector should not set the agenda for the basic.[7] Our rulers should constantly keep in mind another Baconian maxim, from his *Novum Organum*: *Scientia non nisi parendo vincitur* – 'Science cannot be commanded unless it is obeyed'.

The above are not arguments for the scientists in the basic sector to eschew the activities of the applied one. On the contrary, there is every reason for close contact between the two, and a regular traffic in good people and ideas. I can cite many innovations from my own experience, having learned much from my industrial contacts: thus, for example, polythene would not have been discovered if scientists at ICI had not been persuaded by thermodynamic arguments, advanced by academic consultants, that the application of high pressure would favour the formation of long-chain polymers because that reaction would involve the greatest volume decrease. I therefore find it little short of insanity that the university research and teaching base in the UK has been allowed, through chronic government underfunding, to decline in quality to its present position, where science-

---

7. We should always remember the disastrous consequences of the top-down planning of the command economies of the pre-1990 Eastern bloc, which ignored scientifically-based safety and environmental considerations and permitted the disaster of Chernobyl and the pollution caused by plants like the steelworks near Kraków. Take programme policy decisions out of the hands of true scientists and place them in the hands of second-rate scientists who covet power, and they will become influenced by absurd views. I well remember the USSR before the war acting on the erroneous genetic ideas of Lysenko with his notions of 'vernalisation' of the steppe, which had catastrophic consequences for the economy and for individuals.

based industrialists are increasingly heard to complain that 'urgent reform is needed to reverse the passive neglect of university infrastructure'.[8]

The conventional counter-argument of government is 'we can't afford it at the moment', with the fallacious claim that it is more urgent to invest in bringing technological research and development to a higher standard. Policies which deny resources for basic research, because technology is weak, will ultimately ensure the country's economic decline.

Slogans such as the 'white heat of the technological revolution' may have been simplistic and misleading, generating expectations which could not be fulfilled. Nevertheless, Britain cannot afford to miss the gains which may result from the future application of basic science now being pursued: the remorseless reduction in the resources available for curiosity-driven research is closing down options for the years to come. The amount of money required to keep such options open is tiny, far less than one per cent of GDP per annum, and the investment will almost certainly be repaid in abundance through the creation of new science-based processes or enterprises, and their associated employment of skilled people. The fact that I cannot say what those benefits will be, other than that they will be based upon some of the discoveries made, does not invalidate the argument. If asked where the money is to come from today, I would reply with the question 'Where has the money gone from the peace dividend, or the sale of formerly nationalised assets?'

It is easy to write about science policy by concentrating on the resources which government is prepared to provide, especially at the 'basic' end of the spectrum. But neither the science base nor the government *per se* creates wealth. In the process of enrichment there are three players, not two, the third and actual wealth creator being privately-owned industry. None of the three sectors will perform well unless their staffs include many able, well-trained scientists, engineers and technologists. The nation's ability to educate and mobilise such brain power will critically influence its economic performance. The people concerned circulate and interact within the trio of linked players, and are the oxygen which is essential if the national science capability is to remain alive and function well: without such people the economy will eventually wither and die.

---

8. The words are those of George Poste, as chairman for Research and Development in SmithKline Beecham Pharmaceuticals.

CHAPTER 9

FIVE YEARS AT THE INTERFACE BETWEEN GOVERNMENT AND THE UNIVERSITIES

...no one appreciates more fully than myself the vital importance of preserving the liberty and autonomy of the universities within the general lines laid down by the constitution. The state is, in my opinion, not competent to direct the work of education and disinterested research which is carried on by universities, and the responsibility for its conduct must rest solely with the governing bodies and teachers. This is a principle which has always been observed in the distribution of funds which Parliament has voted for subsidising university work; and as long as I have any hand in shaping the national system of education I intend to observe this principle...

H.A.L. Fisher (1865-1940)
President of the Board of Education[1]

A Sideways Transition?

The body entrusted by the government for seventy years (1919–89) with general responsibility for universities and their funding was the University Grants Committee (UGC). It received its money directly from the Treasury until 1964, when the newly created Department of Education and Science (DES) became its paymaster, and then twenty-five years later changed it into the more dirigiste

---

1. The quotation comes from a letter to the vice-chancellors of Oxford and Cambridge dated 16 April 1919. Fisher had a remarkable career, during which he was Vice-Chancellor of the young University of Sheffield and Warden of New College, Oxford. He published widely on historical subjects, and was President of the British Academy as well as the Board of Education. He was elected FRS in 1920.

Universities Funding Council. This in turn was supplanted in 1993 by the Higher Education Funding Councils for England, Scotland, Wales and Northern Ireland. As I have already described, I became chairman of the UGC on 1 October 1973 – a post I held for the next five years. Despite my best efforts, historians may well regard this period as marking the end of what had become the most generous system in the world of state provision for university education.

For me the transition from the Advisory Board for the Research Councils to the UGC marked a further broadening of my education, in which I lost none of my scientific contacts and gained a new perspective on the type of institutions that had employed me for 34 years of my life, and to which I felt a strong allegiance. I expected that the sideways transition from the scientific arm to the mainstream university arm within the Dual Support System would be relatively simple, and that the UGC would not be too dissimilar from the Council for Scientific Policy, also a non-statutory body. In the event this assumption proved to be ill-founded, largely because of the centuries-old concept of universities as independent, self-governing corporations, each controlling the admission of its own students and appointing its own staff who, unlike the *fonctionnaires* of France or the *Beamte* of Germany, were not civil servants and expected full freedom to determine their own teaching and research programmes; and also, between them, the way in which students were to be admitted, taught and examined. At this point it may be helpful to the reader if, at some cost of repetition, I put the work of the UGC in context by describing how British universities developed and how government became the source of a major part of their incomes.

How the University Grants Committee was Created, and Evolved

Britain's first two universities, Oxford and Cambridge, initially comprised just masters and scholars who found what accommodation they could. Over the years wealthy benefactors, often ecclesiastical or royal, founded colleges as an act of piety (or merely to exercise their patronage). From the beginning colleges were independent, self-governing communities, with the masters responsible for teaching the scholars, and so they have remained. The university was simply the corporation of masters, and its major function was to examine and certify successful candidates in the subjects of the *trivium* (grammar, rhetoric and logic) and *quadrivium* (arithmetic, geometry, astronomy and music). During the great expansion of learning of the Renaissance this narrow curriculum was reformed in all European universities, and Oxford and Cambridge also had to contend with the difficulties of the Reformation when the monarch, Elizabeth I, began to take a direct interest in their affairs: she remodelled their constitutions in 1571. Despite the disturbances of the Civil War, the beneficial effects of the Renaissance continued: for example, science began to develop as names like Newton, Hooke, Boyle, Halley and Wren testify. Alas, towards the end of the seventeenth century the two universities began to sink into a state of sloth and corruption which continued throughout most of the eighteenth century. Both the universities and their colleges remained closed communities with religious entry tests, jealously defending and enlarging their territories, possessions and temporal powers. Edward Gibbon's well-known disparagement of Magdalen College, Oxford (where he claimed to have spent the most idle and unprofitable fourteen months of his whole life) merely reinforced the opinion of a tough-minded Yorkshire Quaker and prominent London physician, John Fothergill, who commented sadly in 1769, 'I do not think anything would give me more pain than to reside a few months in Oxford. There I should find men of the first rank of understanding engaged in an idle round of that which the lowest of mankind can enjoy as much as themselves: eating, drinking and sleeping'.

In so far as they had a clear purpose, both universities saw their prime function as simply to educate the sons of the ruling class, or those who wished to enter the learned professions such as law, medicine and the church. Research and scholarship were not recognised as a duty. Reform had to come, but it waited until the nineteenth century when 'honours schools' were established with prescribed courses of study and properly conducted examinations, and the colleges became more outward-looking. Even so, it required three Acts of Parliament (in 1854, 1856 and 1877) to reform their administration. Neither university made any significant contribution to the creation of national wealth during the Industrial Revolution: to a very large extent the builders of Britain's roads, railways, canals, ships, docks, bridges, and engines for pumping, traction or power tools were not graduates of either Oxford or Cambridge.

Scotland was quite different. By the early seventeenth century it had twice as many universities as the much more populous England, and they were unitary and non-collegiate. Their ideal was practical service to the community, producing the people to enable society to work, many of them going on to teach in a school system which was also far in advance of that in England. The Scottish institutions represented a route for able children, whatever their origins, to proceed to the highest levels of knowledge. The professors were valued for what they knew and could transmit to others. They educated good doctors, lawyers and clerics and, when Gibbon was complaining about Oxford, Adam Smith was writing *The Wealth of Nations* in Glasgow and Joseph Black was lecturing on chemistry in Edinburgh – not just to students of medicine from the University but also to apprentices from the factory or the workshop, who often had little or no preparation for such a course but were willing to work hard in order to better themselves. Black also busied himself with chemical research, largely ignored by others apart from the Unitarian minister Joseph Priestley (who himself used Black's burning glass to heat mercuric oxide, and thus discovered oxygen).

The creation of new English universities had to wait for the early nineteenth century, when reaction against the Oxbridge religious tests led to the establishment in 1826 of the 'godless' University College, London, which was non-residential and excluded theology from its curriculum. Reaction from the church followed with the foundation three years later of King's College. Durham came into being shortly afterwards, in 1832. It was surprising that the capital city of an empire had to wait until 1836 for a University of London, and even then its only powers were to examine and confer degrees on students attending approved institutions in the United Kingdom. However, once established it grew rapidly, became a federal university of colleges and, through its power to grant 'external' London degrees to those studying elsewhere, it effectively nursed into university status many young colleges in England and the overseas dominions. Later it became possible for students to secure their degrees independently by private study, provided they satisfied the London University examiners.

Meanwhile the perception was growing that if Britain was to become what was claimed for her, that is, the workshop of the world (which the Great Exhibition of 1851 was supposed to bring to a public focus), then there was a need for more higher education. A few of the leading citizens of our manufacturing and mercantile cities saw this need and they started colleges in cities such as Manchester, Leeds, Bristol, Sheffield, Birmingham and Liverpool: by the end of the nineteenth century, often by combining with local medical and technical schools, these had evolved into university colleges. Collectively these institutions had few students and little in the way of resources, and could rarely be said to have made much impact, except by providing trained doctors, teachers and technical staff to meet largely local needs. If, as some claimed, these colleges were universities in embryo this could only have been in the sense of Groucho Marx, who in a letter to Sam Zolotow wrote, 'My plans are still in embryo. In case you have never been there, this is a small town on the outskirts of wishful thinking.' That England and Wales needed such colleges was beyond doubt; it was equally certain that without help from the Exchequer the embryos would never become adults.

A good precedent for financial help from the state was to be found in Scotland. The four Scottish universities were of some antiquity: St Andrew's, Glasgow and Aberdeen were all ecclesiastical foundations of the fifteenth century, while in 1583 the Edinburgh Town Council established a college which became a university in 1621. These four universities enjoyed small grants from the Scottish government, and after the Act of Union Westminster continued the payments, finally consolidating them into a total sum of £5,000 per annum in 1831. Although the University of London received a subvention of £4,000 when founded five years later, the government turned deaf ears to all appeals for money from other institutions south of the border until 1882, when it made a small grant to University College, Aberystwyth. That this was achieved even then was largely due to the steadfastness of purpose of Sir Hugh Owen and the support given by thousands of ordinary Welsh folk in that part of the Principality, who had contributed their mites to the establishment of the college and were determined it should not fail.

Two years later W.M. Hicks FRS, Principal of Firth College, Sheffield, and William Ramsay FRS, Principal of University College, Bristol, and later a Nobel Laureate, were returning home by ship from their attendance at a meeting of the British Association for the Advancement of Science in Montreal. They had ample opportunity to discuss their and other colleges' financial predicaments, and they decided to launch a campaign to secure government help. Many eminent scientists were vociferous in their support and the Master of Balliol College, the remarkable Dr Benjamin Jowett, who was a staunch friend of University College, Bristol, stated in a letter to *The Times* in 1887 that a sum of £100,000 per annum would ensure the continuation of these colleges. Deputations were sent to London, the support of local and national MPs was enlisted, and slowly the Treasury walls began to crumble. In 1888 £2,000 per annum was allocated to the Victoria University, a federation of the colleges in Leeds, Manchester and Liverpool, and the following year a terse press announcement was issued:

> The Chancellor of the Exchequer has finally decided to allot an annual sum of £15,000 in aid of local colleges. The amount will appear in the Estimates for the coming year. The sum asked for was £50,000.

On the same day the Treasury issued a minute setting up a committee to select the institutions which were to benefit, and to recommend the sums each should receive. The committee did its work well and admitted to its grant list ten of the first eleven supplicants for financial aid (the exception was from Southampton).

From the correspondence between the committee and the Lords of the Treasury many of the elements of the later UGC system can be discerned. It was recognised early on that the universities must have some stability in their funding to help them to plan wisely and effectively, if possible having major changes only at five-year intervals. It was also agreed that institutions should provide information about what would now be called staff complement and student load, as well as the revenue received from all other sources; and that they should be visited on a regular basis by distinguished academics who would make some kind of inspection. The evident wisdom and practicality of the decisions of the first committee, and its successors, ensured acceptance of the idea of such a body standing between government and individual institutions as a permanent feature of higher education in the United Kingdom. By 1905 the committee's grant had grown to £100,000 per annum and its chairman was the redoubtable Richard Haldane. Predictably, he was indefatigable in his representations to government and he persuaded his fellow committee members to propose that there should be a permanent entity – executive as well as advisory – to which the government would allocate a sum of money for distribution directly to the universities. As a result, in 1912 the Treasury handed over some of its responsibilities for universities to the Board of Education.

It was an extremely fortunate circumstance that H.A.L. Fisher was appointed President of the Board of Education in 1916. As Vice-Chancellor of Sheffield University for the previous three years, he fully understood the problems of the 'civic' universities (as they were now known) with their relative lack of endowments. It was his and Haldane's advocacy that led to the establishment by the

Treasury of the University Grants Committee in 1919. Looking back, it is surprising that this most important figure should deliberately detach his department from responsibility for the universities. Perhaps it was in the spirit of the time because, as I explained in Chapter 8, Haldane and Addison were equally firm in their determination to have the Research Councils funded directly by the Treasury and not by any particular department of government.

The First Fifty-four Years

I shall not embark on a history of the UGC, because there are already adequate accounts.[2] Therefore in what follows I shall only pick out those features of the earlier UGC which are germane to events during my chairmanship.

The original terms of reference set by the Treasury consisted of the single sentence: 'To enquire into the financial needs of University Education in the United Kingdom and to advise the Government as to the application of any grants that may be made by Parliament towards meeting them'. These sufficed for twenty years, at the end of which the total number of full-time students was a mere 50,000, of whom 6.2 per cent were postgraduate. Immediately after the war the numbers of students were swelled by demobilised servicemen and women seeking to begin or complete studies from which they had been precluded by war service. It was also clear that with only two per cent of young Britons entering higher education, the universities were falling well short of meeting the needs of the country for graduates. The terms of reference of the UGC were therefore changed in 1946 to ensure that it made a proper contribution to the planning process and ceased just to *advise* on the use of any grants, but had the authority to allocate funds to universities without going back to the government. The committee's duties were spelled out in some detail:

> To collect, examine and make available information relating to university education throughout the United Kingdom; and to assist, in consultation with the universities and other bodies concerned, the preparation and execution of such plans for the development of the universities as may from time to time be required in order to ensure that they are fully adequate to national needs.

2. See, for example, John Carswell, *Government and the Universities in Britain* (Cambridge University Press, 1986).

The Butler Education Act of 1944 and the raising of the school-leaving age to sixteen meant that more pupils stayed on in school to the sixth form. Together with the ambition of parents to secure for their children an education which they had not enjoyed themselves, this led to a steady increase in the numbers of school leavers wishing to enter universities, and having prima facie qualifications. At the beginning of the 1960s the number was given a powerful boost by the acceptance of the Anderson Committee's recommendation that young people accepted by a university or a college of advanced technology should in most cases be entitled to a local education authority award (actually paid from central government funds). Small wonder that by 1963 the number of full-time students then in universities was two and a half times that of 1939.

Pressure for expansion of the student population came not just from parents but also from the government, which wished to reduce shortages evident in the professions (especially doctors to staff the expanding National Health Service) in a period when full employment was not only a slogan but the norm. Furthermore, it was plain that the surge in the birth rate in the immediate post-war years would lead to a bulge in the proportion of 18-year-olds in the early to mid-1960s. Sir Keith Murray, chairman of the UGC in the period 1953-63, not only realised that more university places must be provided but, as I know from a conversation I had with him in 1961, positively welcomed the expansion of the university system and was convinced that additional universities would be both necessary and beneficial. Under his chairmanship the UGC was reorganised and re-energised to mastermind as much expansion as he could persuade the Treasury to fund.

In 1961 the Treasury established its well-known committee under Lord Robbins, which had the following terms of reference:

> To review the pattern of full-time higher education in Great Britain and, in the light of national needs and resources, to advise Her Majesty's Government on what principles the long-term development should be based. In particular, to advise, in the light of these principles, whether there should be any changes in that pattern, whether any new types of institution are desirable, and whether any modifications should be made in the present arrangements for planning and co-ordinating the development of the various types of institution.

At the time I was too busy in Leeds to pay much attention to this decision or to see in it the implied rebuff to the UGC, then the Treasury's own adviser on universities, which *a priori* might well have been judged fully capable of undertaking such a review. When, two years later, the report appeared I took advantage of Charles Morris' decision to provide a copy for every member of the University Senate who wished to receive one. A quick glance satisfied me that it was a vote for expansion of both sectors of higher education, and within that for more university places for students in science and technology. I was content with this until twelve months later when the unexpected, and then inexplicable, downturn in applications to study chemistry in Leeds became only too evident, as I described in Chapter 5. The acceptance by government of many of Robbins' recommendations added impetus to the UGC's own programmes, and there were few persons in that body or elsewhere who saw the flaws. The flaw concerned with science and technology expansion came to haunt me when I myself joined the UGC because, in accordance with its own and Robbins' wishes, and with government backing, it had provided more places in universities for science and technology students than there were suitably qualified candidates coming forward.

The Rhythm and Style of the UGC's Work

When I joined the UGC it consisted of twenty members apart from myself, all appointed by the Secretary of State for Education and Science after consultation with the Secretaries of State for Scotland and Wales. It was made clear to each member on arrival that he or she served in an individual capacity, and was not rep-resentative of any institution or organisation. Their collective expertise covered the whole range of faculties within universities, together with a knowledge of other parts of the educational system as well as business and industry. The Scottish Education Department, the Welsh Office and the Department of Health and Social Security, as well as the Research Councils, were entitled to have assessors attend meetings of the Committee and certain of its sub-committees: they contributed to the discussions but did not take part in the decision-making. From time to time the Committee met the Secretary of State or Minister, or both, and the initiative for such meetings could come from either side. As in the CSP, there was one case of a Minister who thought he should come to all the meetings he was able to attend, on the same erroneous premise that the Committee existed solely to advise him on his policies for the universities. There was a regular system of sub-committees covering agriculture and veterinary studies, medicine, mathematics, physical sciences, biological sciences, social studies, technology, arts, dentistry, education, business studies, and university–industry collaboration. In addition, ad hoc committees were appointed to study particular problems, such as accommodation capacity, research funding, or the creation of a policy for the management of university libraries. Each sub-committee was chaired by a member of the main committee, and its remaining members could be drawn from the universities or other sectors of employment, as seemed most appropriate to the matter in hand.

The UGC met every month except August and also held one weekend meeting a year, usually in September, when time could be given to thorough, wide-ranging discussions of major policy issues. There was also at least one meeting a year with the Committee of Vice-Chancellors and Principals, and with the Association of University Teachers. There was much traffic with various government departments, Research Councils and individual institutions, and a regular cycle of meetings ensured that each university was visited once every five years – the 'quinquennial visitation'. On these occasions the Committee would meet senior officers, groups of staff, students, and members of statutory committees such as the Senate and Council. No subject was excluded from debate, except the confidential advice which the Committee was likely to give to government. These discussions were facilitated by each group submitting papers beforehand and, of course, the Committee had a range of issues on which it wished to know the mind of every university with which it had a meeting. Topics considered included academic developments, industrial relationships, how the university foresaw the development of its research and teaching, whether library services were adequate, the extent to which welfare provisions were satisfactory, and so on. Such encounters, whether involving the whole Committee or one of its sub-committees, were quite invaluable as a means of determining the temper, cohesiveness and sense of common purpose of an institution. Although not designed to assess quality, nevertheless they often provided valuable pointers which registered in members' minds and were the basis of any consensus reached and recorded. These visitations also served another useful purpose, in that members of the Committee were in one another's company for two or sometimes three days on end, and this gave ample opportunity for the kind of in-depth discussion which is not possible when members come together for a single meeting. *Esprit de corps* is an old-fashioned term, but nevertheless a reality which was built up in considerable measure by the shared experience of the many visitations we undertook in the five years I was chairman.

The two major tasks of the Committee were to advise government on the needs of the universities and to allocate, from money which the state provided, grants to individual universities. These were of three kinds. First, there were non-recurrent allocations for the purchase of sites and properties, and to meet the costs of approved building projects and the initial furnishing of new accommodation. Secondly, another type of capital grant was given to enable a university to replace, as necessary, worn out or obsolete furniture and equipment. (Universities had discretion as to when they could spend capital grants, but monetary virement to some other purpose was not permitted.) The third and largest type of award was the annual recurrent grant intended to allow the institution to meet general running costs, including staff salaries (both academic and non-academic), library purchases, laboratory consumables, maintenance of premises, and so on. In all cases, the amounts given were closely related to what is known as the student load.[3]

It was apparent to the proto-UGCs towards the end of the nineteenth century that long planning horizons were required by universities to ensure the best use of the funds allocated to them. Normally the period involved was five years (about the length of the longest degree course) so that, following UGC approval of new developments, universities could assume that money for them had been built into the block grant during the next quinquennial period. Towards the end of a quinquennium, planning began for the next five years. Universities were asked to submit their proposals for new developments in as complete and quantitative form as they could. These were then considered by the UGC to see whether in its view each plan was appropriate for the university concerned and whether, in summation, they could provide a basis for making a credible bid to government for funds, or whether they required modification. In addition, the UGC's total bid had to be reconciled with national policies – for example, any plan to increase the number of doctors or to ensure that the overall costs of higher education in the next five years would not exceed a certain value. None of this work could be satisfactorily accomplished

3. Student load is a measure of the number of 'full-time equivalent' (fte) students taught or supervised in the area concerned: for example, a student taught equally by two departments represents 0.5fte to each of them. Use of fte figures also allows proper account to be taken of part-time students.

without the collection of a wide range of statistics about university numbers and costs, and careful analysis of the data. It also involved the UGC's officers in continuing dialogue with universities, both individually and through the CVCP, and also with the various arms of government.

The culmination of all this work was a letter sent to each university, specifying the recurrent grant for that institution and including a statement of the student numbers on which its funding for the next quinquennium had been calculated. The numbers were subdivided into undergraduate and postgraduate, arts-based and science-based categories. Sometimes, for newly created departments such as medicine, the money would be earmarked for a limited period; otherwise the university was entirely free to use the grant as it thought best. The letter would also contain comments on the proposals submitted, indicating those parts of the plans that the UGC wished to encourage or discourage; for example, the Committee might make full provision for the university's proposal to develop subject X, or only partial provision, or no provision. But whatever was said in the letter, it was understood that the university ultimately had the right to use its money in any way it wished, unless sums had been specifically earmarked. The rationale behind this flexibility was twofold. In the first place it served to protect university autonomy, and in the second place experience had taught the UGC that it had no monopoly of wisdom or experience in these matters; indeed, I can still remember a number of instances in which, despite our lack of encouragement, universities embarked on particular developments which subsequently flourished. Finally, there was always attached to the letter a memorandum of general guidance indicating how the whole university system was expected to develop in the forthcoming five years.

What I have written above is the merest outline of the major activities of the UGC and the way in which it operated. It was all a far cry from the line-item budgeting of many state university systems in North America, and was therefore much envied for the way in which it seemed to liberate the creative energies of academic staff and administrators in Britain, and to foster new developments of perceived value (and discourage those of lesser worth). I also believe that the resulting sense of 'ownership' of individual universities by their academic staff increased people's commitment to their own particular institution, and diminished the chance that they would develop the sterile attitude of merely being an employee of a management whose policies they were unable to shape.

My First Month: A Baptism of Fire

After a hectic month of preparation I felt rather breathless on entering the UGC offices at 14 Park Crescent, near Regent's Park, on 1 October 1973. However, I was made to feel very welcome by the staff, and found waiting a most kind letter from my predecessor, Sir Kenneth Berrill, a friend from my St Catharine's days at Cambridge, whose characteristic generosity and encouragement did a great deal for my morale. I spent a busy day introducing myself to as many colleagues as possible, and that evening had dinner with representatives of the Association of University Teachers. The following day was filled by chairing a staff meeting to prepare the agenda for the main Committee session some three weeks later, and also accompanying my elder daughter, Mary, to University College Hospital Medical School, where she was embarking on the clinical part of her course in medicine.

So far so good, and on the morning of 3 October I entered my office in a cheerful mood, ready to answer the questions which I felt sure Professor J.S. Rowlinson, who was being considered for the chair at Oxford which I had just vacated, would put to me. Our conversation was interrupted by my secretary asking if I would see the Committee Secretary, Ralph Fletcher, as soon as possible on a matter of urgency. I drew my meeting with John Rowlinson to a close as quickly as I could without, I hope, giving him the impression that I was according less attention to his problems than he might consider they deserved. If I failed, here is a rather belated apology! When I entered Ralph's room his first words were, 'We cannot approve any more tenders for buildings', and he went on to explain that this government fiat was likely to be only a prelude to more draconian measures as part of changed economic policies in response to rising inflation and concern over the supply of oil from the Middle East (and its price to the western world). This was indeed disastrous news, particularly because we both knew that many students enrolled in their first year under the expansion programme were already in grave difficulties over securing suitable accommodation, with halls of residence full and private lodgings not affordable. After talking with Ted Moss, the UGC's Under-Secretary in charge of the Capital Division, Ralph and I decided we must lobby hard, and that while he would tackle the civil servants my job would be to persuade Ministers.

As luck would have it, I had to attend a dinner party at Admiralty House the following evening, hosted by Mrs Thatcher, and I also saw her in Oxford two days later when she and I were guests of the University's Alembic Club (and indeed were both speakers). The immediate outcome of Ralph's and my efforts was that on the Friday of the next week I was able to send a letter to all vice-chancellors informing them of the government's decision to rephase the public building programme and stating that the only tenders that could be approved by the Committee would be those for student residences. Vice-chancellors, who had learned from the media of the government's moratorium on building some four days earlier, were greatly relieved by this letter and, more to the point, many students subsequently had adequate accommodation who otherwise would have had none. However, it was also necessary to insert an item entitled 'building programme' in the already agreed (and crowded) agenda for the meeting six days later. This item in fact appeared for discussion at just over half the UGC's meetings in the academic year 1973-74 and, for reasons I shall shortly explain, was soon joined by another recurrent feature known as 'planning numbers'.

Four days after my first full UGC meeting I had, at his request, a talk with Sir David Pitblado, the Comptroller and Auditor General, Head of the National Audit Office and an Officer of the House of Commons, who carried considerable statutory power to examine the efficient and economical working of organisations in receipt of public funds. I was naturally somewhat anxious. Fortunately we soon established common ground, but that did not disguise the seriousness with which he viewed the problem of 'vacant places', which was to be the subject of our discussion. This term was used to denote the situation which had arisen because of Keith Murray's expansionist tendencies and the Robbins Report, which together had caused the UGC to develop building plans that would provide a capacity to admit in 1973 about double, and in 1980 over treble, the number of science and technology students recruited in 1962. I was in a difficult position because the report of the CSP working party which I had chaired (published in 1968) had indicated beyond any doubt that these targets were probably quite unattainable; and this report had been ignored. Inevitably, by 1973 there were several tens of thousands of empty places in these subjects in universities, a fact which no Comptroller and Auditor General could ignore. This problem is still with us, and is directly linked to the shortage of suitably qualified mathematics and science teachers. After thirty years of concern over this problem and its inevitable adverse consequences, I still wonder whether any government has the will to tackle it.

There seemed to be an unending stream of visitors to 14 Park Crescent. Many were vice-chancellors with particular problems, often of a financial kind. Even some chairmen of university Councils would call. The first was Stephen de Bartolomé, Chairman of Sheffield University Council, bearing the news that Sir Hugh 'Norrie' Robson, Vice-Chancellor of that university and also Chairman of the CVCP, was moving to Edinburgh as Principal at the end of the session. Mr Bartolomé's visit was to seek advice in the search for a successor. Neither of us could guess that five years later he would telephone again to ask if I would be willing to become his university's Chancellor.

Although we had leased a flat in Prince Albert Road, on the north side of Regent's Park, Barbara was able to make very little use of it – especially during the Oxford University terms, when her duties as a Teaching Fellow of St Hilda's College kept her out of London. Consequently, if there was no official evening engagement I would either stay late at the office and have a light supper of my own devising at the flat, or drive to the Athenaeum and, having dined, return to do some more work. Such a packed week, leaving Oxford no later than 7am on Monday and departing from the office after 7pm on Friday (times chosen to avoid the worst of the traffic) meant I felt a great sense of relief when I arrived at Fieldside to be greeted by Shep, who seemed to know when I was coming home and was always alongside the car door before I could open it. Barbara and I often found ourselves tired but in time adjusted to the new regime. Despite the attendant anxieties and problems, the pattern of life seemed less burdensome as I became more competent in the job and therefore more confident.

By the end of my first month at the UGC I felt thoroughly 'broken in' and accepted by the staff, so that together we could continue to discharge the remit given to the Committee in 1946.

The Illusion of Normality in a Changing World

As November 1973 began I still imagined that the government's precipitate action over capital programmes was a temporary phenomenon. The first two weeks of the month seemed to confirm this, in that there were useful and enjoyable visitations to two constituent parts of the University of London – the Courtauld Institute of Art and Bedford College – which also served as good practice runs for visits to larger establishments. Altogether there were about seventy institutions to be visited by the Committee during the quinquennium, which meant an average of almost five per academic term. To reduce the time wasted in travel, a visit to one major institution would immediately be followed by that to a neighbouring university, combining for example Nottingham and Leicester, Edinburgh and Heriot-Watt.

Within the 1973-74 programme of visitations, the dates of 28 and 29 November had been set aside for Southampton and Reading universities. In accordance with the general rule, members of the party had been provided by the UGC staff with a considerable dossier about each institution, including a report of the Committee's findings from five years earlier, and any relevant observations generated by subject sub-committees. Each university had also submitted papers prepared by the various groups we were to meet, so the groundwork was well laid for useful exchanges of information and views.

Alas, 'the best laid plans o' mice an' men gang aft agley'. Whilst we knew the Southampton students were not sending any representatives to meet the Committee (their Union had passed a resolution to this effect), we were not prepared for the orchestrated series of demonstrations they had arranged for us. In the afternoon these took the form of trying to prevent our progress to the meeting room. No member of the Committee could tolerate this and, with the help of some university staff, we forced our way physically through the crowd and attempted to conduct our business. Tactically this proved to be unwise, because the room had no door other than the one by which we had entered. After some time, during which the students' noisy demonstrations made it impossible to have any proper discussion, it became clear that it would be difficult for the next group, which consisted of the University Council representatives, to enter and we therefore decided to abandon the rest of the visitation.[4] This posed the question of our exit from the room, but there was no telephone by which we could summon help. Fortunately, the Vice-Chancellor, L.C.B. (Jim) Gower, was a slim, athletic man who squeezed through the window, made his

---

4. The next month members of the Council of Southampton University came to the UGC offices in London to resume the meeting; they were naturally upset and most apologetic for the inconvenience we had been caused. On behalf of the Committee, I had written a letter to the Union President pointing out that we were sorry not to have met the student representatives, that we did not set the level of the fees they had to pay – which they claimed had been the proximate cause of their demonstration – and that by absenting themselves they had also deprived the student body and the UGC of the benefits which we knew could result from such meetings. I do not recall receiving a reply.

escape and called the police to our assistance. So it was that we left Southampton and boarded our coach for the journey to Reading.

There was a milder demonstration at Reading, but it did not impede our business. I began to wonder whether we would encounter other disturbances as disruptive as that at Southampton, or whether student unrest was in fact in decline. Our visit to Essex in February 1974 had all the makings of another upset and I felt sorry for the vice-chancellor and his wife, who lived in the centre of the campus and who had been considerably harassed by the militants. Of course the media made much of the disturbances, and doubtless this contributed to the decision of the House of Commons to establish committees to visit some of the troubled universities. Based on my own experience at Nottingham, I considered this unwise, for radicals thrive on publicity and the media love a 'scene'. Looking back on all the UGC visitations (and I only missed one in five years), I consider that once the students had settled down, a process taking ten or fifteen minutes, the discussions were usually well worth while from our point of view at least. Some of the students we met were of very high quality, deeply serious and devoted to their universities and the cause of higher education in general. I remember mentioning to Norrie Robson during the Edinburgh visitation, apropos the Student Rector's performance, 'I bet he is a son of the manse and that once he gets over his premature gravitas, he'll go far. I wonder where.' Norrie confirmed my first conjecture but disagreed with my prophecy. The young man was Gordon Brown, now Chancellor of the Exchequer.

With hindsight, I think that our meetings with students could have been better arranged so as to make them more productive. As it was, these young people entered the room to sit opposite a line of almost twenty UGC members and officials. Neither group had met the other before and the setting must have suggested to inexperienced students a confrontation, if not an inquisition. On three occasions the timetable allowed us to mingle with the students before the formal meeting, which was much easier and less stilted as a result. I also remember an occasion at Loughborough in 1976 when, at the request of the vice-chancellor, I sacrificed my lunch in an attempt to quieten a few hundred foreign students who wished to protest against the government's recent decision to raise 'overseas' tuition fees. I moved among them, trying to answer a barrage of questions, and soon realised that my responses and arguments could be heard by only a few though I wished to transmit my message to them all. I was much surprised when a large black student with whom I had been talking suddenly seized my left wrist in the manner of a boxing referee, and in a voice with all the richness and power of Paul Robeson called for quiet and then roared 'I have talked with this man. We can trust him. Let him speak'. They did so and when I had finished, having pointed out that the fees decision had not been made by either the UGC or the universities where they studied, they put their questions politely and in an orderly way, without any hostility. Even so, I was not amused when one member of the Committee commented, as I was sorting my papers for the afternoon session, that he and his colleagues had enjoyed an excellent lunch!

The End of Innocence, and of the Quinquennium

As a young professor at Leeds, having met the UGC on its visitation in the early 1950s, I wondered how the members were so well informed and how their chairman radiated such courteous omniscience. This in turn caused me to ponder whether their monthly meetings were also conducted with such efficiency. From my later experience I can answer that question affirmatively. The staff clearly understood and valued the work which universities did, and therefore were themselves highly motivated. Two days before each regular UGC meeting I would hold a final briefing session with some of them, armed with the papers sent to all the members, to ensure that any question which might be put could be answered adequately, and that relevant information was available to enable the Committee to come to clear conclusions. A fortnight earlier, the same group would have met to draw up the agenda and to assign to individuals the preparation of any necessary papers. The UGC monthly meeting itself began at 10.30am, and would usually extend beyond lunch. The office machine ran very smoothly, both for these regularly spaced occasions and for the more broken rhythms of the visitations. When I had lunch early in 1977 with Keith Murray, chairman between 1953 and 1963, he stressed how much he had enjoyed this regularity of events – 'almost soothing', he said – and he hoped I had too. He was 73 then and had himself prepared a delicious lunch for the two of us, and I simply had not the heart to tell him the truth. The reality was that from December 1973, while the meeting and visitation rhythms remained, the business conducted suggested nothing of the controlled, well-oiled, smooth progress over which he had presided in his two quinquennia. Instead, the

1972-77 quinquennial plan had by *force majeure* been largely abandoned, and the best I could hope for in its place was a quasi-triennium.

In fact, during my five years at the UGC there was change at every level. Prime Ministers changed from Heath to Wilson (1974), from Wilson to Callaghan (1976); the Secretary of State for Education and Science changed from Mrs Thatcher to Reg Prentice (1974), from Reg Prentice to Fred Mulley (1975), and from Fred Mulley to Shirley Williams (1976); while at Permanent Secretary level Bill Pile moved to be Chairman of the Board of Inland Revenue in 1976 and was succeeded by Jim Hamilton. Closer to home Ralph Fletcher, the Secretary of the UGC, died in 1974 and was replaced by John Carswell, who resigned in 1977 to become Secretary of the British Academy, his successor being Geoffrey Cockerill. The changes of Secretary caused minimal disturbance because they were all able colleagues who became friends. The real disruptive force was the economic crisis of double-digit inflation and balance of payments deficits, and the financially stringent measures used by successive governments in their attempt to remedy the situation. These in turn undermined the conventions which had informed governmental relations with the UGC, and which made that body such an effective instrument in securing from universities their best responses to its paymasters' stated needs.

1973-74 was the second academic year of the 1972-77 quinquennium, which had been planned on the basis made explicit in the White Paper *Education: A Framework for Expansion* (Cmnd. 5174). The contents of this document, as far as they affected the universities, were known to my predecessor before publication in 1972, and I understood that they underpinned all the UGC's quinquennial plans, as well as those of individual institutions. The White Paper provided for a total of 254,000 undergraduate and 52,000 postgraduate full-time students by 1976-77, to which were to be added some part-time and 'sandwich' students, making 321,500 in all. This was just a step in the bullish programme of higher education expansion which, including polytechnics and colleges of education, was meant to reach 200,000 new entrants per annum by 1981, that is, 22 per cent of the age group as compared with 7 per cent in 1961. Brave words were written to justify this, for example 'The government considers higher education valuable for its contribution to the personal development of those who pursue it. At the same time they value its continued expansion as an investment in the nation's talent, in a time of rapid social change and technological development'.

Both capital and recurrent financial provision for the quinquennium assumed some economies of scale (for example, a reasonable degree of slippage in student–staff ratios). When I joined the UGC there were about 250,500 full-time students and the plan seemed feasible as well as justifiable. It was this which accounted for my sanguine mood on 1 October 1973, so sharply dented two days later by Ralph Fletcher's news which resulted in the dispatch to universities of my letter of 12 October. My confidence soon returned and so, somewhat more slowly, did Ralph's. However, in December the government issued another White Paper, which painted a sombre picture and stated in paragraph 10 of chapter 10: 'the government has decided to withhold half the supplementation of recurrent grant, and not to supplement equipment grant in respect of one year's increase in prices for the academic year 1974-75 and for subsequent years of the quinquennium'. Supplementation here means the addition of extra cash to compensate for the loss in purchasing power due to inflation (as defined by the Tress-Brown Index for university expenditure).[5] This was a very serious blow because the inflation rate was already high and rising, and in fact rose to 29.4 per cent for the 1974 calendar year.

From my knowledge of the finances of universities – including the fact that staff tenure and incremental salary creep meant that, even with no staff recruitment, costs were bound to rise – bankruptcy seemed a near certainty for some with few reserves or endowments available. I put this position to Mr Reg Prentice, the new Secretary of State, expressing our well-founded deep concern and the fact that although we were prepared to use our reserves (despite the fact that they were already earmarked for other urgent purposes), they would not be enough to save the situation. He produced an extra £15 million, for which all universities should be eternally grateful because this sum, together with the lesser amount the UGC was able to provide, ensured that no institution failed financially.

I counted that episode as 'the end of my innocence'. From then on the name of the game changed. Quinquennial planning had to all intents and purposes gone, though we tried to preserve the illusion of its continued existence so as not to shatter the morale of those in universities whose faith in the UGC was understandably

---

5. The Tress-Brown Index had been devised to reflect the essential pattern of university spending, with the major part of the budget necessarily devoted to staffing. Because of this, it always gave an inflation figure above the national average used by the Treasury.

bound to the idea of such a horizon. But from that time forward the system of funding moved steadily into a regime closely tied to the annual public expenditure survey mechanism, in which money voted for the UGC in the forthcoming year was certain but cash-limited, while sums for subsequent years were merely indicative. No guarantee existed that hope would become reality; nor was there any realistic likelihood that cash figures would be supplemented for inflation (rather, quite the reverse). In effect, the starting point was no longer that of the UGC advising government and producing plans for the university system to realise the advice given, with the government considering the UGC's observations before deciding what it would be prepared to accept in the economic conditions prevailing. Instead, the point of departure had become an overriding consideration of the economy, including what the government was prepared to spend on education in the public sector. Government would set the essential parameters of student numbers and costs, based on some assumed capitation figures, in much the same way as was done for schools.[6] On this basis the UGC would effectively have become a mere unit of the DES, charged to execute government policy within prescribed cash limits. Gone would be any real forward planning, with the associated stability which the UGC's begetters rightly saw as essential for a well-run university system. From this state of affairs it would have been an easy step to curtail the academic freedom so vital for effective teaching and research, even if with good intentions.

At the time I was so busy with many day-to-day problems that I did not fully appreciate the slippery slope on which we had been forced to step, even when the DES began to take on the role of planning student numbers – an act which should have been a warning to us, because it was a job which our terms of reference specifically allocated to the UGC. Nor do I think the DES officials with whom we dealt had any devious notions of usurpation of our powers. It was simply the realisation by government that, as John Carswell eloquently put it, 'once the state had plucked up the courage to reach for the tap [controlling money supply] it was found to lie remarkably ready to hand'.[7]

---

6. Some wit suggested that in this scenario universities might change their names to Degree Offering Government Schools, or DOGS, to match the old CATS (Colleges of Advanced Technology).

7. John Carswell, op. cit.

Eleven years after I left the UGC it had disappeared, not just in name but in substance, having been replaced by an entirely statutory and executive Universities Funding Council (UFC), which could be directed by DES officials at the behest of the Secretary of State. It and its successor bodies became the instruments of government, not the trusted advisory planning and executive body represented by the UGC. This change of status signalled the disappearance of a splendidly civilised era in the history of university education in any country. However, these later developments did not form part of my working life, except that I later witnessed the passage of some ten or more Education Bills put before the Houses of Parliament in as many years. I must now return to other aspects of my UGC experience.

The Dons' Pay Anomaly

I have already described how the economic crisis of the early 1970s helped to erode the specially protected position of the UGC in planning and executing university development. This is particularly well illustrated by what was known as the 'dons' pay anomaly', which was a running sore with university teachers for most of my time at Park Crescent.

The mechanism which had developed for settling dons' pay was one in which the UGC played a dual role. On the one hand, when the Association of University Teachers was engaged in discussions with the employers' representatives, the UGC acted as a neutral source of authoritative factual information which was accepted by both sides. (The UGC was not in any way anxious to interfere in a matter which was primarily the concern of the employers and their employees. To have become involved beyond this point would have been to exceed the powers conferred by the UGC's governing minute, to compromise its impartiality, and to diminish the trust which both the universities' governing bodies and the dons had in it.) On the other hand, the government was the ultimate paymaster and therefore was, quite rightly, able to give or withhold any extra money which the UGC might advise would be necessary, if the outcome of the negotiations between the universities and the AUT implied salary increases greater than a particular value, which of course could only be set by the Treasury.

However, as I explained in Chapter 5, there was another and growing institutional sector in higher education, namely, the polytechnics; the salaries of their staff were dealt with by government alongside those of teachers generally. Part of Harold Wilson's electoral baggage when he came to power in 1974 was a promise to examine teachers' pay, which the teachers considered had fallen behind that of other professions. His Secretary of State for Education and Science, Reg Prentice, set up a Committee of Inquiry into the Pay of Non-University Teachers, making it plain that his view was the same. Douglas Houghton, MP for Sowerby, then aged 76, was appointed as chairman. His own mind seems to have been strongly focused on school teachers, for his self-description in reference books such as *Who's Who* and *Dod* was always 'Chairman, Teachers' Pay Inquiry 1974'. In due course the government accepted the recommendations of the review group, which included very large increases of salary (especially for senior staff) and even backdated their implementation to April 1973. As a result of this decision, polytechnic staff benefited enormously at a time when their university counterparts received only 8 per cent – and even that increment was to be delayed until October 1974, a period in which inflation was beginning to rise towards its peak of almost 30 per cent. The UGC had to remain silent on this matter, but privately felt that the situation was manifestly unjust – a view with which the Arbitration Service, to whom the AUT applied, agreed in their judgment. But the government by then had become preoccupied with the rising inflation rate and had decided to adopt an incomes policy, which involved a 'pay freeze' for those receiving more than £8,500 per annum and a maximum of £6 per week extra for those receiving less (corresponding to about a four per cent increase at the critical salary).

As chairman of the UGC, having no *locus standi* in salary matters, I found this situation irritating; particularly as I knew that for many subject areas common to both sectors, the student–staff ratios were smaller in the polytechnics than in the universities. I was also aware that the contracts of the polytechnic staff, which had been negotiated by their union – the National Association of Teachers in Further and Higher Education (NATFHE) – specified in detail the hours per week to be spent in contact with students, in preparation for that contact, in administration, and so on. This was wholly inconsistent with the notion of a professional person totally dedicated to education and research, and trusted to allocate his or her time and effort to the best advantage of those aims. All I could do was to talk with ministers informally, as a private individual. This was part of my purpose in inviting Reg Prentice and his wife in February 1975, and Fred and Joan Mulley in August that year, to lunch at home in Oxford. As I have mentioned in Chapter 3, I had been a colleague of Fred Mulley nearly 30 years earlier, but in this exercise I made less headway with him. This was in part due to the fact that he wanted cast-iron evidence from me that universities were not breaking the pay freeze by giving annual increments to vice-chancellors, who would be the only members of staff whose salaries might exceed the magic £8,500. Although I knew some but not all vice-chancellors' salaries, in order to preserve the separation of UGC from pay matters I refused to give any information. I also emphasised that the individual universities were the legal employers of the vice-chancellors, that their books were open to inspection by the Comptroller and Auditor General, and that I was sure no institution would break the law in this respect.

By the following April Harold Wilson had resigned and James Callaghan had replaced him as Prime Minister. In the ensuing Ministerial shuffle, Fred Mulley became Secretary of State for Defence and was succeeded in Education by Shirley Williams. This was a great stroke of luck because I had known her as a Minister in the DES in the late 1960s, when she had understood clearly the nature of the threat to the Research Councils, which I saw developing by virtue of my membership of the Central Advisory Council on Science and Technology (see Chapters 5 and 8). She had also quickly grasped the impact of the report of the National Libraries Committee. It did not surprise me that, with her strong sense of fairness, she saw at once the inequity of the treatment of dons and strove mightily to get it rectified. Against the odds she succeeded, but the magnitude of the adjustment necessary to restore some kind of parity was so great that it had to be applied in two stages.

Financial Restraint Does Not Preclude All Improvement

Mrs Williams' background and sympathies were academic. Her father, Sir George Catlin, had been a professor of philosophy; her mother, Vera Brittain, had written a remarkably sensitive book, *Testament of Youth*, which had a very moving effect on the inter-war generation of students. Mrs Williams had been a Scholar of Somerville College, Oxford, and from her former experience in the DES fully appreciated the value of the universities as bulwarks of intellectual liberty and freedom of expression, as well as the importance of the UGC. She took an expansionist view of higher education, but also saw the financial constraints which must apply even in a favourable economic climate. Indeed, in the late 1960s she had challenged the universities with her famous 'thirteen points' – indications of ways in which she thought savings might be achieved. Her understanding of such matters, and her accessibility, were not only a comfort to me but a benefit to the universities, while for my part I could sympathise with the fact that she was also in charge of funding the polytechnics, which undertook some activities in common with universities and others which, being more vocational, were wholly their own. The polytechnics were directly financed by local authorities through the 'rate support grant', in which was included an element of central government funds given for this specific purpose. In addition, the polytechnics were largely governed by their individual local authorities and Ministers had no overarching body comparable to the UGC to define a policy for this so-called 'public sector' of higher education – a title I disliked because of its implication that universities were private or exclusive and in some way not serving a public purpose.

The easy relationship between the UGC and Mrs Williams was productive of many benefits beyond the resolution of the dons' pay anomaly. I have space to refer to only four examples, the first of which concerns libraries. Thomas Carlyle considered that 'the true university ... is a collection of books', and it is certainly the case that unfettered access to recorded information and thought is indispensable to all serious students, scholars and scientists. It is also true that the annual rate of publication of such material grows year by year. Therefore, even in universities of constant size there will always be pressure for larger libraries, and corresponding demands for more capital and revenue resources: for the whole system, these could be of frightening proportions. Clearly it was important for the UGC to have a national policy on university libraries. As money for capital development was in especially short supply we decided to set up a working group which we hoped would provide a basic policy proposal, and also criteria allowing the UGC to draw up a list of library building projects in order of priority. I was convinced that without such careful examination to justify our plans the chances of securing any money for new university libraries, or significant extensions, would be negligible.

The working group was established in 1975, under the chairmanship of Professor R.J.C. Atkinson, and its report was published in April 1976 (just as Mrs Williams assumed office). It discharged its mandate well but shocked the library and academic communities by introducing a novel principle, that of the 'self-

renewing library' of limited growth, in which acquisitions would be offset to a considerable extent by withdrawals to a local reserve store in the first instance, and ultimately for disposal to the Lending Division (now called the Document Supply
Division) of the British Library. The UGC recognised that this change of policy
would present administrative problems, for example in identifying the right material for withdrawal, but also accepted that to do nothing would greatly delay the
establishment of an order of precedence for new building work.

We published the report, which carried a foreword from me stressing the pro-
visional nature of the recommendations and inviting comment and suggestions. As
is so often the case with a new idea which appears to threaten the old order, the first
to respond were the objectors. Most wrote to the UGC but the princes of the world
of learning, such as Sir Isaiah Berlin, President of the British Academy, and Lord
Todd, President of the Royal Society, aimed higher – at the Secretary of State –
while courteously copying their letters to me. By writing to her they unwittingly
contributed to the dangerous notion that the UGC was simply the servant of the
DES. Shirley Williams not only asked me to make the substantive replies but skilfully used the report as an argument for extra capital funds for universities, so that
we were at last able to tackle the problem of improving university library provision
and services. I am convinced that this would have been impossible without the
Atkinson Report and the positive support of the Secretary of State. It was also fortunate that 1977 was the centenary year of the Library Association, the body whose
qualifications were sought by professional librarians, and, as its president, I gained
many opportunities to talk to staff of all kinds and to make it clear that the UGC's
aim was to support libraries by making them more effective. The idea slowly
became acceptable, both to the professionals and to the universities.

However, this was not the end of the library problems facing the Secretary of
State, as she made clear to me shortly before I retired from the UGC. The nature of
her other problem was that in 1972 the British Library Act had been passed, establishing that entity with a structure and responsibilities largely along the lines advo-
cated in the National Libraries Committee Report (which had also urged very
strongly the necessity for a new building). Unsurprisingly, the Board of the new
British Library began to press for a start on the proposed development, designed by
Colin St John Wilson, on a site which had become available alongside St Pancras
station. Although the economic situation in 1977-78 was slightly easier than it had

been earlier, the money in the Secretary of State's hands for capital projects remained very limited. This was the position she laid out in a private meeting to which she had called me, before putting her leading question: 'You know better than anyone the problems of the British Library, as well as those of the universities. To which of these two should priority be given?' I took my time before replying, during which pause I had mixed feelings of gratitude that my opinion had been sought and dismay at being asked to make such a difficult choice. In the end I responded by saying that on balance I would give priority to the British Library, on the grounds that if the new building were not to be provided then many of its problems would never be satisfactorily resolved. I also considered that if a start were made on such a large project it would be difficult to stop it if the government had a change of heart. Moreover, whilst a large number of academic staff used the British Library, it also served a much larger readership within the country and outside it. At the same time I pointed out to her the grave disadvantages of deciding that no capital funds should be available for the UGC to put towards the solution of its library problems, when there had been such a furore about the proposals of the working group. She did not tell me her decision there and then, but from what happened subsequently it was clear that she accepted the validity of my arguments: the British Library was given authority to go ahead (authority which was withdrawn by the Conservative government when it came to power in 1979, as I will relate in Chapter 11), whilst the UGC was given some modest resources to make a start with the university library building programme.

During the period of great tightening of belts in the universities in 1974 and immediately afterwards, we came to recognise, in considerable measure due to the representations made to the Committee or its sub-committees at visitations, that there were often costs attached to research in the humanities which neither the institutions nor their academics could meet (because of the prevailing economic crisis and the incomes policy). The sums required to make the research possible were, on average, much smaller than for social scientists, scientists, technologists or medics, all of whom could turn for help to their relevant Research Councils (with which the UGC had close and mutually beneficial relationships). We fully appreciated that something like a Humanities Research Council was needed, but knew that this was a kite which would not fly with the DES. So discussions were opened with the British Academy, to see if it would administer a small grant scheme if we provided the money; and this was agreed. The obvious objection raised by Fred Mulley at our lunch in August 1975 – that the UGC was empowered to make grants only to universities – was easily dealt with by my explanation that the British Academy was simply acting as an agent for this part of our work, and that universities would be the ultimate recipients of the money, in much the same way that we used professional caterers to provide lunch for the Committee. This was a slightly tongue-in-cheek remark, because he and Joan had expressed their satisfaction with the meal Barbara had prepared for their delectation! The British Academy was fortunately unaware of this unintended affront to its *amour propre*, and welcomed the prospect of £125,000 per annum for three years, beginning in October 1976, from which to make small grants (not exceeding £1,000) to individual scholars in the humanities. Furthermore, from this initiative were later to spring other schemes to assist such research, including fellowships and research professorships, with money provided by government or charitable foundations.

The problem of 'vacant places', with which the Comptroller and Auditor General had faced me in my first few weeks at Park Crescent, continued to haunt me. As a result of discussions within the UGC, we began to settle on an area in which we thought we might make useful progress. The scheme reflected my long-held contention that if courses at universities are made harder, longer, or both, then success in them is likely to lead to a more diverse and rewarding career; they will serve as a magnet for the most able and ambitious students, and will deter the weaker ones. It seemed, therefore, that it would make sense to apply this principle as a remedial strategy for subjects in which the vacant place phenomenon was prominent. This was agreed at one of the UGC's September weekend meetings in Oxford, using engineering as the subject area. We envisaged new courses (which we thought would need to be at least four years in length) as rigorous and demanding as existing three-year honours engineering degree programmes of high repute, incorporating subjects such as technological economics, accountancy, management, communication skills, industrial relations, possibly a modern foreign language and, of course, an element of industrial experience – all areas of knowledge we considered to be of value to those seeking 'fast-track' careers in industry. The Committee then invited all universities it judged to have the necessary engineering base to submit proposals for such courses which, if accepted, would attract an appropriate additional sum to that institution's recurrent grant. The response was gratifyingly enthusiastic and practical. I chaired a selection panel which included external members such as the Chief Scientist and Engineer of the Department of Industry. We had several stimulating meetings with representatives from various universities, and in the end selected seven to launch the new scheme. One anxiety was that the prospect of delayed wage-earning might deter students from poorer homes. I raised this problem with Shirley Williams, suggesting that there might be a system of national engineering scholarships for which able students would be eligible, and that companies should be urged to have a stake in the courses and, if possible, to 'adopt' students taking them. She readily agreed. I recall both of us addressing groups of industrialists at Elizabeth House, then the headquarters of the DES. The responses from students and from industry were excellent; indeed, industrial sponsorship rendered a national engineering scholarship scheme largely unnecessary and the programmes, some of which were eponymously named 'Dainton courses', were a great success.

Another problem area was medicine. Not only was it as expensive in the pre-clinical phase as the pure sciences, and even more costly in the clinical phase, but there were structural flaws in the national provision for the education of doctors (which had been highlighted in the Report of the Royal Commission on Medical Education, published in 1968). The first of these concerned the numbers of medical students to be admitted to British medical schools each year. In principle this is not a difficult calculation to make, since it is based on the existing stock of doctors in the Health Service and the number considered necessary to maintain a reasonable standard and scale of healthcare (which in the United Kingdom means a ratio of about 11 to 13 doctors per 10,000 population). The estimate also needs to take account of how soon it is desired to reach the target, allowing for the fact that at least six years must elapse between the date of entry and the student receiving a licence to practise, that there is wastage from the course, and that there are predictable rates of retirement from the profession.

Britain's immediate post-war record in making such calculations is not very creditable. In 1944 the Goodenough Committee recommended that the appropriate intake should be about 2,500 students per annum, corresponding to an output of 2,100 graduates six years later. Thirteen years after this committee reported, another enquiry under Sir Henry Willink's chairmanship recommended to the government that there should be a reduction in the intake so as to avoid a surplus of doctors, despite the known increase in size of the population and the long, steady, upward trend of the doctor-population quotient. This report had a bad effect. Both the number and the quality of the intake into medical schools fell and, shortly after Willink reported, there was an insufficient number of British medical graduates to fill junior hospital posts, a deficiency which had to be made good by immigration. Eight years after Willink the Royal Commission was established. So concerned was it with the shortage of doctors that it offered interim advice to Ministers over two years before the publication of the final report, stating that in order to remedy the shortage and to meet rising expectations the intake into British medical schools should reach 5,000 by 1990. The situation when I joined the UGC was that there were 31 undergraduate medical schools, of which 12 were in the University of London, 13 in English provincial universities, one in Wales and five in Scotland (one of which had only preclinical studies). The total number of students entering these schools in October 1973 was 3,276.

The reasons for continuing the expansion in medical student numbers despite the economic crisis were many and obvious, and require no repetition here. The problem was not just a simple one of finding recurrent money for the universities. Because much of the instruction is at the patient's bedside in NHS hospitals, the student–staff ratio must be lower in the clinical years than in the preclinical phase, and it was necessary to liaise closely with the Department of Health and Social Security to ensure that adequate accommodation was available for clinical teaching, properly furnished and equipped. That was our overriding priority. The challenge facing the government, however, was how to meet changing needs in London necessitated by a migration of people away from the centre of the city, plus a corresponding requirement to build up hospital resources in the provinces, where there was an underprovision. The problems associated with harmonising the UGC and the Department of Health programmes were solved largely through meetings every six months between myself and the Permanent Secretaries of the DHSS – successively Sir Philip Rogers and Sir Patrick Nairne. It was a successful and cordial relationship, and despite financial constraints on both sides we were able to increase the numbers entering medical schools by 20 per cent in five years.

The Royal Commission had identified another problem of medical education. It was a common assumption that the medical schools in the capital must be the best in the country: the redoubtable R.B. Haldane, chairman of the commission appointed in 1910 to enquire into the workings of the University of London, and the facilities there for advanced education and research, told the distinguished American medical educator, Dr Abraham Flexner, that he had decided not to consider the field of medical education 'because we have been informed that medical education in Great Britain is the best in the world'. This statement attracted the sceptical and laconic response, 'By whom?' Flexner was asked to submit a memorandum, and made it clear that his vision of a good medical school was not matched by the arrangements in London. The 1968 Royal Commission report also commented on the weaknesses of the London schools – mainly in their limited basic science education compared with their provincial counterparts, and their relatively small intakes (although, collectively, these added up to about 40 per cent of the total medical entry in the United Kingdom). Both these considerations were strong arguments for bringing the London medical schools together, and into conjunction with multi-faculty university institutions. Among the suggestions was that St Bartholomew's Hospital Medical College and the London Hospital Medical College should combine, and have Queen Mary College as a new multi-faculty base. The idea was always to have a preclinical school embedded in the Queen Mary site, as near to the basic sciences as possible. In my first year at the UGC, an opportunity came up to purchase for Queen Mary College the adjacent Jews' Cemetery. That purchase was made, and over fifteen years later I found myself in retirement chairing a committee to amalgamate the two medical schools. By 1995 this operation was complete: other mergers have since been effected.

Sufficient examples have now been given to indicate how the economic crisis, and the government's response to it, dislocated the carefully laid plans of the UGC for the 1972-77 quinquennium – which had been intended to be a period of consolidation, but which became one of improvised salvage. I have described a few low-cost, ingenious schemes by which some progress was made to ameliorate the situation; however, in addition there were unforeseeable disasters and opportunities which had nothing to do with government policy. At the University of Kent, the Cornwallis Building subsided because of a disused railway tunnel beneath it. At Leicester, the deficiencies of high alumina cement as a constructional material were revealed, causing action to be taken in seventy other university buildings as well. At Warwick, facing tiles fell off buildings; at Sussex, dangerous leaks appeared in the hot water ring main, and so on. None of these buildings was insured, because the premiums would have cost more than the actual expenditure on repair under the Treasury's building indemnity scheme; but, under pressure, that department was understandably becoming deafer to our appeals. Happily, opportunities arose because universities became more enterprising in their efforts to secure capital funds from elsewhere, with the 'Anonymous Donor' to student residence projects in London a notably generous example. Sometimes, however, donors could not or would not meet the whole cost of a development: one such case concerned the acquisition and conversion by the London School of Economics of an old W.H. Smith building next door, facing onto Portugal Place. Because of its location and its high load-bearing floors it was an ideal structure in which to house the internationally important British Library of Political and Economic Science (of which more will be written later), at that time inefficiently scattered over several sites. This was an opportunity not to be missed, and although the building grant we were given for 1975-76 was only £8 million, as compared with a list of outstanding projects amounting to well over £50 million, the Committee did not hesitate to promise a contribution which enabled the moment to be seized.

I also became increasingly adept at risk taking, one example arising when the Vice-Chancellor of the University of East Anglia, Dr Frank Thistlethwaite, came to tell me there was a prospect that David Sainsbury would donate £3 million to construct and endow a centre for the visual arts. This would house the art collections of Sir Robert and Lady Sainsbury, which they were prepared to give to the University. However, a condition of the gift was that the academic department of Fine Art should be accommodated as an integral part of the centre, something for which the Sainsburys would not pay. The University could not afford the cost, and the Vice-Chancellor pressed me for a quick and favourable intervention. This I could not make, because the UGC did not have the money either. But he did persuade me to meet the architect for the scheme, Norman Foster, which I did in April 1976. Not only was his exposition convincing in every respect, but he gave me some guidance on the probable dates when payment of bills for the departmental part of the centre would be due, if the major project started on time. Without the authority of the Committee, but in the belief that we would be very unlucky indeed if our building grant in the next two years was so emasculated that we could not help, I gave sufficient assurance for the Vice-Chancellor to convince the donors to go ahead. It is an action I have had no cause to regret.

The Ebb Tide

Towards the end of 1975 I began to sense what seemed to be a more permanent shift of attitude in government circles towards the UGC, something which went beyond the changes that always happen during the management of economic crises. I had joined the UGC full of admiration for its past achievements and also the modes of working it had devised, which had enabled it to gain a remarkably clear understanding of the needs, aspirations and capabilities of individual institutions, unmatched in other countries. For their part, the universities were willing to place their trust in it, and to accept UGC decisions as reasonable. This was because the Committee was seen to be independent, its members not faceless bureaucrats but experienced academics of good judgment, leavened by eminent persons from commerce, industry and other parts of the educational sector; and because the Committee had rules, such as that of never having a vice-chancellor as a member. The universities also knew that the Committee would stoutly defend academic freedom, and they were prepared to respond positively to UGC policy statements – not just in good times but in bad ones as well, such as the depression of the 1930s when university funding was severely restricted.

In some ways it was remarkable that the universities did behave in this way because, as I have explained, both Ministers and high civil servants in the DES naturally felt responsible for the whole of the education service; and it was an easy step to view the UGC as just an instrument for ensuring that the university sector conformed to a policy which fitted into the larger picture. From 1919, when the UGC was founded, until 1964, when the Treasury was its direct paymaster, such a situation could not arise because the Treasury did not have responsibility for other aspects of educational policy. Mrs Williams fully understood these points, but by the time of her arrival there was ample evidence that the planning function for universities was already slipping out of the UGC's grasp. Following one meeting with an Under-Secretary of the DES, I became so concerned at the general trends as I saw them that in May 1976 I decided to send a personal minute to John Carswell, an unusual procedure which I adopted to get on the record my anxieties and my thoughts on how we might try to improve the situation. His response, as ever, was judicious and succinctly put. He saw, as I did, that 'the biggest risk is of a lurch off the narrow, sometimes imperceptible, path between the role of an independent body and the role of a government agency'. He went on reassuringly to add that 'at present this danger seems to be more theoretical than real...' At that time he was right, of course, but three months later his perception had sharpened and hardened considerably. In retrospect, I see the slow loss of influence of the UGC on the planning process as inevitable, once it ceased to be freestanding and became part of a department of government.[8]

I will give just two of many possible examples to illustrate this point. The first was in July 1976 when Gerry Fowler, then Minister of State in the DES, asked me to accompany him to the Cabinet Office to meet a committee chaired by Michael Foot and charged with developing a policy for the devolution of various powers from Westminster to Scotland and Wales. The issue was one which had been raised with us during visitations to universities in both of these countries but, as I explained then and again at the meeting, the UGC had not formed a view on the matter – we had much more urgent things in hand. It seemed to me that the upper echelons of the DES must already have discussed the issue and that their view would probably be rather relaxed, not least because the Scottish Office had its own Education Department dealing with schooling in Scotland. However, the main point is that I was quite unaware of any conclusions which might have been arrived at within the DES, and it would have been useful to have known something about them in advance.[9]   As it turned out the meeting itself was not very satisfactory. I left disappointed, feeling that the committee either had been briefed inadequately (not by me, for I had not been asked to submit a paper) or had not fully digested its background information, because I had to explain the role of the UGC and correct some misconceptions about it. One striking example stands out in my memory. Mr Brian McElhone, MP for Glasgow, Queen's Park, claimed that young Scots were being short-changed as regards university education, and averred with some force that 'the universities of Scotland should be brought under proper democratic control'. The chairman sought my observation on this, to which I responded that if by control was meant detailed regulation of what was taught and researched, then that

---

8. Lord Beloff never fails to remind me that this was always his view.

9. Later on I related this episode to Keith Murray, UGC chairman for ten years from 1953. His response was crisp: 'You should have been invited in your own right to give your opinion of the pros and cons of devolving responsibility for the universities.' With hindsight, I realise that Keith's attitude was absolutely correct.

was anathema to the UGC and the Scottish universities alike. For good measure I added that Scotland was favourably treated in relation to university education, in that the age participation rate for Scotland was somewhat higher than that for England, and that because the degree courses were on average one year longer in Scotland the per capita spending from the British Treasury was significantly higher there than elsewhere.

Another example arose later in 1976, after Mr Fowler left the DES and his place had been taken by Gordon Oakes, a man with considerable experience of local government who had served in the DES in an earlier Labour administration. It was decided that he should chair a departmental committee to look again at advanced further education, the pattern of which Tony Crosland had set in the 'binary system' which he outlined in his famous Woolwich speech ten years earlier. I imagine that it was because of his heavy duties that he appointed as his *alter ego* for this work Sir Philip Rogers, who had retired twelve months earlier from his post as Permanent Secretary to the DHSS and whom I knew well.

It was clear to me that such a committee could not function properly without taking account of the experience of the university sector, and considering the effect its conclusions might have on that sector. I therefore expected that the UGC would be asked to give evidence. No invitation came, however, so I took it upon myself to put down my private views in a letter to Sir Philip early in June 1977, and a few days later had a working lunch with him. It quickly became evident that although the polytechnics were involved in a considerable amount of degree level teaching, albeit often with a more vocational emphasis than in the universities, the implication that there should be a national forum to arrive at a clear policy for all tertiary education – including the universities, to me a necessary corollary – was unlikely to be something which his committee would wish to consider. Whether that was evidence of a protective attitude towards the universities or of inertia in the face of strong local authority interest in the polytechnics I do not know, but I remained convinced that both the advanced further education sector and the universities would need to expand, and that a coherent strategy on the funding for each would have to be a concern of central government. In the event the necessary steps were not taken until more than a decade later, when the UGC was replaced by the Universities Funding Council, and the Polytechnics and Colleges Funding Council was established alongside it.

Saying Goodbye

Although I have touched on only a small fraction of the UGC's work, I hope I have given an impression of its pace, range and diversity while I was chairman. At the time some friends commiserated with me on the difficulties and disappointments, and opined that I would be glad when I demitted office. But despite all the problems I enjoyed my five years, and as retirement beckoned I did not relish the prospect. Had it been offered, I would cheerfully have accepted an extension, provided my loss of visual acuity could have been halted or, better still, reversed. The main reason for my regret was that the whole of my life experience as a teacher, scientific researcher, university administrator and public servant, combined with my upbringing, had reinforced my conviction of the benefits to individuals and society of strong, independent, high-quality universities. To be allowed to help sustain and develop such institutions, and to make them more accessible in good or bad times, was to me a particularly satisfying occupation. I do not claim to have discharged my duties any better than anyone else, but I did feel a sense of privilege in being involved in such a worthwhile enterprise. Moreover, the UGC, staffed by like-minded colleagues, many of whom I felt I could count as friends, was a very pleasant place in which to work.

At my last formal meeting at Park Crescent, on 21 September 1978, and equally at the last weekend 'retreat' at Oxford, I felt deeply sad to be going, but also much touched by my colleagues' kindness. These were feelings which recurred when the UGC staff held a splendid farewell lunch party on the last Thursday of the month. Even this was not the end of my leave-taking, because I had promised to attend the annual CVCP residential meeting, the theme of which was 'British Universities in the 1980s and 1990s'. I doubt if those present had any inkling of the fact that the reality was to be so enormously different from what we then envisaged or hoped for. Old friends such as Arthur Armitage, Norrie Robson, Derman Christopherson and Edward Boyle were there, all of whom I had come to know well when they were chairmen of the CVCP, and with whom I had always shared knowledge in a way which made our tasks that much easier.

The CVCP meeting was held at Leeds University and I stayed, as I had done several times before, with Edward Boyle in the house which the University had offered us on lease fifteen years earlier. At the final dinner there were speeches, and the finishing touch was the surprise presentation to me of a lovely print of the old Radcliffe Observatory, now part of Green College, Oxford, which formed one of the illustrations of Ackermann's *History of Oxford,* published on 1 April 1814. Edward could not have chosen more appropriately. Not only is the observatory most graceful, resembling a greatly enlarged copy of the Tower of the Winds in Athens, but it is a mason's delight with its variety of stone from Clipsham, Weldon, Taynton and Headington, each chosen for its particular function and effect. The building is also decorated with beautifully carved bas-relief zephyrs and signs of the zodiac. It still gives me pleasure to look at this print and remember those old friends, and to imagine the satisfaction which my father as a craftsman would have found in that splendid building, completed just over two centuries ago.

The following day, 1 October, was the start of the academic year and the vice-chancellors bade me goodbye as if I were a free man at last. I did have a sense of release as I stepped into Alec Merrison's car with his wife Maureen, because I knew we would be driving down to the Black Mountains, at the southern end of which Barbara would be waiting for us with Shep, ready to follow as Alec led us up the lonely valley of the Afon Honddu to their weekend cottage. There, in an idyllic setting, we spent the next few days – an interlude which marked the end of another important phase of my life.

Spin-offs at Home and Abroad

By virtue of the office he holds, the chairman of the UGC has ample opportunity to engage in a variety of other activities which enrich experience and often lead to new friendships – by no means the least of their benefits. I took advantage of the opportunities offered whenever possible, and in concluding this chapter I shall mention just a few of the experiences which came my way as a result.

Human beings identify one another by distinctive characteristics of physique, personality and place in society. An important part of the recognition process is learning what a person does and has done. Having engaged in a variety of occupations, I had acquired several labels including physical chemist, professor, university administrator, science policy adviser, civil servant, librarian, and, perish the thought, educationalist. Indeed, there was one university public orator, Brian Morris, a former professor of English literature at Sheffield and thereafter Lord

Morris of Castle Morris, who gave poetic point to my multifarious activities by quoting the following two lines from Dryden's allegory *Absalom and Achitophel* when presenting me for an honorary doctorate:

> *A man so various that he seem'd to be*
> *Not one, but all mankind's epitome.*

That Professor Morris did not quote the next four lines:

> *Stiff in opinions, always in the wrong;*
> *Was everything by starts, and nothing long:*
> *But, in the course of one revolving moon,*
> *Was chemist, fiddler, statesman, and buffoon*

was something for which I was particularly grateful, because I was known to be a chemist and formerly a willing but indifferent performer on the violin. I feared that the cap was close-fitting enough for listeners to think that the last word, too, was undesirably appropriate.

Barbara has reminded me without acerbity that apart from a week in Malta to recover from a back injury, we took no deliberately planned holiday when I was at the UGC; and that even in later years, one secretary complained to her that she had difficulty in arranging staff holiday rotas because I would not, or could not, tell her when we were taking a summer break. The fact of the matter was, of course, that experiences different from the common round and daily task – even when they involved work – often acted as mental refreshment and stimulus, so that I did not really feel the lack of leisure time.

Wearing a purely chemical hat, I continued to lecture in various places. In Britain the venues tended to be universities. I still remember having to deliver the Faraday Lecture to the Royal Society of Chemistry at Imperial College, London, and the Edison Lecture to young scientists in Schenectady, New York – both in early 1974 and both with pleasure, because preparing them was a satisfying release from the pressing financial worries which dominated my UGC work at that time. Some lectures were works of supererogation: for example, in what were essentially missions concerned with science policy or higher education in Romania, Bulgaria and Israel, I also gave chemistry lectures. Each place and each occasion had a special and characteristic atmosphere.

McMaster University in Hamilton, Ontario, was kind enough to give me an honorary degree in 1975, and while there I had a splendid time with the chemists. Moreover, after the degree congregation I learned that the University library had acquired a collection of Bertrand Russell's papers and I felt I must see them. I found this a rare privilege, and after perusing some of them I commented on Russell's very characteristic, somewhat high-pitched voice and precise articulation. Not sure that I had conveyed a true picture, I asked if the library had any sound recordings of him. Immediately several were produced, and as the first one was played I could not contain my excitement. It was of a family tea party, which I would guess was in the inter-war period. From the quality of the sound the party could have been *al fresco*, but what startled me was hearing a familiar and characteristic voice which sounded exactly like that of Charlotte Williams-Ellis, whom I knew well because she had been a fellow research student with Barbara in the Cambridge zoology laboratory so many years before. Her father was the architect who built the extraordinary romantic holiday village of Portmeirion in Gwynnedd, overlooking Tremadoc Bay, where I had once stayed during a Miller Conference. Prompted by the recorded conversation, I was soon explaining the mores of an educated upper-class tea party in the UK, including the mannerisms and accents of those participating; my small audience seemed captivated, but I suspect they were also very puzzled. The incongruity of listening to Bertrand Russell's voice in a steel town in Canada was not lost on me.

Two years later, and nearly forty years after my previous visit, Barbara and I were in Uppsala – again for an honorary degree ceremony. This formed part of a week-long quincentennial celebration of the founding of the University. There were numerous receptions and lectures, of which I gave one, and great pomposity which involved wearing a white tie and tails, together with orders and decorations, for three or four days – even in the daytime. There were many memorable events, including my splendid gaffe when, having heard the oration by my Promoter, Professor Stig Claesson, I received from him a large scroll with seal attached. He placed a gold ring on my finger, and then a laurel wreath was lowered onto my head. At the moment of contact of the wreath with my forehead a 25-pounder gun was fired outside the hall. The unexpected noise drove all procedural instructions out of my head, except that I knew I must acknowledge the King of Sweden, who had graced the proceedings with his presence. Not knowing where he was sitting,

I bowed to the most splendidly garbed person in my near vicinity with all the sense of occasion that a former praelector of a Cambridge college could muster. In no time at all, hidden firm hands turned me round to face a man in plain civilian dress and I bowed again, this time I suspect rather less elegantly.

Altogether it was a somewhat bibulous few days but we managed to see the Cathedral, the Old Anatomy Theatre, the Linnaeus Garden and other sights, and we met English academics I had not seen for many years (including the biochemist Sandy Ogston, who was a physical chemist and taught electrochemistry in Oxford when I was an undergraduate; and the biochemist and prolific sinologist, Joseph Needham from Cambridge, whose black beret was especially becoming when worn with evening dress!). I am sorry to record that I paid little attention to one rather silent orthopaedic surgeon who was also honoured – John Charnley, from whose total hip replacement procedures I was to benefit nineteen years later. Most interesting of all was a Russian honorand who came with his 'minder': neither of them knew quite where to place his numerous Soviet decorations on the unaccustomed costume he was wearing. As we dined the honorand sought my views on a number of chemical matters, explaining that he had read my book on chain reactions. He turned out to be Yakov Zeldovitch, whom I knew to have worked on the theory of explosions in solids. When I enquired if he knew Yuli Khariton – who had been a protégé of Semenov, and had done some early work on the phosphorus-oxygen branched chain reaction before turning to the theory of solid explosives such as lead styphnate – Zeldovitch beamed and became positively expansive. But when I asked him where Khariton was now and on what research he was engaged Zeldovitch became very secretive, and so did his otherwise friendly companion; in fact, both seemed rather distant from then on. It was not until I mentioned this incident to Lord Penney over lunch at Goldsmiths' Hall about a year later that the reason for the sudden cessation of conversation became clear. Bill Penney had been at Los Alamos in the last twelve months of the war, and on his return to the UK had become head of the Atomic Weapons Research Establishment at Aldermaston. Bill explained the important role that both Khariton and Zeldovitch had played in the Soviet A-bomb and H-bomb development: both had been recruited in early 1943, and spent many years in the atomic weapons establishment at Sarov Monastery, some 250 miles east of Moscow. The work prospered, not merely due to their own high abilities but also because of the helpful information they received through the good offices of one Klaus Fuchs, the long-time Soviet spy, who was eventually tried and convicted in Britain in 1950.

My 'science policy' label proved to be unusually adhesive, and was sometimes accompanied by 'higher education' as a form of recognition. This was particularly the case in North America, but also came to be of interest in Eastern Europe and the Middle East. Early in 1974 I was approached by Sir William Harpham (who had been ambassador to Bulgaria a decade earlier, and was then director of the Great Britain/East European Centre), and was asked to lead a small UK team to exchange knowledge with our Romanian counterparts. I agreed, and in May a group of us set off for Bucharest in a British Airways Trident aircraft.

We landed as scheduled at Sofia and a fellow passenger, the Bulgarian Ambassador to the UK, who was known to Bill Harpham, invited us into the VIP lounge for coffee and plum brandy while the aircraft was refuelled. When summoned back to the plane we made our goodbyes, resumed our seats and waited for the engines to start: however, the centre one of the three failed to do so. In due course we disembarked and were locked in a transit lounge for five and a half hours, which allowed ample time for Steven Bragg, Vice-Chancellor of Brunel University and formerly an engineer with Rolls-Royce at Derby, to explain the angle of thrust of the engine which had failed. Eventually we took off in a Romanian aircraft and were met on arrival by a delegation comprising the Deputy Minister for Science and Technology and Professor Penescu, designated as my co-chairman in the colloquium, to whom I gave some books we had brought as he talked ruefully about our missing the banquet that evening. After the formalities our interpreter got us through customs and immigration and into the bus for the Ambassador Hotel, which we reached at 10.30pm local time. We should have been in the Hotel Athenée, and the Ambassador was a disaster. My bedroom had no wardrobe, no chest of drawers, no table at which to write, no hot water and a hole in a sheet, and was dirty and unbelievably noisy. I finally fell asleep at 2am when the last tramcar ran, and woke at 4.30am when the racket again became intolerable. After washing I launched an assault on the problem of getting my room changed. The battle is too involved to relate, but ended in victory only after I had persuaded the staff that their Foreign Minister would be dissatisfied and displeased unless I was adequately housed. I was then moved to a room which was not much better but was at least bearable, and I reflected that I would only have to be there for four more nights.

Comparing notes with my colleagues on the way back home, I found that they were all uneasy, each feeling that their Romanian opposite number could not express criticism in front of others. It was most noticeable that whereas the British team members would often argue among themselves, the Romanians looked on in silence. They made constant reference to 'plans' and 'programmes' but little mention was ever made of outcomes. We all sensed that they were being careful to speak and behave correctly, as if we were all being watched – as was perhaps the case. We had little time at our disposal for really significant conversations, and even that was eroded by unnecessary visits to some of the local sights.

In trying to draw up a report, it seemed to me that the whole exercise lacked real purpose; we gained little, and I have often wondered what the Romanians thought. The countryside which we saw was pleasant and the towns had some lovely old buildings, but there were also depressing, geometrically disposed, identical tower blocks of flats and, where there was industry, it seemed old-fashioned and highly polluting. Given the rich mineral and oil deposits and the fertile soils of the northern parts of Romania, the country should have been much more prosperous than it evidently was. That there were food shortages is inexplicable, unless there had been under-investment in agronomy in order to spend money on rapid industrialisation, and possibly over-industrialisation.

With this experience behind me I was less than enthusiastic when, the following year, Bill Harpham asked me to lead another British team, this time to Bulgaria. I felt that a reconnaissance was necessary, and Bill agreed with little demur. I carried this out between 4 and 8 October 1975. The Bulgarians had prepared my reception very thoroughly; I had useful meetings with key individuals such as Nacho Papazov, chairman of the Committee for Science, Technical Progress and Higher Education, a man of abundant energy and experience including a spell as ambassador to Japan. These were followed by an efficiently-run general meeting in the University of Sofia, where I was given a clear picture of the organisation of higher education, including the role of the institutes of the Academy of Sciences and their links with the universities. A visit to the Institute of Chemistry was especially valuable: its director, Academician Bogdan Kurtev (a slightly built, intense and sensitive person who had left his sickbed especially to meet me) gave a lucid account of the Bulgarian plan for the education and employment of scientists and the management of their work. The discussion was lively, possibly because his colleagues' initial reticence had been eroded by the informal way I had conducted a discussion lasting forty-five minutes, after a tough lecture I had given in the morning. Although he was obviously disconcerted, and perhaps even upset, when I appeared a little sceptical about top-down research planning, his junior colleagues plainly but tactfully indicated that they shared my opinions, and fully understood the reasons for the UK's flexible Dual Support System, which I had explained. Indeed, relationships became so relaxed that Professor Michaelov was emboldened to ask me if I was 'Ceiling Temperature Dainton' (*sic*) and on my admission to this charge he insisted that I should sign a book for him.

Altogether it was a busy and informative four days, during which I was hospitably housed by our ambassador Eddie Bolland and his wife: he was the son of a Yorkshire miner who went up to Oxford to read history, and so we had much in common in our background. On the flight home, drafting out a few notes, I had no hesitation in recommending that a joint colloquium would be worthwhile because our potential hosts were serious, intelligent, and had a high regard for what went on in science and education in the UK. Moreover, the people I met in Bulgaria, in complete contrast to the Romanians, had shown good qualities of self-confidence and competent organisation, which augured well.

The colloquium took place in Varna (reputedly Arthur Scargill's favourite holiday haunt) in late September of the following year. We fielded a very strong team, and I think it is appropriate here to quote from the first paragraph of my report:

> ... the genuine desire of all the participants to learn and discuss, combined with a pervasive sense of humour and willingness to acknowledge past failures, quickly removed all barriers and the discussions were extremely frank and open, answers were rarely evasive and difficult questions could be fully probed without giving offence. These factors – together with the opinion, fully shared by all participants, that the devising of sound policies for research and development and for higher education, and their successful implementation, are important problems in all countries whether large or small, with or without strong science-based industries and well-established higher education systems – ensured a very successful meeting. We soon discovered that despite the euphoric official pronouncements about fulfilment of various plans, the Bulgarians are faced with several problems, some of which we share (e.g. swing in student choice away from science and engineering towards law and medicine, a shortage of agricultural labour) and others which we do not (e.g. lack of indigenous producers, and therefore service engineers, of sophisticated equipment). The general impression which we gained from visits to institutes and laboratories, as well as from

our discussions within and outside the formal meetings, was of an energetic and lively people who have made remarkable progress from the low income, largely agrarian economy towards an industrialised society enjoying a much higher per capita income, and who have coped intelligently with the teething troubles which are inevitably attendant on such a rapid transition.

Aharon and Ephraim Katchalsky were two brothers who made significant contributions to polymer chemistry and biochemistry respectively. My brief contacts and correspondence were with the former, because his interests overlapped with some of mine. I was therefore greatly surprised and honoured to receive a visit at 14 Park Crescent from Shmuel Bendor, the Director of the Israel Academy of Sciences and Humanities, who asked me whether I would be prepared to give a lecture *in piam memoriam* of Aharon Katzir. I had not realized that on immigration to Israel the brothers had changed their surnames to Katzir; nor did I know that Ephraim had become President of Israel. I took a liking to Shmuel Bendor from the moment we first met. He was a graduate of Liverpool University and deployed his persuasive powers with great skill and humour. He knew that I had spoken at an annual dinner of the Leeds Friends of the Hebrew University and he argued how appropriate it would be if I, as 'a former dynamic member of the Senate of Leeds University', would come to Israel – not just to give the memorial lecture but also to hold meetings with those responsible for science and higher education policy, and 'in so doing emulate if not excel an earlier dynamic member of that university's professoriate, Brodetzky'. If clinching argument were needed that was it, for Selig Brodetzky, who had been a First Wrangler from Trinity before the First World War, was a legend in Leeds University for his enormous vigour and had been accurately described by one historian of that institution as having 'all the brilliance and speed of a comet'. He too had migrated to Israel, and became President of the Hebrew University.

Our arrival at the Ben-Gurion Airport in June 1974 was memorable for the warmth of Bendor's welcome, but also for the awesome realisation that it was here that Aharon Katzir met his death in what the English newspapers called the 'Lod Airport Massacre'. A car was waiting, and Barbara and I sped across the coastal plain and up the western flank of the range of hills which separates that plain from the Jordan valley. Rusted military ironmongery left over from the 1967 war formed prominent roadside debris, reminding us how that war terminated the division of

Jerusalem between Israel and Jordan. Equally noticeable was the intensity of culti-vation of temperate and sub-tropical food crops. Within an hour and a half we were starting to unwind in our room at the King David Hotel, with a panoramic view of the walls of the Old City of Jerusalem.

To do justice to our experiences in the week we spent in Israel would require a much longer chapter, if not a separate book. I was busy from early morning lec-turing at the Academy, and conferring with the National Planning Group and with Israel's equivalent of our UGC and CVCP. We also met the Rectors of Tel Aviv and Bar-Ilan universities, and visited the Hebrew University of Jerusalem, the recently-created Ben-Gurion University outside Beersheba in the Negev, the Haifa Technion (the Israel Institute of Technology) and the Weizmann Institute at Rehovoth. It was hard work trying to note, organise and memorise all the information put before me, and at the same time keep the conversation going on the right track. I concluded that a tape recorder is an indispensable adjunct if full benefit is to be gained from such intense and voluble encounters!

Our hosts were determined that we should see as much of the country as poss-ible, experience something of its history and of the pioneers' life, and appreciate how Israel is geographically overlooked and symbolically menaced by Syria. So on the Wednesday, with packed bags, we left the King David Hotel at 6.30am and descended by a winding road to the northern end of the Dead Sea, nearly 1,300 feet below sea level. In the bright sunshine the 50-mile journey down the west shore by car, with occasional short stops and a longer one to visit Masada at midday, was a thoroughly fascinating but extremely hot experience. Merely to survive in such an environment would be a victory; to have constructed Masada and to have hidden the famous scrolls speaks volumes for human tenacity. While I sat and tried to make notes, Barbara bathed like a cork in the highly saline and therefore dense waters of the Dead Sea. After crossing the Negev and spending three hours in discussion at Ben-Gurion University, we were glad of a simple dinner and a quiet evening at the Dan Hotel in Tel Aviv.

Our second major tour started at the end of our visit to the Haifa Technion, when we were driven via Nazareth and the high parched ground of Qarnei Hittin towards the fresh, clear waters of the Sea of Galilee. We descended slowly so as to absorb fully the welcome sight of vegetation which, in the rays of the late afternoon sun, made Galilee seem like a shining jewel in a green setting. On reaching the shore we drove south through Tiberias, where the remains of the baths were evidence of the Roman Empire. We made a brief stop at Rabbi Meir's tomb and then arrived at what seemed to be an early kibbutz at Ginossar, where we hastily donned bathing costumes and, as the sky darkened, swam in the clear waters of the lake whilst biblical stories I had learned at Sunday school came flooding back into my mind. We were most cordially received at our guest house, and listened intently to accounts of the pioneer settlements and the construction of the conduit carrying Galilee's fresh water to the west, to make otherwise arid lands 'blossom as the rose', as the prophet Isaiah so elegantly put it.

Next day we rose up betimes in order to drive north, seeing sights and hearing words which brought to life the stories of the Old and New Testament, which had been such a feature of my upbringing. I understood from my itinerary that we were bound for Acre and the shores of the Mediterranean, and was therefore much surprised when we took a right fork and were stopped by a military checkpoint at a bridge over a river which I assumed, and our guide confirmed, was the Jordan. After a period of negotiation we were allowed on to the East Bank and went a short distance to a vantage point, from which we could see the Golan Heights. The strategic importance of this area as a buffer against seizure and control of Israel's highly important water supply was at once obvious, and we left Jordan's banks in a suitably sombre mood.

As we refreshed ourselves before dinner that evening, back at the Dan Hotel, we heard voices through the locked door connecting our room with the next. Initially we were too busy to pay attention but I did notice that American English was being spoken, and as we dressed the unmistakable realisation came that the speakers were Israeli and US security men going over arrangements to cover the arrival of President Nixon the following morning. Before he appeared, however, Shmuel Bendor came to ensure our departure in time to catch our flight for London. As VIPs we were whisked through the customs and immigration formalities at high speed and, having bidden a sincere and thankful farewell to Shmuel, we were quite relaxed as the aircraft taxied out on time: we looked forward to a restful Sunday afternoon at home in the garden, which seemed much nearer as the aircraft moved slowly forward. Just over half-way down the runway, however, the engine noise changed as reverse thrust was engaged and the brakes were applied. We came to rest and were escorted back to the terminal building, joining many other passengers whose embarkation was also delayed due to the imminent arrival of the plane carrying President Nixon. Moreover, for obvious security reasons we were kept well away from the windows. Several hours later, and hot, hungry and thirsty, we were relieved to be airborne and on our way home at last. But 'troubles come not in single spies but in battalions': our Oxford house had been burgled. Fortunately the theft was not serious and most of what was stolen, including a spare car key, was discovered just a field away.

Two and a half years later we had another foray into the Middle East, this time to Iran: some 17° of longitude to the east of Israel with over ten times the population, eight times the area (though mostly arid tableland), encircled by mountains on three sides, peopled largely by Muslims of various sects, with an entirely different language and calligraphy, and ruled by a Shah. I was there as part of a team of university administrators, including Clark Kerr, lately president of the University of California, and Jim Perkins, retired president of Cornell University. We were charged, rather vaguely, with advising on higher education in Iran. We arrived on what officials described as our 'magic carpet' on 6 December 1976 and left four days later, not having been inside a single university department or research institute. Most of the time was spent indoors in Tehran closeted with officials, only a few of whom had any experience of western universities. Though we may have shared a common language with them, and they often mouthed the right words, I did not feel that many of those we met had any well-found assessment of the country's real needs in respect of higher education, nor did I sense that they held in their hands any genuine reins of power. This latter impression was confirmed some years later by two Englishmen I met who had worked for long periods in that country, one for the Anglo-Iranian Oil Company and the other involved in the production of locally-manufactured copies of the ubiquitous Hillman Minx saloon car. They considered that the actual power lay in the network of the Shah's nominees, distributed in key posts in institutions, including universities, throughout the country. Our experience was certainly consistent with this description, and as we left I reflected that the only person we had met who seemed to have any real understanding of the plight of the youth of the country was the Shah's wife, who, by definition, was powerless. To cap it all, at the airport we bumped into Austin (E.A.G.) Robinson, a Cambridge economist and Fellow of Sidney Sussex College, where I had known him before the war. He was much more knowledgeable than I about Iran, and his perceptive remarks deepened my gloom and sense of impending catastrophe. Just over two years later the Shah was ousted and the Ayatollah Khomeini seized power; by September 1980 Iran was at war with Iraq.

Shangri-La in the States[10]

I cannot remember all the visits I have paid to Canada or the USA but I always feel thoroughly at home there, partly because I do not have to wrestle with a foreign language. There is also an openness of approach, a willingness to take the visitor for what he or she is, a lack of posturing, and a positively North of England warmth and friendliness that puts Britons at their ease. When I joined the UGC I feared that I might lose some of the connections which had previously taken me to North America and broadened my horizons, both scientifically and socially. If that did in fact happen the losses were few, and were more than compensated for by new causes for visits. I shall mention only two, the first of which began in 1974 when, as I have mentioned in Chapter 7, I accepted Arthur Armitage's invitation to join the UK committee which selected persons to receive Harkness Fellowships.

Financed by the Commonwealth Fund of New York, and for many years known as Commonwealth Fund Fellowships, the Harkness awards could be held for one or two years, and their distinctive feature was a requirement for the Fellow to travel extensively in the USA for a significant period of his or her tenure. Acceptance was based on the applicant's record of past performance, the written opinions of referees and a lengthy interview, which many successful candidates later told me they considered to be very searching (some said they felt intimidated). The overriding criteria in the minds of the committee members were high quality, as evidenced by actual achievement and referees' opinions; a clear sense of purpose; the personality and potential for leadership of each applicant; and whether the candidate, the United Kingdom or the United States was likely to derive benefit from the large investment which a two-year Fellowship represented. Areas of past or proposed study were of lesser importance, although the UK committee tried to achieve a good spread without sacrificing quality. Whilst there was an age limit in

---

10. As many readers will know, Shangri-La was a mythical near-paradise created by James Hilton in his 1933 novel *Lost Horizon*.

the late twenties for applicants who had never left the groves of academe, that for people in other work was higher. In this way the net was cast wide enough to include able people in industry, the creative arts and the public services – a most enlightened arrangement.

I found the Harkness work quite demanding, especially when I became chairman, because all the applicants' papers arrived around Christmas Day and shortlists had to be prepared as quickly as possible. The interviews themselves occupied several days and it became necessary to stay overnight in the London house occupied by the Fund in Upper Brook Street. My encounters with these young and able people were both stimulating and encouraging; the question one was always asking, however, was whether the considerable effort of selection was justified by the results, or would a better outcome be achieved by a more dirigiste policy concerning the precise areas of work or study which could be undertaken by a Fellow. I was never particularly enthusiastic about such a restriction, and towards the end of my chairmanship I was involved in discussion of such matters with the Board in New York, after I had previously elicited the views of my UK colleagues. Eventually, in the early 1980s, a policy of targeting was indeed adopted and it will be for others to determine if this was the correct route to follow.

One of my duties as chairman of the committee was to tour the USA, visiting the centres where most of the Fellows were stationed (such as Princeton, Yale, Harvard and MIT on the east coast, Berkeley and Stanford on the west coast, and Chicago in the midwest). At each venue, Barbara and I hosted a reception for all the Fellows, their spouses and sometimes faculty; I also held individual interviews to assess progress and listen to problems or complaints. A detailed report had to be prepared, which I always managed to do before we left the hospitable shores of the USA. It was invariably a pleasure to meet the heads of the universities, not just to give them feedback from my interviews but to hear from them how much they valued having Harkness Fellows as members of their institutions.

My second North American example came about in an entirely unexpected way, which might well have been connected with my chairmanship of the UGC. It began with a letter from J.E. Slater, President of the Aspen Institute for Humanistic Studies. Both the name and the organisation were quite unknown to me. A quick glance at the letter revealed that it was an invitation to take part in a ten-day workshop, entitled 'The Educated Person in the Contemporary World', and the enclosed briefing statement quickly convinced me that the project was a long way down in my order of priorities. But the word 'Aspen' stayed in my mind because it brought back memories of a meeting at Snowmass in the summer of 1970, organised by the American Chemical Society Educational Division, which Ron Nyholm and I had attended. I had spent all the free afternoons covering as much ground on foot as I could, and I fell in love with that part of Colorado. The terrain was somewhat like the Cairngorms, except that the valley floor was some 5,000 or 6,000 feet further above sea level than the forest of Rothiemurchus. I had longed to go back to Aspen but had put the matter out of my mind. Now, four years later, I was presented with an opportunity to return, and after some further correspondence I decided to accept Mr Slater's invitation.

Seen in retrospect, that was one of the most fortunate decisions I ever took. For five successive years we spent about four weeks at Aspen, and Barbara and I came to look on that place as our Shangri-La. A few days after the July meeting of the UGC we would fly to Denver airport and change to an Aspen Airways piston-engined plane for the 40-minute trip of just over 100 miles, skimming the Rocky Mountain peaks to land in a delightful upland valley 7,000 feet above sea level. The participants in the various Aspen Institute programmes were housed either in very comfortable, well-planned wooden chalets close to a swimming pool and tennis court on one side and the tumbling Roaring Fork River on the other, or in houses in the little town of Aspen. Near the chalets were a restaurant and health centre, the latter designed for supervised physical exercise programmes, volleyball and sauna. This complex of buildings was called Aspen Meadows, from which it was only a short walk to the brick-built Paepcke Memorial Building which housed the Institute's offices, a library, a large auditorium, and a range of seminar rooms. Close to this there was also the Music Festival Amphitheatre which, being a marquee, was inevitably dubbed 'the music tent'. Here soloists and whole orchestras of young musicians, who were students at the independent Summer Music School, would join their internationally renowned teachers, such as Daniel Barenboim and Pinchas Zukerman, in giving concerts that were a great joy to us.

Whether staying in the Meadows, a town house or a private house in Aspen, we could walk or ride bicycles to get everywhere we wished, and we soon slipped into a regular routine. Even the weather seemed to have a nearly standard morning pattern, for the sun appeared over the mountains in a clear sky about 7am, at which time we were having our lonely swim in the pool, but by the coffee break white clouds would gather and then coalesce into larger grey ones. It would be rare if by lunchtime rain had not dropped like mercy upon the place beneath, blessing us as we walked to lunch and refreshing the air and the flowers. Barbara and I made a practice of going to different seminars, though we might meet for lunch; after dinner we would talk with friends or attend a lecture in the auditorium. Saturday afternoons and Sundays were reserved for whole-day outings in the mountains with friends such as Dan and Ruth Boorstin, or if I wished to do something more strenuous I would go off for a long hike, getting above the timber line and occasionally into the snow. Barbara, who had fewer commitments, might sometimes take a whole day off for an excursion as, for example, when she went rafting on the white waters of the Colorado River. There we were, in delightful mountains with agreeable friends, music, good conversation, and enough thought to prevent mental atrophy and to make us feel appropriately virtuous.

It was an idyllic existence for us, but I often wondered what the fast-track rising company executives from all over the New World, and sometimes from the Old, made of reading the carefully contrived pot-pourri of excerpts from the Bible, Aristotle, Sophocles, Locke, Franklin, Marx, Engels, de Toqueville et al, as part of their preparation for seminars in which each had to lead at least one debate on a particular reading or group of readings. For that matter, how did the moderators feel who were guiding the discussion for the nth time, always aiming for each group of executives to finish the course with their beliefs in 'humanistic values' (with an appropriate American slant) subtly reinforced? My words here may suggest that I am dismissive of the outcome, because as a specialist scholar commented to me, 'deep down the process was superficial, and therefore an intelligent moderator was bound to be cynical': this is an easy, superior, mocking attitude to take, but I do not believe that it was generally the case. Nor is that conclusion evidence of gullibility; even my worst enemies would not accuse me of that. My view is in large part based on listening to intense and serious conversations between American participants after Henry Steele Commager, the eminent historian, had spoken in the auditorium to an absolutely silent audience and had done so brilliantly, movingly and almost without a script, as he dealt with the constitutional crisis which Nixon's unprincipled behaviour had created. This event presented citizens with issues of bedrock national importance, which they handled admirably and in a way which I felt was probably significantly better for having attended the seminar. That impression was the proof of the pudding which weighed with me.

There was no doubt that Aspen in August attracted a real galaxy of talent, including distinguished university presidents, scholars, scientists, writers, politicians, public servants (including ambassadors), media personalities and musicians. Britain was well represented, and it was possible to have leisurely conversations with compatriots such as John Maddox, editor of *Nature*, Asa and Susan Briggs, Alan and Nibby Bullock, Shirley Williams, her daughter Becky and nephew Tim, the ebullient and brilliant BBC producer and director Huw Wheldon, and others; at home there never seemed to be 'time to stand and stare' or just to talk. Outstanding among the Americans were the young Mellon Fellows, introduced by their 'fairy godmother' Jessie Emmett, and it struck me that Aspen would be an admirable place for Harkness Fellows to spend part of their travel time. A few did so before I ceased to be chairman of the selection committee, and several of them told me how enjoyable and valuable an experience it had been for them. I do not know whether the practice has been continued since my time.

Auditing the education workshop in 1974 was an especially friendly, intelligent and agreeable man named Marty Kaplan. He came from the Big Apple and had won a scholarship to Harvard, where he majored in biology with distinction and also edited the undergraduate paper *The Crimson*. I am sure he could have been accepted for a PhD anywhere, but instead he chose to go to Cambridge to read for the English undergraduate Tripos at St John's College under the guidance of George Steiner, finally returning to Stanford (I think) to take a research degree in double-quick time. I felt that the somewhat geriatric workshop needed input from at least one person under the age of thirty-five, and would greatly benefit from Marty's quality of mind, wit and perceptive judgment. He was invited and contributed to the proceedings, and it was he who prepared a book about the whole workshop.

Each year we met new, interesting and friendly people who made life especially pleasant at Aspen, but I must exercise restraint if this chapter is ever going to end and forbear writing about them. I am not sure whether those omitted or those named deserve the greater apology – the former on the grounds of my seeming discourtesy by excluding them, the latter by contaminating their good names with mine in a single sentence. Instead I think I should try to impart some sense of the cut and thrust of workshop proceedings.

After breakfast on Monday 29 July 1974, I took my seat for the morning session; my neighbours were the novelist Saul Bellow and the historian H.S. Commager. Some of the scheduled talks had been circulated in print, and what I read and what the first speaker said convinced me that I must remain silent, take notes and use what spare time I could find to try to understand what was going on. By the end of the day I was rather miserable, overawed by the verbal fluency of most of those present and dismayed by my inability to get to grips with the under-lying ideas, most of which were entirely new to me. I alone seemed to be tongue-tied; all the others verged on the garrulous. An auditor,[11] evidently from the *New York Times,* later recorded in that paper that he was not surprised by this: 'The con-ferees were no strangers. They were wizened veterans of the conference circuit ... they knew each other's lines like actors in a travelling repertory company, and quickly began to construct a complex web of intellectual alliances that is the *sine qua non* of any major academic symposium'. I certainly did not fall into that cate-gory; I had no idea what anyone was going to say and I was not part of any alliance. In fact I was not alone – the only other scientist present was the Harvard theoreti-cal physicist Dr Steven Weinberg, and he also was silent.

The next day was much the same as the first, and there was little on the morn-ing of the third day to relieve my sense of isolation. However, one co-chairman, Stephen Graubard, encouraged me to speak and at lunch I found myself sitting next to Frank Keppel, whose laconic conversation revealed a man with a healthy scepti-cism. When I mentioned my embarrassment he encouraged me with the words 'Just say what you think', to which I retorted 'Well, I think we could do with a few basic definitions; like what constitutes education'. 'Go right ahead', he urged me again, and I answered 'It will all have to be *ab initio*'. He simply smiled.

After dinner I wrote about three paragraphs. The following morning I had the notes typed and duplicated, and a copy placed on the table in front of each seat before we began. To my pleasure and surprise this action was well received when, at an appropriate moment late in the morning, the chairman drew attention to it for comment. The same *New York Times* auditor, Robert Reinhold, gave his view in the 10 August edition of his paper, and on balance I think it was a fair statement:

---

11. Auditors were non-participants who sat in at the back of the room.

> It was Sir Frederick Dainton, a British chemist, who described himself as an 'illiterate scientist', who gave the conference its first real focus by listing a series of 'minimum expectations' for an educated man. Among them: enough knowledge to acknowledge one's own ignorance, some understanding of the relationship between one's own field and other categories of knowledge, a feel for the ethical problems of the application of one's knowledge, and a sense of duty to issue an 'attractive invitation' to learning to others.

My sobriquet seemed to appeal to some of my colleagues in the workshop, and I think it was Frank Keppel who drew my attention to another journalist who wrote a little piece, I have forgotten where, with the heading 'Self-styled British illiterate scientist wows (*sic*) the Brahmins' – a superb example of punchy American journalism, which I greatly enjoyed. I was not alone in wishing for a little more precision, for a day or two later my neighbour Saul Bellow posed the rhetorical question 'What am I doing here?' and then walked out, while the distinguished historian Dan Boorstin, an undergraduate contemporary of mine at Oxford whose books have been a constant delight to read, commented with accuracy, 'One of the problems with educated people is that they talk too much'.

This brief morale-boosting episode, though personally welcome, did nothing to enlighten my ignorance. I continued to make detailed notes as people spoke, and I did not respond to several invitations from the chair to comment – except accidentally on one occasion, which led to a deeply embarrassing situation. This concerned Dr Mortimer Adler, a philosopher who seemed to be well known to many in the audience and who, I subsequently discovered, had been a powerful influence in the establishment of the Institute: the notion of the young executives reading excerpts from books was probably his.

On the day in question Dr Adler presented a very dense, closely argued paper which I had some difficulty in following. I had a few misgivings, but he delivered his words with such complete self-assurance that I felt they must be important. I therefore paid particularly close attention in order to get his thoughts down on paper as accurately as I could. When he had finished speaking and I had stopped writing, my hand was rather stiff and I loosened my joints by a little finger wiggling. This digital activity caught the eye of the chairman Stephen Graubard: perhaps out of desperation because of the resolute silence of other conferees, he chose to interpret my action as a signal that I wanted to speak. I certainly did not, but I had a feeling that everybody expected it of me and, having looked at my notes, I paused and fell into the trap of saying something roughly along the lines of 'I am not sure that I have understood Dr Adler's points – certainly not completely – but it seems to me that what he has said rests upon three pre-suppositions, none of which look either axiomatic or provable' – a faithful reflection of my views at that moment. The ensuing silence was broken only by the noise of Dr Adler picking up his papers and pushing back his chair before leaving it. I sensed that it was my words which had hurt him, so I too left the room. By the time I got outside he had vanished and therefore I went over to the Meadows for a stiff drink before lunch, thinking to myself that once again I had put my foot in my mouth, albeit with harmless intentions. There was a queue at the bar and before long I was joined by others with similar designs, including a smiling Frank Keppel: the first two or three insisted they would buy me a drink, remarking that they disliked Adler's arrogant attitude. I suddenly realised that there were some of the conferees who, far from regarding my words as presumptuous, were grateful for what I had said.

I hoped that would be the last time I would meet Dr Adler, but this was not to be. Earlier in this chapter I mentioned that I was President of the Library Association in its centenary year: part of the celebrations consisted of my receiving gifts from various organisations to mark this occasion. I was aware that I was to be presented with a complete set of the latest *Encyclopaedia Britannica* by its general editor, but was quite unprepared for the shock of discovering that the person who appeared before me in this role was none other than Mortimer Adler. Our eyes met in mutual recognition. It took a few seconds before I could recover from my stunned silence and thank him formally, though not addressing him by name.

In subsequent years at Aspen many other subjects were discussed, covering a range of topics such as 'science, technology and humanism', 'scientific literacy' and 'energy', to which I felt I could make a contribution; but with others like 'aid to developing countries', 'economic growth and the environment' and 'international educational development and human choice necessitated by advancing scientific knowledge' I learned far more than I could ever have contributed. Barbara too found the workshops an invigorating activity. Naturally, we compared our different experiences when we were alone together, and this led to many amusing exchanges. One afternoon she electrified me by saying that Diana Trilling (the wife of the well-known academic and writer Lionel Trilling) had declared to her during lunch, 'I am having an intellectual love affair with your husband'. If that were indeed the case, her comments in the seminar room on what I had said had very effectively concealed her devotion.

Those five summers we spent at Aspen left us with abiding impressions of the beauty of that part of the Rockies, of the mental stimulus we experienced, of the sense of well-being when liberated from pressures and able to exercise both mind and body pleasurably, and last but not least of the friendliness, helpfulness and generosity of the Americans we met there. When all else is gone that last memory will remain. They sought only the flimsiest of excuses to help: thus in 1974, when we were invited to stay on for a further week after the education workshop, the son of one of the Music Festival Directors (a physical chemist concerned with science policy, who knew of my similar interests) insisted on taking us in his Jeep for a day-long excursion over rough mountain tracks above the tree line. Another offered us the loan of his car for a day, which enabled us to revisit Snowmass, go to a nearby Trappist monastery (the last thing we expected to find), and explore on foot Maroon and Crater Lakes; and because we had so enjoyed ourselves he lent the car a second time, so that we could visit abandoned mining towns, crossing the Independence Pass and the Continental Divide, and capturing some sense of the difficulties the westward-moving pioneer settlers must have experienced.

A Touch of Royalty

In the same year we decided to see something of the real American West by travelling overland to San Francisco, and then on to Los Angeles for our flight home. Accordingly, Saturday 17 August saw us driving from Aspen to Glenwood Springs to catch the 12.35pm Vistadome, the only westbound passenger train on the Denver and Rio Grande Western Railroad. It was a glorious ride, beside the Colorado River, until we branched northwards through mile after mile of desert country dotted with brownstone mesas of huge proportions, carved by wind erosion into highly unusual shapes and displaying a glorious, warm orange refulgence in the light of the setting sun. We arrived somewhat late at Salt Lake City and the bus, which we had been assured would be waiting to take us to Ogden, was either non-existent or had already departed; so instead we took a taxi there to catch the Amtrak train which would bear us through the night to Reno, Nevada.

Next morning we rose early in order to view the sunrise in that dry state. It was spectacular, but we were appalled by the dull, expressionless faces in the gaming halls; we felt we must get out of Reno as quickly as possible, and drove in our hired car along traffic-free roads to Yosemite National Park. There we spent two days walking on Tuolumne Meadows and beside the Merced River, absolutely fascinated by the geological formations which gave rise to such spectacular structures as the Half Dome, El Capitan, Sentinel Rock and, of course, the Falls. Once again we were moved by the generosity of the Americans, because on arriving at the park we showed our passports and no entrance charge was levied.

After a night sleeping in a tent we rose early and drove north west, on back roads from Yosemite to Sacramento. There was much evidence of ghost towns, and from these and the mine tailings my thoughts turned to the 1849 gold rush and the surge of immigrants into California, which must have included my mother's elder brother Tom. Barbara's mind was on other things. It was warm and we wanted a place to stay, and for her that meant somewhere with a swimming pool. We found a suitably equipped and welcoming motel: in the morning, when we had paid the bill and were just about to leave, the proprietor wiped his hand on his apron and approached us, with his wife just behind, and to my astonishment said, 'Sir, may we shake you by the hand?' Naturally we obliged, and expressed our appreciation of all they had done for us. Suddenly, by way of an explanation which he seemed to think necessary, our host said, 'You see, Sir, we have never seen Royalty before'. Not wanting to spoil his pleasure I gave Barbara a pretty firm dig, which was meant to indicate that she should say nothing to destroy the illusion, and when we were in the car and out of earshot I said, 'For God's sake give them a queenly wave', or words to that effect. I drove off slowly, observing their broad smiles in the driver's mirror, and just prayed that they did not notice the little yellow disc betokening that we were in a Hertz rental car.

What To Do Next?

In 1977, as I pondered how I would occupy my days after finishing as chairman of the UGC in a year's time, I became aware of some spontaneous temporary colour changes in the field of view of my left eye. These gave me the more concern because I was also aware of declining visual acuity. It was clear to me that the colour changes were not characteristic of refraction phenomena and must be occurring at the back rather than the front of the eye. For this I knew I needed the help not of an optometrist but an ophthalmologist. I turned to the only living man in the latter profession who had been elected FRS – Professor Norman Ashton. He at once recommended that I should see Professor Alan Bird at Moorfields Eye Hospital in London, who kindly took me under his care and diagnosed the disease called preretinal fibrosis in both eyes. The cause of this is unknown and it is progressive in all but a few cases. He told me there was a surgical procedure, but after discussion we did not feel it was justified and adopted a 'wait and see' approach.

Professor Bird kept me under regular supervision, and while my eyesight continued to deteriorate I learned to use visual acuity aids to read the papers for any meeting which I had to chair. I found that I could train my memory to retain the essential points, and could take part in the discussion: I think that few people were aware that during my last eighteen months at the UGC I was not reading the closely-typed material in front of me but was relying on my memory.[12]

In the course of one of my regular ocular examinations, Alan Bird announced that cataracts were developing in the lens of each eye. I already suspected this, because when I looked at a point of light in darkness I saw about five instead. I devised a little experiment in which I looked at the light through a pinhole I had drilled in a brass disc placed close to my eye, and observed that by moving the disc laterally through small distances I could make the original light spot disappear and be replaced by one of the others. This convinced me that some element of my eye's refracting system, either the cornea or the lens, was not only relatively inelastic but segmented, each segment producing a different focus on the retina. Alan did not suggest surgery, which I took to mean that the fibrosis was continuing, and this did nothing to lift my gloom about the future; nor, however, did it weaken my determination to continue working. Then at a later examination he announced that the fibrotic process had stopped in my right eye, and that after a lens implant on this side I should see quite well. It was wonderful news and when, a year later, the operation on my eye was carried out the result in terms of brightness, colour rendering

12. The exceptions were of course those close colleagues who made sure that I received papers in good time – John Carswell, Geoffrey Cockerill and Sheila Thorpe (my secretary, who also made my hospital appointments). To these three persons I owe a great deal.

and acuity was dramatic, and allowed me to extend my range of activity. I asked to be given my natural lens, which I have kept in normal saline. Its brown colour and fibrosity are all too evident and account for a lot of my past visual difficulties. The whole incident gave me a new insight into T.S. Eliot's preoccupation with the mystery of beginning and ending, so evident in the lines from *Four Quartets*:

> What we call the beginning is often the end
> And to make an end is to make a beginning.
> The end is where we start from.

I need not have concerned myself about future boredom, because during the latter part of 1977 and the early part of 1978 it became clear that other people felt I had some useful work left in me, and several approaches were made. I think the first was by Sir Brian Windeyer, chairman of the National Radiological Protection Board. He asked me if I would join the Board and I gladly agreed, because I felt it was a worthwhile task and I did have just a little knowledge of parts of the subject. What I did not know, until I had lunch with him and the government's Chief Medical Officer, Sir Henry Yellowlees – whom I already knew because of our joint concern for the MRC's Clinical Research Centre at Northwick Park Hospital – was that the two of them thought I should succeed Sir Brian when he retired at the end of September 1978. The timing was perfect and I accepted the invitation.

Also in my last year at the UGC my interests became refocused on libraries, and not just because of my presidency of the Library Association. I was asked by the British Council if I would conduct some seminars on libraries in Cologne. These were a success and put a number of thoughts in my mind, and I was also able to go and see the new Staatsbibliothek in Berlin. I had not been to Berlin since 1932 and after visiting the new library, which was still under construction, I asked if I could see the Reichstag. The authorities agreed to this, and from the back of a still ruined building I was also able to observe the Berlin Wall in all its enormity. Libraries even surfaced in Aspen: I was asked by the Governor of the State of Colorado if I would chair a group to draw up the elements of a document for a forthcoming White House conference on library provision, to which each State was expected to submit a paper. This was clearly an activity which had nothing to do with the Aspen Institute for Humanistic Studies, so I asked a walking friend, the Columbia physicist Heinz Pagels, if I might borrow a room in the American

Physical Society's little building where they held their summer theoretical work-shops. Happily one was free, and I had a great week trying to bring to a focus the varying views of the different people on that committee. But this had nothing to do with my future: the next invitation did.

It took the form of a request from Shirley Williams, the Secretary of State for Education and Science, which was awaiting my return to the office on 3 October 1977 after our brief excursion to Uppsala. The note was simply to ask me if I could call on her on Tuesday 11 October to discuss libraries. At once I feared the worst, that the capital programme for university libraries was to be cut in some drastic manner, even after all the careful study which had led to the development of our clear policy for them. When we met she came straight to the point, which took me completely by surprise, and simply asked me whether I would be willing to chair the British Library Board after Viscount Eccles retired at the end of November 1978. I accepted at once, filled with enthusiasm to carry forward an institution in whose creation I had had an important influence. I knew that it was absolutely essential to get all the diverse parts of the library brought together under one new roof. The dispersed arrangement of the collections prevented it from giving the quality of service it should, and also ensured the steady deterioration of its holdings – stored as they were in unsuitable buildings, and frequently transported by van across London to be used in the Round Reading Room at the British Museum. Shirley Williams must have acted quickly too, because less than four weeks later I met with the Chief Executive of the Library, Dr Harry Hookway, to discuss details.

Several other offers were made, but I accepted only two of them; both have occupied a great deal of my time ever since I left the UGC. The first of these was from the Royal Postgraduate Medical School, which is located at Hammersmith Hospital. The Dean, Dr Malcolm Godfrey, asked me if I would be prepared to join the Council of that institution. I was delighted to do so: the School is a national asset which must not be allowed to fail for lack of money, or any mistakes on the part of government. A year later, in 1979, I took over as chairman of the Council: I have never asked, but I suspect that it was always in the Dean's mind that this transition should take place.

As I have already mentioned, in my last month at the UGC I received a tele-phone call from Mr Stephen de Bartolomé, to ask whether I was prepared to become Chancellor of the University of Sheffield in succession to 'Rab' Butler.

I tried not to let my delight be too evident over the telephone, but in fact I was very well pleased because it would give me an opportunity to renew my connections with my native city, and to repay some of the debt which I owed. That duty I have continued to perform willingly ever since.

I have always enjoyed foreign travel, and during my last year at the UGC I accepted two invitations which ultimately led to many visits east of the Indian subcontinent. The first was to attend a lunch given by the Foreign and Commonwealth Office in honour of Lee Kuan Yew, the Prime Minister of Singapore, at which I found myself sitting almost directly opposite to him. He was taller than I expected and spoke with great self-assurance which, however, did not hide from me the fact that when he began to talk about higher education his statements were not soundly based, either in reason or in fact: I therefore entered into the discussion to make that plain. That I had done so was evident from the shocked look on the face of an aide whom he had with him, who had probably never heard his Prime Minister addressed in such blunt terms. A young Foreign Office official, whose name I never got, approached me when the function was over to show his disapproval, maintaining that I had not helped but had damaged the purpose for which the lunch had been held. Having studied Lee Kuan Yew's face throughout the meal I disagreed, and reminded him of de Toqueville's phrase as I remembered it: 'Men will not hear truth at the hands of their enemies. Therefore I have spoken it.' Despite this show of confidence on my part, I returned to the UGC offices in Park Crescent feeling that I might have made a mistake. The reverse was the case: Lee Kuan Yew invited me to Singapore to review higher education in that Republic. My first visit was in 1979, and my link with Singapore continues.

The second invitation – also, I imagine, at the prompting of the Foreign and Commonwealth Office – took the form of an invitation from the Japan Foundation to establish and chair a committee to advise it on how best to assist the development of studies of Japanese language, life and institutions in British universities. Several meetings were held at Park Crescent and because of these (and possibly with hidden help from Hugh Cortazzi, later Ambassador to Japan, and the Japanologist Ron Dore of Sussex) both Barbara and I were invited to be guests of the Japanese government for two weeks in 1979. It was a fascinating experience for both of us and was followed by an equally interesting week in South Korea and a short stay in Singapore, as described in the next chapter.

CHAPTER 10

SOME TRAVELS OF AN ELDERLY COUPLE

And what should they know of England
who only England know?

Rudyard Kipling (1865-1936)

An Unfulfilled Curiosity

Although my father had worked on many buildings in Yorkshire, Lancashire and County Durham, he lived for the last 40 years of his life in or near Sheffield (to which he had moved from Sunderland with his growing family). He did of course know Merseyside, with its rich seafaring tradition, from his period of service as a stable lad there, but I am not aware that he ever left his native shores other than to attend Ernie's wedding in Douglas, Isle of Man, shortly before he died. His reaction to the brief sea crossing certainly suggested to me that this was his first voyage on a steamship; indeed, I think I may have made the same Liverpool to Douglas crossing before he did, when I attended my first school camp at Groudle Glen. Despite – or perhaps because of – this total lack of first-hand knowledge of foreign countries, he enjoyed my reading to him from books with an overseas setting. This was, I believe, much of the attraction for him of Kipling's works, set in India, and David Livingstone's *Last Journals from Central Africa*. He also rather obviously shared these authors' Victorian views about Empire. When I got a Sunday school prize, he encouraged me to choose Mungo Park's *Travels in the Interior Districts of Africa*, with its vivid accounts of the Dark Continent.

My desire to travel was naturally aroused by such readings, but until my penultimate year at the Central Secondary School, when I went to Hohenlychen in

Germany, my only non-local excursions were to the Isle of Man, Scarborough, and the village of Watford in Northamptonshire. The Pennines were accessible from home on foot or by bicycle, and my forays into them at least revealed that there were other ways of living than in terrace houses in grimy cities. They also told me much about geomorphology and something of history and prehistory, and could have taught me a good deal about natural history had I been a little more attentive.

My first real outdoor adventure – and with hindsight that word appears pretentious, but so it seemed at the time – was my walking tour with Robert Thompson when I was sixteen, encompassing the Cheviots, the Roman Wall and the Lake District. From then on I was hooked on hill walking. I began to acquire second-hand copies of books about mountaineering and exploration, many of which I still have, including much-used and treasured Scottish Mountaineering Club guides. But, apart from the Anglo-German Friendship School, my brief trip to Paris in 1937 and the curtailed visit to Scandinavia in 1938, my first long-distance travel from the British Isles had to wait until I was 31. From then on I took every opportunity I could to go abroad, much of it, alas, by myself when invited for scientific or other reasons; though when the children grew older we had family holidays overseas. However, the best visits of all were when just Barbara and I were exploring different parts of the globe together. The watershed was the summer of 1968 when the two of us made our first round-the-world trip, something to be repeated twenty years later by a slightly different route (made possible by a generous financial gesture from my former Australian co-workers in research). In both cases our journeys covered mainly Anglophone countries populated with our friends, but the most mind-expanding travels have been to those foreign countries of whose native languages and customs we knew only a very little.

Japan, Korea and Singapore in 1979:
Capitalism and Religious Diversity

I first went to Japan in 1973 and returned – this time with Barbara – in 1979, at the beginning of a wider trip to the Far East. The London staff of the Japan Foundation and the Japanese Embassy were meticulous in their preparations for our visit, and just eleven days before we were due to fly, the Ambassador and Madam Fujiyama gave a dinner party which was not only a pleasant social occasion but also enabled me to gain many useful tips from other guests. Whether by good luck or our hosts' prescience, Roderick MacFarquhar, a distinguished sinologist and at that time Labour MP for Belper, was among those present: his comments on the differences of attitude between the Chinese and Japanese people I found especially interesting, and they recurred to me constantly when, three years later, we were in China. At the party everyone told us of the desirability, almost amounting to a necessity, of being well loaded with gifts for those whom we might meet in Japan. One present, the bulkiest of all that we took, was a framed facsimile of part of the Magna Carta, which the British Library had previously loaned to the USA for the celebration of the bicentenary of the Declaration of Independence. I now took it as an outright gift from the British Library to the Japanese National Diet Library. As we lugged this large and heavy object aboard Flight JAL 422 we were inclined to regret the decision, but the cabin crew were most attentive and relieved me of any anxiety. This helpfulness from all whom we met was what, in human terms, I found most memorable about the whole of our tour.

The first leg of the flight was transpolar to Anchorage in Alaska. Not only did it feel very odd to arrive at 2pm on the same day that we had left London at 3.35pm, but there was no darkness. An enduring memory of our refuelling stop is, alas, the amount of rubbish which was frozen into the ice at the sides of the runway. Later in the flight, however, our conversations were punctuated by expressions of pleasure as the country that we were visiting for two and a half weeks slowly made itself evident, first by the snow-covered flanks of Mount Fuji and then Yokohama harbour, and finally Narita airport where we were met by Mr Norihiro Ito of the Japan Foundation and Miss Yuko Yoshimi, who was to be our almost constant companion and helpful friend throughout our stay. Modern Tokyo seemed like any other big city, except for the occasional glimpse from the highway of a street of small houses, or a temple with prayer papers wafting in the draught of the passing cars. The only real change from my earlier visit seemed to be the greatly diminished number of yen which a pound would buy!

Our first morning in Japan was grey and wet but I gave in to the urge, which always comes over me when I arrive in a new location, to explore on foot the immediate environs of the hotel. As I was returning a familiar voice from the past shouted my name. There, under an umbrella, was the smiling face of Don Ramsay. Don had been a pupil of mine in Cambridge over thirty years earlier, and was then visiting

Tokyo as a distinguished scientist from the National Research Council of Canada. It seemed an auspicious beginning, and my spirits were raised even further by the courtesy of Mr Hideo Kagami, Director General of the Japanese Foreign Office Information Department, who called with two colleagues to tell us who we would meet that evening at a reception to be given by the Japan Foundation at International House. These details were quickly dealt with, and the talk turned to other more general matters while we were served with green tea in beautiful china. I recall a moment when I was a mere spectator, observing the incongruity of Barbara sipping her tea and trying to explain the concept underlying the English system of magisterial justice, administered by people who, for the most part, have no training in the law and rely on clerks to provide the necessary information. The natural politeness of the Japanese nearly, but not totally, concealed our companions' understandable sense of incredulity.

Back at the hotel we were joined by Yuko and Mr Ito, who explained the detailed itinerary for our time in Japan. It immediately became clear how much our hosts wished to make the experience enjoyable for us and, so it seemed to Barbara and me, how little we could give in return. When evening came we found it quite impossible to remember the names of the people we met at the reception but it was very reassuring, when we encountered them a second time in their offices, to be able to recognise their faces. The guests were not limited to Japanese nationals, but included British people serving with the Embassy or the British Council. Barbara and I moved around separately, and compared notes when we were back at the hotel. She had expected that the Japanese sense of decorum and ceremonial would have reinforced the natural tendency of parties of this kind to be a mere exchange of banalities, and therefore was enthused by a vigorous conversation she had engaged in on the pros and cons of whale-hunting.

The following morning we were called upon by Mrs Hotsuki, a charming lady who came with us to the National Diet Library for the presentation of the facsimile of the Magna Carta. She interpreted exceptionally well, making notes in a mixture of Japanese and English while I was talking; as far as we could judge from the expressions on the faces of Mr Minoru Kishida, the Director of the Library, and his colleagues, she caught the spirit as well as the meaning of what I was saying. As in all meetings in Japan where there is the slightest touch of ceremony, we were seated symmetrically around a rectangular table, at the head of which was Mr Kishida, with Barbara, myself and the interpreter on one side and other Japanese representatives opposite us. After the formal introductions I presented the facsimile and the accompanying little book written about the Magna Carta especially for the American bicentenary, together with a small commemorative document in Japanese which I signed in their presence. This was read aloud by Mr Kishida, and to our relief the Japanese agreed that the calligraphy was excellent. I tried to set the Magna Carta in the context of British political history, but our hosts were much more interested in developments in contemporary Britain; for example, when would the British Library be rehoused, why did we have so much industrial unrest, and so on. It culminated in a query as to whether Mrs Thatcher and her government would survive, given that so many previous administrations had had such a short life. I had to remind myself that for over thirty years following the end of the war Japan had been governed by conservatives, almost without interruption, ruling with an absolute majority in both houses for nearly a quarter of a century. I suppose it was in this context that our hosts seemed to be treating with some complacency the national elections at that time taking place in Japan.

After lunch we were driven to the Imperial Palace to be received by Crown Prince Akihito and his wife, the Crown Princess Michiko. On arrival, an official conducted us into a typical waiting room, bare except for rectangular furniture and one exquisite Japanese vase. He explained that the Princess had just returned from presenting Nightingale awards to nurses and was dressed accordingly, and needed time to change. After a few minutes we walked through a square hall, containing little except a harp and a stone dulcimer, to a larger symmetrically furnished room where we were received by their Imperial Highnesses. They were in western dress, and both spoke very good English; it was inevitable that our conversation should begin with Florence Nightingale but it quickly passed to ichthyology, on which the Crown Prince was an expert, having described several new species. From this it was an easy transition to Barbara's research interest in slugs and snails before we turned to the real discussion of what my activities were to be in Japan. Our conversation became animated, and went on considerably longer than planned.

That evening I went to the Tokyo Club for dinner with Hiroshi Kida, who I think had chosen this venue because the last time we met he was my guest at the Athenaeum. Meanwhile Barbara had gone her own way. For two years at St Hilda's her rooms had been adjacent to those of a Fellow in Mediaeval History, Dr Sally

Harvey, who had married an Englishman named Fielding employed by the European Community and serving in Japan. Meeting now in Tokyo, Sally drove Barbara to her flat where they sat for an hour and a half drinking champagne until Sally's husband came home, and then all three moved on to a Japanese restaurant. One of us therefore spent the evening eating Japanese food and discussing English manorial rolls while the other was having dinner in the Tokyo Club, where my host had thoughtfully arranged for English food as an alternative, and discussing Japanese attitudes to western educational research. That neither of us considered this abnormal convinced me that Barbara and I must have made a satisfactory adjustment to life in Japan.

I spent the next morning with members of the Japan Academy and the afternoon with Sogo Okamura, Director of the Japan Society for the Promotion of Science and a former Dean of Science at Tokyo University. For Barbara the day was one of the high points of the visit because she was taken by Yuko to Tokyo Zoo. Through their shared liking for zoos, Yuko and Barbara became firm friends and after a Japanese lunch they visited the Sensoji Shinto shrine, the approach to which was flanked by many gaily decorated stalls in a narrow street which reminded Barbara of the bazaars in Egypt (though by comparison they were very clean and tidy). They went through all the ritual of purification at the shrine, and Barbara maintains that the shock of going into a large modern store afterwards, and returning to the Palace Hotel by underground, added to the incongruity of her diverse experiences that day – a feeling only strengthened by the fact that our host for dinner that evening, Mr Kishida of the National Diet Library, took us to a Chinese restaurant by way of a change.

The next day was devoted entirely to the Tokyo Institute of Technology where Shigeo Tazuke, a former research student of mine, was an assistant professor. In the evening he and another former research student, Rooky Yashiro, together with their wives Hiroko and Resuko, entertained us to dinner at the Barons' Club. It was a delightful evening, following a busy day.

By 10am on Saturday 29 September Barbara, Yuko and I were aboard the Shinkansen Hikari bound for Nagoya. We were favourably impressed with the speed, cleanliness and comfort of this 'bullet' train, not to mention the jets of water which appeared occasionally from the sides of the track to wash the windows and keep the carriages clean. On arrival in Nagoya we took a 'limited express' to Toba, following a picturesque route round the southern shore of the bay. Our planned tour of the local scenery in Toba was thwarted by inclement weather, which subsequently developed into a typhoon, leaving us time to talk with Yuko about her family and upbringing. She seemed to us the very model of a liberated, modern Japanese lady, and we were taken aback to learn that when she was living at home an arrival after 10pm meant that the doors of the house were closed to her and she had to take overnight refuge in the garage!

Viewed in retrospect, the next day seemed to be devoted to Shinto and pearls. The native religion of Japan is something I had often argued about with colleagues in the past: its nationalistic overtones, its association with ancestor worship and its notions of military chivalry (within the army, but not towards its enemies), which permeated Japanese troops even in the Second World War, had long perplexed me. What also fascinated me was the fact that the priesthood is hereditary, and there is a great deal of ritual purification. It was difficult to get Yuko to express a clear view of her own attitude to Shinto, but she certainly approved of its disestablishment as a state religion. Our pilgrimage began immediately after breakfast, and notwithstanding the wet weather we toured a number of shrines. Barbara also took advantage of a gap in the bad weather to photograph an old Japanese hotel, which turned out to be a modern reconstruction: nevertheless it was still referred to as the 'old' hotel and we learned that 'old' in Japan, when applied to a building, means constantly renewed but always faithfully copied from the original, or any successor to the original. Indeed, we were informed that a small, well-kept, open space beside one of the shrines was set aside for the god, who had to have somewhere to stay while his shrine was being rebuilt.

I was brought up to believe that pearls were a natural product of oysters in which some foreign body had become lodged, but had not known the history of how Kokichi Mikimoto had set out to see whether he could deliberately place some small object into a living oyster, to act as a nucleus for the development of a pearl. Within three years he had discovered that the best way was to take a particle of the mantle membrane of one oyster and insert it into another oyster, when in what I imagine to be an immune reaction the encircling membrane would secrete many layers of pearly substance around the irritant. Nowadays, such seeded oysters are put into cages and returned to coastal waters; the cultured pearls are removed between two and five years later.

We left Toba on Monday 1 October and again boarded our little train, which arrived at Kyoto promptly after another scenic journey, but one in which we were never out of sight of groups of small houses. It was also evident that every inch of land which could be cultivated had been planted with rice, vegetables or tobacco, the rice being in various stages – some recently sown, some ready to harvest and some actually harvested, with the rice straw at times carefully hung up to dry, but otherwise left to rot in the paddies.

Although Kyoto is now a bustling city of some one and a half million people, it prides itself on its refined culture and the arts it has nurtured in its long history. Over several centuries it was important as the capital of Japan; what is more, all its historical buildings escaped destruction during the Second World War and it has a large number of temples and gardens, covering the whole of its 'capital' period. It was explained to us that the tea ceremony was really developed and cultivated in Kyoto, as well as various domestic arts, including in particular that of flower arrangement. I had told Yuko of my earlier visit and she had thoughtfully arranged a programme which supplemented that experience, so as soon as possible we drove to a viewpoint on the top of a hill to get our bearings: we lingered longer than per-haps we should have done, simply to enjoy the warm sunshine and clear views (the first we had had in Japan). Thus acclimatised, we were driven to a most delightful street full of attractive shops selling many things we would have liked to have bought, but for the difficulty of getting them home. At the top of the street was the large Kiyomizu Dera, a temple founded by the shogun who subjugated northern Japan. It was an imposing wooden structure which seemed to be built into the side of a hill and was approached by a large flight of steps. We were assured that no nails had been used in its construction. Close by were several minor temples where one could drink water from different streams to ensure health, wealth or happiness. As we drove back to the hotel I pondered yet again that the Japanese mind, supremely successful in the application of science through technology, could also accommo-date so easily the traditional beliefs which they held, whereas in my mind I could see only an unbridgeable gap.

The next day was devoted to a visit to the Shugaku-in Imperial Villa, which we reached by a scenic drive along a mountain road east of Kyoto. The immediate environs were idyllic, having been chosen eight centuries earlier as the site of a temple which was destroyed in the civil wars of the fourteenth century. Even now, so many years later, I still find a great sense of peace and quiet engendered by my memory of the simple architecture, the lovely artificial lakes and cascades, the variety of trees including azaleas, cedars, cypresses and the omnipresent maple and cherry, the contrived but beautiful arrangement of stones in the dry gardens; and always with the magnificent view of the hills which lie to the north.

During our visit to Japan we were frequently impressed by the immense amount of care taken in the maintenance of the buildings and their surroundings. This attention to detail was nowhere more powerfully evident than when we went to the Urasenke Tea House where, after taking part in the tea ceremony which is dedicated to the notion of the beauty of natural simplicity, we observed a gardener picking up pine needles from a path with tweezers! I have wondered many times how long this meticulous attitude will successfully withstand the impact of Japan's technological success, and the western culture and ideas increasingly finding their way into Japanese life nowadays.

One thing however is certain: despite the vast differences between West and East, it is still possible to have genuine, unreserved, warm relationships between individuals and families drawn from these very different cultures. The classic case in our lives, to which I have referred in Chapter 7, is the friendship we made with Shigeo Tazuke, his wife Hiroko, and his parents and sister. This is why, on my earlier visit to Kyoto, I insisted on finding time to meet Shigeo's father before leaving for Osaka. It is also the reason why in 1979 we felt we must call and see Shigeo's mother, now a widow, and his sister in their home in Kyoto. To our surprise this was a substantial brick villa which might have been constructed by a Victorian builder for a middle-class London family, although at least one room, in which we sat, was fully Japanese in style with long sliding windows and cushions on which to squat. In another room Shigeo's mother, Mrs Sadako Tazuke, showed us the house shrine to her late husband in the form of a photograph, in front of which stood a bowl regularly replenished with fresh fruit. We drank tea with them and spent a most enjoyable hour with two people who, like Shigeo himself, seemed to span the two worlds with an ease and grace that we could not muster.

On our last day in Kyoto we toured a factory where we were shown the traditional method of painting on silk and the more modern stencil method, and then boarded a train for Tokyo. During the three-hour journey we revisited in our minds all that we had done in Kyoto and, with Yuko's help, were able to fill in some of the details. By this time our relationship with Yuko had become very informal and friendly, and she had gained in self-confidence so that, because my actions often made her smile, she christened me 'Mr Peculiar' – a designation which persisted for the rest of the trip and throughout the correspondence which we have maintained ever since. We were sad when the time came to part from her.

In Tokyo we stayed at International House in the Minato district, where our welcoming reception had been held just eight days previously. Looking out from the building, the eye was led by a sinuous white path through an immaculate lawn studded with the most carefully groomed shrubs, to a pavilion standing in a small round pond with lovely flowering shrubs, carefully placed stepping stones, aquatic plants and stone lamphouses, all clear evidence of design by someone steeped in the traditions of Japanese architecture. It was a garden in which we took great pleasure, where once again we saw gardeners on their knees teasing out individual weeds with great thoroughness and precision. Some of the roofs which were overlooked by neighbouring buildings were covered in the same meticulously weeded grass.

The next few days seemed to be entirely occupied with meetings on a range of topics, and a courtesy visit to the Ministry of Foreign Affairs. On the Friday morning I conducted a seminar on science policy at Monbusho (the Ministry of Education); and in the afternoon was billed to give a lecture at Tokyo University Library on 'administrative policy on libraries'. I was astonished by the size of the audience until I learned that word had gone out to all the library schools in Japan, and also that the National Libraries Committee Report, with which I had been so deeply involved, had been translated into Japanese and for many of the library schools was a set book. At the end of the lecture I was presented with a copy: it was only on riffling through the pages that I recognised some of the diagrams and realised what it was. The lecture itself took a long time to deliver because it was translated sentence by sentence, which I am sure made my language somewhat stilted and certainly inhibited any attempt at levity; but I had already judged that the audience was far too seriously minded for jokes to be told.

Happily, in these last few busy days there were still opportunities for evening events, including some enjoyable dinners at the British Embassy and an outing to the opera where, to our surprise, we heard *The Magic Flute* performed in German by the Royal Opera Company under the baton of Colin Davis. The cultures of the world may be very different, but there are unexpected points of contact!

On Wednesday 10 October at 7am we were ready to be driven out to the International Airport for a flight to Seoul in Korea. Alas, as were were loading our car someone noticed that the radiator was leaking, and although another English person was leaving in a British Council car for the same airport and offered us a lift, Yuko felt she could not allow this; she thought her credibility would be harmed if we were not delivered properly in a Japanese vehicle. We were therefore taken to a garage in central Tokyo and transferred into another car for the long drive to the airport, through what Barbara described as 'the most featureless and unrelieved mess of concrete buildings I have ever seen'.

Our first visit to Korea, the 'Land of the Morning Calm', came at a time when that country had just adopted its fourth five-year plan intended to liquidate the adverse balance of payments which had followed rapid growth to satisfy an internal market. Korea aimed to do this by substantial research and development investment in high added-value export industries, and the plan called for a strengthening of higher education in areas of science, education and technology. I suppose this was why a visitor such as myself, with interests in higher education and in scientific research, was made especially welcome. The plan was successful, for ten years later the balance of payments deficit had been transformed into a huge surplus.

We were met at Kimpo airport by Professor Wan Kwoo Cho, Vice-President of the Seoul National University, and Dr Lee, an expert in linguistics. Professor Cho had spent some time working in Cambridge and Dr Lee had been at University College, London, for many years. Both spoke excellent English. They saw us safely into the Shilla Hotel in Seoul and suggested a 'sky-line drive' that would take us to a café and observation point on the south side of the 30-mile-wide demilitarised zone (DMZ) close to latitude 38°N. It was an exhilarating experience, first because I realized that the Korean paintings of mountains, which to my innocent eye had seemed highly unnatural, had in fact fully caught the essence of their topography and flora; and secondly because the DMZ is now effectively a vast nature reserve virtually untrodden by humans.

Although the first settlements at Seoul took place in the fourteenth century and it was once the seat of the kings of the Choson dynasty, its explosive population growth occurred in the twentieth century, especially after the Second World War. This was in part caused by the flow of refugees from the so-called Democratic People's Republic of North Korea, with its old-style Communist dictatorship.

When we were there the population of South Korea was about seven million and that phenomenal growth has continued apace, so that twelve years later it was over ten million. This growth was only too evident, for the skyline was dominated by tall buildings, and tall cranes set up for the purpose of building yet more tall buildings. Even so, in the heart of the city there were still ancient palaces and gardens which would have been quiet sanctuaries, if only there were not so many tourists.

Unfortunately, because our programme was packed with activities we could only get brief glimpses of the ancient walled city in between other appointments. Our first call was on the President of Seoul National University, Professor Byong-ik Koh, an historian who had been designated as our official host. The University is the largest and most prestigious in the country, and was created as late as 1946 by amalgamating the old Imperial University, founded twenty years earlier, with nine public and private specialist tertiary colleges. As we drove in through the traditionally-designed entrance gate, I could hardly believe my eyes at the ranks of four-storey 'cloned' student residences regularly disposed along the major contour lines; their sheer ugliness seemed all the more stark against the magnificent slopes of Mount Kwanak which formed the backdrop. Only the main library (of special importance as it contained the largest collection of books in Korea) had a setting, architectural shape and detailing which raised the spirit of the observer.

The following day we were shown over this library by its Director, Dr Kim, and I was particularly interested to see some examples of early printing, because the Koreans invented movable block type about 1230 AD – some two centuries before Gutenberg. Nobody I asked seemed to know what material was used at first: I suspect it may have been wood, but since bronze had already been used for 2,000 years in the making of tools and weapons, it seems possible that the type was metal. When I mentioned my connection with the British Library great smiles appeared, and the evident veneration of its collection of oriental manuscripts and printed books was heart-warming.

Seoul National University had its own teaching hospital and I was well received by the General Director, Hyack Kwon. On seeing a statue of Florence Nightingale, I mentioned to him that people living in the Far East seemed to have a greater veneration for this lady than those in Britain. After a general discussion about healthcare provision, I was taken to see the radiological and radiotherapy facilities: someone had evidently done their homework about my interest in these areas. This proved to be a memorable occasion because in the course of the conversation I was asked about the work of Godfrey Hounsfield, the inventor some ten years earlier of the first computerised transverse axial tomography scanner; just then someone burst into the room, smiling broadly, and told us that Hounsfield had been awarded a Nobel Prize in Medicine that very morning. We drank his health in orange juice! Despite the lack of alcoholic stimulus, I was buoyed up by the news and lectured with confidence about the chemistry of the electron, while students demonstrated on the pavements outside.

As we were driven around Seoul we could not fail to notice the church spires, and when on Sunday we went by train to Kyongju there seemed to be scarcely a village without one. They stood out because their gothic architecture appeared so incongruous among the traditional houses with their characteristic tiled roofs. We were told that more than one-third of the population were Christian, in part as a result of missionary work which began with the Catholics in the eighteenth century. Because Catholicism had a special appeal for the oppressed, the Korean rulers of the eighteenth century sought to suppress it. Much of the Christian proselytisation occurred in the second half of the nineteenth century when North American Protestants, largely Presbyterian and Methodist, arrived. They were impelled by a progressive democratic spirit and founded many schools, paid for hospitals and brought modern medicine to Korea. That such missionaries were opposed to the anti-democratic rule of the Japanese must have added to the appeal of Protestantism, for its adherents now outnumber Catholics by four to one. One Methodist mission established the Ewha Girls' School in 1886, the country's first school for women. By 1910 it had become a Liberal Arts College, and in 1946 it was granted full university status as Ewha Woman's *(sic)* University. We were received there by the president and learned that, in its brief twenty years as a university, Ewha had produced more than 42,000 alumni – just over 40 per cent of all the Korean women graduates: only technology and engineering do not feature in the curriculum. Our hosts were interested to learn that Barbara was a graduate of an all-female college in Cambridge and a Fellow of a women's college in Oxford.

We paid visits to numerous other institutions and met with many dignitaries – government ministers, industrialists, and members of professional groups such as the Korean Advanced Institute of Science, the Korean Institute of Science and Technology, the University and Industry Foundation, and the Korean Traders'

Association. All recognised their vulnerability to attack from North Korea, which seemed all the more likely because of the widening economic gap due to failures in the North and outstanding successes in the South. In everyone we met there was a will for change and an intense desire for new knowledge, combined with a drive for innovation. We were showered with presents for ourselves, as well as a generous gift to support Korean studies at the University of Sheffield.

Before concluding this section I must describe some idiosyncratic features of Korea which we were privileged to enjoy. The programme arranged for us generally included a couple of hours each day for 'sightseeing', when the indefatigable Dr Lee would conduct us to places of interest. He wished, and perhaps he had been instructed, to show us the National Museum in the Kyongbok Palace gardens, but the latter were so magnificent that we declined to enter the building. We also wished to see how a late twentieth-century Korean lived and so we persuaded Dr Lee to take us to visit his home and family, for whom we had a small gift. The visit was a great success once I had melted everyone's reserve by mystifying his two daughters and small son with some string tricks, which have never yet failed me in a foreign country. Characteristically, the item which dominated the furniture was an enormous radio and music centre, an icon signifying much about modern Korea.

Our hosts had planned a visit to a folk village at Suwon, some 30 miles south of Seoul. I longed rather to see something of what I was sure would be the spectacular peaks and ravines of the T'aebaek mountains: I had been told that these had some lovely pre-Cambrian granites, gneiss and other metamorphic rocks. However, I had to eat humble pie, for the folk village turned out to be a delightful place to spend a Saturday afternoon in early autumn. Although largely a modern construction, it contained a range of old-style buildings with life-like wax models of men and women engaged in daily tasks and playing games, of course traditionally dressed and provided with period tools. We learned much about the history of Korea and its language, which is markedly different from Chinese or Japanese: philologists consider that it should be classified with Hungarian and Finnish. Korean writing is phonetic, although nowadays it accommodates the use of many Chinese characters. No one knows for certain where the Korean people originated. One theory is that they arrived in the peninsula by sea, though nobody knows whence; another is that they are the descendants of a people who inhabited Eurasia before the arrival of the Chinese (who are known to have come from the west). It is tempting to imagine that the people whom the Chinese displaced were driven north into Finland, south into Hungary and eastwards into the Korean peninsula, with a corresponding evolution of the language they spoke. What is certain is that the Koreans developed an advanced state before they adopted Chinese civilisation. In the twentieth century the Japanese attempted to suppress the pre-existing Korean culture, but only with limited success.

On Sunday 14 October we caught the train to Kyongju, the cradle of the Shilla kingdom. We were greeted with great warmth and honour by the stationmaster and then were driven to the royal burial mounds, one of which we were able to enter. Over dinner that evening our hosts explained how in the middle of the fourth century AD the leader of the Saro tribe assumed kingship over Shilla, which in the mid-seventeenth century unified the peninsula; Buddhism replaced the previously dominant Confucianism and the dynasty survived for about six centuries. It is the kings of this line who lie in the burial mounds.

Monday was a complete contrast, with visits to the Ulsan College of Engineering, of which the President, K. Lee, was a Liverpool PhD graduate. The Union Jack was flying in our honour and President Lee proudly introduced us to staff who had experience of postgraduate work at Imperial College, UMIST, Strathclyde and Loughborough. Having taken our leave we moved on to the huge Hyundai company, where we were conducted round the car factory and parts of the shipyard. The former was not particularly notable, being like any other such plant with its own characteristic work rhythms, but I did notice many crates labelled 'Perkins Diesel Engines, Peterborough' and my enquiry elicited the answer that Hyundai's two-ton vans were powered by these splendid units. The dry and wet docks for tankers and supertankers were staggering: I had never seen a shipyard so vast, with so few signs of rust and clutter or such great evidence of advanced machinery. Barbara sadly noticed British ships being repaired there at a time when our own yards were without work.

The next day, as we flew to Singapore, I began to reflect on our visits to Japan and Korea. We had learned that in the nineteenth century each society had suddenly been exposed to the impact of western thought and technology, and both had begun to make use of this knowledge for their own development (though each at a different pace, because the Japanese hegemony delayed progress in Korea). Although lacking natural resources, both have competed successfully with western industries and have been genuine innovators in manufacture. Yet their conspicuous economic and materialistic success seems not to have eroded the old cultural and religious values; indeed, the discipline implicit in the latter seems to have been used successfully as a motivation for company loyalty in the factory. Thinking about this, I recalled how the Buddhist missionaries built their temples close to Shinto shrines and emphasised the beliefs which were common to both: to this day, many Japanese are married according to Shinto rites and buried according to Buddhist ones. This religious co-existence contrasts sharply with the intolerance of the Christian proselytisers who tore down idols and shrines to indigenous gods. The eastern civilisations seem to have been for all time much more willing to recognise the good in other religions, and successful in absorbing much of the old into the new. Their attitude is in marked contrast to the way in which the Soviet Union and the European countries it controlled officially abandoned the past, economically and in terms of religious belief, and have now failed. China perhaps remains a 'riddle wrapped in a mystery inside an enigma', to use Churchill's words: it claims to have sidelined religion but, as my old pupil Tsao commented later when we met him in Shanghai, 'Chinese culture is very persistent'.

In Chapter 9 I described my first meeting with the Prime Minister of Singapore, Lee Kuan Yew, and his invitation for me to advise him about the development of university education in the Republic. In 1979, which was our first visit, we were there only long enough for me to make some courtesy calls and to go over certain issues relevant to the enquiry I was making. However, we have since made many trips to Singapore and have witnessed the transformation of the Nanyang Chinese University – first into the Nanyang Institute of Technology and then into the Nanyang Technological University. One thing that always impressed us was the mutual tolerance of the three major ethnic groups – Chinese, Malays and Tamils – with their varied religions, a state of affairs not often achieved in the world in which we live. Barbara and I have often reflected on the wisdom of Lee Kuan Yew in making English the language of commerce and education. Singapore is such an international trading port that this choice was clearly good for trade: certainly the shops were always full of everything from Chinese silks and English ceramics to French gloves and African batik. Moreover, the fact that all education is in English means that everyone, whether Chinese, Malaysian or Tamil, can speak to one another: in this context, one cannot help being reminded of the wisdom of the founding fathers of the USA. Two other facts must also have contributed to the apparent racial harmony. The first and probably the more important is the fact that there was no real indigenous population to be disturbed at the time when Raffles arrived. Secondly, the way in which different races live in groups with like-minded people must also have helped: everyone still seemed to us to be enjoying his or her own culture, with freedom to practise it and, at the same time, to share that of others. There are now relatively few English people living on the island, but evidence of the former connection is still around in many ways.

Barbara and I grew very fond of Singapore and we were delighted when the University of Sheffield started holding presentation ceremonies there for its Singaporean graduates, because this led to additional visits to that city state. Although these were primarily for business, in my role as Chancellor, we were also able to take some time off: I recall with particular amusement our participation in a game of musical chairs on the playing field of the local Methodist boys' school, which lasted so long that it achieved a mention in the *Guinness Book of Records* (though we left well before the end, because of the heat and humidity).

Other special memories relate to August 1989 when I was in receipt of the Lee Kwan Yew Fellowship, and we spent a marvellous twelve days in the city; and April 1997, when we were entertained by Lee Kwan Yew in his home and he said that his country regarded me as the 'father' of its two universities. This was a very heartwarming statement, and one we will always treasure.

Hong Kong and China, 1982: Contrasts and Coexistence

The background to our visit to Hong Kong and China in 1982 was the increasing role of the Royal Society overseas, in formal relations with corresponding national academies of science. As far as China was concerned, my predecessor but one as Dr Lee's Professor of Chemistry in Oxford, Sir Cyril Hinshelwood, had visited in 1959 at the invitation of the Chinese Academy of Sciences (CAS), while President of the Royal Society. Sir Cyril had taught himself some Chinese, and had developed a keen interest in carved jade pieces: the Chinese people are always delighted when westerners take some trouble to understand something of their language and culture, and it was clear to us that his presence in China had been much appreciated. Since that time many visits had taken place in both directions, sponsored by the Royal Society and CAS. I was told that the frequency of such exchanges dropped during the Cultural Revolution, but by the end of 1978 it seemed possible to negotiate a proper agreement between the two bodies. In 1981 Sir Michael Stoker, then Foreign Secretary of the Royal Society, enquired whether I would be willing to go to China: I agreed with alacrity, not least because I wished to see the land in which my 'big brother Bill' had worked for almost one and a half decades.

Sir Michael demitted office at the end of November 1981 and his successor, Sir Arnold Burgen, decided he also wished to make the trip. I think it was he who suggested it would be sensible to return via the USSR so that we could see something of that country's Academy of Science, and make contact with its principal officers. We both felt the irresistible attraction of travelling overland across the great Mongolian plateau, and experiencing something of railway travel in these vast countries. The obvious plan was therefore to fly to Hong Kong, which we could use as a springboard for the People's Republic: this suited Barbara and me particularly well, because we also had other fish to fry in Hong Kong. St Hilda's College had been led to believe by one of its medical graduates, a Chinese lady named Deanna Rudgard, that her father – Mr Richard Lee, successful Hong Kong businessman, alumnus of Pembroke College, Oxford, and head of the charitable Lee Hysan Foundation – wished to donate money to the College to enable a Chinese woman from the mainland to study or conduct research in Oxford. It was felt that if good candidates were to be selected the College must have a significant input into the selection process, and not simply accept annually an individual nominated by CAS or the Chinese Academy of Medical Sciences (CAMS). As the Zoological Fellow of St Hilda's, Barbara knew exactly what the College wanted, and it was agreed that we should arm ourselves with a suitable background briefing from Deanna and her father, and then hold discussions during our visit with the relevant mainland Chinese (identified by officers of CAS and CAMS in Beijing).

On the morning of Monday 5 April 1982 Barbara and I met at Gatwick with Sir Arnold and Lady (Judith) Burgen and John Deverill, a Russian language speaker on the Royal Society staff, whose help in the USSR was to prove invaluable. Our minds were not entirely focused on our journey, because Argentina had invaded the Falkland Islands on the previous Friday and, in common with many other UK citizens, we had given much thought to the possible responses open to Britain. While waiting in line at the check-in desk we heard of the decision to dispatch a military task force to recover the islands. Apart from the limited information our ambassador, Sir Percy Cradock, was able to give us in Beijing, that was the last authentic news we had until five weeks later when we boarded the flight to London at Moscow airport and a stewardess greeted us with the news of the sinking of the Argentine cruiser *General Belgrano*.

Our descent to Kai Tak, the Hong Kong International Airport at the eastern end of the Kowloon peninsula, was dramatic. Below, there opened up to our view the Pearl River, Macao, the New Territories and the island of Hong Kong with its sky-scrapers thrusting up towards us, plus numerous smaller islands. We looked down at a mass of shipping, from large tankers to sampans, some at anchor, some arriving and others departing, some in dry dock or tied up at the many wharves and jetties. As the aircraft came in to land we also became aware of the dense road traffic, and soon experienced its reality as we were driven to our hotel in Kowloon. After breakfast and unpacking we went out on a reconnaissance on foot and by ferry. We were overwhelmed by the sense of being in a human beehive or, perhaps more aptly, a colony of sea-birds nesting on a cliff face, because no possible space was left unoccupied by human beings – all seemingly engrossed in some gainful occupation. People even seemed to be living in wooden huts perched on the flat roofs of office or apartment blocks. The phrase 'teeming millions' immediately acquired a whole new meaning for us.

That evening Richard Lee and his wife Esther gave a delightful dinner party for which, with great thoughtfulness, they had assembled many interesting people. These included the Vice-Chancellor of the Chinese University, Ma Lin, who said he had attended my lectures in Leeds; his wife, a pathologist who had trained in London at the Royal Postgraduate Medical School; and Judge T. Liang Yang and his wife Barbara, both graduates of University College, London, in law and medicine respectively (the Judge later became Chief Justice of Hong Kong and Chairman of the University and Polytechnic Grants Committee). The personality among the guests who struck us most forcibly was Fei Yiming, a member of the Chinese Communist Party, who described himself as 'a democratic socialist'. As we talked and I learned not only of his extensive travels but also that he was a Chevalier of the Legion d'Honneur, I began to see him as a true world citizen. More importantly, his presence suggested that the Establishment of the Communist Party, doubtless due to Deng Xiaoping's influence, was becoming a 'broad church', able to accommodate a wider spectrum of more tolerant views: this realisation strengthened my resolve to take all whom we met in China at face value and not to make any assumptions about their beliefs and attitudes, but merely to let the facts emerge as we talked to each other.

The next thirty-six hours were to be packed with activity. We were able to admire the beautiful campus setting of the Chinese University at Shatin in the New Territories, which gave us superb views of sea inlets into many narrow valleys: our guide took us into the library, the art gallery (to which the Lee Hysan Foundation had made generous gifts), the science centre and even the chemistry department. The highly functional multistorey buildings of Hong Kong University, which we also visited, are perched on a steep hillside; they are generally less elegant than those of the Chinese University, apart from the Staff House, which is in a pleasing classical style with columns, arcaded quadrangles and a lovely cupola roof over the senior common room. We repeatedly reconnected with our past in the shape of former colleagues and students, and in the evening we were joined by Pauline Chan, a high-powered lady who had expressed some interest in St Hilda's. Our discussions over an exquisite dinner must have been to her satisfaction, because she subsequently made generous gifts to establish both a Fellowship in Physics and the Pauline Chan Fellowship in Economics.

The Hong Kong grapevine must have been very efficient because we were sought out by several other people during our short visit, including staff in the Queen Elizabeth Hospital, where we spent an hour and a half discussing scientific aspects of radiotherapy and radiological protection. Those Hong Kong Chinese people we met clearly valued the British connection, its values, style and special qualities, but not to the point of diminishing their strong sense of cultural identity. We speculated on how they would fare after the handover of the Territory to China in 1997, and decided that those who stayed would survive because it was the commercial drive and entrepreneurship of such people that had caused Hong Kong to become a vital node in the world of international relationships. The new China would need to secure Hong Kong's economic success, so we felt that the lifestyle of the Hong Kong Chinese might not alter very much; and possibly their approach to life would, by its success, diffuse back into China itself.

These and other thoughts were in our minds as we flew to Beijing at the end of our brief stay in Hong Kong. We wondered, for example, whether during our visit we might get any glimpses of the feelings and opinions of individual Chinese we encountered, or whether there would still be a reticence to declare views openly. The political developments which followed the death of Mao in 1976 were clearly real and not cosmetic: we were conscious that China was opening herself to the world, inviting foreign capital and restoring diplomatic relations with the USA, but had there been any concomitant change in the hearts and minds of the people? We were confident that we would have easy relationships with the scientists we were due to meet because they would probably know English and we would therefore not require interpreters, and we would also share common professional interests; but we were somewhat uncertain as to how we would be received and regarded by other people. In the event there was always an easy transition from the first smile to more serious, friendly and open discussion, though because we had to concentrate on business we had few opportunities for conversation about the deeply held beliefs and motivations that made individuals 'tick'. Naturally enough, the scope for free discussion was greatest with our interpreters.

The drive to our hotel was reminiscent of our first visit to Poland twenty-five years earlier, in that the roads were flat, straight and tree-lined, with very few cars but occasional flocks of sheep, ample evidence of ducks and many horse-drawn farm carts, each horse equipped with a little bag to catch its droppings. As we came closer to the city pollarded trees began to line the roads; behind them were factories, drab blocks of Soviet-style flats and occasional pear orchards. Wind and dust were everywhere, and everything seemed to be sand-coloured apart from a few trees just coming into leaf. We had no sense of passing through suburbs: the straight roads simply broadened, becoming enormously wide in the centre of the city, where they were filled with thousands of cyclists and pedestrians through whom the few car drivers negotiated their way by vigorous use of the horn and what appeared to be a good deal of luck. The contrast with life in Hong Kong was striking.

Hong Kong housing had been almost entirely high-rise flats, but in Beijing most citizens apparently still lived in relatively primitive one- or two-storey houses crowded together. Hong Kong streets were brash and noisy, brightly lit, flanked by garish advertisements and thronged with motor vehicles of all kinds, as if the whole city flaunted the consumer ethic. Beijing had no such 'buzz' and its citizens looked puritanical. The vast majority were dressed in blue Mao suits and caps which proclaimed the enforced orthodoxy of earlier years and which, for whatever reason –

cost or psychological conditioning – they seemed to have found difficult to put aside. However, we were assured by our guides that change was occurring, and indeed their own clothes exemplified this.

Once installed in the Peking Hotel we assembled with the Burgens and John Deverill to be briefed on the programme which had been arranged for us. In the main this reflected the briefing sent weeks earlier by the Royal Society, but despite my best efforts I was unable to find out at that stage what lectures I was supposed to give, and at which institutions. In the event the talks took place in several laboratories and two libraries: the library services were parlous, even in comparison with the poor state of the laboratory equipment,[1] but despite this certain institutions were evidently able to acquire by purchase or other means books and journals from overseas. This was brought home to me rather forcefully during a meeting at the Institute of Photographic Chemistry. When the group was called to order and I was introduced, I wrote my name on the board as F.S. Dainton, at which point one person left the room. This disconcerted me somewhat, but he returned a minute or two later with a little volume which he presented as a gift. It was in fact my book on chain reactions, of which 10,000 copies of a Chinese version had been printed in 1957, although this was the first I knew of it! Interestingly enough, this piracy and breach of copyright raised my eyebrows, but not those of my local audience.

As we moved round various institutes and universities, we were constantly reminded that the scientific community inhabits a relatively small world. For example, in one laboratory we met a British couple who had been pupils of Dorothy Hodgkin. They had adopted Mao suits, which I took to be psychologically protective clothing: the wife, Rosemary Stewart, explained that 'in western dress we would be regarded as Martians'. Another connection was evident when we visited Peking University and were greeted very warmly by Professor Han Degong of the Chemistry Department: he had read my book in his younger days and was now conducting research on oscillatory reactions, a matter of considerable interest to my old student and successor at Leeds, Peter Gray. Again, the Deputy Director of the Department of Biology and Professor of Biochemistry at the University of Peking (a lady called Gu Xiaoqing, who was working on the preparation of crystalline

1. Since our visit the World Bank has made a grant of $200m US to enable China's 26 major universities to purchase modern apparatus, with an equivalent sum promised by the Chinese government.

proteins) turned out to have secured some money to come to Oxford: we were able to arrange for her to join St Hilda's and, having been there and learned something of British universities, she was well placed to help the college later in selecting suitable candidates for research support.

The President of the Chinese Academy of Sciences was a physical chemist named Lu Jiaxi who had worked before the war with Samuel Sugden at University College, London, and with Linus Pauling at CalTech in the United States. After pleasant reminiscences with him and others we discussed the proposed exchange agreement with the Royal Society, especially a series of collaborative projects on which they were keen (plus a proposed joint expedition to Tibet, about which they were much less enthusiastic). At our first meeting I also discovered that the Vice-President of the Academy, Li Xun, had once spent fourteen years in the Metallurgy Department of Sheffield University. Unfortunately he was away, but we managed to meet later for dinner: we reminisced about Sheffield, and he sent a message to Professor A.G. Quarrell, Emeritus Professor there.

Looking back, it seems extraordinary that I learned so little in my youth about the history of the most populous nation in the world, occupying a land area approximately the same as that of Canada or the USA but with 50 times the population of the former. I do not think I was unduly ignorant for a British youngster, and indeed I had a privileged source of information about China in the form of my elder brother Bill – both in the letters he wrote and when he was home on leave. However, his comments had been largely about the internecine quarrels of the warlords and their periodic assaults on the territorial 'concessions' held by the western powers. If he knew of it, he said nothing of the UK's disgraceful role in the export to China of opium in exchange for tea, although I did hear a little about this from the occasional Methodist missionaries who preached at the Banner Cross chapel in Sheffield. I knew something of the craft skills of the Chinese from the artefacts which Bill brought back, but there was never any questioning of the privileged position he and other Britons enjoyed and which seemed to him quite natural. The person whose enthusiasm for matters Chinese really influenced me was Barbara's mother, and I suppose I paid extra attention to her utterances because I hoped to become her son-in-law! I imagine her interest had a twofold origin: first, her brother-in-law had spent many years as headmaster of the Queen's School in Hong Kong; and second, although a biologist by initial training, she lectured in geography at Manchester University and had special interests in the Far East. From her I learned something of the Palaeolithic Peking Man, and about the city of that name, which began to develop in the second century AD into a trade centre for the whole of the middle basin of the Yellow River, as well as for Mongolia and Korea. She told me how Peking (now Beijing) came to be the capital of larger and larger territories over the years, how it was almost completely destroyed by the Mongols and then rebuilt as a walled city in the mid-thirteenth century AD by the Yuan Dynasty. Kublai Khan controlled the vast Chinese empire from Beijing, which was then called Khanbalik – Khan's Town. When the Mongols were expelled by the Ming Dynasty the latter abandoned Beijing as their capital, but the third emperor returned and began the reconstruction of what is now called the old city. That, and the fact that Marco Polo was employed by Kublai Khan, was, I am ashamed to admit, all that I knew about Beijing: I realised that I had much to learn on our non-scientific excursions.

Our visit to the Forbidden City, so named because it was the home of the emperors from which ordinary people were excluded, and also the imperial seat of government, took place on a Saturday afternoon when it was thronged with Chinese visitors. For the most part the adults were dressed in drab Mao tunics and trousers, but their children often had white shirts or blouses graced with bright red Young Pioneer neckerchiefs, and they frequently dressed their round-faced, apple-cheeked babies in bright red and blue clothes. I had caught a glimpse of the City's reddish-golden roofs in the morning sunshine from the top floor of the hotel earlier that day, and was amazed by the area it covered (nearly 200 acres) and what appeared to be an extraordinarily symmetrical disposition of the buildings, all surrounded by a crenellated wall. That it contained more than 40 palaces and halls and had been constructed over a mere three years defies belief. We went in from the the north side of Tiananmen Square, through 'The Gate of Heavenly Peace' – a name which has a somewhat hollow ring, given that the square was the site of such brutal application of authoritarian power in the student massacre of 1989.[2] Once beyond the gateway,

---

2. The names of the halls, pavilions and palaces fall beautifully on the ear but to a European are redolent of the Chinese preoccupation with states of being. For example, there are halls of *complete harmony*, *preserving harmony*, and *supreme and eternal harmony*; of *earthly tranquillity*, *imperial tranquillity* and *benevolent tranquillity*; of *nurtured happiness* and *prolonged happiness*; of *cultivation of the character* and *culture of the mind*, of *literary glory* and *literary profundity*; and what particularly appealed to me, of course, were the halls of *peaceful old age* and *vigorous old age*.

our eyes were transfixed by many architectural wonders as we passed through a succession of great halls to the Imperial Garden, and finally, feeling very virtuous, through the 'Gate of Perfect Rectitude' into the barracks of the Imperial Guard which line the inside of this northern perimeter wall.

That evening we talked over our impressions. The visions which floated across our inward eye were of massive structures of wood and stone arranged with great regard for regularity and symmetry, gold-covered bronze urns and lions, and intricately carved stone walls and trellises. Thinking of these images, we speculated on the thoughts that might have been passing through the minds of the many Chinese visitors that afternoon. We knew that little was taught to them about Imperial China at school, and Barbara had observed that there were very few exhibits within the National Museum in Tiananmen Square which related to that long period; we wondered whether this was a deliberate act of obfuscation on the part of the authorities or whether, at least as far as the museum was concerned, many of the artefacts had found their way overseas (perhaps to Taiwan). Since we had encountered a corresponding ignorance of Britain's imperial past in the youth of today at home, we finally decided that such questions were unprofitable and that maybe the Chinese were just enjoying a family outing, away from their unreformed hovels or Soviet-type blocks of flats.

The following day, Easter Sunday, we went to visit the Great Wall. My first thought, as I saw it snaking over the crests of the hills as far as the eye could see, was what an enormous enterprise its construction must have been – comparable with that of the pyramids – and I was not surprised to be told that much of it had been built by conscript labour, the military or prisoners. It was started under the Qin dynasty from 214 BC, when its purpose was to keep the Mongols and Huns from entering northern China. Not surprisingly, once Mongolia and China were united under the Yuan dynasty the rulers then were not interested in maintaining it in good condition, and it was left to the Ming dynasty to rebuild much of it. Over the centuries it has largely fallen into decay again, and only recently has it been properly restored at a limited number of places.

After our trip to the Great Wall, and to the Ming tombs nearby, the final visit we made together was to the Summer Palace. This lies to the north-west of Tiananmen Square and comprises a large walled estate on the banks of an artificial lake; the original buildings were destroyed by Anglo-French troops and were

113, 114. Flanked by my old friends Frank Kearton (left) and Burke Trend, I was introduced to the House of Lords in July 1986, having been made a Baron in the New Year Honours List. I took for my title Hallam Moors, as a reminder of my childhood in and around Sheffield. The pastel of those moors was a present from the artist, Jill Lauriston, who works in the University of Sheffield.

115-117. Three portraits, spanning a quarter of a century: *left,* as Vice-Chancellor of the University of Nottingham (painted in 1970 by William Narraway); *above,* as Chancellor of the University of Sheffield in 1984, with the artist, Trevor Stubley; and *below,* 'working' for June Mendoza in 1991.

118. Artistic licence from the cartoonist Trog in 1991.

119. Some of my medals. *Clockwise from top left*: Faraday Medal of the Royal Society of Chemistry (1974); Semenov Centenary Medal of the Russian Academy of Sciences (1996); Curie Medal of the Polish Society for Radiation Research (1983); President's Medal of the Institute of Physics (1997); Davy Medal of the Royal Society (1969); Tilden Medal of the Chemical Society (1950).

120-123. I have been fortunate to receive honorary degrees from many universities, including Strathclyde (Lord Todd conferring, *above*) and Leeds (with the Duchess of Kent, *left*), as well as from the Council for National Academic Awards (in conversation with the Princess Royal, *below*).

For obvious reasons, the honorary degree I received from Oxford has a special place in my affections. The facing page shows me in the Canterbury Quadrangle at St John's College, after the conferment in 1988.

124. My association with the University of Sheffield dates back to my schooldays, when I made use of libraries in the Chemistry Department and the octagonal Edgar Allen Building, seen here on the left of the picture. The original red-brick buildings at Western Bank had hardly changed by 1978, when I was elected the University's sixth Chancellor.

125. My formal installation as Chancellor took place in March 1979, in the splendour of the City Hall.

126. From the outset, I took every opportunity to spend time in the company of students. This photograph was taken in December 1983.

127. Presiding at a higher degree congregation in Firth Hall (named after Mark Firth, the Sheffield industrialist who in 1879 founded Firth College, the forerunner of the University).

128. Helen Sharman graduated in chemistry before going on to higher things as Britain's first astronaut. She was a worthy recipient of the Chancellor's Medal, which I instituted so that outstanding achievements could be recognised.

129. Over the years the University of Sheffield has been well served by its Vice-Chancellors. Geoffrey Sims (*centre*) was in post when I became Chancellor, and is pictured here with his successor, Sir Gareth Roberts, after receiving an honorary doctorate in 1991.

130, 131. I was honoured when the University decided that its Chemistry Building should bear my name. As on so many other occasions, Barbara was present at the opening ceremony to share in my pleasure.

132. The University marked my 80th birthday with a special reception at which I was presented with a congratulatory message and a cheeky cartoon.

133. Barbara took centre stage when she formally opened the roof garden in the University's Division of Adult Continuing Education, June 1997.

134. Fieldside was our Oxford home for 23 years. Here, an ageing Shep sets out across the fields.

135. The building of a dual carriageway just 150 metres from the front door of Fieldside precipitated our move in 1993 to this house nearer the centre of the city.

136-140. Moments of relaxation. *Clockwise from above*: with Shep in Derbyshire, during our Nottingham days; mowing the lawn at Fieldside; at Dunkery Beacon, Exmoor, in 1996; in reflective mood; and opening my 80th birthday cards.

141-144. Scenes from family life. *Clockwise from top left*: Mary and John at a family party in 1996; with Rosalind, her husband Christopher and daughter Anna, at Fieldside in 1992; early driving lessons for Anna; Mary's daughters Harriet (*left*) and Penelope entertaining friends.

145. In September 1989 some of my former colleagues and students came together to celebrate my 75th birthday. 'The Dainton Symposium' was held in the School of Chemistry at the University of Leeds: on my right in the group photograph is Arthur Salmon, who succeeded me as Director of the Cookridge Radiation Research Centre, and next to him is Jerzy Kroh, who had come all the way from Poland.

146. After a day of academic seminars, I was able to relax at a most convivial dinner. I was glad that I did not have to tackle 75 candles!

147, 148. On the second day of the symposium we went to Malham in North Yorkshire, scene of many happy group expeditions when we were all a lot younger. *Above*, the former professor, still in declamatory mode; *below*, walking near the field centre with Bill Seddon *(left)* and Keith Chambers.

149. *Left:* A reflective moment in the College Library at St John's, Oxford. Archbishop Laud looks on.

150. *Right:* I was inspired in my choice of career by my gifted chemistry teacher, Alf Ridler. He stayed on in Sheffield after retirement, and we have remained close friends. In 1997, when this photograph was taken, Alf was in his 92nd year.

151. *Below:* After my father died in 1930 my mother gave his stonemason's tools to his last apprentice, Charles Gibbs. Sixty years later Charles presented them to me, and they are now displayed in the Chancellor's Room at the University of Sheffield. Charles and I are seen here outside the Town Hall, with a mallet and chisel used by my father in its construction.

152. *Overleaf:* Back where it all began: enjoying a summer's evening in my native Sheffield.

rebuilt by the Empress Cixi in 1873. The palace is full of mural paintings in the temples, halls and corridors; and evidently empresses are not allowed to get wet, because every building is connected to the next by a covered way. At the end of the half-mile-long frontage on the lake there stands incongruously a marble boat, and as I looked at it I wondered whether that was what gave Clough Williams-Ellis the idea of building a stone boat at the dockside in Portmeirion.

Whilst I was busy with meetings and lectures, Barbara had more time to explore Beijing with Judith Burgen. One activity on which they spent a good deal of time was hunting in museums for Chinese embroideries. Barbara's quest had its origin in some presents which her uncle had given to her mother. As a fluent Chinese speaker he was able to shop around successfully, and on one occasion returned home with beautiful sashes of the type favoured by mandarins. He also brought her a dress of the kind worn by a lady of high birth: plain amber-coloured silk with rectangular panels of embroidery framed by embroidered edges. Slowly the dress itself deteriorated, and Barbara's mother arranged for the embroidered parts to be mounted for preservation and display, as she had already done with the mandarins' sashes. It was Barbara's hope to find similar embroideries, or at least someone who knew something about such things. To this end she and Judith visited the Forbidden City and the National Museum, but unfortunately there was nothing from the nineteenth century, the age to which Barbara suspected her uncle's embroideries belonged; everything had disappeared as a result of the activities of the Red Guards during the Cultural Revolution. Eventually Barbara fell back on the Victoria and Albert Museum in London, where she did find some interesting examples but not the answers to many of her questions.

Our last social occasion in Beijing was a reception and dinner given by the Royal Society party at International House on the evening before we departed for Xi'an. We entertained our guests in a huge, gaunt dining room where European and Chinese dinner menus were offered at different tables, an arrangement which augmented the tendency of those speaking only one language to segregate. However, I was lucky in that two of our guests made a bee-line for me. The first was George Wu, whom I had met when he came to England on business for the International Commission on Radiological Protection (ICRP). I told him that my laboratory visits had made me concerned about the apparent disregard of radiological protection in China (in contrast to Hong Kong), and that when I had mentioned this to colleagues at the Chinese Academy of Sciences they had simply avoided the question. George confirmed that there was no real determination in China to implement ICRP recommendations, and that the Academy people must have known this: he suggested that their reluctance to discuss the question with me was almost certainly due to their sense of shame. He also admitted freely the lack of insistence by employers that their employees should wear personal dosimeters, and their failure to record regularly the doses gained by those who did wear them. This was the first time I had occasion to reflect on the paradox that the governments which claim the highest proletarian credentials are in fact those least likely to be concerned about the health and safety at work of their proletariat.

The second person who came to sit with me at dinner was the chairman of the Chinese Academy of Medical Sciences, Huang Jiasi, because he knew that I was chairman of the Council of the Royal Postgraduate Medical School (of which he retained fond memories and a high regard). He told me about the exceptionally high incidence of oesophageal cancer in China, albeit with substantial disparities between regions: because of the marked dietary differences, these provide ideal opportunities for exploring whether there is any association between diet and susceptibility. Huang was still a practising surgeon, and since Barbara and Judith had just witnessed for the first time the use of acupuncture in a hospital they had visited, I asked Huang if he used this method for anaesthetic purposes. His answer was a firm negative, on the grounds that acupunctural anaesthesia is of uncertain duration and wears off quickly, and that its maintenance by the repeated vibration of inserted needles gets in the surgeons' way.

The Renmin (People's) Hotel in Xi'an, our next port of call, consisted of two enormous stuccoed blocks with a dome in the centre. Inside there were very high bare rooms, devoid of any decoration and with the most uncomfortable rectangular furniture. The corridors were long and ill-lit, and the whole reminded me of an old-fashioned British high school with dark brown paint everywhere.

Barbara had a temperature and was glad to go straight to bed. Since there was nothing I could do for her, I went out with the others and our interpreter Xiao Ma to see the Big Wild Goose Pagoda built in 652 AD, a seven-storey construction with twin 'double helix' staircases powerfully evocative of DNA. It houses the Buddhist sutras, translated and brought back from India by the celebrated monk Xuanzang – arguably the act which established Buddhism in China – and has plaques on the stair walls bearing the names of candidates successful in the Imperial Civil Service examinations. That these were still so carefully preserved by the Communist regime seemed rather surprising.

The pagoda is surrounded by pleasant gardens in which flowering trees were in bloom. One huge weeping lilac was so gloriously scented that I pressed my way through the outer canopy to find, sitting cross-legged, his back supported by the bole of the tree, a young man with an open book in front of him. Immediately I apologised in English for disturbing him. A broad smile appeared on his face and he replied in the same language. I had a curious sensation of being in a quite private conversation in a fragrant room occupied only by the two of us and unseen by anyone passing by. I asked what he was reading, to which came the reply 'economicals'; he then began a very interesting conversation about the differences between England and China, carried out in an open manner that strengthened the feeling of absolute privacy. I left him with reluctance to rejoin the others, with whom I wandered through streets teeming with pedestrians and cyclists, before returning to the hotel for dinner with Professor Hua Shenjun, Vice-President of the Xi'an branch of the Chinese Academy of Sciences (a physical chemist, strongly argumentative and with a marked political commitment). We had much to disagree about but he still remembered with pleasure Sir Cyril Hinshelwood's visit to China in the early 1960s, and this did something to bridge the gap between us.

Only one day remained in Xi'an, and although both of us now had bad colds I was determined to see how ordinary folk lived, and so went 'walkabout' among the lanes and hovels. It was an amazing experience. Clothes were being washed in the street, with cold water and tiny rubbing boards, and then hung over the pavement on bamboo poles or on lines joined to the nearest tree. Men were playing cards or Chinese chequers, sitting cross-legged on the pavement. Youths were batting shuttlecocks over any barrier they could find or invent. With such primitive accommodation and facilities, how the Chinese remained so clean and tidy seemed nothing short of a miracle; sometimes they even went to the lengths of wearing white gloves while cycling. The small children were always beautifully turned out, and appeared remarkably obedient.

The following morning we caught the plane to Shanghai, being struck during the flight by the greenness of the terrain beneath us – a marked contrast to the dry dusty brown of the Beijing district. As we walked down the gangway on arrival we saw waiting a smallish man in a Mao tunic, smiling broadly. He advanced, held out his hand and enquired, 'Remember me?' For a moment I could not place him, or recover his name: then the years dropped away, and in my mind's eye I saw again the Chinese undergraduate Tsao from Gonville and Caius College, Cambridge, to whom I had taught physical chemistry some thirty-six years earlier. It was an unforgettable, delightful moment in my life. By 1982 Tsao had become Deputy Director of the Shanghai Institute of Biochemistry in the Chinese Academy of Sciences, and was married to Xie Xide, a solid-state physicist at Fudan University: they had a son carrying out postgraduate work in Chicago. We had many enlightening conversations about the Cultural Revolution, starting as we waited for our luggage and concluding when he came to dinner during a later visit to Oxford.

On the way to the city every inch of land between the hamlets seemed to be cultivated and sprouting fresh green shoots, but as we approached the centre of this great seaport the traffic density came to resemble that of Beijing. In other respects there were marked differences between the two cities. In central Shanghai the streets were more winding and a great deal narrower, and for those reasons the cycle traffic seemed correspondingly heavier and slower. Most striking of all was that the proportion of Mao-suit wearers seemed far lower than in Beijing, and there were more blouses and skirts among the girls. My greatest surprise was to see many 'Stockbroker's Tudor' half-timbered villas with surrounding gardens enclosed by walls. I wondered who lived in them, since the foreign population of Shanghai was said to be much less than in the earlier parts of the twentieth century, when I guessed many of these houses must have been built.

Once settled into the Jing-an Guest House, I indulged my usual wish to see more of my immediate environment. My first visit was to the Friendship Store to buy a few gifts, including a Mao cap with red star for myself, and then I took a long walk down the Bund which stretches along the west bank of the Huangpu River. It was an eerie experience, because apart from the pedestrians it seemed like a cross between the Embankment in London and the Liverpool waterfront as it was before the war. Later on I asked to be taken to the fire station in Bubbling Wells Road which my brother Bill had designed, but the driver did not recognise the address and I was told afterwards that many of the streets had been renamed. Nor could he find his way to the house where the Chinese Communist Party was founded in 1921, so I asked to see some shops instead. I was reminded at once of the small independent traders I knew in earlier times in the lanes of Sheffield and the arcades of Leeds, except that here there seemed to be a lot of talk before a purchase was made (which my interpreter said was 'bargaining'). By this time I was exhausted and, feeling the effects of a rising temperature, returned to the sanctuary of the Guest House. I did not leave it in the next two days; an attempt to divert myself with statistical thermodynamics proved mildly comforting, but I was sorry not to see Tsao's laboratories, which Arnold Burgen considered to be of high quality.

On our penultimate day in Shanghai I was fit enough to enjoy a visit to two large, well-run institutes, namely Organic Chemistry with 1,300 staff and Cellular Biology with 350 staff, in both of which the discussions were illuminating and informative. By the evening I was ready to enjoy a splendid meal talking to Tsao on my left side and, on my right, an organic chemist who had taken his doctorate with Robert Robinson at Oxford. The next day was to be a holiday in Suzhou, which I looked forward to seeing because I had heard it described as 'the Venice of China'. We were up at daybreak in order to catch the 6.50 train, and on arrival we rushed off to Tiger Hill and the seven-storey brick pagoda of the same name. Thereafter my memory is of endless gardens and craft centres, with almost nowhere to sit and an increasing awareness that I had not conquered my cold after all. By the end of the day I felt I could not subscribe to the romantic description of Suzhou. I do remember filthy, polluted canals flanked by factories or hovels from which various effluents were being discharged, ensuring a pervasive malodorousness. Even the gardens created by scholars – paradoxically described as 'humble administrators' – had lost any sense of serenity which they might originally have possessed, destroyed by the milling thousands of citizens visiting them and endlessly photographing one another. I prefer to think of that trip as just 'a day out' and leave it at that, an experience to have had but not necessarily enjoyed.

The following day I felt much better again, and we were on our way to Shanghai airport by 10.30am, accompanied by the devoted Tsao and the Director of the Foreign Affairs Bureau of the Shanghai branch of the Chinese Academy of Sciences. On arrival back at Beijing we were taken to Qinghua University, widely regarded as the MIT of China – an inspired decision on the part of those who had planned our visit, because it meant that we left this vast country on a high note. The name itself signifies 'beautiful landscape', and the university is pleasantly situated in ample grounds. Based on a high school founded in 1900, Qinghua became a university on this new site in 1925: when in 1952 all Chinese universities were reorganised, it lost its arts departments to Peking University in exchange for the latter's engineering faculty. At the time of our visit Qinghua was re-establishing itself after the disruption of the Cultural Revolution, and we were given a two-hour account of what it had tried to achieve in the previous six years. By a happy chance, when we visited the library the Vice-President was able to lay his hand on four bound volumes of Shakespeare's works, which he told us had been presented by the University of Oxford over fifty years ago.

The long journey into Russia on Train 19, the Beijing to Moscow express, allowed plenty of time for reflection on our experiences in China and Hong Kong. The visit had not been given over entirely to conversations with scientists in laboratories, nor yet to sightseeing and the enjoyment of warm hospitality. In China we had had serious policy discussions with the President and other members and officials of the Chinese Academy of Sciences, with the Vice-President of the State Commission on Science and Technology, and with various senior members of the Chinese Association for Science and Technology. The State Commission was *de facto* a powerful ministry of science which not only made long-term policy in many areas (other than defence), but also coordinated research carried out by other ministries: in other words, it was more powerful than any British ministry of science has ever been. There were also several academies for specific sciences – for example, agriculture, forestry and medicine – financed by the relevant departments of government. Each academy in turn funded and controlled several institutes, whilst universities were overseen by the Ministry of Education. It was noticeable that when, in my seminar on science policy, I stressed the value and importance to British eyes of the Dual Support System for the universities, there was a favourable reaction among those present. Several people in the audience told me that for many years universities in China had been regarded primarily as teaching institutions and had neither the apparatus nor the staff for research at the highest level, but that this appeared to be changing; for example, half of Qinghua University's research funds were by then drawn from industrial enterprises, one-third from the State Commission and only one-sixth from its own budget. Such views were echoed in our discussions with the Chinese Academy of Sciences; indeed, major structural changes in government were agreed at the Twelfth Party Conference a few months after we had left the country.

The Chinese Association for Science and Technology (CAST) was a rather different body from the others, because although it received state funds its role was to be an advocate for science, in the sense of increasing its popularity and acting as a conduit to convey the opinions of scientists to government departments and the Party. Its nearest analogue in the UK is the British Association for the Advancement of Science, and a few years later, when I chaired the working party which established the International Federation of Associations for the Advancement of Science, I took particular pains to ensure that CAST became a member.

In some ways our most interesting meeting at government level was an hour which we all spent in the Great Hall of the People on the west side of Tiananmen Square, when we were received by Wan Li, the Vice-Premier and Minister of Agriculture and a prominent figure in the Chinese Communist Party. I sensed that he was pragmatic and cosmopolitan (he had been a student in France before the Second World War) rather than an ideologist, and therefore that he would be a natural supporter of Deng. Certainly the fortunes of the two men rose or fell together. Thus in 1966, at the beginning of the Cultural Revolution, Deng was disgraced and Wan Li was publicly branded as a 'bourgeois reactionary'– which endeared him to me, because only a couple of years afterwards I had been labelled a 'bourgeois obscurantist' in the Nottingham students' revolutionary newspaper *Red Blob*. By 1976–77 their star was in the ascendant when Deng was recalled and Wan Li re-emerged after the purge of the Gang of Four. Looking ahead, by 1990 Wan Li had become chairman of the influential Standing Committee of the National People's Congress and an ardent supporter of Deng's economic liberalism. Though he could not use the word capitalism, the slogan he urged for action by the people was 'rich peasants are a model for poor peasants', which speaks volumes for his views. Our talks in 1982 covered many of the issues raised in earlier meetings, on the substance of which he had doubtless been briefed by some of the officials who had been in attendance. He seemed keen to increase the exchange of scholars and scientists between our two countries, and we emphasised that we in the UK derived as much benefit from such exchanges as the Chinese.

It is always difficult to assess what has been achieved by visits such as ours, but I am confident that mutual goodwill and respect, so necessary as a basis for further collaborative relationships, were enhanced. I am also sure that both sides gained a much clearer understanding of the structures for 'managing' science and technology in the other's country, and the reasons for the selection of policy objectives. At the personal level, both Barbara and I found our trip a fascinating learning experience, which we would hate to have missed. Moreover, we came to like personally many of the Chinese we met, and especially their ready sense of humour, though at the same time we were left with a paradox: they seemed to be able to accommodate in their outlook what to me was a contradiction (or at least an ambivalence) between a fierce, almost puritanical, belief in socialism founded on the equality of human beings, and the tyranny over individuals which always accompanies such certainty, and which has been plainly evident in China's recent history. On the other hand there were obviously pragmatists such as Deng and Wan Li who professed the belief but acted according to the dictates of practicality, to achieve material gains for their country.

Our interpreters in China were all young, friendly and good at their jobs, and, as in Japan and Korea, their accent showed little American influence. In each case they asked at the outset if I knew a Miss Flower (I think that was the name) who from their remarks I judged to be the best known Briton in China – far more so than Mrs Thatcher, for she was a regular broadcaster teaching English as a foreign language. That I did not know her quite clearly lowered me greatly in their esteem. When the interpreters were not exercising their skills but were simply acting as our companions during sightseeing visits, their conversation could be quite revealing. It seemed to me that whilst they admired what Mao had done to liberate them from what they regarded as the oppressive and corrupt Kuomintang, they thought that he and his cronies were entirely wrong in the Cultural Revolution of the 1960s; and this had shaken their hitherto unquestioned respect for the opinion of their elders, so long an article of faith in China. With my English background I put to them Baron Acton's maxim, usually rendered as 'All power corrupts; absolute power corrupts absolutely', but they were not prepared to accept this proposition and countered, in what I thought was a rather feeble way, by saying 'Mao was not like that in the 1950s'. It was also clear that while they hoped to achieve the rising living standards which economic liberalism could bring about, they were far from wanting a slavish copy of western institutions.

I came away from China with a strong impression that the young people we met were intensely proud of their 'Chineseness', which distinguished them from all other nations, and were looking for better ways of realising the high potential which they profoundly believed their country had, almost regarding it as a destiny. To my mind they have a major task on their hands in trying to achieve this goal, and it would be to the rest of the world's advantage to assist in this process. Of course, I worry about what appears to be blatant aggression in Tibet, but then I remember the inaugural lecture of Owen Lattimore, the first professor of Chinese Studies in the University of Leeds, in which he maintained that China's aggressive forays beyond her borders are intended not to conquer and create Chinese hegemony but merely to test the security of those borders. I hope that his assessment was right, and since that security can now be verified by other means such as remote sensing, the proof of the pudding will be that there should be no more warlike excursions. At the very least, I believe that the foreign policies of Europe, North America and Japan should encourage and welcome the emergence of China, and help to give her a degree of self-confidence which will reduce her militant instincts and make her instead into a more beneficent power.

The USSR in 1982: Still Living Under Communism

On arrival at the immense and grandiose Beijing railway station there was a slight delay while our interpreter verified that our tickets were in order and that the compartments designated for our party were vacant and properly prepared.[3] It was a moment in which I could move quickly to the head of the train to see the power unit which would haul us north through China to enter the USSR. I am not a railway buff, but I could not conceal my delight at the sight of a splendid steam locomotive ready to go. That pleasure, and the prospect of joining the Trans-Siberian Railway for the latter part of our journey, were somewhat dimmed as we inspected the compartment which was to be our home for the next three nights and days. It seemed something of a period piece with good hardwood fittings, but we never succeeded in opening the window; it had lower and upper bunks, but with a broken ladder; and we were forbidden the use of the shower and lavatory shared with the adjacent compartment, because a water pipe was broken. The service ducts which ran over the

---

3. I was somewhat puzzled by the fact that while, as one might expect, Chinese and Russian were two of the languages in which essential information was given on the tickets, the third language was German. This was all the more surprising as, in the course of the journey, we met people of many nationalities, including American, Australian, British and one Italian-speaking Swiss, but no Germans.

corridor at the level of the upper bunk were not airtight, so that we also had the dubious benefits of the solid-fuel heating system's effluent vapours. My chemical knowledge told me that these would contain carbon monoxide, and therefore I felt it necessary to wrap round the faulty part of the ducting something which I hoped would exclude that lethal gas.

Despite these inefficiencies we enjoyed a good night's sleep and woke up ready for whatever delights the morning might produce. However, our first full day of railway travel turned out to be flat in every sense: from morning to night the bare landscape was relieved only by a few spindly trees. The land was sometimes tilled, sometimes provided poor grazing for sheep, and sometimes seemed like the salt pans of South Australia. Mile succeeded mile of dirty, brown, miserable wilderness, interspersed with some surprisingly large towns: the buildings rarely had any charm or grace, except occasionally for the railway station facades. There were no temples and no pagodas but plenty of chimneys, water towers and desolation. After dinner we went to bed early!

It was obviously colder when we woke, at 5.30am, and the ground was more hilly. Within the hour we pulled up at the Chinese border station just beyond Manzhouli, where our documents were checked. We alighted and changed some of our yuan to US dollars, while Barbara spent her small change on sweets and hand-kerchiefs. Back on the train and in motion again, we soon became conscious of barbed wire and armed soldiery in grey overcoats and hats, with uniformly Caucasian faces. When the train came to a halt again a guard was posted on the ground by each of the four exit doors, whereupon immigration officials entered for an examination of our bags which was as inefficient as it was officious. Every one of my hundred or so irreplaceable lecture slides was scrutinised, and a knitting pattern of Barbara's was taken away for half an hour, presumably so that it could be checked for possible codes. I fell back on ramming tobacco into my pipe to relieve my irritation, and achieved only a trifling revenge by insisting that our tormentors search a bag which I knew to contain only dirty washing. Though they spotted the stratagem, they could hardly refuse.

After the officials had at last completed their checks we were off again, going slowly through poor grazing country with few cattle and rather more soldiers and weaponry. In the townships through which we passed there were now more motor vehicles, more TV aerials, more blocks of standard Russian flats. After a while we encountered ice-covered pools, and later on snow. We had plenty of time to meditate on these changes, which seemed to us in every respect to be a case of 'from smiling Chinese spring to scowling Soviet snow'; by now we were on an electrified line, but the speed was a good deal less than under steam. Rolling country and trees, mainly birch and conifer, began to replace the barren environment to which we had become accustomed. Next day, on our left-hand side, the mountains with their snow canopies became more prominent; and finally on our right was Lake Baikal, ice-covered and stretching as far as the eye could see.

We arrived at Irkutsk several hours later than scheduled, but looking forward to meeting some scientists with common interests. Our first shock was that there was no one to meet us, probably because our hosts had not been told of the delayed train's arrival. We decided to wait on the station forecourt and were soon rescued by the voluble local interpreter, Tamara, a lively young lady anxious to display her colloquial English, which was full of action-packed phrases like 'let's go!', presumably acquired by watching too many Hollywood films. She was accompanied by a tall man who never spoke, and by another (very accomplished) interpreter called Nellie; the latter had been sent over specially from Novosibirsk, where she worked in the headquarters of the Siberian Branch of the Academy of Sciences in Akademgorodok, or 'Science City'.

My schoolboy knowledge of Lake Baikal was that it was about 400 miles long and very deep, contained one-fifth of the world's fresh water (even more water than the Baltic Sea), and that many of its aquatic organisms were not found anywhere else in the world. Of the city of Irkutsk I knew nothing. Our timetable allowed us only about 36 hours there, of which four had already gone, so as soon as we had deposited our bags in the Intourist Hotel – which, as we entered, seemed as silent as the grave – I wanted to be off exploring.

Irkutsk is about 40 miles west of the lake and straddles the outflow, which is known as the Angara River.[4] The city grew out of a settlement by Russian Cossacks, who built a fort there some 300 years ago, and its subsequent development owed much to its strategic position as a trading post on the route eastwards to Mongolia and China. We were driven to the central Kirov Square, where Nellie extolled the non-existent beauties of the regional government headquarters whilst dismissing as

---

4. 336 rivers and streams are said to flow into the lake, but it has only the one outlet.

'under the protection of the state' two rather handsome Orthodox churches, and as an 'organ hall' another church which we later found to have been built by Polish patriots exiled to Siberia at the end of the nineteenth century. After this we managed to slip from our guides' clutches for a short time to admire the layout of the square and its gardens, until we were called to order and taken by car along Lenin and Karl Marx Streets to a mineralogical museum where the display was certainly fabulous, showing beautiful specimens from all over eastern Siberia. The only noticeable gap was that there were no uranium minerals, although they are found in the area: this was not satisfactorily explained.

By this time Barbara and I had had enough and, desperately wanting a quiet walk, refused to be driven back to the hotel with the others, thereby creating some consternation. We walked over the bridge crossing the Angara River, ambled along the other side and returned by another bridge. The following day we again seized a chance to walk alone and saw the handsome opera house, a perfectly charming arts museum and the university library, known by everyone as the White House. We were not surprised to be told that it was late eighteenth century and built to the design of an Italian architect with a large practice in St Petersburg. We also enjoyed strolling past delightful wooden houses, all set in gardens behind timber fences and with shuttered casement windows. As a result of our meanderings we were a trifle late for dinner; however, our guides were not only mollified but also taken aback when I asked why the embankment on to which the hotel fronted bore the name Gagarin. When in the course of conversation I mentioned having had lunch with the world's first astronaut (only because at the time I was a member of the Council of the Royal Society) their attitude verged on the respectful.

Next morning we went to the imposing headquarters of the local Akademgorodok, which is responsible for nine major institutes employing a total of 1,200 scientists. We had wide-ranging conversations with Chairman Logachev and other senior staff: it was clear that much of their work quite naturally had a special relevance to eastern Siberia's resources and industries. About 11.30am we departed in cars for a delightful drive through the taiga, very reminiscent of the Canadian highway near Deep River. After an hour or so the forest gave way to fenced meadows, a few single-storey log cabins and a lemon-coloured church with a tower, on which was poised a slender spire, then finally some laboratory buildings looking out over a sea of ice. We had arrived at the Academy's Limnological

Institute, and were greeted by the large and enthusiastic Director. He was in all senses a stout defender of both the taiga and Lake Baikal against would-be encroachment and exploitation by industry, no less environmentally unfriendly here than in any capitalist country.[5] On our return to the hotel we had dinner in the same room as the large retirement party of a female post office worker: haunting songs were sung beautifully by some of the women present, and their sense of harmony and expressiveness created just the right atmosphere. Finally we departed for the airport soon after midnight, and in due course took off for Novosibirsk without the slightest word on safety measures.

I remember being told by Mr Campbell, my old geography master at the Central Secondary School in Sheffield, that Novosibirsk meant New Siberia and was the place where the Trans-Siberian Railway engineers successfully bridged the River Ob in 1897. I also knew it as part of the address of the Academy's Institute of Kinetics, the source of many papers in my field of chemistry, but I had no mental picture of the place. Nor had I realised that the railway and the bridge had led to an economic boom: Novosibirsk must have been one of the fastest growing cities in the world, and at the time we were there the population was approaching one and a half million. The Akademgorodok here is about 18 miles to the south; we had hoped we might see something of the city on our drive to 'the house of the scientists', but for some bizarre reason we found ourselves back on Beijing time, so that the journey was taken in the dark.

After breakfast the Secretary of the Siberian Branch of the Academy of Sciences, who doubled as a professor of econometrics at the Novosibirsk State University, explained its structure and its importance within the national organisation. In all the Branch consisted of some fifty research institutes, of which half were in Novosibirsk and half were distributed over places such as Irkutsk (as we knew), Yakutsk, Tomsk and Krasnoyarsk, with a total staff of 25,000. Roughly a quarter of them were professionals, and of these 100 were either full or corresponding

---

5. I wrote this just before I received a copy of the *Royal Society News* for July 1997 and read with great pleasure that the Royal Society had reached an agreement with the Russian Academy of Sciences enabling researchers to work at Lake Baikal, assisted financially by British Petroleum. The report further said that UK scientists in the last four years had raised over three quarters of a million pounds from various agencies and had carried out a large amount of research on the biodiversity of diatoms, mathematical modelling of lake mixing processes, remote sensing, and the origin of a virus which was killing the freshwater seals.

members of the Academy. I was struck by the close relationship between the Siberian Branch and the University, which facilitated collaboration and helped to raise the standard of teaching and research above the national average. This was the only occasion in either China or the USSR that we found any evidence of a strong commitment to this kind of university–government alliance.

I spent the whole of the rest of the day very happily in the Institute of Kinetics and the Institute of Catalysis. I was favourably impressed with the layout of the laboratories, the quality of the instrumentation, the arrangement of the workshops and the skills of the technicians in them. As always, the Russian scientists were well grounded in theory, and this had led them to predict that the combination of free radicals would be retarded by strong magnetic fields; now they were testing their hypothesis experimentally. This was long before the important role of free radicals in cellular processes had been accepted, a matter of central significance in the later study of any possible effects which the oscillating magnetic fields might induce in people living close to high tension power transmission lines.

The following day I took the long drive into Novosibirsk to see what was described as the 'State Public Scientific and Technical Library of the USSR Academy of Sciences, Siberian Branch'. The notion that there should be a state scientific library originally emerged at the end of the First World War and went through various transitions until 1958, when the library was made a part of the Siberian Branch specifically in order that research establishments, universities and industrial enterprises in Siberia and the Soviet Far East should have access to a powerful information base. In the next seven or eight years a new library was planned and built in Novosibirsk and the collections, the catalogue, and all the documentation were transferred to it. The library is specially designed to meet the severe climatic conditions of Siberia and, like the British Library, it has four underground storeys. I never understood why it was located such a long distance from the Akademgorodok, which clearly could make good use of the collections. As the Librarian took us around his reading rooms, rare book rooms and stacks – and especially when he explained the library's right to receive a copy of every book published in the USSR – I began to realise that it was not, as I had first thought, simply the analogue of the former UK National Reference Library of Science and Technology, but that the word 'science' was used there in the Baconian sense, to mean the whole of human knowledge.

Saturday was May Day and everyone seemed to have got up early and dressed in their best; there was a strong sense of excitement. At breakfast the restaurant was full. Families with brightly-clad young children tugging coloured balloons were moving around in the streets before nine o'clock. At 10.15, following a delay of fifteen minutes because the television cameras were not working, the parade started. It was headed by noisy go-carts bearing red flags, followed by marching groups with banners from the institutes, faculties of the university and so on. As each passed the podium its name was announced over the loudspeakers with a call for 'Hurrah!': the response, never strong, got more feeble with time. The whole thing reminded me of an old bank holiday Sunday school parade, a cross between a day out and an expression of local solidarity. As comradely foreign visitors (*sic*) we had been invited to join the local dignitaries on the platform, but were afraid that we would be manoeuvred into making speeches; we declined politely, on the respectable proletarian grounds that we wished to mingle with the workers and share their happiness. The army lorries which had distributed the balloons at the beginning of the day appeared again in due course with fizzy drinks for the children. We were then taken off to a nearby ski resort where we walked in the woods for a couple of hours and also drank rising birch sap, said to be very salubrious.

In one respect at least the Soviet Union puts Britain to shame. I know of no single city of reasonable size which does not have a good theatre and a fine opera house, and Novosibirsk was no exception. The theatre building dominates Lenin Square, and must be one of the largest in the Soviet Union. We were treated to a performance of the ballet *Gaiana* by Khachaturian. It was electrifying: we were in the front row and the music with its fire, drama and percussive effects was a magnificent accompaniment to extraordinarily athletic male dancing, with much use of impressive swords and sticks.

After breakfast on Sunday 2 May we set off for Moscow and our last night in the Soviet Union. It was a long flight, traversing some 46° of longitude, but because of the time zone change we arrived early enough to have lunch in the palatial dining room of the Sovietskaya Hotel. We had been allocated an apartment of four rooms, including a huge bathroom with its own ante-room, and the old hardwood furniture gave us great pleasure because of its good workmanship. With a TV set, two radios, room service and a few books we could happily have spent the whole day relaxing there but our interpreter, a fair-haired lady who stood out at the airport because of her colourful modern clothes, had other plans. She told us she had tickets for a performance at a newly-built circus, and I was able to persuade her to take us there by a route which passed some of the places I knew from my 1965 visit. The journey had few surprises and, as usual in Russia, the circus turned out to be not so much a performance by animals as by humans, partly on ice and also of course on the high trapeze. The lighting and the music were brilliantly synchronised with the movement of the acrobats and skaters. The evening was completed by a congenial reception at the British Minister's apartment.

The next day Arnold and I had talks at the Praesidium of the Academy of Sciences, while Judith and Barbara went off to explore the Kremlin. Our business did not take long, so I enquired after old friends and asked if it would be possible to see any of them in the period before lunch. My wish was granted, and I spent a happy 40 minutes walking and talking in the drizzle with my old friend Victor Talrose. Our conversation gave me much food for thought, and brought to a pleasant end a trip which had lasted four weeks in all and was one of the most educative we have ever made. Despite the cordiality of almost all our hosts, however, it was a relief to be back on a British Airways jet and to know that we could once more speak our minds freely. It cannot be denied that as a result of those four weeks the idea of a 'free society' acquired a much deeper significance than before, and an irresistible appeal for us both.

After our return, recurrent questions came to my mind concerning the attitudes of Chinese and Russians to one another, and to us. The Chinese in particular had been very friendly, and some of this was undoubtedly due to their high regard for UK universities. Many people in senior positions had had postgraduate experience in Britain: the lesson for the UK government is, I feel, 'do not underestimate the value to this country of overseas students, who often go on to hold influential positions in their own country, where they can exercise a benevolent attitude towards Britain'. On the other hand, it became clear to us that the Chinese had considerable reservations about the USSR; the Soviets who had come into China to help in modernisation programmes had not endeared themselves (as we knew they had not in Egypt either) or gained the respect of the Chinese, who saw in their activities and motives a latter-day colonial spirit. The Russians we talked to, in their turn, had a widespread interest in what China was like and what was really going on there. This was all the more striking because at no stage during our visit did they ask me about

Poland, Czechoslovakia or Hungary, even though many of them knew I still had contacts in those countries through scientific friends and former pupils.

Undoubtedly, our own reception in both countries was helped by the fact that Britain is no longer a significant colonial power, and has neither the will nor the resources to become one again. That does not mean, of course, that we cannot be influential. English is now the world's first language for traffic in knowledge and ideas, and the United Kingdom is still respected for some of its professed values, its reputation for fair dealing, probity, practicality in public administration, its free press and, finally and somewhat surprisingly, for the Commonwealth.

While we were in China we did not realise that the ferment of discussion and power struggle within the Party, so much hidden from the public, was as close to resolution as became apparent at the Twelfth Party Congress in September 1982. But even that is not the whole story, because seven years later the army put down the student demonstrations in Beijing, just when the Communist dictatorships in Europe were showing the cracks which presaged their own collapse.

Poland, 1983: Indomitable in Adversity

In April 1983 Barbara and I arrived in Warsaw, a mere four months after martial law had been withdrawn. Poland could not then have been described as a happy, democratic, economically successful country, and in theory we should not have relished going there. In fact the opposite was the case, because the many visits we had made since 1967 had each strengthened our admiration for the Poles' national spirit. All their setbacks seemed only to unite them more. They have a single language with no dialects peculiar to regions or to social class; and they cling to Roman Catholicism, I suspect in part as an affirmation that they are neither Russian Orthodox nor German Protestant by religion. Indeed, it seems that all attempts to bully the Poles have failed. Despite six centuries of foreign domination, they have remained great individualists with a strong sense of belonging to their homeland, always willing to unite against external threats. They are also enormously proud of their cultural heritage. All the citizens we met seemed to be well aware of famous figures such as Copernicus, Chopin, Paderewski, and especially Marie Sklodowska Curie, twice a Nobel Prize-winner (once in 1903 for physics, the prize shared with Henri Becquerel and her husband Pierre, and again in 1911 for chemistry, in recognition of her work on the isolation of radium from pitchblende). Her commemoration by the Polish Radiation Research Society was the immediate cause of my welcome invitation to visit the country again in 1983.

We were met at Warsaw airport on Easter Monday by Roman Broszkiewicz, who had worked with me in Leeds some years earlier. I subsequently learned that Roman, who had formerly been a scientist in the Institute for Radiation Research, had been elected by the Institute's Communist Party to be their Secretary. As such he had a permanent place at the discussions held by the president of the atomic energy authority, a very able man named Sowinski, where matters of policy were settled; Roman was also a member of the Central Committee of the Communist Party. Over the years I had had many talks with him and had come to the conclusion that, although he was a communist, he was cynical about politics and was primarily just a Pole, markedly anti-Russian and pro-British, with a striking capacity for personal and institutional survival. He was clearly affluent, and when Barbara asked him about the future of Poland he said emphatically, 'I have no wish to be liberated again. I have already been liberated twice in my lifetime'. In the end perhaps it could be said of him that, politically, he simply backed the wrong horse.

To the superficial observer all might have seemed quite normal in Poland. Buses, trams and cars were abundant on the streets; the people going to and from work, or strolling in the parks on Sunday, looked reasonably clothed; the coffee houses were full; there were not that many militia or soldiers in evidence; and prices seemed low compared with those in the United Kingdom. However, looking a little deeper one saw ample evidence of meat rationing, with butchers' shops closed; much external woodwork was unpainted because paint was unobtainable; buildings in Warsaw lay unfinished and unoccupied; and many other projects had been discontinued. In laboratories and libraries there were shortages of equipment, periodicals and western books. Permission to travel abroad, even to Eastern bloc countries, was difficult to obtain. There was an extensive black market and, we were told, hard currency (often sent in by relatives overseas) could buy anything, including queue-jumping. This was evidently tolerated, because it appeared that no enquiry about the depositor's method of acquisition was made by the banks at which the hard currency was paid in.

The economy seemed curiously mixed. People told us there were plenty of private medical practices and that 50 per cent of the homes were owned through housing associations, or individual purchase; there was an immense amount of moonlighting, and it was quite clear that society was organised hierarchically. The part that was played by Communist Party membership in ascending this hierarchy was not easy to discover, but that it had a role I had little doubt.[6]

The morale of many of the scientists to whom I spoke was somewhat low, in considerable measure due to the defeat of the 'Solidarity' trade union to which many of them had given their support. They felt abandoned by the rest of Europe, and this had induced a mood of despair: nevertheless they remained firmly western-oriented and anti-Soviet. It was much the same story at the National Library, where I had a frank talk with two deputy directors who had spent three months at the British Library in 1979, and therefore were anxious to see me. There seemed to be little provision for bibliographic services, which are essential for the proper and full use of a library; there was little automation; and the library's grant had been cut so badly that it was virtually impossible to obtain foreign material except by exchange. Although the library had BLAISE (British Library Automated Information Service) terminals, they were quite useless to them while direct telephone dialling between Warsaw and the western world was suspended.

During the scientific meetings there was plenty of opportunity to talk with academics, who told me of the government's vindictive stance after the 'Solidarity' episode. Not only were university resources cut beyond what might reasonably be attributed to the economic crisis, but in addition all bar five of the polytechnic university rectors, and all except two of the other university rectors, had been dismissed. Jerzy Kroh, himself Rector of Lódz Polytechnic University (who had worked with me in the late 1950s as one of the first government-sponsored post-doctoral fellows), gave me a vivid account of the meetings of the Conference of University Rectors and their attempts to explain the needs of higher education to General Jaruzelski's new administration. He had been one of the delegates who visited the general and his aides for a discussion which began at midnight and lasted for more than two hours, at the end of which Jaruzelski – who had not taken any part at all – simply announced that the Conference was to be dissolved.

---

6. We were invited to a dinner party by one particularly ruthless *apparatchik*: the menu, and the maid service, were opulent beyond all reason. Even the exorbitantly expensive caviar was replaced instantly and lavishly after a skilful raid by the dog.

While I was saddened by much of what I heard and saw on this visit, I also felt that our friends were trying to tell us something of fundamental importance. The programme seemed to be arranged so that we met Poles who shared those values without which no human society can be civilised and harmonious, and so that we could see something of the nation's heritage. Perhaps the organisers were taking all possible opportunities to ensure that the Polish situation was known and appreciated beyond their own frontiers. Thus, while in Wroclaw, we were given a special tour of the Ossilineum. This is essentially the library of the bibliophile Ossilinski, a privy councillor and librarian to the Austro-Hungarian Emperor in Vienna, who built up a special Polish collection and persuaded the imperial authorities that it should be located in Lower Silesia. Wroclaw was agreed as the site, and we were shown some of its treasures by staff who did not conceal their pride in the library or their faith in its future, however bad the 1980s might be. My feeling was that they wished to affirm their claim to be part of the western tradition of civilisation, and their pleasure in the role their countrymen had played in defending it.

It was just the same in Lódz when Jerzy Kroh and his wife Barbara showed us the Institute of Radiation Chemistry, and its new accelerator. They also made sure that we visited the lovely seventeenth-century Vilanôw Palace and gardens, home of the national hero Jan Sobieski, who is credited with saving Europe from the Turks (and, moreover, was descended from another great Polish warrior who once brought the Tsar of Russia captive to Warsaw). What place could have been more symbolic of Polish patriotism?

On our last day in Warsaw we spent the early part of the morning at the Academy of Sciences, which is housed in the modern Palace of Culture and Science. The workmanship and maintenance were deplorable. One lift refused to work, a door-handle came away in my hand, and I nearly tripped on a threadbare carpet; but Scientific Secretary Katzmarak was a good scientist (a hydrologist), and had an excellent command of English which he used with charm, intelligence and humour. He seemed to have all the qualities necessary in his difficult post as chief executive officer for 70 institutes with 11,000 staff. He was also responsible for the allocation of one-quarter of his resources to universities for research, and finally, of course, he had to negotiate with the government for the necessary funds. Fortunately he also sat in as an observer at the meetings of the Council of Ministers, so he was particularly well informed.

Roman Broszkiewicz and his wife Krystina came to the airport to see us off. For her it was obviously an emotional moment but he, as always, kept me guessing. On the flight, recalling the events of our week in Poland, I felt we must try our hardest to give all possible practical help to its scientists by facilitating their travel, getting them better access to the literature, and simply keeping in touch as friends. I was quite clear in my own mind that the lack of open unrest betokened a merely superficial stability, and that one day the hitherto firmly suppressed instincts and longings of Poland's citizens would be given expression.

China had already espoused economic liberalisation and had also excluded much Russian influence; but Poland had only one-thirtieth of the population of China, could be much more easily controlled by force, and was vital to Russian defence as a member of the Warsaw Pact. Similar arguments would also apply to Czechoslovakia, Hungary, the Baltic states and Germany, and therefore it seemed to me that little if any change would come without some significant political developments in the USSR. I could not then see how these might happen, but my first inkling was to come sooner than I thought, in December 1984, when I met Mikhail Gorbachev – even then a Soviet politician with a difference. What took place five years later is, as they say, history.

A Few Final Thoughts

The journeys described in this chapter enabled us to see, at closer quarters than the casual or holiday visitor, several countries whose political systems were either copied from western capitalist economies (notably Japan) or, like Russia, were *de facto* dictatorships but were beginning to show cracks. Our visits to China, the USSR and Poland were compressed into twelve months and convinced me that all their political systems were inherently unstable.

If despotism has no long-term stable future, what are the alternatives? Unless succeeded by despotism of another hue, the immediate effect is likely to be anarchy. Shelley regarded anarchy and despotism as equal dangers to the state and likened them to Scylla and Charybdis, monsters between which a nation must steer a careful political course. In Far Eastern countries there is a further consideration, which was put into my mind by Barbara. She saw more hope because of their distinct and enduring cultural backgrounds, and she suggested an alternative quotation from Oliver Goldsmith's *The Traveller*: 'There may be equal happiness in states which are differently governed from our own'. On that philosophy I would see Japan and South Korea as embracing and sometimes surpassing western technology, whilst also trying to adapt western ideas of parliamentary democracy in a way which takes proper account of their own histories and traditions. Hong Kong had technology brought to it by its colonial exploiters and used it to its own advantage, thereby becoming indispensable to China. The latter has been different in its recent development in that its political ideas have come from Marx. However, traditional Chinese culture is 'very persistent' and, despite the excesses of the Cultural Revolution, China has been able to pull back and develop some economic freedom, and a greater openness to the west. It is also strong enough to resist any possibility of a Soviet take-over. Russia, on the other hand, was a real communist dictatorship when we were there, and never became in any sense democratic until the upheavals of the late 1980s and early 1990s. Our travels in that country showed how far from a free society it was: its economy was in relative decline and its satellite states, as exemplified by Poland, could not be fully controlled.

CHAPTER 11

LIFE AS A CASUAL WORKER

It is impossible to enjoy idling thoroughly
unless one has plenty of work to do.

Jerome K. Jerome (1859-1927)

Hopes of a Little More 'Space': The Great Illusion

No one could have been more imbued by parents, chapel and school with the 'Protestant work ethic' than myself. This is not to say that there was any lack of fun or conviviality in my life; but leisure, apart from holidays, was something in which one did not idle, and if one were not enjoying outdoor experiences, leisure was a time for reading, playing chess, cards or family games. As a child I read a great deal, often by candlelight in bed in the attic, a habit which attracted many a reprimand from my parents because of the risk of fire. Despite such disapproval, the presents I received from my elder siblings, especially Ernie, were often books. One which he gave me and which I greatly enjoyed was Jerome K. Jerome's *Three Men in a Boat,* the tale of three men and their dog on a rowing holiday on the River Thames. At the public lending library I sought out other books by the same author, from one of which I took the quotation at the head of this chapter. I have chosen it because it expresses exactly my own feeling that work and leisure provide necessary contrapuntal rhythms in life, like yin and yang, and good and evil; neither has meaning if experienced without the other.

During a busy life I had little time to ponder retirement, least of all during my period at the University Grants Committee. My preoccupation with what is often now termed 'crisis management' not only drove out all thoughts about what I should do after 1978, but even obscured some of the underlying causes of the crises. For planning one's retirement, no less than for the judicious assessment of contemporary issues, a longer perspective is necessary, and this demands a change of pace or a shock to induce the right frame of mind. While I was at the University Grants Committee the change of pace was provided by our visits to Aspen; the shocks that catalysed my thought processes were predominantly those engendered by the deaths of people who had featured much in my life, particularly when I was asked to review their achievements for memorial addresses or obituaries. In doing such a thing the writer cannot avoid catching glimpses of his own life seen, as it were, momentarily in a mirror which is someone else's story. I recall two losses which had a specially great effect on me.

The first was the sudden death in 1975 of Jack Linnett. I first met Jack in 1933 at St John's College, Oxford, where he was also reading chemistry but two years ahead of me, and he and I shared lodgings with Henry Fowler in 1936-37. We kept in close contact as Jack's career path led to him becoming Professor of Physical Chemistry at Cambridge and then Master of Sidney Sussex College. In 1973, the same year that I was appointed Chairman of the University Grants Committee, he became Vice-Chancellor (in Cambridge, this is an elected, fixed-term post). I felt I knew Jack well, and I always regarded him as orthodox and conservative in outlook. However, during his first few months in office he surprised me by asking if I would spend a weekend with him at the Master's Lodge, and on the Sunday conduct a seminar for senior Cambridge academics. The subject of this was to be the university–government interface, of which he felt they had little knowledge. In that one act, and in the ensuing discussion, he showed himself much more perceptive of the need for change than I had expected, and much more willing to try to adapt Cambridge to the challenge of an evolving world than most of the colleagues who attended. Afterwards we agreed on a view of both the direction and the means of adjustment, which for Cambridge meant (among other things) giving its Vice-Chancellor longer tenure and greater executive power, while still preserving the University's essential democratic mechanisms to ensure the maintenance of academic freedom – an opinion which I put to him in writing some time later. Many years were to elapse, accompanied by long deliberations in a committee chaired by Sir Douglas Wass, formerly Permanent Secretary of the Treasury, before significant alterations to the Cambridge University governance and administration were to become a reality. It was barely two years later, on 29 November 1975, that I found myself ascending the steps to the pulpit of Great St Mary's Church in Cambridge to deliver the address at Jack's memorial service.

The second sad occasion was of a quite different nature and occurred some two and a half years after Jack's death, when I received an imperious telephone call from the manager of a bank in Cambridge. He did not ask but instructed me to come to see him at once. When I inquired why he had made this demand on my time, he answered that the bank was the executor of the will of Jack Linnett's professorial predecessor and my own former colleague and supervisor, Professor R.G.W. Norrish, who had died a few days previously. His will instructed the manager to hand to me (and only to me) a locked tin document box and its key, and required me to open it in his presence. After some argument, however, it was conceded that one of Norrish's twin daughters might bring the box to our home in Oxford for the ceremonial opening.

Reflecting on this arrangement before she arrived, I became more and more perplexed because, during the years between 1937 and 1950, when I was in his department, there had been many a tense moment in which I had to disagree with her father. He was a colourful character, often acting intuitively and impulsively in his science and in his daily life, and this sometimes led to crises in the Physical Chemistry Laboratory. On those occasions it had frequently fallen on my shoulders to act as both conciliator and interpreter.

Opening the box was actually something of an anticlimax. The contents were a curious mixture of the predictable – such as his Nobel Prize details – and some personal bric-a-brac, which included a couple of postcards sent to his mother in Cambridge when Norrish was a prisoner in the First World War; some strange writings of a religio-philosophical kind; and a note which surprised me by its cordiality, asking me to write his Biographical Memoir for the Royal Society – a duty already assigned by that body to Brian Thrush, so we did it together. I was puzzled that he should ask me, until I remembered that two years after he shared with George Porter half the Nobel Prize for Chemistry (the other half going to Manfred Eigen), Norrish had written me a letter and enclosed a copy of *Les Prix Nobel*, which contained the following inscription: 'With gratitude to my friend Dr Frederick S. Dainton, FRS for his splendid collaboration in research, and for his many personal kindnesses which I shall always remember but cannot adequately repay. From Ronald G.W. Norrish, 22.5.1969.' It had seemed to me then that, considering the arguments and tensions between us, to express such feelings was hardly credible. That the note in the tin box was so similar to the earlier message served to convince me that in both cases the sentiments were not a mere flash in the pan, but that they had been held by him for many years. I felt ashamed that I had earlier shown such little generosity of mind, and had therefore misjudged him.

As I grew older I realised that there were more such reconnections to be made with people and events of the past. This caused me to look forward to retirement from the University Grants Committee and to finding space in that retirement to look at correspondence and photographs, to recall the faces, shared experiences, words exchanged and emerging hopes, ideas, pleasures and disappointments of former days, all matters which are the stuff of life; and also to reflect on the times in which we had lived, how they had affected us and what we then thought. 'When retirement comes I will work no more than a couple of days a week, shared between the National Radiological Protection Board and the British Library Board', I thought to myself, 'and spend much more time at home, get my papers in order and, vision permitting, continue my re-education by doing a lot of reading'. I have failed conspicuously to realise these intentions but, to my surprise, as I write these words nearly two decades later I have no regrets, for those years have been wonderfully enjoyable, educative and rewarding.

With hindsight, I can see that my inability to prevent my free time from being eroded was due first to the fact that I had no definite plans for its use, merely vague aspirations which were essentially backward looking. I had evidently forgotten the Latin maxim given in the preface to this book: 'Life is given to be used'. A second cause lay, I think, in two flaws in my personality. One was a fear that I might in fact never be asked to engage in any new and interesting tasks, and so might merely slip into a limbo populated by memories (and a concern that if I were approached to take things on but refused, then I would be less likely to be considered on future occasions). This testified to a lack of self-confidence on my part. To be invited to undertake any fresh duty was therefore reassuring; but when asked I was all too easily persuaded by honeyed words of blandishment, which suggests a second, unworthy characteristic, namely vanity. Whether I have more or less of this quality than the next person is not for me to judge, but that I benefited from the acceptance of almost every task is beyond doubt.

I must now describe the two 'real jobs' – the chairmanships of the National Radiological Protection Board and the British Library Board – which I knew I was going to take up before leaving the University Grants Committee and which, because they had fixed terms, I would describe in today's jargon as 'contract labour'. I always regarded these appointments as full-time commitments, in the sense that in each case I carried the responsibility for the performance of the permanent body. That is what distinguishes them from the variety of other roles I undertook in 'retirement', described later on in this chapter, where I felt that my personal contribution was much less crucial.

Protection Against the Invisible, Inaudible and Intangible

Despite the horror of the newspaper photographs taken in Hiroshima and Nagasaki in the days immediately following the dropping of the uranium and plutonium bombs in August 1945, and the equally moving newspaper correspondents' accounts of the damage to buildings and the human carnage, most people in Britain welcomed the use of these weapons. Apart from the coal-mining community, Britons were equally enthusiastic about the prospect of unlimited nuclear power for the generation of electricity, ship propulsion and isotope production for radio-therapy, medical and industrial radiography, and 'labelling' in research. The nation rejoiced when the first British reactor went critical at Calder Hall. At the same time, however, there was a vague public perception that the concomitant invisible radiation was dangerous, and therefore that steps should be taken to protect people from exposure by building large radiation shields around the reactors and ensuring there were no leakages of radioactive materials from the plants. By the same token, it was accepted that nuclear industry workers should themselves be protected by the best known scientific means, which in turn implied accurately measuring received doses of different kinds of radiation, and having clear information about the relationship (if any) between exposure and the onset, nature and magnitude of later illness. There were exceptions to the general attitude – for example, in the Campaign for Nuclear Disarmament (CND), in which Bertrand Russell was a pivotal figure – but many people, myself among them, felt they could endorse the use of reactors for power generation while at the same time being opposed to Britain's possession of nuclear weapons. Solly Zuckerman was one of the distinguished advocates of this standpoint within government. It also seemed to me there was a tenable argument, if perhaps a paradoxical one, that an atomic armoury would ensure that neither fission nor fusion bombs would ever again be dropped; in other words, that such weapons were truly the ultimate deterrent.

The 'Windscale incident' in 1957, and the enquiry that followed, were turning points in public perception. Though entirely minor compared with later malfunctions, notably that at Chernobyl, Windscale did exemplify the possibility of the escape of radioactive substances to rivers, the sea and the atmosphere, and thence into the human food chain.[1] In order to assess how much radioisotope dispersal had taken place as a result of the reactor failure, an emergency committee and task force were set up and the Medical Research Council (MRC) was drawn in to advise on the effects on people. The Windscale incident – along with the increasing numbers of nuclear weapons, stockpiles, power generation plants, bomb-testing programmes and consequent airborne radioactivity – all demonstrated the need for some statutory body to be established as the national point of authoritative reference for radiological protection. The body set up was the National Radiological Protection Board (NRPB), which under the 1970 Act was also charged to acquire knowledge about the protection of human beings, and to provide information and advice. NRPB has always played a leading role in setting exposure limits as recommended by international bodies, to whose deliberations it makes a major contribution. However, it does not conduct research in radiobiology, which remains the preserve of the relevant MRC unit. Fortunately, in recognition of the fundamental link between protection and radiobiology, NRPB and the MRC unit are on adjacent sites outside the perimeter fence of the old Atomic Energy Research Establishment at Harwell, in company with other civil scientific research stations such as the Rutherford-Appleton Laboratory.

I joined the Board as a member in 1977 and succeeded the founding chairman, Sir Brian Windeyer, when he retired at the end of September 1978. He was a man I liked and admired and I felt comfortable when his mantle fell on my shoulders, partly because some of my own research interests had given me an understanding of the mechanism of deposition of energy in matter by incident radiation, whether

---

1. Windscale was the site of the Calder Hall reactor, and is now known as Sellafield.

or not this is ionizing; and I was also interested in the physical and chemical effects produced in matter and living tissue. Moreover, it seemed to me that the new buildings which NRPB occupied were well equipped and well suited to their purpose. Nevertheless I had much to learn, not least about cost-benefit analysis, which raises difficult questions such as the monetary value of a human life – particularly when the association between radiation received and apparent effect is either unknown or incompletely understood.

Interesting as such intellectual problems are, I was more concerned with the actual day-to-day issues facing the Board. The first of these was the looming cuts in income from NRPB's parent department (Health and Social Security), as it felt the restriction on public sector spending introduced by the new Conservative government. The second was the scrutiny of bodies such as NRPB – collectively known as quangos, meaning quasi-autonomous non-governmental organisations, now called NDOs (non-departmental organisations) – which was being carried out by Sir Leo Pliatzky, recently retired from the post of Permanent Secretary in the Department of Trade. I had few worries about the outcome of this review because I reckoned that, as a quintessential regulatory body, NRPB was necessary and therefore had nothing to fear – especially from Sir Leo, whom I had known when he was Second Permanent Secretary at the Treasury. This turned out to be the case, but the financial squeeze really began in 1980 and this meant that if the books were to be balanced some staff would have to leave, and that we would also need to seek more external contract income.

This situation could have been coped with had we not already had staff problems at the highest level. Sadly, in March the founding Director, Dr Andrew McLean, was pronounced seriously ill and he died four and a half months later. It was left to the Board Secretary, Fred Morley, and myself to share the chief executive's duties for almost two years until we were able to persuade John Dunster, then a deputy to the Director General of the Health and Safety Executive, to join the Board as Director. This was a great relief to me, because my allotted one day a week had almost trebled. Moreover, John was experienced in atomic energy matters and had been Assistant Director of the Board from its inception up to 1977.

It was also at this time that public confidence in the nuclear industry began to decline. This was partly as a result of the activities of pressure groups such as Friends of the Earth and CND. Other contributory factors having an input were mounting anxieties concerning the supposed cluster of childhood leukaemias around Windscale; the allegedly plutonium-laden wind-blown sea spray in that area (which deeply worried the Secretary of State for Health and Social Security, Patrick Jenkin); radon in houses; and how radioactive waste should or could be stored safely until the activity had declined to an acceptable level. In addition, other matters outside the radioactive field fell within the Board's remit because of public concern. These included the supposed ill-effects of high tension electricity power-lines on those who lived near them; and the ultraviolet component of the sun's rays, which can cause skin cancer and was increasingly reaching the earth's surface as a result of upper atmosphere ozone depletion. In my view, the only workable strategy in such circumstances was to be frank with all enquirers, whoever they were; and to encourage politicians and other influential people, but also representatives of protest groups, to visit the Board and talk with the staff. So it was that our invited visitors included the elder statesmen Edward Heath and Roy Jenkins; the rising political star Norman Lamont; and journalists – among them, because of the increasing interest in radiation hazards among women, Anna Ford.

The bedrock on which good radiological protection policy rests consists of reliable data on the lifetime medical records of as many individuals as possible, whose radiation dosage and other health factors are known. Only then can trust-worthy dose-effect graphs be prepared and recommendations made to keep expo-sures as low as reasonably achievable, taking economic and social factors into account. Among the most valuable records were those held by the Ministry of Defence (MoD), because some of its personnel had been involved in nuclear weapons testing or had served in nuclear submarines. The Board was naturally anx-ious to get hold of this information; but even though the case for having it was clearly made to the Ministry, and the argument as to its value could not be refuted, that body refused to part with the data. (This absurd secrecy seems to have been a set policy for many years because, as recently as 1997, only in the face of incon-trovertible evidence did MoD admit to the exposure of servicemen to organophos-phates in the Gulf War.) Happily, the Ministry did ultimately hand over the relevant database to the Board, but only because the Australian Government was pursuing the matter through the courts on behalf of its own servicemen, who had also been involved in the bomb tests. MoD has since continued to demonstrate its narrow-mindedness by refusing to pay NRPB for keeping the database up to date.

Temple and Warehouse of Knowledge: A New Building
for the British Library

Earlier in this book I expressed my indebtedness to the Sheffield City Libraries, and the St John's College and Radcliffe Science Libraries in Oxford, for the key roles they played at various stages of my career. Not surprisingly, I took a rather keen interest in my duties as chairman of the Advisory Committee on Scientific and Technological Information and later the National Libraries Committee; and also, while at the University Grants Committee, I supported the Atkinson Committee's proposals on university library accommodation. I was therefore much more delighted than I may have shown when Shirley Williams asked me if I would be willing to succeed David Eccles as chairman of the British Library Board in 1978. This new statutory body had come into being as a direct consequence of the acceptance of most of the recommendations of the National Libraries Committee. My pleasure was enhanced by the fact that the Chief Executive of the British Library was Sir Harry Hookway, another chemist, with whom I had worked before. I also knew that the Labour Government had accepted in principle the idea of the Library vacating the British Museum site and bringing under one new roof the collections then scattered all over London; and that it had now bought for this purpose a disused nine-and-a-half-acre railway goods yard adjacent to St Pancras Station.[2]

With this knowledge, I entered the empty chairman's office in the first week of December 1978 in an optimistic mood. It was located on the first floor of a building in Store Street, Bloomsbury, adjacent to the Library Association premises. The building was relatively new, having been constructed just twelve years earlier, and its stacks groaned under the weight of the large collections of the Department of Oriental Manuscripts and Printed Books. My stay there was destined to be short: the professional staff were manifestly relieved to know that mere administrators

---

2. Over thirty years earlier, the Trustees of the British Museum were fully seized of the need for additional accommodation for the proper care and accessibility of their expanding library collections. They considered the matter to be so urgent that in 1944, when the outcome of the war was far from certain and the nation was impoverished by the hostilities, they proposed that additional accommodation should be built on the land south-east of Great Russell Street. By 1967 planning permission for a building designed by Sir Leslie Martin and Colin St John Wilson had been granted and half the site had been purchased for some £2m. The MP for Holborn and St Pancras South, Mrs Lena Jeger, in whose constituency this area was situated, then campaigned vigorously and successfully against the scheme, mainly on the grounds that its implementation

such as Harry and myself, and other headquarters people, were soon to be removed to Soho, where we would occupy Novello House, at the corner of Wardour Street and Sheraton Street. This latter building had been selected from a number of premises which the Property Services Agency (a division of the Department of the Environment) thought would meet the Board's specified accommodation requirements. It was intended that we should occupy part of the topmost floor, above an elaborate cornice, but with the workmen still busily erecting temporary partitions it was difficult to assess how practical my room would be. In the event, it proved to be a very serviceable office base in London for seven years, made all the more agreeable by pleasant and helpful colleagues.

As the nation's principal 'copyright library', the British Library receives by legal deposit a copy of every book published in the UK, and it is today immediately responsible for about 15 million books and periodicals, some 45 million patent specifications, 8 million stamps, 1.5 million music scores, over 50,000 newspaper titles, nearly 300,000 manuscripts and volumes of manuscripts, over 30,000 prints and drawings, and an extraordinarily rich collection relating to the Indian subcontinent (now known as the Oriental and India Office Collections). There are also over a million sound discs and 150,000 tapes, held at the National Sound Archive, and an unrivalled collection of more than 200,000 photographs. All have to be curated, catalogued, preserved, periodically refurbished and made available at short notice for readers. In any one year nearly 5.5 million items are consulted and another 4 million documents or copies of them are sent all over the world from

---

would lead to an unacceptable loss of residential accommodation. It must have been a bitter blow for the Trustees to receive a letter in late October 1967 terminating the designation of this site for use by the British Museum, and also announcing the Government's decision to 'set up a committee to study national library services'. This was the decision which led to Sir Herbert Andrew's Saturday night telephone call to me in Nottingham a few days later, and in due course to the firm recommendation of the National Libraries Committee that the various nationally supported libraries in London and at Boston Spa, including the British Museum Library, should be amalgamated to form a new national library with its own governing body and purpose-built accommodation in London. The report was accepted. The British Library came into being on 1 April 1973 and its Board, under the chairmanship of David (Viscount) Eccles, who had been chairman of the British Museum Trustees between 1967 and 1970, quickly appointed Colin St John (Sandy) Wilson as planning architect. Fortunately, British Rail had decided to close its St Pancras goods yard and the Government bought the site for £6m in 1976. A year later, Sandy Wilson presented a plan to the British Library Board for a new British Library to be constructed on this site in three phases. The Board endorsed this plan and in 1978 it was accepted in principle by the Government. Whether this decision was made before or after I saw the Secretary of State, Shirley Williams, I do not know.

Boston Spa. In addition, the British Library lays on major exhibitions and lectures, publishes extensively, and creates some 400,000 catalogue records annually.

Quite apart from the need to bring collections together in order to give a faster service to readers, the Board was faced with the fact that many irreplaceable items were physically disintegrating because they were not stored and used under conditions of constant temperature and relative humidity, and were being exposed to the atmospheric pollution prevalent in all large cities. Variations of temperature cause alternating expansion and contraction of paper fibres, while oscillations of humidity involve water uptake (which causes their swelling) and evaporation (which makes them shrink), all factors affecting both paper and binding. Oxides of nitrogen and sulphur from the pollution break the fibres by catalysing their hydrolysis and oxidative degradation. In addition, paper made from sulphite-treated pulp retains acidity and thereby signs its own early death warrant; and the vast bulk of the British Library's stock is printed on acid paper. (Many people will have noticed the consequences of fibre deterioration in the fragility, embrittlement and yellowing of pages, especially in old paperbacks.) The best way of minimising decay is to print books on acid-free paper and use them in clean, constant environments: reconditioning copies which have already deteriorated requires very expensive skilled work, and they can never be completely restored to their pristine condition. The case for the new building rested primarily on these two elements of improvement of service and conservation of the vast and valuable collections.

Shirley Williams accepted the Board's agreed development plan but trisected Phase 1 into parts A, B and C, and in March 1978 she authorised a start on the construction of Phase 1A in 1979. Unhappily, the end of 1978 and the beginning of 1979 were marked by much trade union unrest and evident fissiparous tendencies in the government, features which earned for that period the term 'winter of discontent'. To resolve matters a general election was fixed for early May 1979, which marked the beginning of the 'Thatcher years': and a few weeks later the new Minister for the Arts, Norman St John-Stevas, also Leader of the House of Commons and Chancellor of the Duchy of Lancaster, informed the British Library that the decision to start the new building would be reviewed. All bets were off.

Just before the dissolution of the Labour Government in 1979, Shirley Williams had received a letter from Professor Hugh Thomas, the chairman of the Centre for Policy Studies – the Conservative Party's version of a 'Think Tank' –

opposing the British Library's plans. When Norman St John-Stevas was given responsibility for the Arts, Professor Thomas sent him a copy of the same letter. It was largely his own work, aided by discussions with a few friends, and while Professor Thomas accepted in part the need for a 'repository for books', he argued strongly against vacating Panizzi's Great Round Reading Room at the British Museum. In mid-1979 he launched a campaign in the newspapers which showed that neither he nor his supporters understood the real problems to be solved, and either did not care about the Library's duty to preserve material for the scholars of the future or did not understand the nature of the physico-chemical deterioration processes. The chairman of the Trustees of the British Museum, Lord (Burke) Trend, former Cabinet Secretary, and I both felt these arguments must be refuted publicly, and therefore we wrote a letter of rebuttal to the *Daily Telegraph* on 27 July 1979. Our arguments evidently did not satisfy Professor Thomas because – with 32 other people, mainly writers – he produced a pamphlet in mid-December, a copy of which was sent to each British Museum Trustee and British Library Board member. It contained nothing new that I could see, but because it was receiving wide circulation it had to be evaluated by specialists. Their assessment reinforced my own views and also revealed the fact that, of the 33 stout defenders of the Round Reading Room, no less than 19 did not hold one of the reader's tickets required to gain access to that room. I drew my own conclusions.[3]

Despite these distractions, and the fact that the authority to proceed with building had been withdrawn pending the outcome of the new government's intention to review the case, there was every reason to continue the planning process: it was wholly unthinkable to me that the Library's extraordinarily diverse and disparate holdings should not be properly housed, and that the conspicuously successful lending division at Boston Spa, much of it still in wartime concrete and wooden huts, should not have appropriate accommodation. As I looked into the decision-making mechanism, however, I could not help but compare it unfavourably with that which obtained in the university sector. The UGC always took the view, derived from its founding Treasury Minute, that its job was to assess a university's need for a

---

3. Professor Thomas was nothing if not tenacious. At the beginning of September 1986, as Lord Thomas, he returned to the charge in a letter to *The Times,* and on 10 September that newspaper published a riposte from my successor as chairman of the British Library Board, Lord Quinton.

particular capital project and then, when it was satisfied that the need was justified in the context of the quinquennial or other relevant agreed plans, ensure that the designs were sound and economical. Only then would it agree to the bid. If a new building were approved, the UGC would be prepared to fund construction costs, professional fees and furnishings, allowing for what the institution itself was able to contribute – frequently little or nothing. From then on the university, as the future user and therefore ultimate customer, was in charge and policed the process through its own buildings officer. Any cost overruns would have to be met from its own resources, unless there were extreme mitigating circumstances. These conditions put universities on their mettle to get the best they could out of the available money, thereby creating a tautness of supervision of the building work.

The arrangements for the British Library were completely different and much less conducive to a good 'value for money' result; there were too many fingers in the pie and the influence of the ultimate customer, in this case the Library itself, was diluted to a damaging degree. This was because the building was seen by government as a grand national enterprise, which in the old days would have been the responsibility of the Ministry of Public Buildings and Works, whose designing hand can be discerned in many overseas British Embassies and High Commissions. By 1979 the Ministry's functions had passed over to the Property Services Agency. However, if there was any department of government with a real stake in the success or failure of the project it was surely that which dealt with arts and libraries, through whose vote the British Library's grant-in-aid was provided. As the capital cost of the new building constituted a large fraction of that department's total budget, the project inevitably attracted great Treasury interest. It was evident to me that this complex web of relationships was a recipe for delays in starting the project, if indeed nothing worse.

As the months slipped by in 1980, and there was still no Government decision, the Board members understandably became more and more anxious. There was one gleam of light, in that the Education, Science and Arts Committee of the House of Commons had chosen the British Library as one of its subjects of enquiry. We had a satisfactory meeting with its members at Novello House, and first Harry Hookway and then the Minister for the Arts and I appeared before them on a later occasion. Their unanimous conclusion, published in late May, was a resounding endorsement of the Board's plans and we awaited a Government response to the report with renewed optimism. When nothing had happened by July, the Board asked me if I would personally put the Library's case directly to the Prime Minister. This I did by letter, and Mrs Thatcher agreed to see me on 16 September at 3pm. My colleagues gave me plenty of good advice but none of them seemed keen to accompany me, and I decided that I was going to tell the Prime Minister the plain unvarnished facts as I knew them. I arrived well armed with my reasons why any other solution to the problem was impractical; and of course Mrs Thatcher, with her early scientific training, fully appreciated the inevitability of the decay of precious documents if nothing was done. Moreover, I had carefully worked out the cost in camera-man-hours if the much-vaunted option of miniaturisation was adopted, and she accepted this was not viable. I also carried with me specimens of damaged books and she reacted to these with apparent horror, particularly to a dilapidated specimen of a 'Penguin', which fortunately was by one of her favourite authors. She then immediately expressed her opinion that we must have the building. On my return I told my colleagues I was sure that the result would be positive, but that there would be a delay because Ministers would have to consider many other matters over the next six to eight weeks. I gained the clear impression that they deemed me to be over-optimistic, but in the light of our conversation I was confident the Prime Minister had understood the scientific and quantitative points much more clearly than any of our critics.

At the Board's October meeting I presented a verbal report of my visit to 10 Downing Street, and within a month the news came through of a favourable decision. It was arranged that the Prime Minister would come to Novello House on Friday 28 November, where we had invited her to unveil a bronze bust of my predecessor, David Eccles. In her remarks she made the announcement, to be repeated that afternoon in the House of Commons by Norman St John-Stevas, that the construction could go ahead but that, because of government restrictions on public spending, the amount of money available would be less than that which had been promised by the previous administration. I was delighted, the more so because I knew that once building work had begun it would be very difficult to stop, and that therefore this was a real turning point in the fortunes of the British Library.

There was an amusing by-play within the day's drama. We decided to admit the Prime Minister through the main door of Novello House on Wardour Street, because I felt that she should be given as near a royal welcome as we could muster.

As I escorted her to the top of the stairs into the vestibule, walking on a scrupulously clean red carpet, Mrs Thatcher said, 'This place is very grand for you. How did you come by it?' I explained quickly that we had acquired it by the normal means, in other words, through the Property Services Agency. The matter was then dropped as I introduced her to those waiting in the vestibule. That evening, however, Michael Heseltine came up to me at a function we were both attending and asked, 'What did you say to the Prime Minister this morning?' I did not know what he was referring to and said so, to which he replied that he had just received a minute from her seeking an explanation as to why such grand accommodation had been provided for us. I smiled inwardly at this additional evidence of her passion for verification and the economical use of taxpayers' money.

Much had to be done by way of further planning, site clearance and preparation before construction could actually begin, and the seal could then be set on the whole enterprise by the unveiling of the foundation stone by HRH the Prince of Wales. The ceremony could not be an actual laying of the stone, because for months all that the work consisted of was the excavation of a very big hole. The appointed day for the ceremony was 7 December 1982, and a large slab of polished red granite was brought to Novello House and mounted on a stand in the boardroom, from which it was later removed to the vestibule and stayed there for many years before being incorporated in the new building. The inscription had been finely carved in simple Roman lettering by the well-known Cambridge designer craftsman Will Carter. Whenever I passed it in my remaining time as chairman, I felt a quiet pleasure that my father would have approved both of the quality of Will's work and the temple for books which was to be its home.

Indeed it was a real craftsman's day, because I was able to present Prince Charles with two gifts, both splendid examples of human skill and artistry. The first was a book, *Man and his Symbols,* by Carl Jung, an author whose work he admired greatly: this had been specially bound for him by Library staff in russet morocco leather, in the style of the library of Henry, Prince of Wales, eldest son of James I, many of whose books came to the British Museum Library in 1757 with George II's gift to the nation of the Old Royal Library. The boards were emblazoned with the Prince of Wales' Feathers and Arms and the spine bore the interlocking Cs of Charles II's monogram. The second gift was an exquisite paperweight of silver and gold made by the master craftsman Kevin Coates, which brought into conjunction the concepts of the book and the Welsh dragon. It was commissioned by the Goldsmiths' Company, of which Prince Charles had become a Liveryman and I was Prime Warden at the time.

During his visit the Library's architect, Sandy Wilson, showed the Prince a series of poster-sized artist's impressions of how the building would look, inside and outside, when completed. We pointed out that the two major demands were first to minimize the deterioration of the stock (which required environmental control of the whole building, and the exclusion of pollutants and harmful ultra-violet light); and secondly, to satisfy the requirement of scientists and technologists for open access to the stacks, while at the same time meeting the needs of those interested in the arts and humanities by quickly providing requested items from stock held in compact, closed-access storage. There were many other desiderata: for example, that there should be space for exhibitions, seminars, conservation studios, biblio-graphic services and so on, and especially for rapid information outlets to meet enquiries in person or by letter, telephone or electronic media. All these considera-tions meant that the Library would be a heavily serviced structure.

The site also imposed its own constraints. Obviously, to accommodate nearly 200 miles of shelving and provide over 1,200 reader places the building would need to be very large, yet must not rise too high if the view of Sir George Gilbert Scott's masterpiece St Pancras station hotel was not to be lost, and a permanent morning shadow was not to be cast over the flats in Ossulston Street to the west of the site. Clearly there would have to be several floors below ground level, which in that part of London meant going below the water table – giving particular problems in terms of damp-proofing. No fewer than 500 piles had to be driven to support the heavy load-bearing floors, and there were additional difficulties caused by two under-ground railway lines crossing the site, with the associated potential for vibrational damage (and indeed damage to the tunnels as well, if they were to rise excessively when the mass of overlying soil was removed).

Finally, there was the aesthetic problem of how a highly functional and spacious building should be expressed architecturally, to convey to people that it was both a temple and a warehouse of knowledge, offering to all who would enter it an attractive invitation to learning. This argued for an agreeable piazza to welcome visitors in from the Euston Road, rather than a daunting cliff-face frontage. While the Prince asked a number of pertinent questions about the project, I could not divine his reactions, either to the posters on display or to my explanation of the underlying needs which had to be met.[4]

The unveiling was a memorable occasion which gave me an opportunity to thank a lot of people for their work on behalf of the Library, especially Mr Paul Channon, whom I had seen on a regular basis throughout his two years as Minister for Arts and Libraries. He had been a staunch supporter of the new building project. As the day closed I could not help thinking that it was fifteen years, almost to the day, since Sir Herbert Andrew's two telephone calls whch had ultimately led to my involvement in this major enterprise.

As I write, Phase 1 of the St Pancras building is virtually complete. It will, however, fall short of the original plan in having far fewer readers' seats and less shelving than was envisaged for the new Library as a whole. There is a body of opinion that regrets these shortfalls: the opposing view is that information technology has rendered printed matter obsolete and therefore also this additional library space, and that if the contents of old books and manuscripts are to be preserved then it should only be in microform, photographically or on tape or disc. Rational objections to both views can be produced. Before I append my own rebuttals I would just make an observation about the building itself. As a 'hard hat' visitor I made many inspections during construction, and have seen gross structural progress. As sections have been finished I have attended functions and lectures, and I am favourably impressed with the design and interrelationship of the working spaces, the quality of the finishes, the attention to detail in the design of the reader places, and the technology which those readers will command. I am convinced that the building will be a place in which researchers will be well served and find their tasks easy to accomplish, and that the same will be true for the Library's staff. The longevity of the holdings will be significantly increased by a permanent unpolluted environment, whether they are on shelves or on desks. Aesthetic reactions are a personal matter, but I have been delighted to see distinguished visitors – whose eyes are more educated, discerning and informed than mine – acknowledge that they too experience the elevation of mind and spirit which the building produces in me. I believe that

---

4. Some years after his visit, Prince Charles described the rising structure as seeming to be designed as 'an academy for secret police'. I am told, however, that when he first entered the completed building he admitted that he had changed his mind (BHD).

as more and more people use the Library the erstwhile critics will be silenced. A great deal of praise must go to Sandy Wilson, not only for the design of the building (which will speak for itself to its users) but for the steadfast and dignified way in which he has withstood the 'slings and arrows of outrageous fortune' in the shape of ill-informed and unjust criticism, and the stoicism and ingenuity with which he faced each setback and delay in funding.

But is the Library too big or too small? Here, as a scientist, I tread on solid ground. When I went to see the Prime Minister I began by saying that I was not an enthusiast for new buildings, and nothing would have given me more pleasure (though it would not have cheered the British Museum Trustees) than for the Library to remain in the handsome buildings in Great Russell Street. However, we had to face two pressing questions: could a large, diverse and growing stock be miniaturised, and if so what should be done with the original material?

Miniaturisation was easily dealt with. First, the commonest form of bibliographic miniaturisation available in the late 1970s was the microform. For this to be acceptable in quality and durability often involves disbinding, at an overall cost of around ten pence per page at 1980 prices. To miniaturise ten million volumes in this way, each containing (say) 400 pages, would cost more than the construction of a building to house the originals. A little further arithmetic using the figures for maximum output per camera day, with no hitches, shows that 100 cameras would have to work for more than a century to cope with the task. Moreover, the film images do not have an infinite life, and they too require periodic renewal. Undaunted, our enthusiastic proponent of technological solutions might reply to these arguments, as did John Vaizey in a letter to the Prime Minister, that photographic microforms are obsolete and that magnetic tape and disc are the answer. But tapes or discs require for their interrogation a machine available to each reader, and they can only display one page at a time. Some scientists are content with this and already keep up to date with unpublished information through what are often informal specialist networks and e-mail, but typical scholars in the humanities (and many other scientists) are to be found in libraries working with several books or journals open in front of them, something which one visual display unit cannot replicate. Offer the option of a book or a screen to such readers and they will choose the book. Better still, ask the publishers, who have good reason to keep a watchful eye on the market, about the effect of the electronic revolution and they will tell you that the demand for books continues to rise, despite the steadily increasing availability of electronic forms of information. More troublesome is the fact that technology is continually advancing in unpredictable ways, thereby causing the rapid obsolescence of equipment which must be replaced at frequent intervals.

Even taking the optimistic view that technology will one day reach a stage at which the problems mentioned above are solved, what does the nation do with the originals, those first editions, those rare manuscripts, psalters and missals? Do we destroy them, and our original Magna Cartas? To do so would, in my opinion, be the clearest possible proof of the country's descent into philistinism, of the rejection not only of our heritage but of civilised values. If the treasures are to be kept, the obvious repository is the British Library, located in the capital city.

At this point I must return to the arguments of the National Libraries Committee, which determined the physical form of the St Pancras building as originally planned, and the conclusions of the Atkinson Committee (which drew up the UGC policy for university library accommodation). Both bodies posed the question 'How are libraries actually used?' The National Libraries Committee identified a major difference between the scientists, engineers and technologists, who characteristically and predominantly make short visits to consult a particular journal reference for recent information, and the humanists, who tend to stay longer and put greater emphasis on monographs. Also, the former group frequently want a reprint or copy of an article for ready reference at the user's desk or laboratory bench: this fact was a stimulus to Donald Urquhart to invent the document lending library, out of which grew the much-used facilities at Boston Spa. What Atkinson and others observed was that the use of large parts of a library's holdings diminishes with age. As I described in Chapter 9, he took the view that since university libraries cannot accommodate for ever everything they take in, there must be a weeding of the stock; this should be in two stages, the first into a repository of lesser-used material, from which an ultimate discard would take place in due course (with decisions based on criteria such as intrinsic value and rarity of use).

The British Library is, however, the national library and also that of last resort, which carries with it the duty of retention of material. When the St Pancras building was conceived, it was assumed that it would have this duty across all fields of knowledge and that all the stock would be housed on that single site, so the plans made provision for the storage of some 25 million volumes: this decision received general approval. But, given the pattern of usage, the Board was bound to ask itself whether a high quality of service could not be maintained if some of the little-used material was stored under good environmental conditions at Boston Spa, where costs are significantly lower. I believe that it was a wise decision of the Board to construct a storage building on that site, but it will be essential to keep reliable records of patterns of demand: all libraries develop and change over time, and the calls on the British Library's stock and services are bound to grow. It would therefore be foolish for the government to allow the land at the north end of the trapezoidal St Pancras site to be lost.[5]

If this book were a history of the British Library there would be many other matters on which I should comment, but I shall not do so because these paragraphs are essentially the jottings of a casual labourer who gladly gave more of his time to the Library than his secretary, Sheena Routledge, often said she expected. But three matters I cannot forbear to mention. The first is the American Trust for the British Library, with its Director Dr Douglas Bryant. During the Second World War the only serious damage to the British Museum Library was caused by a bomb which hit the American collections. In an act of immense generosity, a few Anglophile American citizens banded together to form a Trust, initially funded by their own donations but also seeking contributions from other individuals and foundations, to replace the items lost. Dr Bryant, recently retired from the Directorship of the Harvard University library system, had served his country in London at the end of the war and he worked tenaciously on behalf of the Trust, on both sides of the Atlantic. His efforts not only helped the British Library but, because part of the programme of work was to prepare microfilm copies of missing publications, there was a reciprocal benefit for American libraries, which wanted copies of these microfilms and could acquire them very cheaply. Especially important for me were the new friendships that I made, especially with Steve Stamas, a devoted Oxonian, and the humorous and warm-hearted William T. (Bill) Golden. The latter was always busy with good works and, though no scientist himself, was fascinated by science, scientists and their interactions with government. The British Library owes a great debt of gratitude to this group of Americans.

---

5. In the future this may become a cause for concern, because in 1990 the government made it a condition of the grant to complete Phase 1 that the residual land should ultimately be sold.

The second great pleasure was that of receiving visitors I would never have met otherwise. They often came bearing gifts from all over the world. In 1985, my last year as chairman of the Board, the Governor of North Carolina paid a visit as part of that State's celebration of the quatercentenary of Sir Richard Grenville's settlement of Roanoke Island, to see some of the contemporary maps and to present a silver medal (which, with Yorkshire caution, I had assayed at Goldsmiths' Hall). There were frequent Japanese, South American and European visitors, and it seemed to be *de rigueur* for senior figures in the USSR Communist Party to make a pilgrimage to London to visit the house in Clerkenwell where Karl Marx lived, his grave in Highgate Cemetery, and the place in the Round Reading Room where he studied, and to see his signature in the Readers' Book.

I well remember the visit of Mikhail Gorbachev on the afternoon of Saturday 15 December 1984. He, his wife Raisa and their retinue were received by Burke Trend and myself at the north entrance of the British Museum on Montague Place. I greeted Gorbachev in my extremely limited and elementary Russian and then stepped back as we walked through various rooms and he was shown items considered likely to be of interest to him. To my horror, as the group entered one large room I heard a disturbance some 40 or 50 feet away: security people were holding back a few protesters. When he became aware of this, Gorbachev immediately left Burke and me and went over to talk with them. I have no idea how long the conversation lasted, because on such occasions one's first thought is not the timing but the probable outcome of the event. In this case the 'confrontation' ended with smiles and handshakes all round, a fact which on its own confirmed the presence of a new brand of Soviet leader. Then we went to the Round Reading Room and, after solemnly inspecting Marx's signature, repaired to the west wing of the museum for tea. This was the cue for me to present the future First Secretary with a copy of *Treasures of the British Library*. In return I received a book from him, after which he leaned forward and inserted a metal badge in the buttonhole of the jacket I was wearing, saying words which the interpreter rendered as, 'I am making you a member of the Writers' Union of the USSR'. Gorbachev then added with a smile words which clearly embarrassed the interpreter as he translated, 'It is Russian. It will break'. Here indeed, I thought, is a special politician, and I smiled back. The whole encounter was unforgettable, and I was not surprised that after she met him Mrs Thatcher said publicly about Gorbachev, 'I can do business with this man'.

It was not only by the spoken word that overseas visitors expressed their high regard for the British Library. I received many letters from foreigners remarking what a treasure-house the library was, frequently the only place where they could find the information they wanted. Sometimes these letters were published in the country of origin. For example, the January 1985 issue of *Literaturnaya Gazeta* from Moscow contained a letter from a Mr A. Maldiss, in which he described how he had come to England to try to find any surviving documents or books from his native Byelorussia, some so ancient that he hardly dared hope to trace them. But there they were in the British Library, dating back to 1429 and going right through to the nineteenth century. He declared the material to be unique, and of inestimable value to all those interested in the history of Russia and the Soviet republics before the time of Peter the Great.

The third point to which I would refer derives from a concern I developed many years ago as a consequence of a delayed train departure from Newcastle to Leeds. Rather than wait on the platform, I took a walk to see something of the city centre. On leaving the station I saw on my right hand a small, well proportioned, attractive stone building which appeared to be public premises, but which was actually the home of the Literary and Philosophical Society (or some such name). No one challenged my entry, and within the building I saw bookshelves bearing periodicals which I think were the property of the North East Engineering and Mining Institution. A quick look in the short time available suggested that they were a goldmine of history about the nineteenth-century mining and engineering industries, which exported coal and built ships, railway lines and engines, bridges and docks for use all over the world, and which were now entering a terminal decline. As I left I wondered who cared for the collection, and at a subsequent meeting of the National Libraries Committee I cited the incident as an illustration of a need which had become apparent, but for which there seemed to be no provision. This was to secure the survival of collections of national importance, whether in public or in private hands, the owners of which did not have the means to maintain them properly. To purchase such material and remove it to a national library would be to take away a source of local pride and identity. It would be much better to leave the collections in their areas of origin, on condition they could be well cared for, conserved and made available to the public. Statute 1.3(b) of the British Library Act empowered the Library to make grants to organisations such as churches, schools and private libraries, helping them to bring their holdings into the desired condition of usefulness, but also relying on individual communities to become involved in fund-raising as a means of generating local interest and pride in their treasures.

It will be clear that I have derived enormous satisfaction from my long association with the British Library. As my last day in office, 30 November 1985, approached I was deeply sad but it was a good time to go, in that the new building had begun and the Board had just agreed its first corporate plan. I was touched by the kindness of many colleagues at my farewell party, and the skill of the craftsman in the book of dedications I was given. Moreover, my fears that my departure would also mark the end of my contact with the British Library, and the library world in general, happily proved to be unfounded. Not only was I invited to chair the Library's grant allocation committee, but in an act of great kindness the Board established an annual eponymous lecture, which at first was presented in the rooms of the Royal Society. I have attended every one, and to my great delight that in 1997 was given in the lecture theatre of the new building at St Pancras.

Solving the Gardening Problem

Much as we enjoyed the large garden at Fieldside, our Oxford home, its maintenance became a problem to us as we grew older. A solution came about as a result of a much more serious matter. The Ministry of Transport secured planning permission to build a northward extension of the A34 road, connecting with the M40 and passing just 150 metres from our front door, thereby blocking our hitherto extensive views across fields to the east. More importantly, the carriageway was to have four lanes and the constructors were allowed to make the surface of transversely ribbed concrete, a sure recipe for creating a most unpleasant, high-pitched 'screech' when traversed by traffic travelling at about the legal limit of 70 mph. When the road was opened we found the noise intolerable and we decided to move. For the same reason, however, the sale value of our house was depressed. Because this price penalty seemed unjustified, I decided to learn how to use a sophisticated noise meter (which I borrowed from the University of Sheffield) and to make extensive readings over two weeks during one summer and one week in the next summer. At the same time we made hourly counts of the traffic flows and established that, among the houses on our lane, the noise was greatest at Fieldside. I studied the legislation concerning permissible noise levels in detail, and confirmed that the actual (measured) readings indeed came in the 'excessive' category.

I sent my first report to our local MP, Douglas Hurd, for onward transmission to the Ministry of Transport. The Ministry appointed the firm of Sir William Halcrow as consultant engineers. They merely made the theoretical calculations which are accepted legally in cases of this kind, as set out in a public document. Why these calculations should be preferred to actual data puzzled me, because this is the antithesis of the scientific method. However, I persisted and the Ministry eventually agreed that neither my data nor my criticisms could be refuted: this allowed us to obtain through the District Valuer a just compensation for the depreciation in the value of our house. This in turn enabled us to move to a house in North Oxford with a more modest garden, thereby diminishing the physical burden on Barbara and myself. In passing, I would comment that the behaviour of certain local estate agents seeking to act for other local residents, whom I knew from my measurements not to have the same basis for compensation, reflected badly on their competence or their probity, or both.

A Lifetime's Fascination With Words

I have often been teased about my desire to know the precise meaning of a word and to learn something of its etymology. Whether in praise or derision I am not sure, but someone once said to me 'You have the mind of a lexicographer'. He could not have known that I do have a secret liking for Samuel Johnson, not least because of his love of chemistry. Perhaps I have a lexicographical aura which makes an impression on other people, for I was twice approached to give help in this field. The first time was to be a member of the Longman Advisory Board to discuss a range of matters relating to the compilation and presentation of dictionaries. It was an extremely eclectic group, under the chairmanship of Asa Briggs, and included the footballer Derek Dougan, Germaine Greer, the trade unionist Clive Jenkins, the indispensable Randolph Quirk, George Murray, Jack Longland and R.D. Laing, whose name I associated with the students of the late 1960s and with whom, if I had ever seen him at any of the meetings, I would certainly have argued. I felt I was of minimal use to this group, but I think we can have done little harm because the *Longman New Universal Dictionary* is one which I find very useful.

The second approach was from Oxford University Press, though I am not sure how it came about. It could have been from the Secretary to the Delegates, George Richardson, a Fellow of St John's, whom I had come to know a little through my membership of that college. It could equally well have been through Robert Steiner, Professor of Radiology at the Royal Postgraduate Medical School – of whose Council I was chairman – because he knew Richard Charkin, a Cambridge physiology graduate who was Managing Director of the Academic and General Division of Oxford University Press. I am, however, clear that Charkin came to see me at home in 1983 and I found him to be an engaging and optimistic individual. His infectious enthusiasm for playing cricket sat happily with an equally dynamic commitment to the production of an immense computerised database from which, by appropriate tagging of the information, it would be possible to extract instantly the entries appropriate for the *Shorter*, *Concise* and full versions of the *Oxford English Dictionary (OED)*, and more user-friendly variants for overseas markets such as Australia and North America.

I heard what Richard had to say sympathetically because I had acquired my first copy of the third edition of the *Shorter Oxford Dictionary* soon after the last war and found it invaluable, and had only recently bought the two-volume revised (1983) edition. I became intrigued as he explained the vast possibilities for exploiting the database, but I also understood the immense problems associated with its creation. For example, some 60 million words would have to be typed in, with each entry appropriately subdivided by font and tags to give full historical references extending over seven centuries, able to be updated at will and to yield on interrogation whatever it might be decided to publish, in whatever format. At Richard's suggestion, I visited the house used by *OED* staff on the west side of St Giles in Oxford to gain an impression of the enormity of the task, bearing in mind that for nearly a century editing work had been carried out using purely manual methods for creating and constantly revising a written record.

The long-term benefits were obvious and compelling, but what about the costs? First, the computer hardware and software necessary to store, manipulate and access the text of the existing *OED*, and its four supplementary volumes, had to be devised and installed. There was much research and development to be done and paid for, and here the chairman of IBM UK, Eddie Nixon, was invaluable in agreeing to provide the hardware and to second experts to come and work with

OED staff in Oxford.[6] Because I was certain that this project, if successful, would carry the United Kingdom's name around the world, I felt it was in the national interest for the government to become associated with it. At that time the Department of Trade and Industry had Mr Kenneth Baker as its first Minister of State for Information Technology. On 27 August 1983, in Wheeler's restaurant on the King's Road in Brighton, I rather diffidently cast a fly over him for help; and was delighted when he rose to the bait with some enthusiasm. Enquiries by officials followed, and in the end the government gave its blessing and sealed it with £300,000 towards the cost of development. I was a little anxious when, in the following year, Mrs Thatcher reshuffled the Cabinet and Kenneth Baker became Secretary of State for the Environment. Happily for me and for the new *OED*, his successor as Minister for IT was Sir Geoffrey Pattie, whom I knew from St Catharine's, Cambridge, and who was supportive of the project.

The keyboarding of the vast amount of existing data was the biggest and most expensive part of the project, and was entrusted to an American subsidiary of Reed International. Their work was checked and found to be exemplary by an army of proof-readers; that enabled the old *OED* and its supplements to be combined into one set of volumes. However, the Press also wanted to publish electronic versions, plus others with illustrations, and to construct a new database accessible in several different ways. The research and development necessary for this work was assigned to the University of Waterloo in Ontario, a relatively new institution which laid great emphasis on IT exploitation.

By May 1984 the essential elements of the project were in place and a public launch took place at the Royal Society, where a target date for publication of the hard copy version was announced. An Advisory Committee was appointed, and in the event the deadline was met with a few days to spare. The venture was a great success in many ways, not least because sales were well in excess of expectations. For me the whole episode was an extremely happy and educative experience, and

---

6. It was also thought advisable to keep IBM in the United States fully informed and on side, and therefore the parent company was invited to nominate someone to come and visit Oxford. To my delight it was Lew Branscomb who was sent, whom I knew well from his time at the National Bureau of Standards and again at Aspen. George Richardson laid on a splendid private dinner in St John's, before which Lew and I walked around Oxford and talked about old times and this new project. Because he mentioned that his father was a Rhodes Scholar at Wadham College, we slipped through the back gate of St John's gardens into Wadham. I think it was an afternoon which gave him great pleasure.

my reward for being a member of the Advisory Committee was a set of 20 volumes of the new *OED*, a gift which went far beyond my wildest dreams. It has been much used ever since, a constant reminder that, as Samuel Johnson put it, 'language is only the instrument of science, and words are but the signs of ideas'. At my suggestion, Kenneth Baker received from the Press a rather gaudy commemorative tie, which was so envied by Neil Kinnock that he was similarly supplied, though it did him little good in the 1992 election!

My Concern With Medical Education

As I approached the end of my term as chairman of the University Grants Committee I received an invitation from Dr Malcolm Godfrey, Dean of the Royal Postgraduate Medical School (RPMS), to join its Council. I accepted gladly, and in 1979 I took over as chairman. This institution, based at the Hammersmith Hospital, was admitted as a School of the University of London in 1934 and the quality of its work is universally recognised. It is unique in that it accepts only students in medicine or related subjects, to read for postgraduate degrees and diplomas in various aspects of clinical practice.

Over and above the general financial troubles which have afflicted university institutions in recent years, RPMS has had to face one particular challenge. This concerned the Clinical Research Centre in Northwick Park Hospital, established in the early 1970s. The then chairman of the Medical Research Council (MRC), Sir Harold Himsworth, had the idea that he would create something like the United States National Institutes of Health at this newly built hospital in Harrow. I had come to know it quite well because for a considerable period I was one of a group of four 'wise men', who also included the Department of Health's Chief Medical Officer, appointed to study the development of this project. I was convinced the main reason it was not progressing as envisaged was that the oversight of the hospital was in the hands of a district health authority: there was no provision for the medical research scientists to have control over admissions, or any inducement for able young doctors to go to the Clinical Research Centre rather than RPMS. (In the latter institution, they would have the benefit of clinical leaders who were also academics, and they could also study for degrees of the University of London.) The message got through to MRC in the 1980s, and it decided to see if a cooperative arrangement could be reached with RPMS. A plan agreed by both parties and approved by the Advisory Board for the Research Councils was rejected by the government at Prime Ministerial level, on very weak arguments. RPMS and MRC then reappraised the possibilities and came to an agreement for a substantial proportion of the Centre's staff, mainly those concerned with molecular medicine, to come to Hammersmith. The Wellcome Trust and MRC gave large capital grants to ensure that adequate accommodation would be available.

When the building was nearing completion, and a new Dean of RPMS had been appointed, I felt it was time for me to retire from the Council. This was not, however, the end of my association with the School, for in 1990 I was appointed as President – a post which carries with it all of the pleasures of office and little of the responsibility, unless the institution faces major challenges. Unfortunately this is exactly what happened following publication in 1992 of the Tomlinson Report on medical care in central London. As a result of this report the Department of Health decided that RPMS should join Charing Cross Hospital, where it would become part of the medical school of Imperial College. This restructuring was duly carried out: I very much hope that Imperial appreciates the jewel which it now has in its crown, and continues to fund RPMS in a way that is appropriate to its status as a world-class research centre.

As can be seen from this tale, it is not always the case that attitudes and actions follow reason as readily and smoothly as in the case of the computerisation of the *OED*. If the action involves change it seems generally less acceptable the older the players, whether these be individuals or institutions. A vivid example of this was provided by another supposedly limited-time commitment to the University of London, which I accepted in the autumn of 1982. The Vice-Chancellor, Professor (now Lord) Randolph Quirk, sent a letter to the Principal of Queen Mary College (QMC) and the Deans of St Bartholomew's Hospital Medical College (always known as Bart's) and the Royal London Hospital Medical College, announcing the setting up of a committee to encourage the three institutions to move towards a common curriculum and examinations in medicine, and to draw up a development plan to achieve these ends. It also stated that I would be the committee's chairman. The letter was dated 25 November, which I took to be propitious – it is the festival of St Catherine of Alexandria, the patron saint of learning. Alas, this was not to prove to be the case, at least in the short run.

The issue was simple. The report of the Royal Commission on Medical Education, published in 1968, had recommended both an increased intake into UK medical schools and the pairing of existing schools in London, each pair being closely associated with a college of the University of London which had a good science base. My commitment to this concept was well known, as was the fact that it was a policy objective of the University Grants Committee. Moreover, in the Royal London–Bart's case the UGC, in my first year as chairman, had authorised Queen Mary College to acquire new land which, *inter alia*, would allow the College to establish a joint preclinical school on its campus. When I accepted this commission I knew I could expect to encounter sensitivities over what might be regarded by the long-established medical schools as a loss of autonomy, and therefore I would need to tread delicately. However, I also knew that there was a pot of gold available for capital development of this kind, so that any new facilities would be an improvement on what already existed. The committee worked hard and issued reports on the feasibility of locating the new preclinical school on the QMC site. It outlined the options and identified which in our opinion was the best; it had the cost implications appraised by a firm of accountants; and it proposed a form of governance which ensured that the joint preclinical school, though located on the QMC site, would 'remain as a wholly autonomous institution independent of QMC, in receipt of grants direct from the Court Department of the University, unless and until it is prepared to move towards a merger with QMC'.

The committee, which had been given the unattractive and cumbersome name of 'City and East London Medical Education Group', had members drawn from all three institutions, with Malcolm Godfrey and myself as independent representatives. Although occasional reminders that Bart's was founded in the twelfth century exposed a particular sensitivity in that quarter, the report was unanimous, something which owed much to the sound judgment and tact of our secretary, Mike Saville, a Sheffield native with whom I had been able to establish an excellent working relationship. I had also gone to considerable trouble to meet and listen to individuals, particularly at Bart's, who were opposed to the planned scheme. I was therefore much dismayed when the governing body of Bart's rejected our proposals, which by then had been accepted by the Dean and welcomed by both the UGC and the University of London. Bart's went so far as to make application to the High Court of Justice for a judicial review of the decisions of the UGC and the University of London – an extreme reaction. But in contentious matters time is a great healer, and it also allows wiser councils to prevail. So it was that in 1997 a full amalgamation of the two preclinical medical schools was finally achieved on the Queen Mary and Westfield site (Westfield College having joined QMC in the interim).

The Worshipful Company of Goldsmiths

I mentioned in Chapter 2 how the Goldsmiths' Company in London twice helped me financially, when I was an undergraduate at Oxford and when I was a research student at Cambridge. I evidently had not vanished from their beneficent eyes, because when I was Dr Lee's Professor at Oxford I received an invitation from Sir Owen Wansbrough Jones (a fellow chemist whom I had known when he was a don at Trinity Hall, Cambridge) to have a talk with him. His purpose, as I discovered, was to sound me out as to whether I would be willing to become a non-trade Freeman. I accepted with great pleasure, and progressed through the various strata of membership to become Prime Warden in 1982-83.

The origins of the Goldsmiths' Company, one of the twelve great City livery companies, date back to the end of the twelfth century, when a Guild of Goldsmiths was established. Unlike most livery companies, it still has real and important duties to perform in testing the currency of the United Kingdom (and New Zealand), in binding apprentices and assisting them with their further education, and in fostering the crafts of goldsmithing, silversmithing and jewellery making. It is rare that one finds a conjunction of such divergent interests as those of the employers, the labour force and the consumers entrusted to one body. The Company is also responsible for the administration of educational and general charities, jobs which it takes seriously and for which it has been my privilege to chair the relevant committees. Its educational activities have been varied, and not wholly concentrated on the trade: thus it created Goldsmiths' College in the south-east of London, now a constituent college of the University of London; it endowed Chairs in English at Oxford and Metallurgy at Cambridge; and it still assists schoolteachers and students in various ways. It has an admirable library dealing with aspects of its trade and craft, and perhaps most importantly it hallmarks articles made of gold, silver and platinum, a duty which it shares with three other Assay Offices in the UK – in Birmingham, Edinburgh and Sheffield.

The Goldsmiths' Company does not go in for pomp and ceremony, and it has been willing to accept suggestions on new ways of using its money that are not necessarily restricted to producing benefits solely in the south (for example, it has helped three Community Trusts in South Yorkshire, Cleveland, and Tyne and Wear to establish themselves in those deprived regions and to achieve a multiplier effect in the charity field). I have greatly enjoyed my long connection with the Comapny, and Goldsmiths' Hall has been a delightful second home for me in London.

One exhibition in my year as Prime Warden particularly sticks in my mind. It was held to celebrate fifty years of the craftsmanship of the silversmith Leslie Durbin, and several owners, including the Queen Mother and the City of Stalingrad, loaned outstanding works by this great artist. The Queen Mother visited the display, and in company with Mr Durbin I conducted her around various exhibits. He said very little, which disappointed me, and I tried my best to draw him into the conversation but with minimal success. At one point, looking at the Sword of Stalingrad [7] which he had designed and executed, I put my key question to him. 'How', I asked, 'do you arrive at such beautiful and appropriate designs?' Very quietly he uttered his longest sentence of the evening: 'I think what it has to do, then I do it'. I was humbled by such simple and powerful directness, and then felt better as the thought crossed my mind that they were words which might well have fallen from my own father's lips.

Another memorable event during my year as Prime Warden took place in my native city of Sheffield. The Guardians of Sheffield Plate, who are the governors of the Assay Office there, asked me if I would lay the foundation stone of an extension to Guardians' Hall, which is in Portobello Street, facing the engineering departments of the University. The guests included the Lord Mayor, the Master Cutler, the President of the Chamber of Commerce, the Vice-Chancellor of the University and many other notables, among whom was the irrepressible and ever-friendly Billy Ibberson. Known locally as 'Mr Sheffield', he was a much respected figure in the cutlery industry who made unremitting efforts to promote his native

---

7. This sword was a gift from the people of Britain to those who had so stoutly defended Stalingrad against the attacking German armies. That city's authorities sent the sword back to London for the exhibition in the care of a Russian custodian, who had very little English and found the brightness and vitality of the London streets quite overwhelmingly seductive.

city, both by his representation of it externally and by good works internally. I had stayed with him and his wife a year or two earlier, and he had shown me round two of the splendid working museums which he had helped to create (and which he continued to encourage). One was the Abbeydale Industrial Hamlet, preserved as a small water-powered steel mill replete with tilt hammers, grindstones and workmen's dwellings, still with craftsmen using their ancient tools on open days. The other was Kelham Island Museum, which is on the River Don and testifies to a later phase of Sheffield's industrial development. Its exhibits include a giant (and fully functional) steam engine from a rolling mill, a massive Bessemer Converter and many smaller evidences of the way in which steel-making and engineering skills were brought together. To stay with Billy and his wife was pure joy, for no two people were more devoted to bestowing the warmest hospitality on their friends or so expert in creating an atmosphere of unreserved welcome.

Barbara and I also paid a memorable visit to Dublin in 1983. Like London, this city had its influx of Huguenot goldsmiths who fled from France at the revocation of the Edict of Nantes in 1685, and who at first tried to evade marking their silver but who also brought new ideas and skills to the craft. The Goldsmiths' Hall there is to be found in Dublin Castle. On arrival we were warmly received by the Clerk, Ronnie le Bas, and two of his Wardens – one the elderly founder of the Waterford Glass firm, who was a diabetic, and the other a local goldsmith who had a shop in the centre of Dublin. Because I was Prime Warden of the Goldsmiths' Company they were determined to entertain us royally, and for lunch we were taken to a special restaurant in a delightful Georgian terraced house. When the menu had been decided, Ronnie le Bas said I must choose the wine. Bearing in mind that the goldsmith had to work and the diabetic was unable to take alcohol, I ordered one bottle of red wine but was rapidly overruled by Ronnie with a 'Make that two, will you' before the waiter got out of earshot. The consequence was that when the Clerk and the Wardens bade us farewell at the end of the meal, Barbara and I instinctively took one another's arms, something we rarely do, but which on this occasion seemed necessary for mutual support and stability! As we walked I said to Barbara, 'Before we return to Denis and Marjorie (her uncle and aunt, with whom we were staying) we will find our way to Trinity College, crossing roads only at zebra crossings and traffic lights, and sit in the autumn sunshine until we have reached an acceptable degree of sobriety'.

As we approached Trinity's great gate on that lovely early October afternoon (having made our way there without incident) and thought of the tranquillity we were shortly to enjoy, we were surprised by the amount of noise emanating from the front square. We discovered that it was the day, or one of the days, on which undergraduates registered for their courses. One result was that various student societies had laid out their stalls in the square in an attempt to encourage the freshmen and others to join. Some tables were besieged by enquiring customers, but others had none. One of the latter, near the end of the line, was labelled 'Classical Society' and had sitting behind it two charming girls. They looked somewhat forlorn at the lack of custom and so I gave them a friendly smile, which prompted one of them to say with great alacrity and a lovely brogue, 'Join the Classical Society, young man' with a marked emphasis on the adjective. As it was fairly evident I was approaching my seventies, I gave her full marks and thought to myself that she would surely have a successful career, whatever subject she studied!

General Acting Unpaid Odd Job Man

A long-standing interest in the works of skilled craftsmen led to my involvement in retirement with both the Society of Designer Craftsmen and the Crafts Council. While I felt a natural affinity with the former, I did not necessarily think I had much to offer the latter – certainly nothing by way of expertise. The Society of Designer Craftsmen, founded by William Morris and Walter Crane over a century ago, is a body of wholly delightful people earning their living by making beautiful objects, which might be practical, such as a chair or table, or largely decorative, such as a tapestry. The Society is entirely self-supporting from fees paid by its members, who are admitted to the two grades of membership on criteria which involve critical scrutiny of the quality of their work. I found this connection delightful, firstly because of my father's craftsmanship, and secondly because everyone was so friendly and unpretentious. When invited to become President in 1985 I had no hesitation in accepting, and I have been delighted to serve in that capacity ever since. To mark the centenary of the Society's foundation in 1988 I asked the Goldsmiths' Company to commission a silver medal, which was designed by Leslie Durbin and shows the heads of Morris and Crane; a copy of it is now offered to a member of the Society annually, on the results of a competition.

I joined the Crafts Council largely because of the persuasive powers of David Mellor (the distinguished Sheffield designer craftsman, not the politician), who was its chairman in the early 1980s. Funded by the Department of National Heritage, the Council is the national body for promoting the crafts. I never felt really comfortable in that organisation: the loquacity of some of the members bordered on the pretentious, and I had a sense of cross-currents that were not wholly productive. David Mellor's resignation in 1984 came as no great shock, and I was pleased when the Council left its rather expensive premises in Lower Regent Street and moved to more practical, if less salubrious, accommodation in Islington. Visiting it again while Nigel Broackes was chairman, I sensed a healthy change of attitude.

In my last year as chairman of the British Library Board I agreed to become a member of the Museums and Galleries Commission, having served earlier as a trustee of the Natural History Museum for a period of ten years from 1974. The Commission acts as the official adviser on museum and gallery matters of all kinds, ranging from facilities for disabled visitors to the conservation of artefacts. It keeps a constant eye on museum policy, both nationally and at the level of individual establishments. At first I was rather reluctant to join because I had had a previous encounter with the Commission when I was chairman of the University Grants Committee (the Commission had produced a report on university museums which it sent to me for comment, and which seemed to me to be singularly ill-informed: since I am not a person to mince my words, I said so). However, both the Chairman of the Commission, Brian Morris, and the Director, Peter Longman, assured me that it had changed since that time, and indeed I found it was a workmanlike body with a strong sense of collegiality and responsibility. There was a particularly enjoyable annual event, when we carried out a 'progress' of museum activities in a particular part of the country. This helped to bring the members together as well as to inform them. I thoroughly enjoyed my seven years on that body and was reluctant to leave in 1992, but I had already well overshot the age limit for membership.

Shortly after demitting office as chairman of the UGC, I was approached by the Director of the London School of Economics and Political Science to ask whether I would agree to become a member of the Court of Governors. My feelings were mixed. On the one hand I was attracted by its reputation as a high quality institution, and I knew from past experience that its library – the British Library of Political and Economic Science – had outstanding collections. On the other hand

I was somewhat wary because, being a natural scientist, I did not see how I might contribute to academic deliberations in the School. Having slipped in at the back of two lectures and a seminar, I realised that while the quality could be outstanding (Professor Maurice Cranston was my ideal lecturer) it was not uniformly so, and a little more humility in the self-estimation of certain staff would have become them better. That said, I found one or two niches where I could be helpful and came to enjoy my long association with the School – especially the ten years I spent as chairman of its Library Panel, which began shortly after I left the British Library. The problems to be tackled were obvious and depressing. As the unit of resource shrank the reaction of the Librarian was to preserve jobs, and inevitably the unavoidable cuts fell on the acquisitions budget, a sure recipe for failure. Change was necessary and was made possible by the appointment of two outstandingly good Librarians in succession. The first was Chris Hunt, a Manchester University graduate in history and a man of gentle but firm disposition, who came to the School from the University of Queensland. Aided by consultants, he wrought a culture change which enabled staff costs to be contained and the acquisitions budget to rise, while at the same time increasing morale and giving an improved service. When he left to become Librarian of his alma mater the good work was continued by Lynne Brindley, who added IT policy and implementation to her responsibilities.[8] All that the School's library needed now was better accommodation, and when outline plans for this had been prepared by Norman Foster and accepted by the Court of Governors, I felt I could step down.

Whilst I was still involved with the Advisory Board for the Research Councils it became clear that genetic manipulation was a rapidly evolving science. There had been a conference in California to examine the probable and possible hazards of work in this field, and the safety precautions that should be adopted to protect the workers and also the public at large. An appraisal of the risks and benefits was obviously called for, and I suggested to ABRC that Lord Ashby be asked to look into this matter. He produced an utterly convincing report which led to the formation of the Genetic Manipulation Advisory Group. Its role was to establish the levels of

---

8. Lynne Brindley subsequently became Brotherton Librarian and Pro-Vice-Chancellor in the University of Leeds, before taking up the post of Chief Executive of the British Library in 2000. These appointments would have delighted Fred, who spotted Lynne's potential early in her career (BHD).

containment under which work in various categories of risk should be performed, and to pave the way for more general regulations to be enacted by Parliament. When I retired from the University Grants Committee in 1978, I was asked by the Committee of Vice-Chancellors and Principals if I would serve on this group: doing so proved to be a liberal education in this field, and I watched with interest some of the debates involving people as diverse as Hans Kornberg, Donna Haber (now Hans' wife), Bob Williamson, an American molecular biologist at St Mary's Hospital, the trade union doctor Ron Owen, Mark Richmond, who later became chairman of the Science and Engineering Research Council, and my lively former pupil Bernard Langley. It was a body which seemed to me to display both reason and passion, but also one which I felt strongly should have been brigaded under the Health and Safety Executive, as ultimately it was.

The work of the Genetic Manipulation Advisory Group was in some ways similar to that of the National Radiological Protection Board, but in one respect quite different. The latter body had only come to exist because of the palpable evidence that radiation could cause adverse effects on the human body, a notable example being the death of Marie Curie from persistent aplastic anaemia. Unfortunately, the regulation came in rather late, as radiation had been used for therapy and diagnosis for several decades. In the case of genetic manipulation, the risks could largely be defined before the experiments were carried out, and so it could be said that scientists were perhaps too cautious in the beginning and imposed conditions for themselves which, in some cases, proved to be unnecessary. However, the Group was useful as one of the early examples of the increasing inter-action of scientific and medical practice with ethics, which is bound to present society with problems for many years to come.

My interests in education and medicine, and my experience with the charities of the Goldsmiths' Company, were probably the reasons for my being invited to work with other such bodies. These included the Arthritis and Rheumatism Council for Research, the Jacqueline du Pré Memorial Fund, the Edward Boyle Memorial Trust, the Wolfson Foundation, and the Arkwright Society. However, these charities were very different from one another.

The Arthritis and Rheumatism Council attracts large sums of money by all sorts of means, including bequests and the tireless activities of thousands of people. It forms part of that cluster of medical charities which together dispose of funds for research exceeding those of the Medical Research Council. I have been honoured to serve as its President, and Barbara and I always look forward to the Council's annual meeting, at which we meet representatives of the many fundraisers and hear about the research that is being supported by their endeavours. I particularly remember one occasion in Blackpool, when a young police officer and his girl-friend decided to raise money by getting married at the top of the Blackpool Tower and then abseiling to the ground after the ceremony. They invited us to attend and we were delighted to do so. Alas, it began to rain immediately after the ceremony, which considerably reduced the size of the crowd waiting at the bottom of the Tower, from whom we had hoped to make a substantial collection. Although the weather did not co-operate, nothing could detract from their generous thought or the original form of their wedding.

I first met Jacqueline du Pré in 1980, when the University of Sheffield resolved to confer upon her the honorary degree of Doctor of Music. Seriously ill with multiple sclerosis, she was too unwell to travel to Sheffield and so, as Chancellor of the University, I decided that the degree should be conferred somewhere that was more convenient for her. The Goldsmiths' Company generously co-operated and the ceremony went ahead in Goldsmiths' Hall. I was much taken with her bearing and courage, as indeed were all the other people present. Subsequently I was approached to join the Board of Trustees set up under Lord Goodman to admin-ister her memorial fund. This venture had two main aims: to build sheltered accommodation for musicians smitten by her debilitating disease, and to construct a Jacqueline du Pré Music Building in the grounds of St Hilda's College, Oxford (of which Jacqueline was an Honorary Fellow). Here I served as chairman of the Executive Committee, which became the driving force of the Fund because of the ill-health of Lord Goodman.

Both goals were achieved and Oxford, the city of Jacqueline's birth, now has an acoustically superb auditorium seating 200 persons and a suite of practice rooms in the college which honoured her. One of the most gratifying features of the fund-raising exercise was the uniformly positive response of musicians in schools, colleges and universities, who responded to our appeals by presenting special performances. A pleasant by-product was my election as a Privilegiate of St Hilda's College, which carries with it all the benefits accorded to an Honorary Fellow, to which St Hilda's, being a wholly women's institution, was debarred by its statutes from electing me! I also served on the Newnham College Trust, which raised money for the essential repair of its beautiful buildings in Cambridge, and Barbara has always maintained that one of the best things she ever did for her two colleges was to arouse my interest in them.

I came to know Edward Boyle, the Tory politician and Education Minister who went on to become Vice-Chancellor of the University of Leeds, during my time as chairman of the University Grants Committee. Sadly, he died in office in 1981, and shortly afterwards the Edward Boyle Memorial Trust was founded to commemorate his name. It was hoped to raise funds which could be used to promote music, education and learning. For most of the Trust's lifetime I served as its chairman and found it an absorbing duty, not least because of the people I met and the demonstration of how a little money properly applied can have a powerful effect, often catalysing the flow of other resources. When the Trust was wound up in 1997 a considerable sum was passed on to the Jacqueline du Pré Music Building project, where the concert hall has been named the Edward Boyle Auditorium.

The Wolfson Foundation is very rich but it has a peculiar set of articles of association which led me to leave in 1988, after I had been a trustee for almost ten years. These articles permitted the chairman, Lord Wolfson, to dismiss out of hand distinguished trustees such as Lord Zuckerman (responsible for my nomination), Lord Bullock, Sir Cyril Clarke and Sir Jack Plumb, and to behave in an idiosyncratic, if not to say irrational, manner. Nevertheless, the work was interesting and led to my involvement with the School of Environmental Sciences at the University of East Anglia, of which Lord Zuckerman had been one of the founders. This is something for which I shall always be grateful, because it reconnected me with former students and colleagues on the University's staff; and it educated me in aspects of geomorphology and climate, including the vexed question of global warming and the public policy issues which it raises.

As an historian interested in industrial archaeology, Christopher Charlton founded the Arkwright Society in 1971 with the aim of preserving Cromford Mill in Derbyshire, long disused and certain to deteriorate further. He realised that it could be made into a monument to the achievements of its founder, Sir Richard Arkwright, who pioneered the use of machinery in the production of textiles, using both water power and some of the early steam engines. So Charlton set about this gargantuan task, raised several million pounds, and then spent it imaginatively and economically. I have been happy to serve as one of the Society's Vice-Presidents, to which office I was also able to recruit Sir George Kenyon (who was subsequently President in succession to the Duke of Devonshire) and Brian Morris (Lord Morris of Castle Morris). The old mill, widely regarded as one of the birthplaces of the Industrial Revolution, is of considerable educational value and has now developed into an attractive visitor centre.

In between my various 'retirement' commitments, I made time for two new publications. The first of these was prepared at the invitation of an Oxford contemporary of mine, the extraordinarily gifted Barbadian Sir Hugh Springer, whose notable career of public service included the posts of Governor General of Barbados and Secretary General of the Association of Commonwealth Universities. He asked me to write a text which would be helpful to applicants for Fulbright and Marshall Awards contemplating study in British universities. I hope the resulting booklet, *Choosing a British University* (published in 1981), was useful. It certainly was a re-education of myself, as I had to look at British universities with the eye of a North American graduate and think carefully about how the common language and academic traditions might conceal some of the subtle but important differences which, if they remain unexplained, can lead to an academic visitor's stay being less rewarding than it should be. I had in mind the kind of coded messages from Oxbridge tutors which are difficult to comprehend for North Americans, who are more accustomed in their own universities to numerical marks in a weekly quiz or, as it is comically called, 'recitation', as a guide to their progress.

My other publication, a book entitled *Reflections on the Universities and the National Health Service*, appeared in 1983 and was the required outcome of my tenure of the Rock Carling Fellowship, provided by the Nuffield Provincial Hospitals Trust. It necessitated my probing into the histories of the university system and medical education, the origins of the UGC and the Research Councils, and the changes which had taken place in the NHS since its inception in 1948. If I were to be charged with writing such a book today, I would subtitle it 'two case histories of government attempts to curb expenditure on increasingly expensive public services'. In retrospect, it seems strange that in my book I should be criticising the management of the NHS for having both area and regional health authorities, whose members seemed to be chosen more for their representativeness than their knowledge: for now that these bodies have been swept away, I find the new style of so-called managers depressingly driven by the jargon and precepts of second-rate business schools. They have all too evidently lost sight of the fact that the only personal interface which really matters in medicine is that between the practitioner – whether it be doctor, nurse or other professional – and the patient. The manager's primary role should be to create a setting in which these transactions are optimised, and this requires more humility and willingness to listen than most of them seem to me to display at present.

I had no need to convince Barbara of the relevance of the work of the British Association for the Advancement of Science, for she started going to its Annual Meetings at a much earlier age than I did.[9] For several years I was at the centre of its affairs, which included in 1981 the sesquicentennial celebrations at York (the city in the grounds of whose Philosophical Society it was founded in 1831). My involvement was especially rewarding because it coincided with an important period for the Association, which quite rightly was seeking a larger role, particularly in relating science to public affairs. As ordinary members, both Barbara and I have attended the Association's week-long meetings in places as disparate as Strathclyde and Sussex, Bristol and Belfast. We have always found much to interest us, but student hostel life (which has usually been the norm, as far as accommodation is concerned) becomes less easily accepted the older one gets.

In retirement I have also had time to ponder other issues and then to write up lectures about them: for example, the probable effects of information technology on educational and social structures in advanced nations. The many invitations I have received to speak on matters so different from the subject of my formal training have led me to conclude that there must always be audiences willing to listen to people, however ill-qualified, who are prepared to address them on a subject in which they are unafraid to expose their ignorance, and to show clearly that, like their hearers, they are trying to learn. Nor have I lost contact completely with my own fields, because I continue to take certain chemical journals and to accept occasional invitations to lecture on scientific topics. Each is a spur to relearning and updating. I became (and still am) lost in admiration of the way in which younger chemists, skilfully deploying ever more sensitive spectroscopic techniques in

---

9. Barbara's first 'BA' was in Leeds in 1927, when she was eleven years old. On that occasion she went with her parents and Donald her dog; she has been a regular attender ever since.

combination with ultra-fast instrumentation, have unravelled the details of the trajectories and energies of atoms in activated and reacting molecules; and are now, in Dick Zare's evocative words, 'choreographing chemical reactions'. My enthusiasm for their achievements could have led me to undervalue the excitement which past scientists also felt, were it not for the fact that I was recruited by the late Leslie Sutton and Mansel Davies, both former colleagues and friends, into reading and discussing with them their contributions as co-authors of the *History of the Faraday Society*. This pleasurable task caused me to reflect on the development of physical chemistry throughout the twentieth century, and allowed me to recapture some of the excitement of previous Faraday Society Discussions. I had been present at many of these, and therefore found myself a living witness of the emergence of important new ideas and techniques.

Maintaining My Links With Sheffield

My appointment as Chancellor of the University of Sheffield in 1979 has allowed me to re-establish and strengthen contacts in my native city which had inevitably grown weaker during the time when my day-to-day interests lay elsewhere. To give just one instance, I have described in Chapter 1 the joy I felt in getting to know Charles Gibbs, my father's last apprentice, and in receiving from him the tools which he had been given by my mother in 1930.

I have always believed that the big civic universities do an excellent job in 'adding value' to the students who enter their doors, and my time as Chancellor in Sheffield has amply confirmed this view. It has also been thoroughly rewarding in purely personal terms. Degree ceremonies have been my most regular public functions, becoming longer in duration and also more frequent as the University has grown in size; in the 1996-97 academic session there were eleven first degree congregations in July, as well as three higher degree ones at other times of the year. The preparation of my addresses for these occasions has become something of a preoccupation, especially on long railway journeys. Though the message I want to deliver is essentially the same, I obtain great satisfaction from attempting to tailor individual speeches to topics I imagine will command the attention of students from the different faculties as they appear before me. As the number of ceremonies has increased, so too has the groundwork, but I have resisted the temptation to repeat past speeches lest the new graduates do not find them relevant, and also so that I do not get bored delivering them. All in all I have admitted over 57,000 graduands to their degrees, never missing a summer degree congregation and only a few of the higher degree ones. Over this long period I have observed interesting and important trends among the graduands, most notably the increasing proportion of mature students and the growing numbers of female engineers. I have always enjoyed meeting students, though I have grown wary of asking ostensibly overseas students, identified as such by their appearance or their name, where they come from since I started getting answers such as 'Brixton' or 'Birmingham'!

Barbara's dedication and commitment to the University, and her distinction as a scientist in her own right, were movingly acknowledged in the University's award to her of an honorary degree in 1992, the year of our golden wedding anniversary. Another delightful occasion which will never be forgotten was when a more than usually mature student appeared before me and whispered 'Caddy, Form 3A'. After a short hesitation I recognised in him a former classmate at the Central Secondary School, and memories of those happy years came flooding back. Though he was clever at school he left before I did to train as a laboratory technician, and had worked in Sheffield all his life. After retiring he found himself watching an Open University history programme and thought 'I could do that'. He duly studied history at the University, and after graduating took an MA by research. I asked him 'what next?', to which he replied immediately 'a PhD, of course!' – a rather refreshing attitude, as we were both approaching our eighties.

I have managed to visit a good number of University departments since my installation, whilst only interfering in the institution's affairs when I thought it absolutely essential. Probably the most important occasion was when I helped to secure Gareth Roberts as a first-rate successor to Geoffrey Sims when he retired as Vice-Chancellor at the end of 1990. It had been good to watch the University grow under Geoffrey's leadership and to witness the appearance of many new buildings on the campus, including the multi-purpose Octagon Centre which replaced the City Hall as the venue for the University's major degree ceremonies. Gareth arrived in Sheffield in the era of assessment exercises for research and teaching excellence: he has piloted the University through these challenging years with consummate skill and energy, and Barbara and I continue to draw great satisfaction from Sheffield's high ranking in these key areas of activity.

Nevertheless I think that Chancellorships should not be for life, and for this reason I have tendered my resignation every five years. So far the offer has always been rejected. Indeed, my hundredth congregation in 1991 was marked by a completely unexpected fanfare of trumpets and I was presented with a beautiful glass goblet, specially engraved by David Peace. This will, I hope, find its permanent home in the University's Turner Museum of Glass when the family can be persuaded to part with it. We were also greatly touched by the generosity shown on the occasion of my 80th birthday, when we had a delightful party in Goldsmiths' Hall in London and, if it were possible, an even better one in Sheffield, where the University's affection for us was clearly demonstrated.

Involvement with the University has also brought me into close contact with Sheffield City Council, the Cutlers' Company, the South Yorkshire Community Foundation, and local leaders of industry and commerce, as well as representatives of the Catholic, Anglican and Free Churches. I hope I have been able to contribute a little to the city's welfare, and I was honoured to be invited to write a foreword to the splendid three-volume boxed set of books entitled *The History of the City of Sheffield*, published in 1993 to mark the sesquicentenary of the town's incorporation as a borough and the centenary of the granting of its city charter. It seemed especially apposite that the front cover of Volume 1 carried a photograph of the Town Hall, a building my father knew so well.

The House of Lords

I have left the House of Lords to the end of this book, though membership of it has certainly dominated my later years. When I was created a Baron in 1986 I was very conscious of the honour bestowed upon me, but I did not know what their Lordships really did or how effective they were. Also, I had no idea in what way I could make any kind of contribution to the work of the Upper House, assuming that I thought it worthwhile in the first place. In the event, the ensuing years have presented me with more challenges and interest than I could ever have expected. A major reason for this is that for most of the time the Conservative government enjoyed a considerable majority in the House of Commons, and became increasingly arrogant. Its members seemed for the most part to be driven by an ideologically motivated reforming zeal and therefore many of the bills put forward were ill thought out, both in their general purpose and in their practicability. It was often left to the House of Lords – including its Conservative members – to get some sense into these bills, and in certain cases to emasculate them, even going against party colleagues in the Commons. The intensity of the work can be illustrated by the fact that we had to deal with thirteen Education Bills in fourteen years; a Royal Commission report on criminal justice and a Criminal Justice Bill; and numerous bills reforming aspects of the National Health Service. These are all areas in which I have a deep personal concern.

I have also found myself engaged in the day-to-day running of the House through my chairmanship of its Library and Computers Sub-committee, which in turn has led to membership of the Offices Committee, the main executive body of the House, and other sub-committees concerned with staff, finance, buildings and works. In addition, the House of Lords operates a Select Committee on Science and Technology, and I have had the pleasure of chairing three of its sub-committees – dealing with systematic biology research, forensic science, and graduate careers in research – as well as participating in many others as a member. The influence of these bodies has of course been variable but, I would argue, mainly beneficial. From my own point of view, I think I can say that the House of Lords has done more to enlarge my education than almost any other experience in my life, apart from that of reading to my father!

Barbara Dainton writes:

This was as far as Fred had taken his draft before he suffered the unexpected heart attack from which he did not recover. The rest of this chapter is therefore written by me, to round off the story.

I was with Fred when he opened his letter of appointment to the House of Lords. He was genuinely surprised, and obviously felt uncertain about the responsibilities he was taking on: but I did not view this very seriously, because he always reacted to some new activity in this way. The wealth of knowledge and experience which the life peers brought to the Upper House soon modified our previous conviction that it should eventually be entirely democratically elected. However, once Labour came to power in 1997 with its enormous majority, abolition of the hereditary principle became a certainty: we often discussed the nature of the body which would result, and how the change might best be brought about. Fred would have liked a commission appointed to review the functions of the Upper House before its composition was considered. He also felt that the restructuring should be carried out in stages, partly because he appreciated the value of the contributions made by at least a minority of hereditary peers.

When Fred accepted his peerage he announced to me: 'I am not going to speak on anything I know nothing about!' Anyone who takes even a cursory glance at Hansard during the years when he was a member cannot help noticing how frequently debates and bills centred on his lifelong interests of science policy, education and healthcare; and he gained great satisfaction from bringing his knowledge and experience to bear on these debates. Several members commented to me, while Fred was still alive, on the evident wisdom behind his speeches and the clarity with which they were presented. I know that he was very gratified by the attention he received when he spoke.

Fred knew at once that he would be an Independent cross-bencher, because he wanted to bring knowledge to the Lords, not party loyalty. Moreover, he liked to work with colleagues from all sides of the House, and he revelled in all-party support when he could command it. He also discovered the important role of the Upper House in scrutinising legislation proposed by the Lower House, which he found was frequently ill-informed. One example will suffice. When Kenneth Clarke was Secretary of State for Health, and one of many bills to reform the NHS appeared in the Lords, Fred and two or three other peers noticed that there was no representation of the universities on the health authorities responsible for the teaching hospitals. This omission also overlooked the fact that buildings provided by the University Grants Committee for medical teaching purposes were sometimes physically embedded in these hospital premises. Together with some of his colleagues, Fred sought a meeting with Kenneth Clarke and his civil servants and, as he told me, they tore strips off them for their oversight. Fred then handed Kenneth Clarke a draft of the changes which they thought necessary. These were later accepted as government amendments, and adopted by both Houses without further ado.

The first House of Lords committee which Fred chaired arose out of reports of the difficulties experienced by the Natural History Museum, Kew Gardens and other national centres in recruiting biologists who could care for their marvellous collections. I was surprised to discover that Fred was chairing a committee on systematic biology, which was a subject I had taught, and so I wrote him a short paper entitled Kindergarten Systematics. He thanked me for this and then said firmly he did not want to hear anything more about the matter, since his mind must remain open to comments from others. In the event, I think that having the committee chaired by a physical scientist, who by definition would be acting independently, was a good thing. I myself got considerable pleasure out of observing him becoming more and more interested in my own academic subject.

The second committee he chaired was on forensic science. It arose out of the miscarriages of justice in the trials of the 'Birmingham Six' and the 'Guildford Four', due to faulty forensic evidence. The profession appeared to react positively to the work of the committee, and action was taken to improve its techniques. Fred was subsequently awarded the Firth Medal of the Forensic Science Society, so they must have felt he treated them fairly!

The career prospects, or lack of them, available for contract researchers in universities formed the remit of the third committee to be chaired by Fred; its report was being implemented when he was taken ill. The whole concept of contract research workers came into existence when the universities were coping with funding cuts and were therefore unwilling to appoint tenured staff. These unfortunate people are recruited for fixed periods, which may be very short even if the contract is renewable; they are left without the usual privileges granted to permanent staff, and no future career structure when they have to move on. At the last meeting he attended, Fred was delighted by the positive response of the Scottish Higher Education Funding Council to a campaign on these matters led by Professor Juliet Cheetham. The Higher Education Funding Council for England followed suit, as a result of representations made by Professor Sir Gareth Roberts some time after Fred had died; money was found to provide contract research staff with much-needed financial help and careers advice.

Earlier in this last chapter Fred commented on his chairmanship of the House of Lords Library and Computers Sub-committee. Coming home after attending one of its meetings, he said to me: 'Today I suggested that Parliament would be better served by its libraries if those of the House of Commons and the House of Lords were combined. This idea fell a like a lead balloon and I shall not propose it again.' Perhaps the reformed Upper House may eventually come to understand the wisdom behind his recommendation.

One of Fred's last activities in the House of Lords concerned the proposed establishment of General Teaching Councils in both England and Wales. These were intended to bring about a necessary unification in the profession, to establish expected standards and to advise on the development of the whole profession, while leaving negotiations over pay and conditions to the trade unions. This would be a parallel division to the long-standing one in the medical field between the General Medical Council and the British Medical Association. Teachers themselves would then be responsible for advising government about standards, and would be able to deal with Ministers directly. Both Fred and I had long believed these changes to be necessary for the proper development of teaching as a profession, and we were pleased when John Sayer and John Tomlinson invited Fred to help steer the appropriate legislation through Parliament. After the 1997 general election the establishment of English and Welsh Councils was included in the Labour Government's Teaching and Higher Education Act (1998). Unfortunately Fred did not live to see the legislation introduced, but he would have been delighted with the outcome: the General Teaching Council for England duly came into being on 1 September 2000, with that for Wales following shortly thereafter.

Fred's final lecture was given in Cambridge in September 1997, at a conference in Churchill College commemorating J.J. Thompson's landmark discovery of the electron. He was the only chemist invited to contribute, and he enjoyed talking to the physicists and meeting many old friends. I am pleased that his last lecture was a scientific one, on a subject so relevant to much of his academic work, and that it was delivered in the university where we had first met.

Early in 1998 I attended the annual dinner of the Institute of Physics with our son, John, at which we were presented with the President's Medal which Fred had known he was about to receive – something which gave him great satisfaction. Later that year, on 25 June, the Queen officially opened the new British Library building at St Pancras, describing it as 'truly worthy of our country's contribution to literature and scholarship, to science and technology'. Our elder daughter, Mary, came with me, and we rejoiced in the architectural splendour of the Library's new home. It seemed a fitting memorial to Fred's life of achievement.

EPILOGUE

If a man will begin with certainties, he shall end in doubts;
but if he will be content to begin with doubts,
he shall end in certainties.

Francis Bacon (1561-1626)

Every book, like every life, has a beginning and an ending; and as I come to the end of my tale some final thoughts come flooding in. The first is one of gratitude to my family – parents, Barbara, children, grandchildren – who above all have defined standards and expectations as well as duties, thereby saving me from myself, and have given me great happiness and support. There are of course many other friends, teachers and pupils who taught me much, although only a few of their names appear in these pages. To all I owe a great debt. In my life I have tried to the best of my ability to repay these debts but, acknowledging human frailty, I must accept that there will be cases – some unknown to me – where I have failed to do so. I can only ask for forgiveness, and perhaps a little credit for good intentions.

In the course of a long and varied life the elegant simplicity of Bacon's words, quoted above, have often come to mind when I have been faced by someone's exposition of their opinion, written or spoken in a manner so confident and assured as to defy (and therefore usually to terminate) calm discussion. Both parts of Bacon's sentence are axiomatic and salutary. They complement each other and reinforce my instinctive distrust of absolute conviction in others, as well as the personal arrogance of which it is so often a manifestation.

Looking back, I think my natural scepticism and my subliminal recognition of the Baconian maxim may have been underlying reasons for my youthful difficulty, which I could not reveal without causing my mother hurt, in complying with the public affirmation of the unknowable required of its members by Banner Cross United Methodist Church. They have certainly been the origin, much later in life, of my mistrust of those devout reductionists (if I may coin a paradoxical phrase) who claim certainty about present theory, when the progress of science lies in the *refutation* of present ideas and their replacement by others more comprehensive, though not necessarily final. In attributing a common characteristic to reductionists and religious believers I am aware that I shall not attract much approbation from either party, but it does not seem to me that atheistic regimes, any more than theocratic ones, necessarily lead to civilised, just and humane societies, or to free intellectual enquiry.

In old age a consciousness of the inevitability of death increases, and with it a tendency to self-questioning and especially a desire to know whether one's life has been worth while. The difficulty in addressing the latter question comes in defining 'worth', for which there is no single criterion which is both comprehensive and universal. My father would have liked to have been judged by the quality of his masonry, much of which survives to this day; my mother by whether she had created a loving home, and brought up and cared for her large family to the highest standards achievable. Neither was given to verbal elaboration of their precepts to their children, beyond brief phrases like 'Think on, lad'; 'Is it any use?'; 'Give him a hand: he can't help hissen', each implying an emphasis on certain qualities such as reflection before action, judgment by utility, and helping others. These examples, and their occasional advice when a choice of action had to be made, were for me a guide without which I could not have managed in good times or bad.

I have little to leave behind that is tangible or durable, like my father's buildings. Even though I played roles, some would say key roles, in important ventures such as the creation of the new British Library at St Pancras and the Queen's Medical Centre at Nottingham, it could be argued that each of these was so necessary that it would have been built one day by someone: and to a certain degree the same may be said of many of the educational initiatives with which I have been credited. However, I think it will readily be accepted that such developments generally met the criterion of usefulness.

Scientific work with which my name is coupled will endure, not least because it is permanently recorded in the literature under my name – often with others. Its utility will be judged, and no doubt re-evaluated, with the passage of time, but some matters only I can record. The first is the great contribution made by both colleagues and students to the ideas, their execution, and their outcomes. Some of these collaborations have featured in this book, but they are only a fraction of the total. To write a short, intelligible memoir involved continuous selection, often painful but absolutely necessary, if the book was to be interesting to the general reader and friends, and a reasonably short 'read'.

Secondly, I am in the best position of anyone to explain my reasons for undertaking the researches concerned. Only in the case of the decisions to investigate the radiation chemistry of water and the oxidation of white phosphorus was the motive external, driven by a practical necessity: active design optimisation in the first case, military aircraft protection in the second. Furthermore, it is certain that if I had continued in an employment having such immediate objectives, I would not have embarked on the more fundamental studies which I believe to have longer-term importance. On the other hand, those projects which were purely curiosity-driven – by an interest which, in almost every case, had been aroused by something that appeared not to fit in with existing ideas – frequently led to a revision of earlier thinking which had an impact on practical, individual or environmental issues, no less than on the basic understanding of the subject.

The last observation illustrates something I believe to be generally true; namely, that whilst work selected to be of immediate practical utility – for example the improvement of a product, a procedure, even a therapy – can, in the current jargon, assist in the 'creation of wealth' or the 'enhancement of the quality of life', it is less likely to contribute to an understanding of the scientific mechanisms involved in such practical gains, and even more unlikely to produce the big breakthroughs which transform both theory and practice. In national scientific policy, as in many other spheres of activity, short-term expediency may give quick, limited, commercial gains, but if pursued at the expense of self-chosen, curiosity-driven ideas it will not only postpone but possibly deny major practical gains for the future. Moreover, the tipping of the investment balance towards the short term is always the greater, the smaller the fraction of its gross domestic product a country is prepared to provide for publicly-funded scientific research and development. This is the position into which the UK has slowly moved over the last twenty-five years, so that now the Research Councils are obliged to pay special attention to politically correct crystal-ball gazing, and even basic research institutes are considered fair game for privatisation studies. *Sic transit gloria Angliae*!

It is important to remember that all the innumerable benefits of modern life are consequences of the uniqueness of man in the animal kingdom, because of the power of his brain to organise knowledge systematically, and his innate desire to know more. Without these faculties, progress from a demanding life as hunter-gatherers would have been impossible. Moreover, the power and desire are auto-acceleratory unless we wish and decide that things shall be otherwise. Science drives progress in the world: it is thus of paramount importance that science should be maintained in a healthy state, and applied wisely.

In the closing years of my life, two lines from the chorus of T.S. Eliot's pageant play *The Rock* often come to mind. They are

> Where is the wisdom we have lost in knowledge?
> Where is the knowledge we have lost in information?

These words recur to me because they reflect a persistent anxiety about the future. The second question of the pair is particularly apposite now that the electronic world of personal computers and the Internet is capable of quenching us with information, and perhaps at the same time to so anaesthetise our senses that we lose our powers of discrimination, indeed become disabled in 'making a right judgement in all things', as Aristotle defined the purpose of education. Will each human being in the years to come have the strength of mind to disconnect from the insistent flow of information in order to think deeply about some aspect of it, seeing in it those incongruities which are the stimuli of new thought?

Combining Eliot's gloomy questions with Bacon's famous and incontrovertible assertion that knowledge is power, we are brought face to face with the key question which should concern us as we enter the third millennium AD. It is simply, 'are we capable of using wisely the knowledge we now possess, or will possess in the future?' When the history of the twentieth century is taken into consideration, the omens do not seem to me to be especially propitious. We have used our powers to allow both the world population and the average annual demand each person makes on Planet Earth to increase, resulting in adverse impacts on the environment, such as global warming and depletion of the protective ozone layer; we still slash and burn forests, destroying ecosystems by ill-sited dams and in other ways so numerous as to justify the appellation of the human race as 'plunderers of the planet'. Feeble attempts to come to grips with some of the problems facing us have been made, for example in 'summit meetings' at Montreal and at Rio de Janeiro. However, we in the developed world are so besotted with economic success – our own selfish national desire for a rising standard of living (which we do not really need), and the dogma that this is only achievable by competition and expansion – that we cannot see that gratifying these wishes simply compounds the problems we face. Instead, in addition to reforming our own practices, we should be helping the developing countries to approach western levels of prosperity without repeating the mistakes of the past. If there is to be a future, it is essential that we stabilise the human population and its per capita demand on global resources at sustainable, non-damaging levels.

That is the challenge. Will it be met? I do not know: but I wish every success to those who commit themselves to the cause.

Only human beings guide their behaviour by a knowledge of what happened before they were born and a preconception of what may happen after they are dead; thus only humans find their way by a light that illuminates more than the patch of ground they stand on.

P B and J S Medawar, *The Life of Science (1977)*

APPENDIX 1

FREDERICK SYDNEY DAINTON:
OUTLINE CHRONOLOGY

1914	Born 11 November at 66 Ranby Road, Sheffield: youngest son of George Whalley Dainton and Mary Jane Dainton (née Bottrill)
1919	Hunter's Bar Infant School and Greystones Elementary School, Sheffield
1925	Scholarship to Central Secondary School, Sheffield
1933	Exhibitioner, St John's College, Oxford
1934	Casberd Prizeman
1935	Casberd Scholar Goldsmiths' Company Exhibitioner
1937	BSc degree with First Class Honours, University of Oxford Research Student, Sidney Sussex College, Cambridge
1938	First met Barbara Hazlitt Wright, Research Student at Newnham College, Cambridge, only daughter of Dr and Mrs W B Wright of Manchester
1939	Goldsmiths' Company Senior Student Departmental Demonstrator in Chemistry, University of Cambridge (1939-44)
1940	PhD degree, University of Cambridge
1942	Married Barbara Wright: one son and two daughters born in 1947, 1950 and 1952
1944	University Demonstrator in Chemistry, University of Cambridge (1944-46)

1945   Fellow of St Catharine's College, Cambridge

1946   Humphrey Owen Jones Lecturer in Physical Chemistry, University of
            Cambridge (1946-50)
            Praelector of St Catharine's College, Cambridge

1949   Visiting Professor, University of Toronto

1950   Professor of Physical Chemistry, University of Leeds (1950-65)
            Fellow of the Royal Institute of Chemistry
            Tilden Lecturer and Medallist, the Chemical Society

1952   Peter C Reilly Lecturer, University of Notre Dame, Indiana

1953   ScD degree, University of Cambridge

1957   Fellow of the Royal Society of London

1958   Sylvanus Thompson Medallist, British Institute of Radiology

1959   Arthur D Little Visiting Professor, Massachusetts Institute of Technology
            Lady Masson Lecturer, University of Melbourne

1961   Honorary Fellow of St Catharine's College, Cambridge
            George Fisher Baker Lecturer, Cornell University

1962   Boomer Lecturer, University of Alberta

1964   Chairman of the Association for Radiation Research (1964-66)

1965   Vice-Chancellor, University of Nottingham (1965-70)
            President of the Faraday Society (1965-67)
            Council for Scientific Policy (Member 1965-72; Chairman 1970-72)

1966   President of the Association for Science Education
            Advisory Committee on Scientific and Technological Information
            (Chairman 1966-70)
            Honorary ScD degree, Lódz Polytechnic University, Poland

1967   Chairman of the National Libraries Committee (1967-69)

Member, Central Advisory Council on Science and Technology (1967-70)

1968   Honorary Fellow of St John's College, Oxford

Foreign Member of the Royal Swedish Academy of Sciences

Honorary ScD degree, Trinity College, Dublin

1969   Davy Medallist, the Royal Society of London

1970   Dr Lee's Professor of Chemistry, University of Oxford (1970-73)

Honorary DSc degree, University of Bath

Honorary DSc degree, Heriot-Watt University

Honorary DSc degree, Loughborough University of Technology

Honorary DSc degree, University of Warwick

Honorary LLD degree, University of Nottingham

1971   Knight Bachelor

Honorary DSc degree, The Queen's University of Belfast

Honorary DSc degree, University of Exeter

Honorary DSc degree, University of Strathclyde

1972   President of the Chemical Society (1972-73)

Chairman of the Advisory Board for the Research Councils (1972-73)

Foreign Member, American Academy of Arts and Sciences

Honorary DSc degree, University of East Anglia

Honorary DSc degree, University of Manchester

Honorary LLD degree, University of Aberdeen

1973   Chairman of the University Grants Committee (1973-78)

British Committee for the Harkness Fellowships (Member 1973-85; Chairman 1978-85)

Honorary DSc degree, University of Leeds

1974   Faraday Lecturer and Medallist, the Chemical Society

Trustee of the British Museum (Natural History) (1974-84)

1975 Foreign Member of the Academy of Sciences, Göttingen

Honorary DSc degree, McMaster University

1977 President of the Library Association

National Radiological Protection Board (Member 1977-85; Chairman 1978-85)

Honorary DSc degree, Uppsala University

1978 Chairman of the British Library Board (1978-85)

Chancellor of the University of Sheffield (1978-97)

Trustee of the Wolfson Foundation (1978-88)

1979 Chairman of Council, Royal Postgraduate Medical School (1979-90)

Honorary Fellow of the Royal College of Physicians

Honorary DSc degree, University of Liverpool

Honorary DSc degree, University of Salford

Honorary LLD degree, University of Cambridge

Honorary LLD degree, University of Sheffield

1980 President of the British Association for the Advancement of Science (1980-81)

Honorary DSc degree, New University of Ulster

1981 Rede Lecturer, University of Cambridge

Crookshank Lecturer and Medallist, Royal College of Radiologists

Honorary DSc degree, University of Kent at Canterbury

1982 Prime Warden of the Worshipful Company of Goldsmiths (1982-83)

Chairman of the Edward Boyle Memorial Trust (1982-97)

1983 Curie Medallist, Poland

Honorary Fellow of the Royal Society of Chemistry

Stamp Lecturer, University of London

Honorary LLD degree, University of London

1984   Honorary Fellow of the Royal College of Radiologists

            Honorary Fellow of Goldsmiths' College, University of London

            Member of the Crafts Council (1984-88)

1985   Knight Commander of the Order of Merit, Poland

            President of the Society of Designer Craftsmen (1985-97)

            Honorary Fellow of Queen Mary and Westfield College, University of London

            Member of the Museums and Galleries Commission (1985-92)

1986   Life Peerage: Baron Dainton of Hallam Moors in the County of South Yorkshire

            Honorary Fellow of the Library Association

            Honorary Fellow of the London School of Economics and Political Science

            Honorary Fellow of Birkbeck College, University of London

            Convocation Lecturer, University of Newcastle upon Tyne

1987   Member of Council, Foundation for Science and Technology (1987-94)

            Honorary Member of the British Institute of Radiology

            Edward Boyle Lecturer, Royal Society of Arts

            Dainton Lecturer, British Library

            John Snow Lecturer and Medallist, Association of Anaesthetists

            Gray Hartley Lecturer, University of Manchester

1988   President of the Arthritis and Rheumatism Council for Research (1988-97)

            Honorary DCL degree, University of Oxford

            Honorary LLD degree, University of Lancaster

1989   Lee Kuan Yew Fellow, Singapore

1990   President of the Royal Postgraduate Medical School (1990-97) and Honorary Fellow

1991   Foreign Member of the American Philosophical Society

            Honorary DLitt degree, Council for National Academic Awards

1993   Patron of the English Place-Name Society (1993-97)

Firth Medallist, Forensic Science Society

1994   Privilegiate of St Hilda's College, Oxford

1996   Semenov Centenary Medallist, Russian Academy of Sciences

Honorary DSc degree, University of Reading

1997   President's Medallist, Institute of Physics

Invited Lecturer, International Centennial Symposium on the Electron, University of Cambridge

Died 5 December, in Oxford

PUBLICATIONS

1956   *Chain Reactions*

1967   *Photochemistry and Reaction Kinetics* (editor and contributor)

1968   *Enquiry into the Flow of Candidates in Science and Technology into Higher Education* (Cmnd. 3541, as Chairman) (Report of the Committee on 'The Swing Away from Science')

1969   *Report of the National Libraries Committee* (Cmnd. 4028, as Chairman)

1971   *A Framework for Government Research and Development* (Cmnd. 4814, including the 'Dainton' and 'Rothschild' reports as appendices)

1981   *Choosing a British University*

The Parliament of Science (contributor)

1983   *Reflections on the Universities and the National Health Service*

2001   *Doubts and Certainties: a Personal Memoir of the 20th Century* (edited by Barbara Dainton)

plus 276 other publications, the majority being papers in learned journals (1937-98)

The Dark Lady:
A Postscript by Lady Dainton

I have been asked by the publishers to include some details of my own life in this book because I keep appearing at intervals in the text, in the guise of 'the Dark Lady' as they put it! I do so with some hesitation, only mitigated by the fact that it adds to the tale of this remarkable century through which we have just lived.

Fred and I came from very different backgrounds. My father was an academic geologist who spent his entire working life with the Geological Survey of Great Britain and Ireland, moving from Dublin to Manchester in 1921 when the Irish Free State was founded. This meant that I lived in England from the age of four. In spite of the differences in childhood experience between Fred and myself, the values imparted by our parents were remarkably similar. They were all based on strict codes of conduct, made easier and more acceptable because they obviously involved the principles which so clearly ruled our parents' own lives. Fred and I both grew up conscious of the Protestant work ethic, though we would not have recognised it by that name: we were taught by example that hard work was always worth while, that everything should be done to the highest possible standard of which you were capable, and that time off was to be spent engaged in something of value which would bring refreshment to the whole person. Time must not be wasted! It was a good upbringing, and one for which I have always been grateful.

Fred and I were also lucky in that we had similar ambitions in life. We were both conscious that we had been fortunate to have attained a university education, Fred because of his family's financial circumstances and in my case because I was a woman (even though I attended an independent school, few girls there went on to university: most parents had no such ambition for their daughters). In this context, my maternal grandfather must have been a remarkable man. He was a medical doctor, trained in Dublin by apprenticeship to another physician in the manner common at that time; yet he put his two elder daughters through university in that city. My aunt studied classics at Trinity College, and my mother read biology at the Royal College of Science, which later became part of the pre-partition National University of Ireland. It was, therefore, quite simply a family assumption that the girls in the next generation should go to university if they wanted to. The family never considered higher education for women to be a waste of time or money, though this was still a widely held view when I was a teenager.

Even before the traumatic experiences of the Second World War, I believe both Fred and I wanted to do something which would provide increased opportunities for people to benefit as we had done; and because we were both scientists we knew that we would find it satisfying to have a chance to increase the sum of scientific knowledge, in however small a fashion.

During the war years Fred continued his teaching duties and also carried out various scientific projects for the government, in Cambridge and elsewhere, whilst I conducted research for my PhD degree on slugs (considered to be legitimate war work, because the slugs were eating the vital potato crop) and also taught long hours in the University and for Queen Mary College, London, which at that time had been evacuated to Cambridge. In addition, I briefly taught chemistry at Cambridge High School for Boys, where I was invariably addressed as 'Sir' and once slapped a very large boy on the cheek for deliberately causing a dangerous explosion in the laboratory. I have no remorse about this particular example of corporal punishment, though years afterwards, when I became a magistrate, I felt glad I could not be prosecuted retrospectively!

I taught at Newnham College, Cambridge, for a short time after the war, but gave up when we started a family. There was strong social pressure on me to look after my children full time, which I believe was encouraged by the Government because it released jobs for men returning from war service. This seems to me to have been a thoroughly sensible policy at the time, but I resented statements such as 'it has been shown by psychologists that the children will suffer if you do not personally look after them for 24 hours every day'. Ideas of this kind were taken very seriously and only began to be questioned in the late 1950s. In my view, they reflected a cruel social compulsion; but the widespread expectation today that (especially if they have a profession) women should *not* stay at home to rear their children seems to me equally wrong. The decision on this matter should surely be one for the parents alone.

When I married Fred in 1942 I did not realise that he was going to have quite such an exciting career, but I began to see this as a possibility soon afterwards. After our third child was born, I came to the conclusion that it would be best for all of us if, in the modern jargon, I prioritised my activities. I did not tell Fred at the time, but I decided that his career should come first. A major factor in making this choice was my own conviction that the things I most wanted to work for were increased higher education opportunities and advances in scientific research: supporting Fred seemed to me the most effective way in which I could achieve these aims. Next, of course, must come the welfare of the children, and I was keen to give them as much of my personal attention as possible because I soon realised that Fred would often be away from home. This certainly happened, though he never missed a chance to be with them and I am sure they all remember exploring the Yorkshire Dales and the Lake District as a family. Thirdly, in whatever time I had left, I would seize every opportunity to pursue my own scientific and educational objectives. I have never regretted my decision, for it has brought me great satisfaction and happiness – and a wide variety of experiences which would not have come my way if I had continued with a full-time career myself.

I sometimes feel unadventurous because all my children read mathematics, physics and chemistry at GCE A-level, and proceeded to scientific careers. As both their maternal grandparents were scientists this was always likely, and Fred and I also felt that school science would leave open to them a wide choice of rewarding future careers. Our son, John, is a professor of physics and is working on subatomic particles, which would certainly have interested his grandfather. Mary, our elder daughter, is a doctor, whilst Rosalind is assistant principal of a large sixth-form college, where she also teaches physics.

After we moved to Leeds, I took on a little part-time teaching in the sixth forms of local grammar schools. This experience proved valuable when, later in life, I was involved in the Oxford University admissions process: I am sure it made it easier for me to separate individual candidates' potential from the effects of good teaching when assessing them. Then, three years before we left Leeds, Professor J M Dodd, who had recently been appointed to the Chair of Zoology, invited me to become his research assistant to work on the function of the thyroid gland in the South African clawed toad, *Xenopus*. The children were now well established at school, and I was delighted to accept: I spent a happy period working in his laboratory on the toads, which my mother conceded were slightly more endearing than slugs. As Fred has mentioned, all this stopped when we went to Nottingham University, where I discovered that I was not welcome in any of the biology departments – presumably, just because I was the Vice-Chancellor's wife: something which I am glad to say would not happen today. Nottingham wanted me to be a social hostess and preferably a cordon bleu cook. The latter role I could never have achieved and, whilst I was pleased and interested to be a social hostess, I did not find this totally satisfying. I therefore made time to become a hospital management committee member and also a magistrate. From the former I learned much about the problems of the National Health Service; and being a magistrate was especially rewarding because it involved dealing with people from completely different walks of life, and discovering that a strong sense of justice is common to all.

When we moved to Oxford my magistracy was transferred to the local bench and then, to my great surprise, I was appointed to the Oxford Regional Hospital Board (which later became the Regional Health Authority). Here I encountered problems at a higher level of NHS management, which seemed to be just as intractable as those facing any individual hospital. Looking back, I feel that the eleven years I spent serving the NHS were largely devoid of achievement, although I thoroughly enjoyed the contact I had with those working at the 'coalface'.

Fred has described how I was invited by J W S Pringle, Linacre Professor of Zoology at Oxford (who had taught me when I was a student and he was a demonstrator in Cambridge) to undertake some part-time teaching in the Zoology Department. This was the first step on a path leading me to become a Fellow of St Hilda's College, where I gained enormous satisfaction. When, in due course, Richard Southwood succeeded John Pringle in the Linacre Chair he suggested I return to the study of slugs, using more sophisticated apparatus to repeat some of the work which had formed the research content of my PhD thesis. This was in some ways a rather frightening proposition and I wondered whether, if I found my previous results to be faulty, I ought to send my PhD back to Cambridge! However, all was well and the findings were similar, this time in a variety of species. They demonstrated clearly the importance of circadian changes in temperature: the onset of activity in slugs and snails coincides with the time at which an evening fall in temperature is perceived in their daytime resting place. In spite of this work I find that many of my biological colleagues persist in believing that slugs' nocturnal activity is directly related to the onset of darkness. They have never succeeded in explaining to me how a slug resting beneath a stone, or buried below the surface of the ground, could be aware that the light is fading.

The changes which have occurred in the twentieth century would not have seemed possible to anyone alive in 1900. My father brought me up to think that the scientific advances of my lifetime would be immense, but even so he did not foresee their real magnitude. I can remember his interest and excitement when the atom was split, but I am also fairly certain that before the event he would have doubted whether this would lead to the release of atomic energy, and that he would have agreed with the frequently quoted opinion of Lord Rutherford – that the very idea was sheer moonshine.

At Cambridge during the late 1930s I was taught that the hereditary material in cells was almost certainly a protein: it was not until the 1950s that the elegant structure of DNA was finally determined and its functional significance appreciated. Like Darwin's discovery of the power of natural selection to account for the diversity of living organisms, this scientific breakthrough was to change not only the possibilities open for future research work but also our whole way of thinking, an influence which nowadays spreads far beyond research scientists to thinkers of all kinds. Alas, looking back over my lifetime, there does not appear to have been a comparable increase in mankind's wisdom which would enable him to cope comfortably with so much new knowledge.

The years have also seen a great change in the position of women in society. When I went up to Cambridge women were not formally members of the University, even though two had been appointed to professorships! This did not detract from our experience as undergraduates but I am sure it was very hard for women dons in Girton and Newnham Colleges, who were debarred from sitting on committees or having any part in the running or development of the University. The qualifications we earned were known as 'titular degrees' and they were never conferred. However, seven months after Fred died I attended in Cambridge a great celebration of the 50th anniversary of the admission of women to full membership of the University. I am sorry Fred missed this occasion, because he was one of those who signed a circular in 1948 supporting the idea of the Grace which made this possible. Oxford was much more advanced than Cambridge in this respect, having first admitted women to full membership in 1922.

Some young people express astonishment when they learn that Fred and I were married for 55 years and that we found it a splendid experience. I am sure that the great happiness which marriage brought us was based on the fact that we were very good friends, who had a lot in common and whose aims in life were similar. We were fortunate to have found one another, and I often reflect that this would not have happened but for the Forster Education Act, which made elementary education available to all; and the foundation of the Irish Free State, which later became the Republic of Ireland. If my family had remained in Dublin I would almost certainly have attended Trinity College, and though this might have been a most rewarding experience, I would not have met Fred!

Subject Index

INDEX OF PERSONAL NAMES

Picture Credits

The majority of the illustrations in this book are from Lady Dainton's collections. Every effort has been made to trace other copyright holders; any errors or omissions are regretted, and if notified will be acknowledged in future editions. The Publishers are particularly grateful to the following, who have provided photographs or given permission for material to be used:

The British Library
The University of Cambridge
Cookridge Hospital
John Donat
Hulton Getty
Imperial College of Science, Technology
  and Medicine
Jill Lauriston
The University of Leeds
Liberty Publishing Ltd
June Mendoza
National Radiological Protection Board
Newark Advertiser Ltd
Nottingham Post Group Ltd

The University of Nottingham
Oxford University Press
The University of Oxford
PA Photos
Mark Rodgers
The Scientist
Sheffield Libraries and Information Services
Ian Spooner
The University of Sheffield
Trevor Stubley
Telegraph Group Ltd
Times Newspapers Ltd
The Worshipful Company of Goldsmiths

FREDERICK SYDNEY DAINTON
11 November 1914 – 5 December 1997